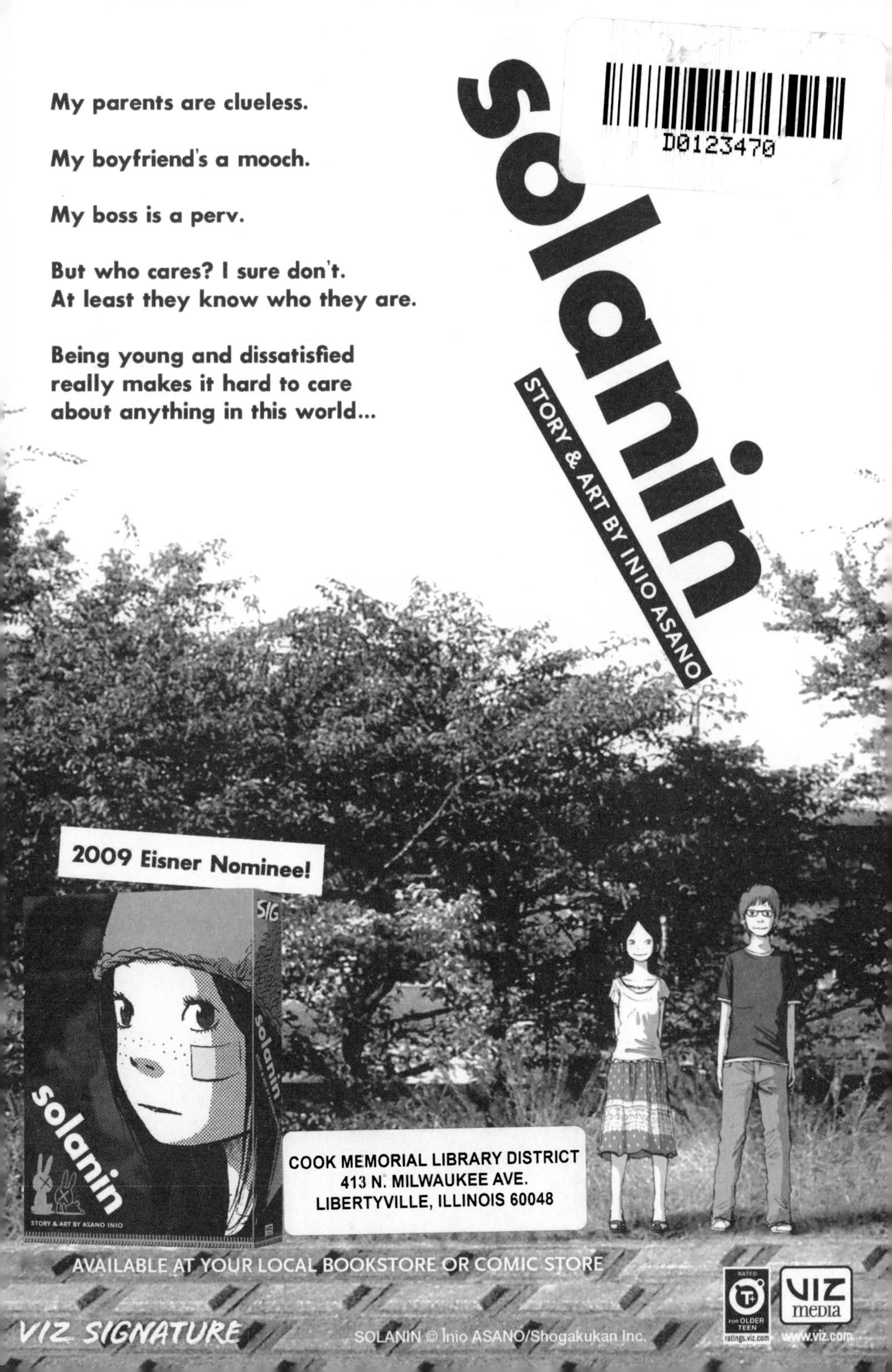
D0123470
My parents are clueless.
My boyfriend's a mooch.
My boss is a perv.
But who cares? I sure don't.
At least they know who they are.
Being young and dissatisfied
really makes it hard to care
about anything in this world...
solanin
STORY & ART BY INIO ASANO
2009 Eisner Nominee!
SIG
solanin
solanin
STORY & ART BY ASANO INIO
COOK MEMORIAL LIBRARY DISTRICT
413 N. MILWAUKEE AVE.
LIBERTYVILLE, ILLINOIS 60048
AVAILABLE AT YOUR LOCAL BOOKSTORE OR COMIC STORE
VIZ SIGNATURE
SOLANIN © Inio ASANO/Shogakukan Inc.
RATED
T+
FOR OLDER TEEN
ratings.viz.com
VIZ media
www.viz.com

SWEET BLUE FLOWERS
VOL. 4
VIZ Signature Edition

Story & Art by
Takako Shimura

Translation & Adaptation/John Werry
Touch-Up Art & Lettering/Monaliza De Asis
Design/Yukiko Whitley
Editor/Pancha Diaz

AOI HANA
© Takako Shimura 2012, 2013
All rights reserved.
First published in Japan in 2012, 2013 by Ohta Publishing Co., Tokyo
English translation rights arranged with Ohta Publishing Co.
through Tuttle-Mori Agency, Inc., Tokyo

Printed in Canada

Published by VIZ Media, LLC
P.O. Box 77010
San Francisco, CA 94107

10 9 8 7 6 5 4 3 2 1
First printing, June 2018

VIZ SIGNATURE
vizsignature.com

viz.com

End Notes

Page 15, panel 5: Glass Mask
A popular manga series by Suzue Miuchi about acting that debuted in 1976.

Page 61, panel 1: Marriage interview
Omiai in Japanese, it is a meeting of prospective partners for a formally arranged marriage.

Page 102, panel 1: Castella cake
A light, sweet sponge cake popular in Nagasaki, where they claim it's been made since the 16th century. The name may come from the Spanish region Castile, though the recipe is apparently Portuguese.

Page 340, panel 1: Coming-of-age ceremony
Coming of Age Day is a national holiday in Japan held on the second Monday in January. It celebrates everyone turning 20 in the coming year. In Japan, 20 is the age at which you can vote and drink.

Sweet Blue
Flowers

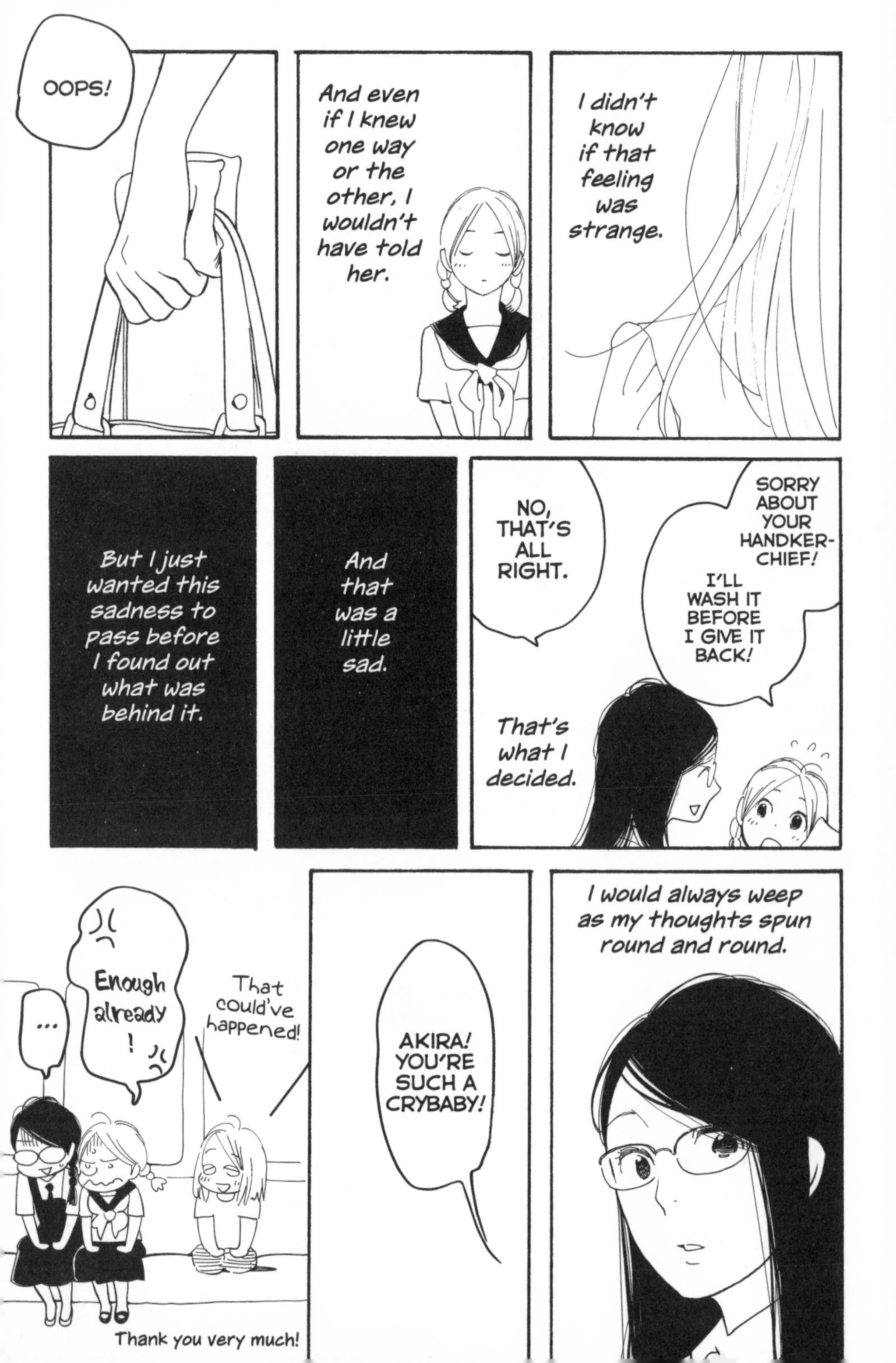
I didn't know if that feeling was strange.
And even if I knew one way or the other, I wouldn't have told her.
OOPS!
SORRY ABOUT YOUR HANDKER-CHIEF!
I'LL WASH IT BEFORE I GIVE IT BACK!
NO, THAT'S ALL RIGHT.
That's what I decided.
And that was a little sad.
But I just wanted this sadness to pass before I found out what was behind it.
I would always weep as my thoughts spun round and round.
AKIRA! YOU'RE SUCH A CRYBABY!
That could've happened!
Enough already!
...
Thank you very much!

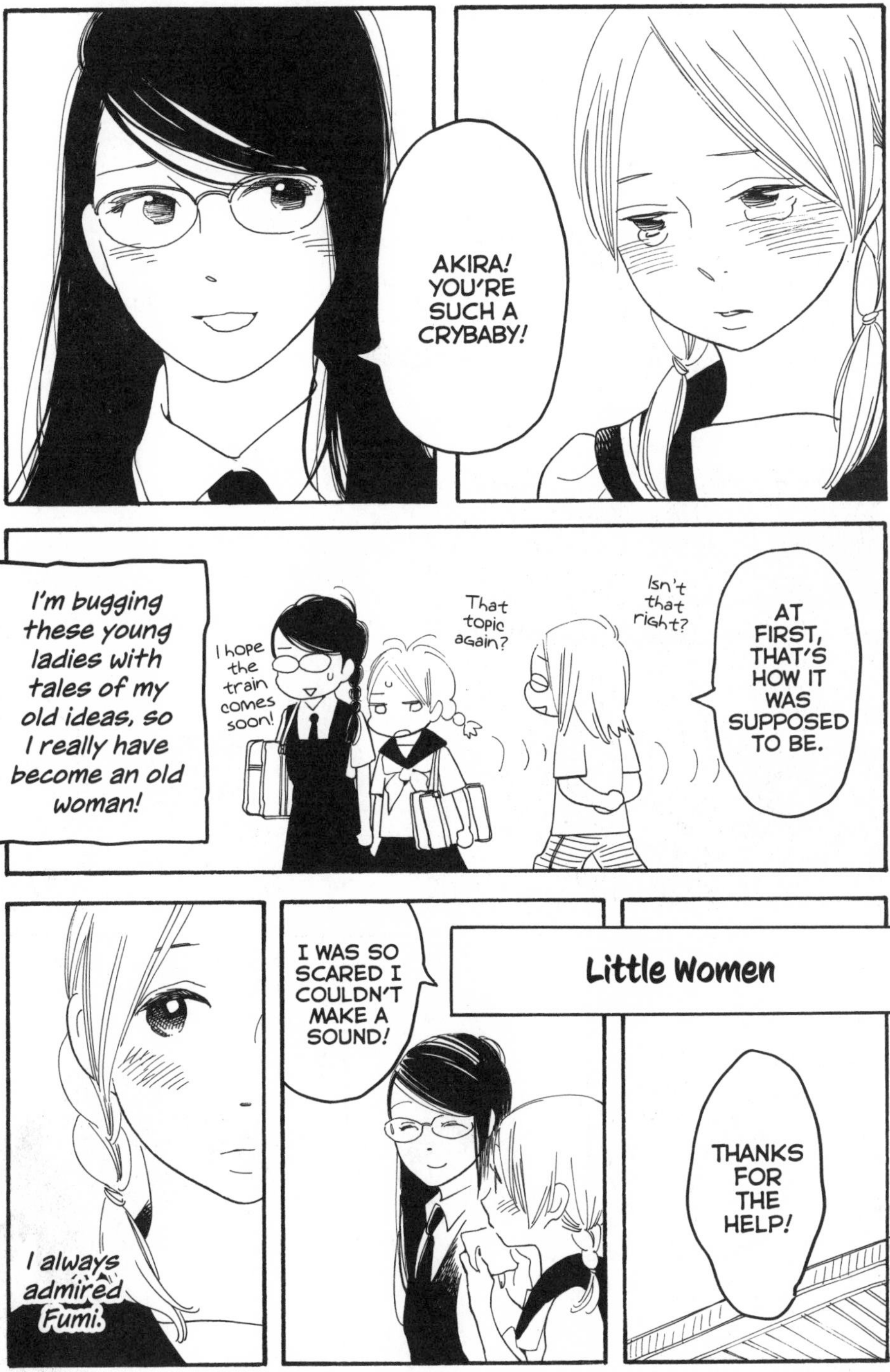
AKIRA! YOU'RE SUCH A CRYBABY!
AT FIRST, THAT'S HOW IT WAS SUPPOSED TO BE.
Isn't that right?
That topic again?
I hope the train comes soon!
I'm bugging these young ladies with tales of my old ideas, so I really have become an old woman!
Little Women
THANKS FOR THE HELP!
I WAS SO SCARED I COULDN'T MAKE A SOUND!
I always admired Fumi.

The End

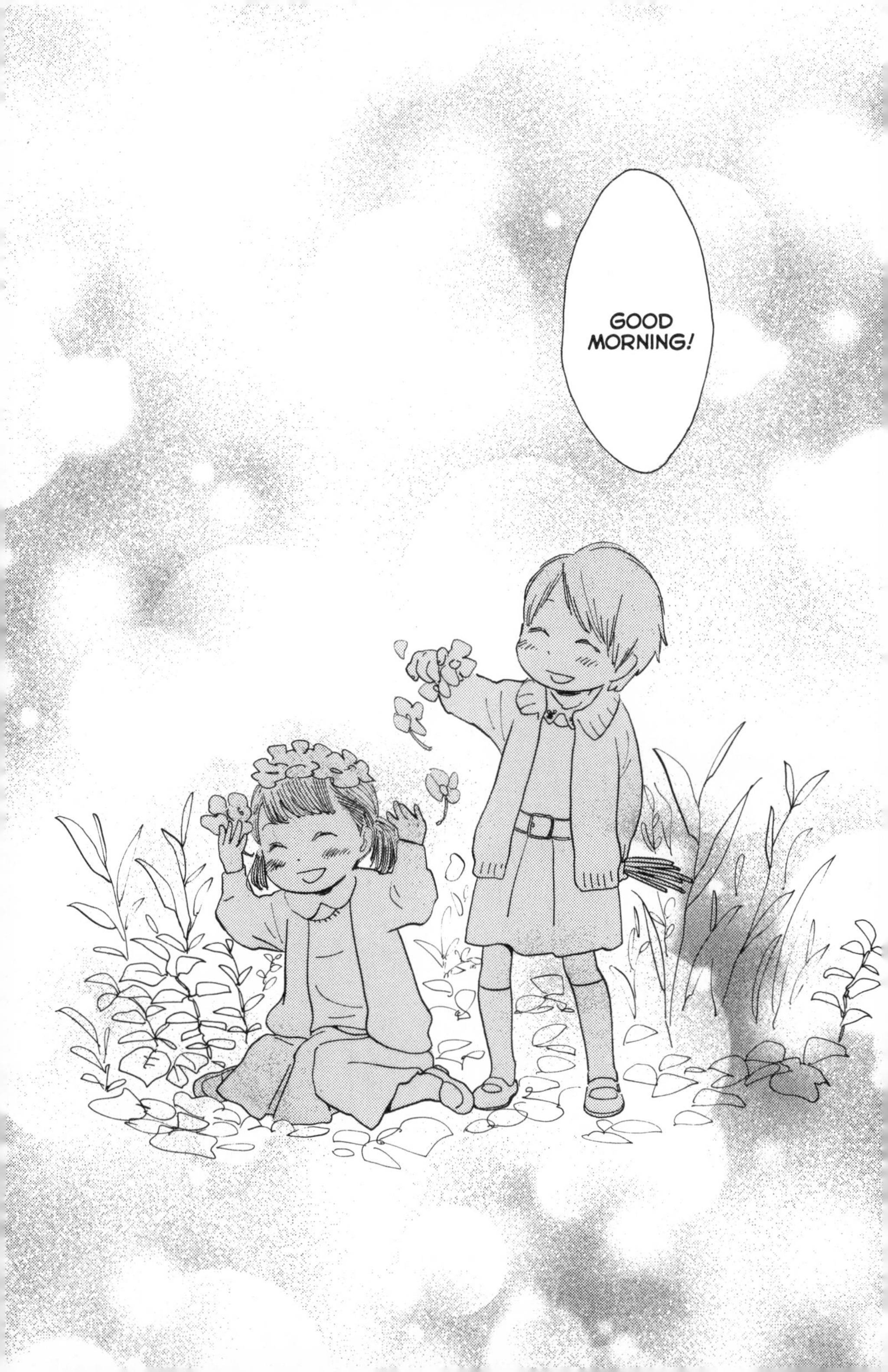
GOOD MORNING!

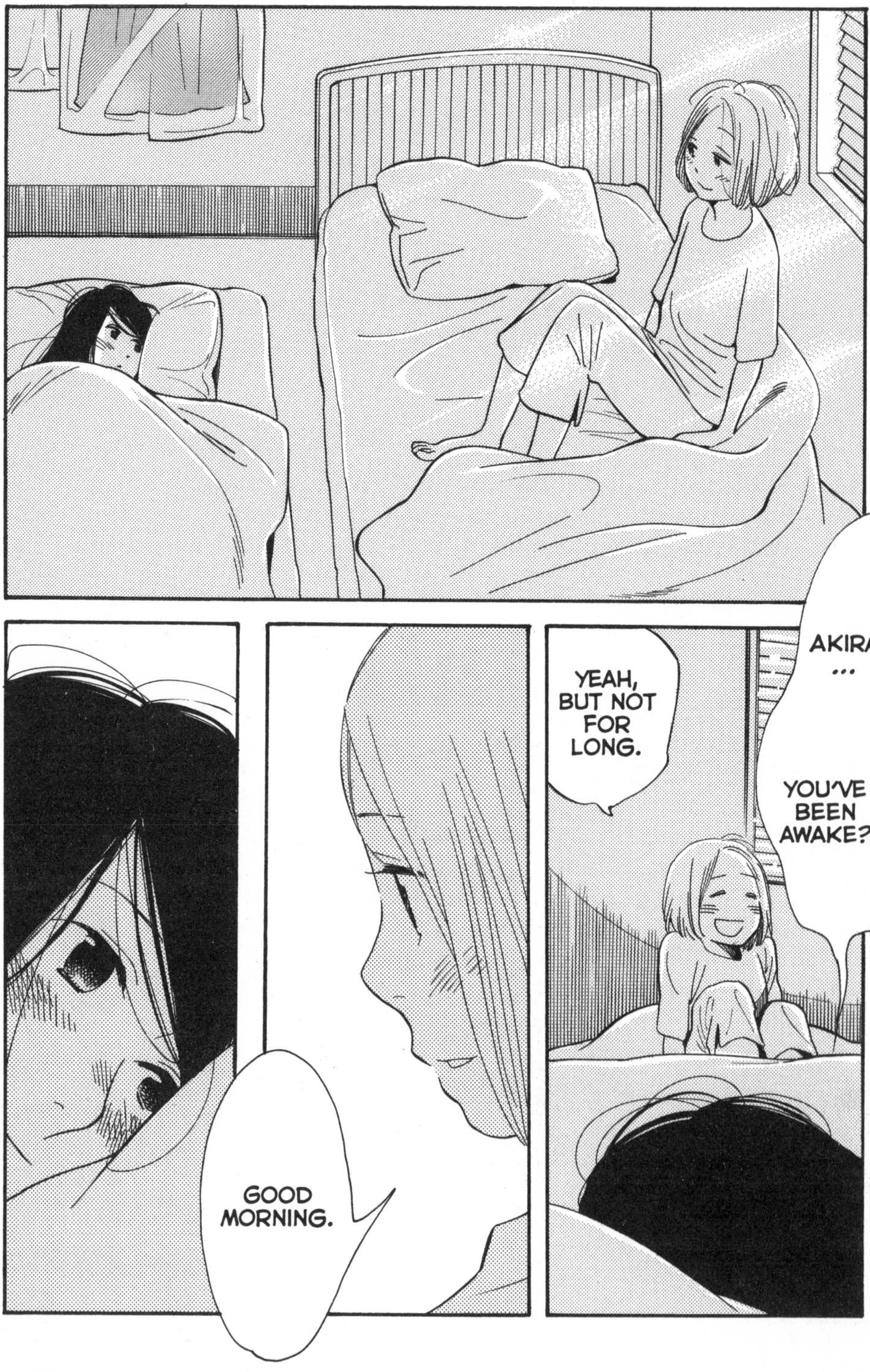
AKIRA ...
YOU'VE BEEN AWAKE?
YEAH, BUT NOT FOR LONG.
GOOD MORNING.

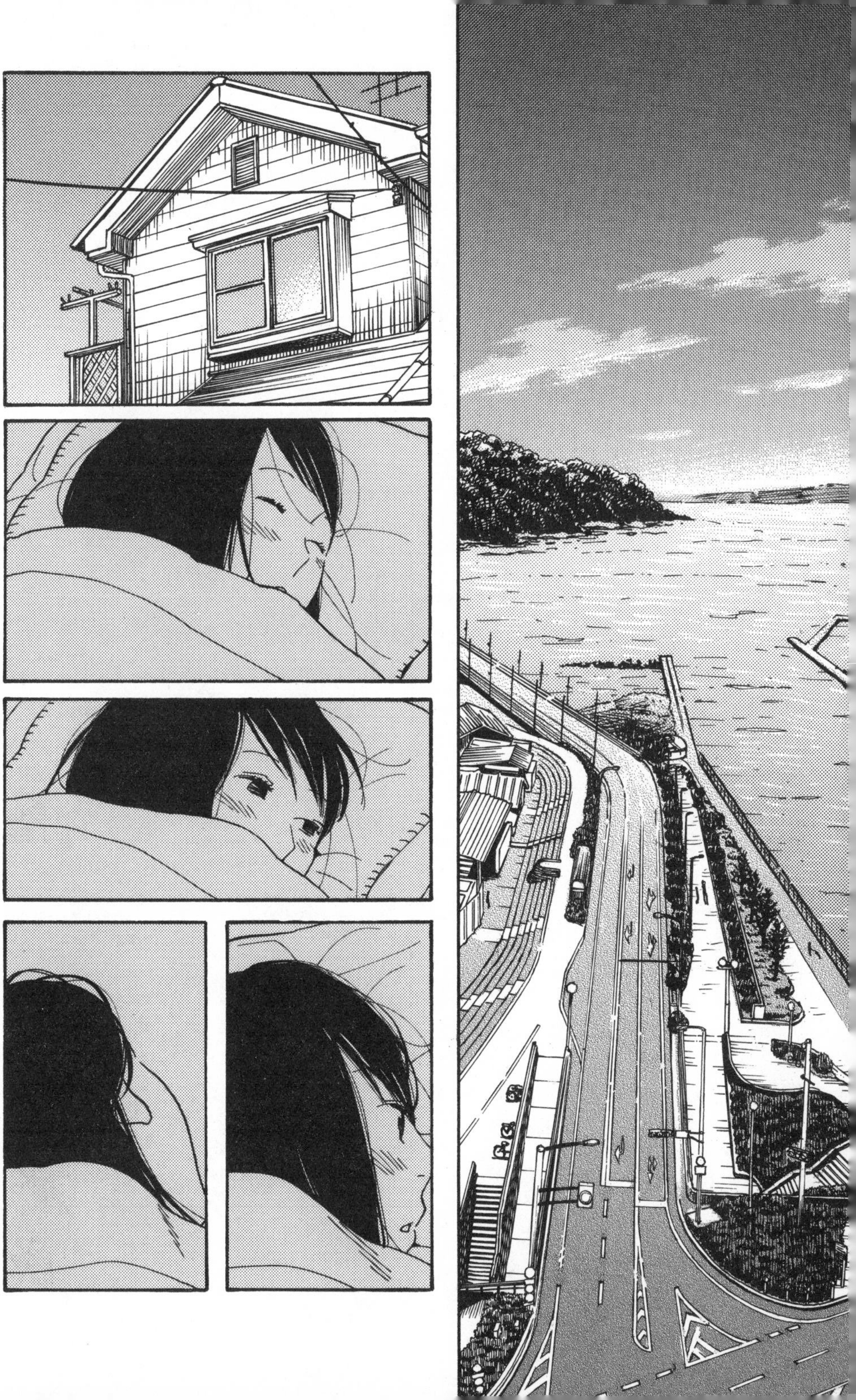

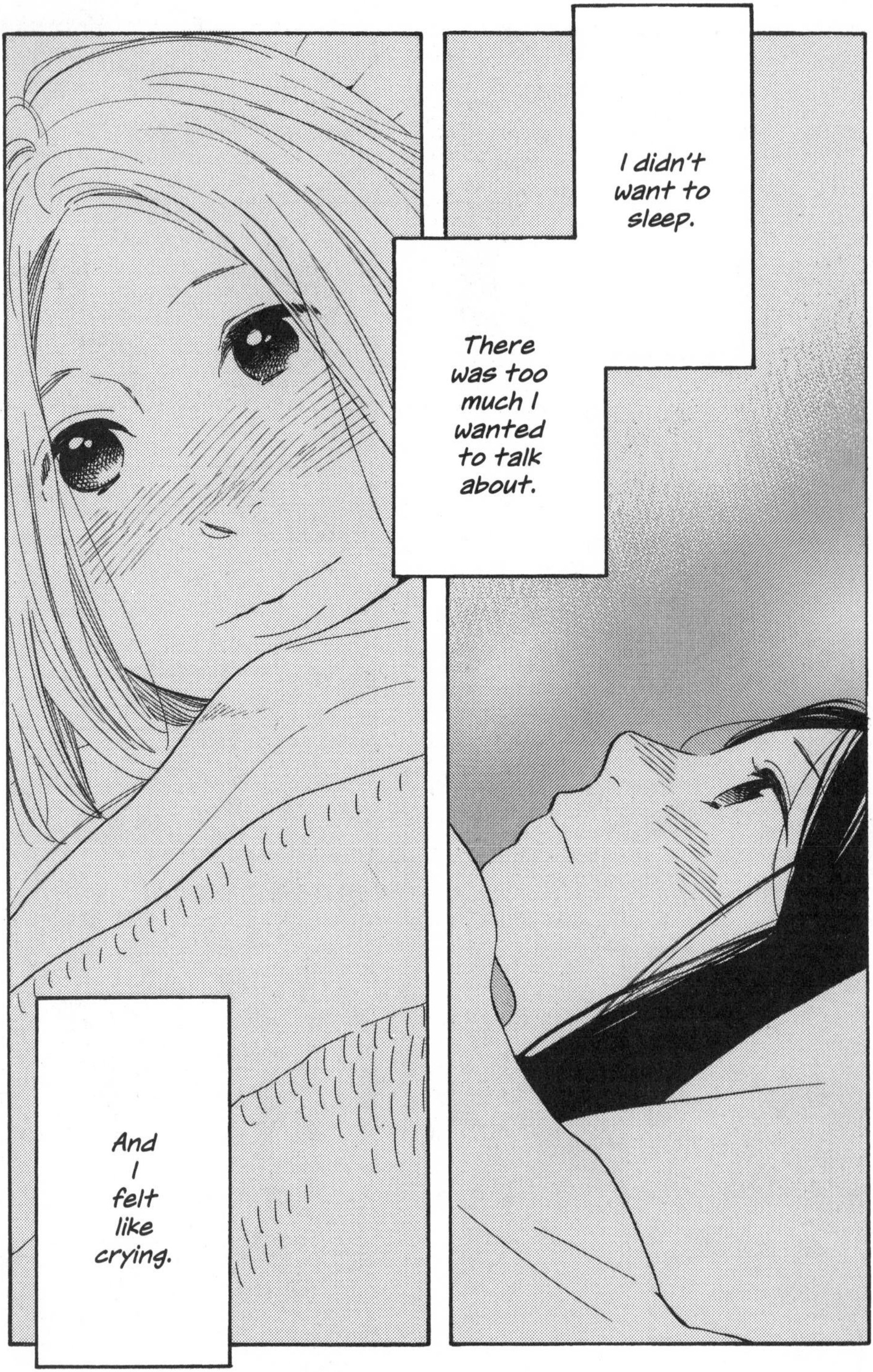
I didn't want to sleep.
There was too much I wanted to talk about.
And I felt like crying.

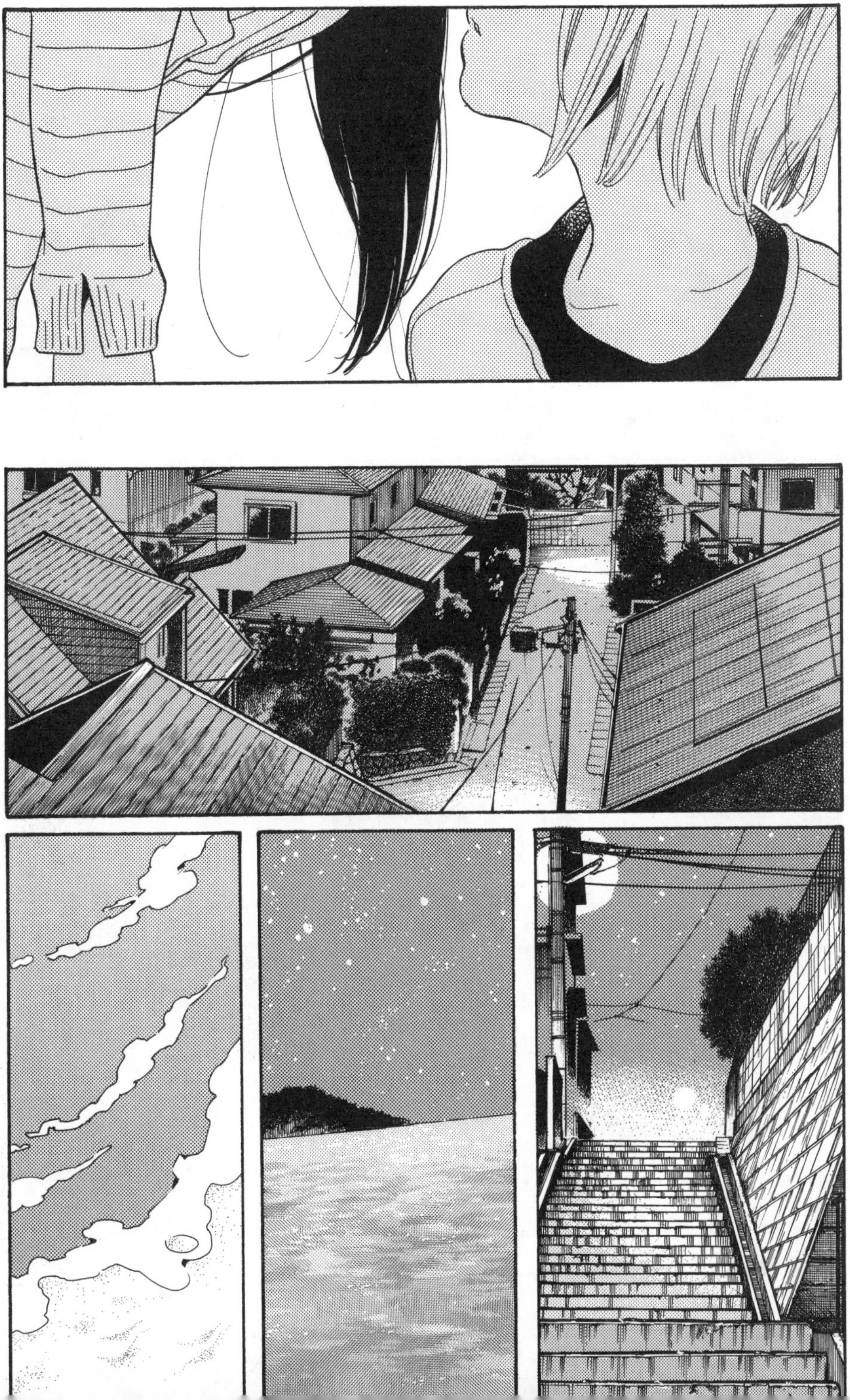

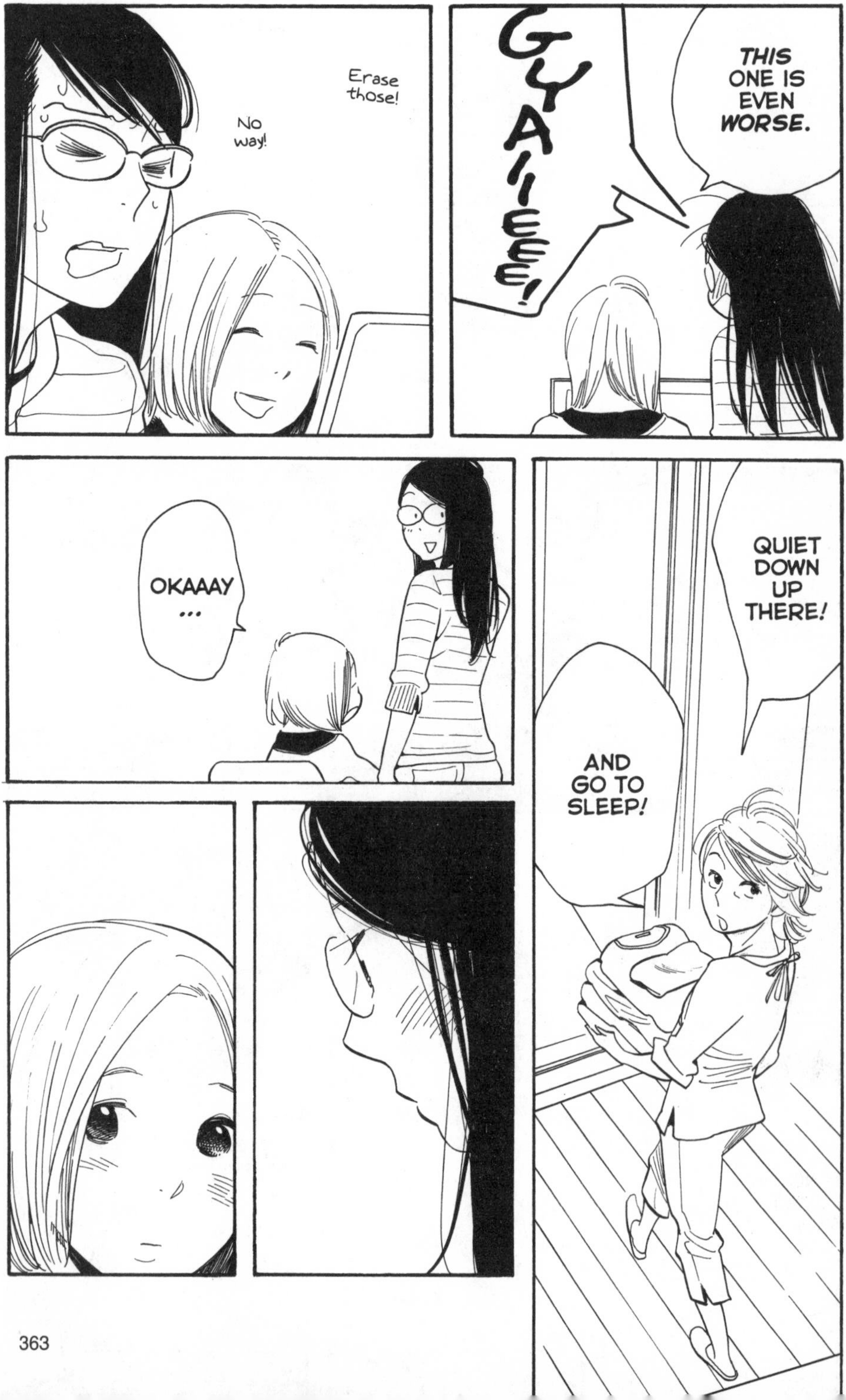
THIS ONE IS EVEN WORSE.
GYAIIEEE!
Erase those!
No way!
QUIET DOWN UP THERE!
AND GO TO SLEEP!
OKAAAY ...

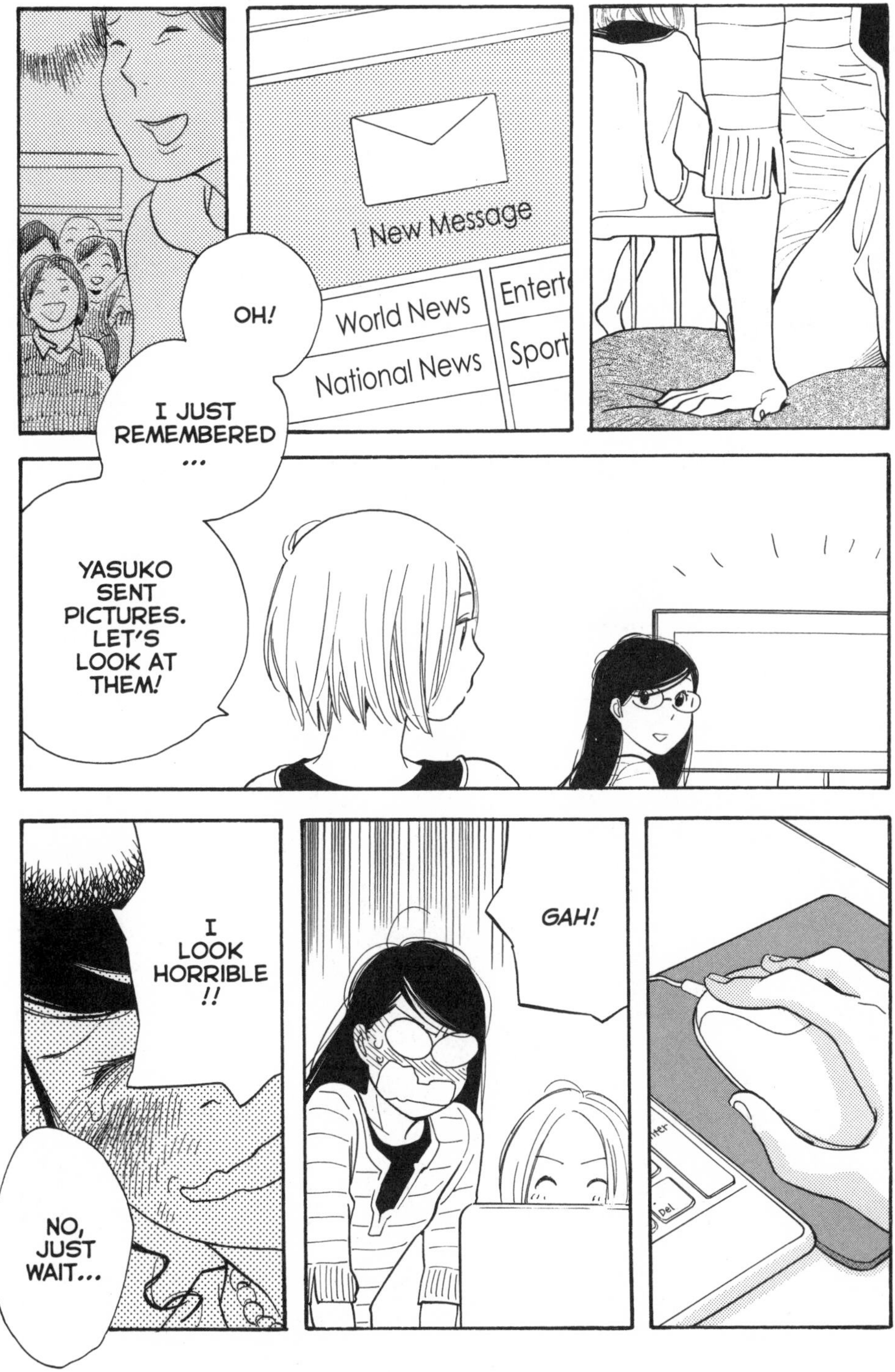
1 New Message
World News
National News
OH!
I JUST REMEMBERED...
YASUKO SENT PICTURES. LET'S LOOK AT THEM!
GAH!
I LOOK HORRIBLE!!
NO, JUST WAIT...

...they would shine a light into my future.

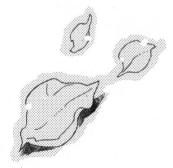

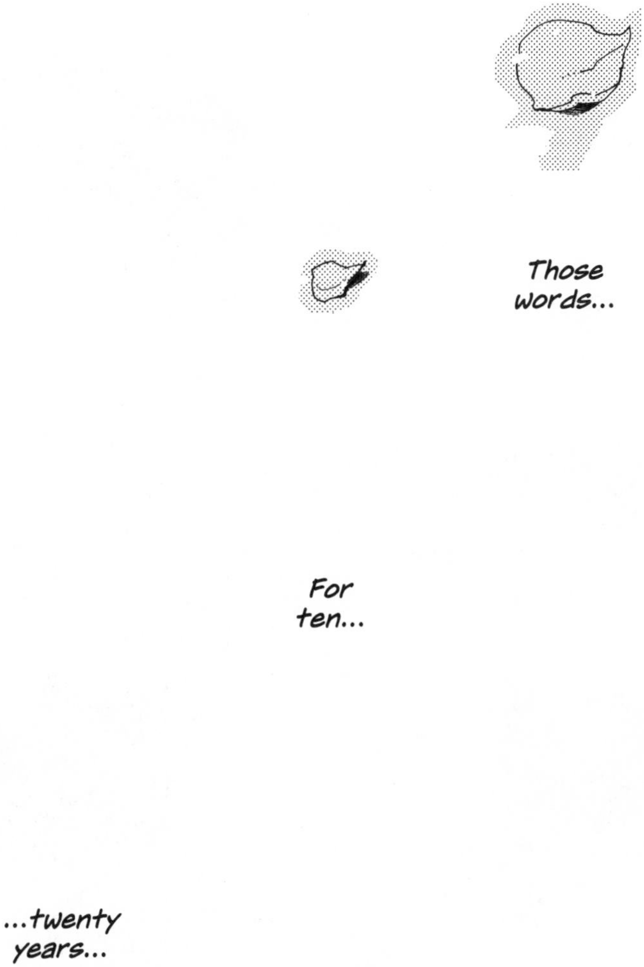
Those words...
For ten...
...twenty years...

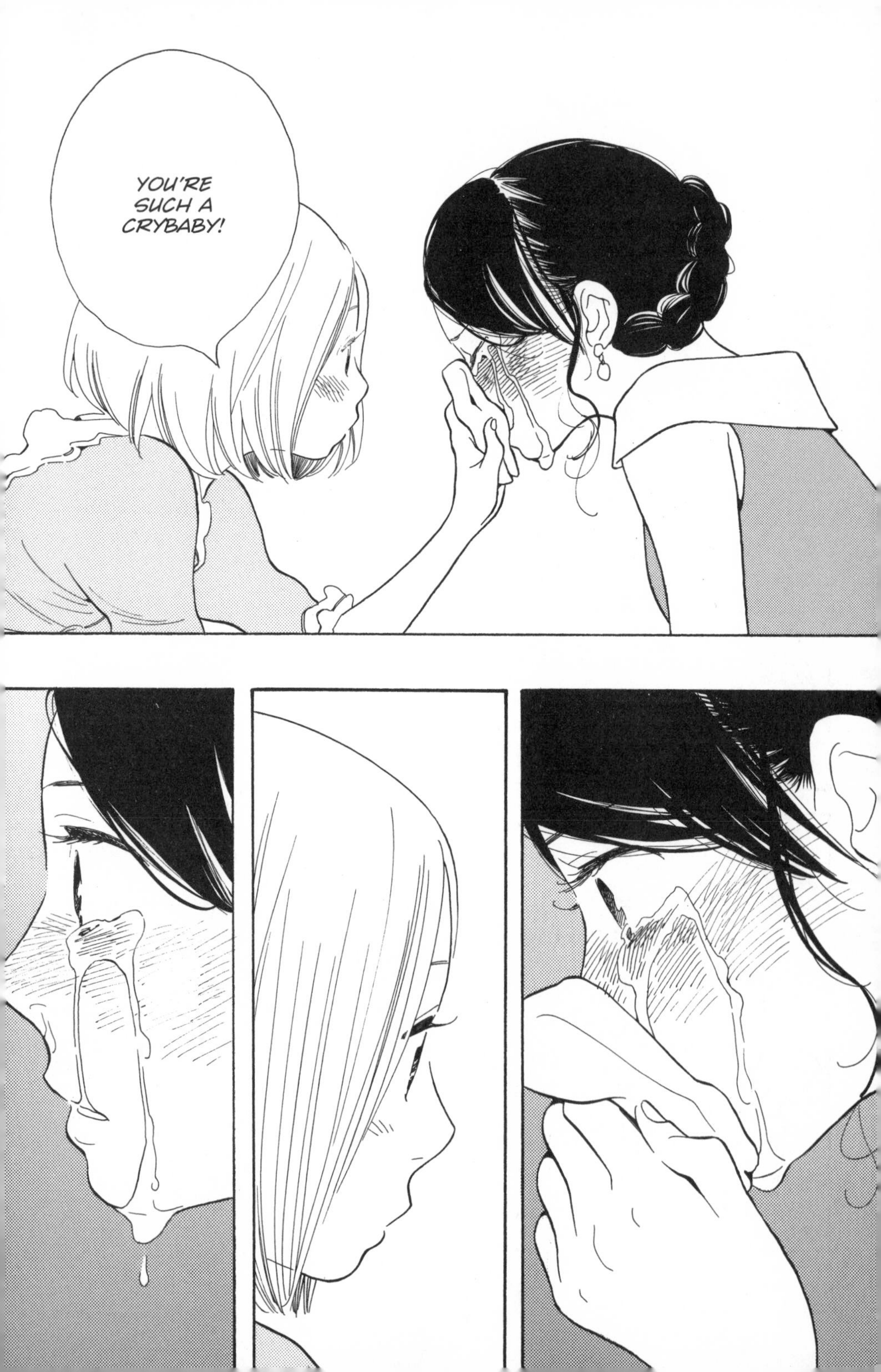
YOU'RE SUCH A CRYBABY!

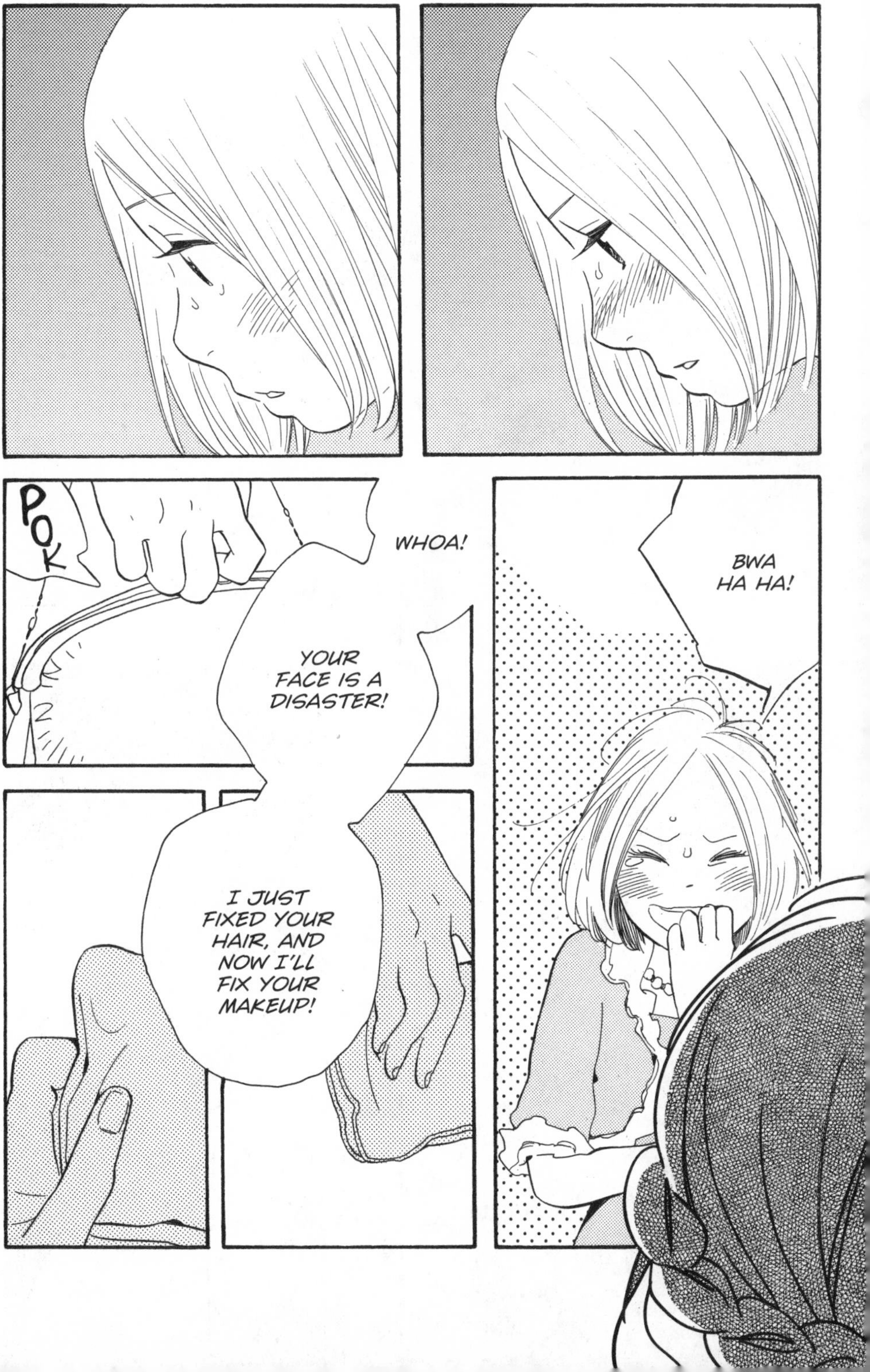
BWA HA HA!
WHOA!
POK
YOUR FACE IS A DISASTER!
I JUST FIXED YOUR HAIR, AND NOW I'LL FIX YOUR MAKEUP!

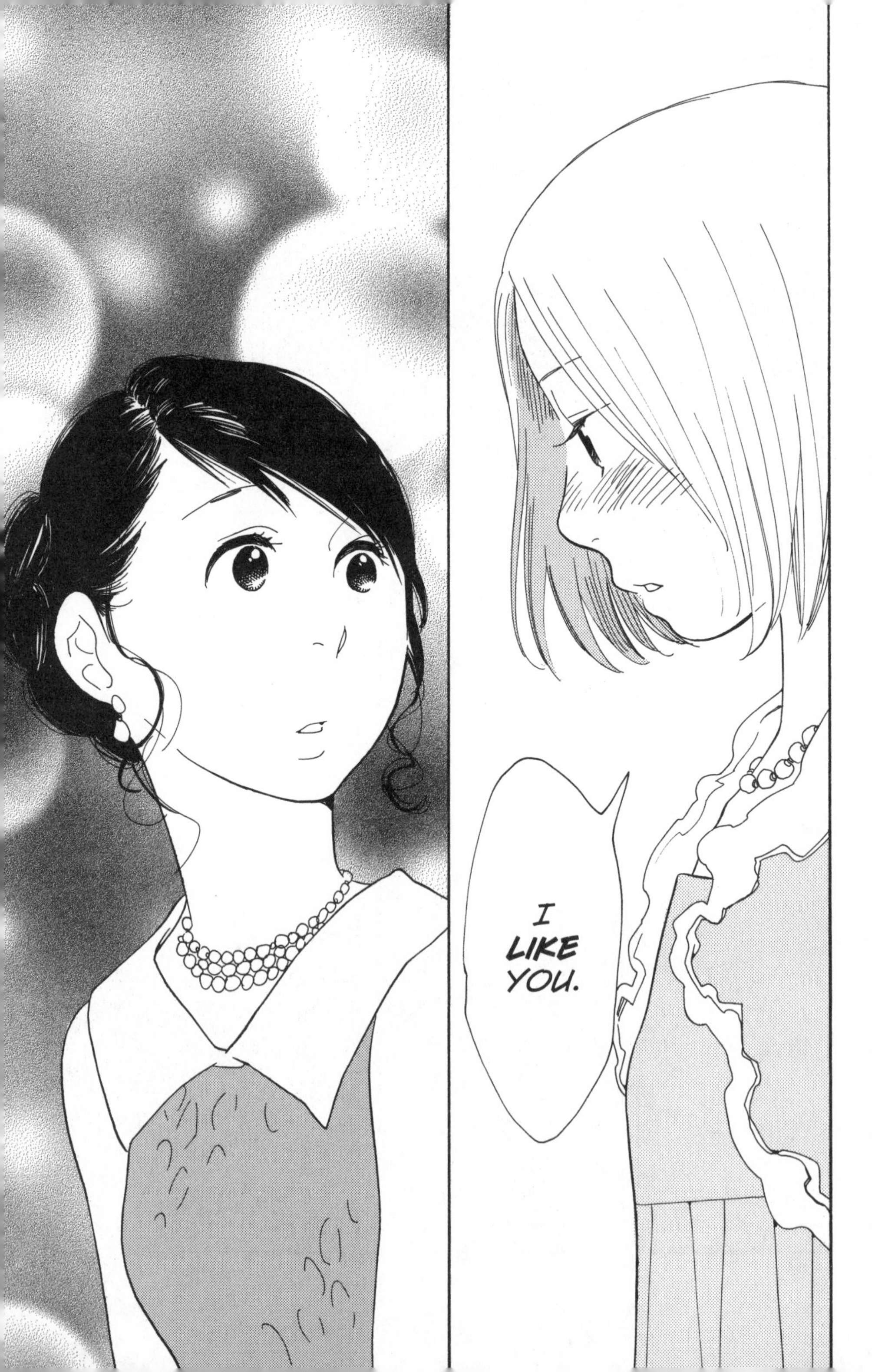
I LIKE YOU.

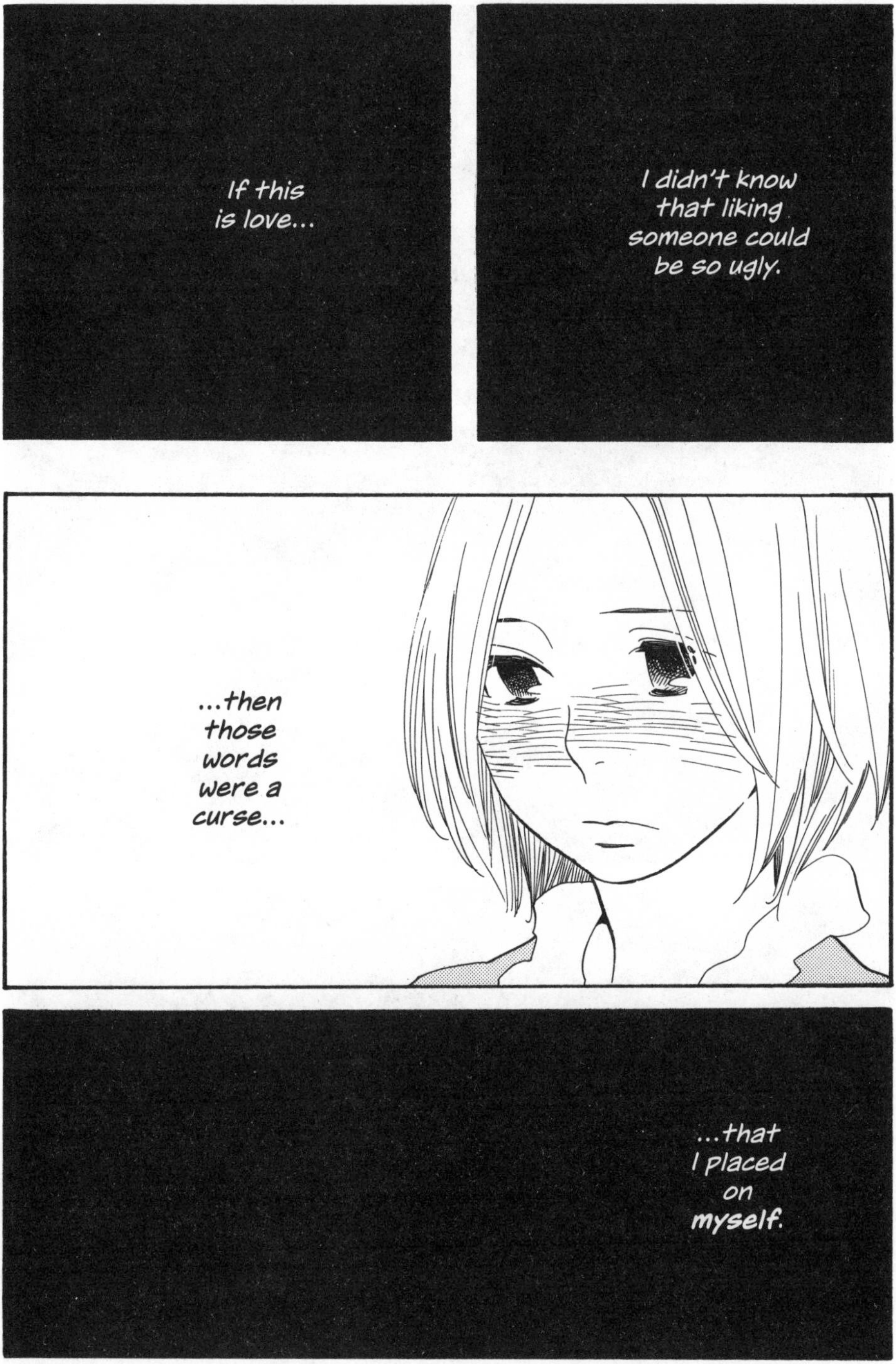
I didn't know that liking someone could be so ugly.
If this is love...
...then those words were a curse...
...that I placed on myself.

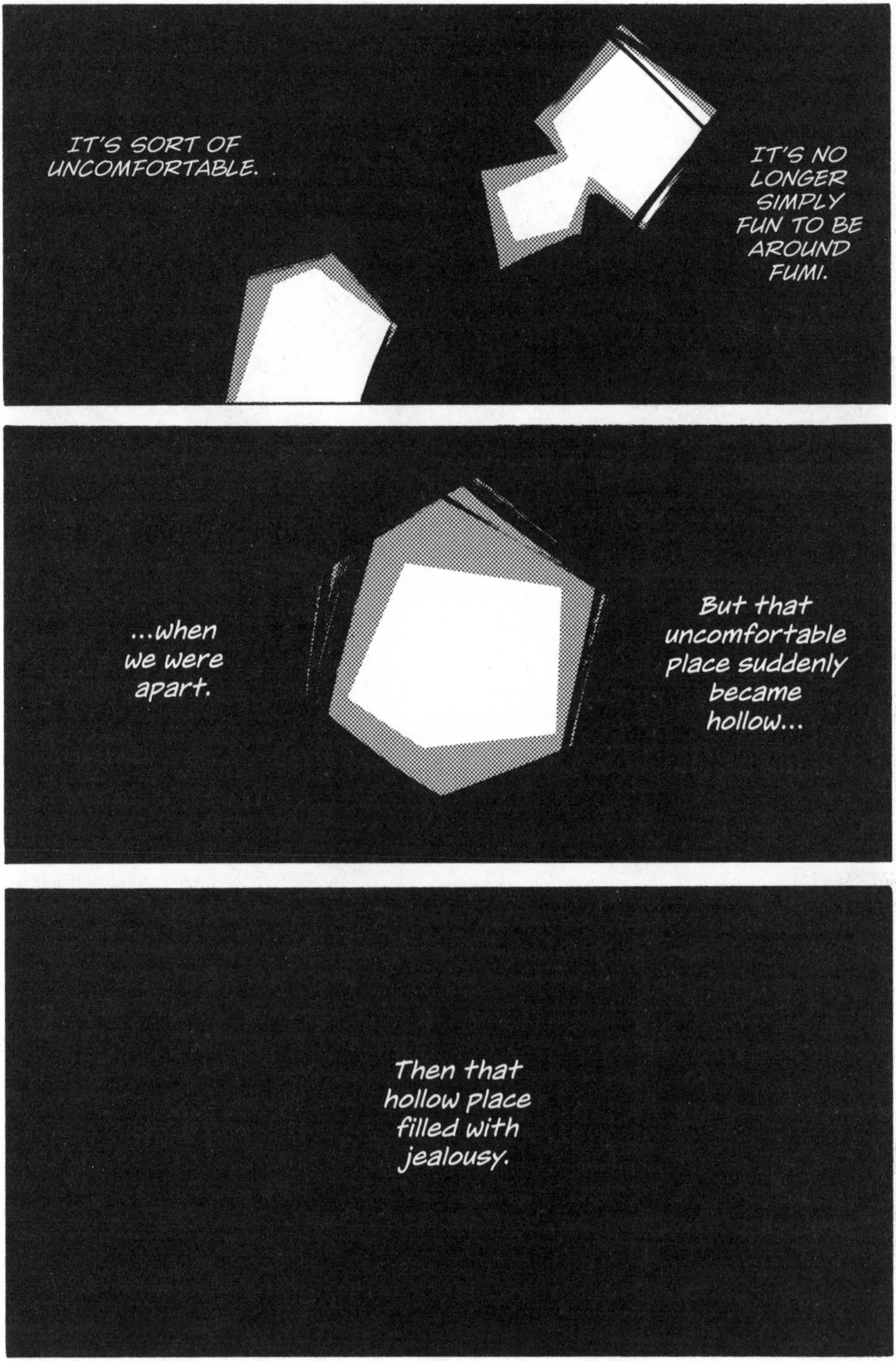
IT'S NO LONGER SIMPLY FUN TO BE AROUND FUMI.
IT'S SORT OF UNCOMFORTABLE.
But that uncomfortable place suddenly became hollow...
...when we were apart.
Then that hollow place filled with jealousy.

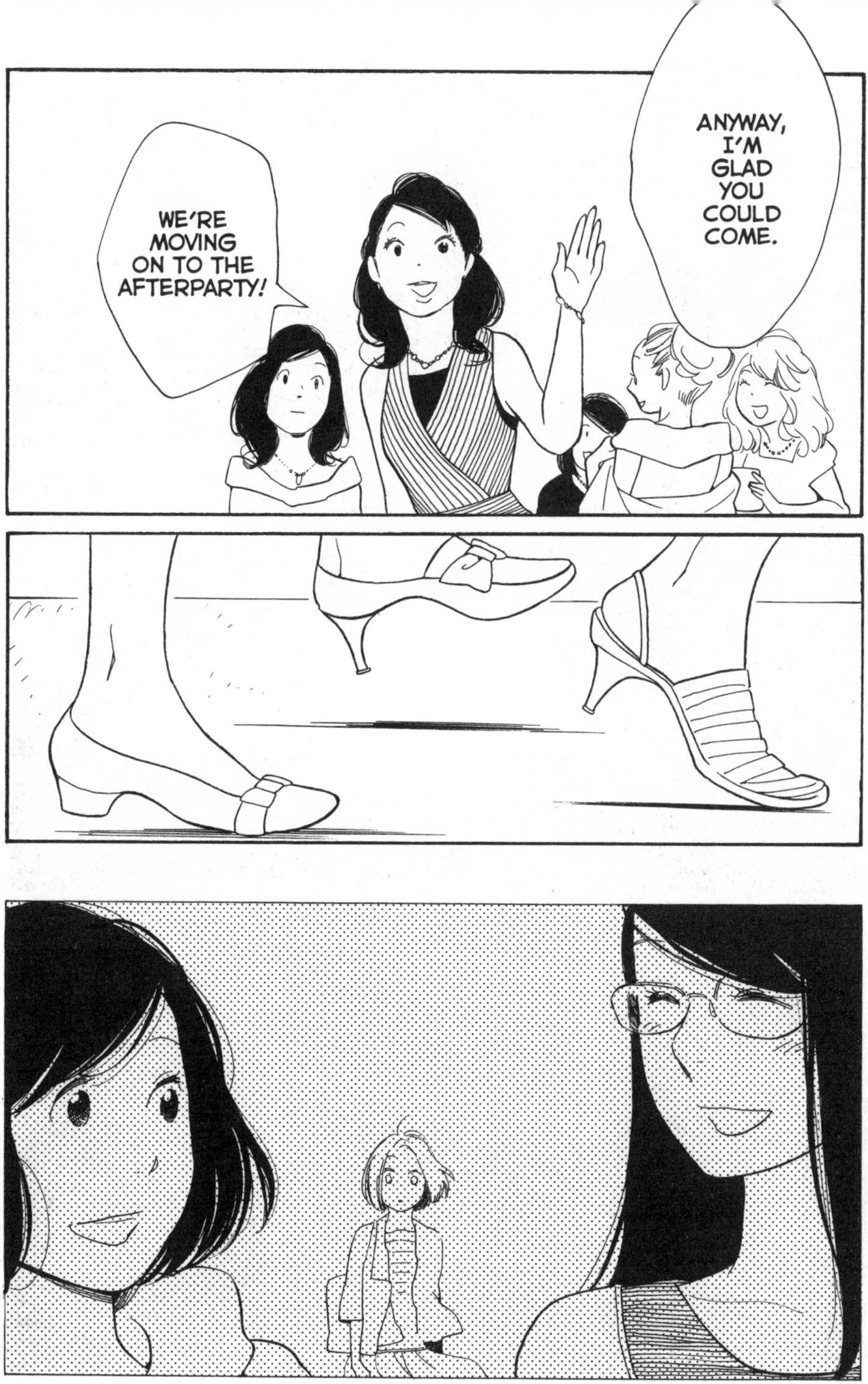
ANYWAY, I'M GLAD YOU COULD COME.
WE'RE MOVING ON TO THE AFTERPARTY!

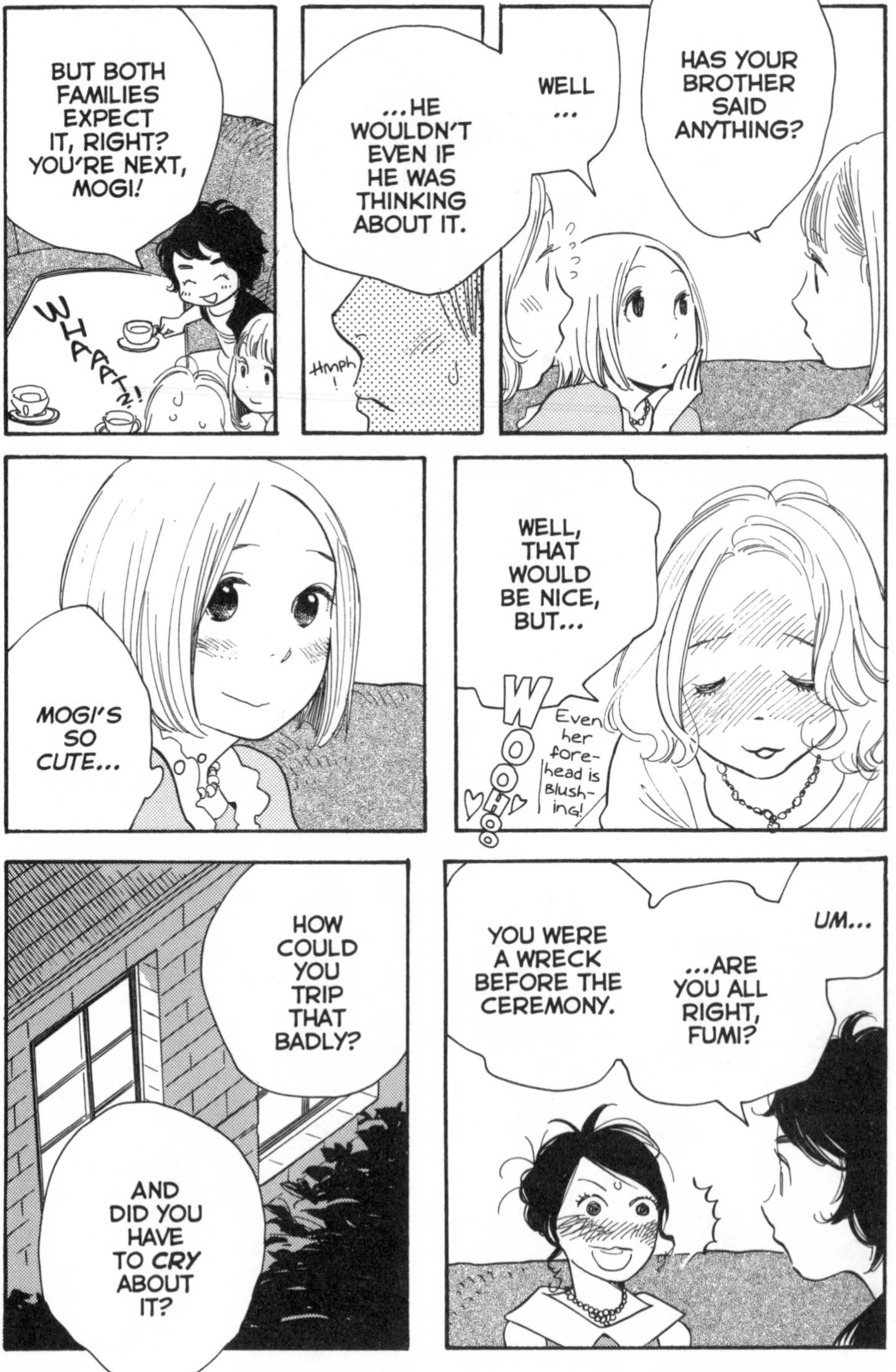
HAS YOUR BROTHER SAID ANYTHING?
WELL ...
...HE WOULDN'T EVEN IF HE WAS THINKING ABOUT IT.
Hmph!
BUT BOTH FAMILIES EXPECT IT, RIGHT? YOU'RE NEXT, MOGI!
WHAAA?!
WELL, THAT WOULD BE NICE, BUT...
WOOHOO
Even her fore-head is blush-ing!
MOGI'S SO CUTE...
UM...
...ARE YOU ALL RIGHT, FUMI?
YOU WERE A WRECK BEFORE THE CEREMONY.
HOW COULD YOU TRIP THAT BADLY?
AND DID YOU HAVE TO CRY ABOUT IT?

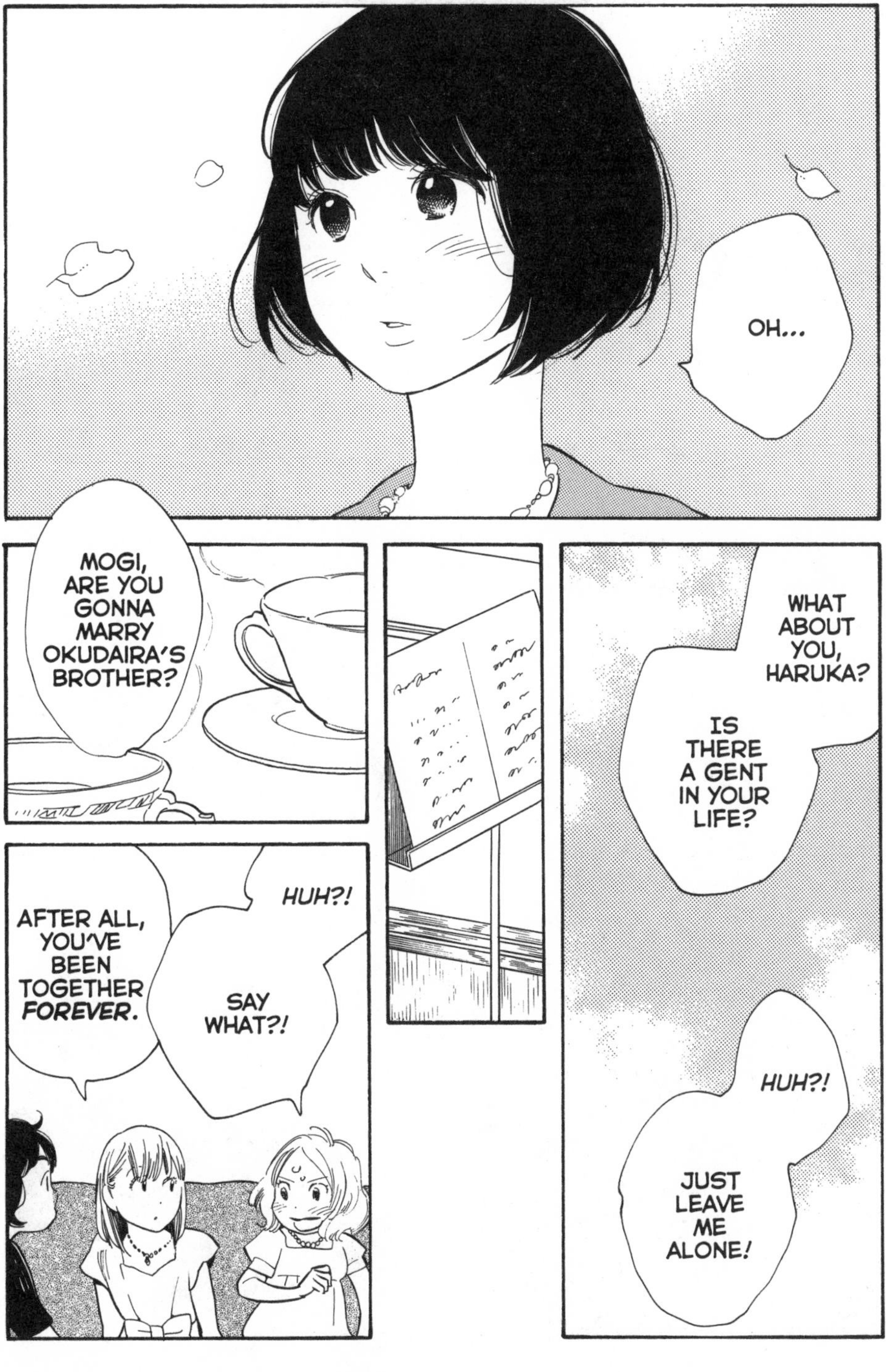
OH...
WHAT ABOUT YOU, HARUKA?
IS THERE A GENT IN YOUR LIFE?
HUH?!
JUST LEAVE ME ALONE!
MOGI, ARE YOU GONNA MARRY OKUDAIRA'S BROTHER?
HUH?!
SAY WHAT?!
AFTER ALL, YOU'VE BEEN TOGETHER *FOREVER*.

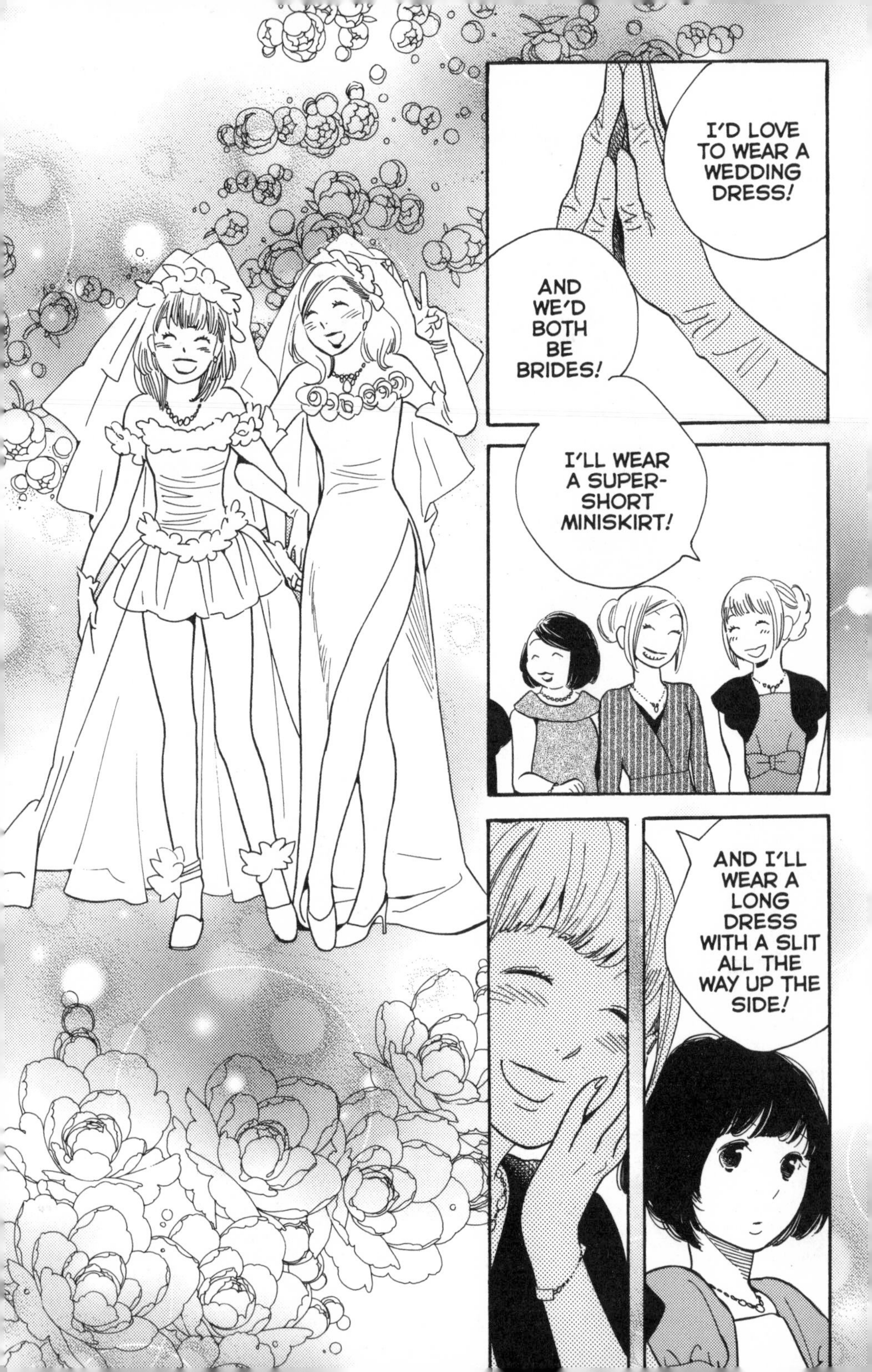
I'D LOVE TO WEAR A WEDDING DRESS!
AND WE'D BOTH BE BRIDES!
I'LL WEAR A SUPER-SHORT MINISKIRT!
AND I'LL WEAR A LONG DRESS WITH A SLIT ALL THE WAY UP THE SIDE!

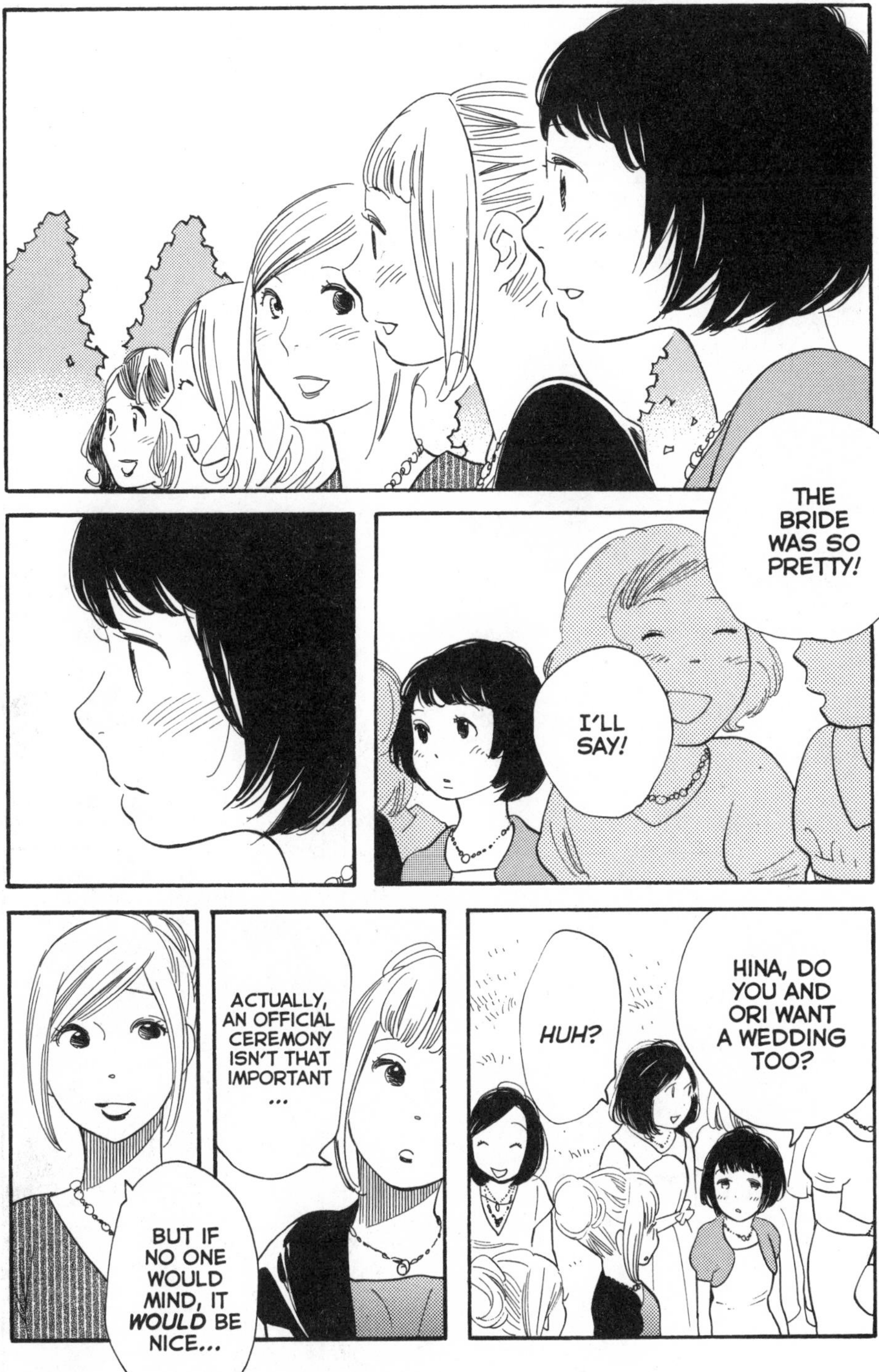
THE BRIDE WAS SO PRETTY!
I'LL SAY!
HINA, DO YOU AND ORI WANT A WEDDING TOO?
HUH?
ACTUALLY, AN OFFICIAL CEREMONY ISN'T THAT IMPORTANT...
BUT IF NO ONE WOULD MIND, IT *WOULD* BE NICE...

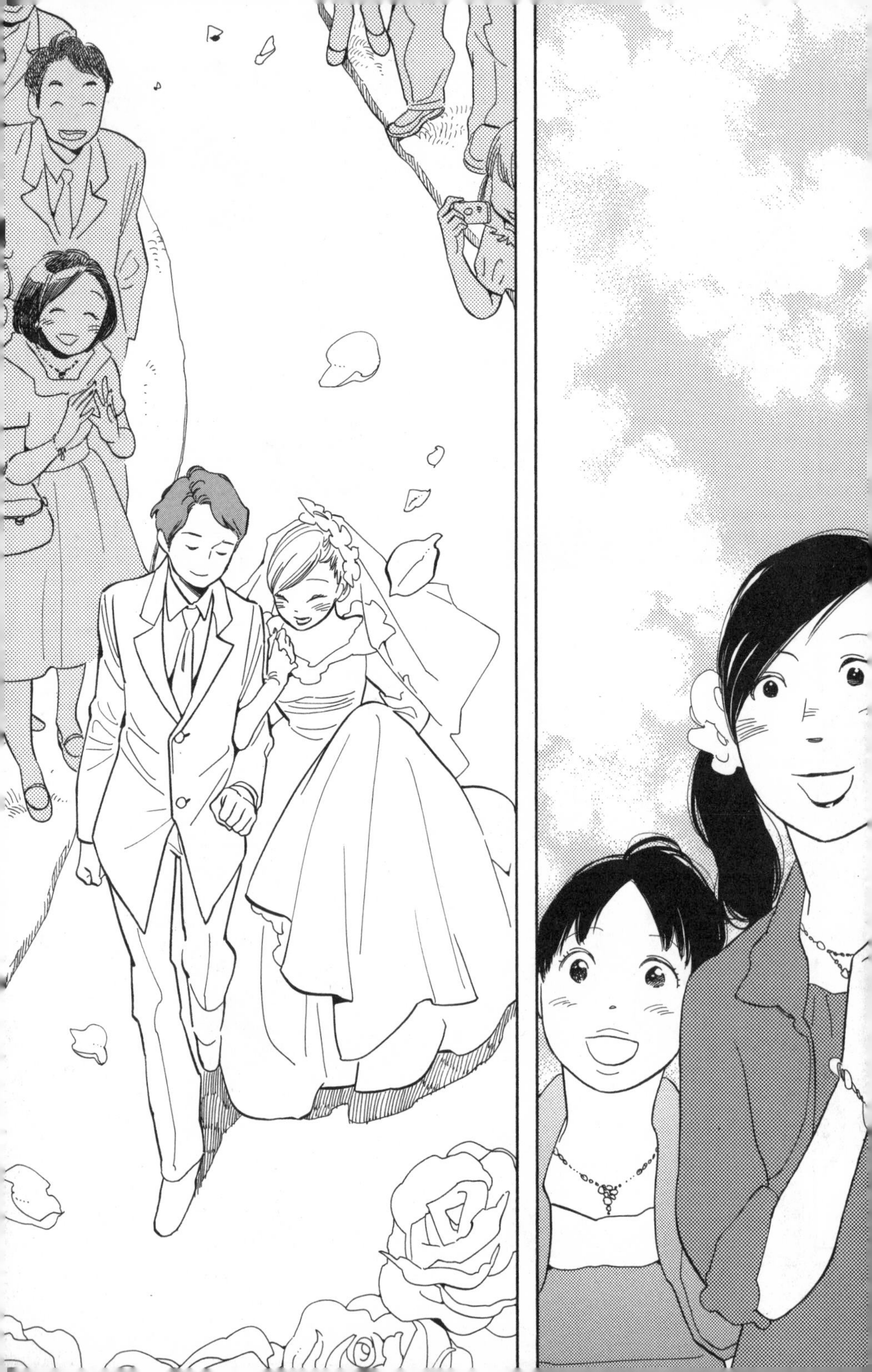

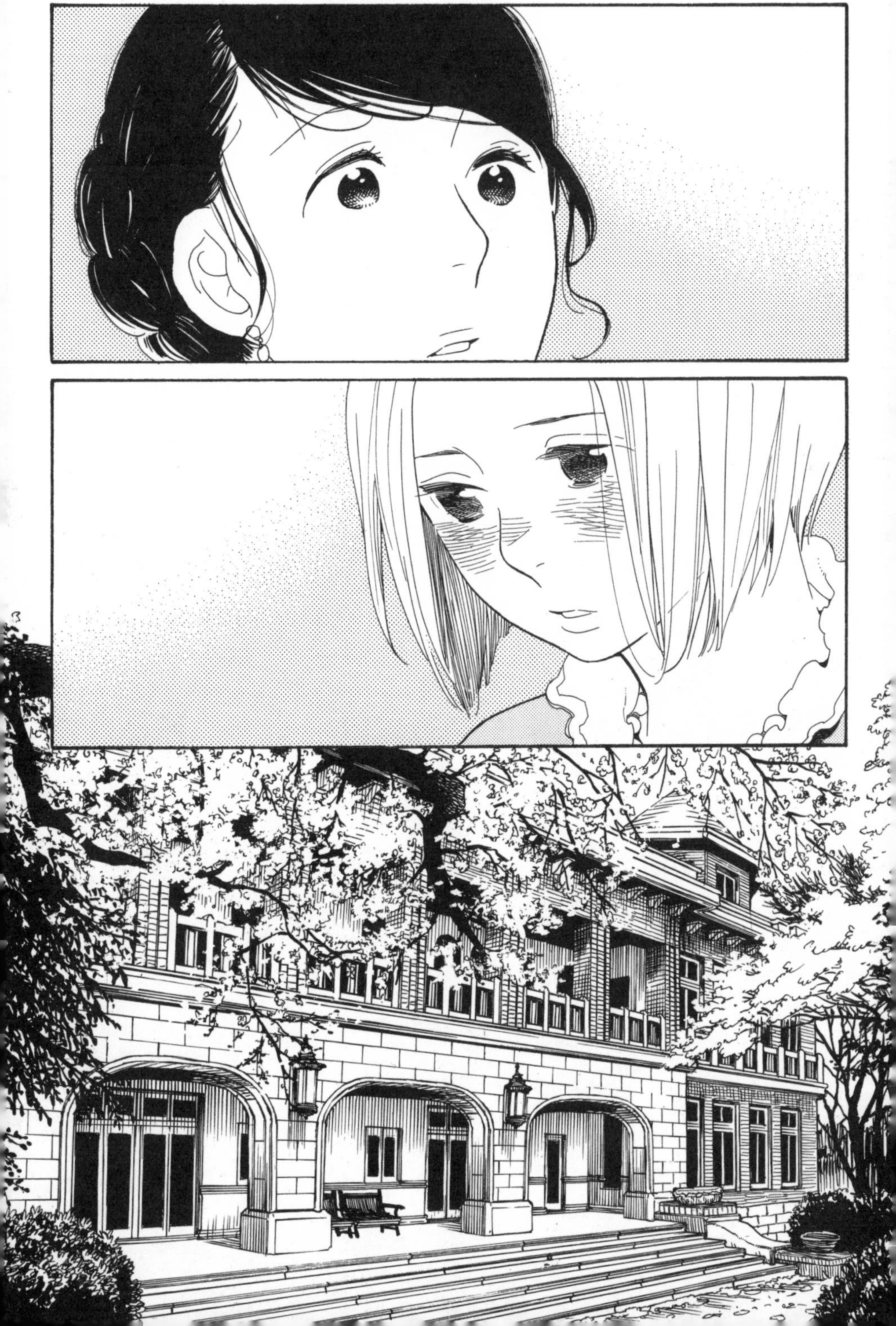

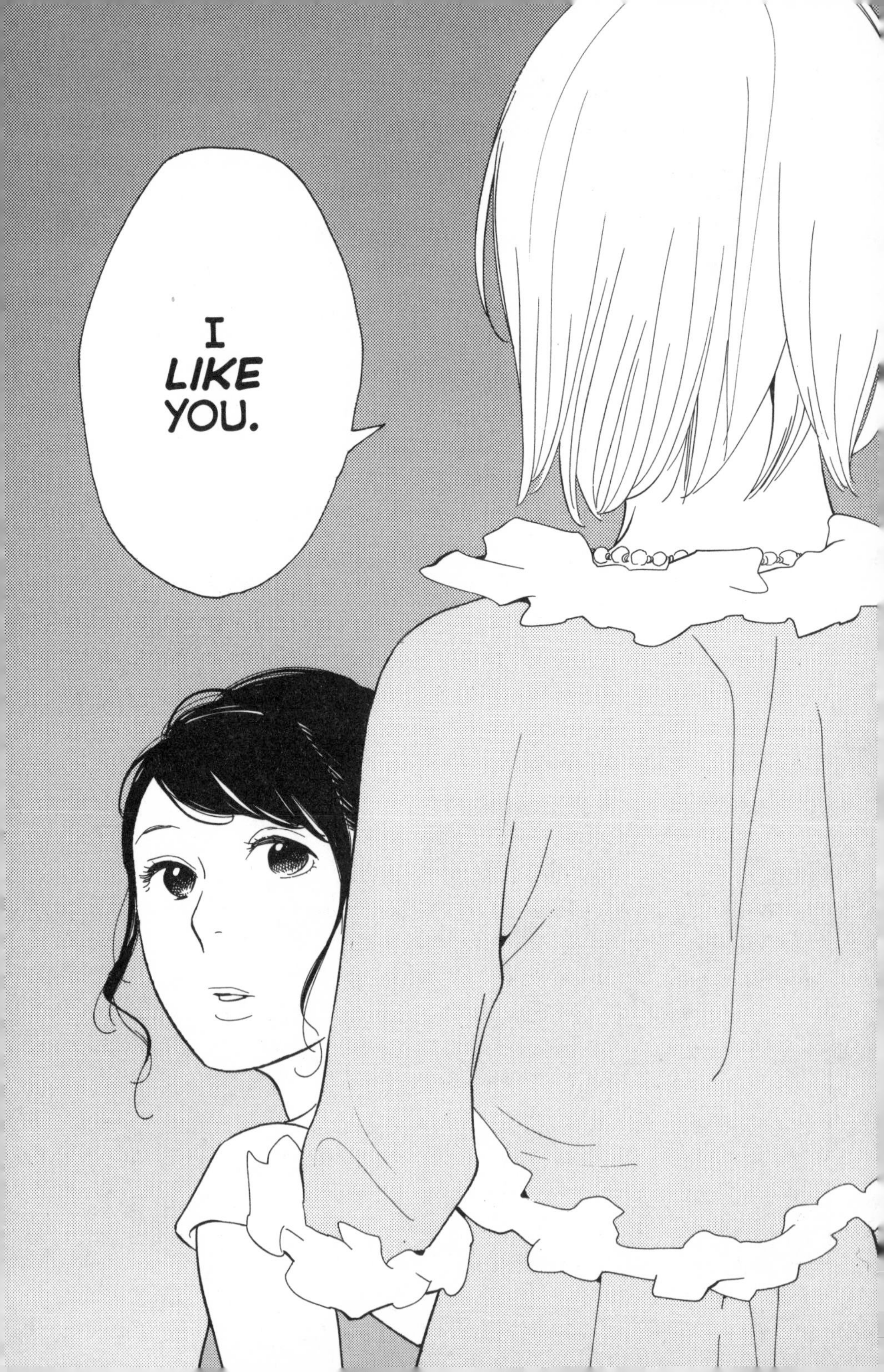
I *LIKE* YOU.

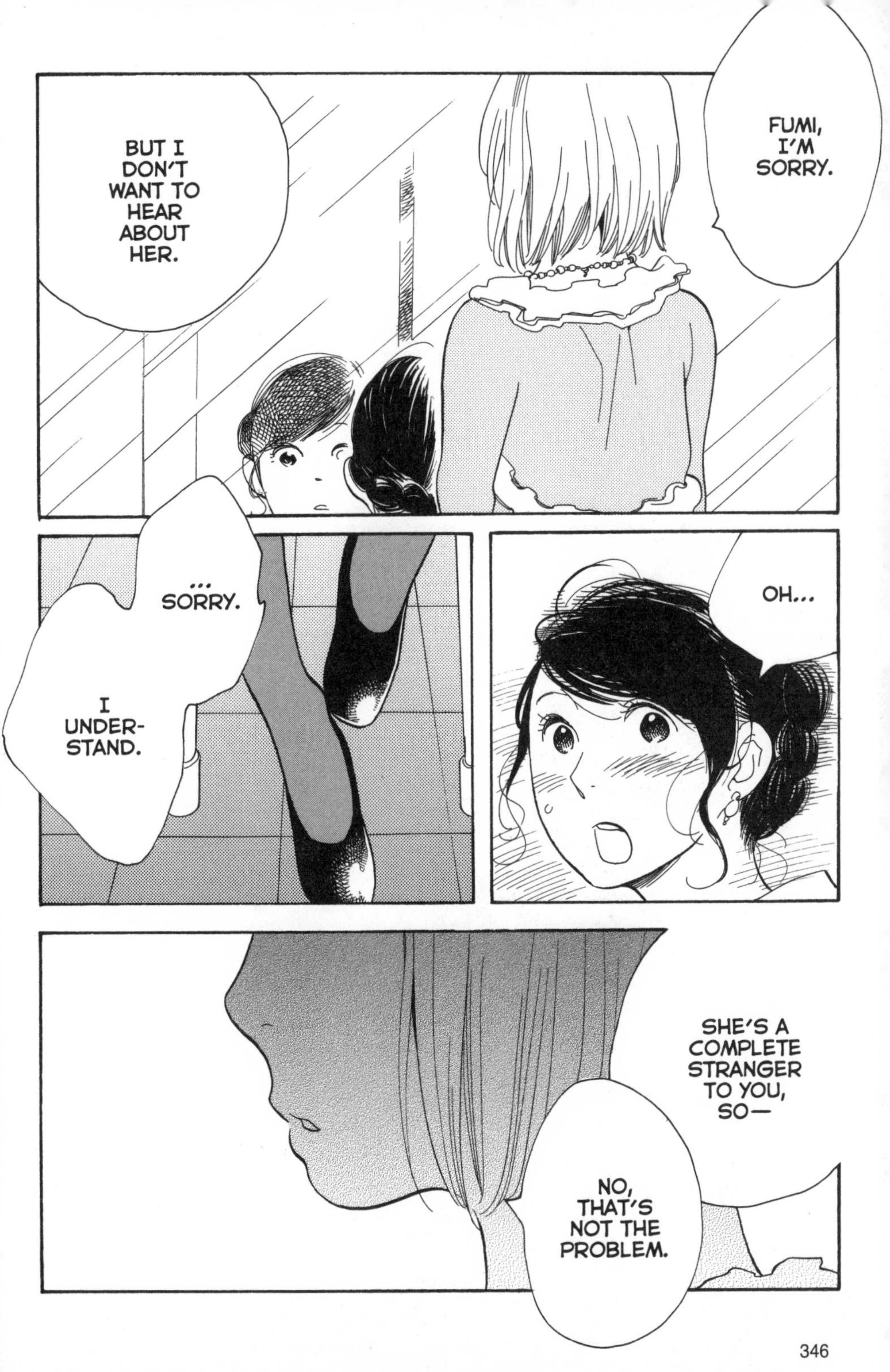
FUMI, I'M SORRY.
BUT I DON'T WANT TO HEAR ABOUT HER.
OH...
...SORRY.
I UNDERSTAND.
SHE'S A COMPLETE STRANGER TO YOU, SO—
NO, THAT'S NOT THE PROBLEM.

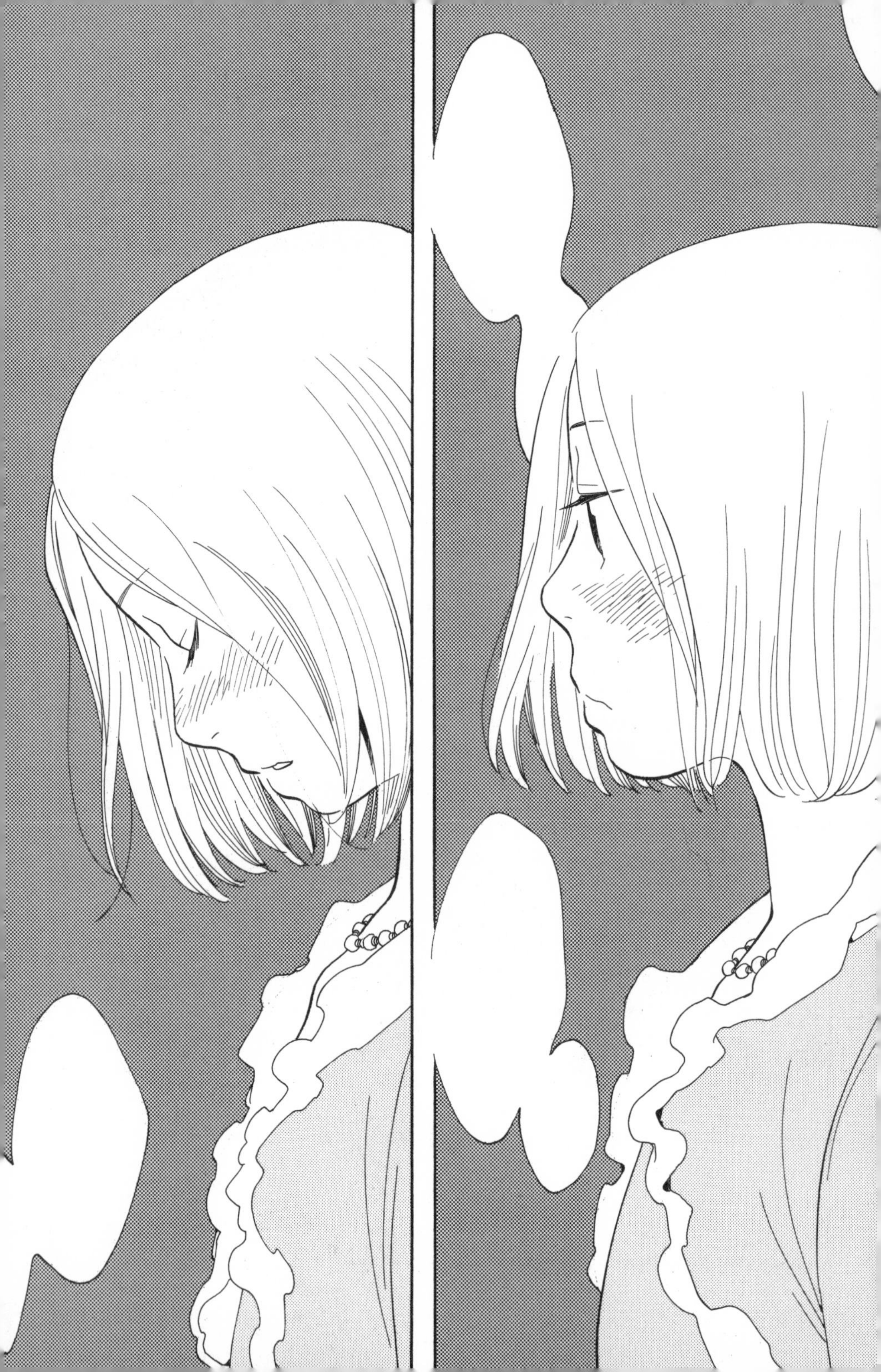

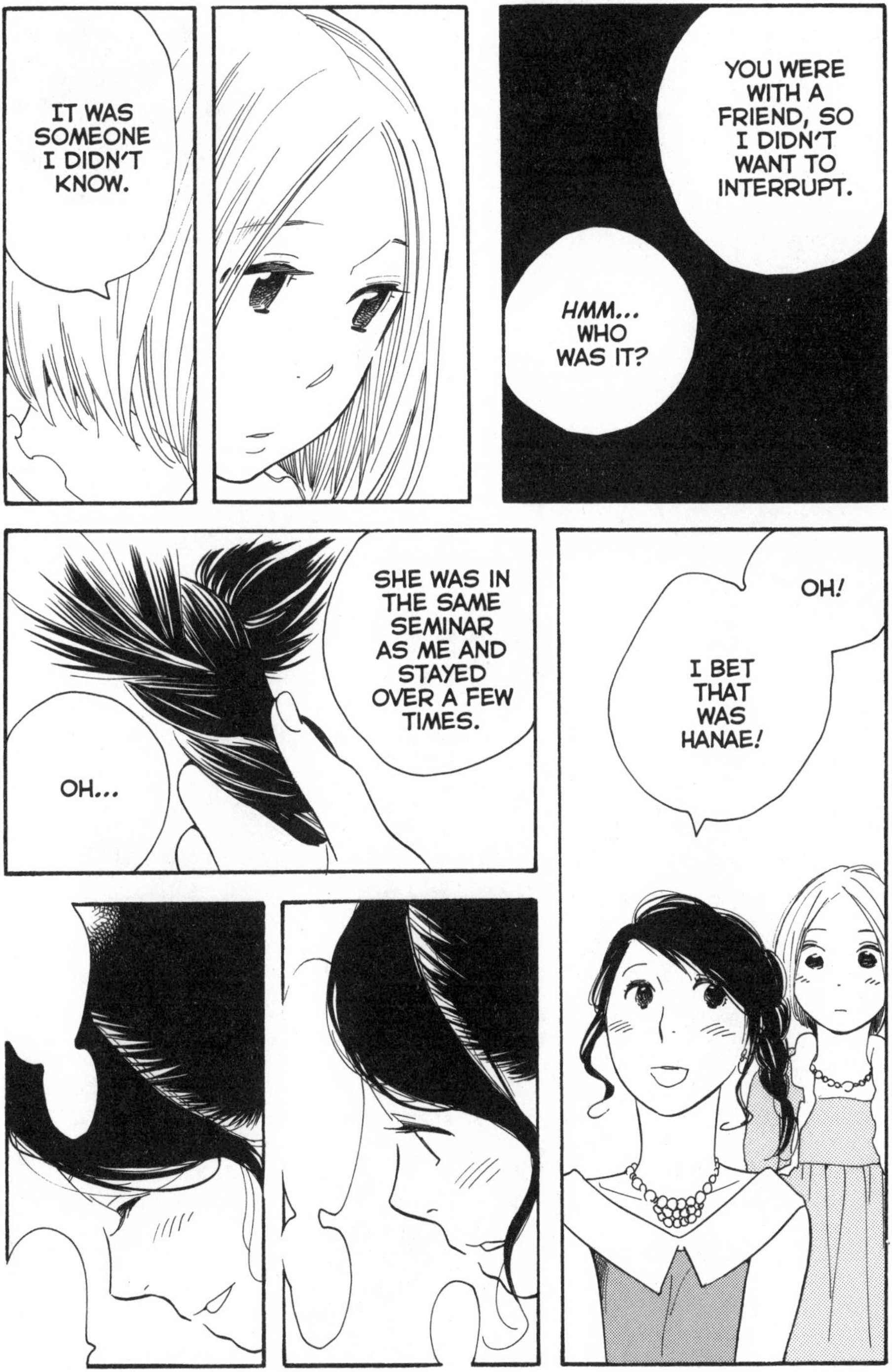
YOU WERE WITH A FRIEND, SO I DIDN'T WANT TO INTERRUPT.
HMM... WHO WAS IT?
IT WAS SOMEONE I DIDN'T KNOW.
OH!
I BET THAT WAS HANAE!
SHE WAS IN THE SAME SEMINAR AS ME AND STAYED OVER A FEW TIMES.
OH...

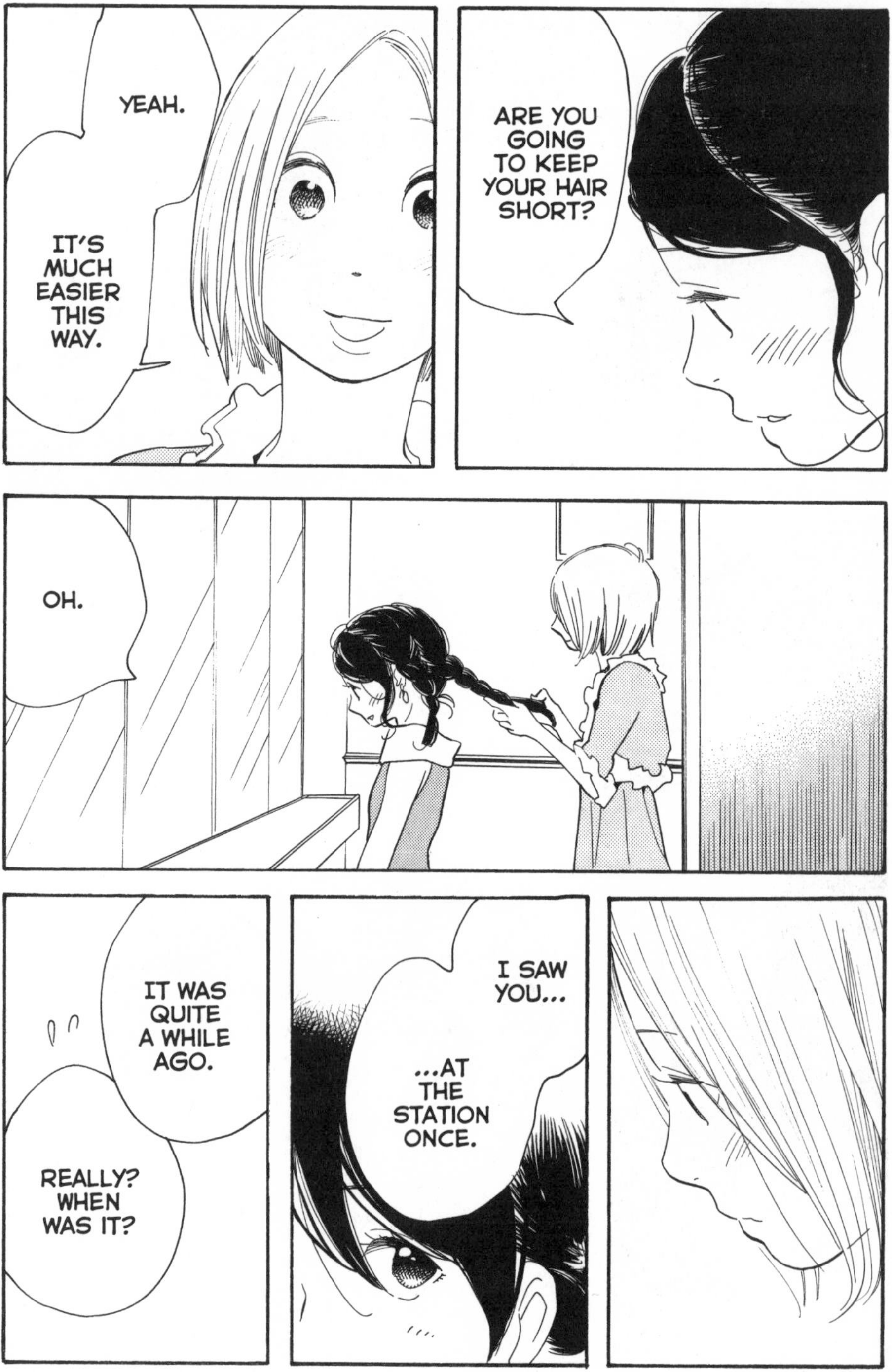
ARE YOU GOING TO KEEP YOUR HAIR SHORT?
YEAH.
IT'S MUCH EASIER THIS WAY.
OH.
I SAW YOU...
...AT THE STATION ONCE.
IT WAS QUITE A WHILE AGO.
REALLY? WHEN WAS IT?

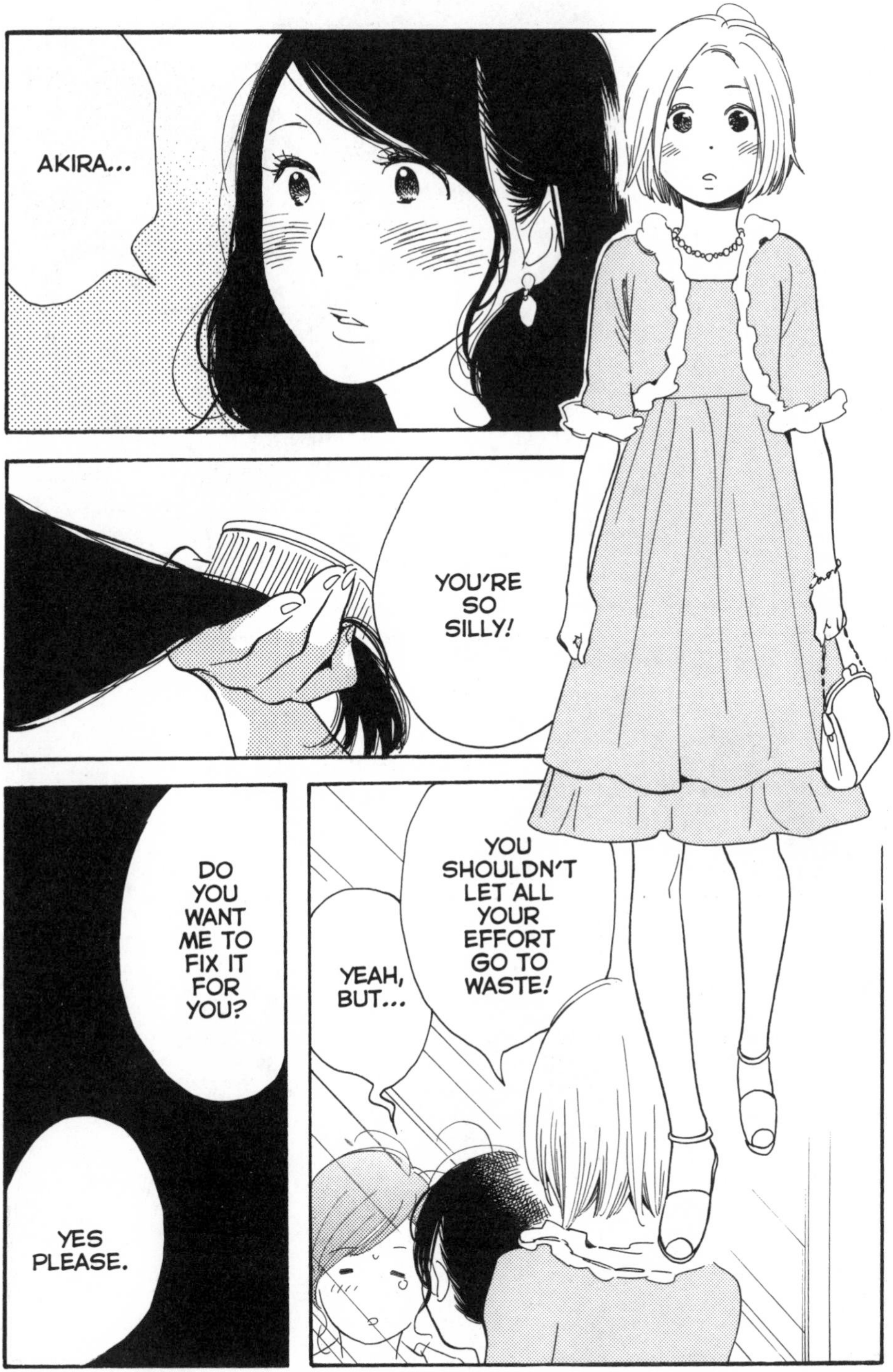
AKIRA...
YOU'RE SO SILLY!
YOU SHOULDN'T LET ALL YOUR EFFORT GO TO WASTE!
YEAH, BUT...
DO YOU WANT ME TO FIX IT FOR YOU?
YES PLEASE.

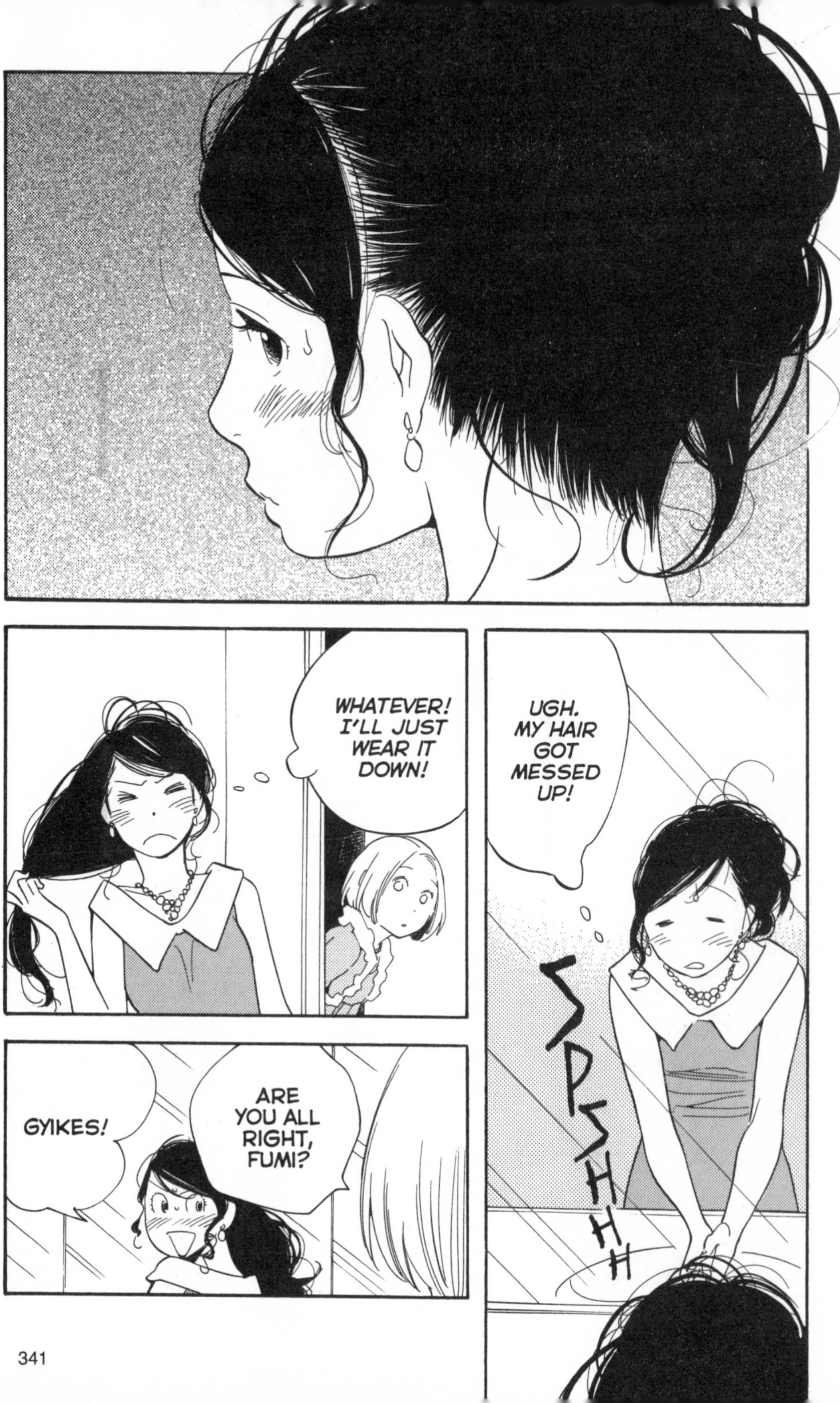
UGH. MY HAIR GOT MESSED UP!
SPSHHH
WHATEVER! I'LL JUST WEAR IT DOWN!
ARE YOU ALL RIGHT, FUMI?
GYIKES!

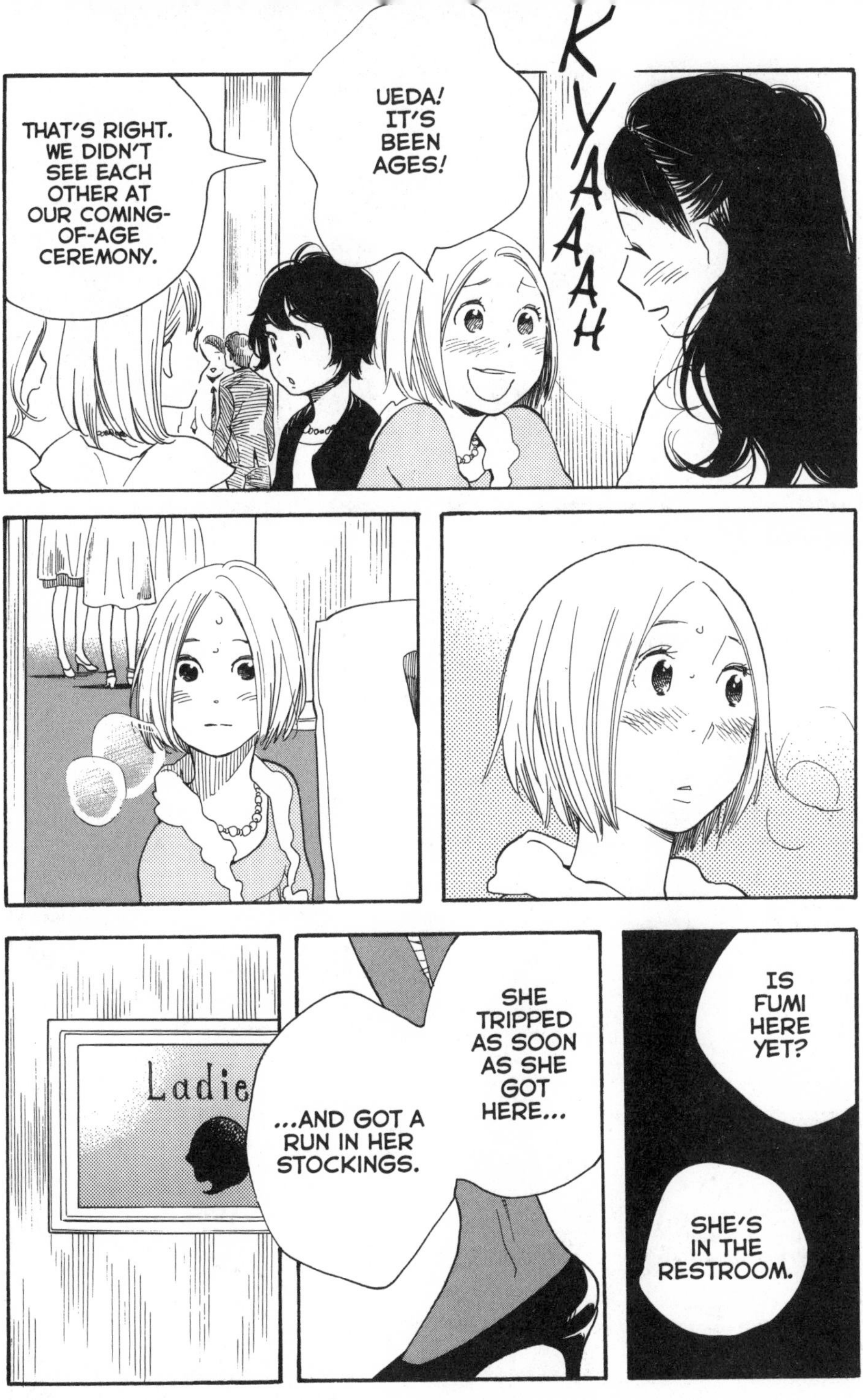
KYAAAAH
UEDA! IT'S BEEN AGES!
THAT'S RIGHT. WE DIDN'T SEE EACH OTHER AT OUR COMING-OF-AGE CEREMONY.
IS FUMI HERE YET?
SHE'S IN THE RESTROOM.
SHE TRIPPED AS SOON AS SHE GOT HERE...
...AND GOT A RUN IN HER STOCKINGS.
Ladie

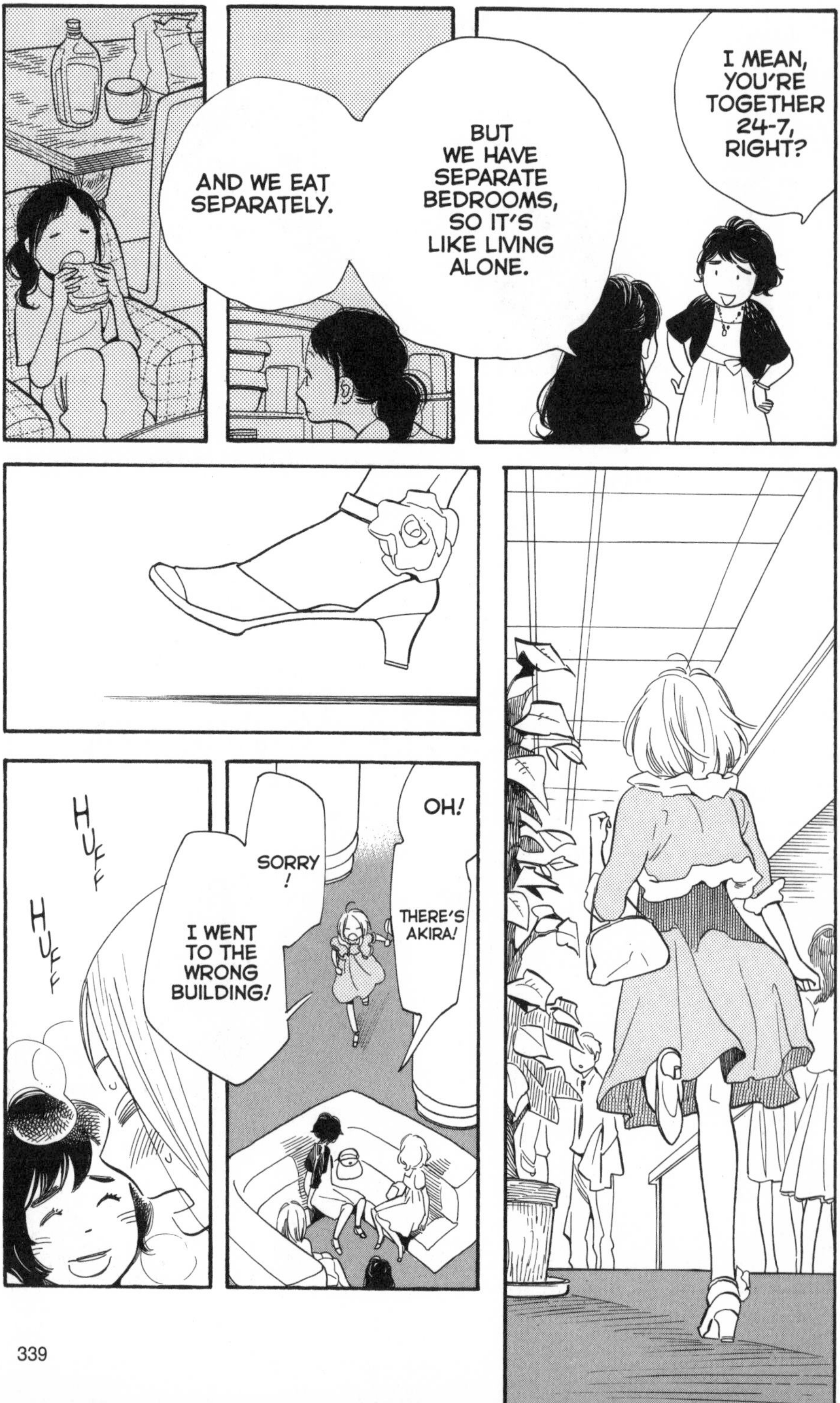
I MEAN, YOU'RE TOGETHER 24-7, RIGHT?
BUT WE HAVE SEPARATE BEDROOMS, SO IT'S LIKE LIVING ALONE.
AND WE EAT SEPARATELY.
OH!
THERE'S AKIRA!
SORRY!
I WENT TO THE WRONG BUILDING!
HUFF
HUFF

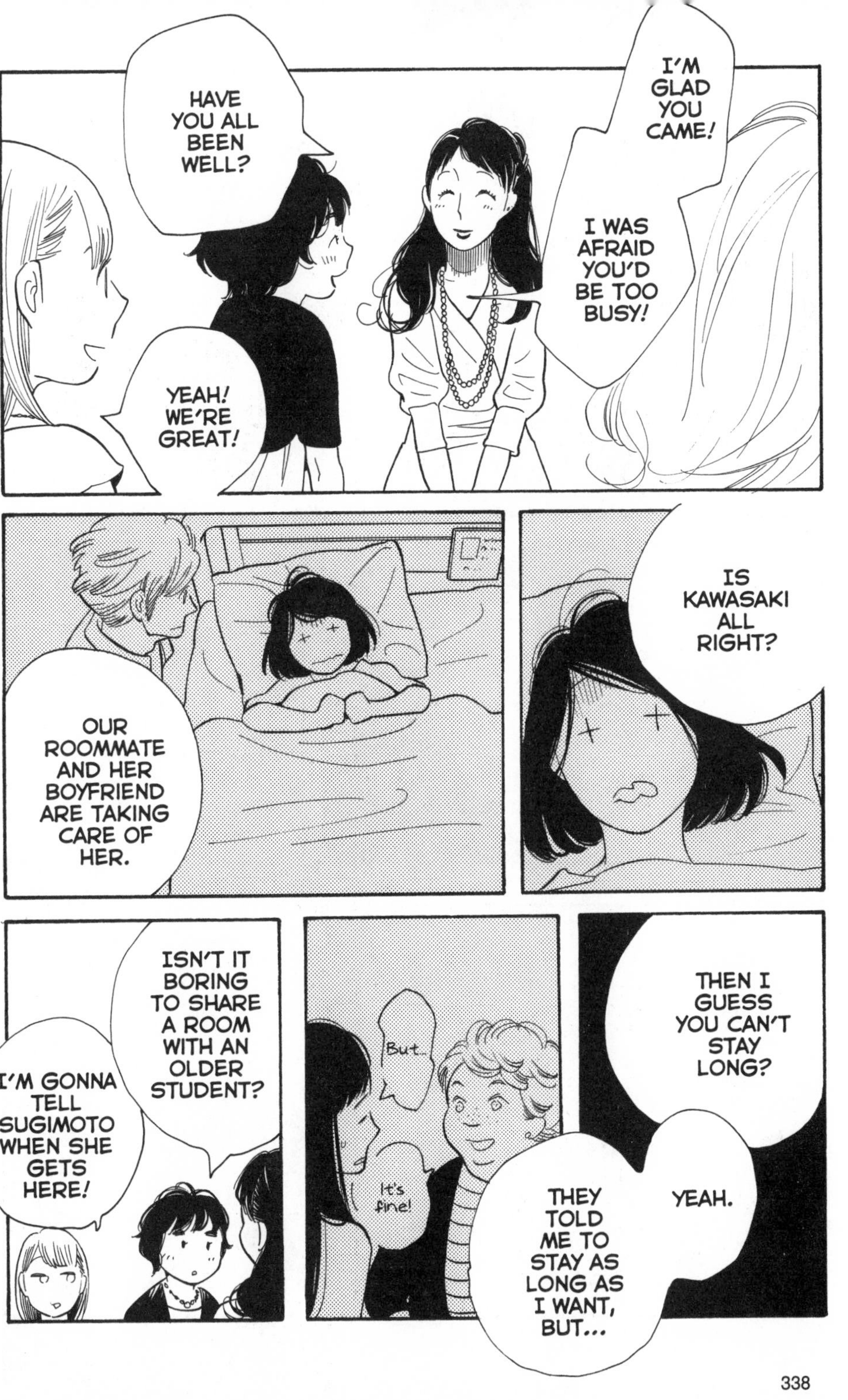
I'M GLAD YOU CAME! I WAS AFRAID YOU'D BE TOO BUSY!
HAVE YOU ALL BEEN WELL?
YEAH! WE'RE GREAT!
IS KAWASAKI ALL RIGHT?
OUR ROOMMATE AND HER BOYFRIEND ARE TAKING CARE OF HER.
THEN I GUESS YOU CAN'T STAY LONG?
YEAH.
THEY TOLD ME TO STAY AS LONG AS I WANT, BUT...
But..
It's fine!
ISN'T IT BORING TO SHARE A ROOM WITH AN OLDER STUDENT?
I'M GONNA TELL SUGIMOTO WHEN SHE GETS HERE!

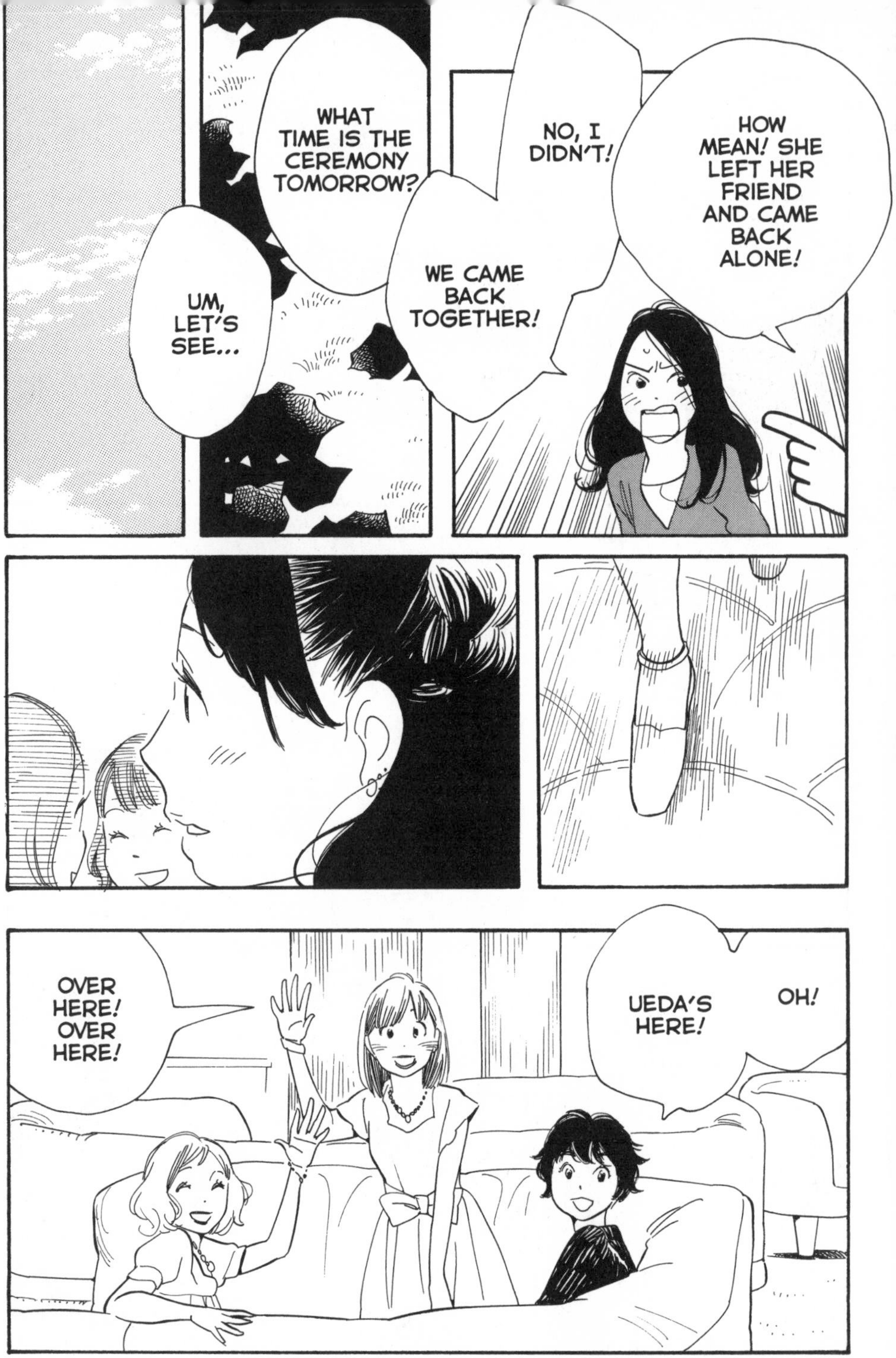
HOW MEAN! SHE LEFT HER FRIEND AND CAME BACK ALONE!
NO, I DIDN'T!
WE CAME BACK TOGETHER!
WHAT TIME IS THE CEREMONY TOMORROW?
UM, LET'S SEE...
OH!
UEDA'S HERE!
OVER HERE! OVER HERE!

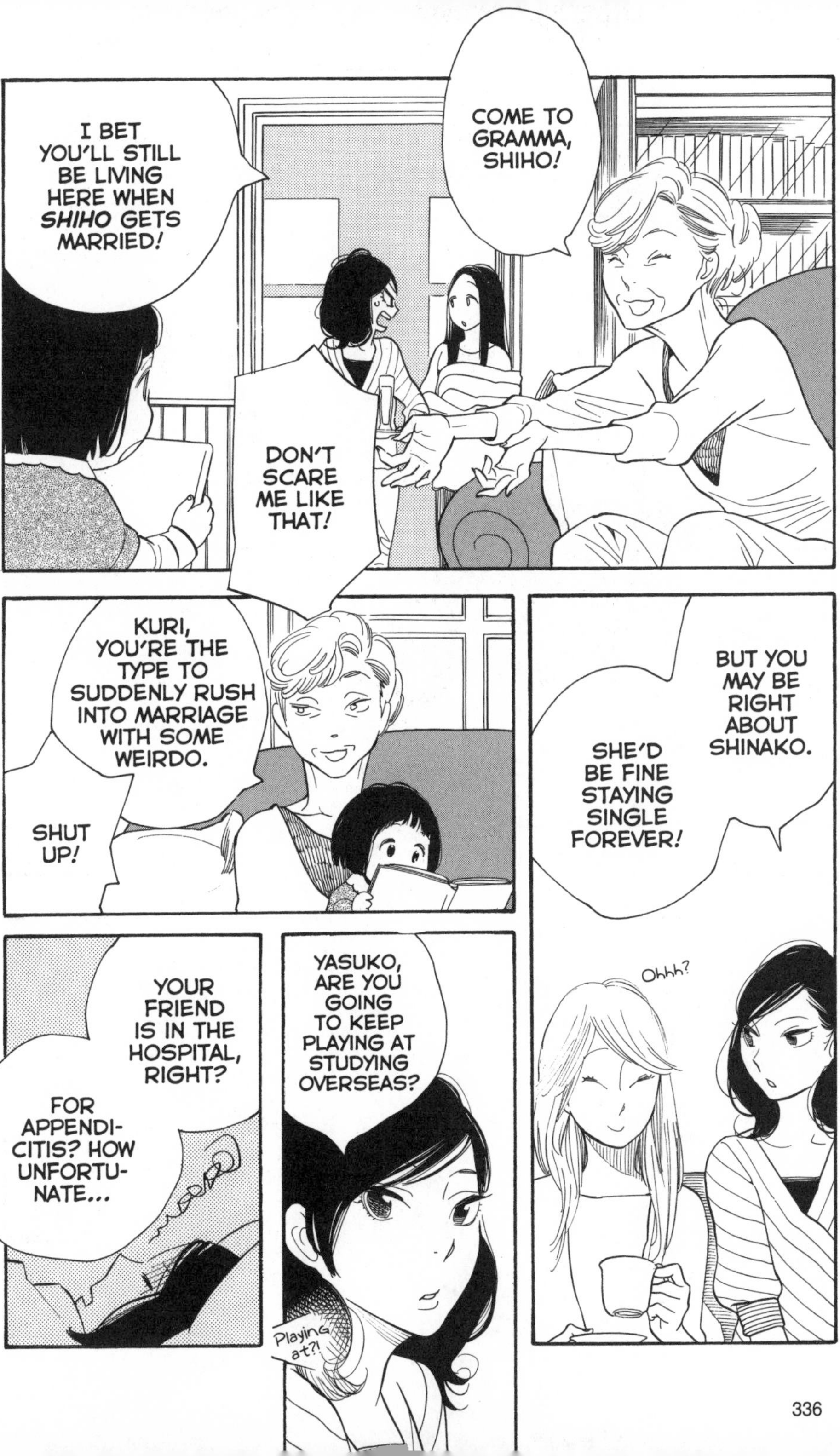
COME TO GRAMMA, SHIHO!
I BET YOU'LL STILL BE LIVING HERE WHEN *SHIHO* GETS MARRIED!
DON'T SCARE ME LIKE THAT!
BUT YOU MAY BE RIGHT ABOUT SHINAKO.
SHE'D BE FINE STAYING SINGLE FOREVER!
Ohhh?
KURI, YOU'RE THE TYPE TO SUDDENLY RUSH INTO MARRIAGE WITH SOME WEIRDO.
SHUT UP!
YASUKO, ARE YOU GOING TO KEEP PLAYING AT STUDYING OVERSEAS?
Playing at?!
YOUR FRIEND IS IN THE HOSPITAL, RIGHT?
FOR APPENDICITIS? HOW UNFORTUNATE...

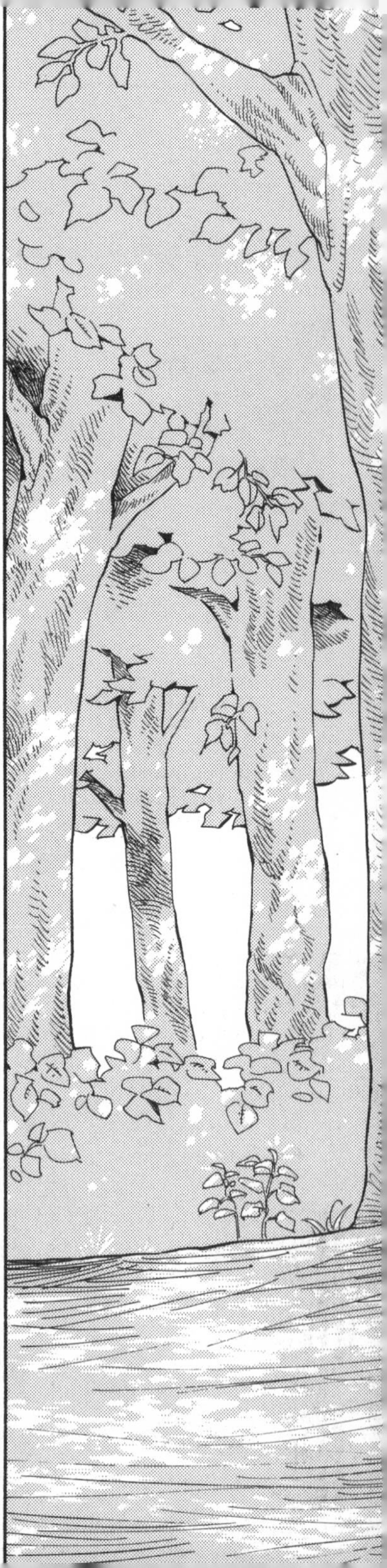

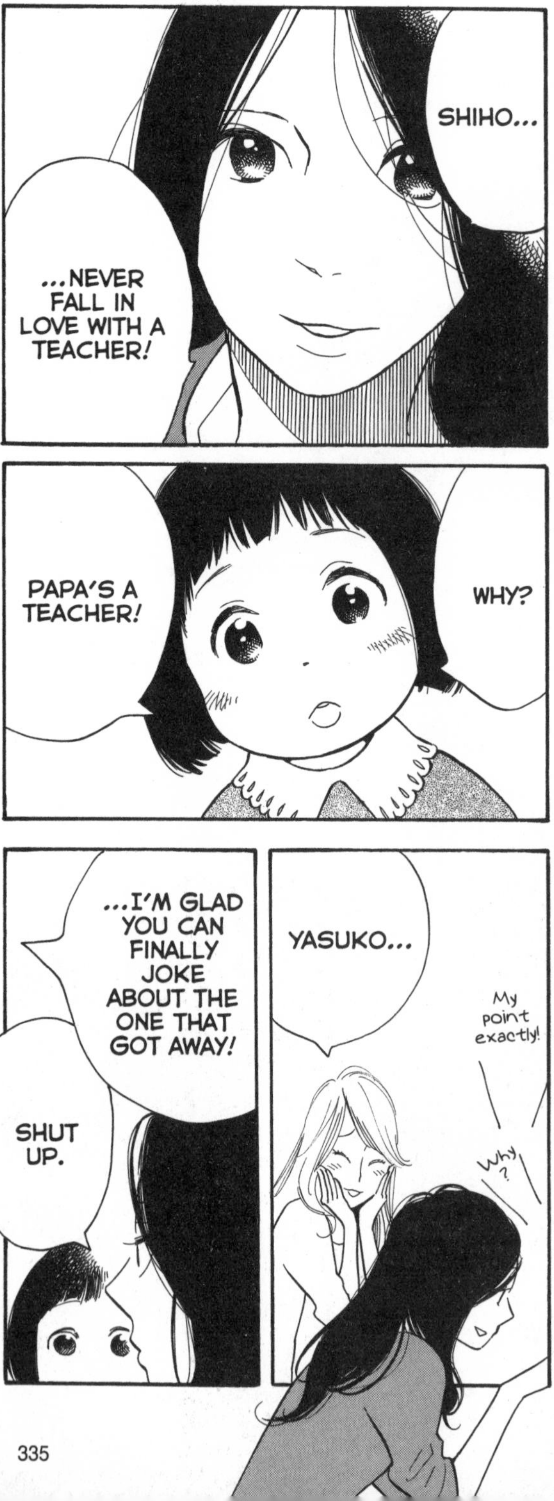
SHIHO...
...NEVER FALL IN LOVE WITH A TEACHER!
WHY?
PAPA'S A TEACHER!
YASUKO...
My point exactly!
Why?
...I'M GLAD YOU CAN FINALLY JOKE ABOUT THE ONE THAT GOT AWAY!
SHUT UP.

WELL, I'M NOT AGAINST IT...

...AND THERE *IS* SOMEONE I'VE ALWAYS LIKED.

OH, TELL ME MORE!

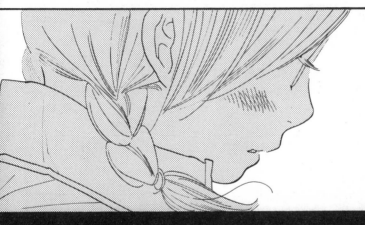

The curse that day was powerful...

...and persists even now that we're 20.

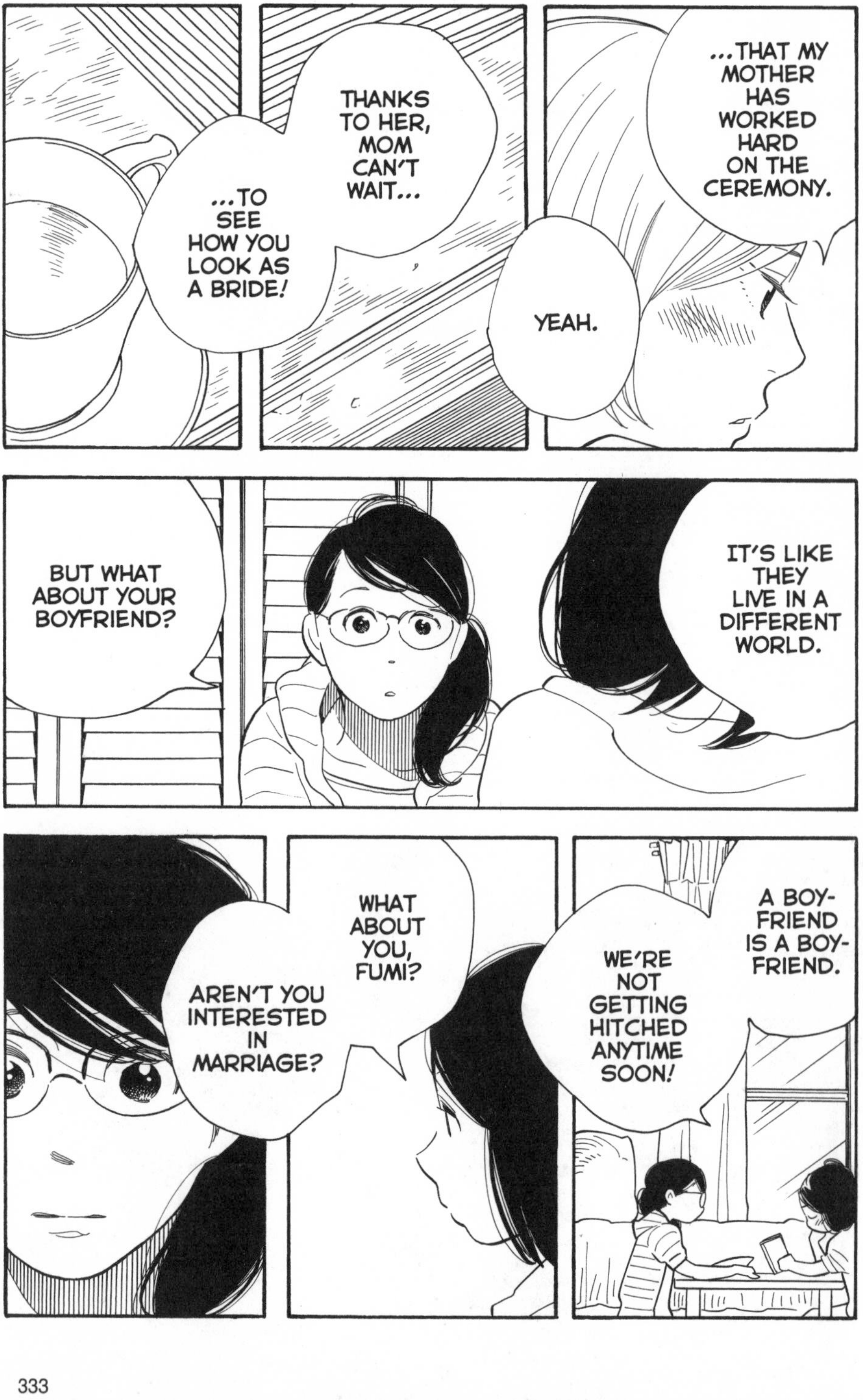
...THAT MY MOTHER HAS WORKED HARD ON THE CEREMONY.
YEAH.
THANKS TO HER, MOM CAN'T WAIT...
...TO SEE HOW YOU LOOK AS A BRIDE!
IT'S LIKE THEY LIVE IN A DIFFERENT WORLD.
BUT WHAT ABOUT YOUR BOYFRIEND?
A BOY-FRIEND IS A BOY-FRIEND.
WE'RE NOT GETTING HITCHED ANYTIME SOON!
WHAT ABOUT YOU, FUMI?
AREN'T YOU INTERESTED IN MARRIAGE?

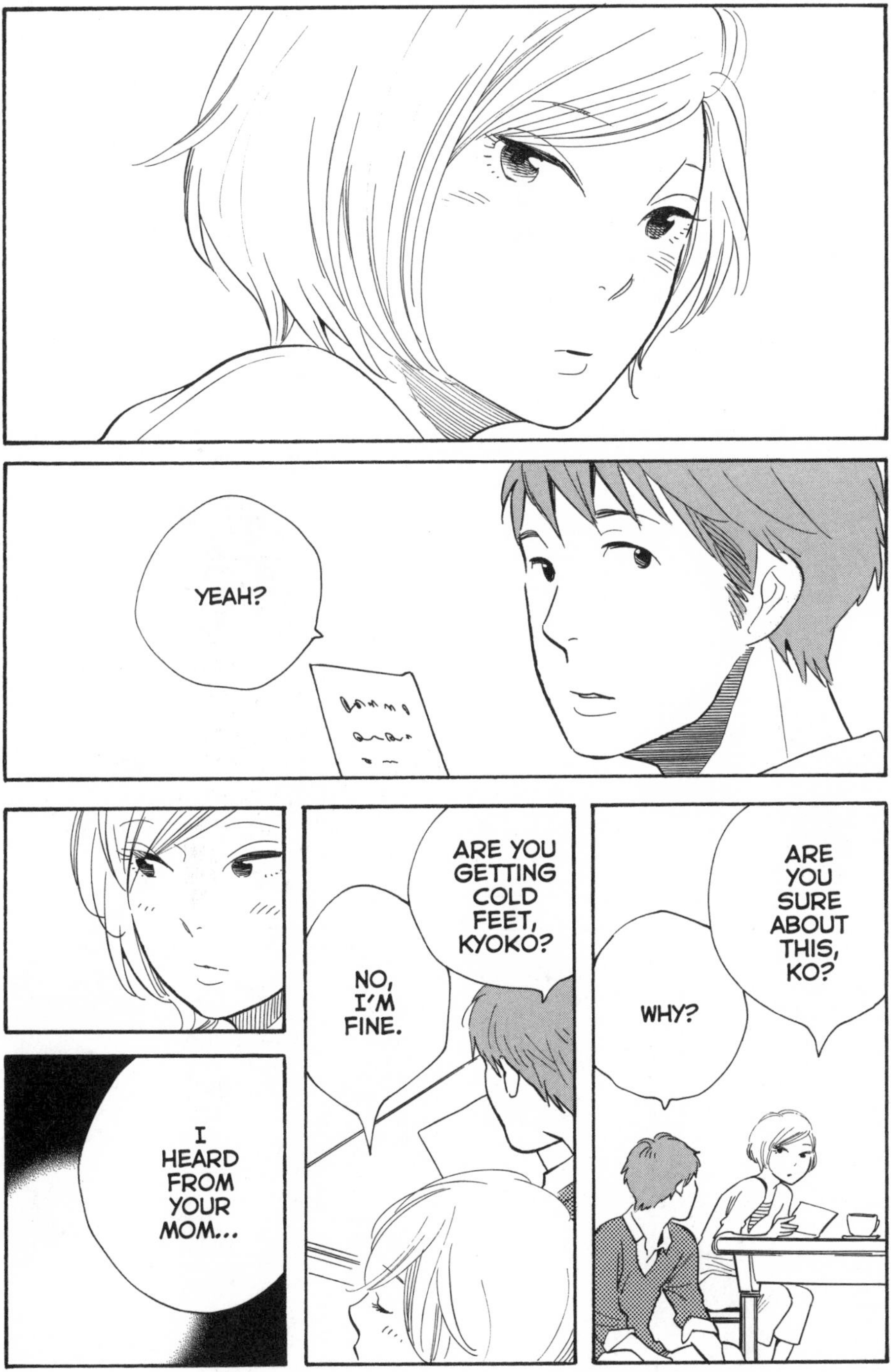
YEAH?
ARE YOU SURE ABOUT THIS, KO?
WHY?
ARE YOU GETTING COLD FEET, KYOKO?
NO, I'M FINE.
I HEARD FROM YOUR MOM...

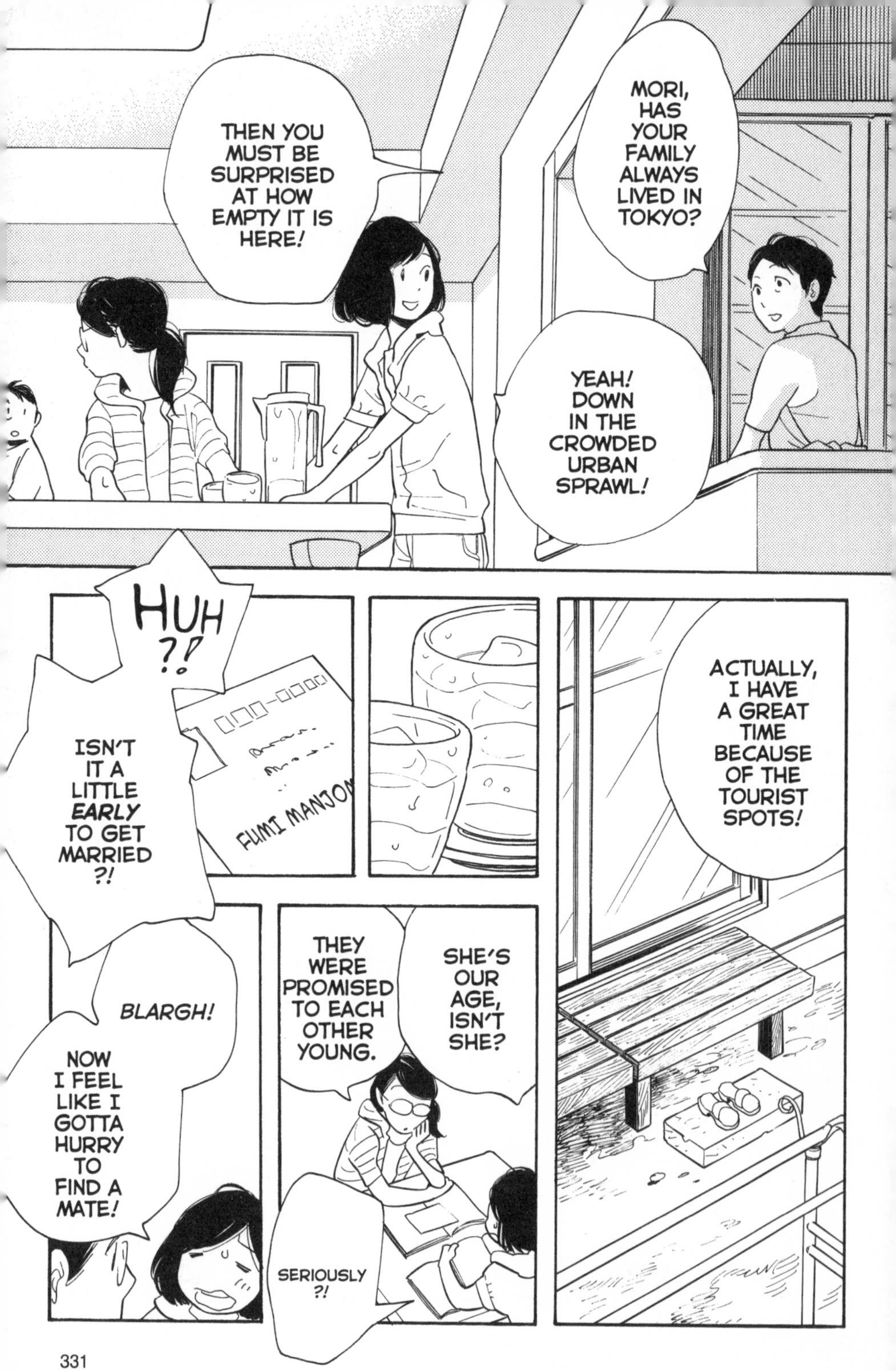
MORI, HAS YOUR FAMILY ALWAYS LIVED IN TOKYO?
YEAH! DOWN IN THE CROWDED URBAN SPRAWL!
THEN YOU MUST BE SURPRISED AT HOW EMPTY IT IS HERE!
ACTUALLY, I HAVE A GREAT TIME BECAUSE OF THE TOURIST SPOTS!
HUH ?!
FUMI MANJO
ISN'T IT A LITTLE *EARLY* TO GET MARRIED ?!
SHE'S OUR AGE, ISN'T SHE?
THEY WERE PROMISED TO EACH OTHER YOUNG.
SERIOUSLY ?!
BLARGH!
NOW I FEEL LIKE I GOTTA HURRY TO FIND A MATE!

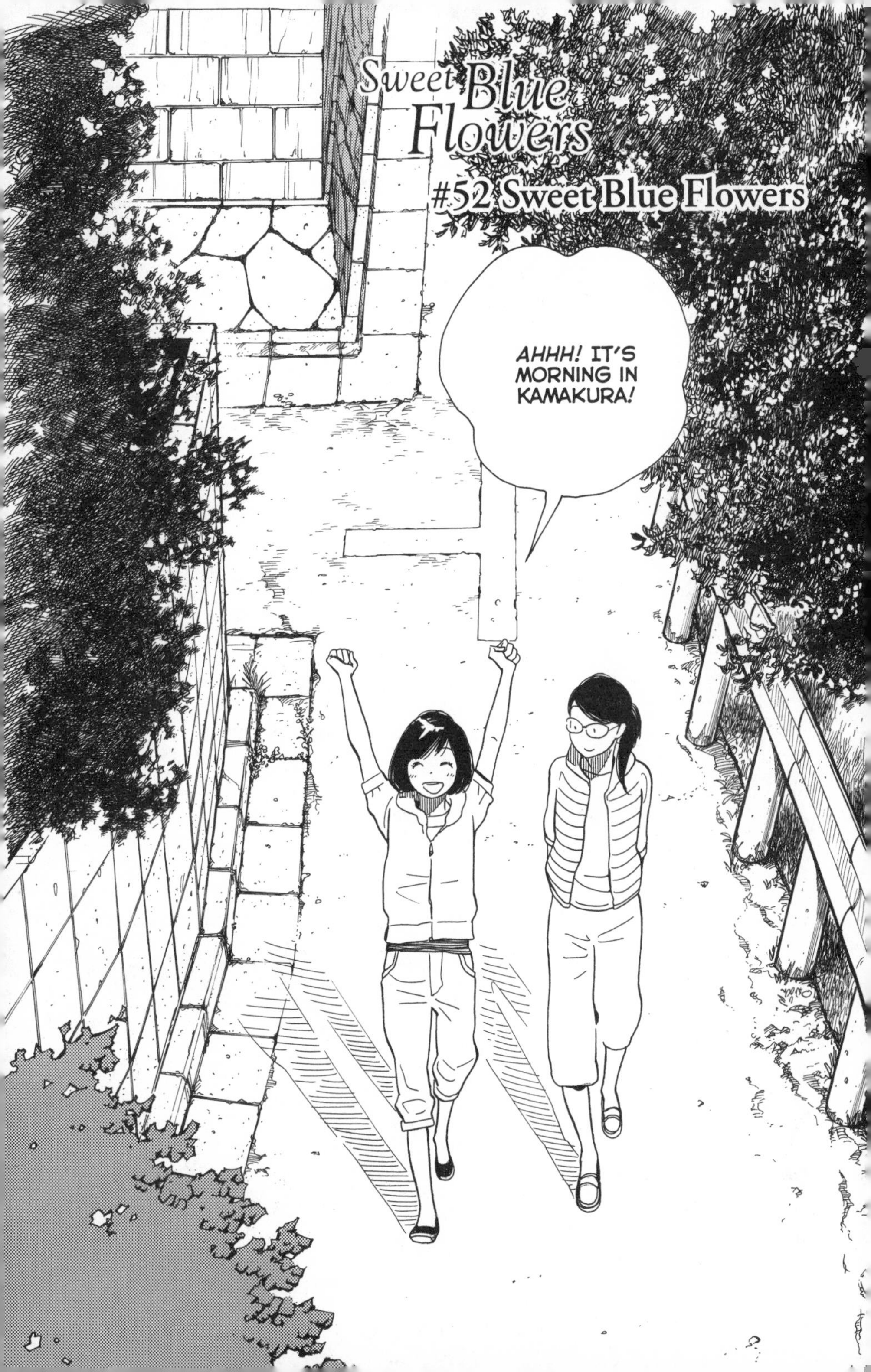
Sweet Blue Flowers
#52 Sweet Blue Flowers
AHHH! IT'S MORNING IN KAMAKURA!

#52 Sweet Blue Flowers

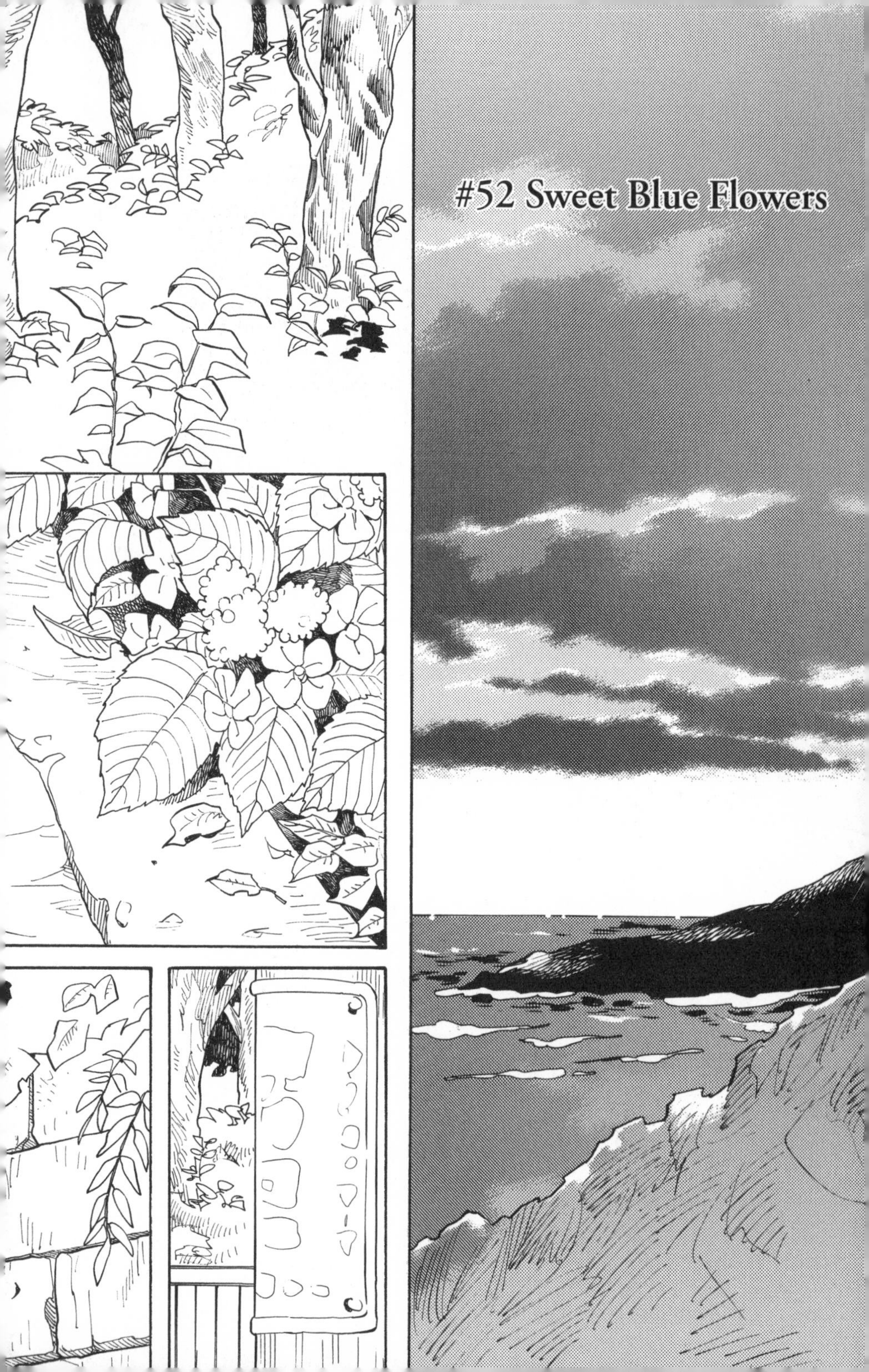

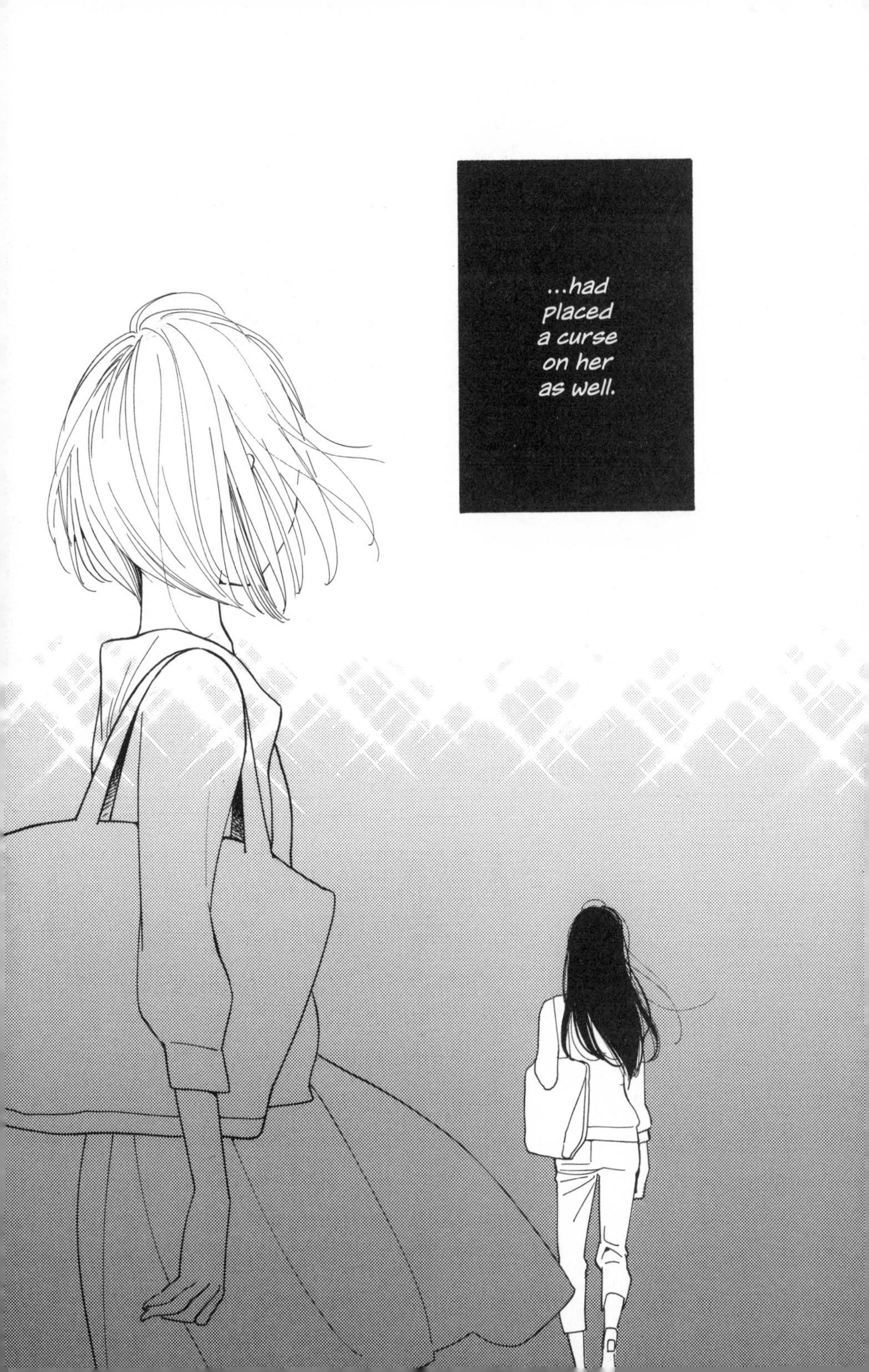
...had placed a curse on her as well.

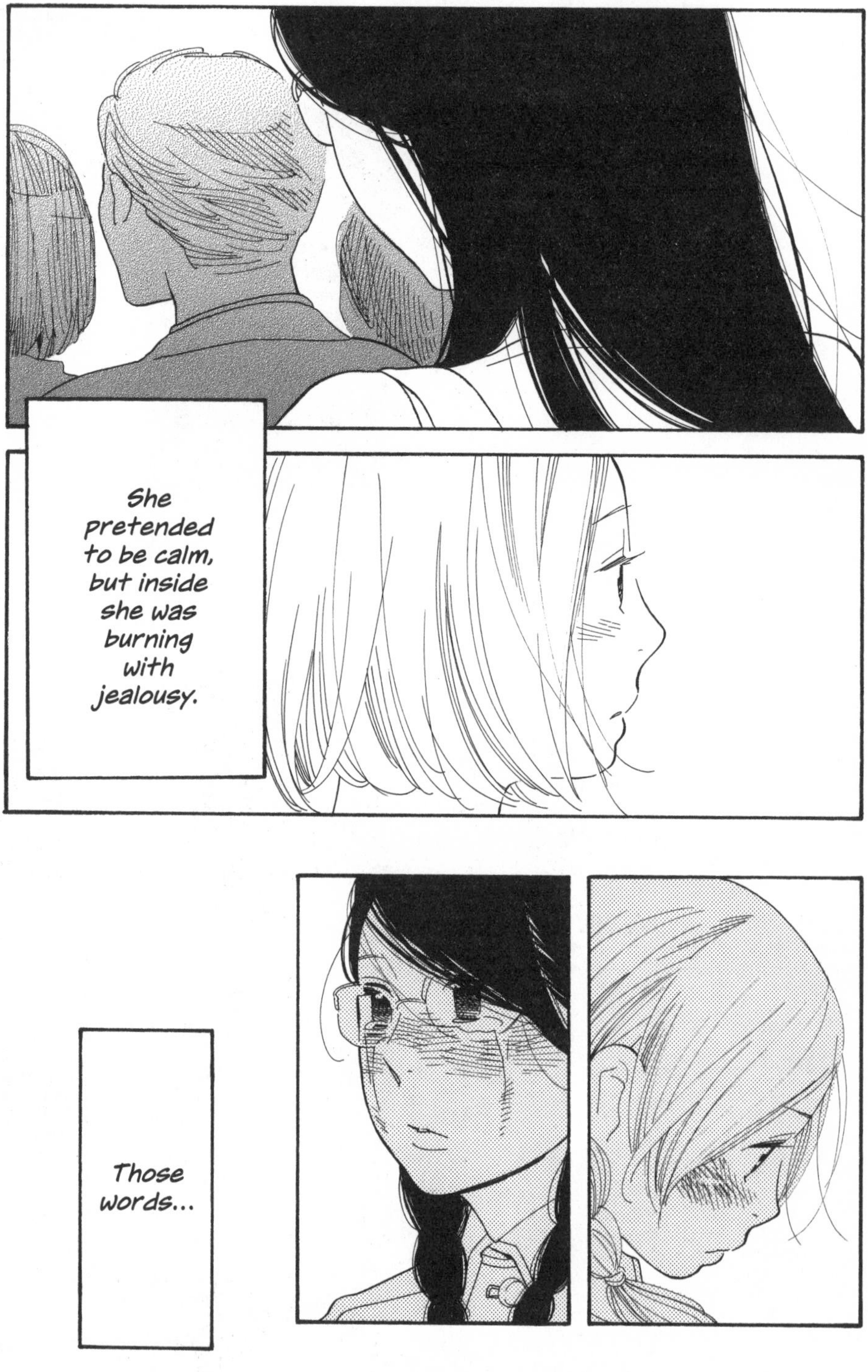
She pretended to be calm, but inside she was burning with jealousy.
Those words...

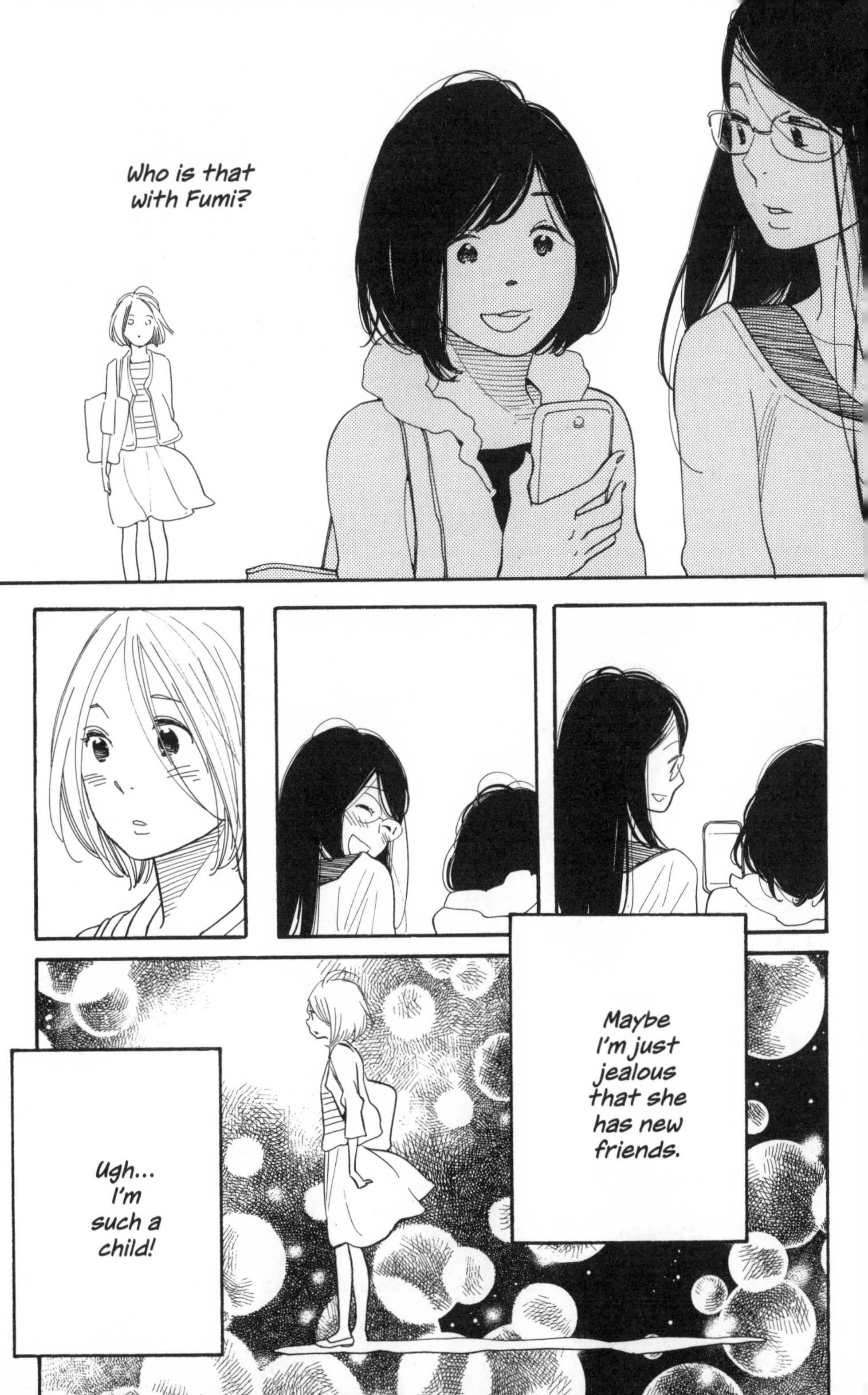
Who is that with Fumi?
Maybe I'm just jealous that she has new friends.
Ugh... I'm such a child!

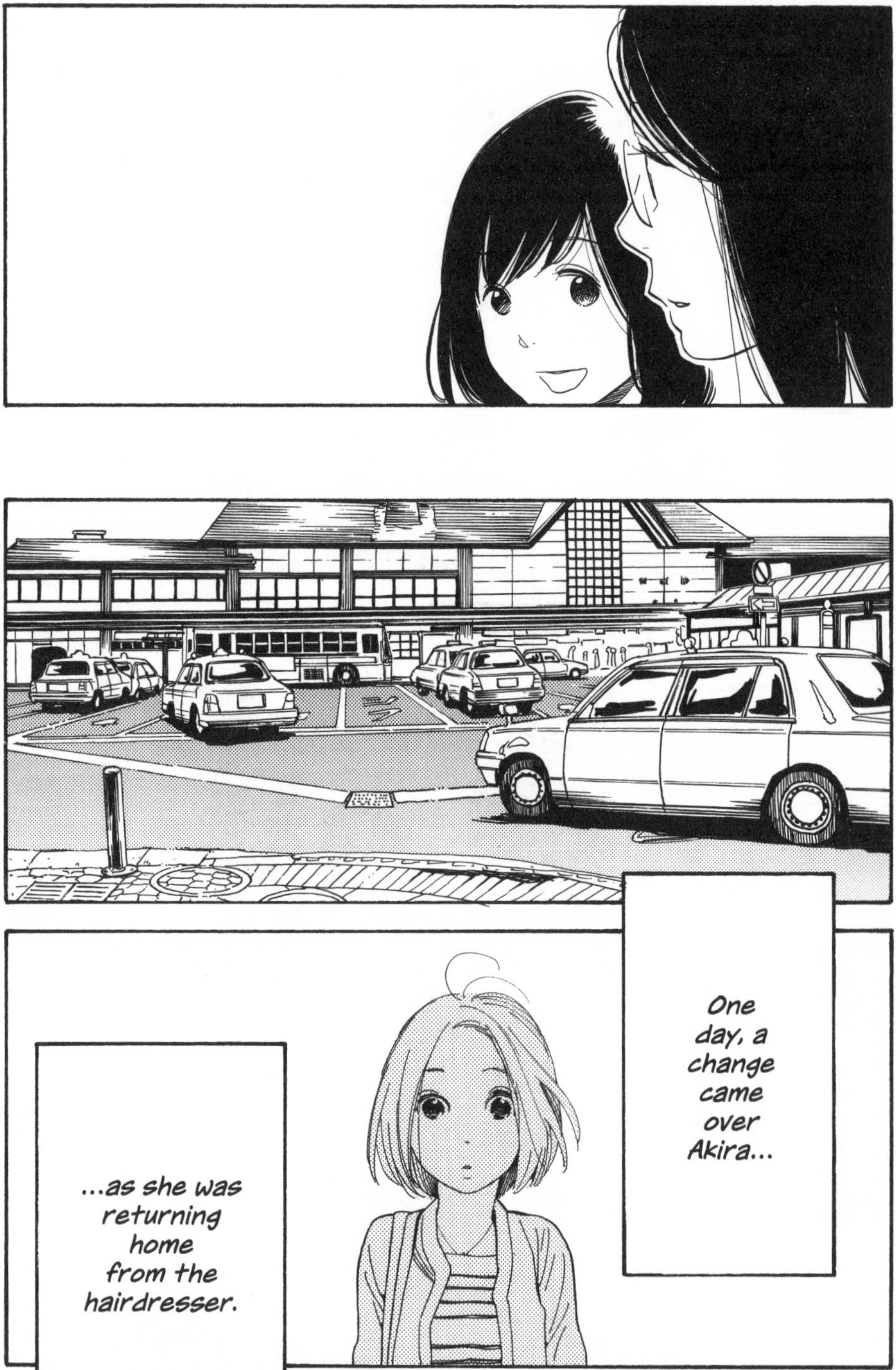
One day, a change came over Akira...
...as she was returning home from the hairdresser.

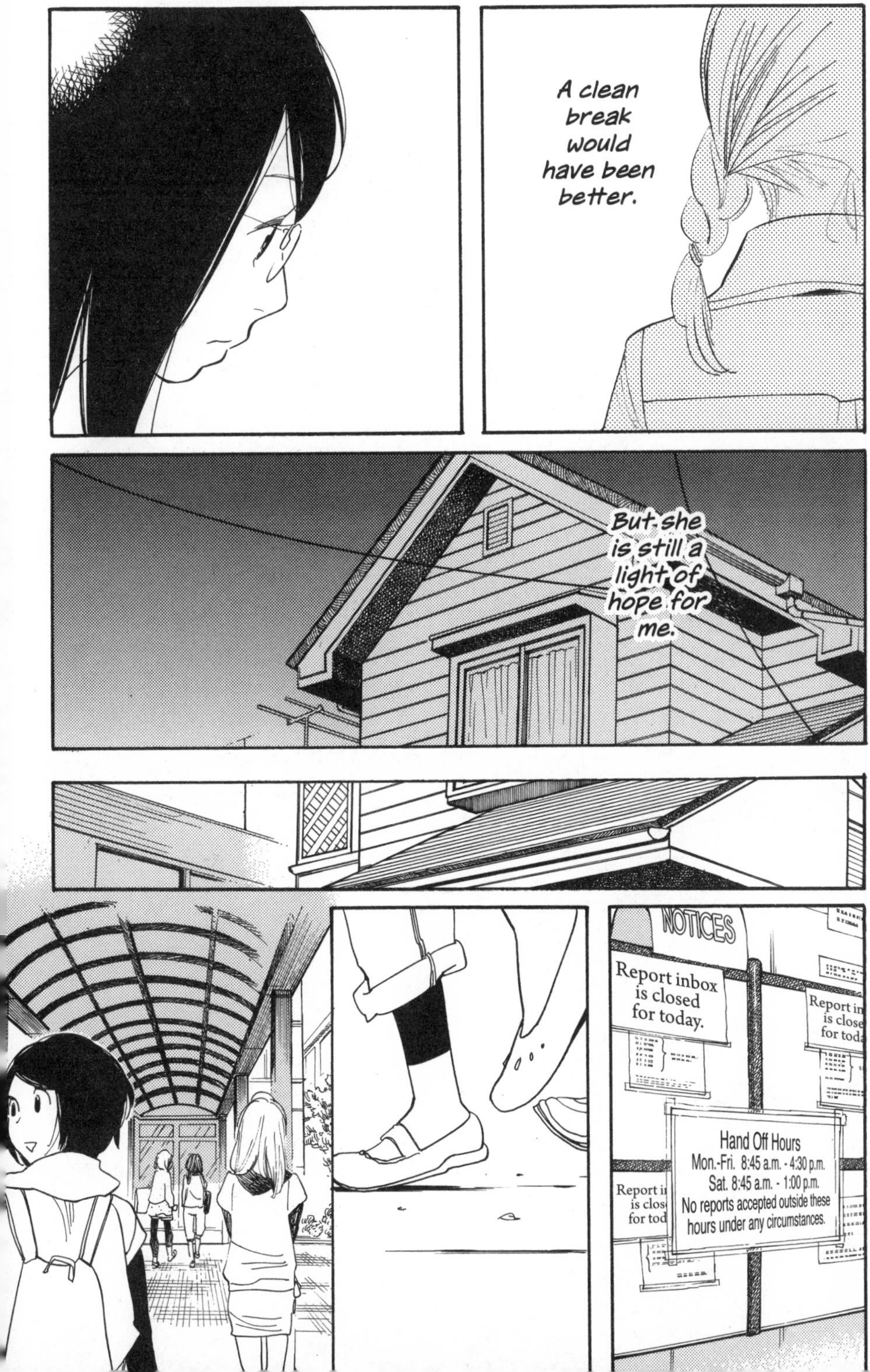
A clean break would have been better.
But she is still a light of hope for me.
NOTICES
Report inbox is closed for today.
Hand Off Hours
Mon.-Fri. 8:45 a.m. - 4:30 p.m.
Sat. 8:45 a.m. - 1:00 p.m.
No reports accepted outside these hours under any circumstances.

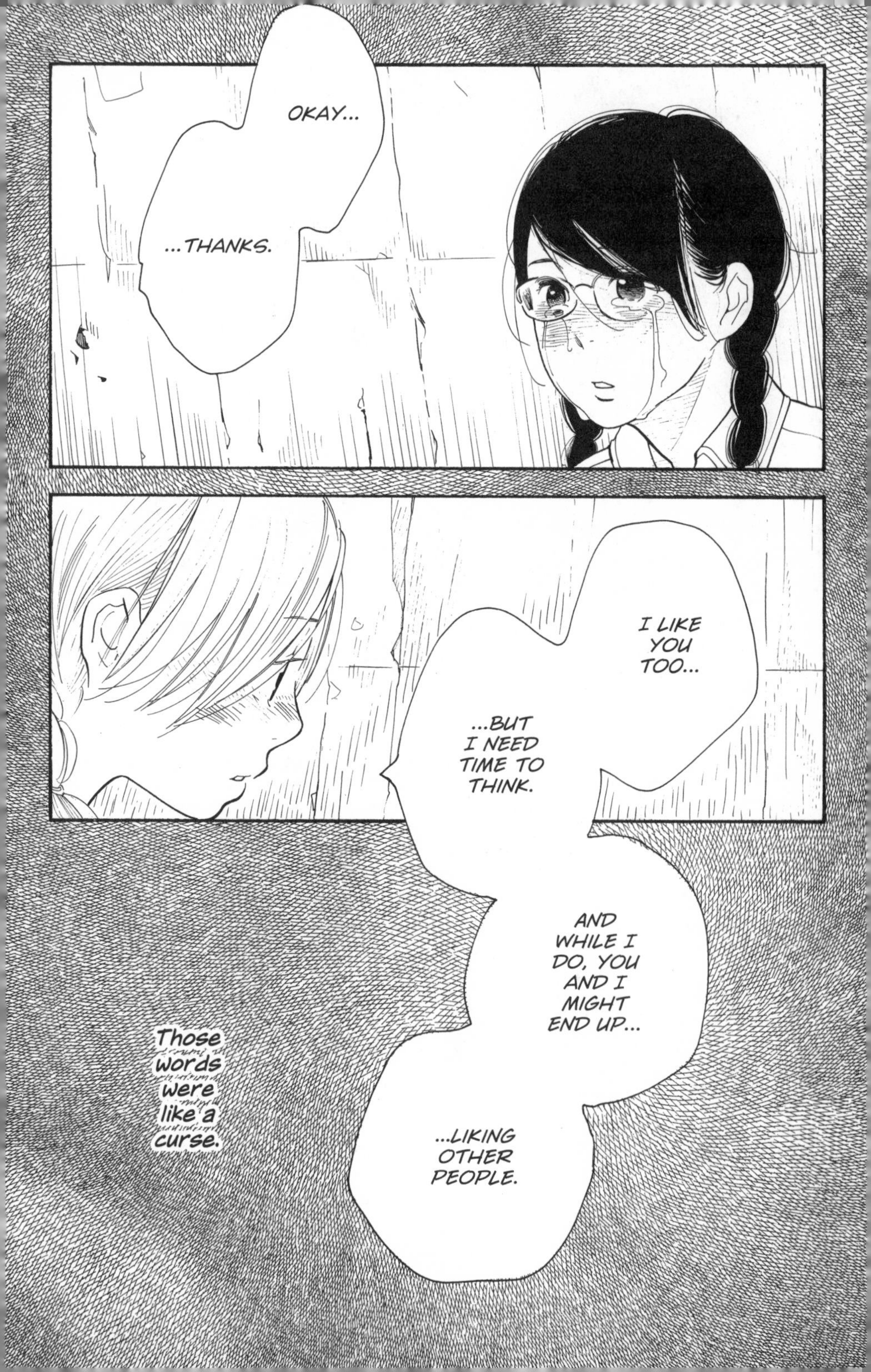
OKAY...
...THANKS.
I LIKE YOU TOO...
...BUT I NEED TIME TO THINK.
AND WHILE I DO, YOU AND I MIGHT END UP...
...LIKING OTHER PEOPLE.
Those words were like a curse.

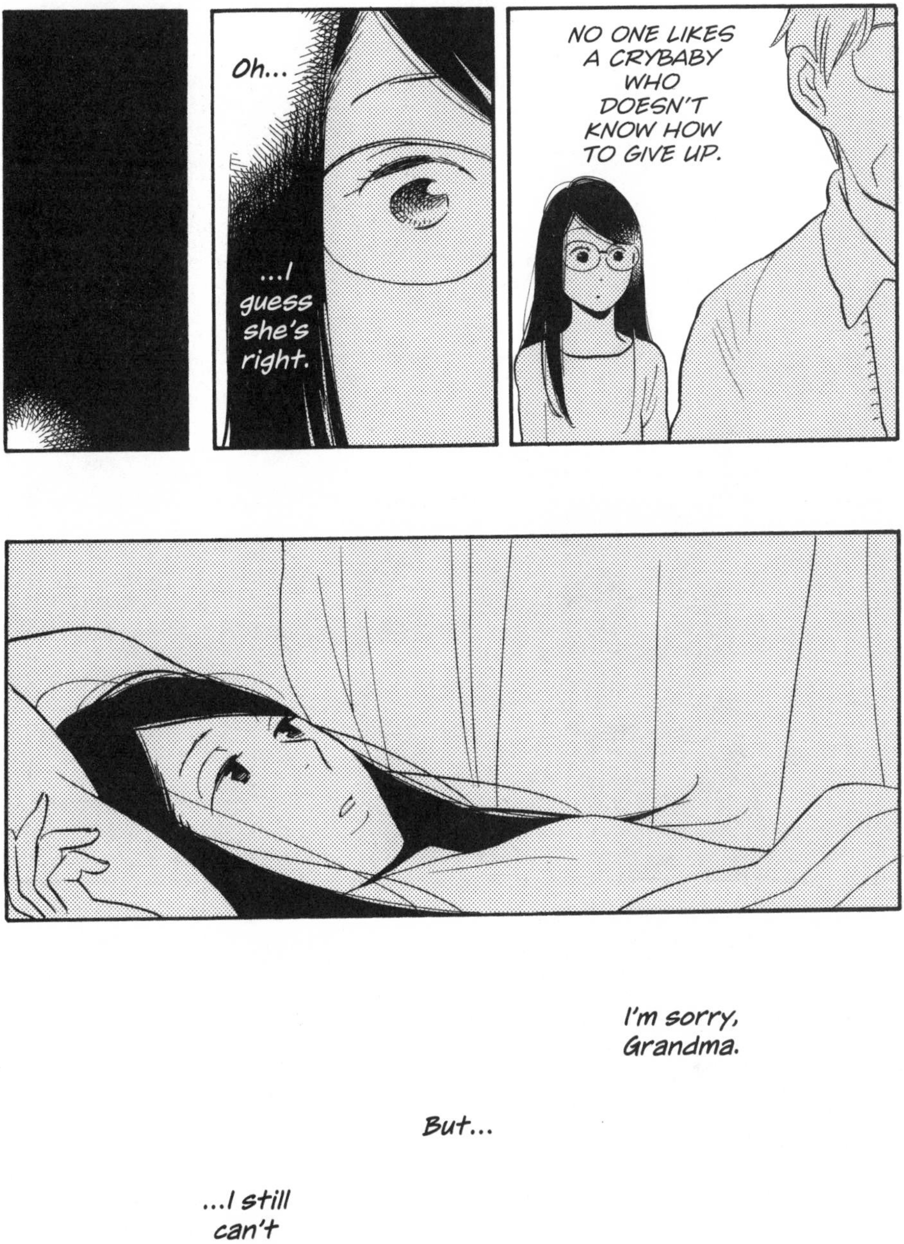
NO ONE LIKES A CRYBABY WHO DOESN'T KNOW HOW TO GIVE UP.
Oh...
...I guess she's right.
I'm sorry, Grandma.
But...
...I still can't give up.

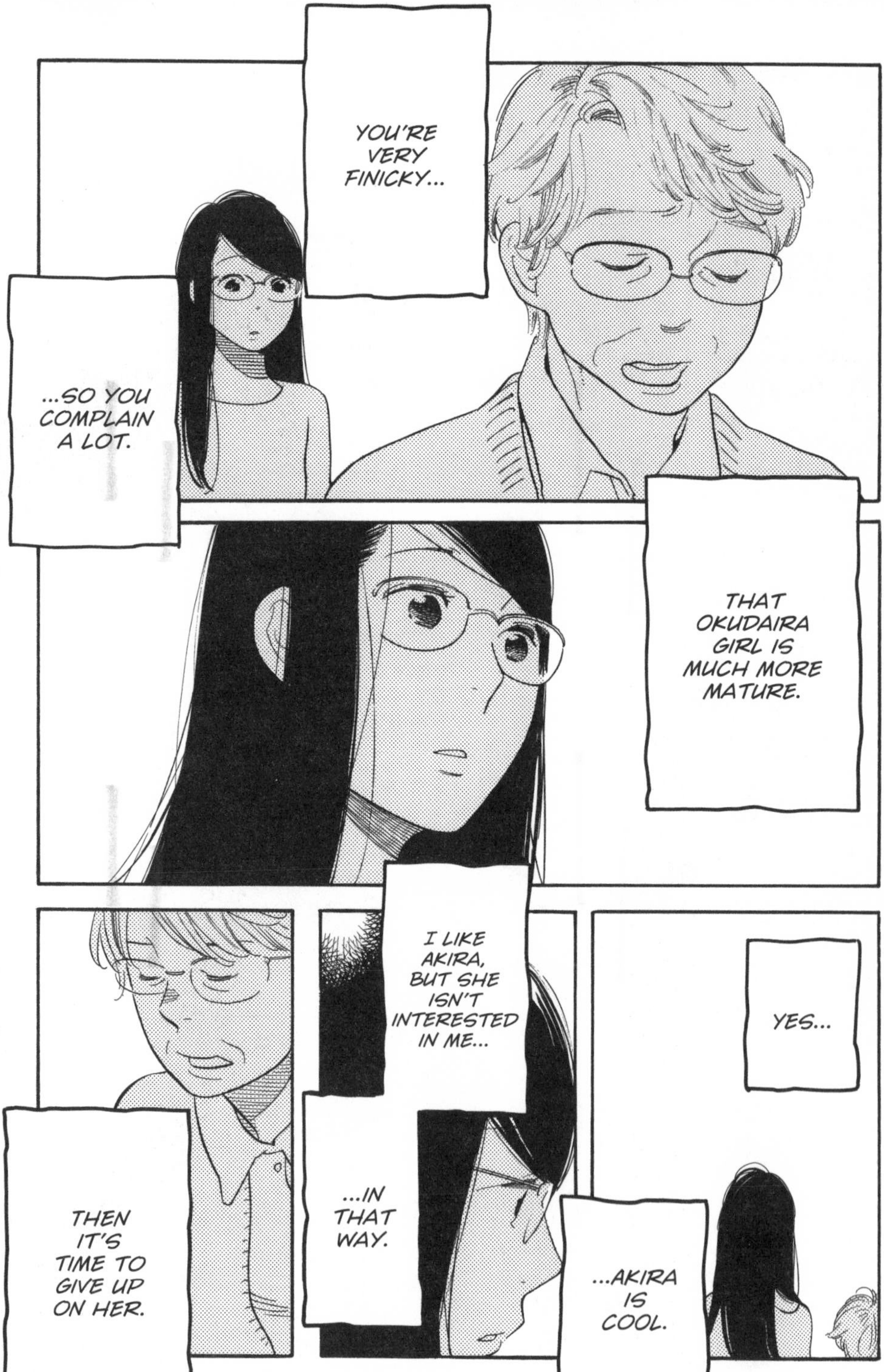
YOU'RE VERY FINICKY...
...SO YOU COMPLAIN A LOT.
THAT OKUDAIRA GIRL IS MUCH MORE MATURE.
YES...
...AKIRA IS COOL.
I LIKE AKIRA, BUT SHE ISN'T INTERESTED IN ME...
...IN THAT WAY.
THEN IT'S TIME TO GIVE UP ON HER.

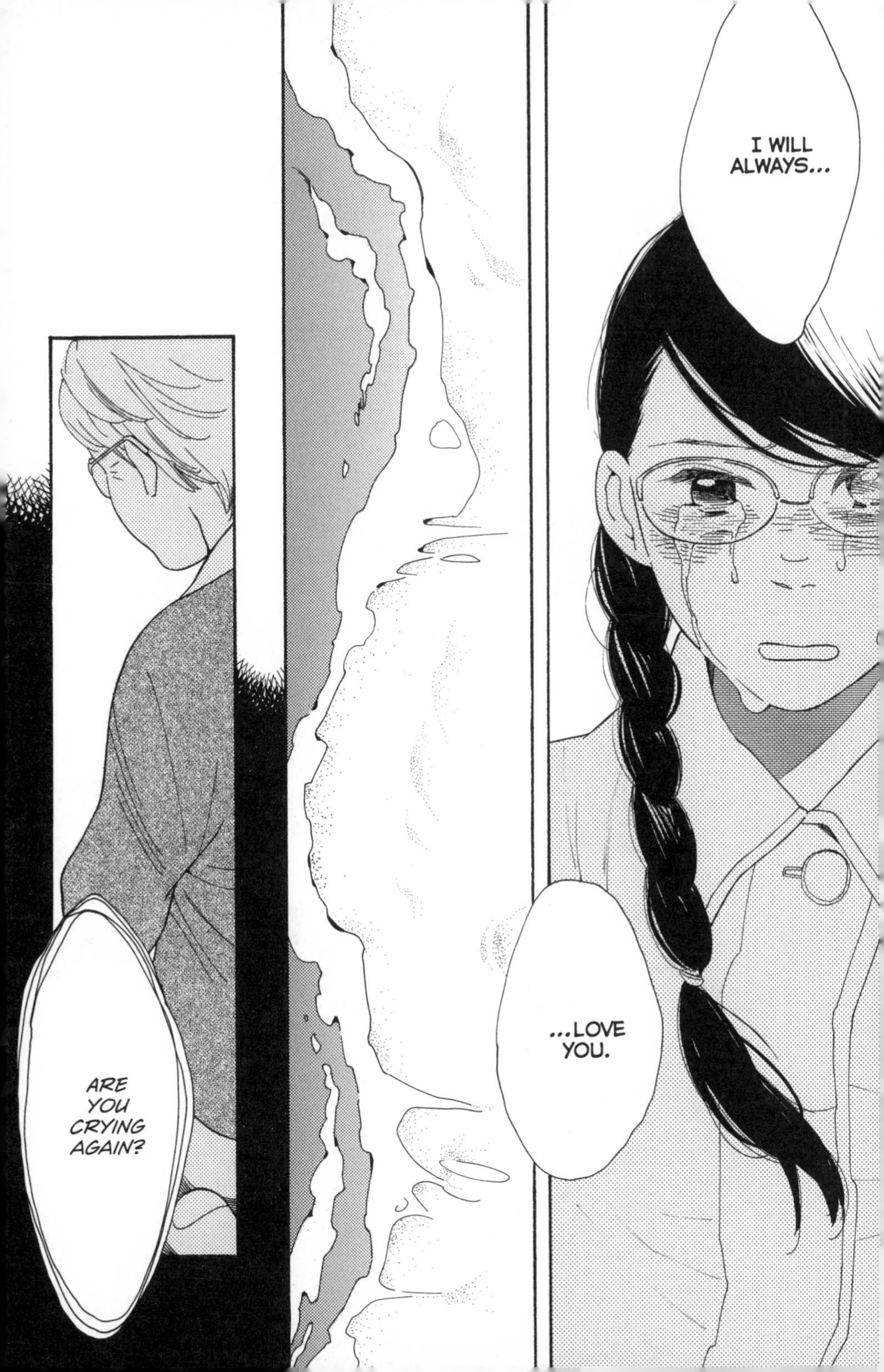
I WILL ALWAYS...
...LOVE YOU.
ARE YOU CRYING AGAIN?

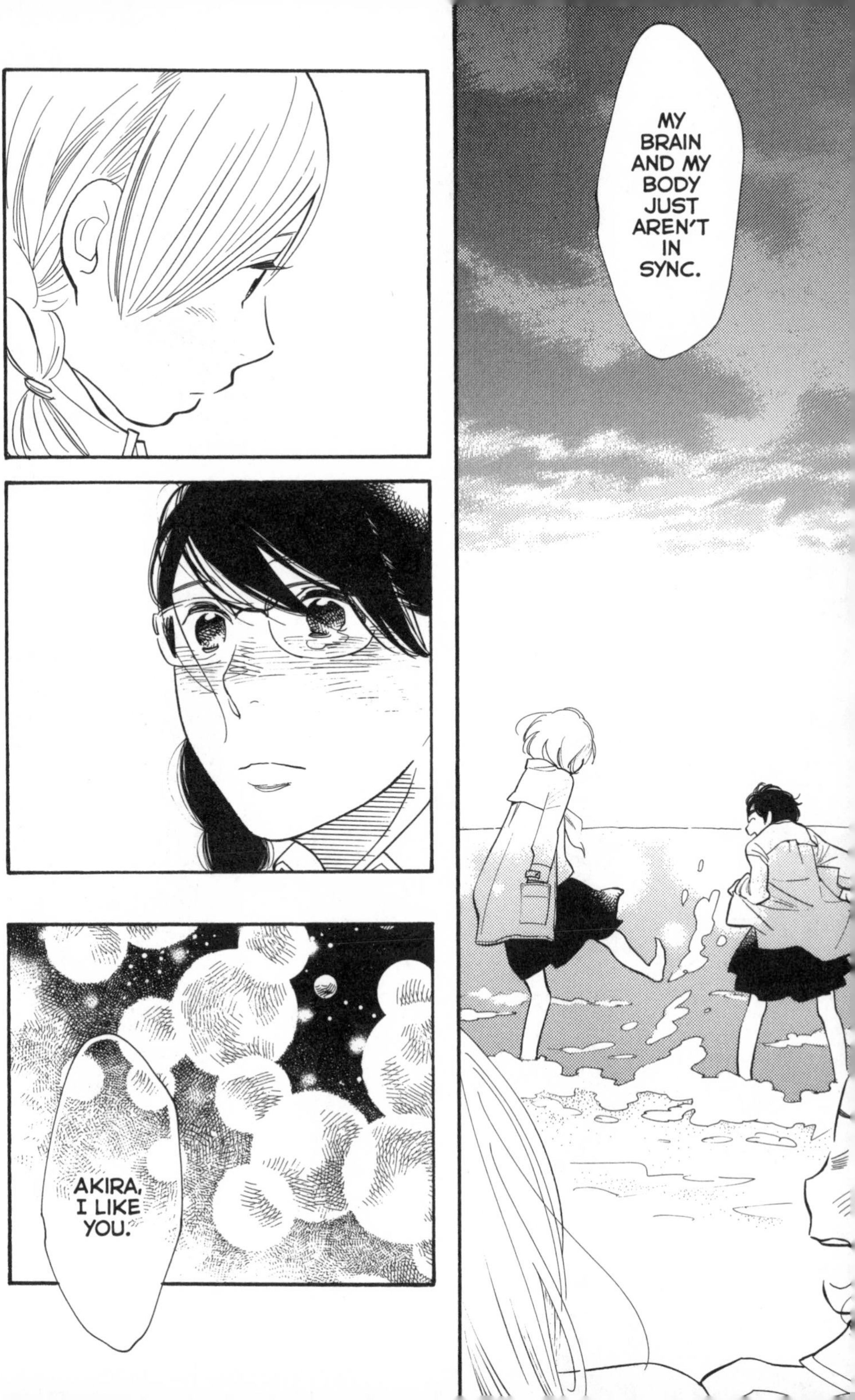
MY BRAIN AND MY BODY JUST AREN'T IN SYNC.
AKIRA, I LIKE YOU.

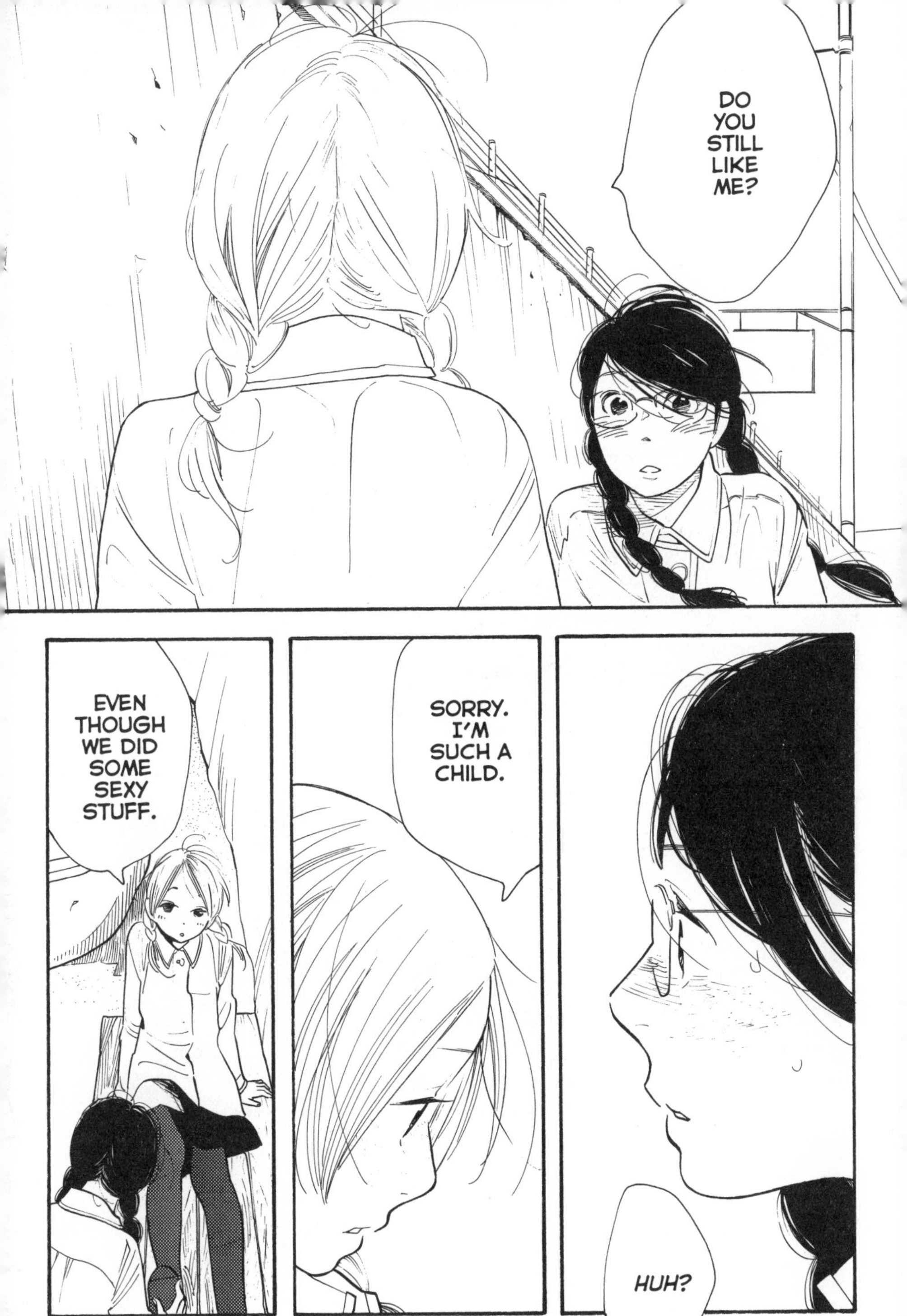
DO YOU STILL LIKE ME?
HUH?
SORRY. I'M SUCH A CHILD.
EVEN THOUGH WE DID SOME SEXY STUFF.

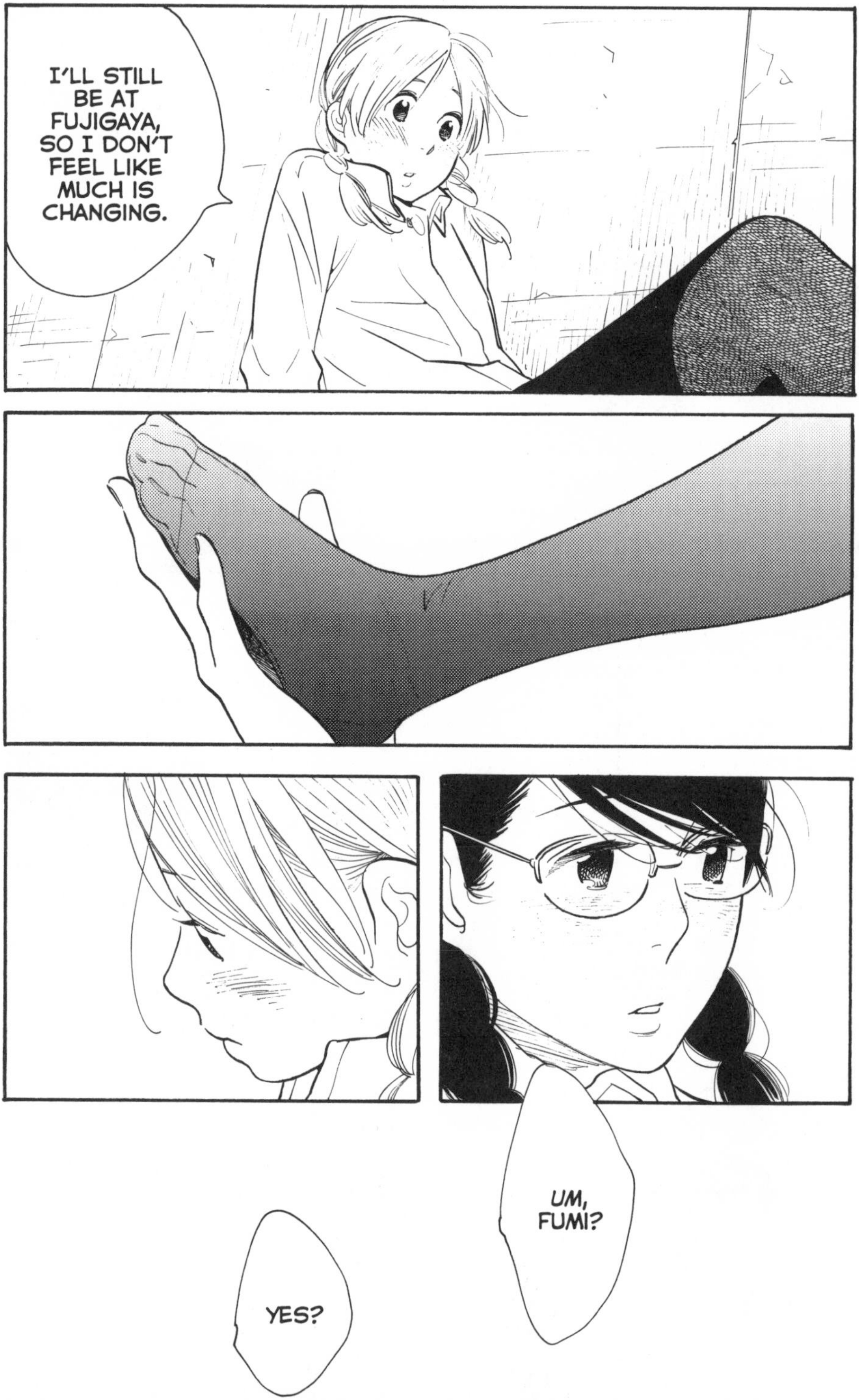
I'LL STILL BE AT FUJIGAYA, SO I DON'T FEEL LIKE MUCH IS CHANGING.
UM, FUMI?
YES?

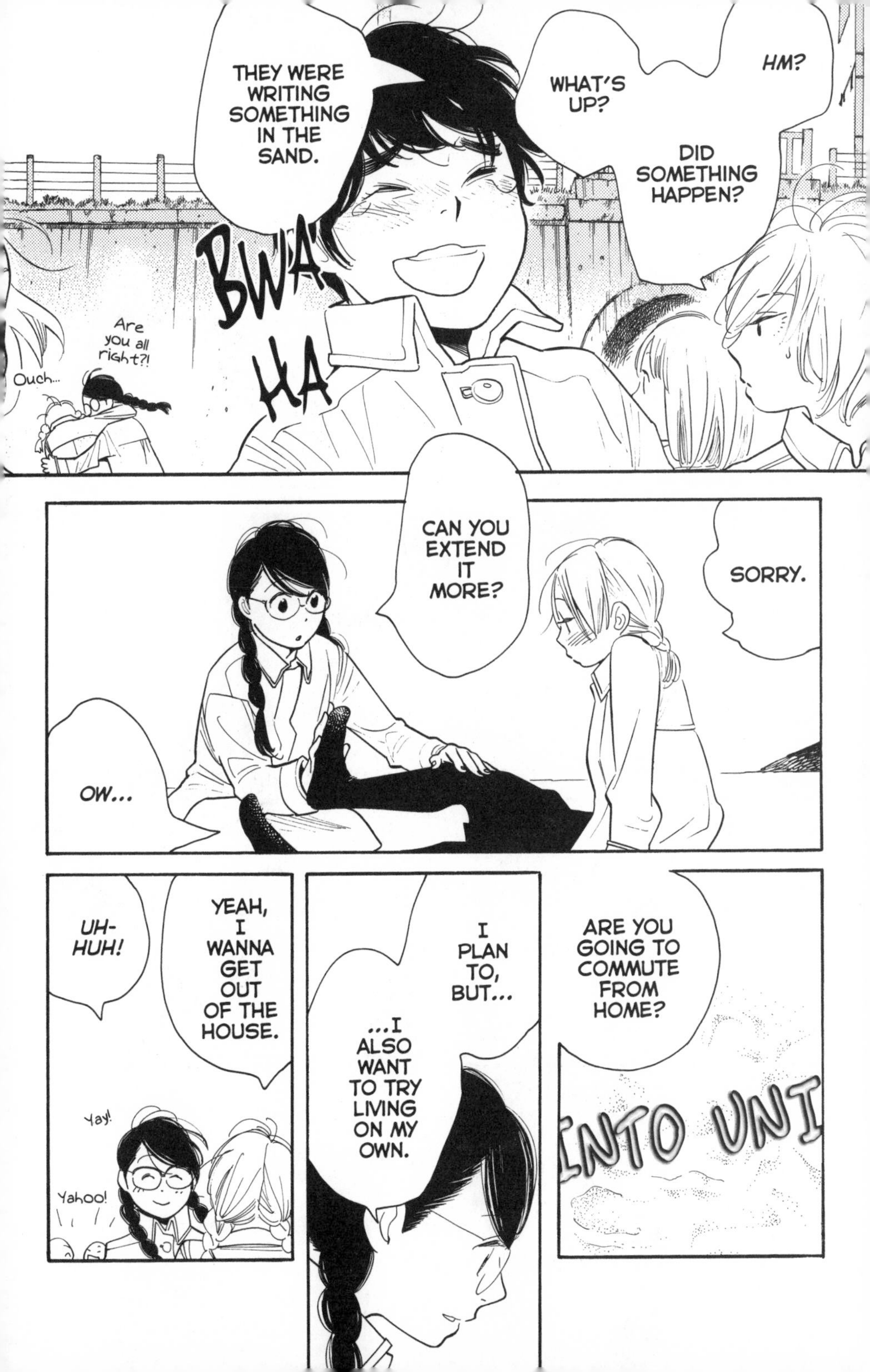
HM?
WHAT'S UP?
DID SOMETHING HAPPEN?
THEY WERE WRITING SOMETHING IN THE SAND.
BWA HA
Are you all right?!
Ouch...
SORRY.
CAN YOU EXTEND IT MORE?
OW...
ARE YOU GOING TO COMMUTE FROM HOME?
INTO UNI
I PLAN TO, BUT...
...I ALSO WANT TO TRY LIVING ON MY OWN.
YEAH, I WANNA GET OUT OF THE HOUSE.
UH-HUH!
Yay!
Yahoo!

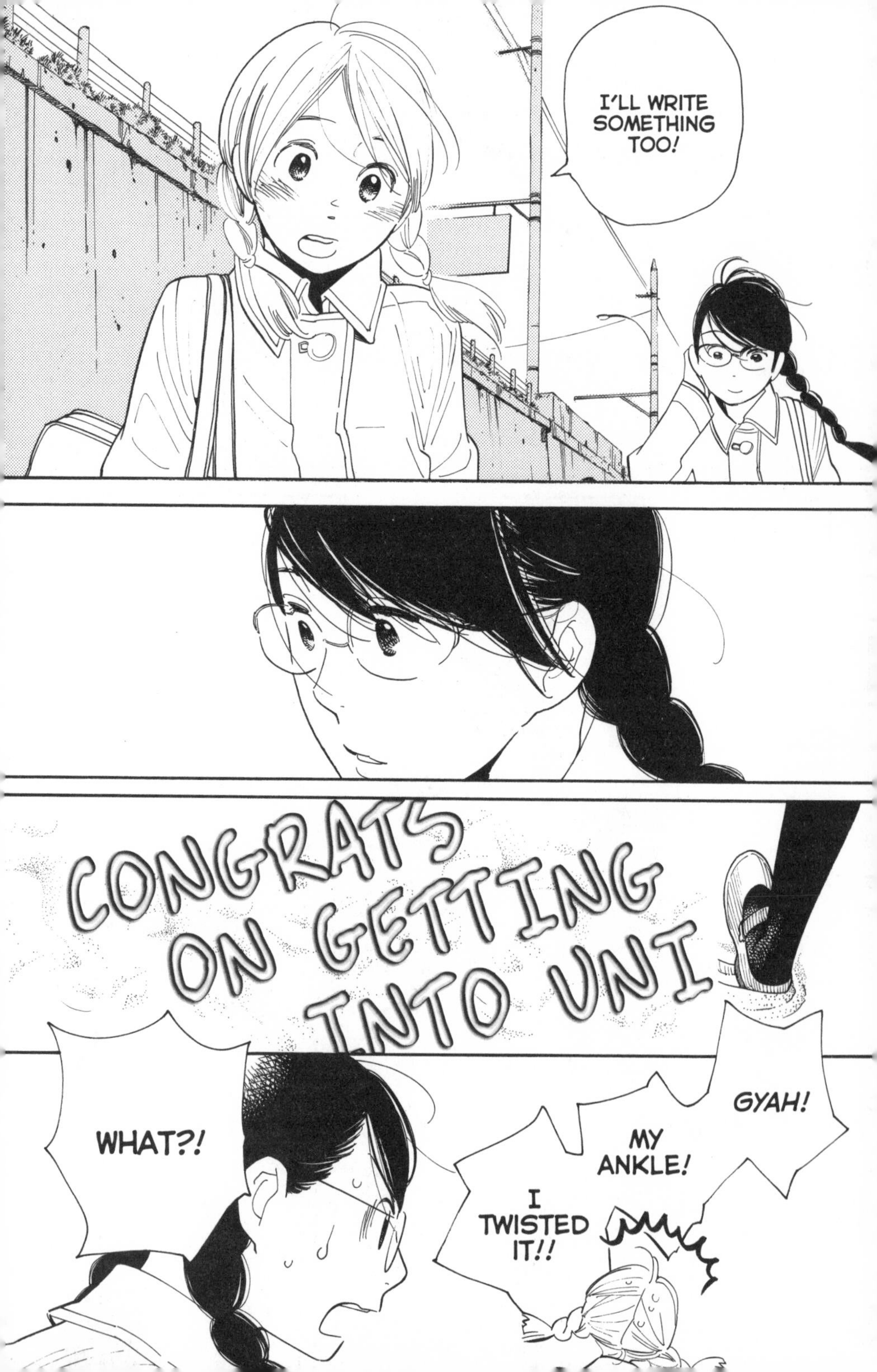
I'LL WRITE SOMETHING TOO!
CONGRATS ON GETTING INTO UNI
GYAH!
MY ANKLE!
I TWISTED IT!!
WHAT?!

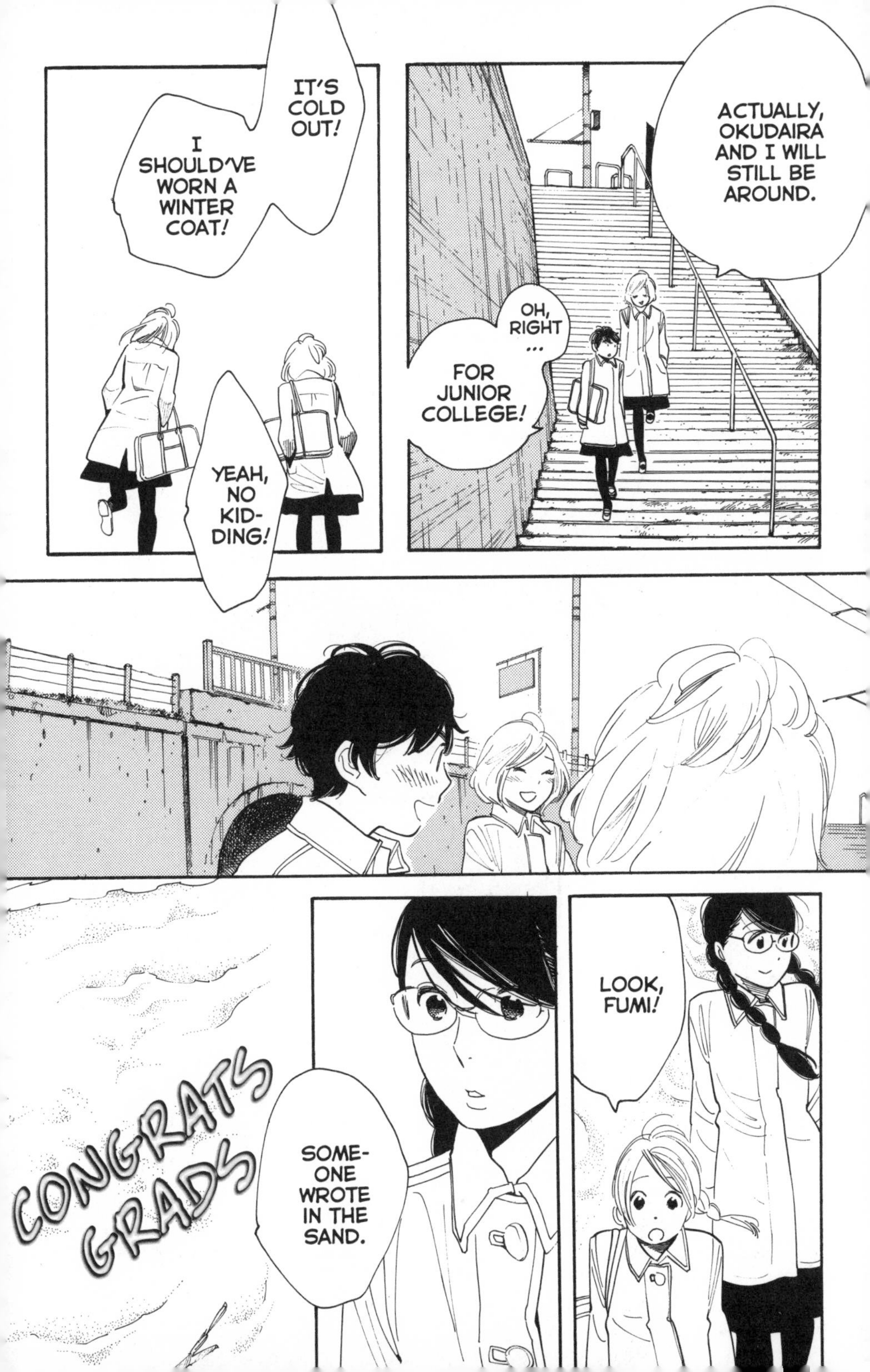
ACTUALLY, OKUDAIRA AND I WILL STILL BE AROUND.
OH, RIGHT ...
FOR JUNIOR COLLEGE!
IT'S COLD OUT!
I SHOULD'VE WORN A WINTER COAT!
YEAH, NO KID-DING!
LOOK, FUMI!
SOME-ONE WROTE IN THE SAND.
CONGRATS GRADS

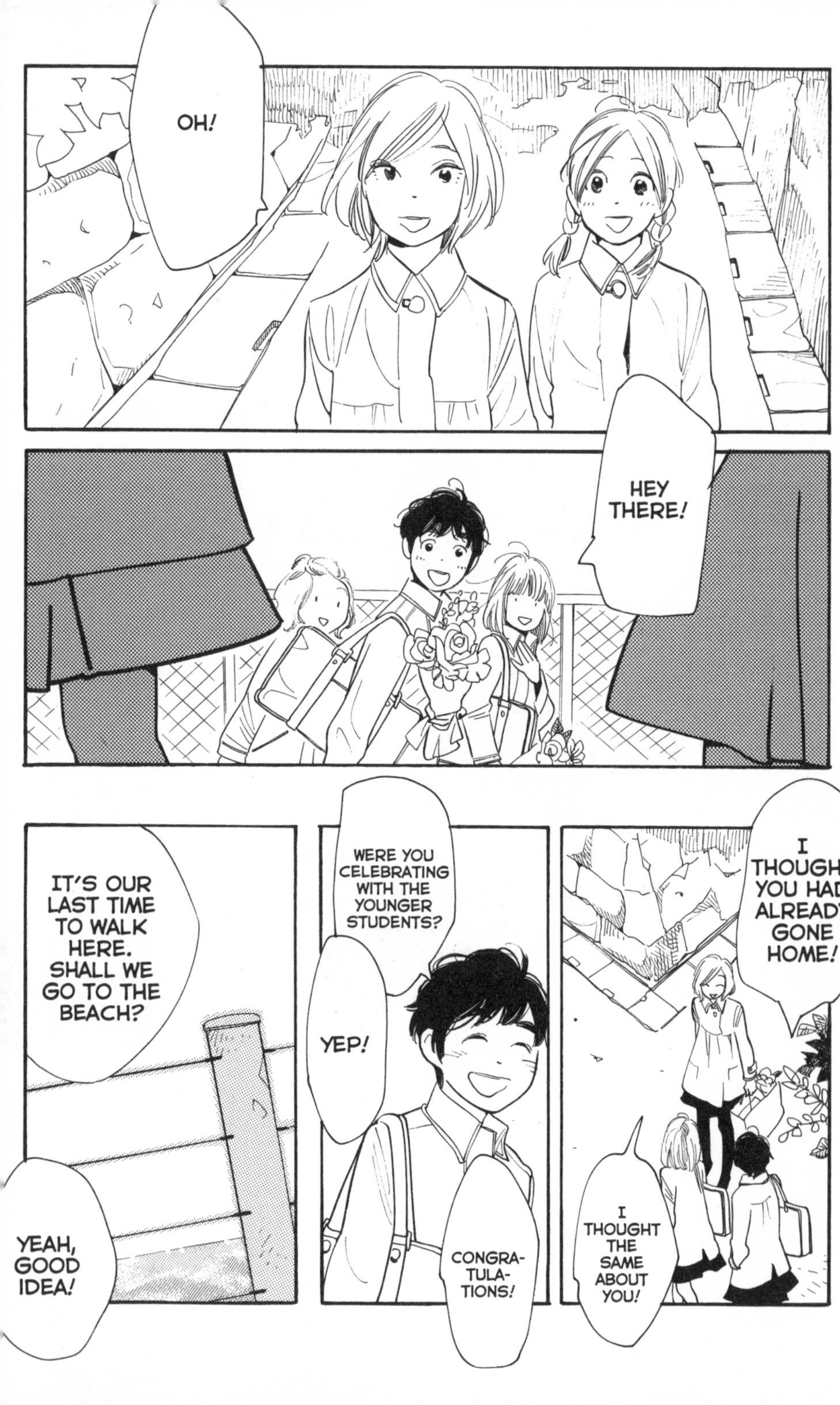
OH!
HEY THERE!
I THOUGHT YOU HAD ALREADY GONE HOME!
I THOUGHT THE SAME ABOUT YOU!
WERE YOU CELEBRATING WITH THE YOUNGER STUDENTS?
YEP!
CONGRA-TULA-TIONS!
IT'S OUR LAST TIME TO WALK HERE. SHALL WE GO TO THE BEACH?
YEAH, GOOD IDEA!

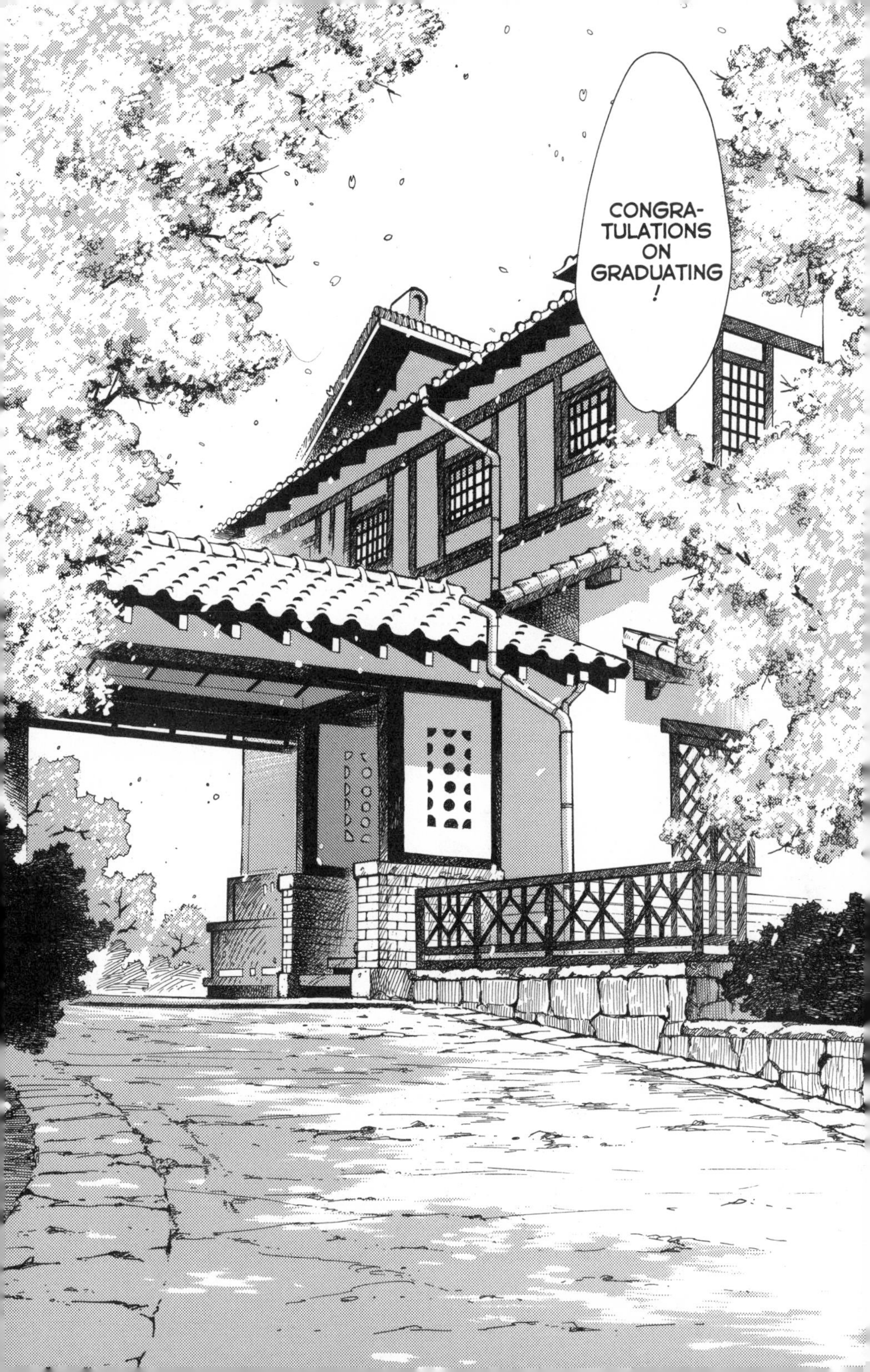
CONGRATULATIONS ON GRADUATING!

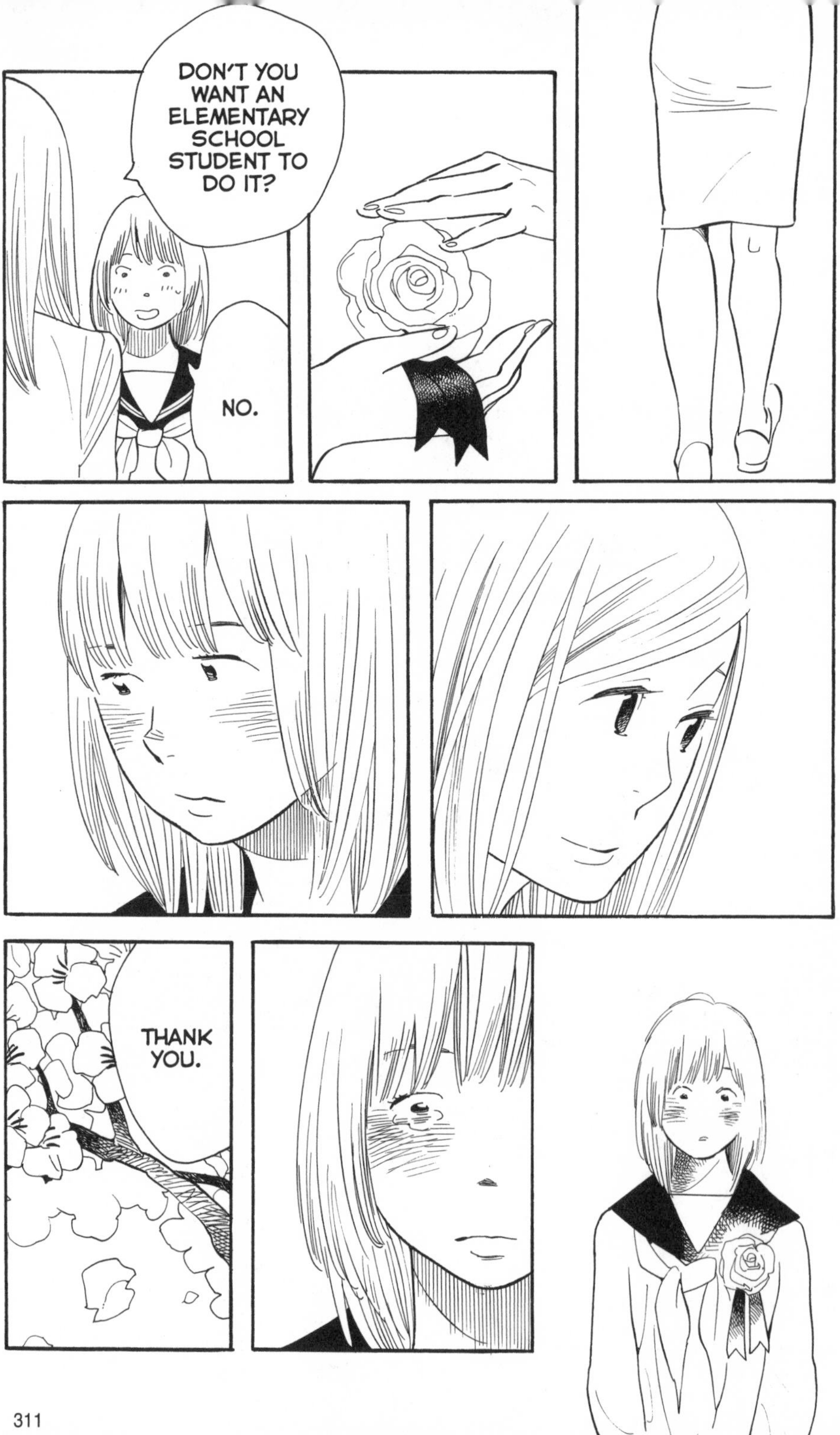
DON'T YOU WANT AN ELEMENTARY SCHOOL STUDENT TO DO IT?
NO.
THANK YOU.

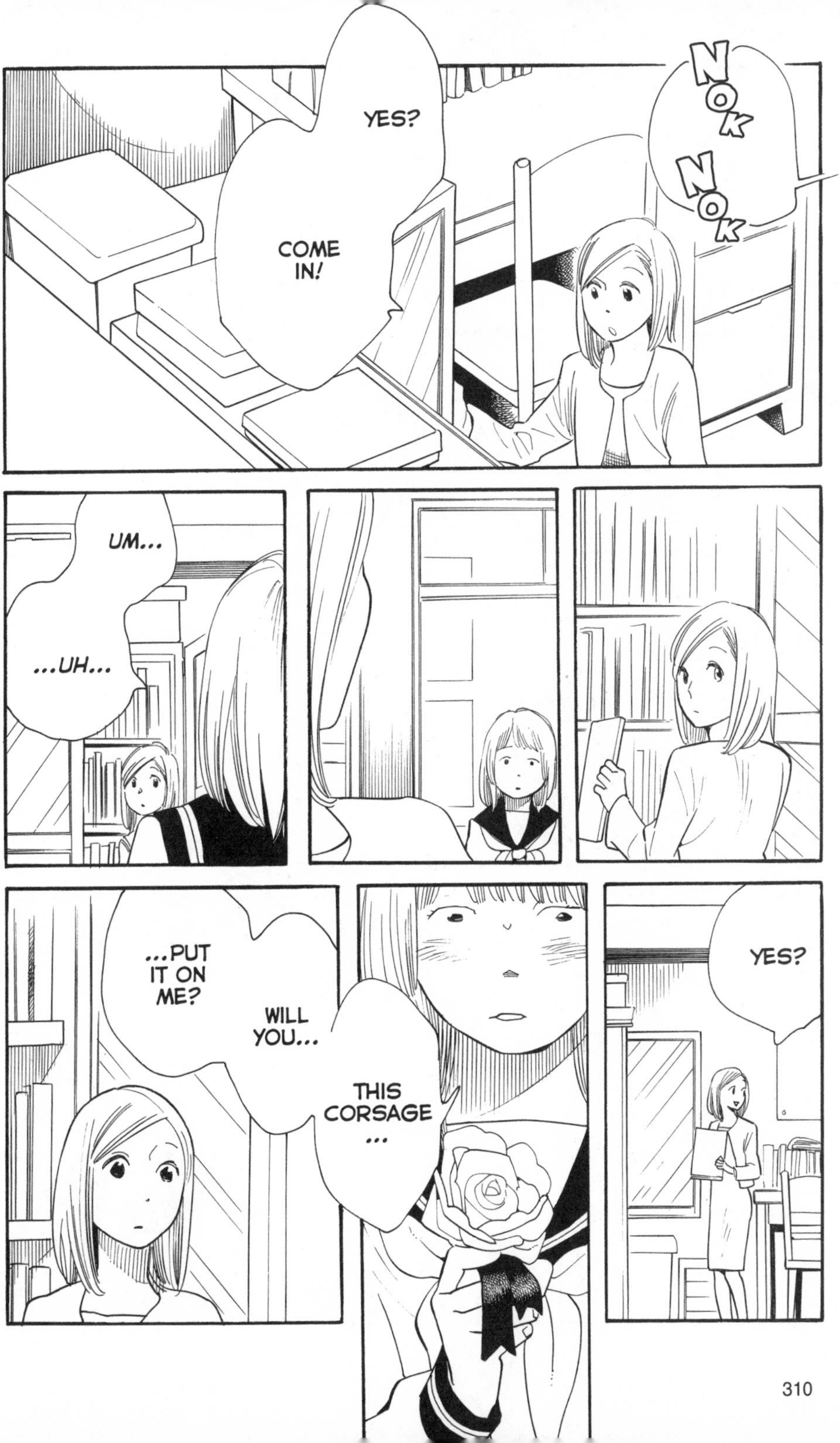
NOK NOK
YES?
COME IN!
UM...
...UH...
YES?
THIS CORSAGE...
WILL YOU...
...PUT IT ON ME?

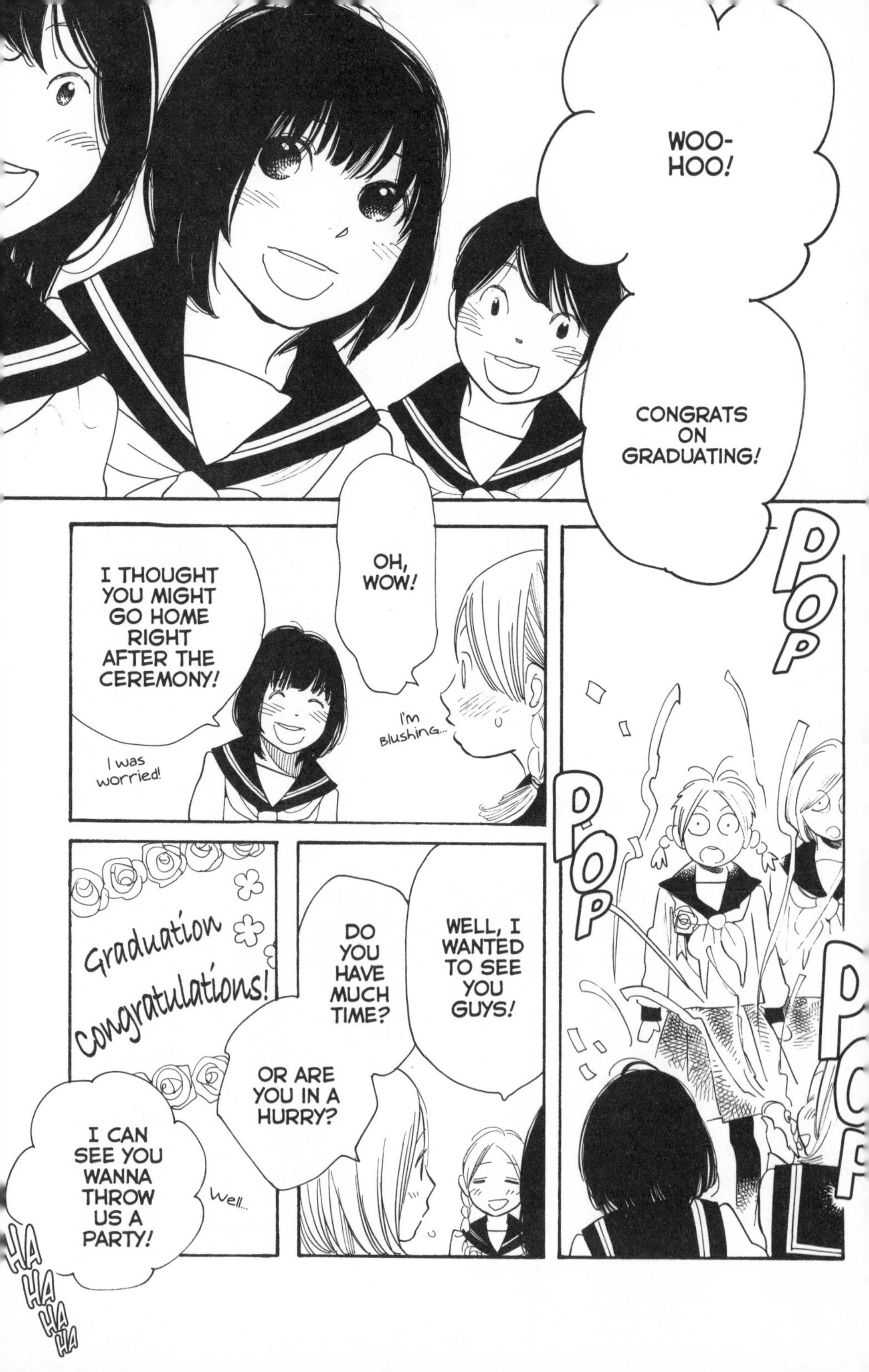
WOO-HOO!
CONGRATS ON GRADUATING!
POP
POP
POP
OH, WOW!
I THOUGHT YOU MIGHT GO HOME RIGHT AFTER THE CEREMONY!
I'm blushing...
I was worried!
WELL, I WANTED TO SEE YOU GUYS!
DO YOU HAVE MUCH TIME?
OR ARE YOU IN A HURRY?
Well...
Graduation Congratulations!
I CAN SEE YOU WANNA THROW US A PARTY!
HA HA HA HA HA

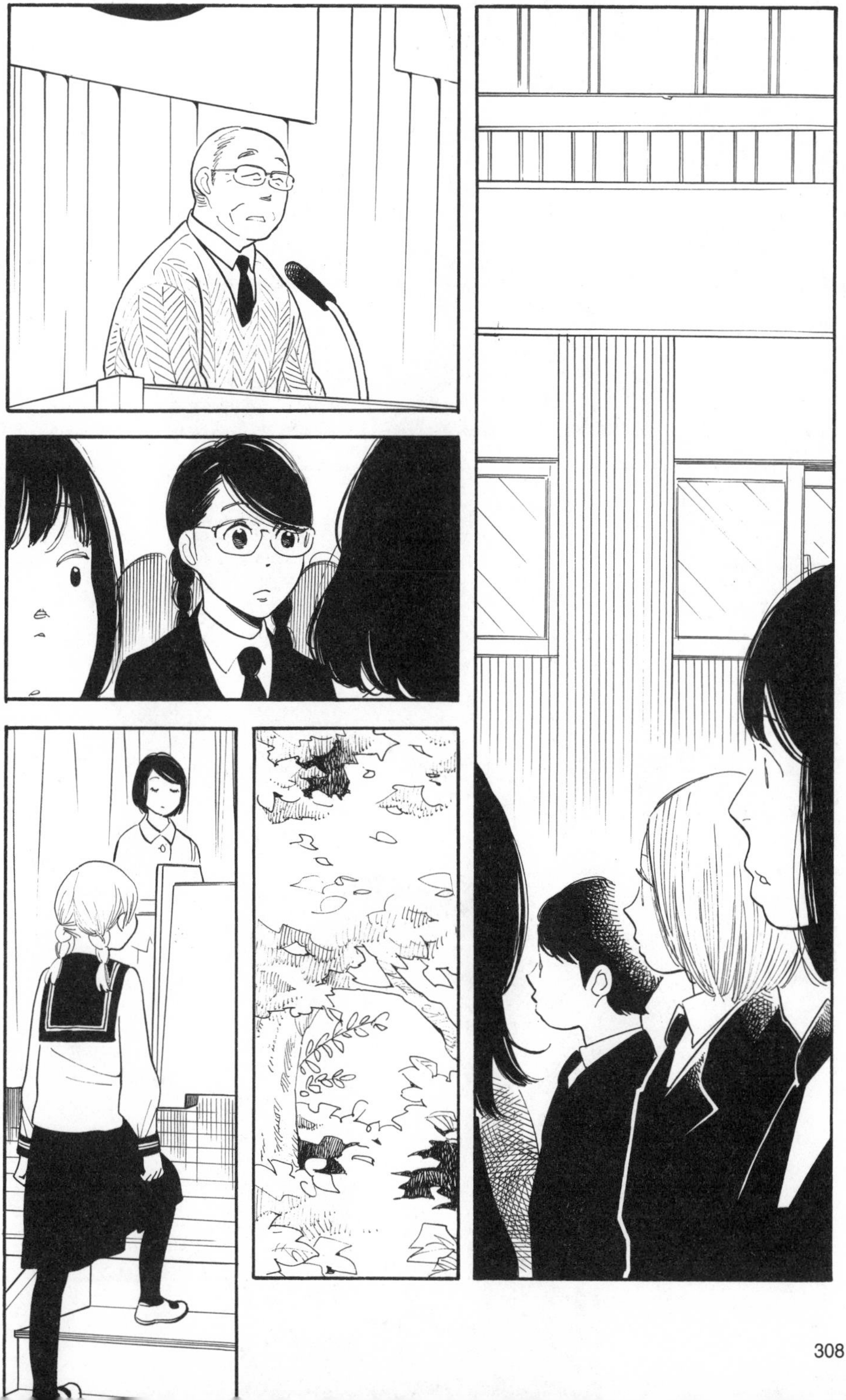

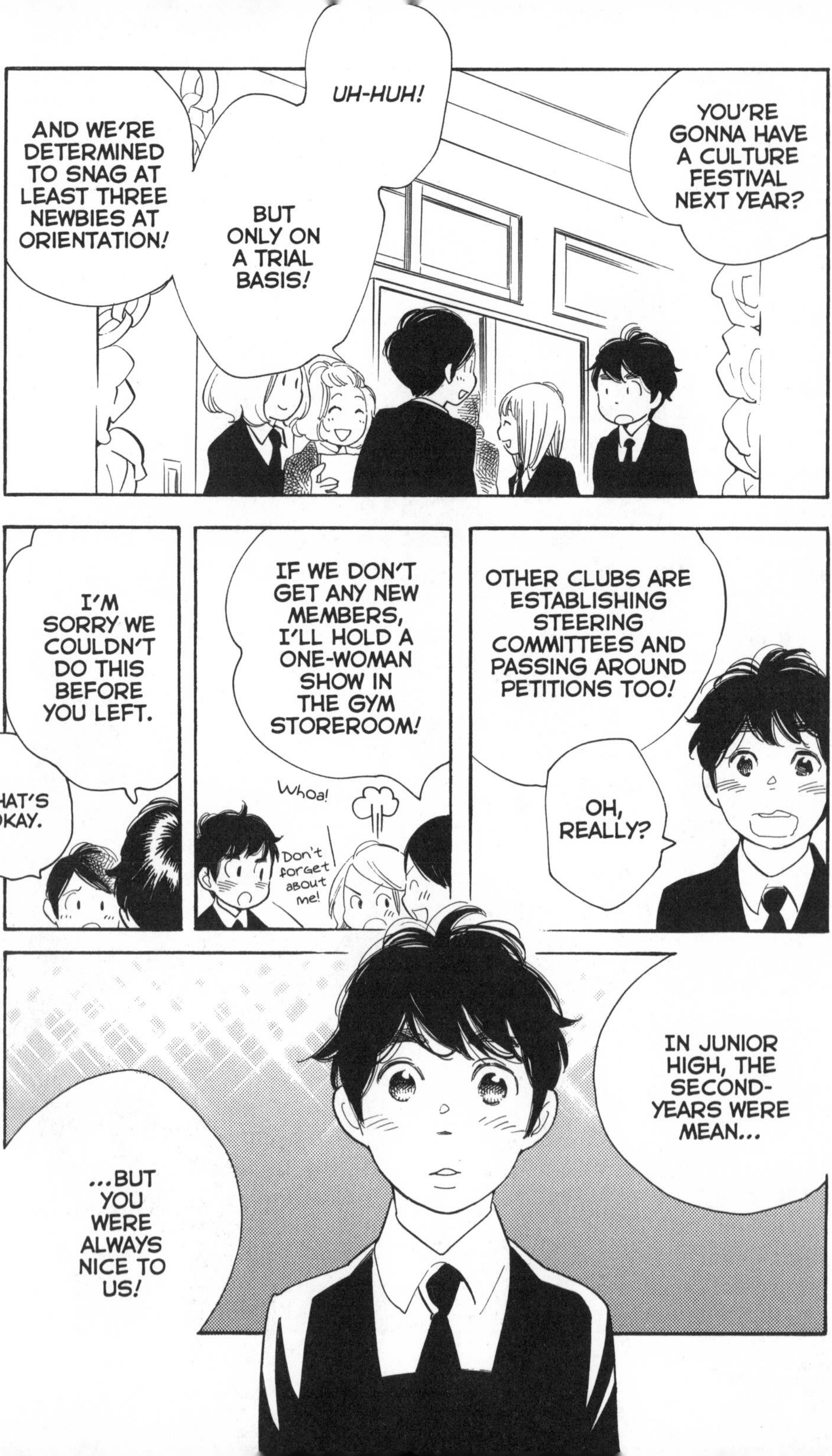
YOU'RE GONNA HAVE A CULTURE FESTIVAL NEXT YEAR?
UH-HUH!
BUT ONLY ON A TRIAL BASIS!
AND WE'RE DETERMINED TO SNAG AT LEAST THREE NEWBIES AT ORIENTATION!
OTHER CLUBS ARE ESTABLISHING STEERING COMMITTEES AND PASSING AROUND PETITIONS TOO!
OH, REALLY?
IF WE DON'T GET ANY NEW MEMBERS, I'LL HOLD A ONE-WOMAN SHOW IN THE GYM STOREROOM!
Whoa!
Don't forget about me!
I'M SORRY WE COULDN'T DO THIS BEFORE YOU LEFT.
THAT'S OKAY.
IN JUNIOR HIGH, THE SECOND-YEARS WERE MEAN...
...BUT YOU WERE ALWAYS NICE TO US!

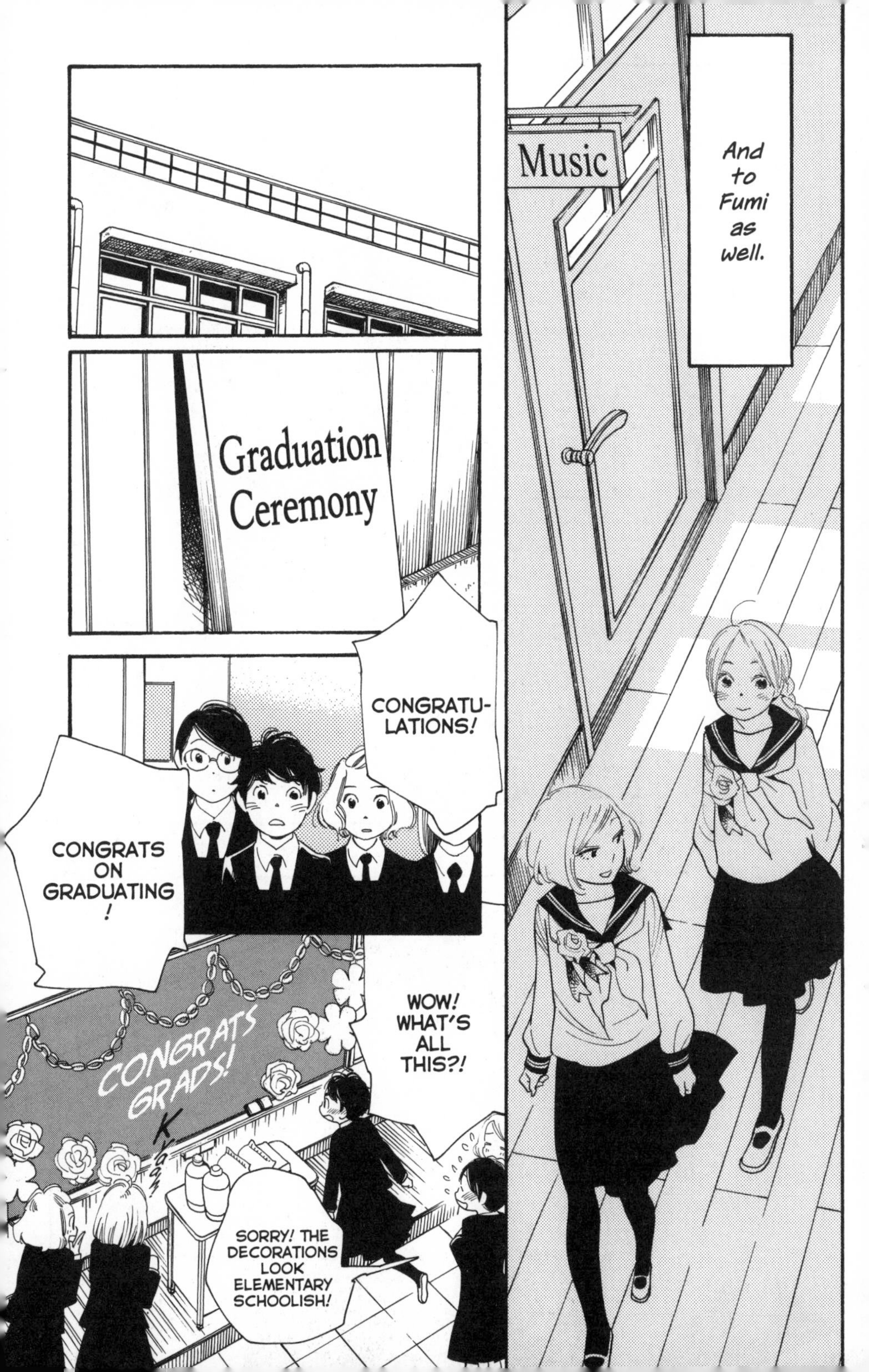
Music
And to Fumi as well.
Graduation Ceremony
CONGRATULATIONS!
CONGRATS ON GRADUATING!
WOW! WHAT'S ALL THIS?!
CONGRATS GRADS!
SORRY! THE DECORATIONS LOOK ELEMENTARY SCHOOLISH!

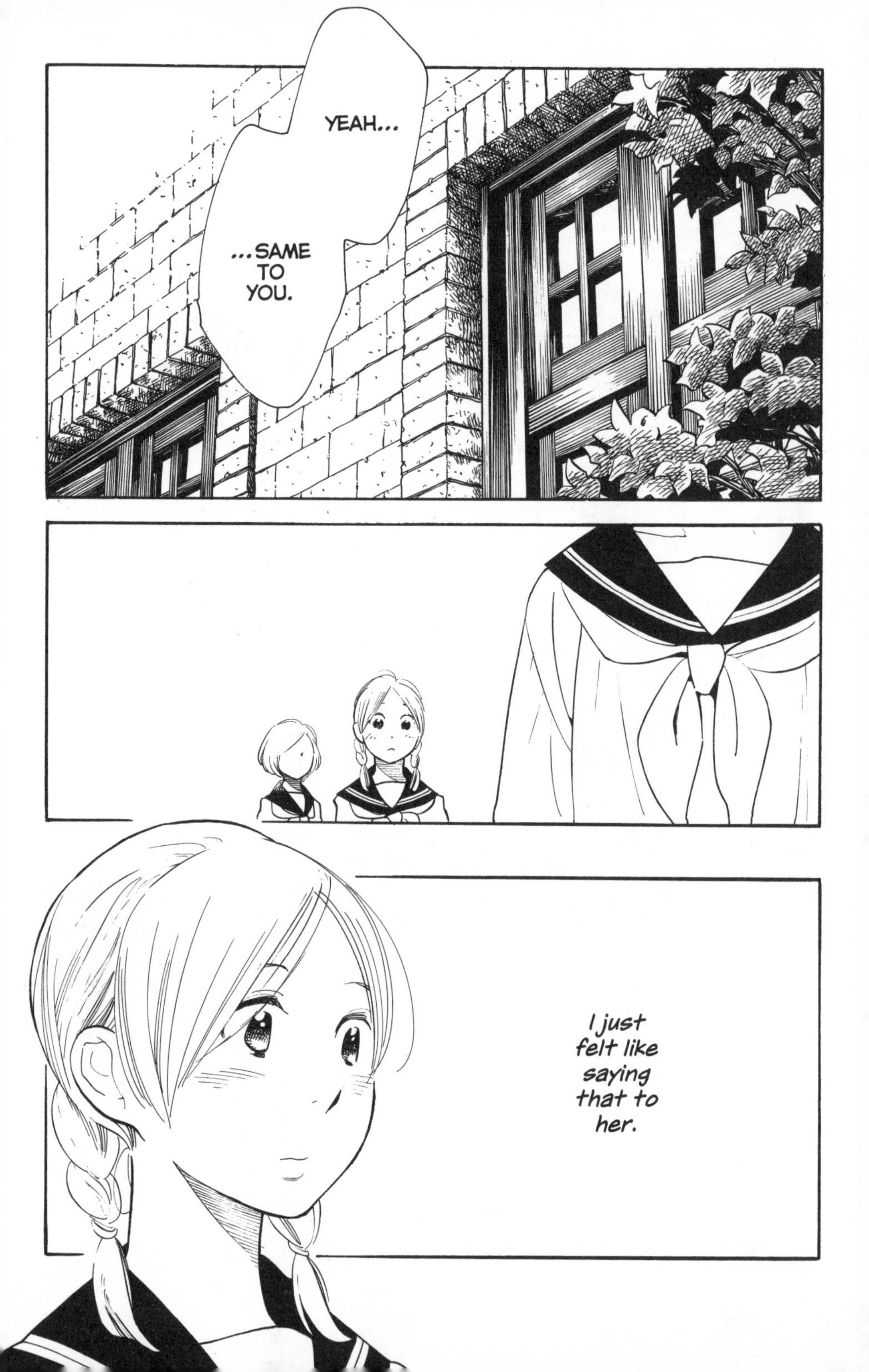
YEAH...
...SAME TO YOU.
I just felt like saying that to her.

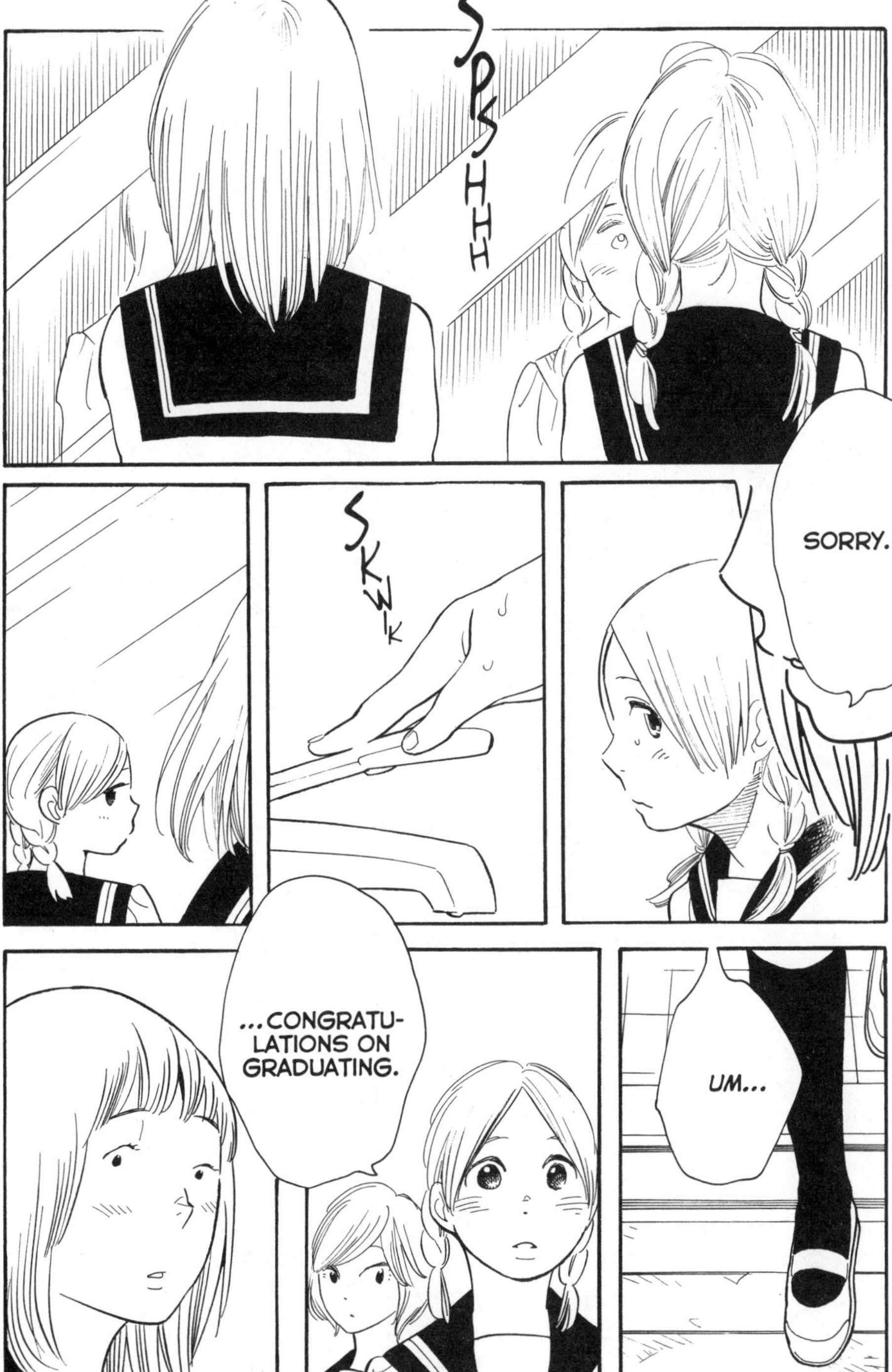
SPSHHH
SORRY.
SKWIK
UM...
...CONGRATU-
LATIONS ON
GRADUATING.

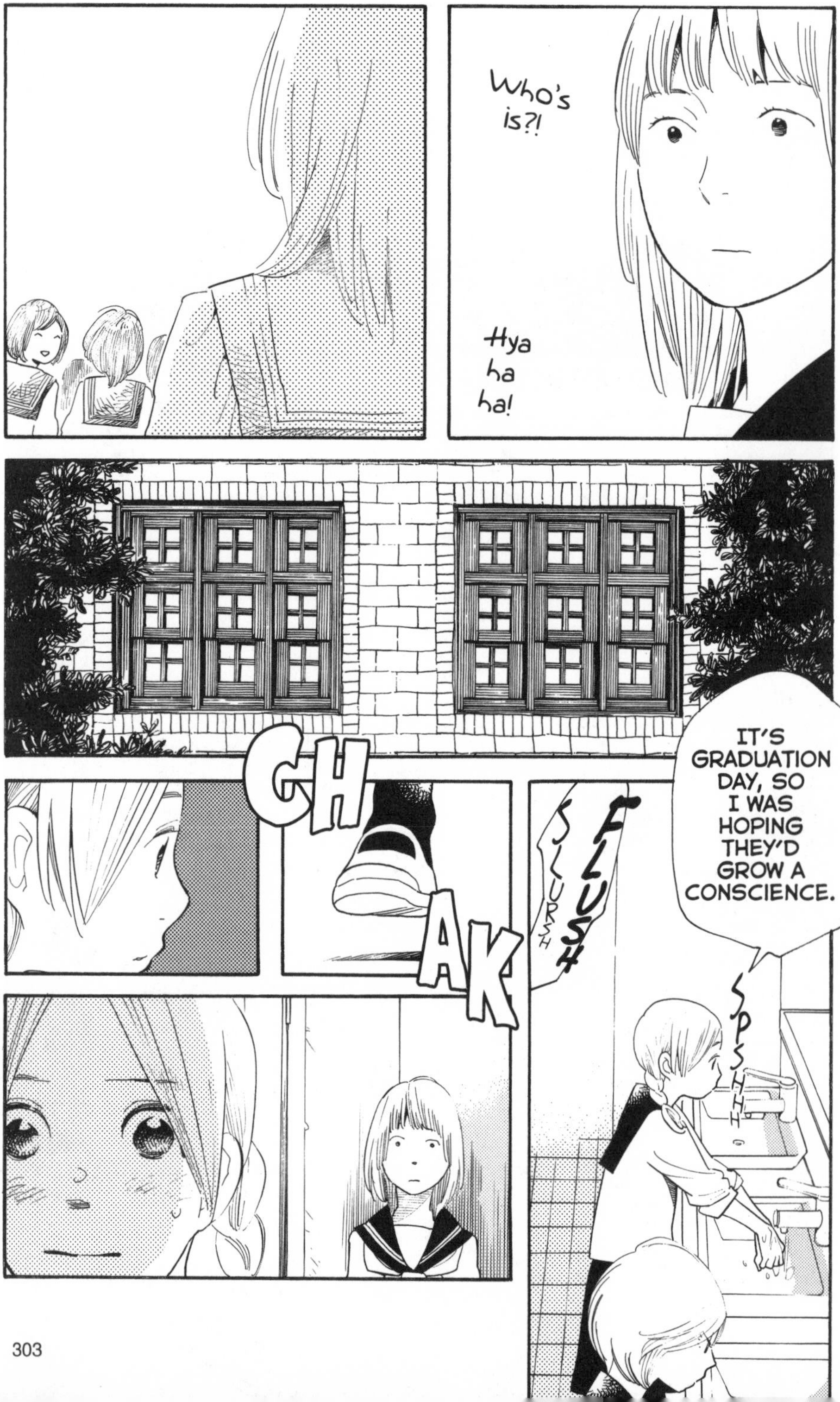
Who's is?!
Hya ha ha!
FLUSH
SLURSH
IT'S GRADUATION DAY, SO I WAS HOPING THEY'D GROW A CONSCIENCE.
SPSHHH
CHAK

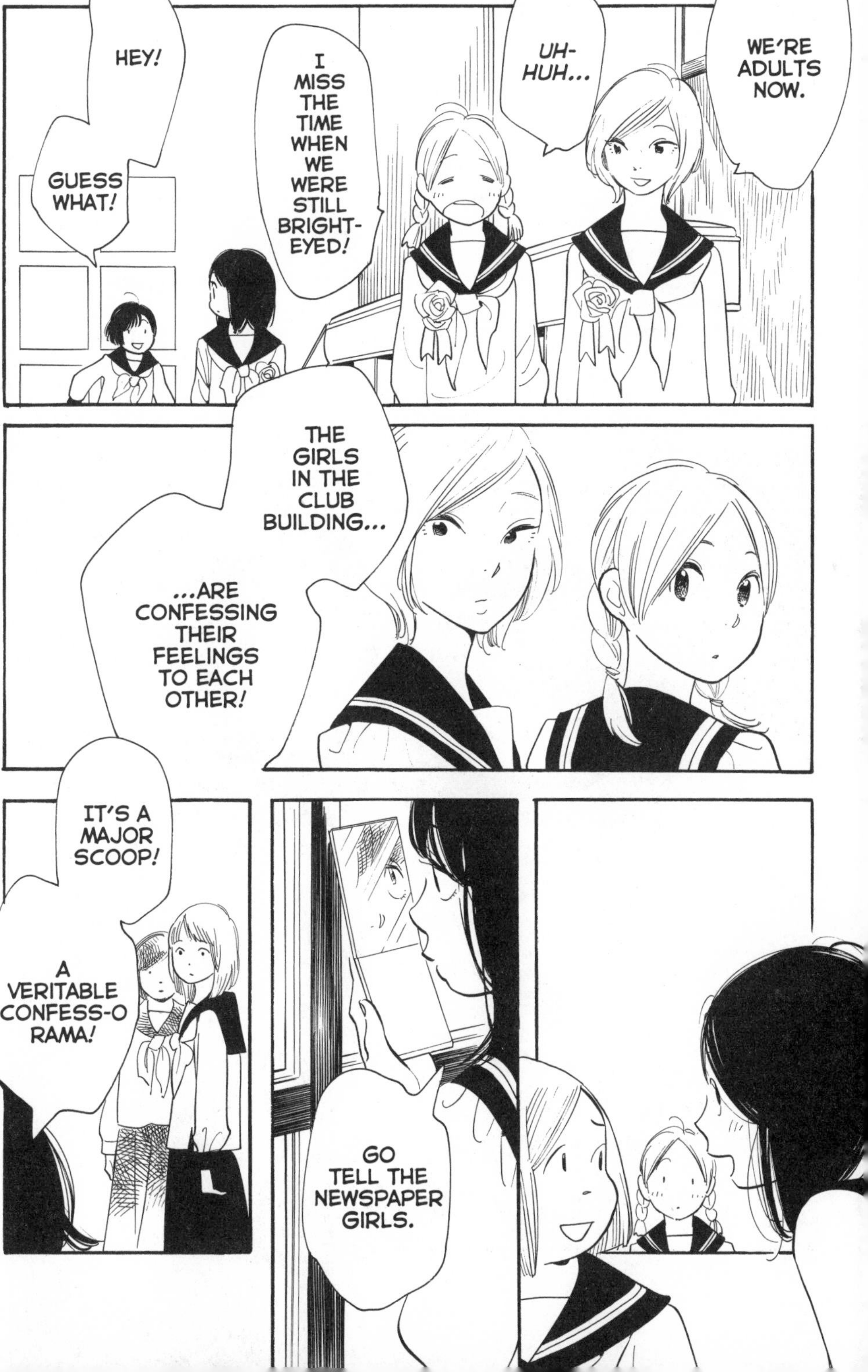
WE'RE ADULTS NOW.
UH-HUH...
I MISS THE TIME WHEN WE WERE STILL BRIGHT-EYED!
HEY!
GUESS WHAT!
THE GIRLS IN THE CLUB BUILDING...
...ARE CONFESSING THEIR FEELINGS TO EACH OTHER!
GO TELL THE NEWSPAPER GIRLS.
IT'S A MAJOR SCOOP!
A VERITABLE CONFESS-O RAMA!

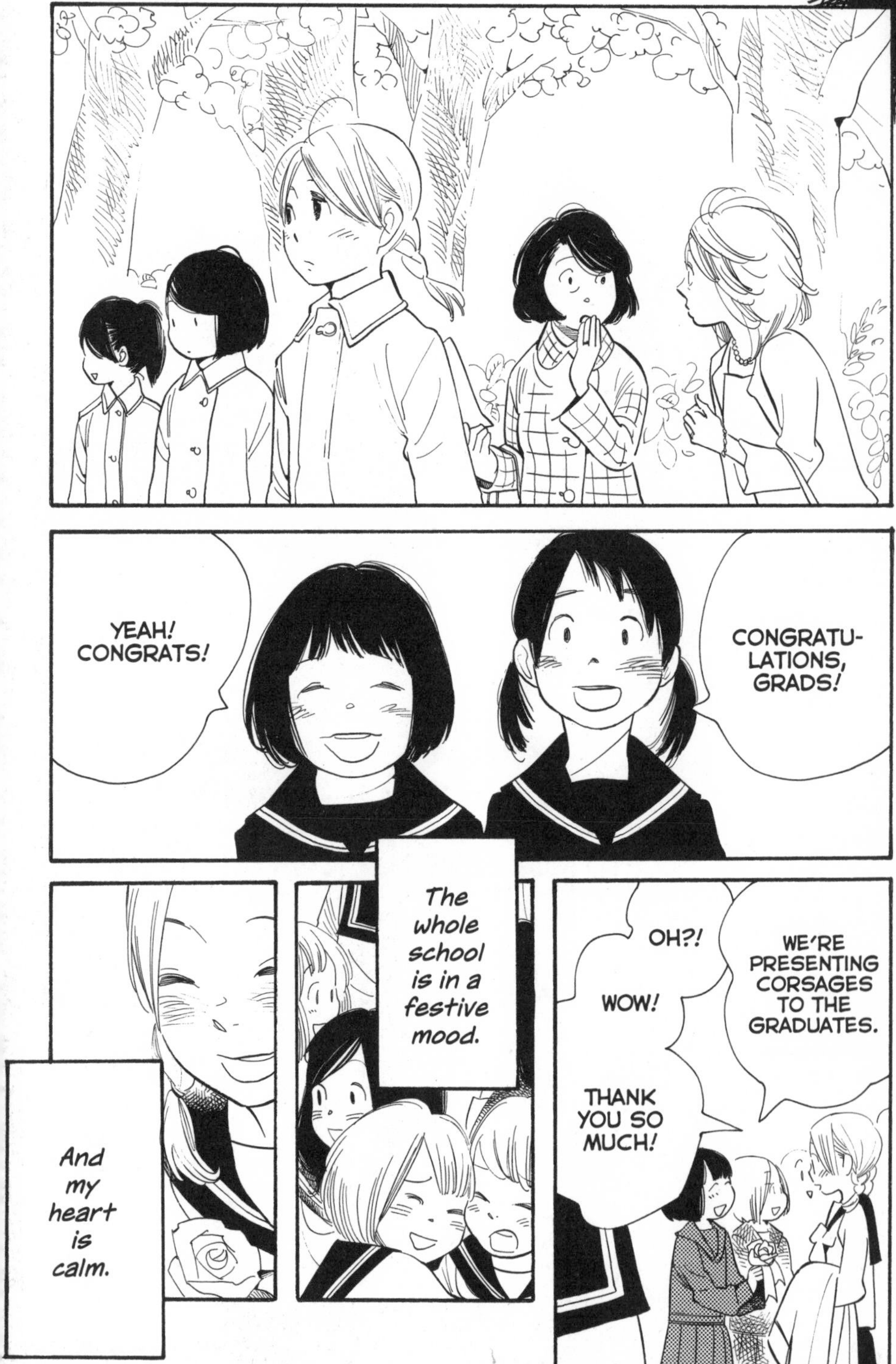
CONGRATU-LATIONS, GRADS!
YEAH! CONGRATS!
WE'RE PRESENTING CORSAGES TO THE GRADUATES.
OH?!
WOW!
THANK YOU SO MUCH!
The whole school is in a festive mood.
And my heart is calm.

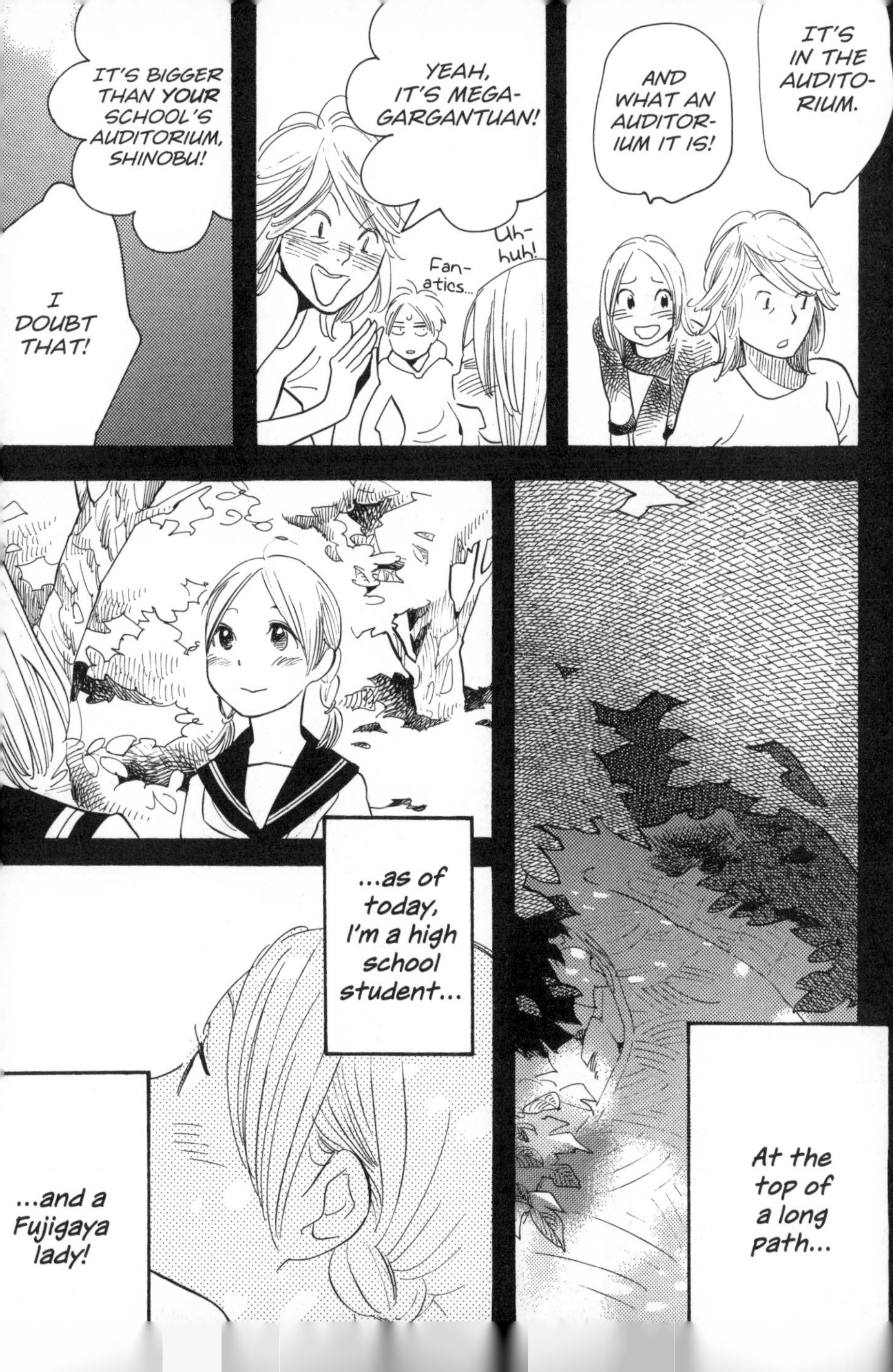
IT'S IN THE AUDITORIUM.
AND WHAT AN AUDITORIUM IT IS!
YEAH, IT'S MEGA-GARGANTUAN!
Uh-huh!
Fan-atics...
IT'S BIGGER THAN YOUR SCHOOL'S AUDITORIUM, SHINOBU!
I DOUBT THAT!
At the top of a long path...
...as of today, I'm a high school student...
...and a Fujigaya lady!

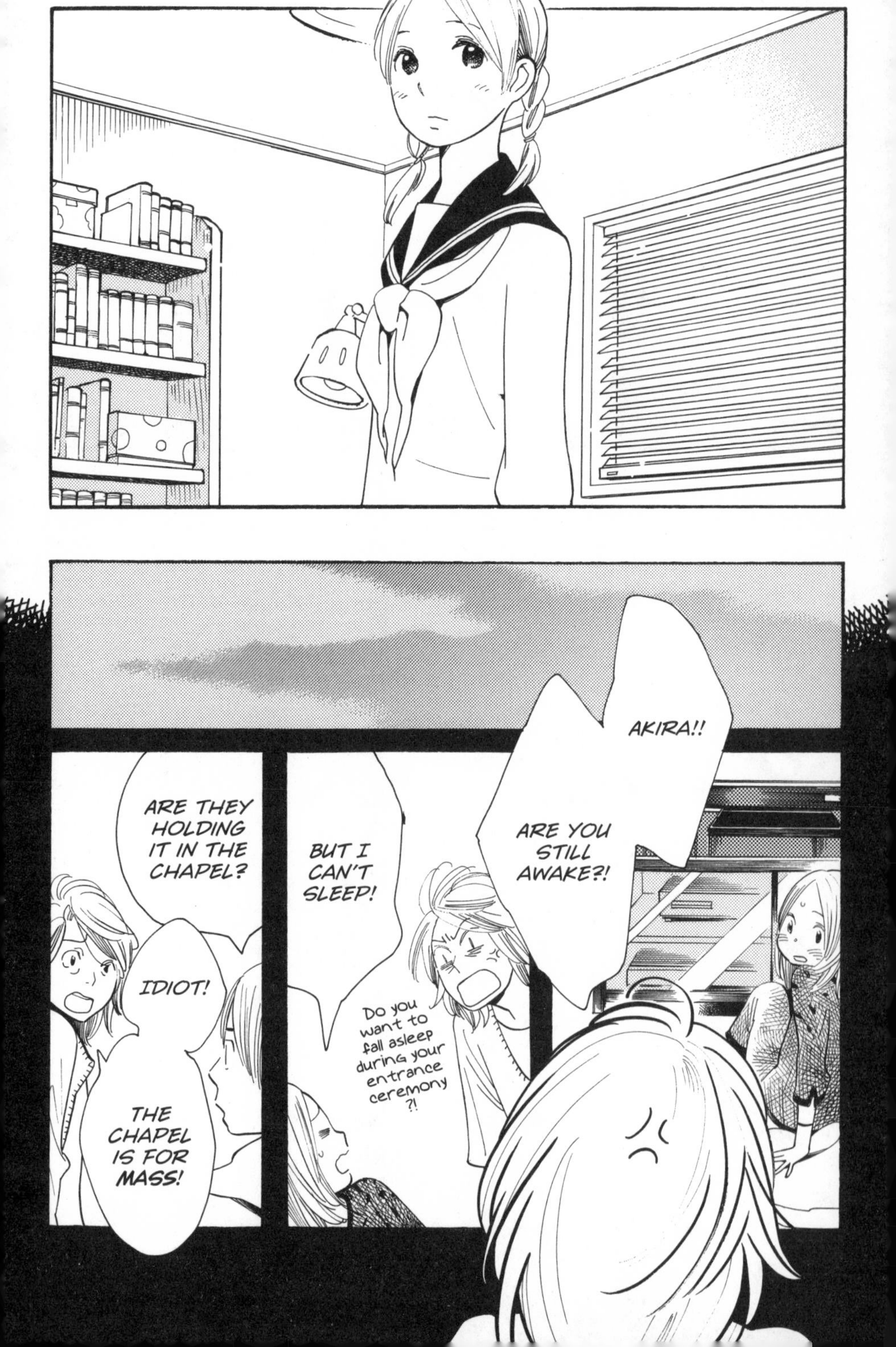
AKIRA!! ARE YOU STILL AWAKE?!
Do you want to fall asleep during your entrance ceremony?!
BUT I CAN'T SLEEP!
ARE THEY HOLDING IT IN THE CHAPEL?
IDIOT! THE CHAPEL IS FOR MASS!

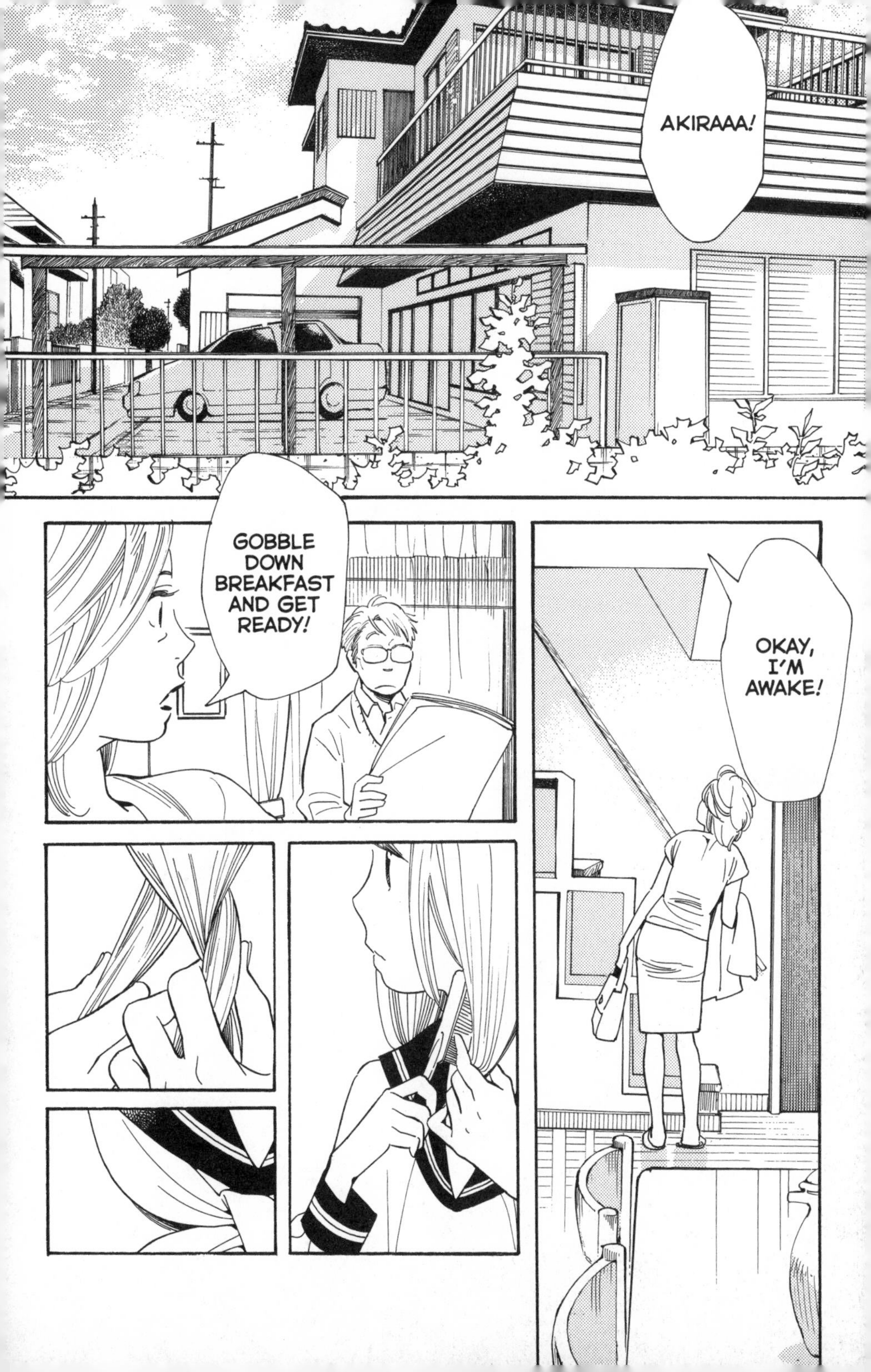
AKIRAAA!
OKAY, I'M AWAKE!
GOBBLE DOWN BREAKFAST AND GET READY!

Sweet Blue Flowers

#51 Wandering the World of the Seventh Sense

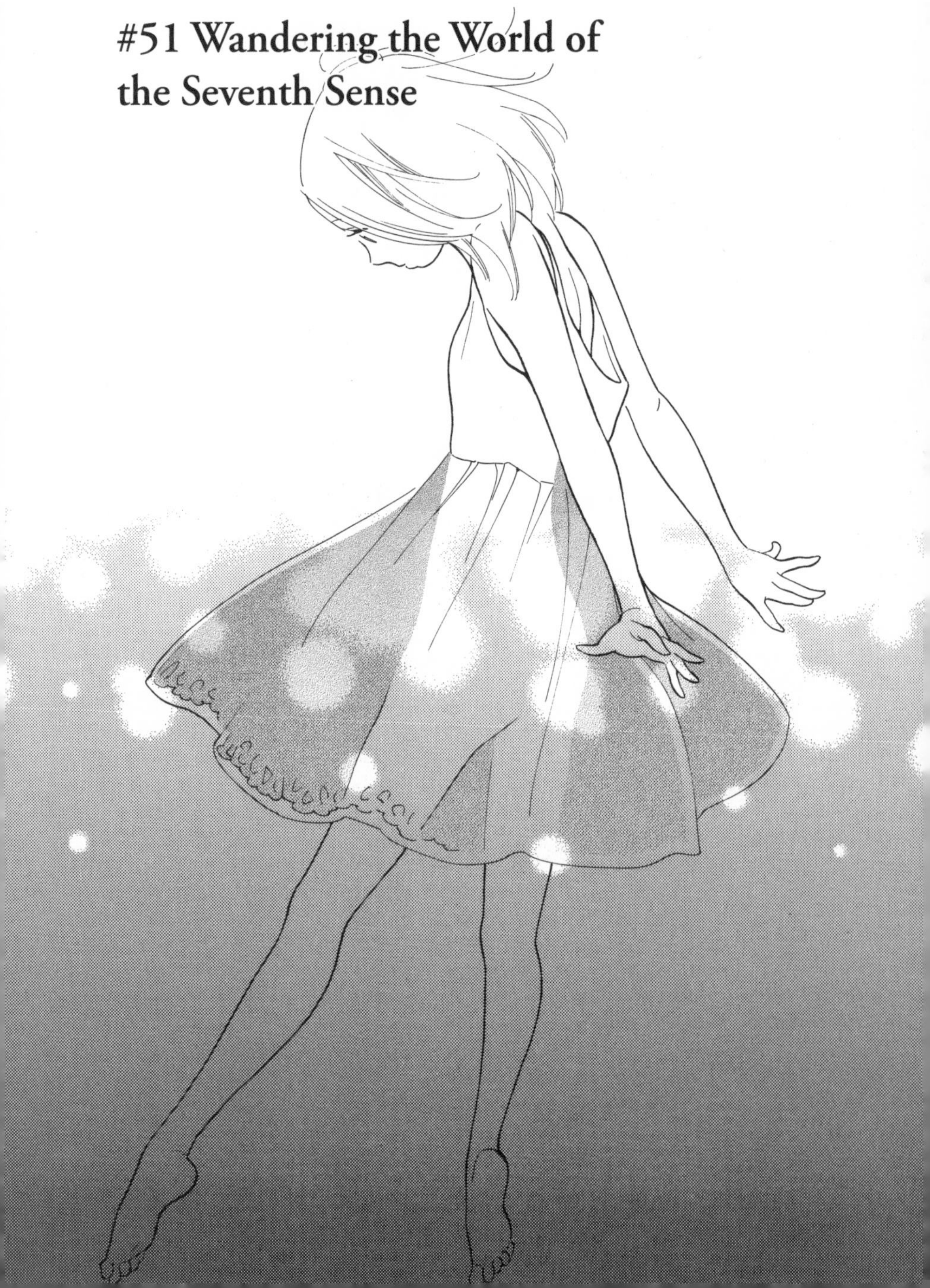

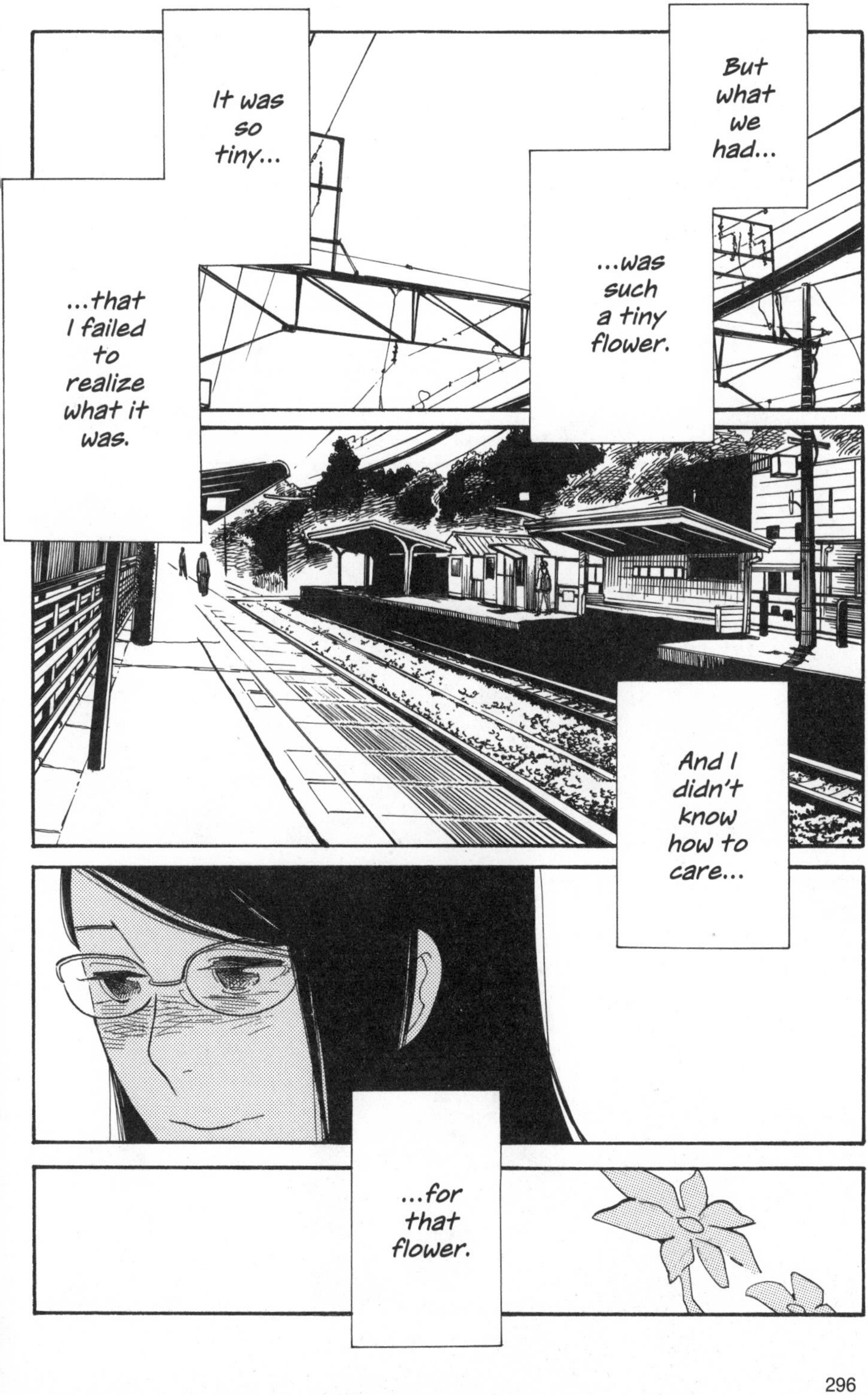
But what we had...
...was such a tiny flower.
It was so tiny...
...that I failed to realize what it was.
And I didn't know how to care...
...for that flower.

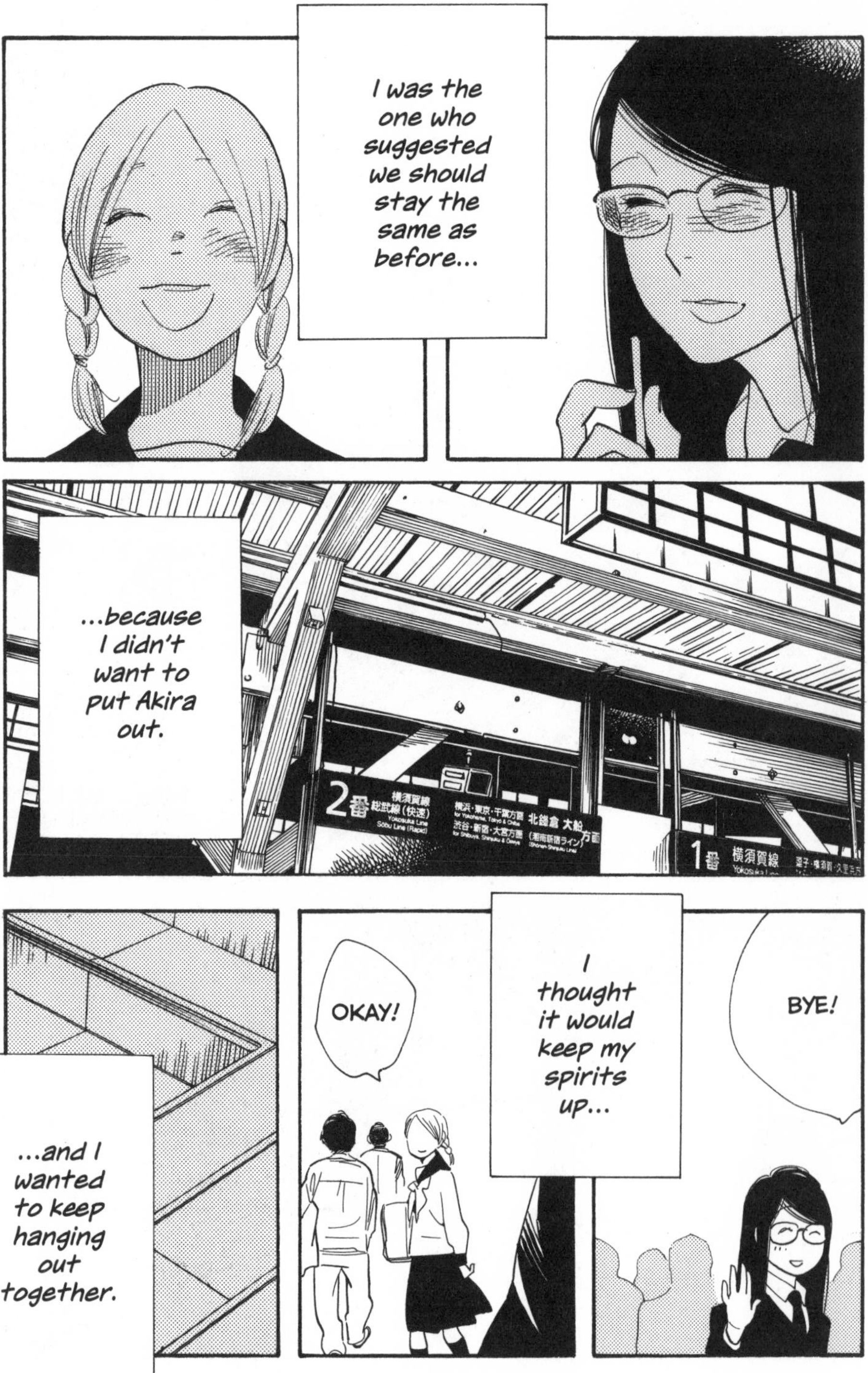
I was the one who suggested we should stay the same as before...
...because I didn't want to put Akira out.
2番 横須賀線 総武線(快速)
横浜・東京・千葉方面
渋谷・新宿・大宮方面
北鎌倉 大船方面
(湘南新宿ライン)
1番 横須賀線
BYE!
I thought it would keep my spirits up...
OKAY!
...and I wanted to keep hanging out together.

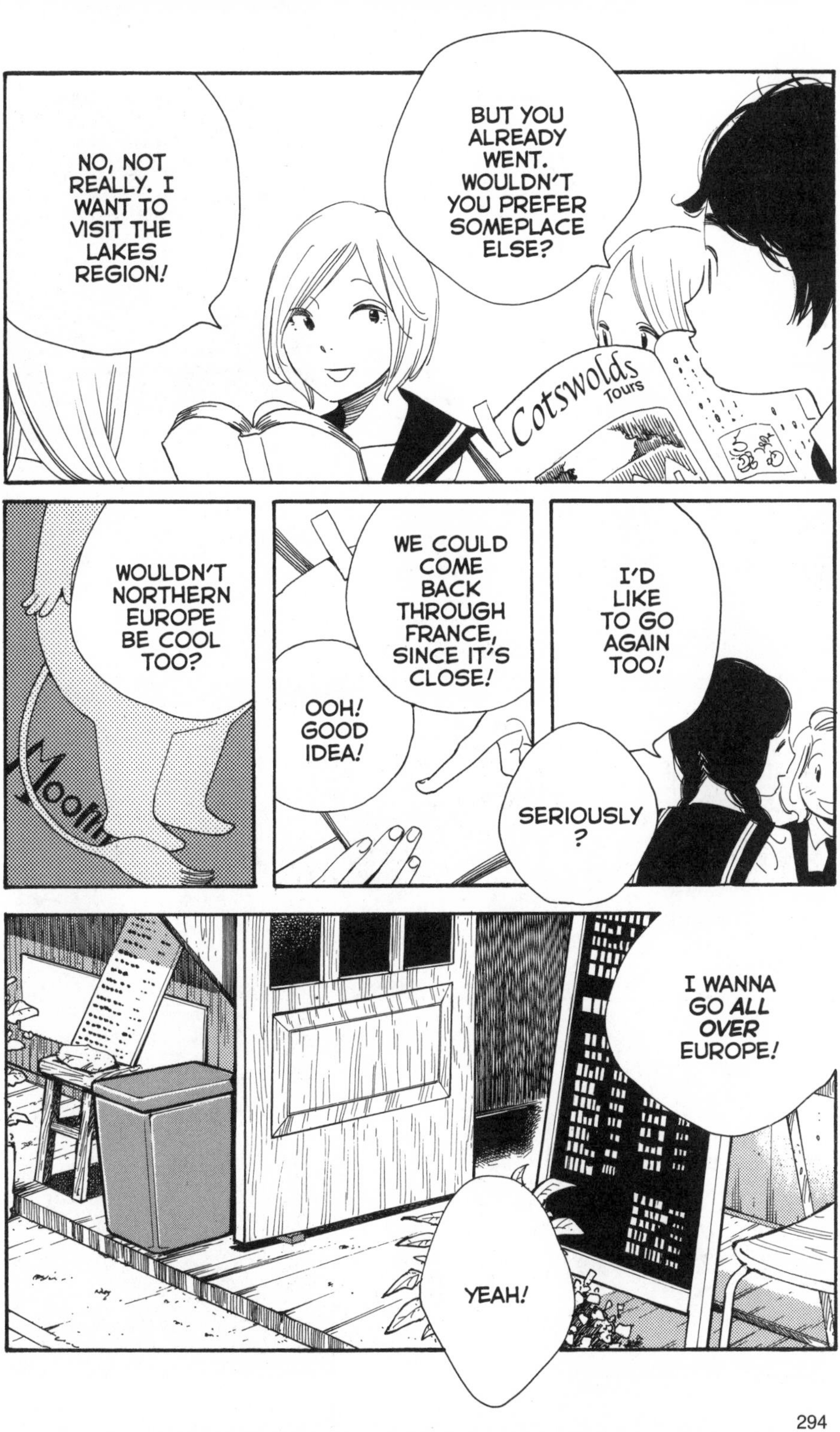
BUT YOU ALREADY WENT. WOULDN'T YOU PREFER SOMEPLACE ELSE?
NO, NOT REALLY. I WANT TO VISIT THE LAKES REGION!
Cotswolds Tours
I'D LIKE TO GO AGAIN TOO!
SERIOUSLY?
WE COULD COME BACK THROUGH FRANCE, SINCE IT'S CLOSE!
OOH! GOOD IDEA!
WOULDN'T NORTHERN EUROPE BE COOL TOO?
I WANNA GO ***ALL OVER*** EUROPE!
YEAH!

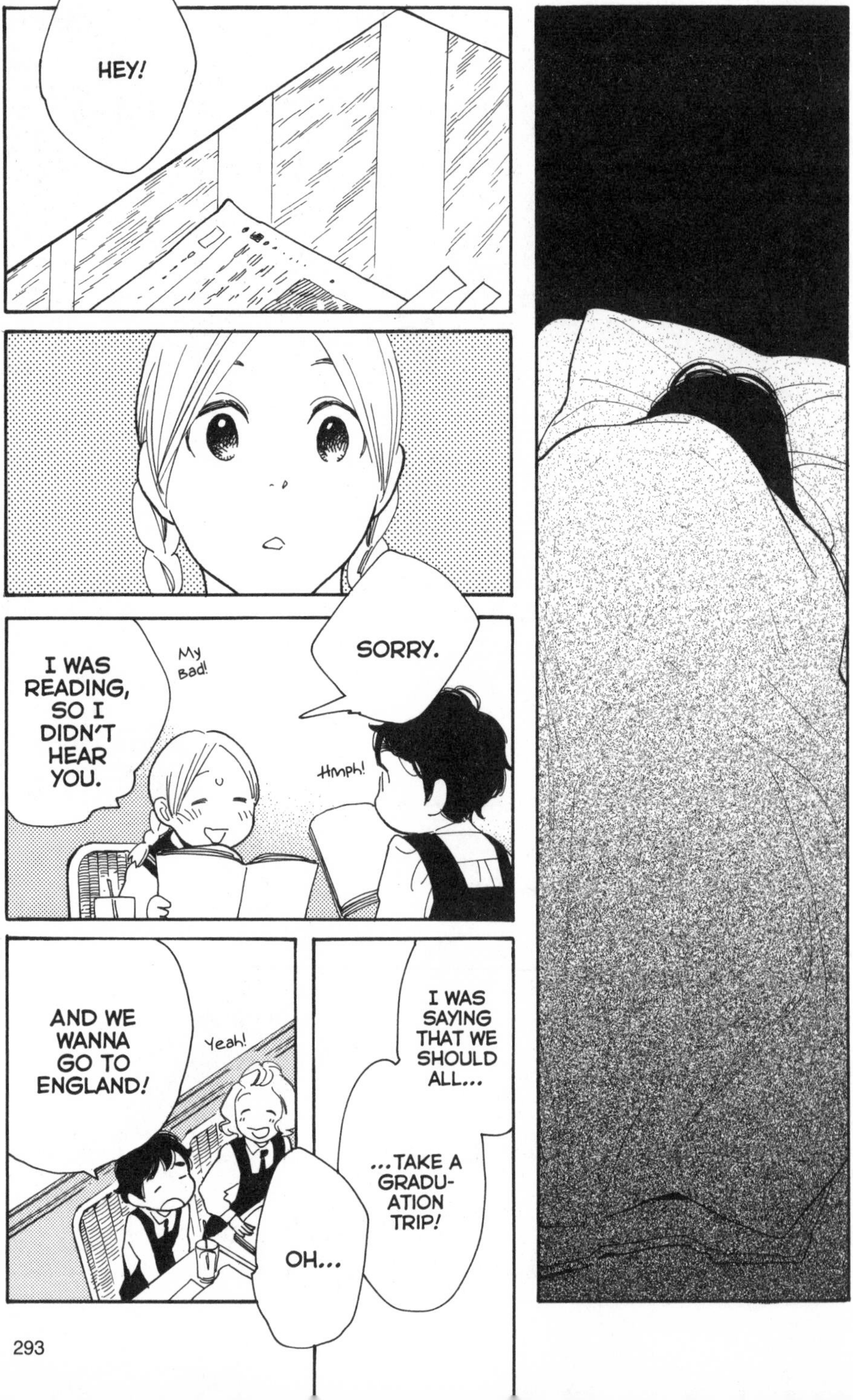
HEY!
SORRY.
I WAS READING, SO I DIDN'T HEAR YOU.
My Bad!
Hmph!
I WAS SAYING THAT WE SHOULD ALL...
...TAKE A GRADUATION TRIP!
OH...
AND WE WANNA GO TO ENGLAND!
Yeah!

STOP THAT,
FUMI!

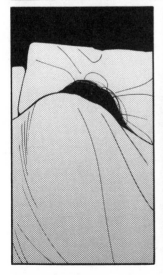

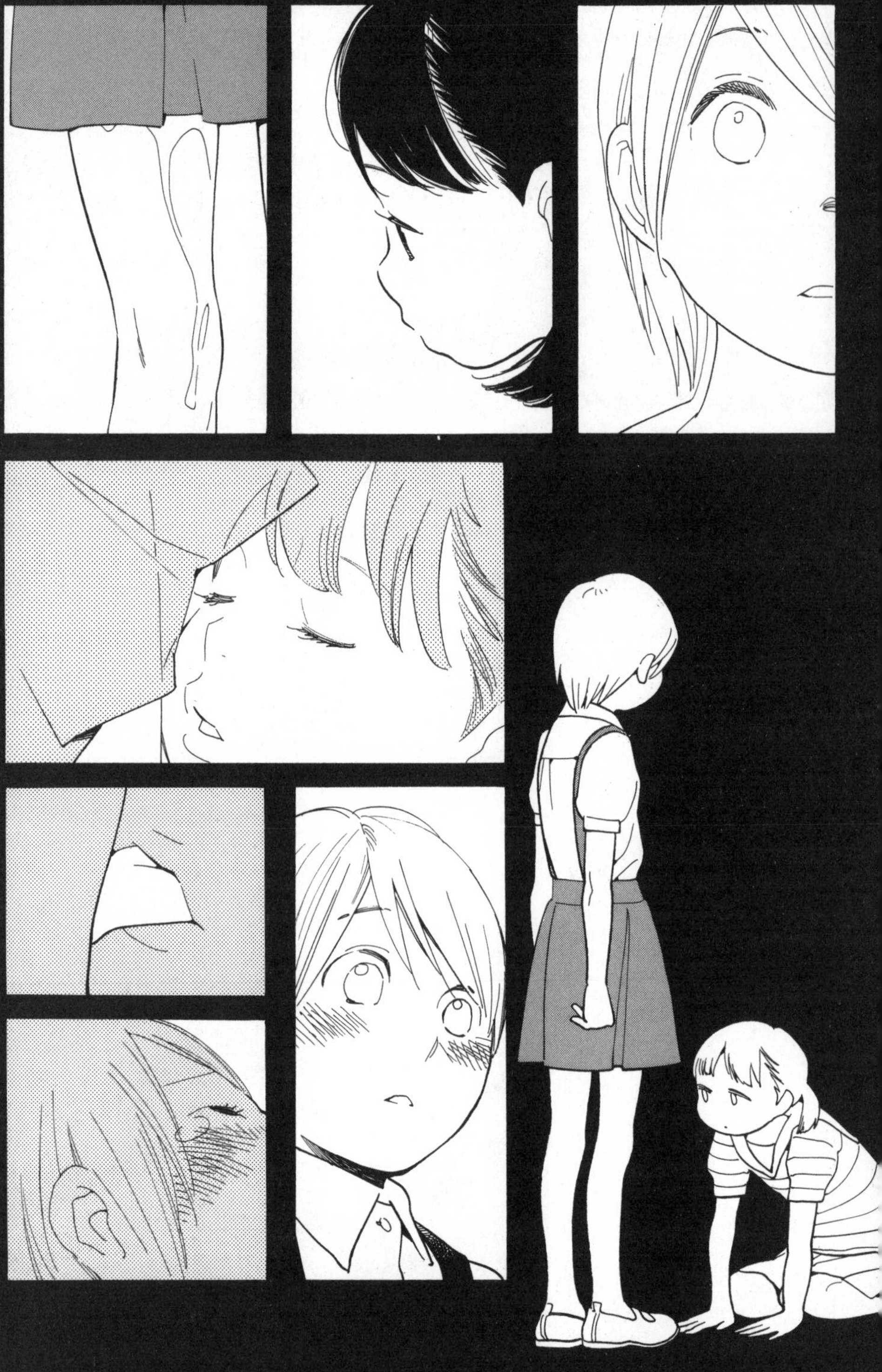

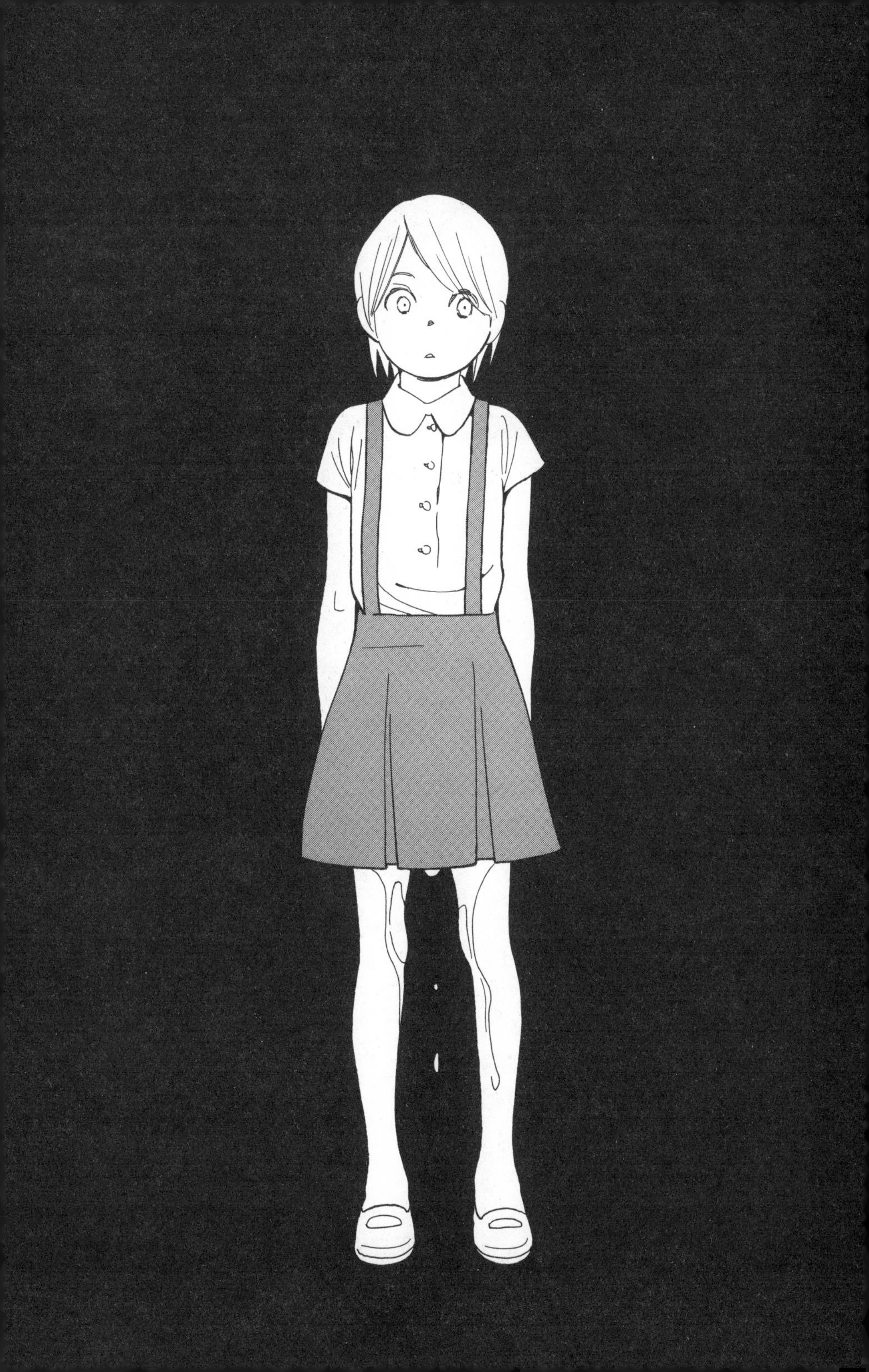

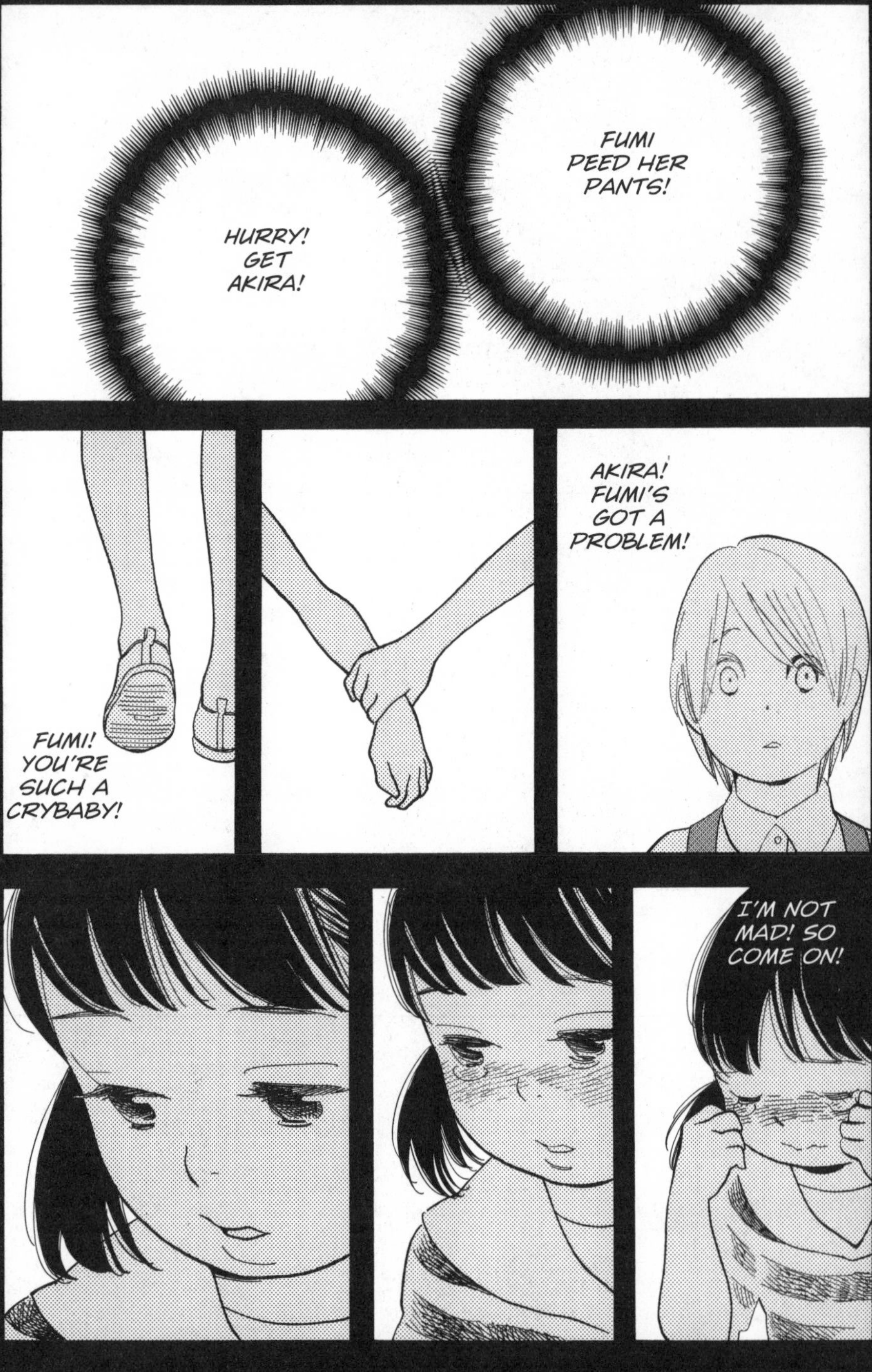
FUMI PEED HER PANTS!
HURRY! GET AKIRA!
AKIRA! FUMI'S GOT A PROBLEM!
FUMI! YOU'RE SUCH A CRYBABY!
I'M NOT MAD! SO COME ON!

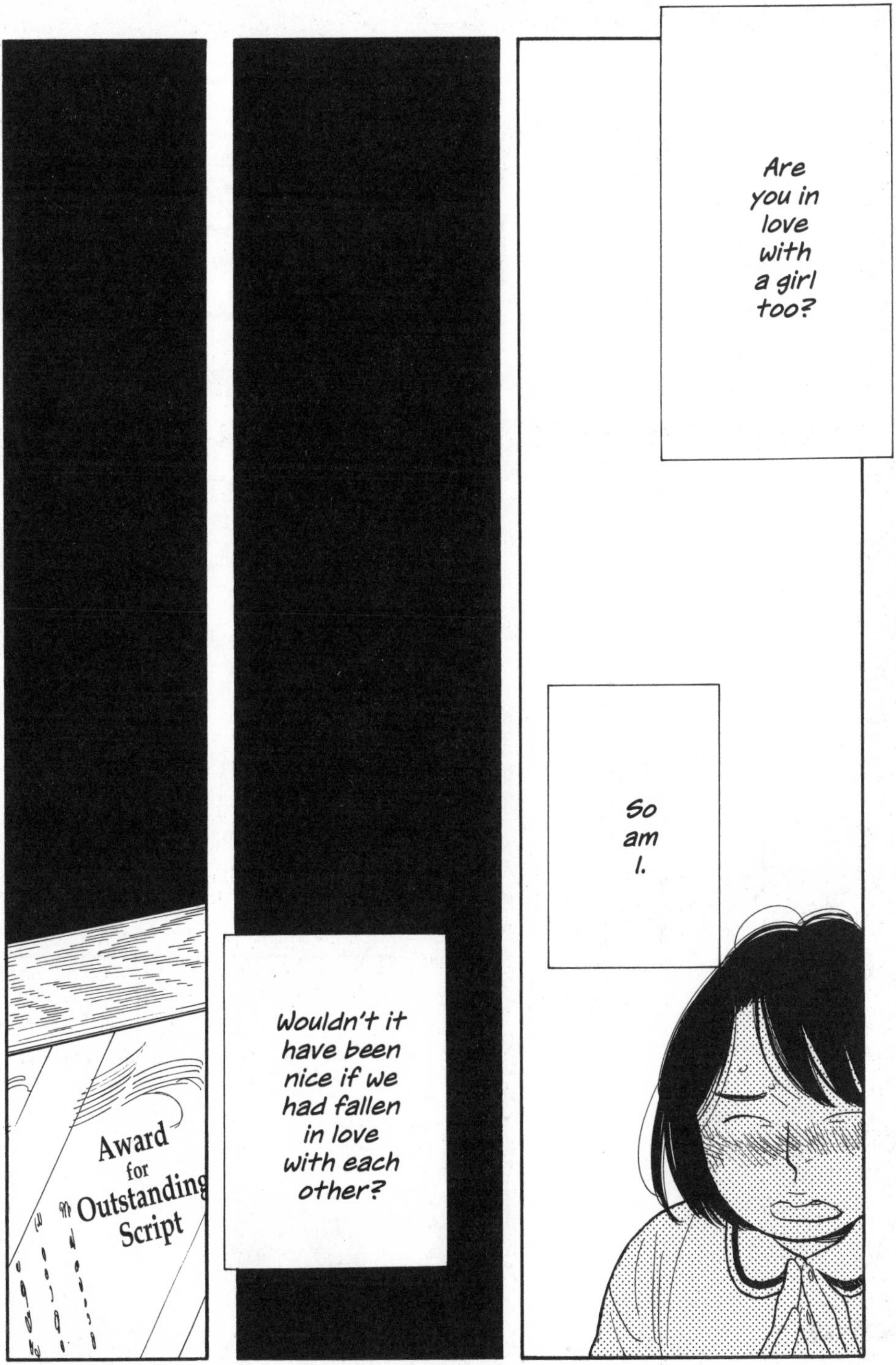
Are you in love with a girl too?
So am I.
Wouldn't it have been nice if we had fallen in love with each other?
Award for Outstanding Script

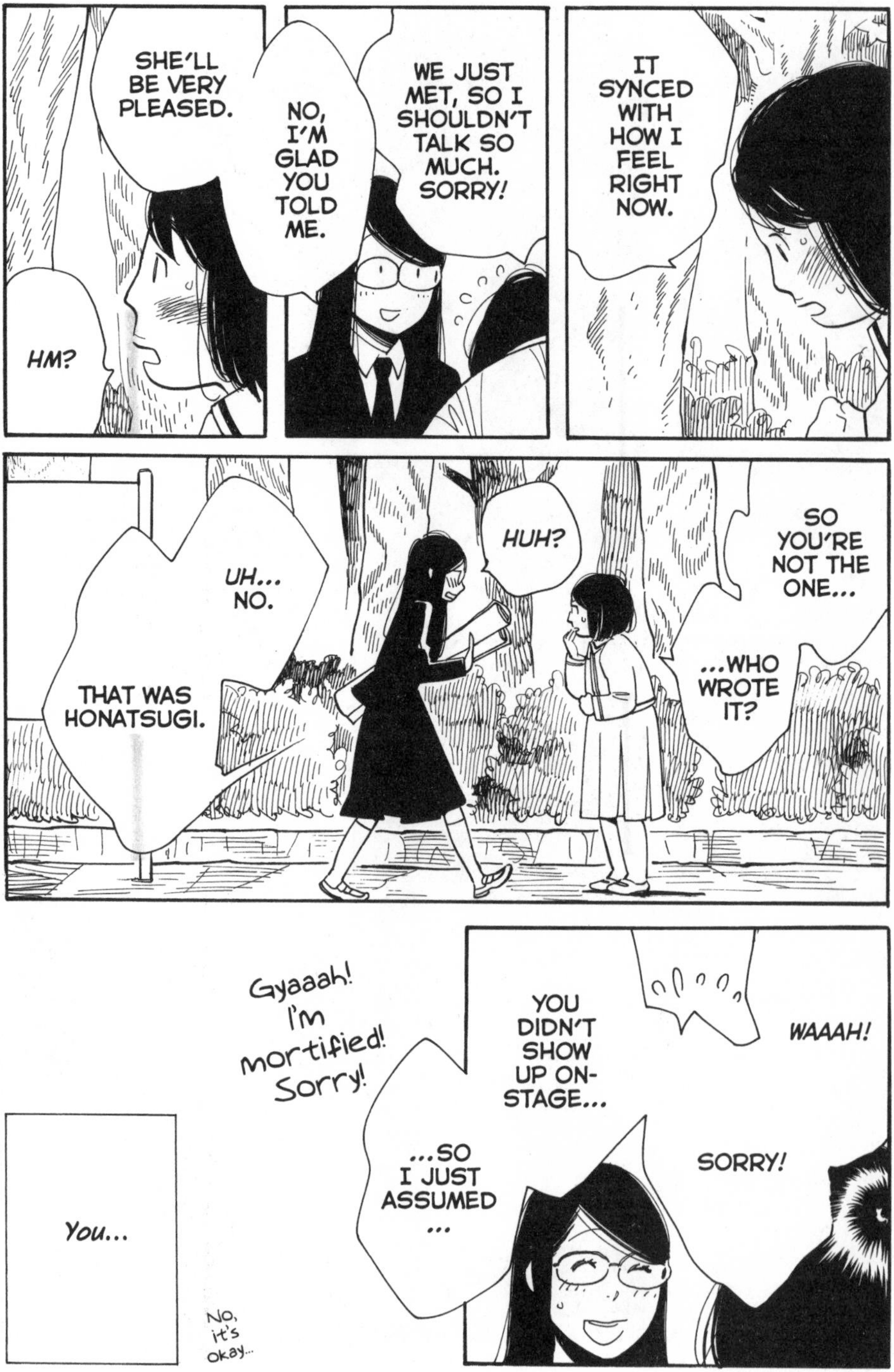
IT SYNCED WITH HOW I FEEL RIGHT NOW.
WE JUST MET, SO I SHOULDN'T TALK SO MUCH. SORRY!
NO, I'M GLAD YOU TOLD ME.
SHE'LL BE VERY PLEASED.
HM?
SO YOU'RE NOT THE ONE...
...WHO WROTE IT?
HUH?
UH... NO.
THAT WAS HONATSUGI.
WAAAH!
SORRY!
YOU DIDN'T SHOW UP ON-STAGE...
...SO I JUST ASSUMED ...
Gyaaah! I'm mortified! Sorry!
You...
No, it's okay...

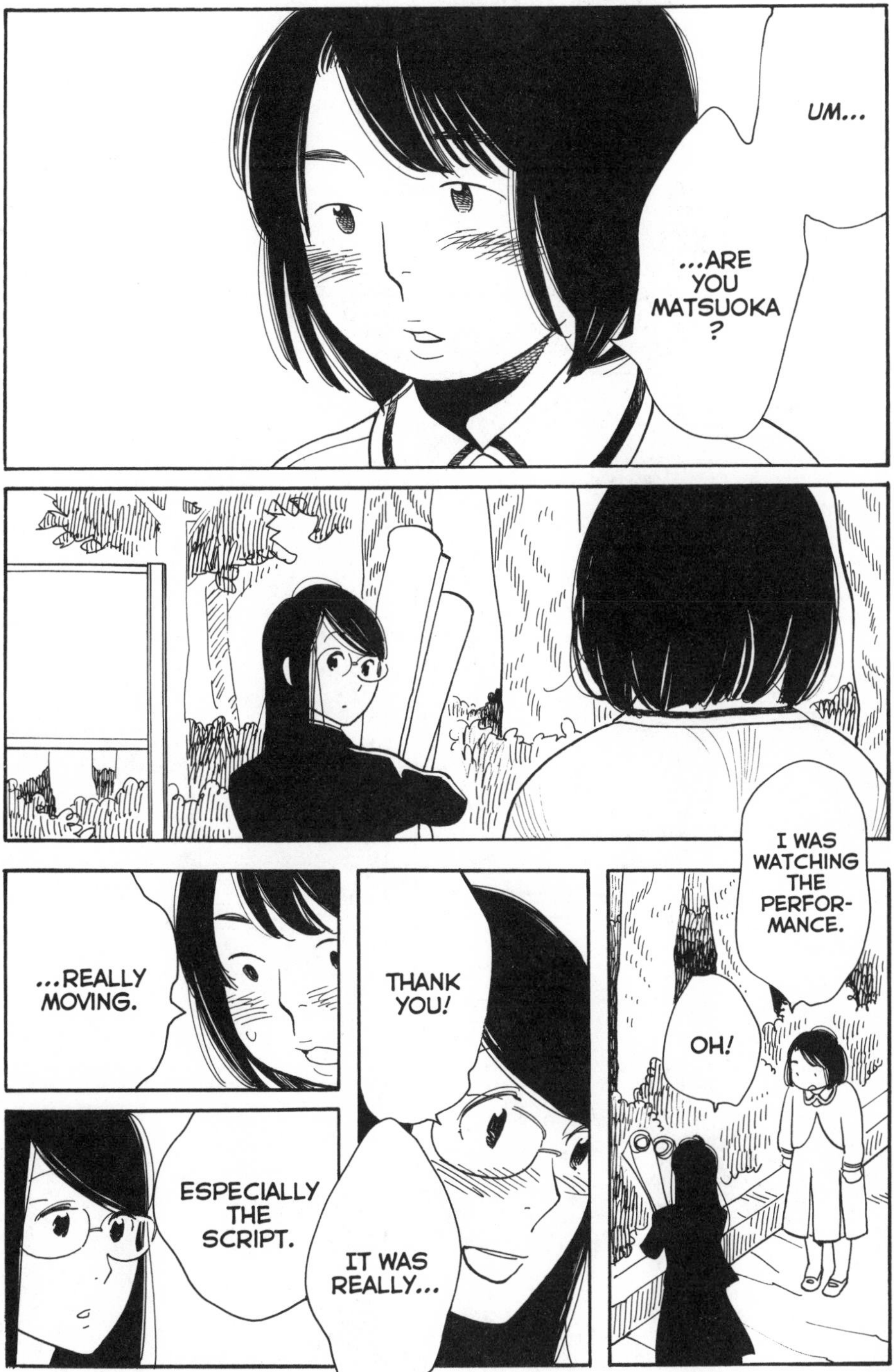

UM...
...ARE YOU MATSUOKA?
I WAS WATCHING THE PERFORMANCE.
OH!
THANK YOU!
IT WAS REALLY...
...REALLY MOVING.
ESPECIALLY THE SCRIPT.

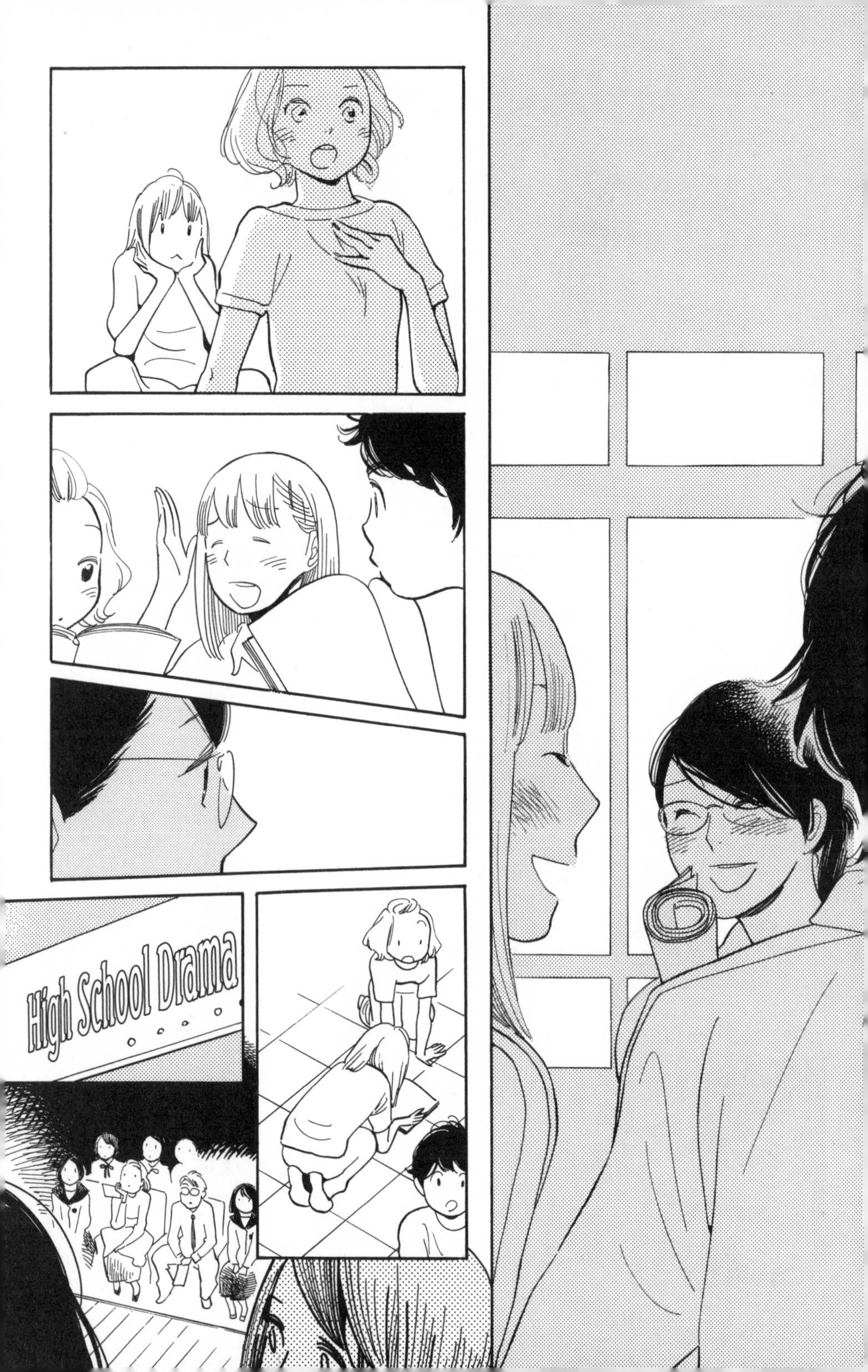
High School Drama

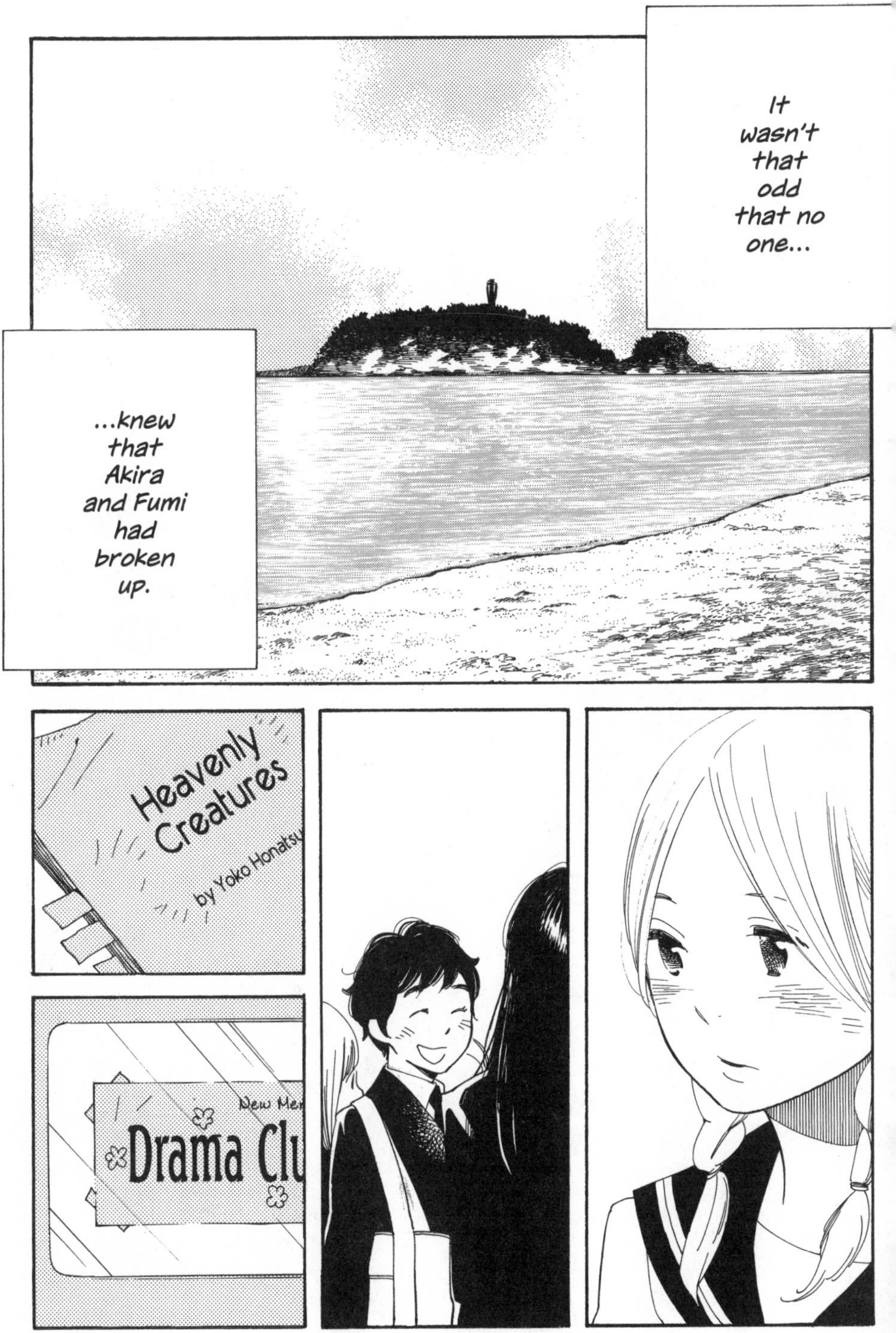
It wasn't that odd that no one...
...knew that Akira and Fumi had broken up.
Heavenly Creatures
by Yoko Honatsu
Drama Clu

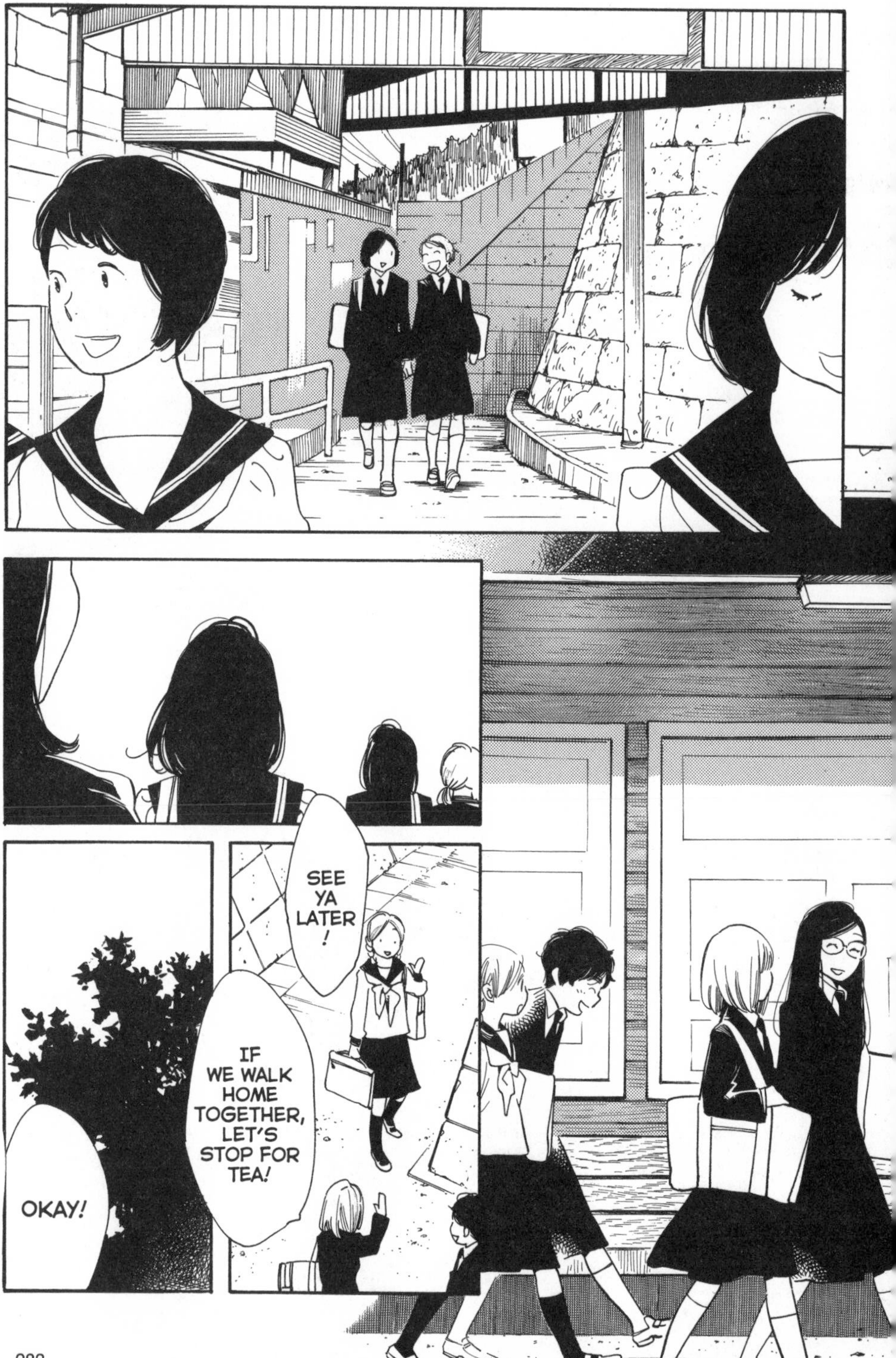
SEE YA LATER!
IF WE WALK HOME TOGETHER, LET'S STOP FOR TEA!
OKAY!

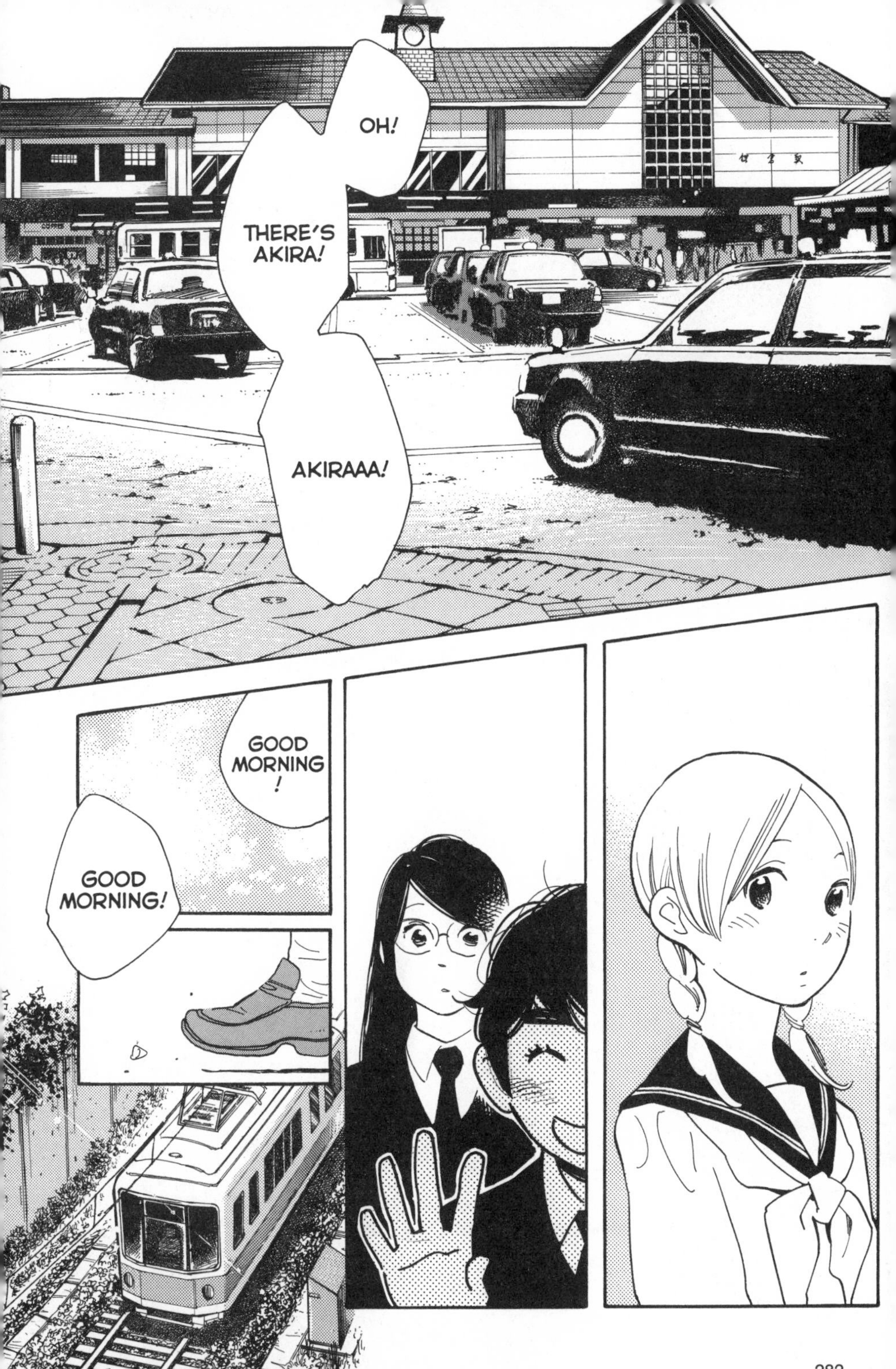
OH!
THERE'S AKIRA!
AKIRAAA!
GOOD MORNING!
GOOD MORNING!

Sweet *Blue* *Flowers*

#50 Even Though
I'm Waiting for You

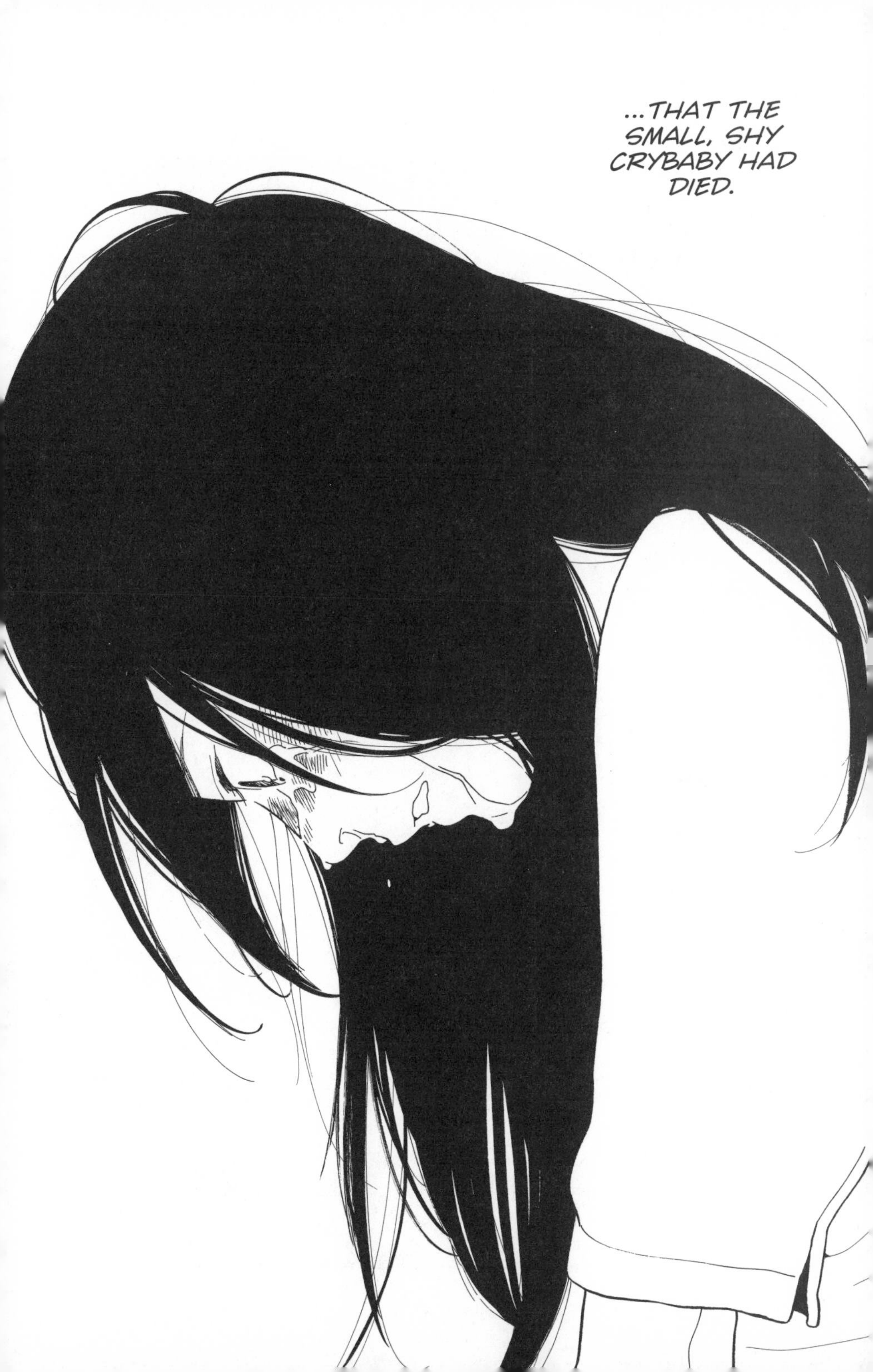
...THAT THE SMALL, SHY CRYBABY HAD DIED.

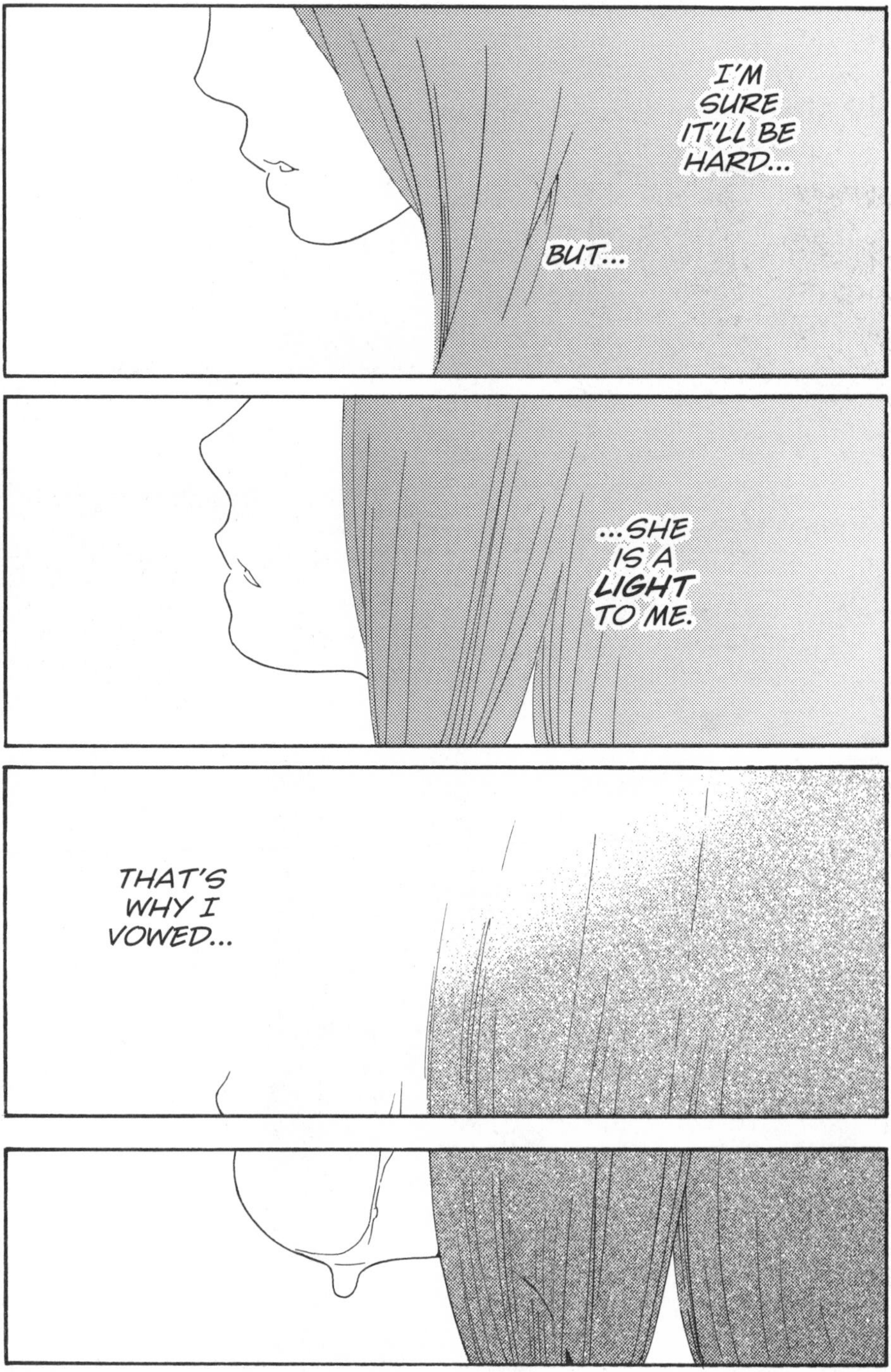
I'M SURE IT'LL BE HARD...
BUT...
...SHE IS A LIGHT TO ME.
THAT'S WHY I VOWED...

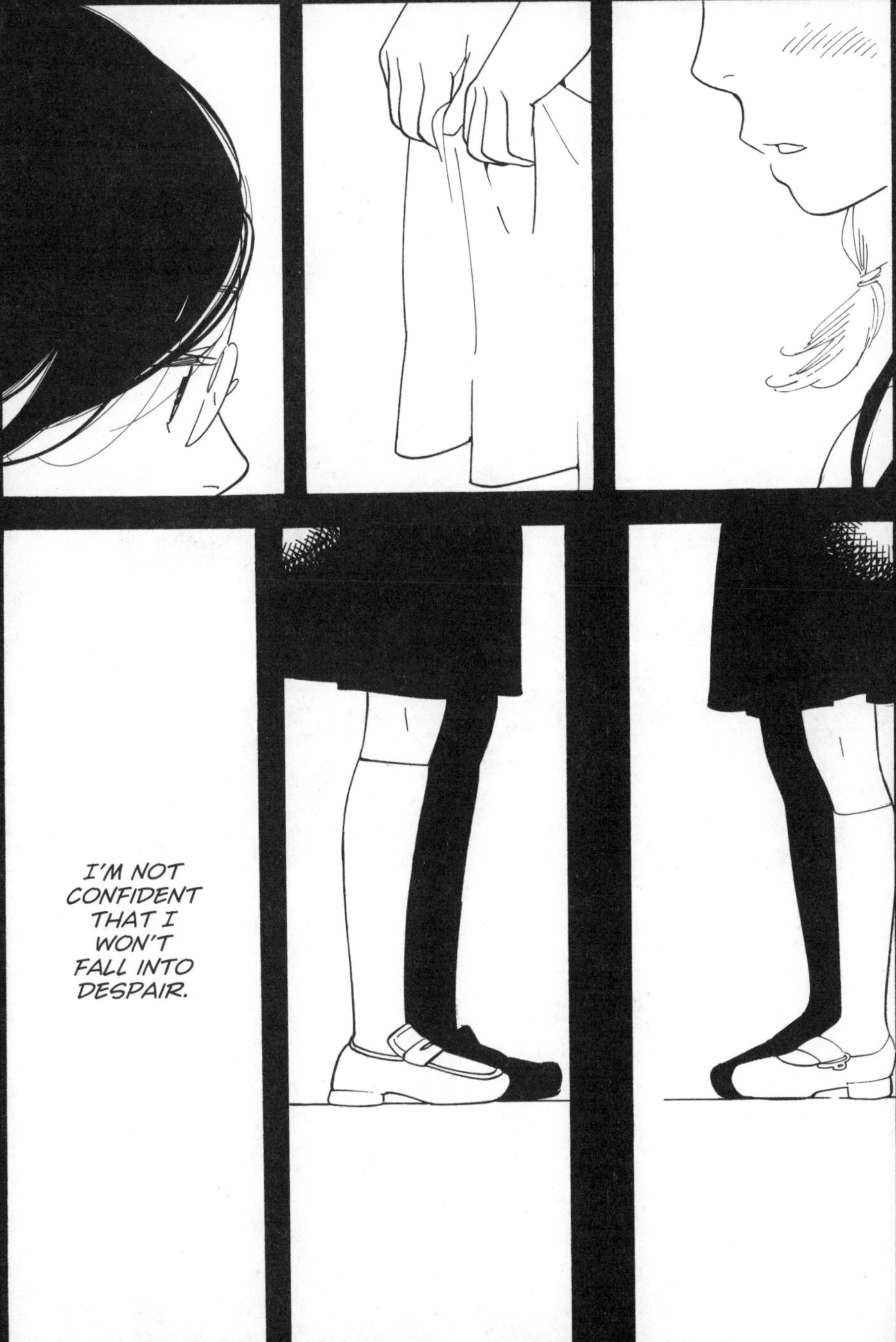
I'M NOT CONFIDENT THAT I WON'T FALL INTO DESPAIR.

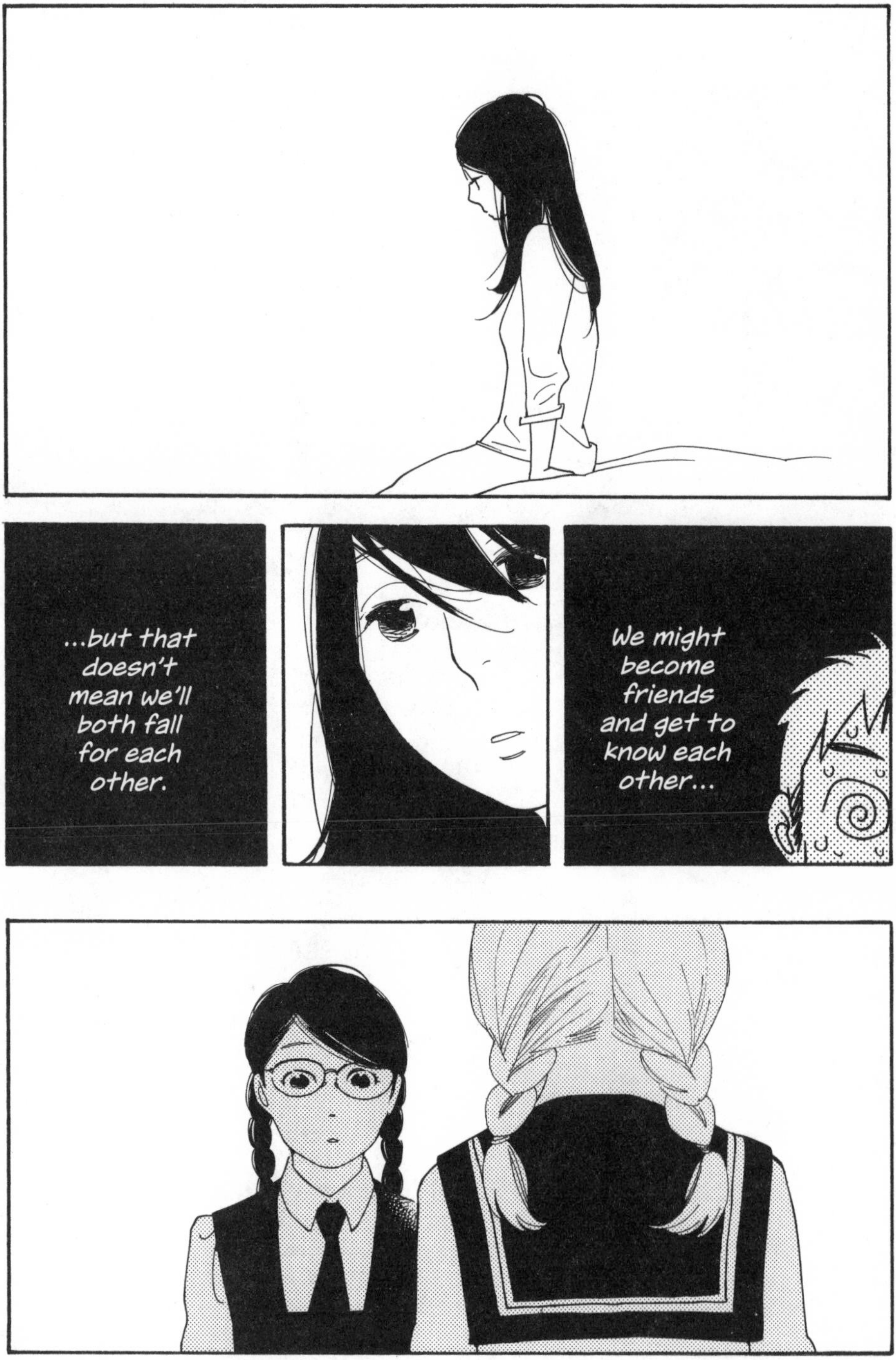
We might become friends and get to know each other...
...but that doesn't mean we'll both fall for each other.

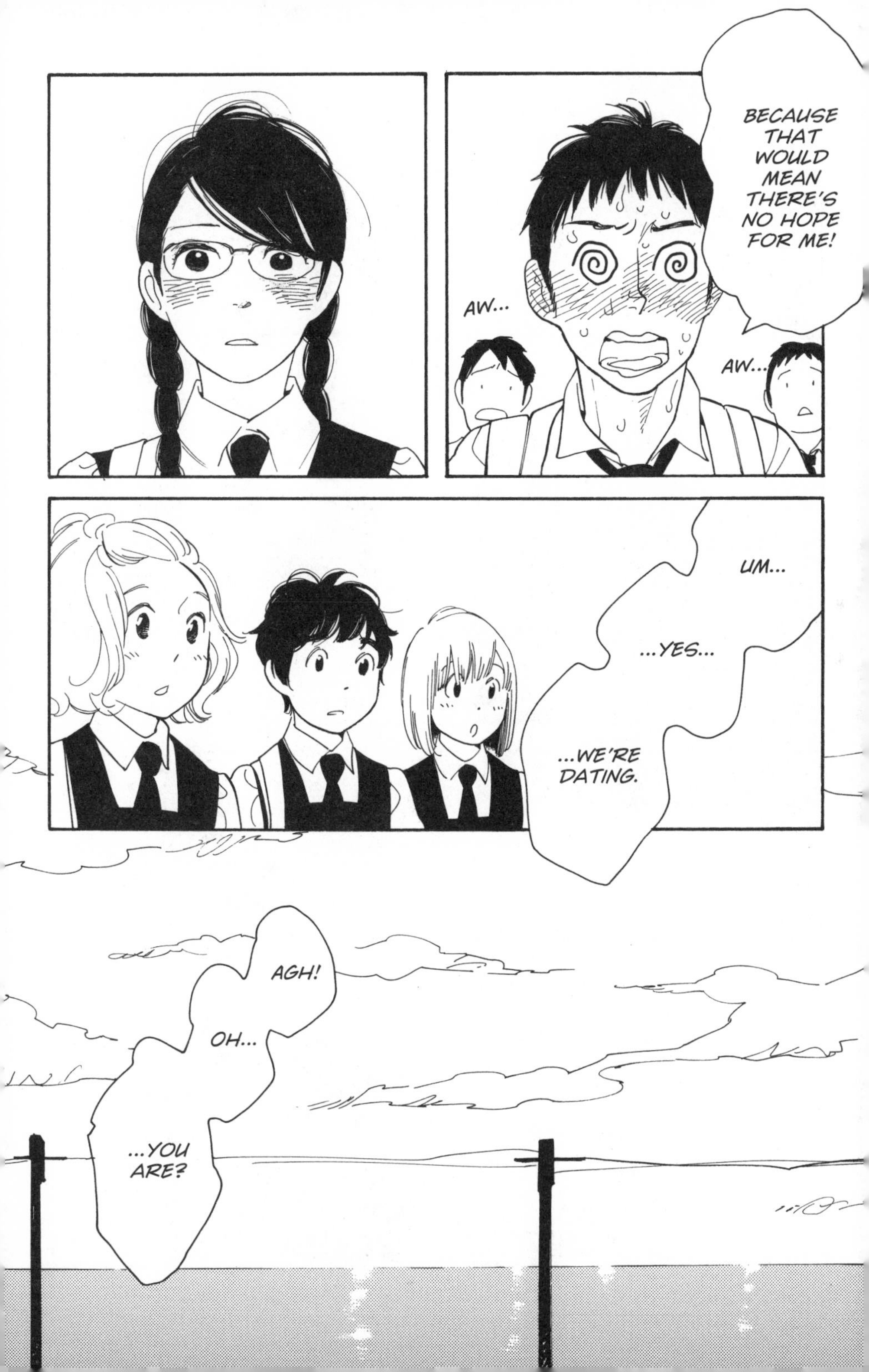
BECAUSE THAT WOULD MEAN THERE'S NO HOPE FOR ME!
AW...
AW...
UM...
...YES...
...WE'RE DATING.
AGH!
OH...
...YOU ARE?

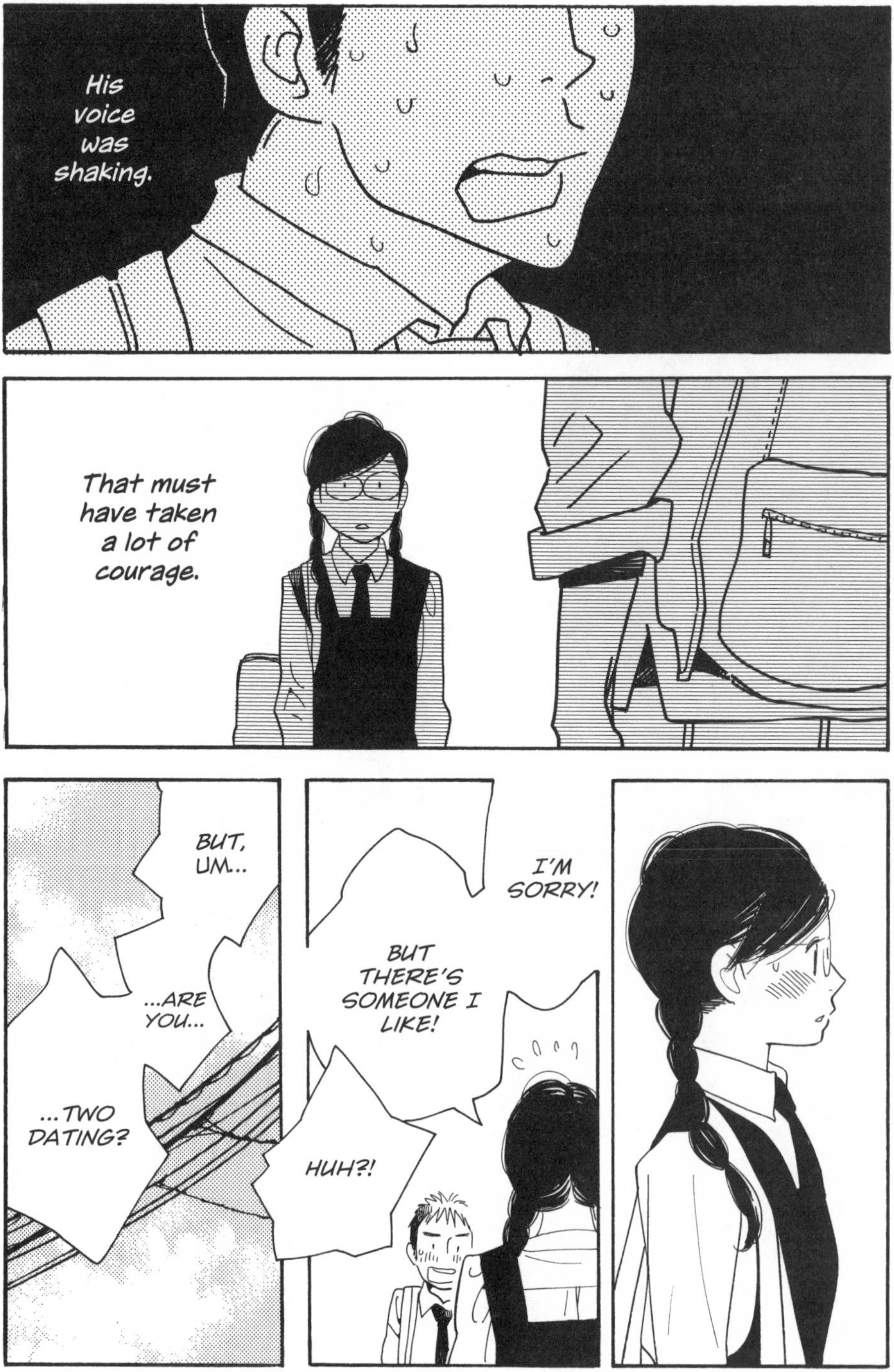
His voice was shaking.
That must have taken a lot of courage.
I'M SORRY!
BUT THERE'S SOMEONE I LIKE!
HUH?!
BUT, UM...
...ARE YOU...
...TWO DATING?

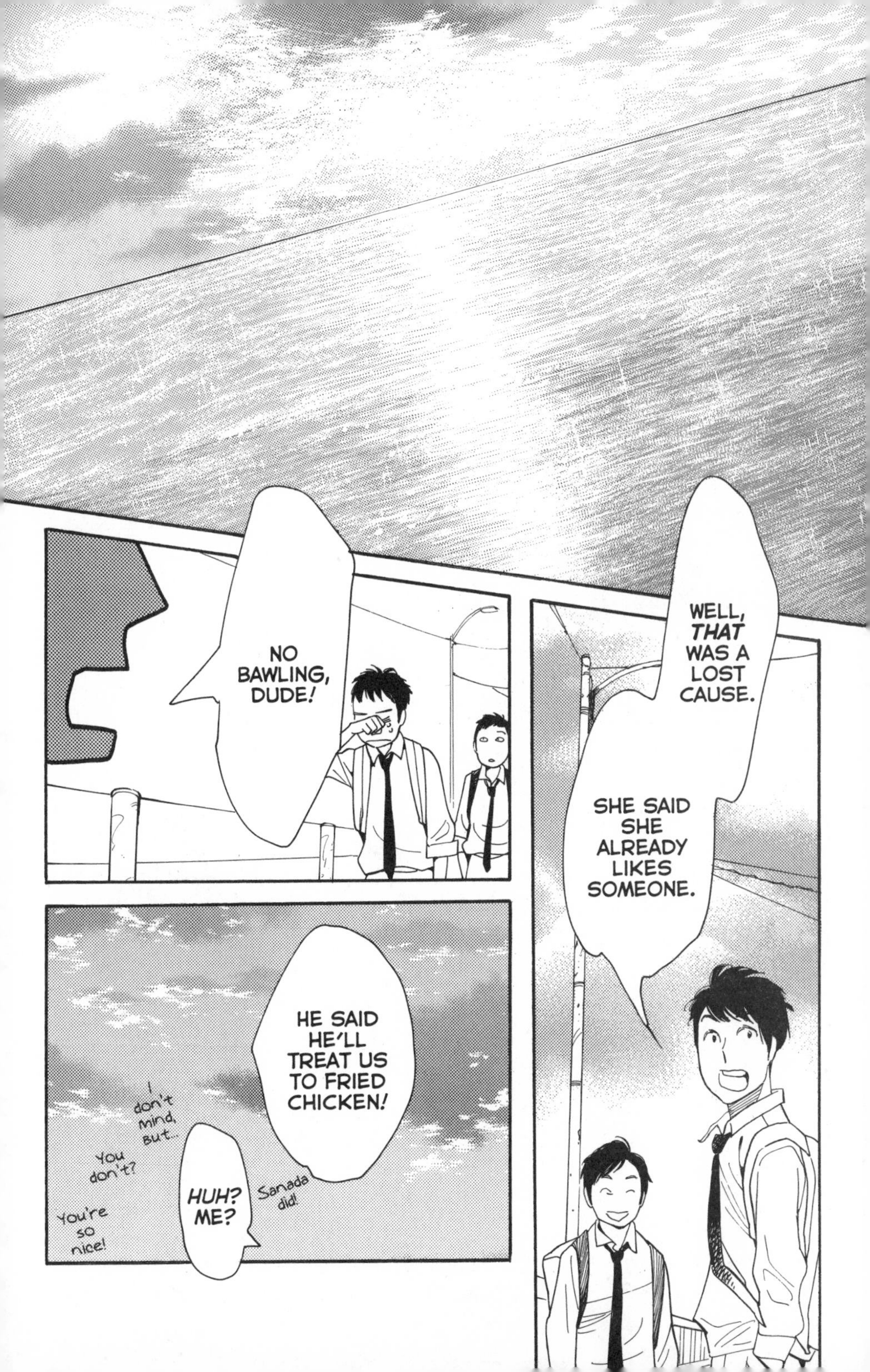

WELL, *THAT* WAS A LOST CAUSE.
SHE SAID SHE ALREADY LIKES SOMEONE.
NO BAWLING, DUDE!
HE SAID HE'LL TREAT US TO FRIED CHICKEN!
Sanada did!
HUH? ME?
I don't mind, but..
You don't?
You're so nice!

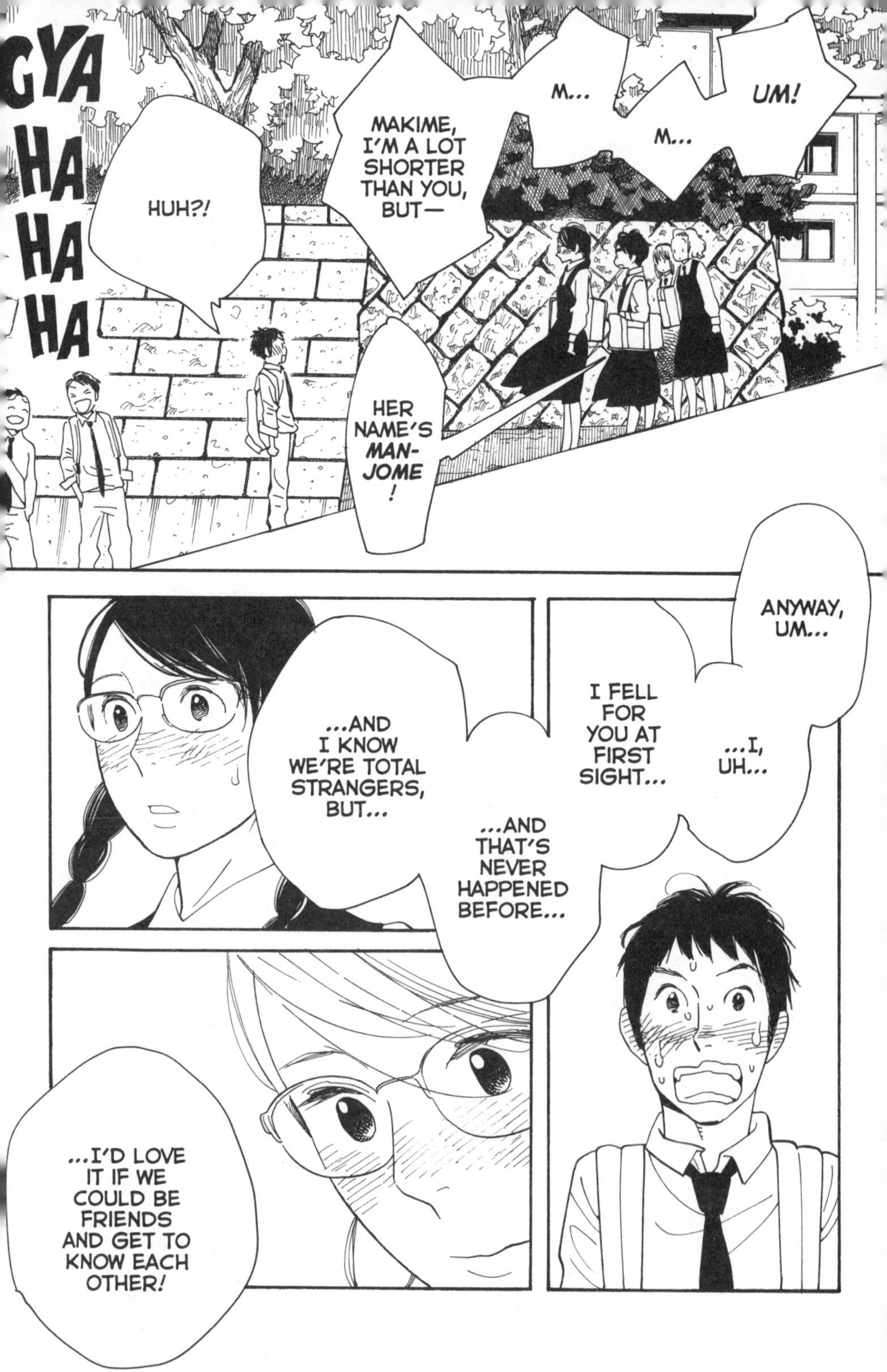
UM!
M...
M...
MAKIME, I'M A LOT SHORTER THAN YOU, BUT—
HUH?!
HER NAME'S MANJOME!
GYA HA HA HA HA
ANYWAY, UM...
...I, UH...
I FELL FOR YOU AT FIRST SIGHT...
...AND THAT'S NEVER HAPPENED BEFORE...
...AND I KNOW WE'RE TOTAL STRANGERS, BUT...
...I'D LOVE IT IF WE COULD BE FRIENDS AND GET TO KNOW EACH OTHER!

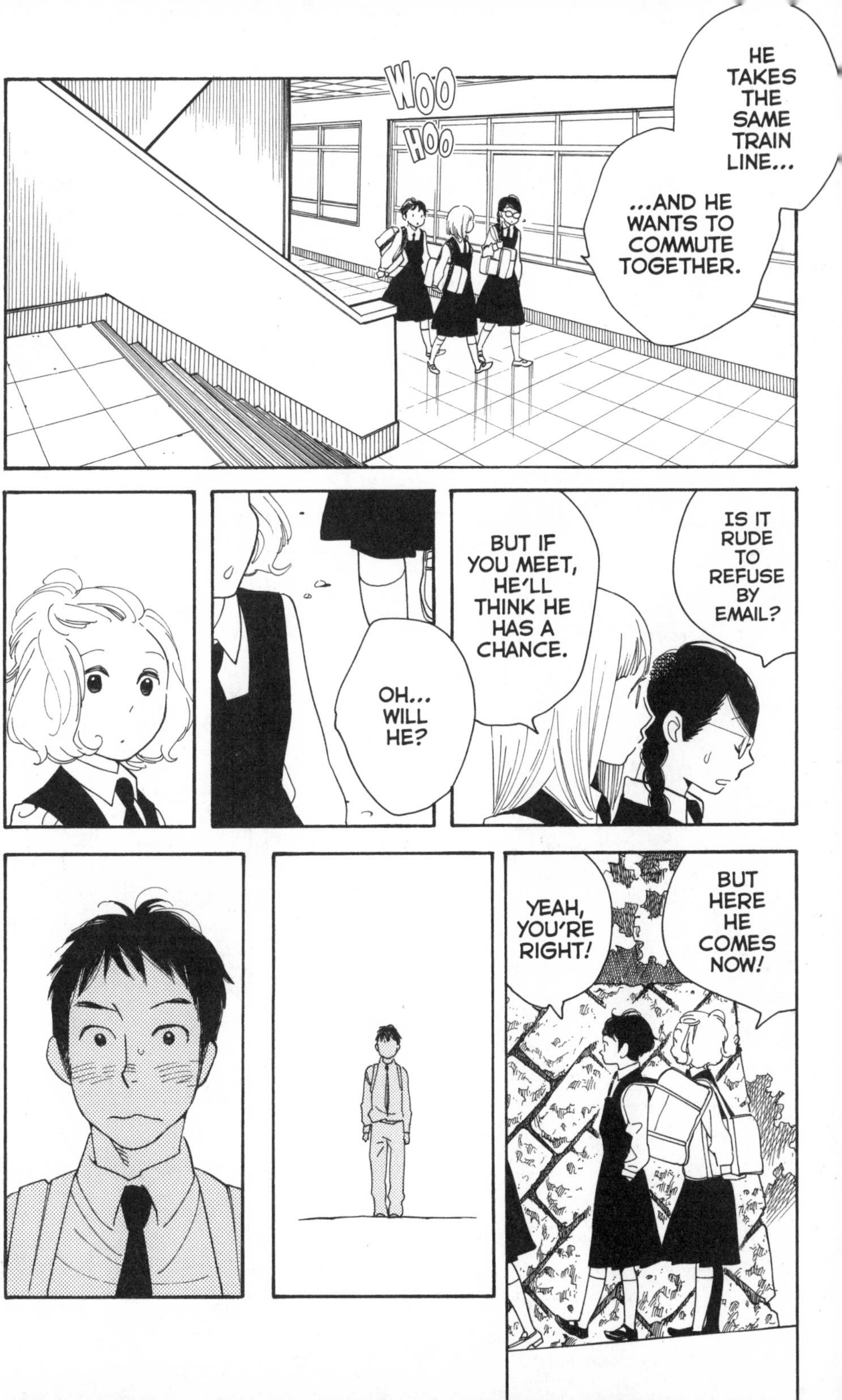
HE TAKES THE SAME TRAIN LINE...
...AND HE WANTS TO COMMUTE TOGETHER.
WOO HOO
IS IT RUDE TO REFUSE BY EMAIL?
BUT IF YOU MEET, HE'LL THINK HE HAS A CHANCE.
OH... WILL HE?
BUT HERE HE COMES NOW!
YEAH, YOU'RE RIGHT!

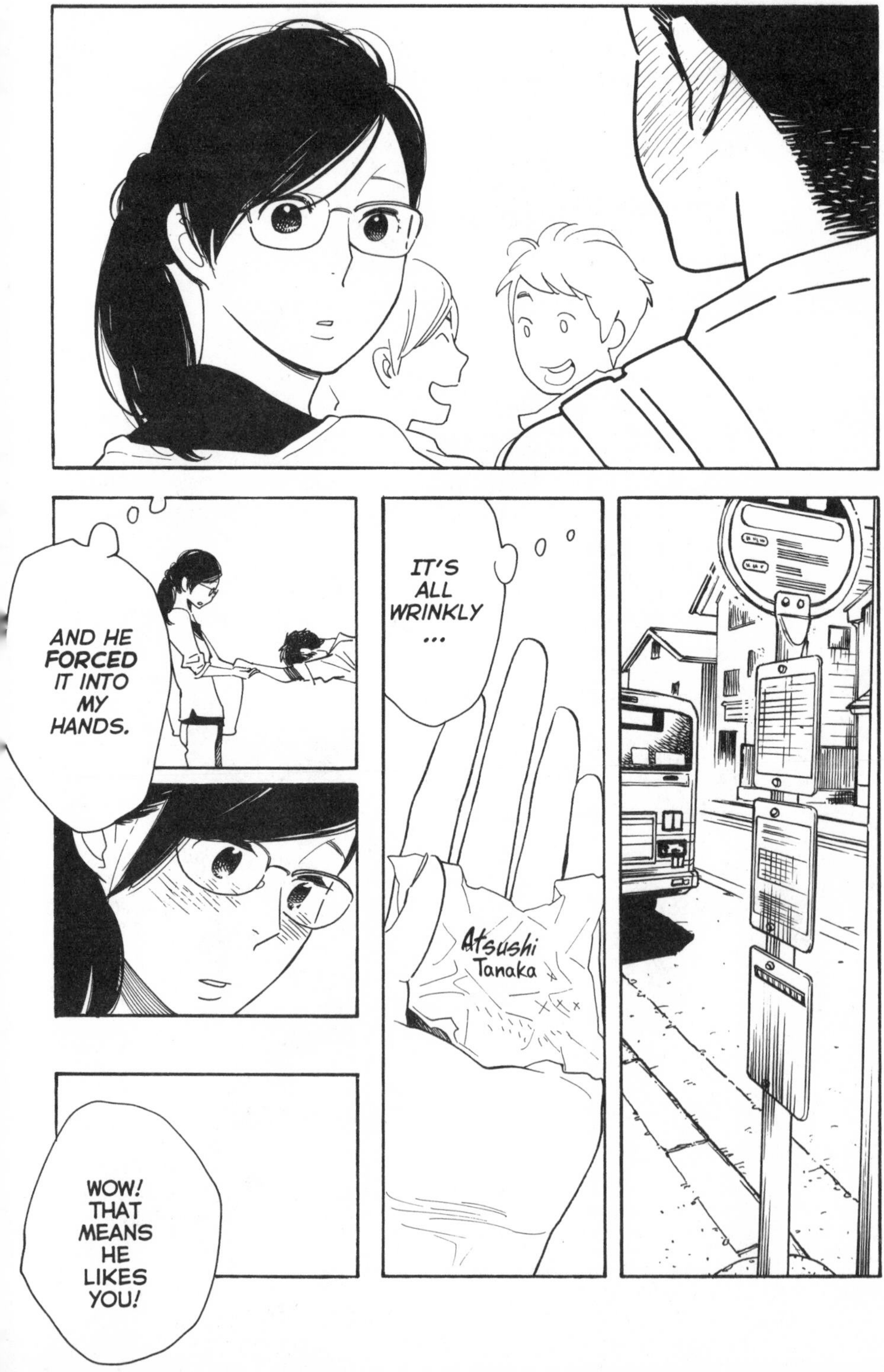
IT'S ALL WRINKLY ...
Atsushi Tanaka
AND HE FORCED IT INTO MY HANDS.
WOW! THAT MEANS HE LIKES YOU!

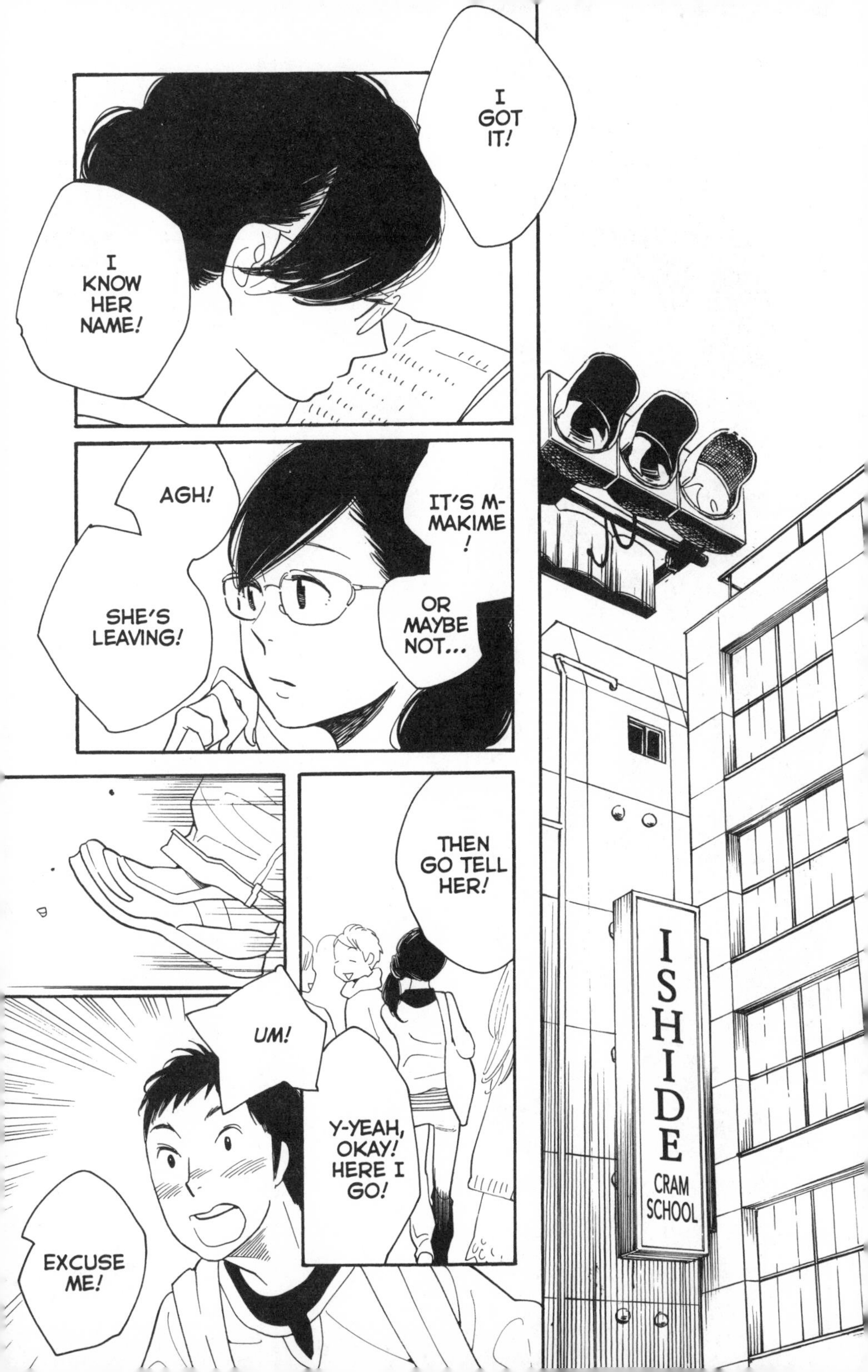
ISHIDE
CRAM SCHOOL
I GOT IT!
I KNOW HER NAME!
IT'S M-MAKIME!
OR MAYBE NOT...
AGH!
SHE'S LEAVING!
THEN GO TELL HER!
Y-YEAH, OKAY! HERE I GO!
UM!
EXCUSE ME!

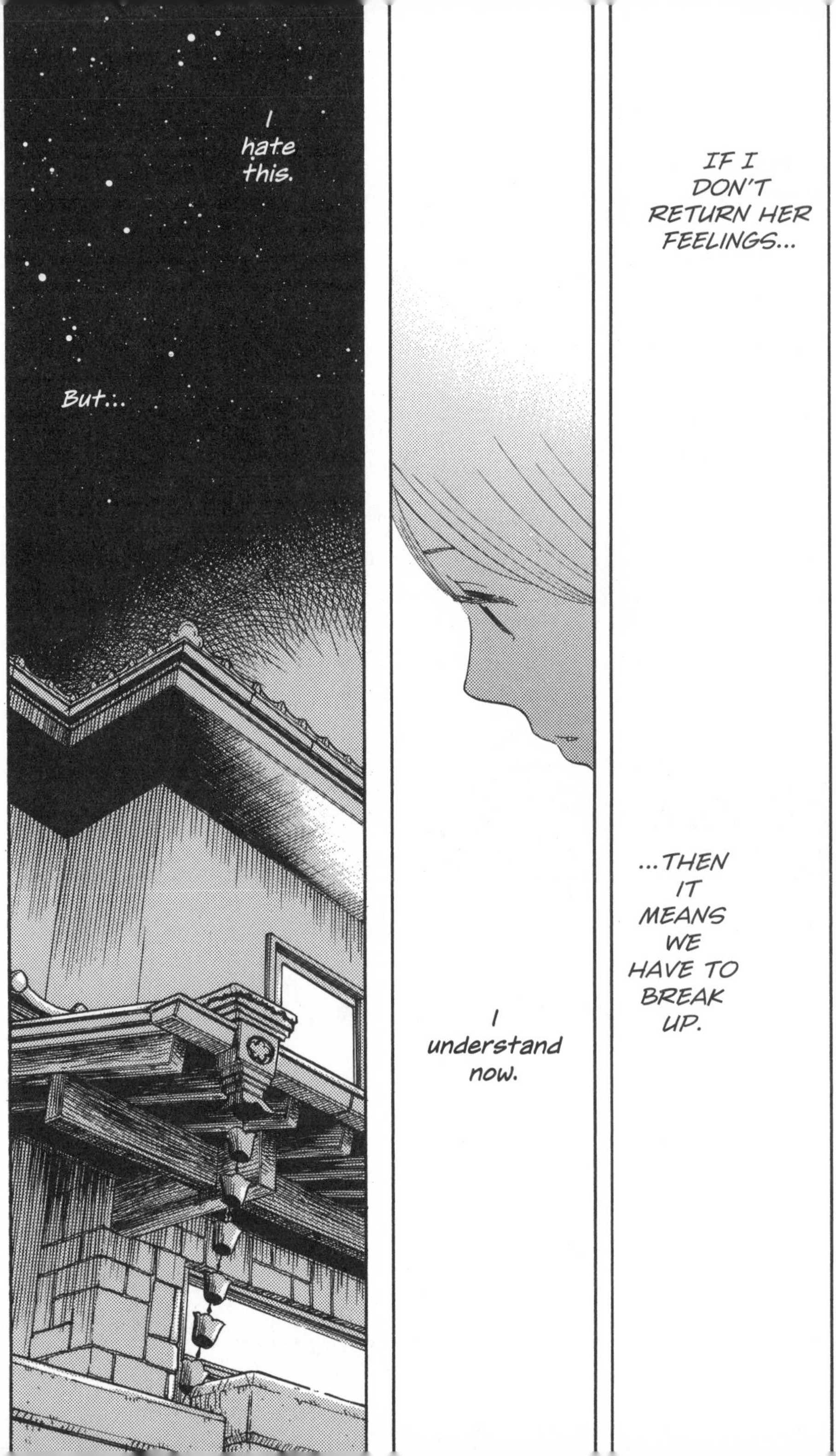
IF I DON'T RETURN HER FEELINGS...
...THEN IT MEANS WE HAVE TO BREAK UP.
I understand now.
I hate this.
But...

Sweet Blue Flowers

#44 On a Spring Night

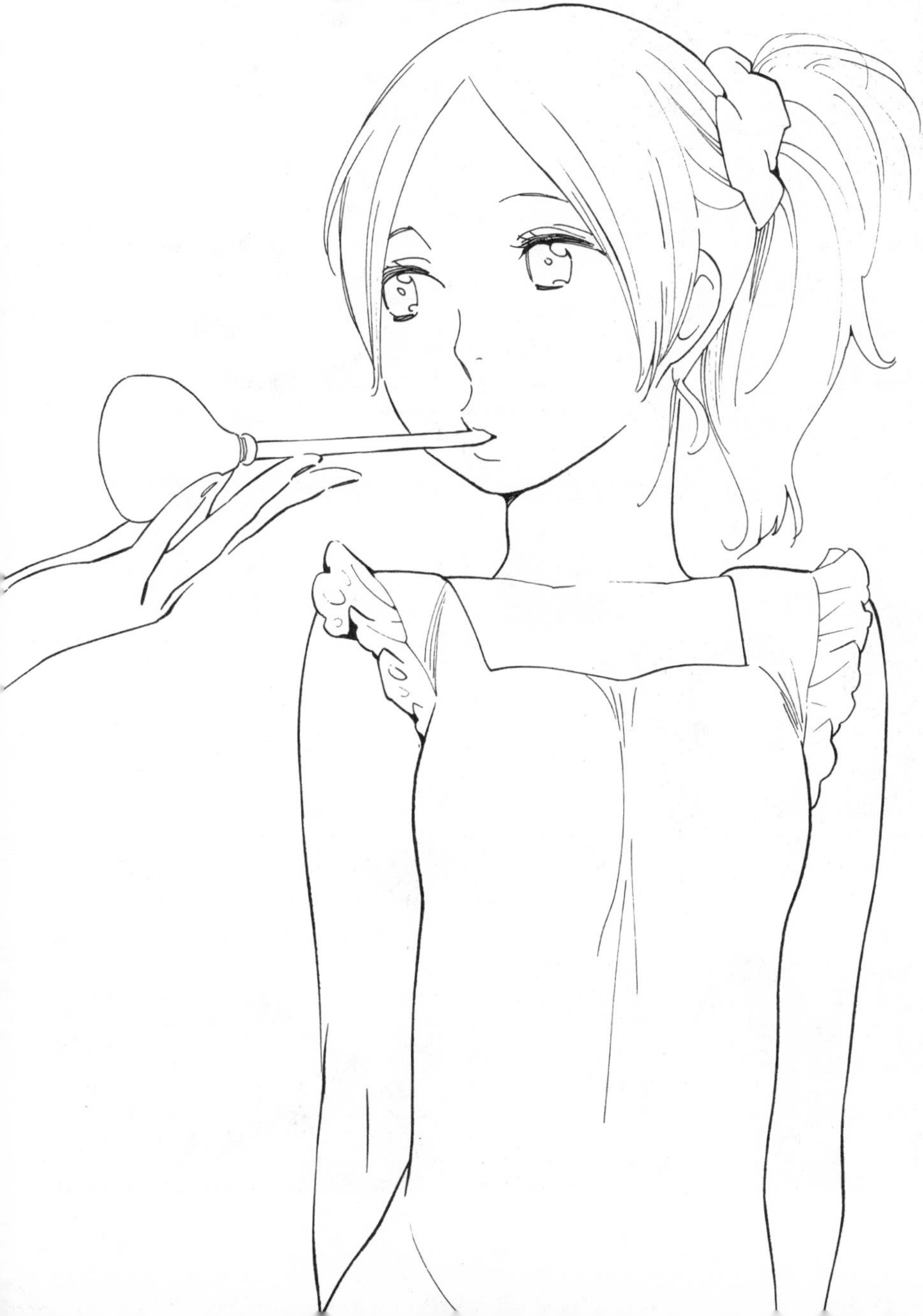

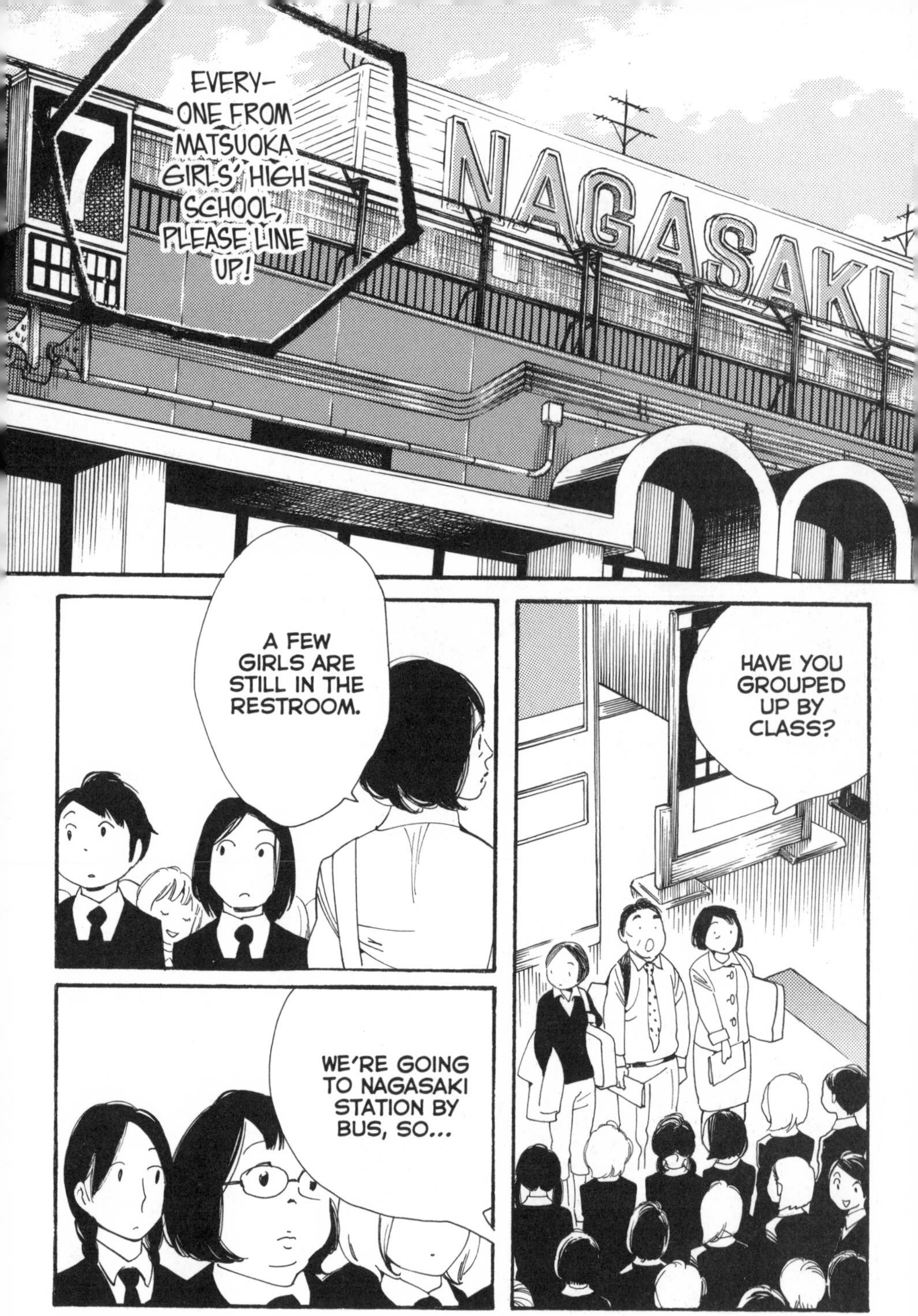
NAGASAKI
EVERY-ONE FROM MATSUOKA GIRLS' HIGH SCHOOL, PLEASE LINE UP!
HAVE YOU GROUPED UP BY CLASS?
A FEW GIRLS ARE STILL IN THE RESTROOM.
WE'RE GOING TO NAGASAKI STATION BY BUS, SO...

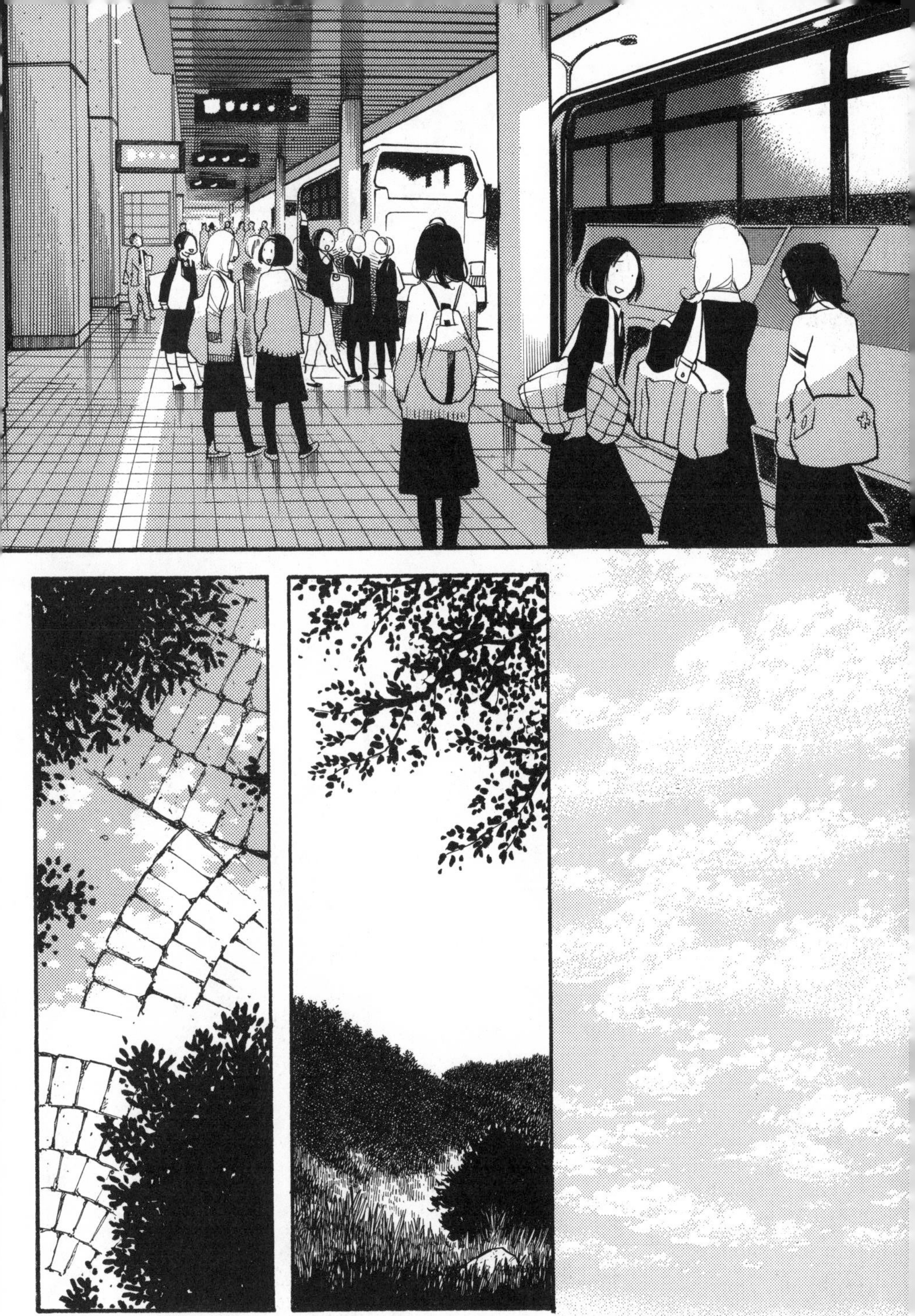

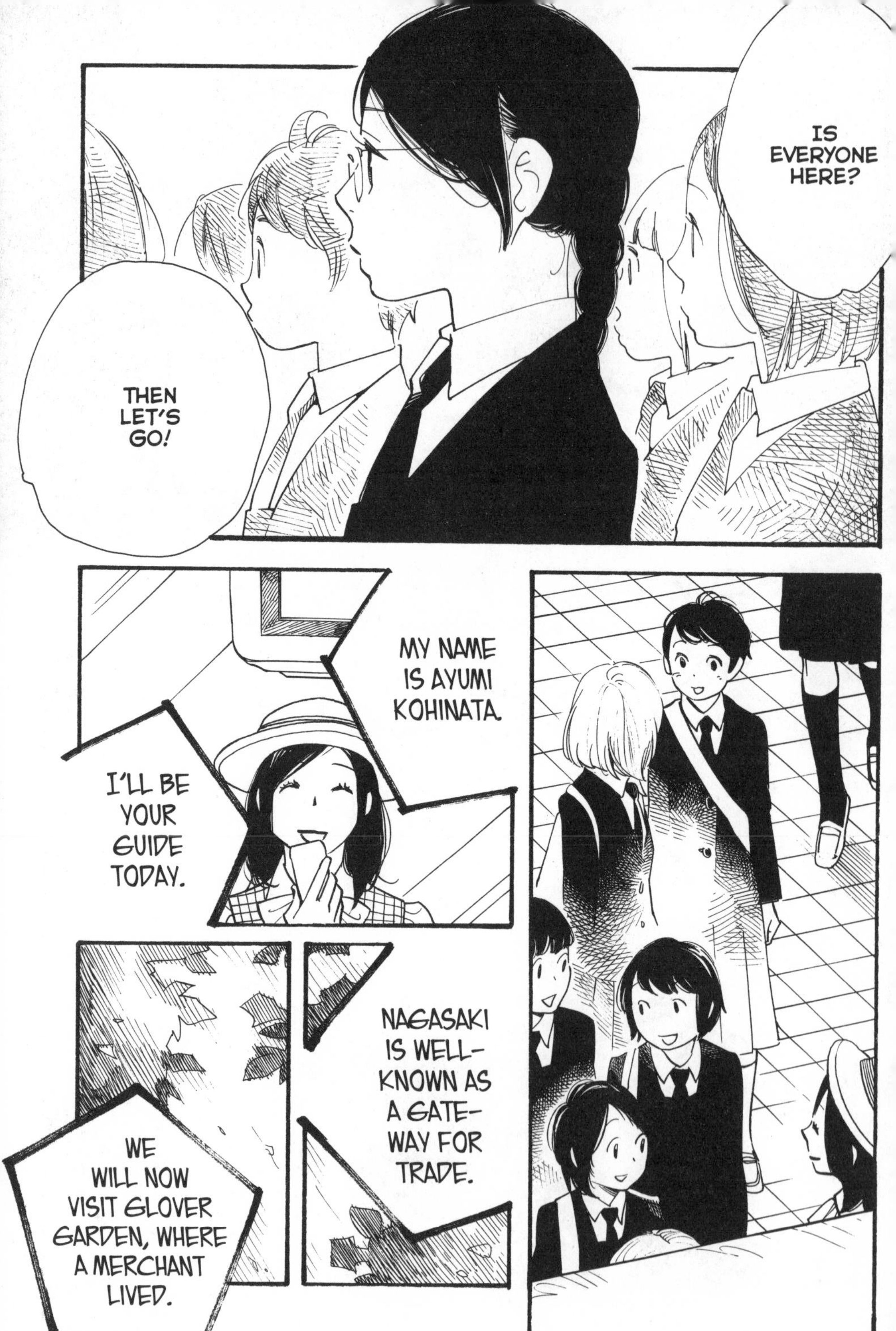
IS EVERYONE HERE?
THEN LET'S GO!
MY NAME IS AYUMI KOHINATA.
I'LL BE YOUR GUIDE TODAY.
NAGASAKI IS WELL-KNOWN AS A GATE-WAY FOR TRADE.
WE WILL NOW VISIT GLOVER GARDEN, WHERE A MERCHANT LIVED.

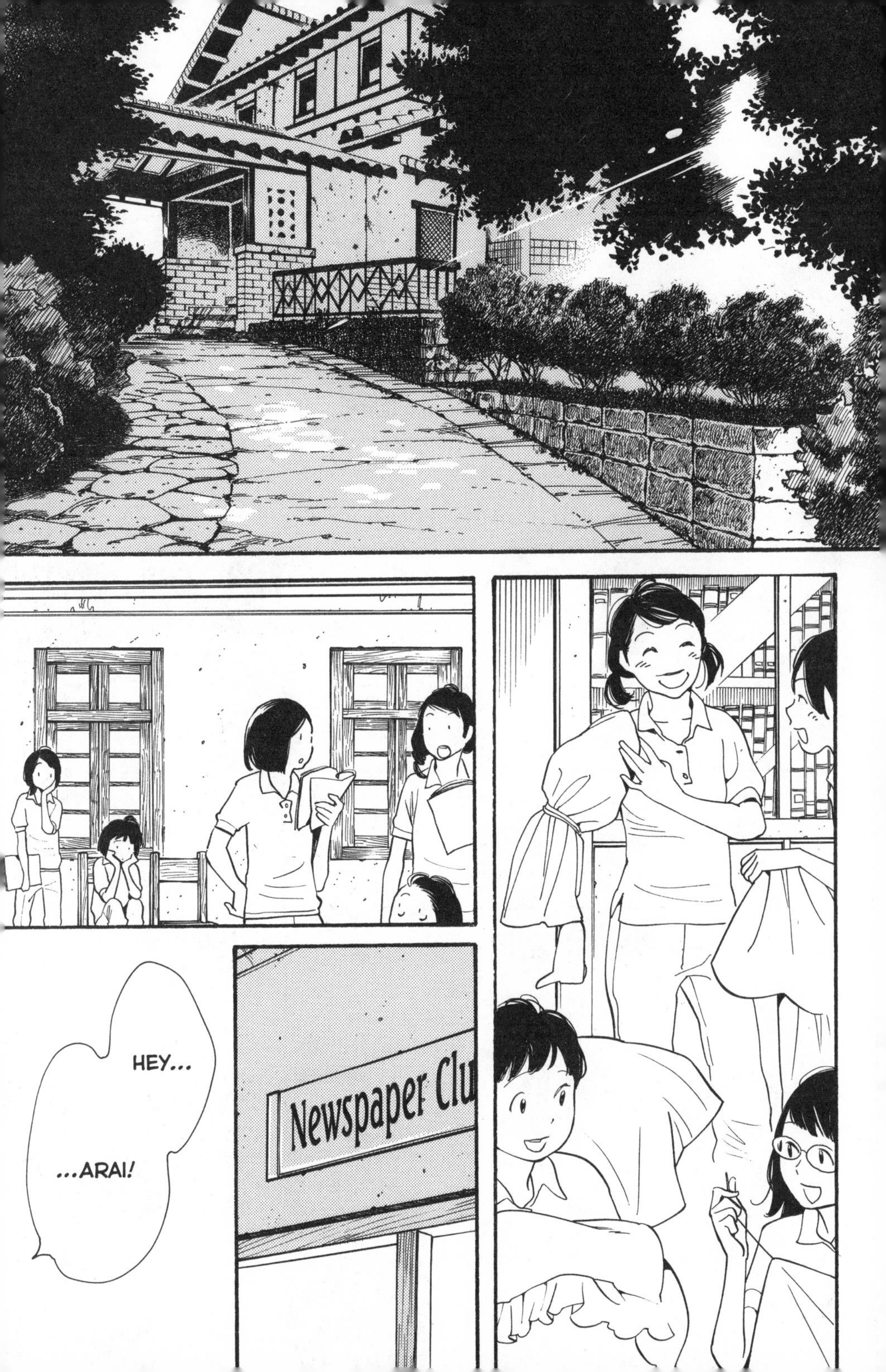
Newspaper Clu
HEY... ...ARAI!

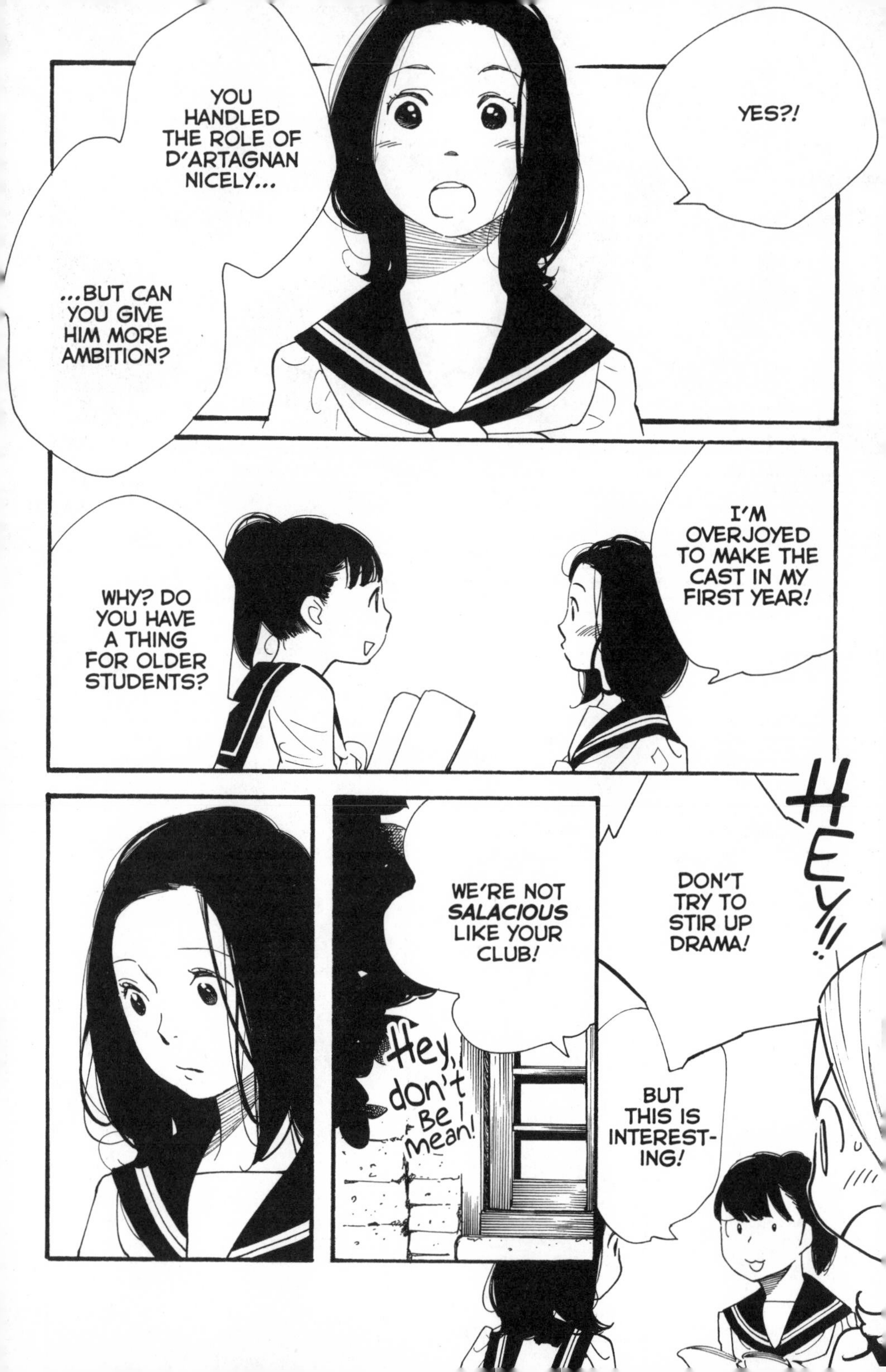
YOU HANDLED THE ROLE OF D'ARTAGNAN NICELY...
...BUT CAN YOU GIVE HIM MORE AMBITION?
YES?!
I'M OVERJOYED TO MAKE THE CAST IN MY FIRST YEAR!
WHY? DO YOU HAVE A THING FOR OLDER STUDENTS?
HEY!!
DON'T TRY TO STIR UP DRAMA!
BUT THIS IS INTEREST-ING!
WE'RE NOT *SALACIOUS* LIKE YOUR CLUB!
Hey, don't Be mean!

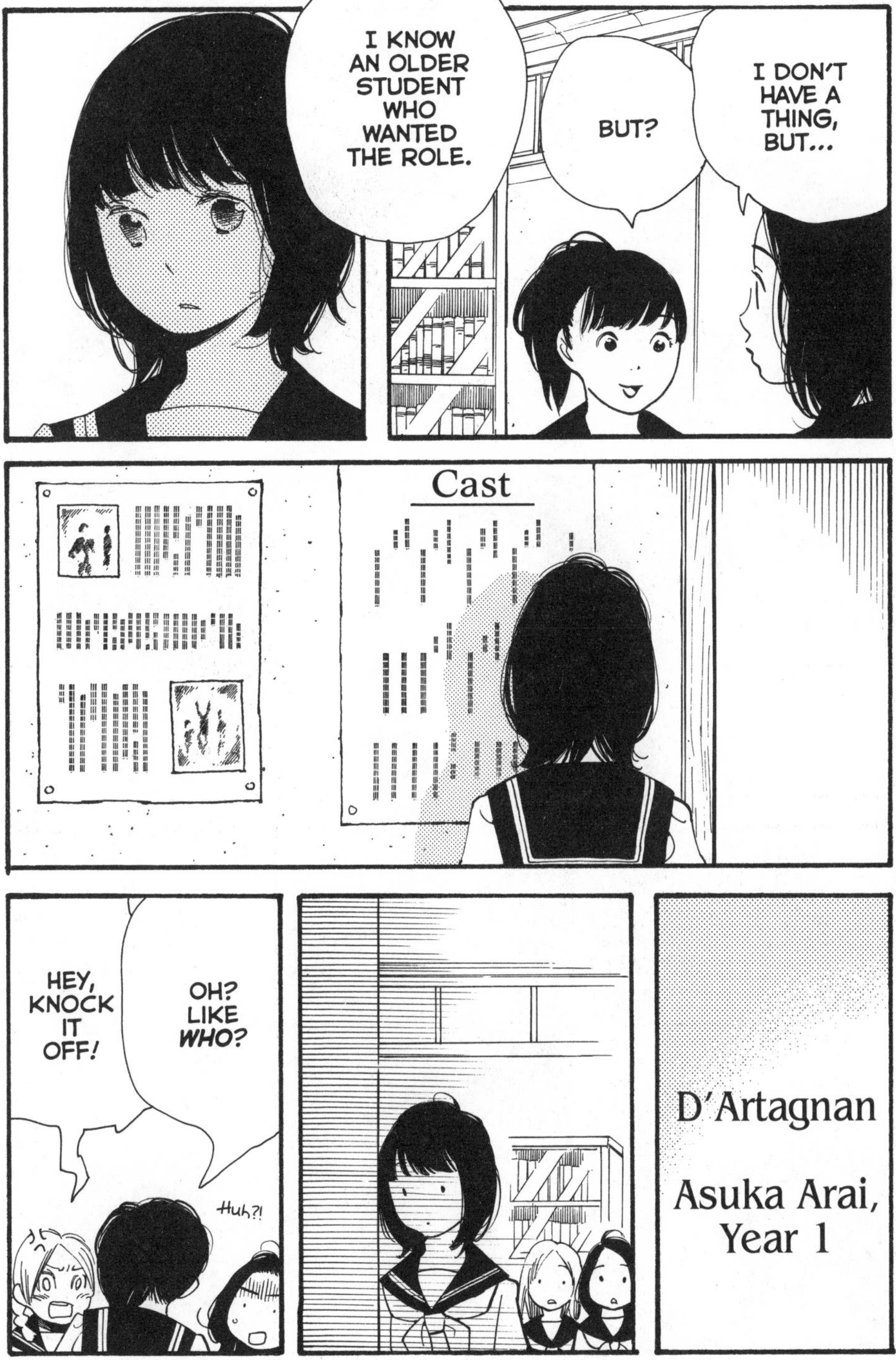
I DON'T HAVE A THING, BUT...
BUT?
I KNOW AN OLDER STUDENT WHO WANTED THE ROLE.
Cast
D'Artagnan
Asuka Arai, Year 1
OH? LIKE *WHO*?
HEY, KNOCK IT OFF!
Huh?!

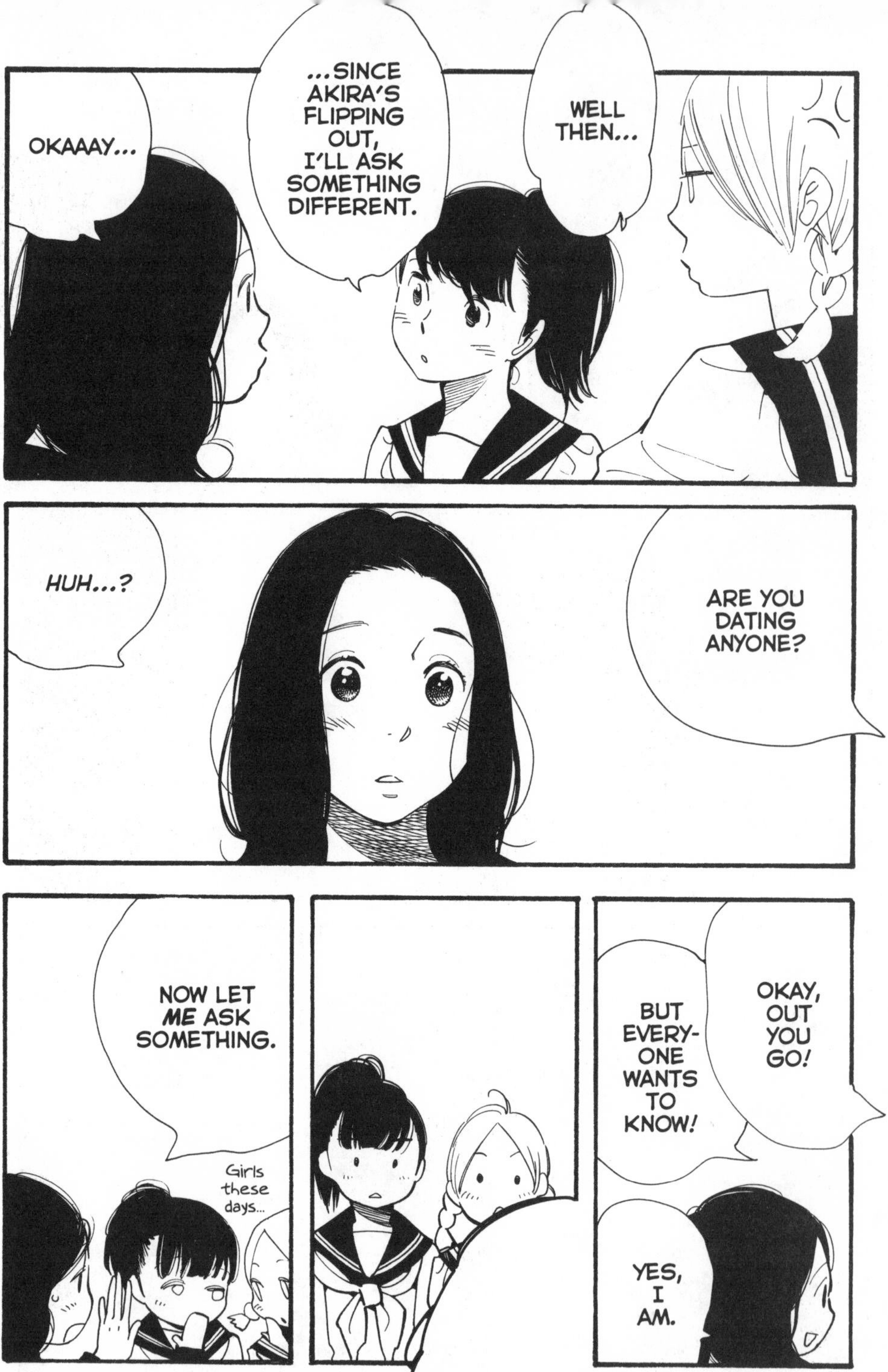
WELL THEN...
...SINCE AKIRA'S FLIPPING OUT, I'LL ASK SOMETHING DIFFERENT.
OKAAAY...
ARE YOU DATING ANYONE?
HUH...?
OKAY, OUT YOU GO!
BUT EVERY-ONE WANTS TO KNOW!
YES, I AM.
NOW LET *ME* ASK SOMETHING.
Girls these days...

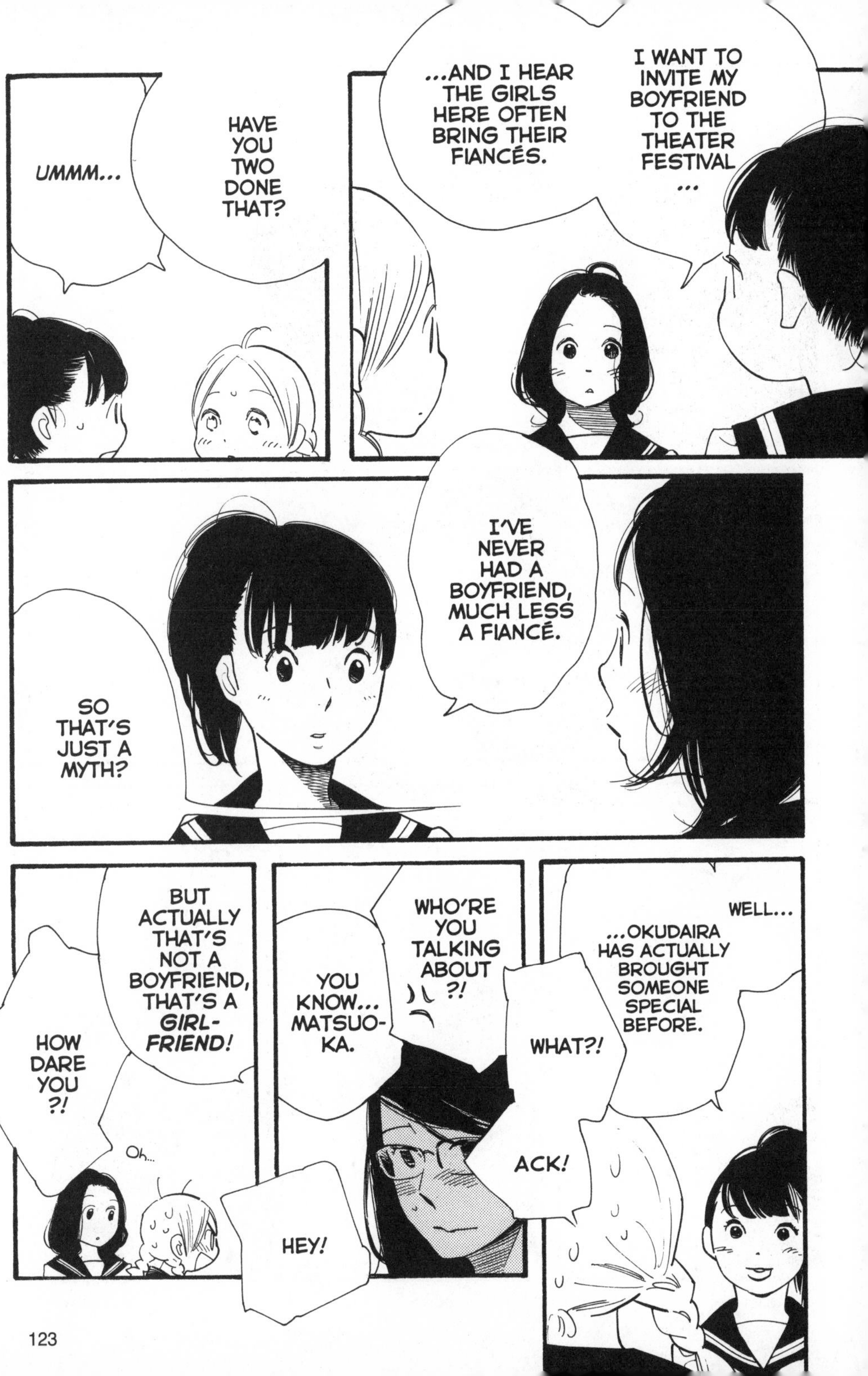

I WANT TO INVITE MY BOYFRIEND TO THE THEATER FESTIVAL...
...AND I HEAR THE GIRLS HERE OFTEN BRING THEIR FIANCÉS.
HAVE YOU TWO DONE THAT?
UMMM...
I'VE NEVER HAD A BOYFRIEND, MUCH LESS A FIANCÉ.
SO THAT'S JUST A MYTH?
WELL...
...OKUDAIRA HAS ACTUALLY BROUGHT SOMEONE SPECIAL BEFORE.
WHAT?!
ACK!
WHO'RE YOU TALKING ABOUT?!
YOU KNOW... MATSUO-KA.
BUT ACTUALLY THAT'S NOT A BOYFRIEND, THAT'S A *GIRL-FRIEND!*
HOW DARE YOU?!
Oh...
HEY!

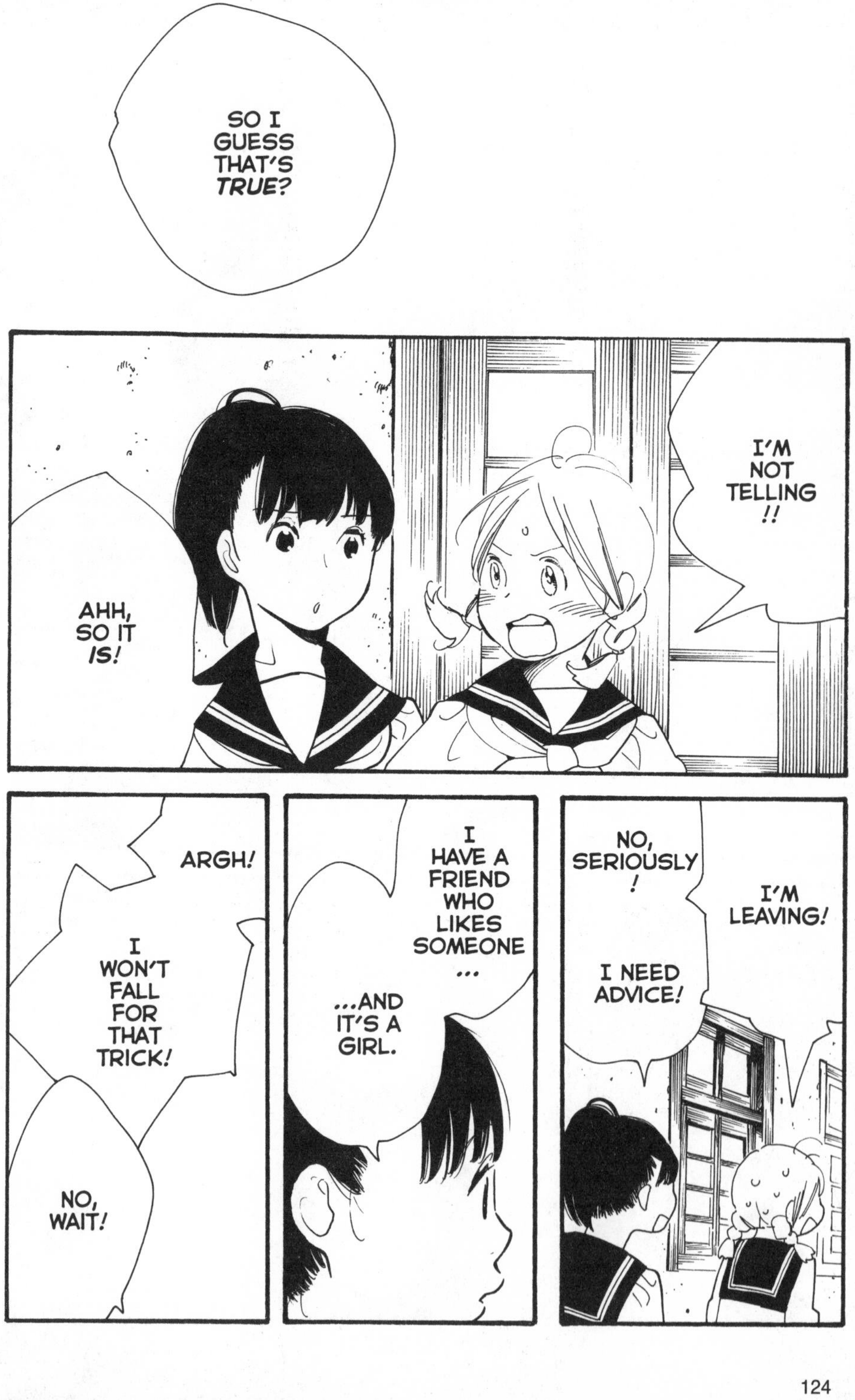
SO I GUESS THAT'S *TRUE*?
I'M NOT TELLING!!
AHH, SO IT *IS*!
I'M LEAVING!
NO, SERIOUSLY! I NEED ADVICE!
I HAVE A FRIEND WHO LIKES SOMEONE...
...AND IT'S A GIRL.
ARGH! I WON'T FALL FOR THAT TRICK!
NO, WAIT!

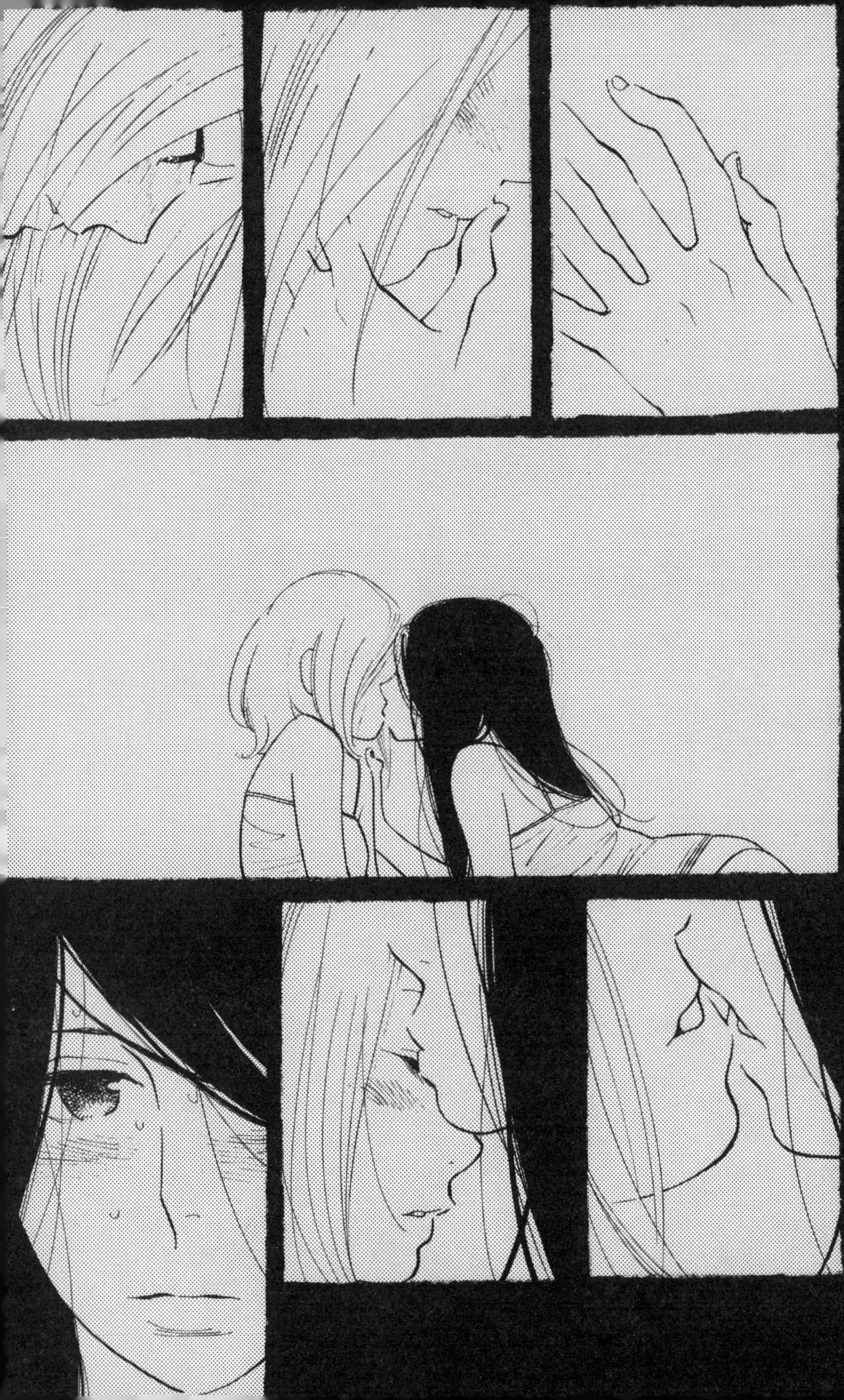

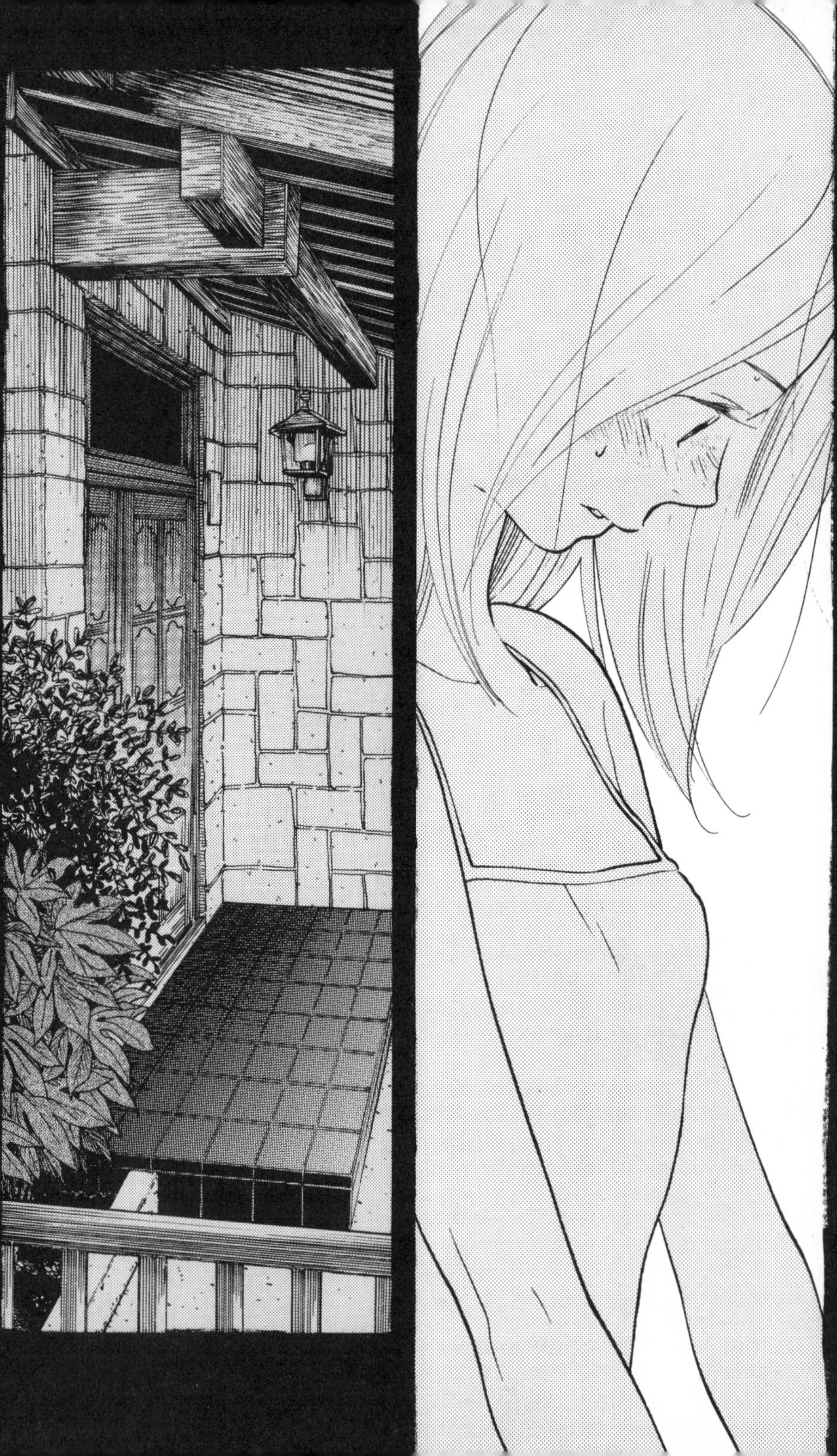

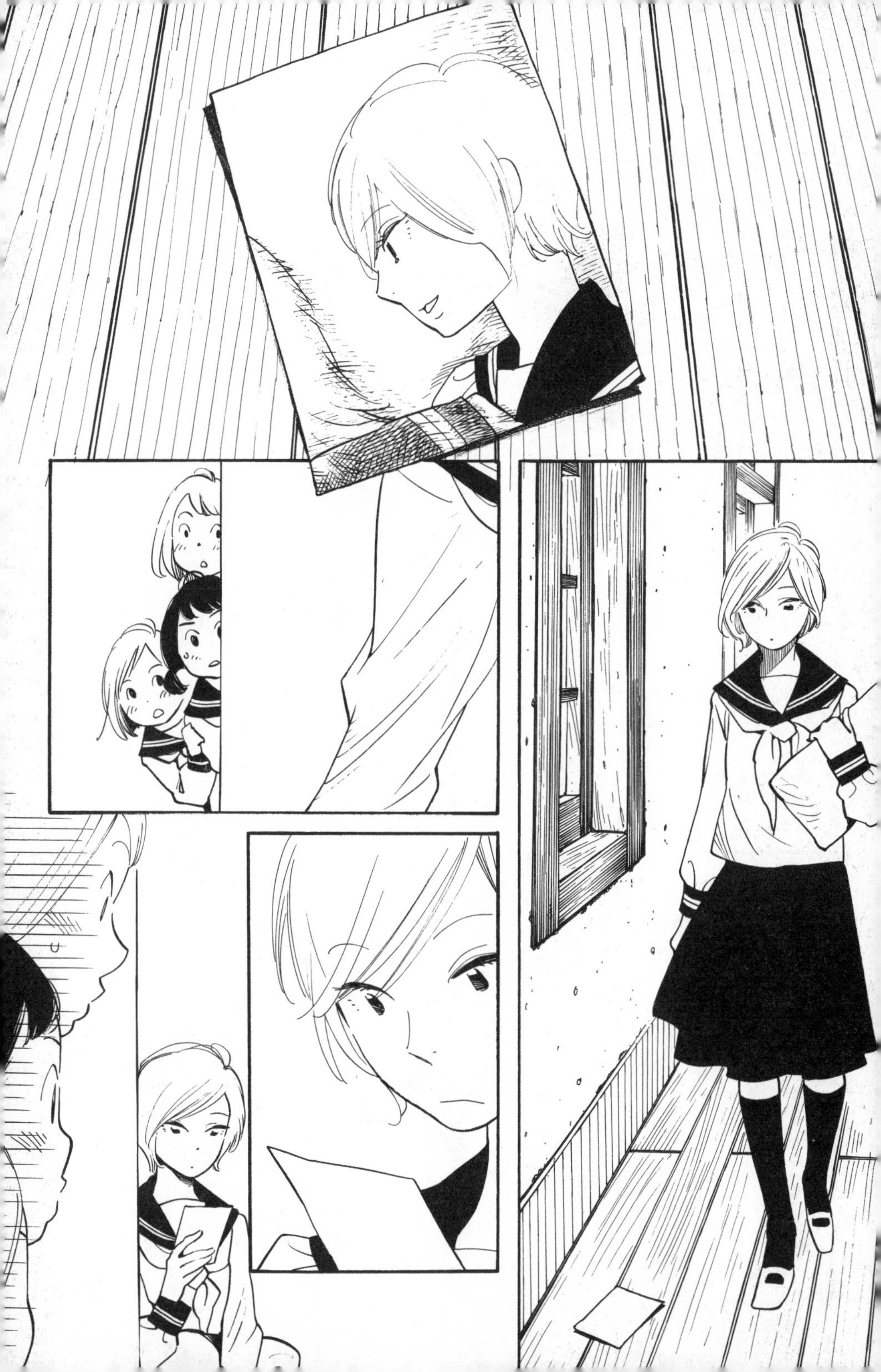

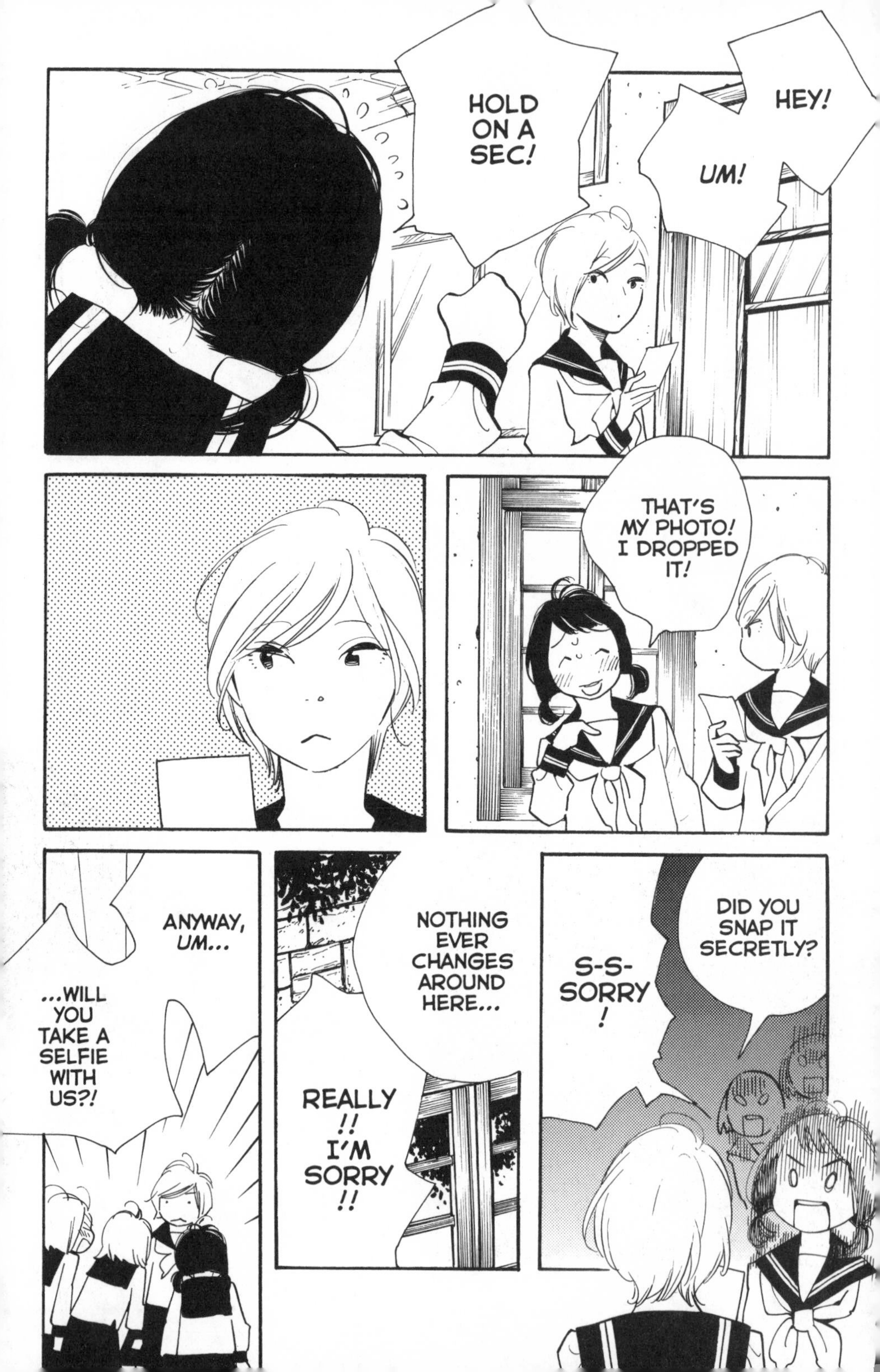
HEY!
UM!
HOLD ON A SEC!
THAT'S MY PHOTO! I DROPPED IT!
DID YOU SNAP IT SECRETLY?
S-S-SORRY!
NOTHING EVER CHANGES AROUND HERE...
REALLY!! I'M SORRY!!
ANYWAY, UM...
...WILL YOU TAKE A SELFIE WITH US?!

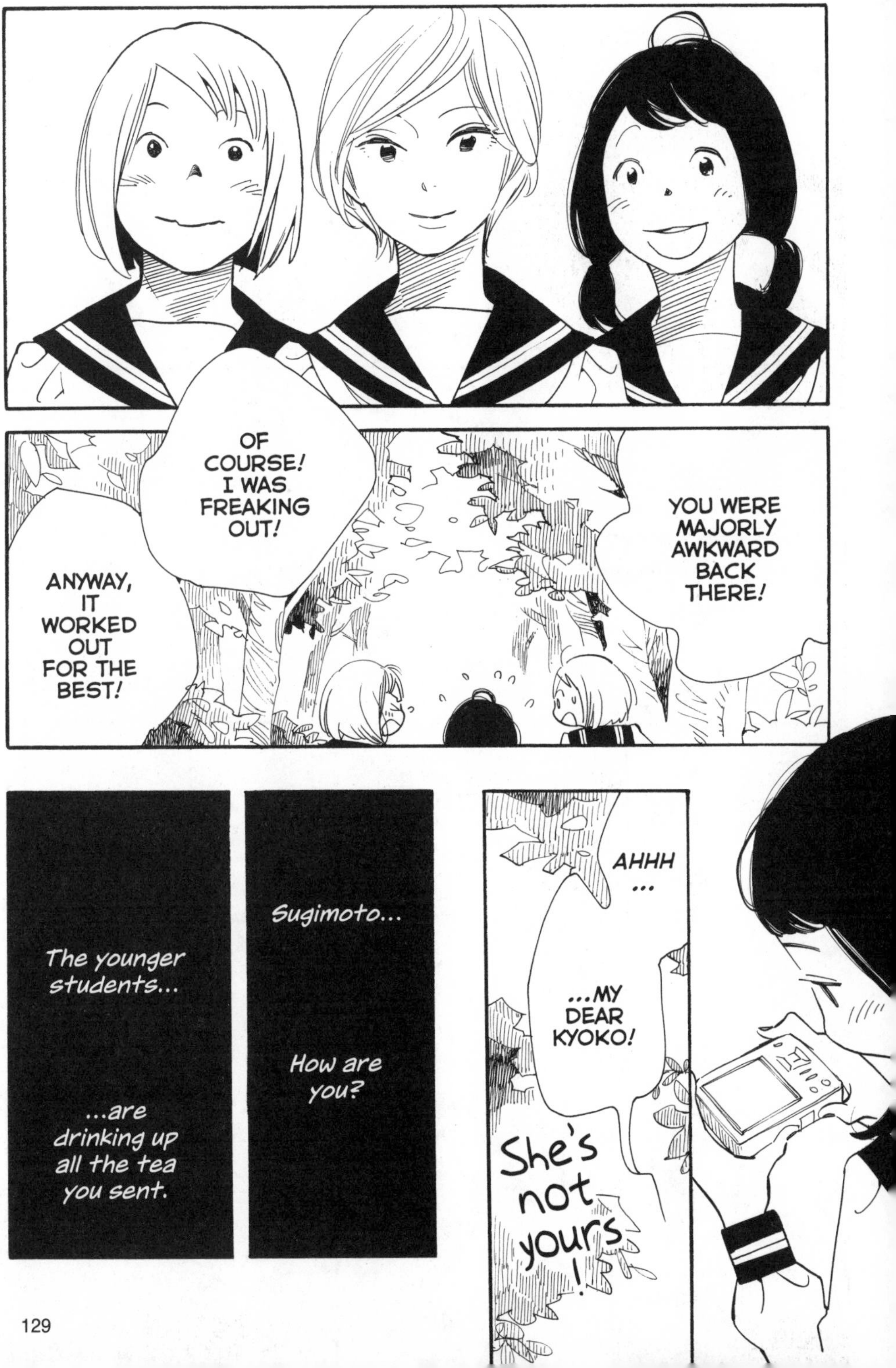
YOU WERE MAJORLY AWKWARD BACK THERE!
OF COURSE! I WAS FREAKING OUT!
ANYWAY, IT WORKED OUT FOR THE BEST!
AHHH...
...MY DEAR KYOKO!
She's not yours!
Sugimoto...
How are you?
The younger students...
...are drinking up all the tea you sent.

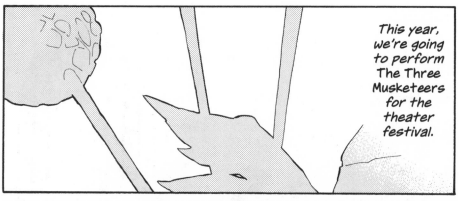

This year, we're going to perform The Three Musketeers for the theater festival.
I'm going to play the musketeer named Athos.
I think you would have made a great Aramis.
HA HA...
I'm looking forward to seeing you during my school trip.
CAN YOU BELIEVE THAT?
HM?

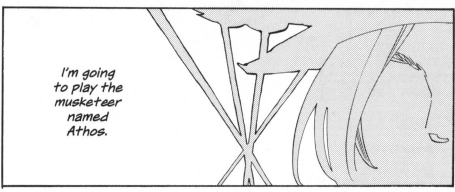

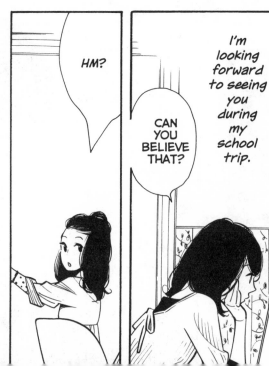

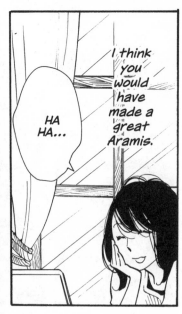

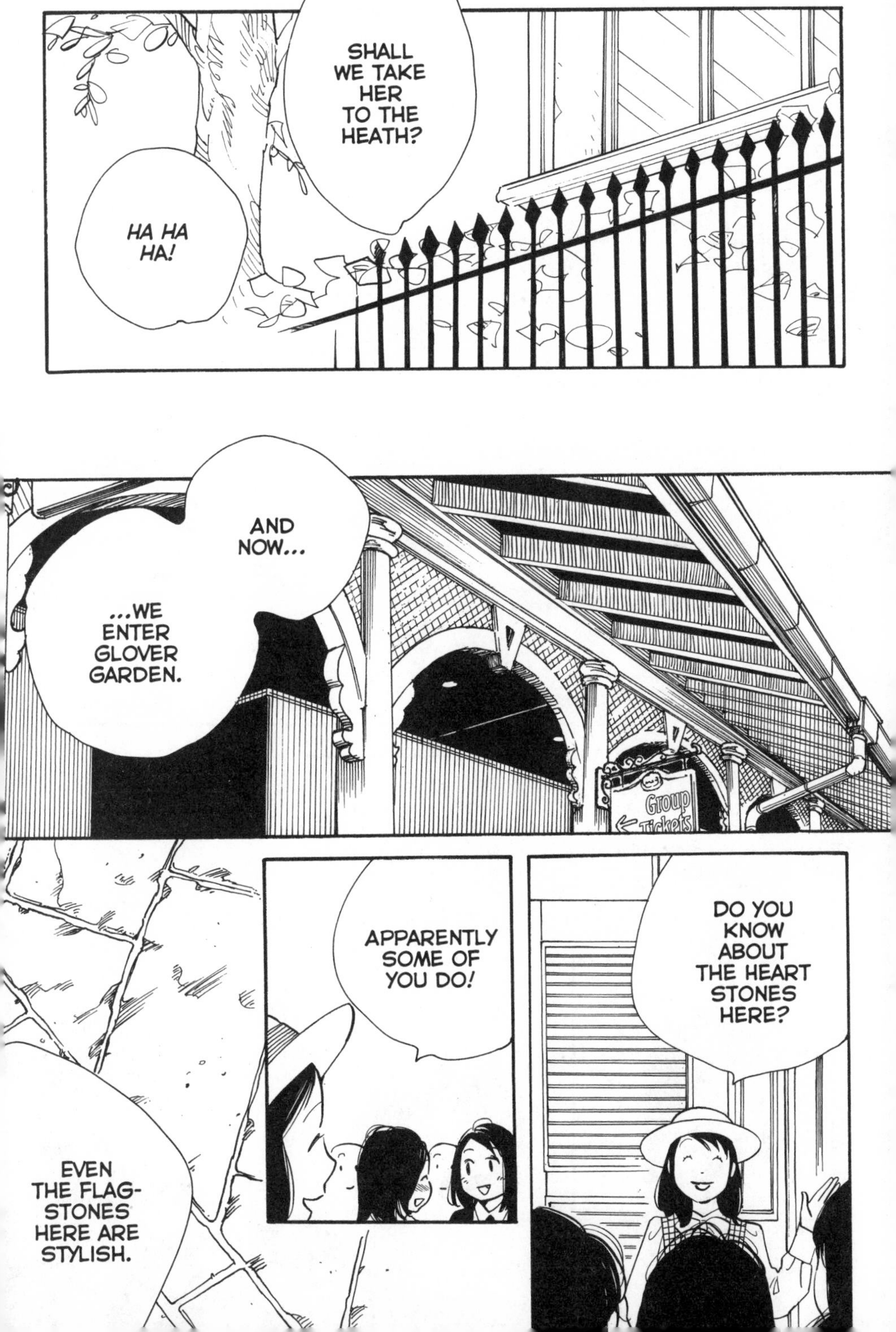

SHALL WE TAKE HER TO THE HEATH?
HA HA HA!
AND NOW...
...WE ENTER GLOVER GARDEN.
Group Tickets
DO YOU KNOW ABOUT THE HEART STONES HERE?
APPARENTLY SOME OF YOU DO!
EVEN THE FLAG-STONES HERE ARE STYLISH.

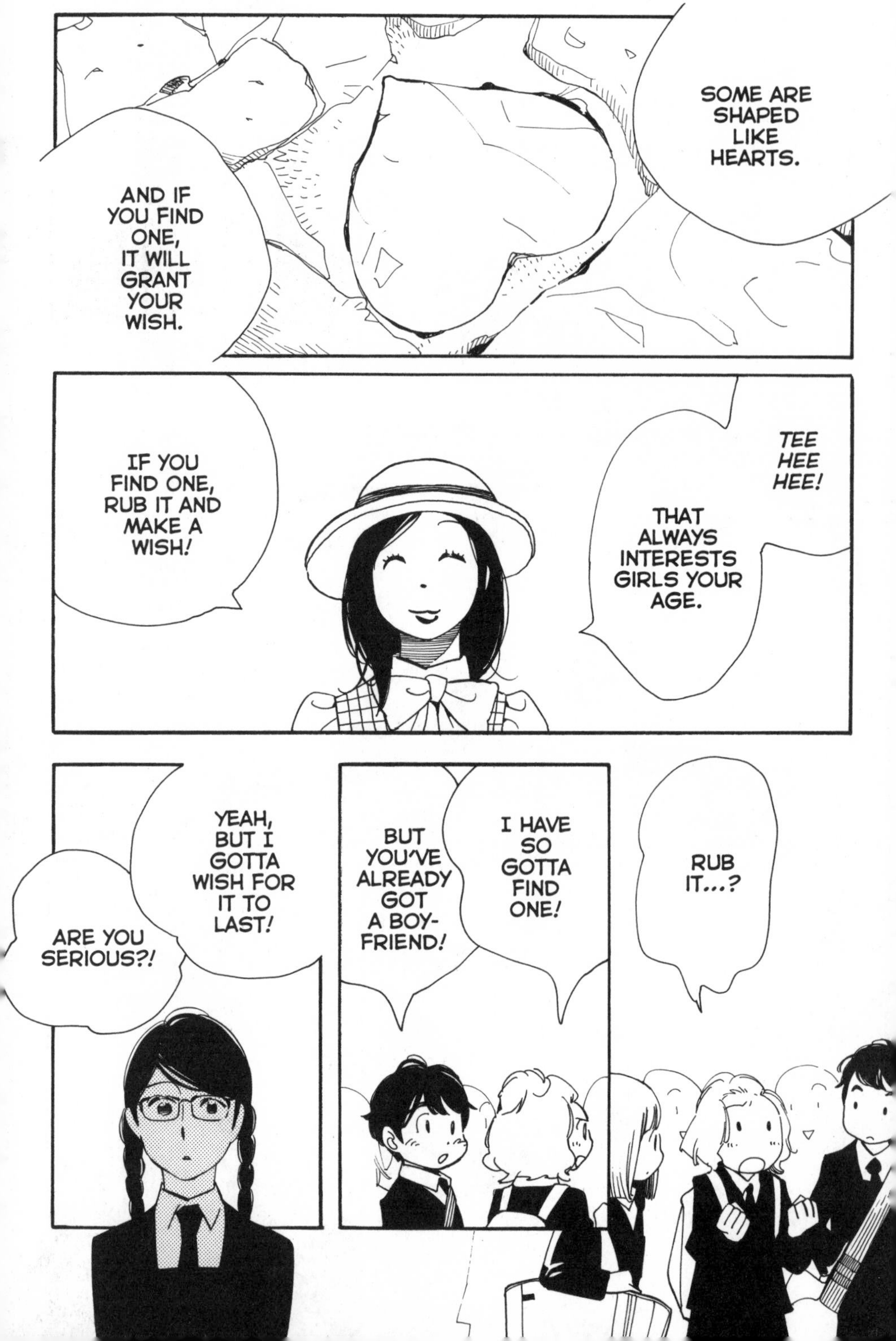
SOME ARE SHAPED LIKE HEARTS.
AND IF YOU FIND ONE, IT WILL GRANT YOUR WISH.
TEE HEE HEE!
THAT ALWAYS INTERESTS GIRLS YOUR AGE.
IF YOU FIND ONE, RUB IT AND MAKE A WISH!
RUB IT...?
I HAVE SO GOTTA FIND ONE!
BUT YOU'VE ALREADY GOT A BOY-FRIEND!
YEAH, BUT I GOTTA WISH FOR IT TO LAST!
ARE YOU SERIOUS?!

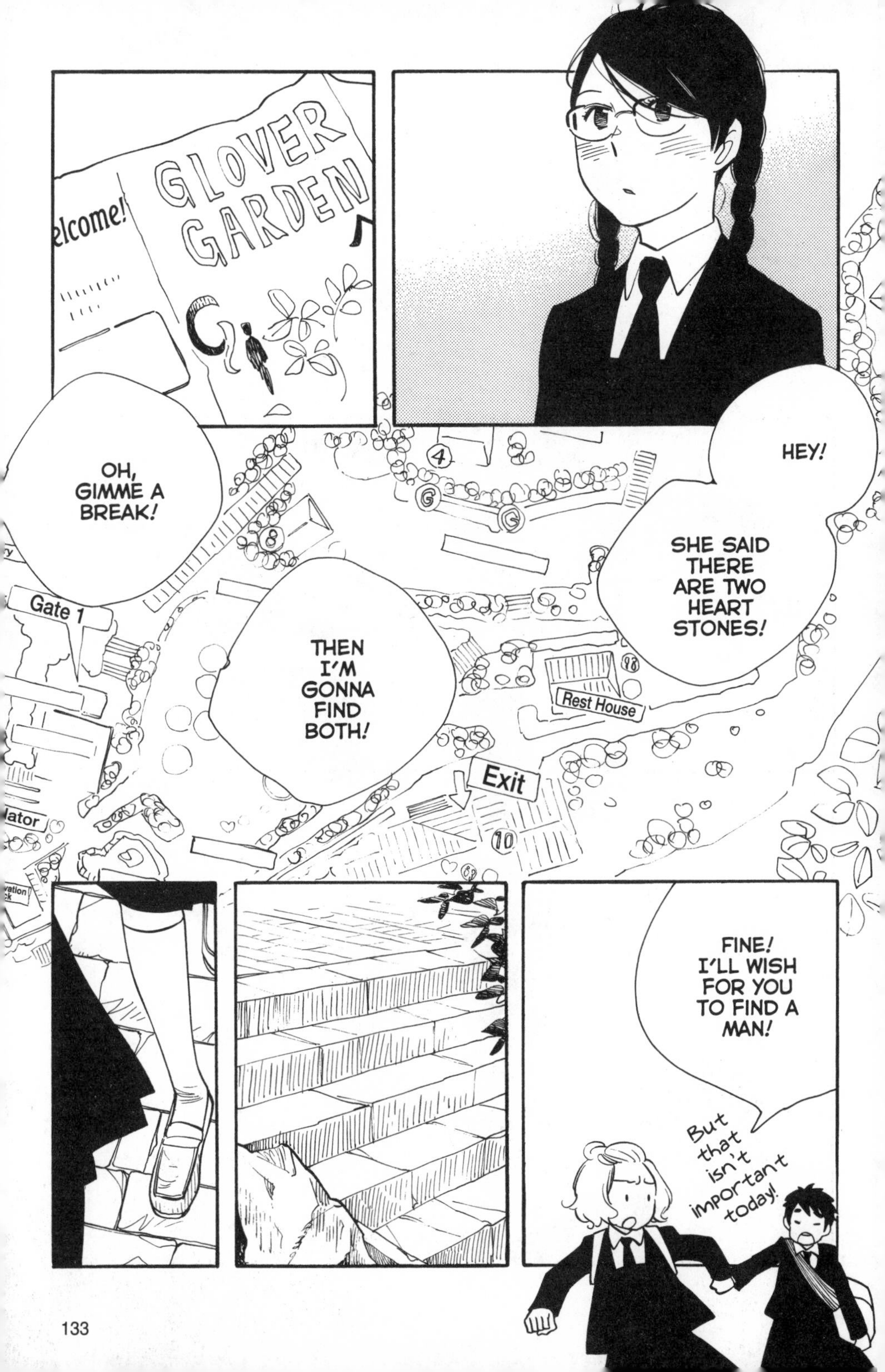
GLOVER GARDEN
elcome!
HEY!
SHE SAID THERE ARE TWO HEART STONES!
Rest House
THEN I'M GONNA FIND BOTH!
Exit
OH, GIMME A BREAK!
Gate 1
ator
FINE! I'LL WISH FOR YOU TO FIND A MAN!
But that isn't important today!

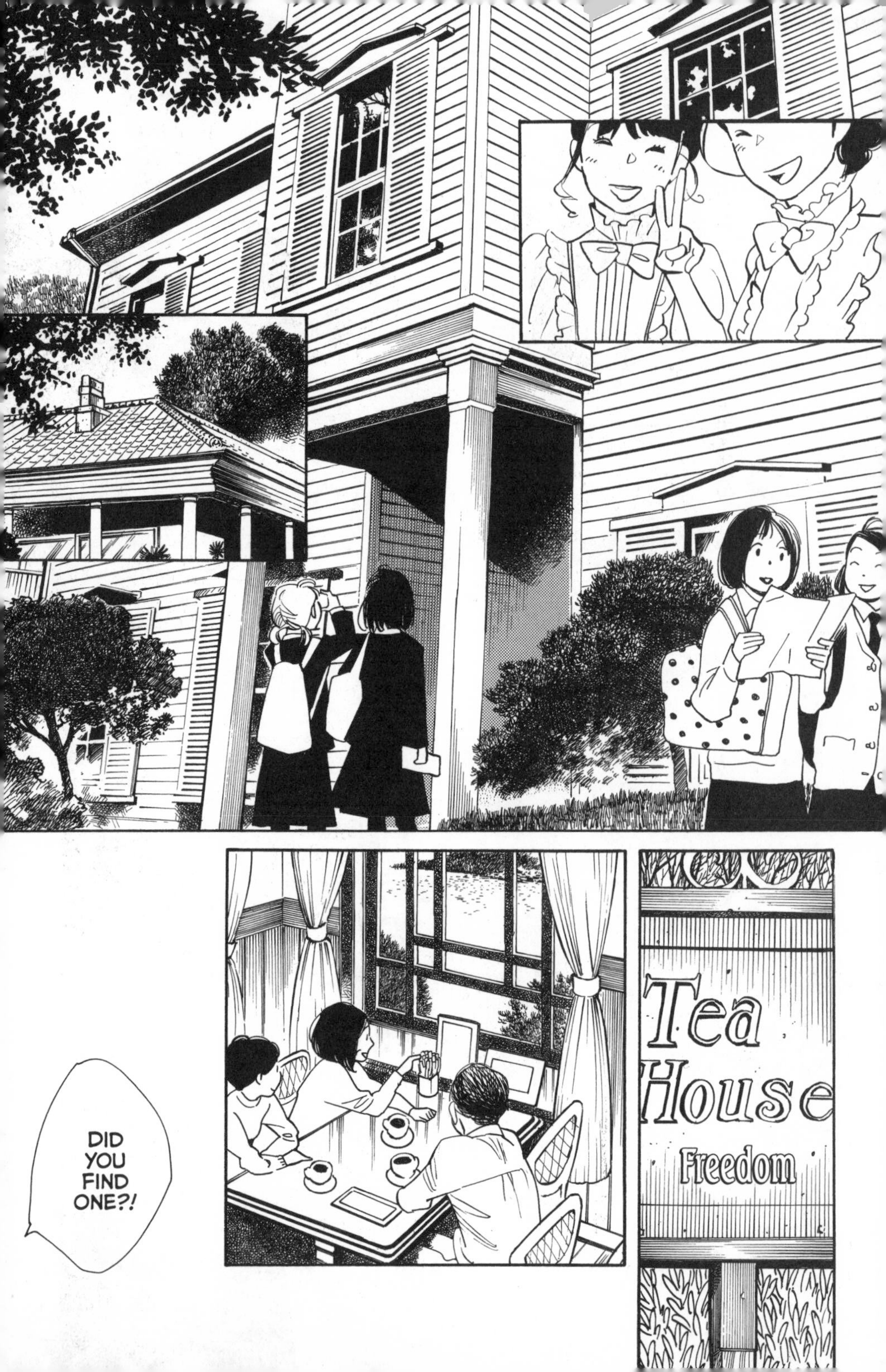
Tea House Freedom
DID YOU FIND ONE?!

KURO AND THE OTHERS FOUND ONE!

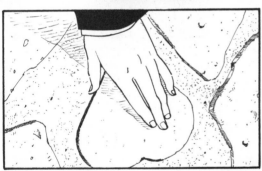

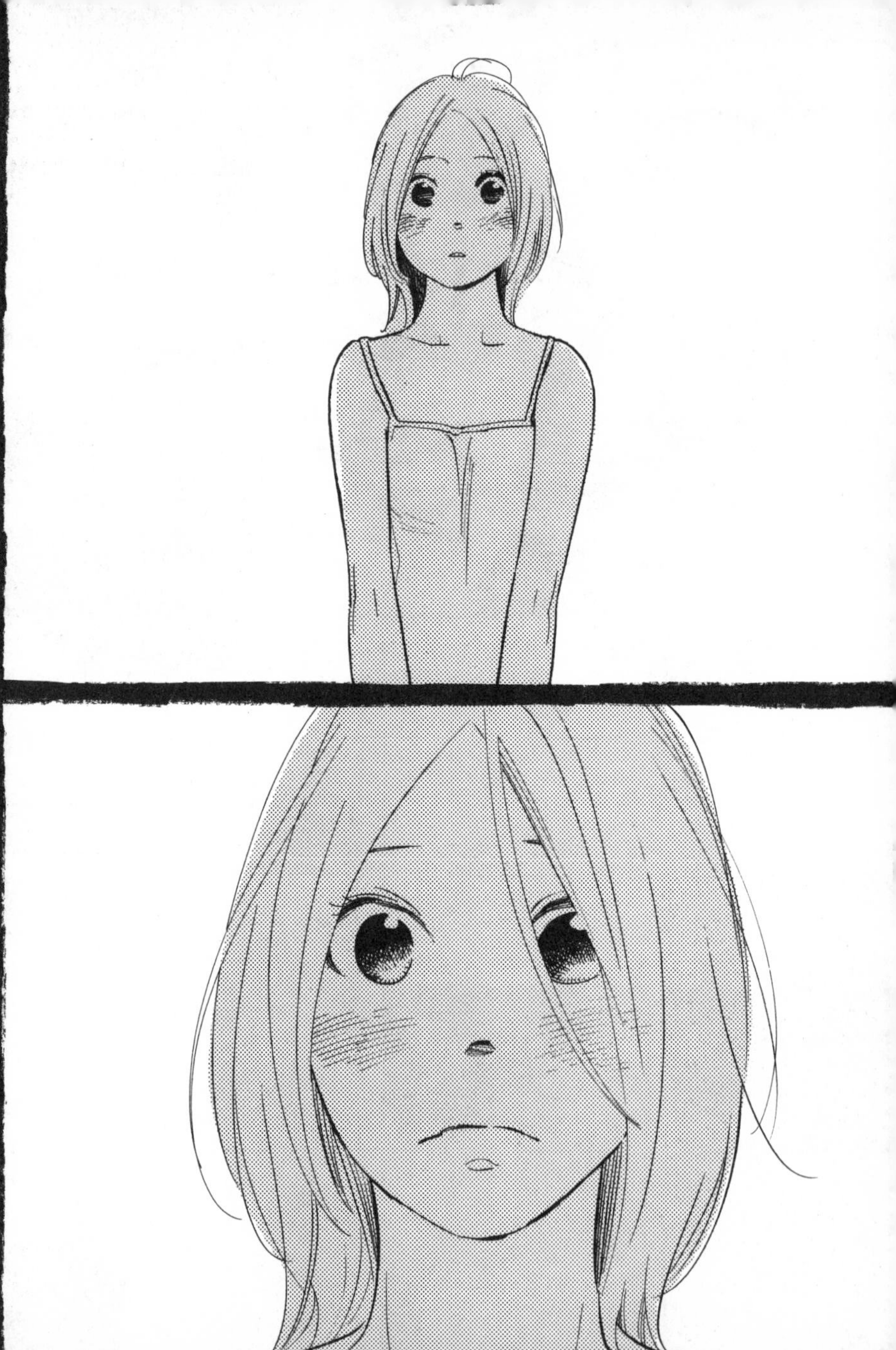

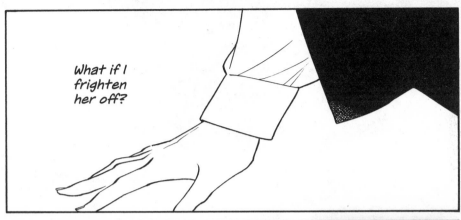

What if I frighten her off?
What if she pulls away from me?
LET'S GO HAVE TEA!
Is what I wanted what Akira wanted to do too?
I'm scared.

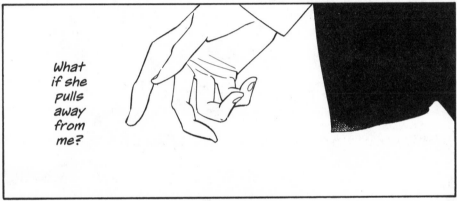

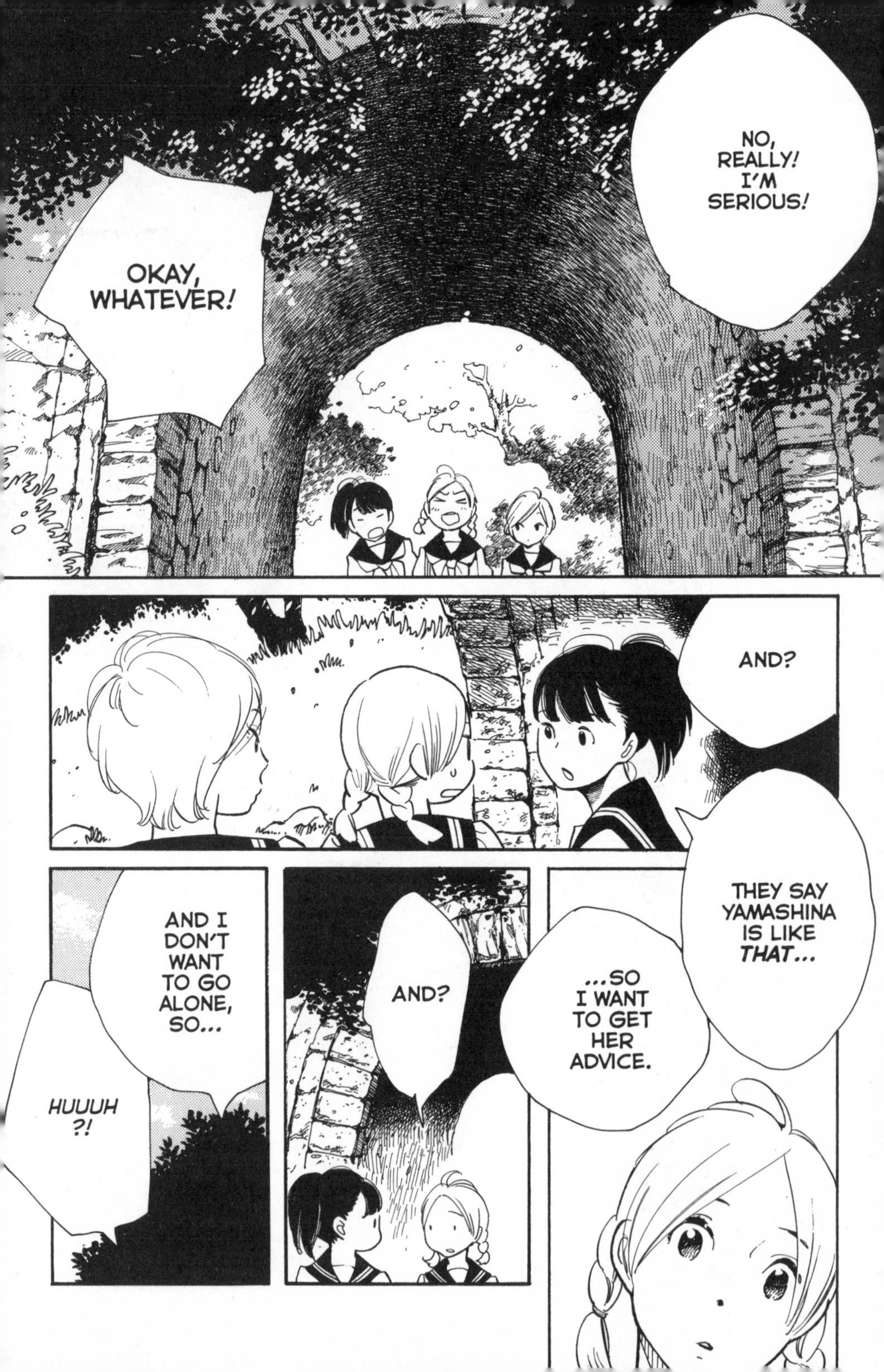
NO, REALLY! I'M SERIOUS!
OKAY, WHATEVER!
AND?
THEY SAY YAMASHINA IS LIKE *THAT*...
...SO I WANT TO GET HER ADVICE.
AND?
AND I DON'T WANT TO GO ALONE, SO...
HUUUH ?!

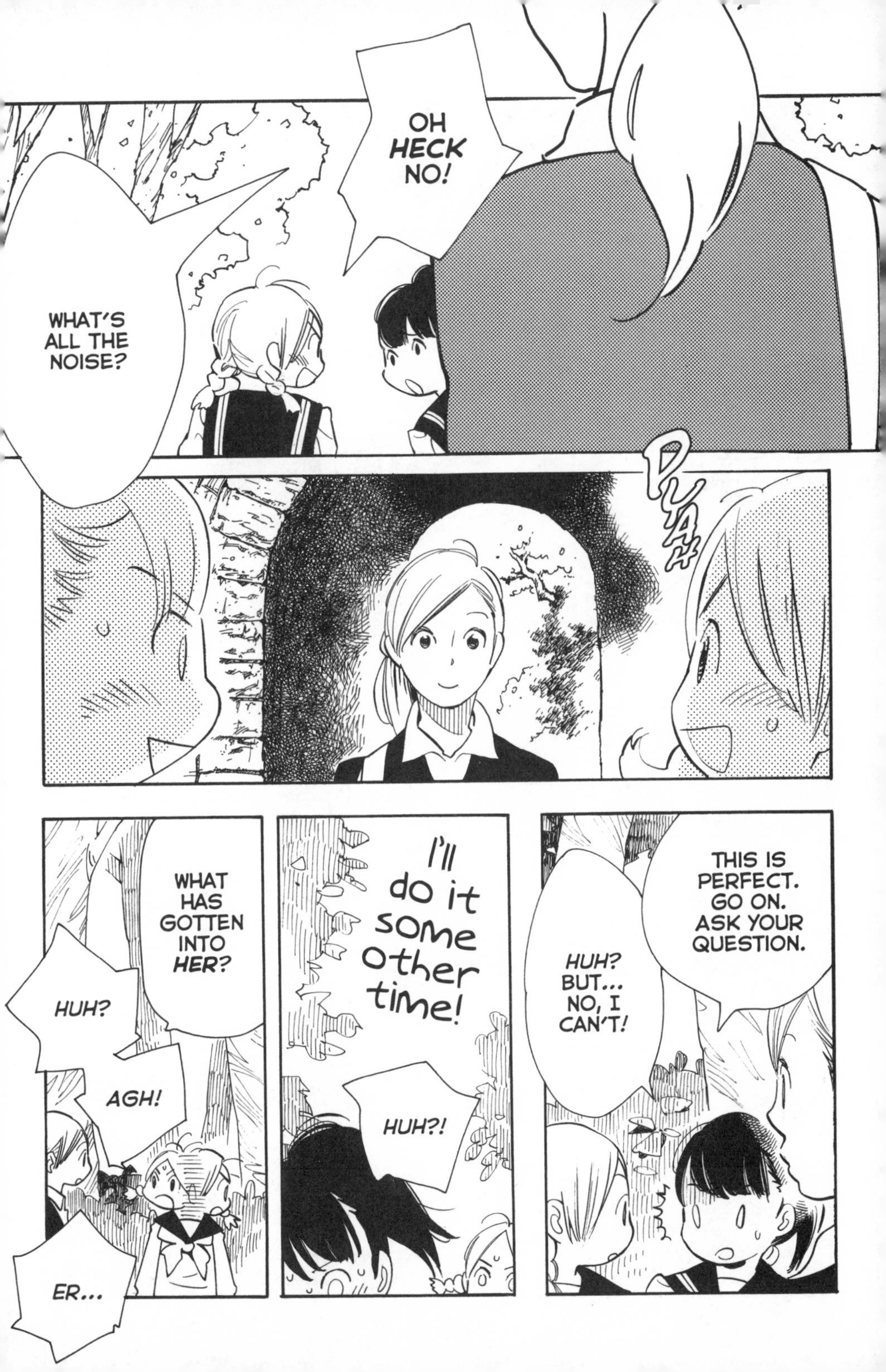
OH **HECK** NO!
WHAT'S ALL THE NOISE?
DUAH
THIS IS PERFECT. GO ON. ASK YOUR QUESTION.
HUH? BUT... NO, I CAN'T!
I'll do it some other time!
HUH?!
WHAT HAS GOTTEN INTO **HER**?
HUH?
AGH!
ER...

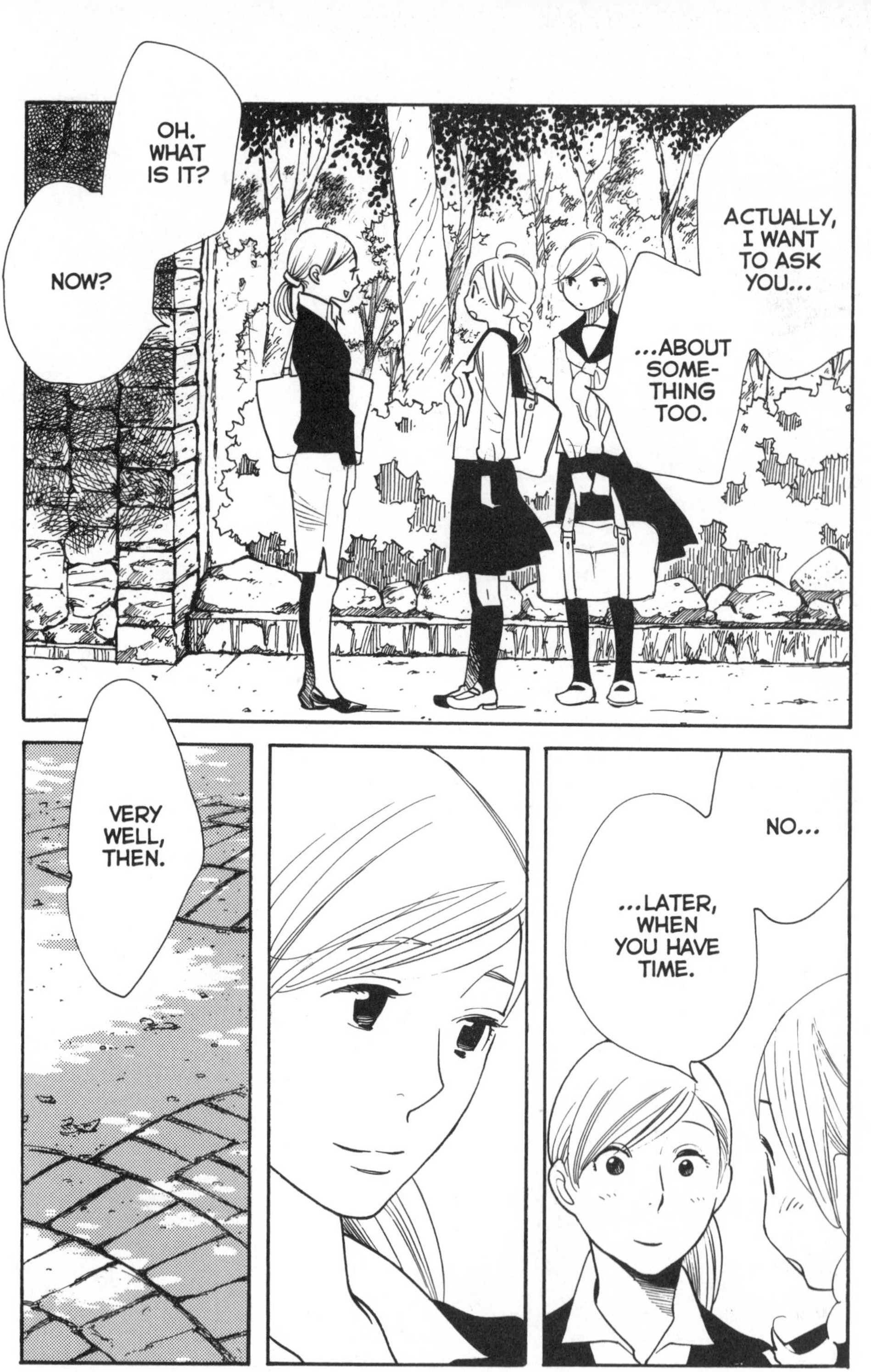
ACTUALLY, I WANT TO ASK YOU...
...ABOUT SOME-THING TOO.
OH. WHAT IS IT?
NOW?
NO...
...LATER, WHEN YOU HAVE TIME.
VERY WELL, THEN.

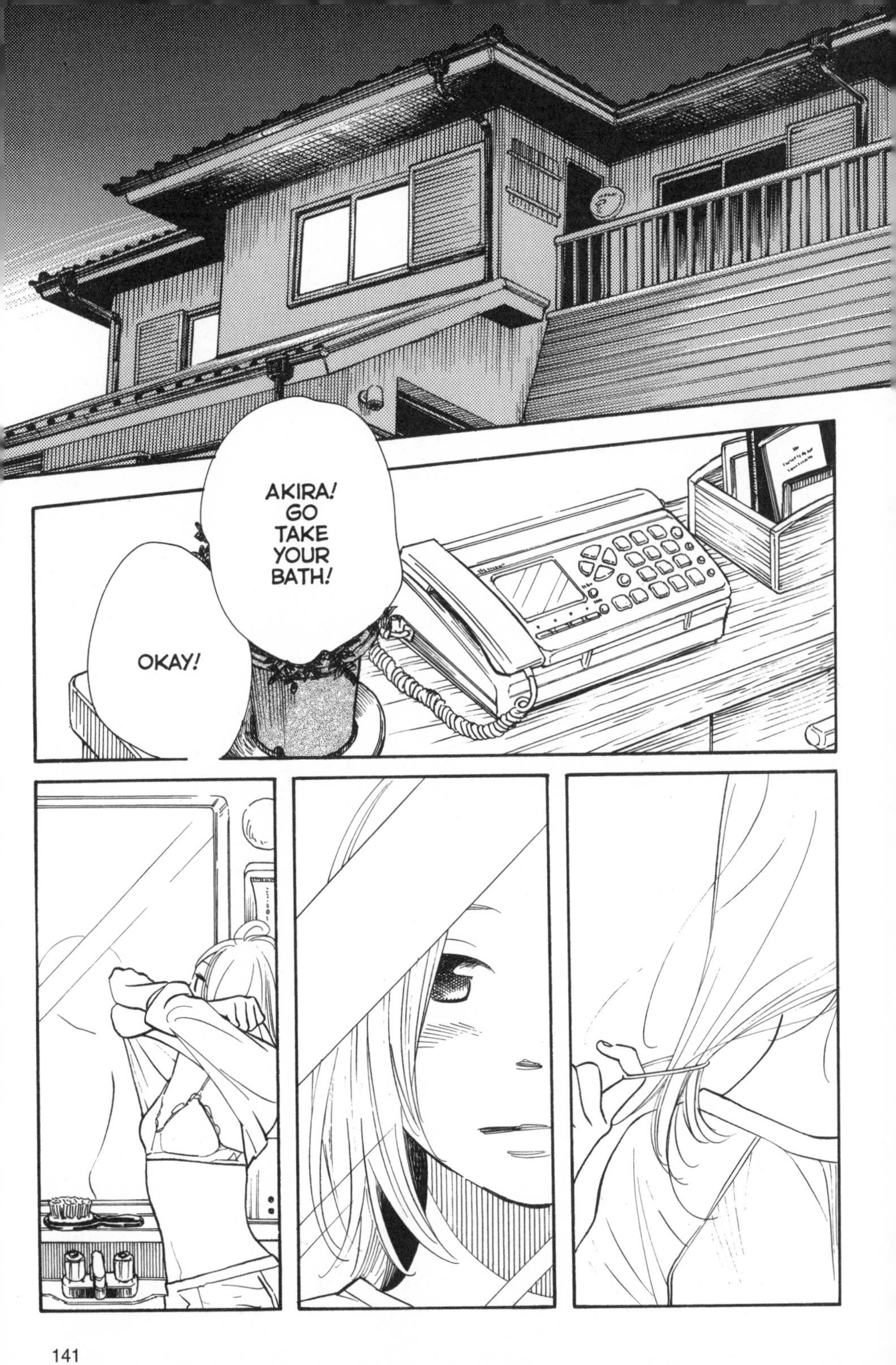
AKIRA! GO TAKE YOUR BATH!
OKAY!

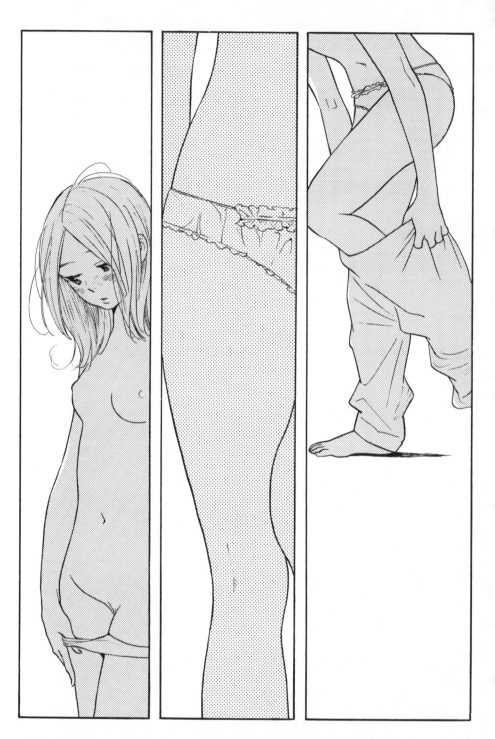

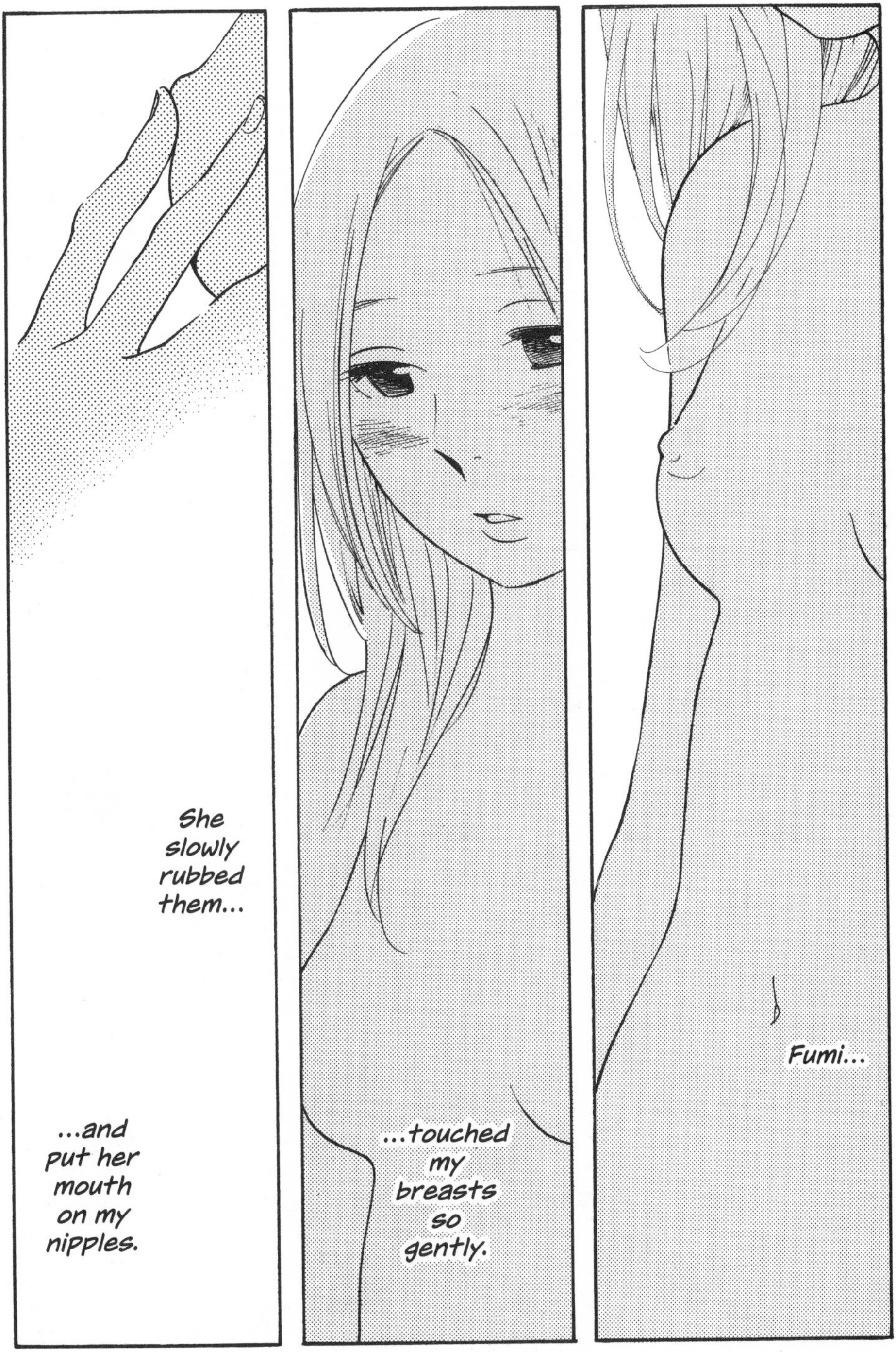
Fumi...
...touched my breasts so gently.
She slowly rubbed them...
...and put her mouth on my nipples.

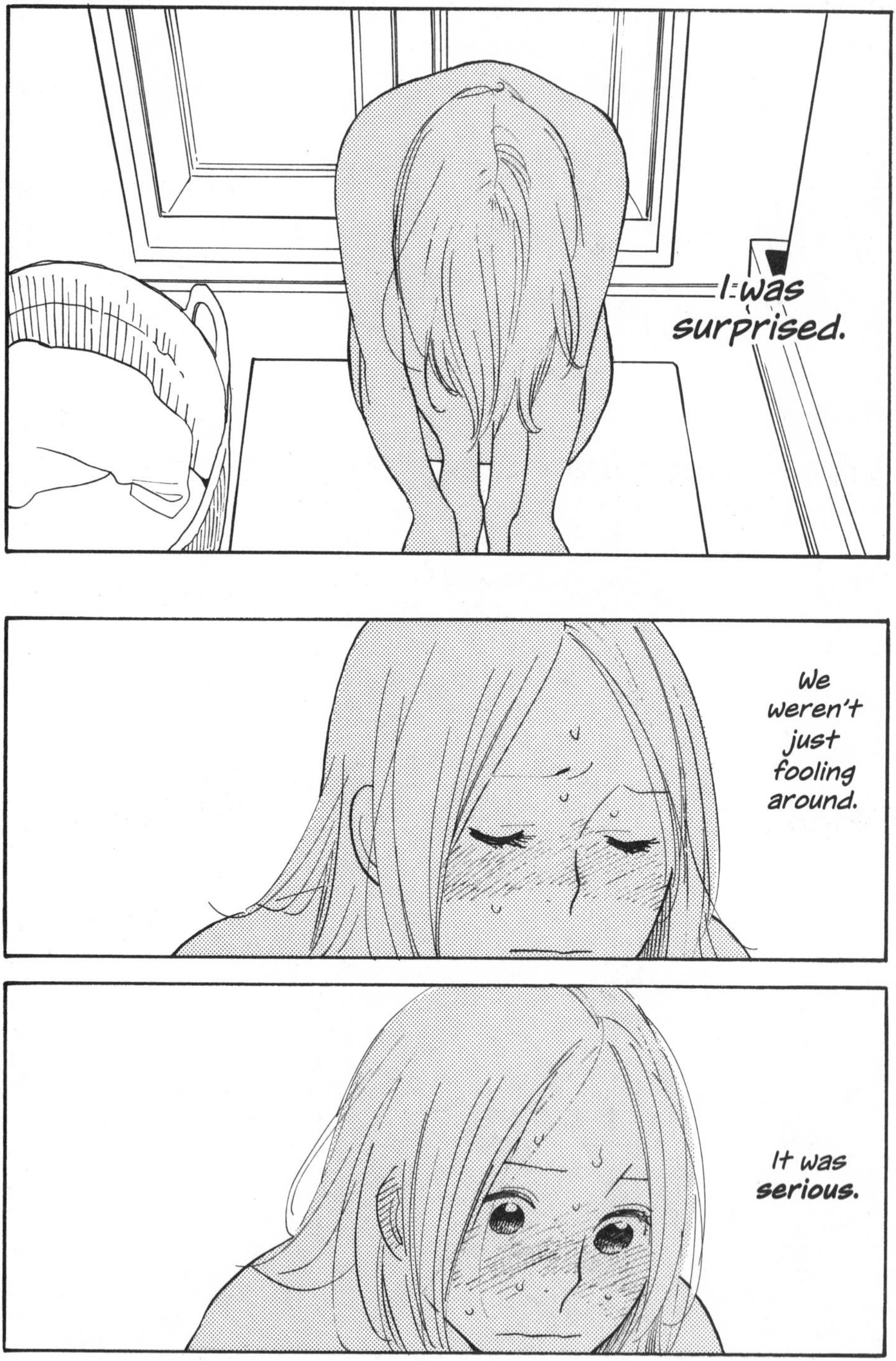
I was surprised.
We weren't just fooling around.
It was serious.

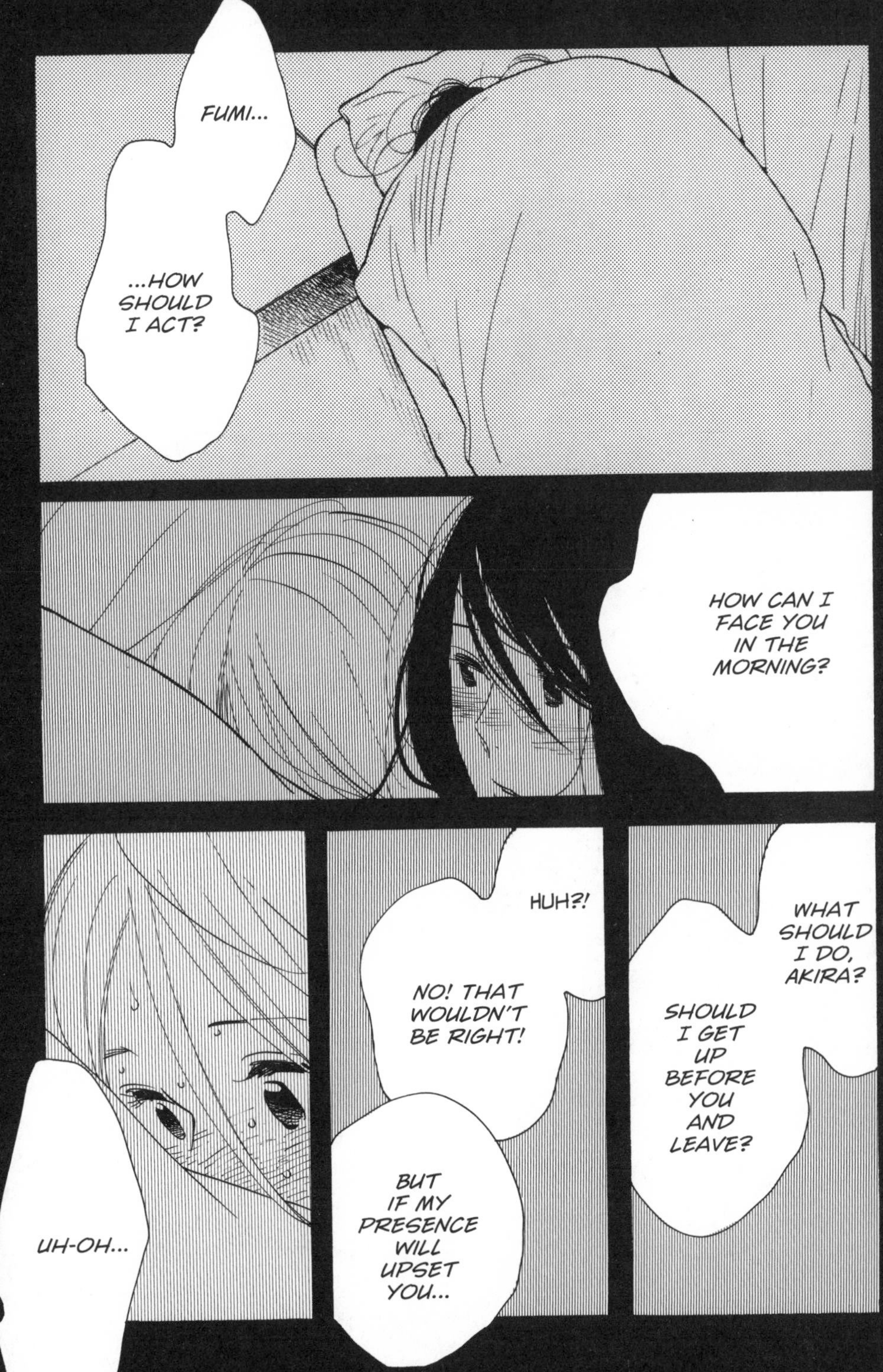
FUMI...
...HOW SHOULD I ACT?
HOW CAN I FACE YOU IN THE MORNING?
WHAT SHOULD I DO, AKIRA?
SHOULD I GET UP BEFORE YOU AND LEAVE?
HUH?!
NO! THAT WOULDN'T BE RIGHT!
BUT IF MY PRESENCE WILL UPSET YOU...
UH-OH...

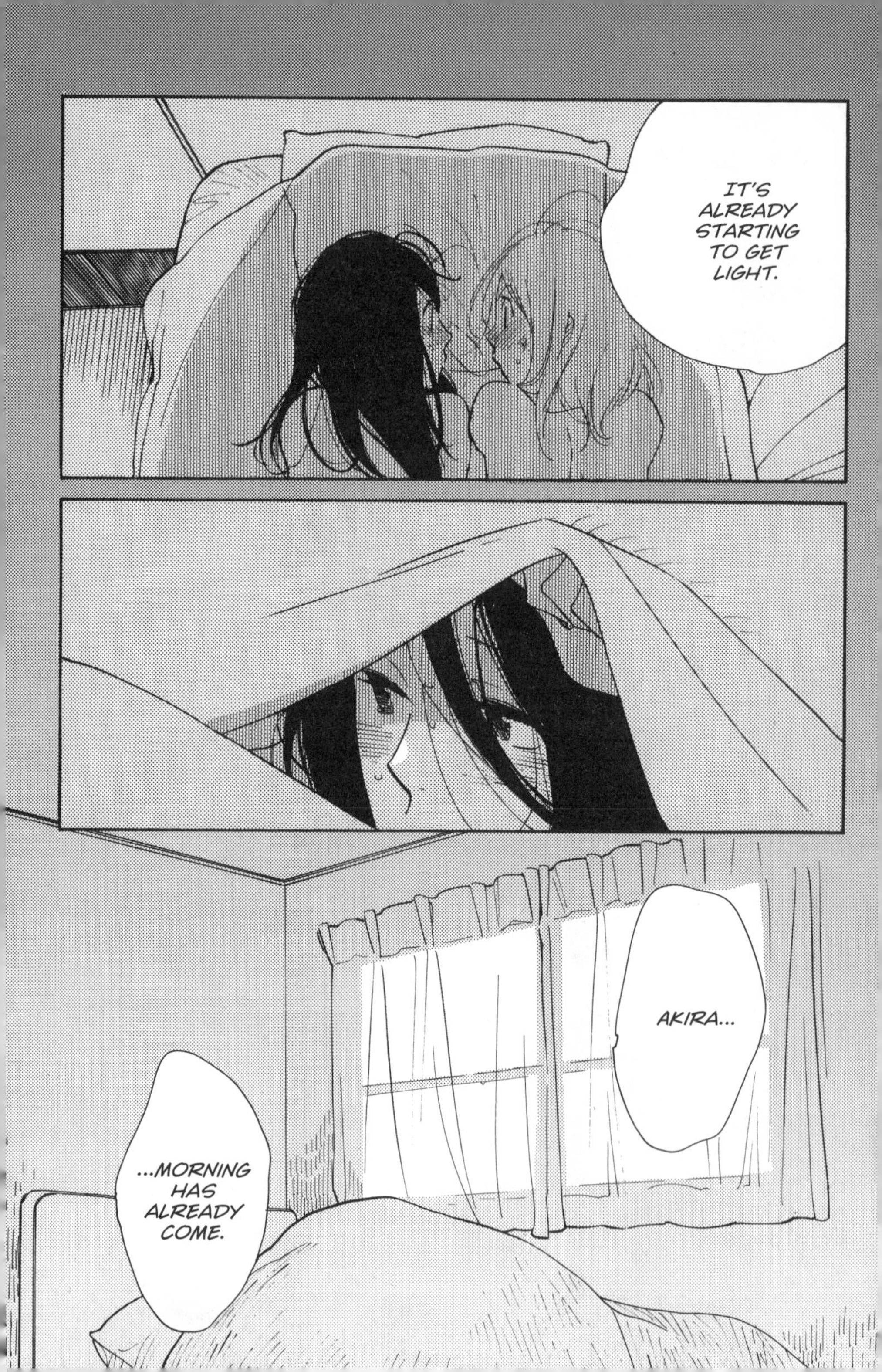
IT'S ALREADY STARTING TO GET LIGHT.
AKIRA...
...MORNING HAS ALREADY COME.

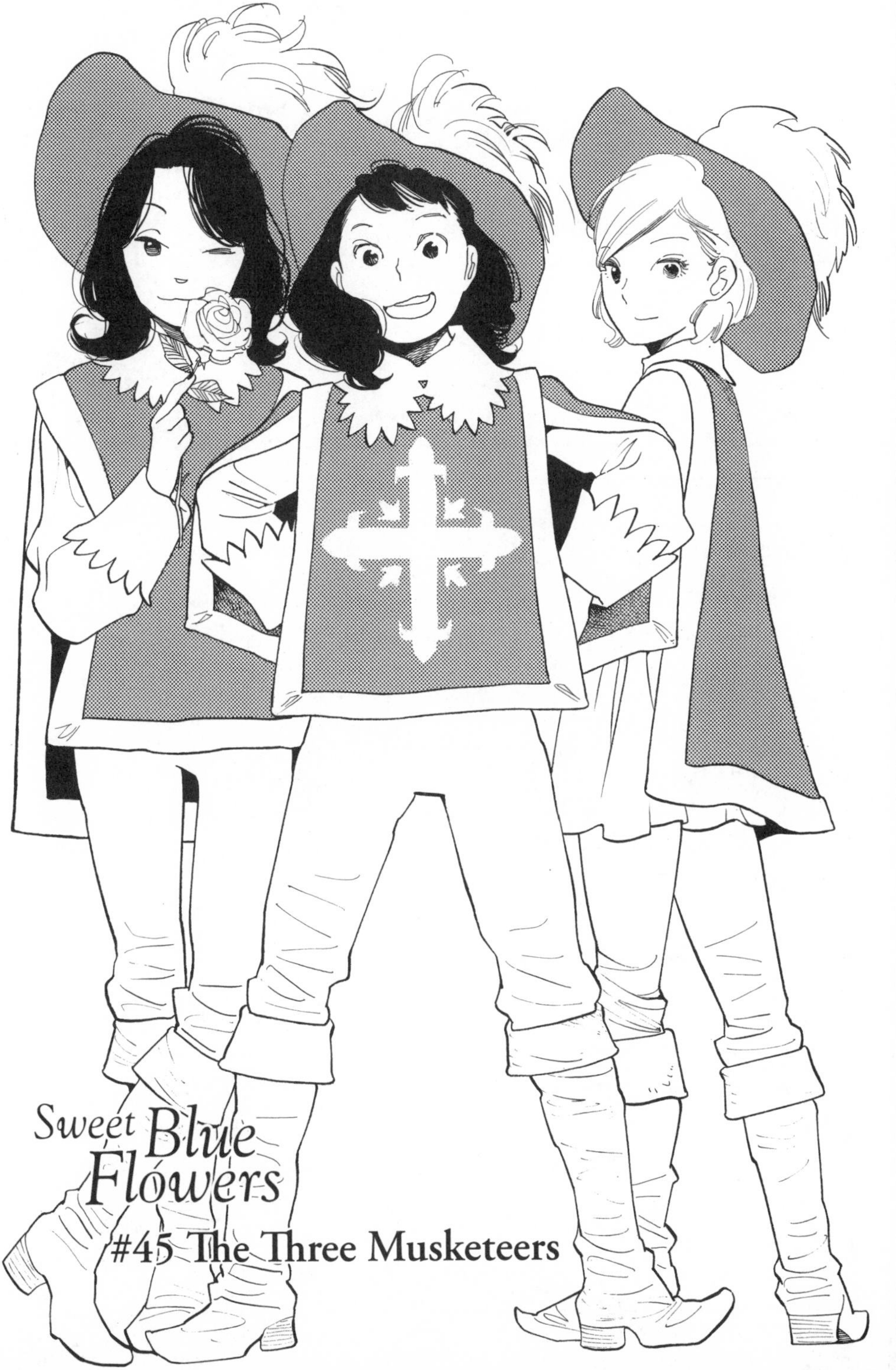

Sweet Blue Flowers

#45 The Three Musketeers

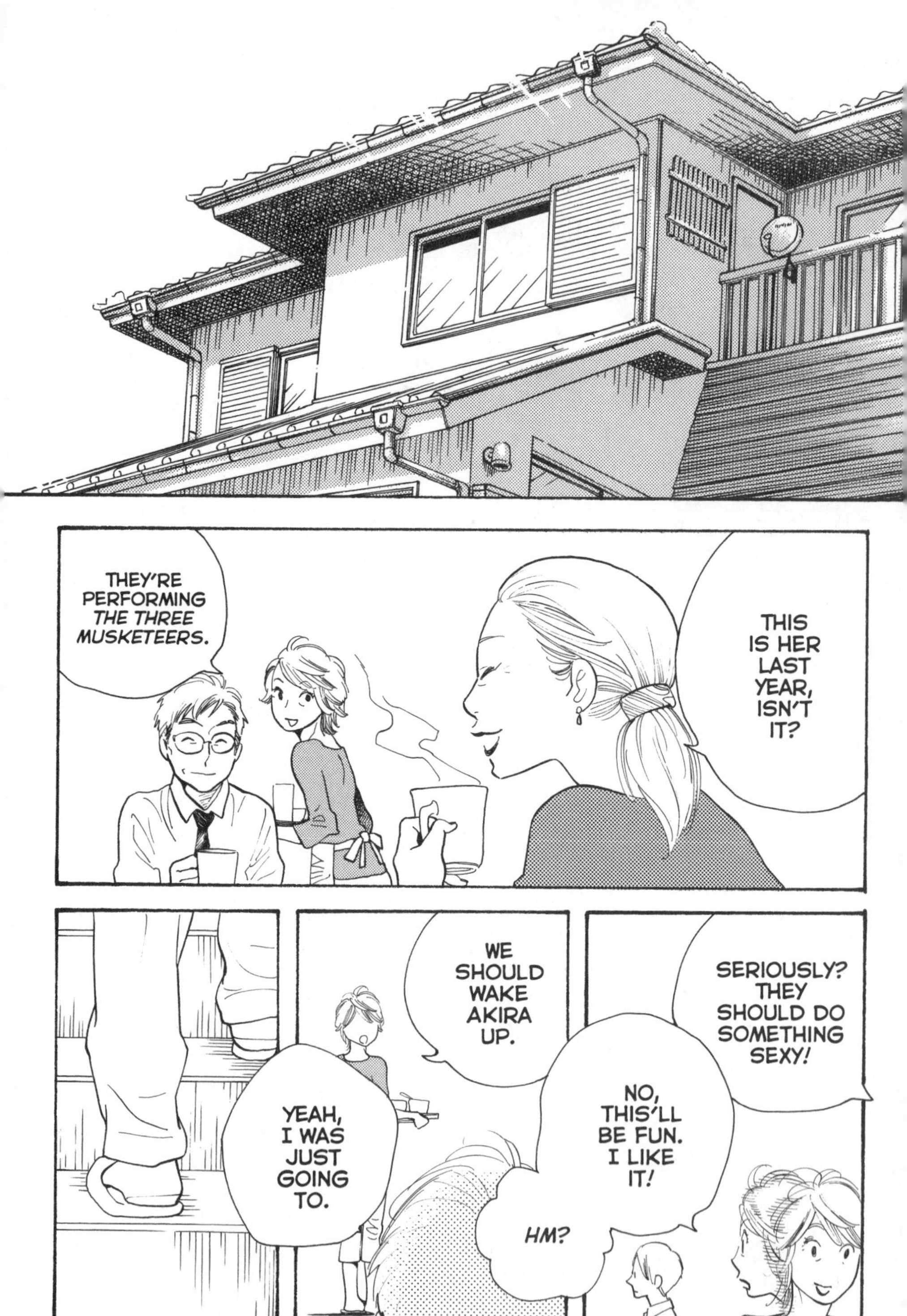
THIS IS HER LAST YEAR, ISN'T IT?
THEY'RE PERFORMING *THE THREE MUSKETEERS*.
SERIOUSLY? THEY SHOULD DO SOMETHING SEXY!
NO, THIS'LL BE FUN. I LIKE IT!
HM?
WE SHOULD WAKE AKIRA UP.
YEAH, I WAS JUST GOING TO.

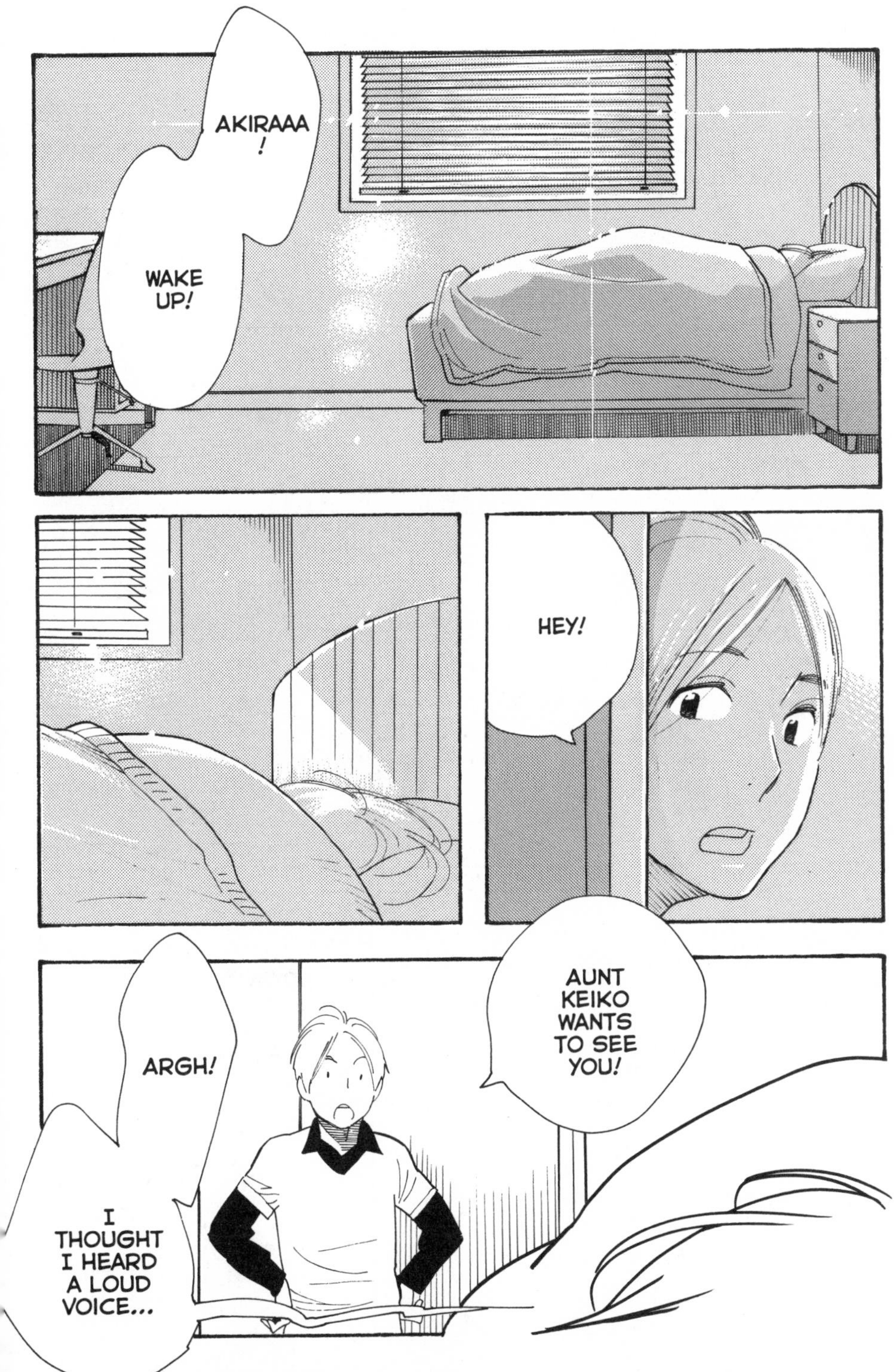
AKIRAAA!
WAKE UP!
HEY!
AUNT KEIKO WANTS TO SEE YOU!
ARGH!
I THOUGHT I HEARD A LOUD VOICE...

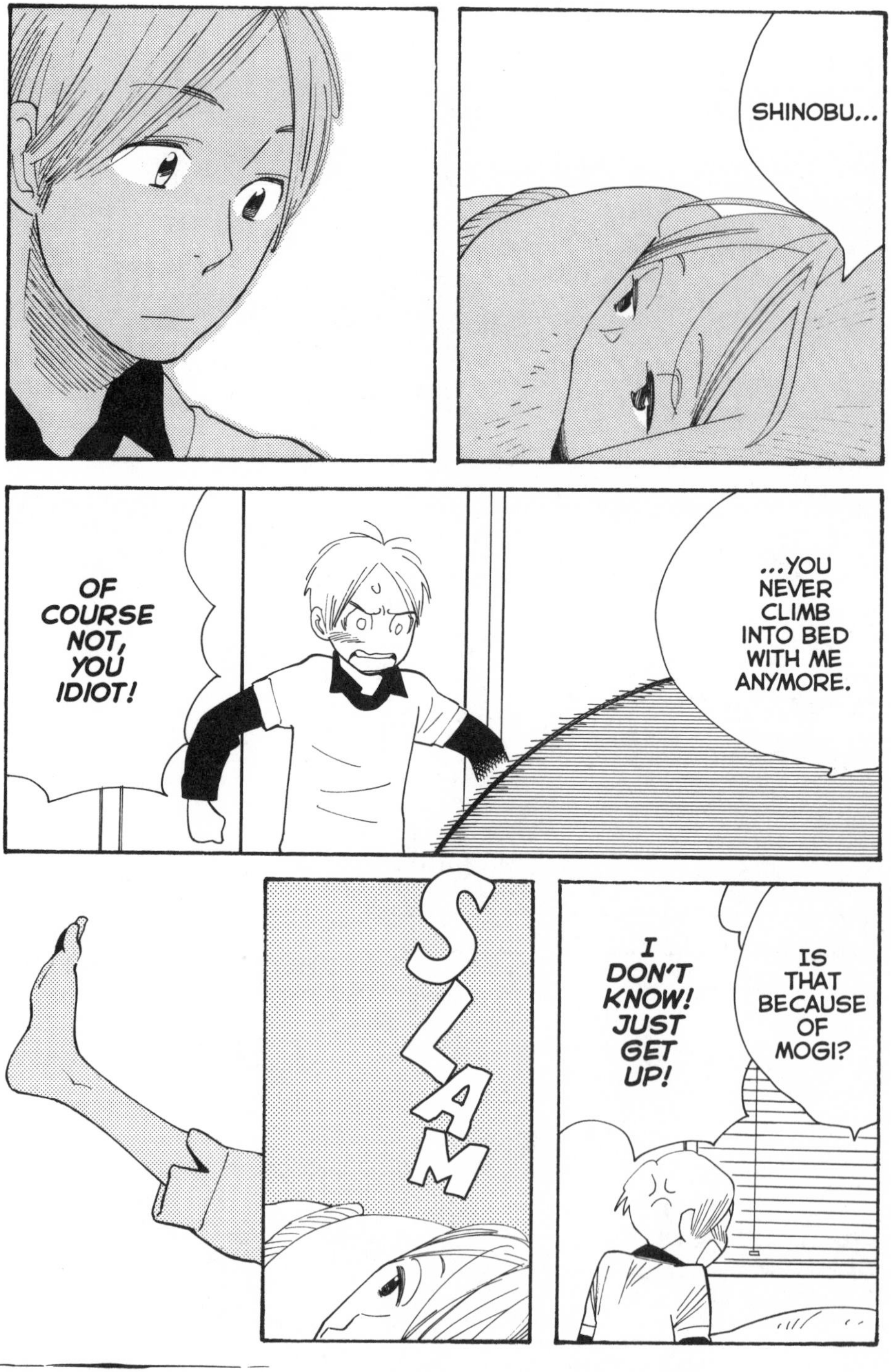
SHINOBU...
...YOU NEVER CLIMB INTO BED WITH ME ANYMORE.
OF COURSE NOT, YOU IDIOT!
IS THAT BECAUSE OF MOGI?
I DON'T KNOW! JUST GET UP!
SLAM

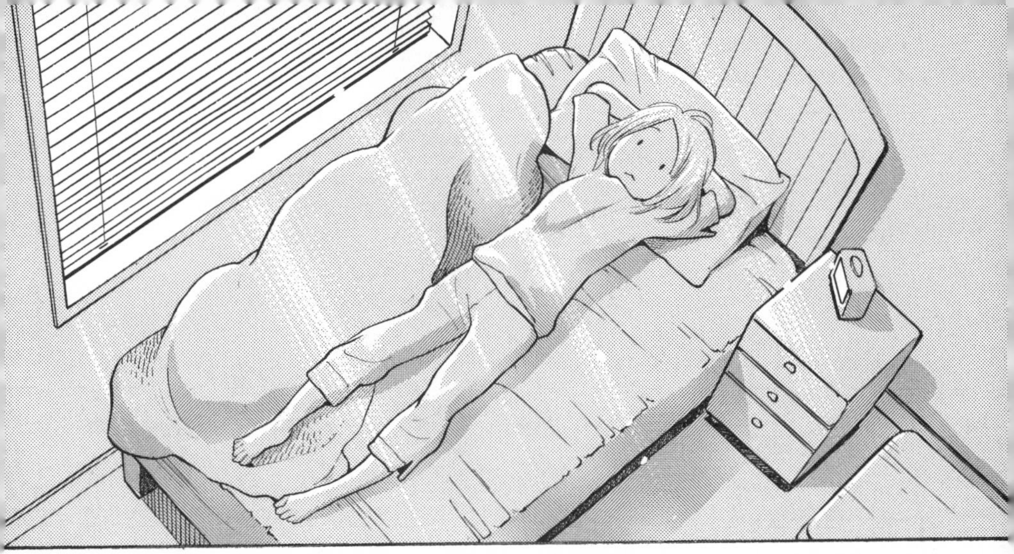

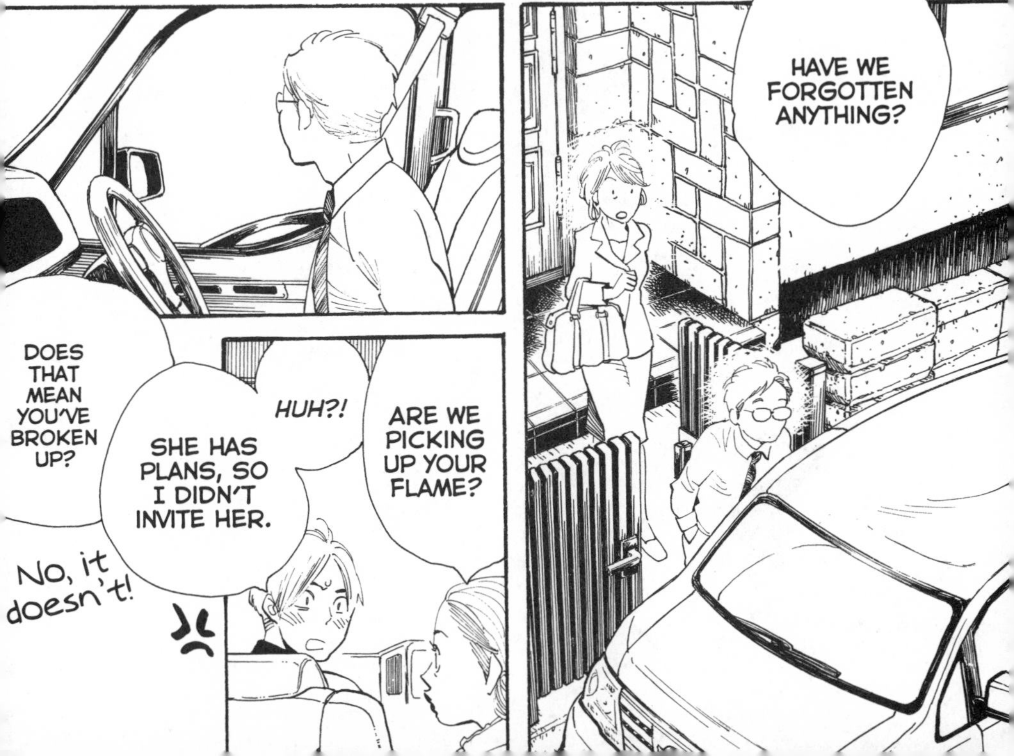
HAVE WE FORGOTTEN ANYTHING?
ARE WE PICKING UP YOUR FLAME?
HUH?!
SHE HAS PLANS, SO I DIDN'T INVITE HER.
DOES THAT MEAN YOU'VE BROKEN UP?
No, it doesn't!

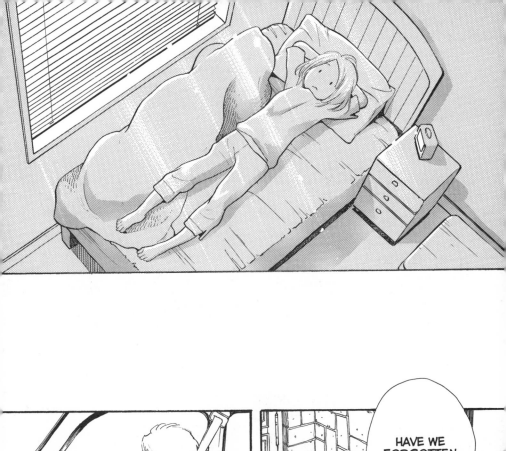

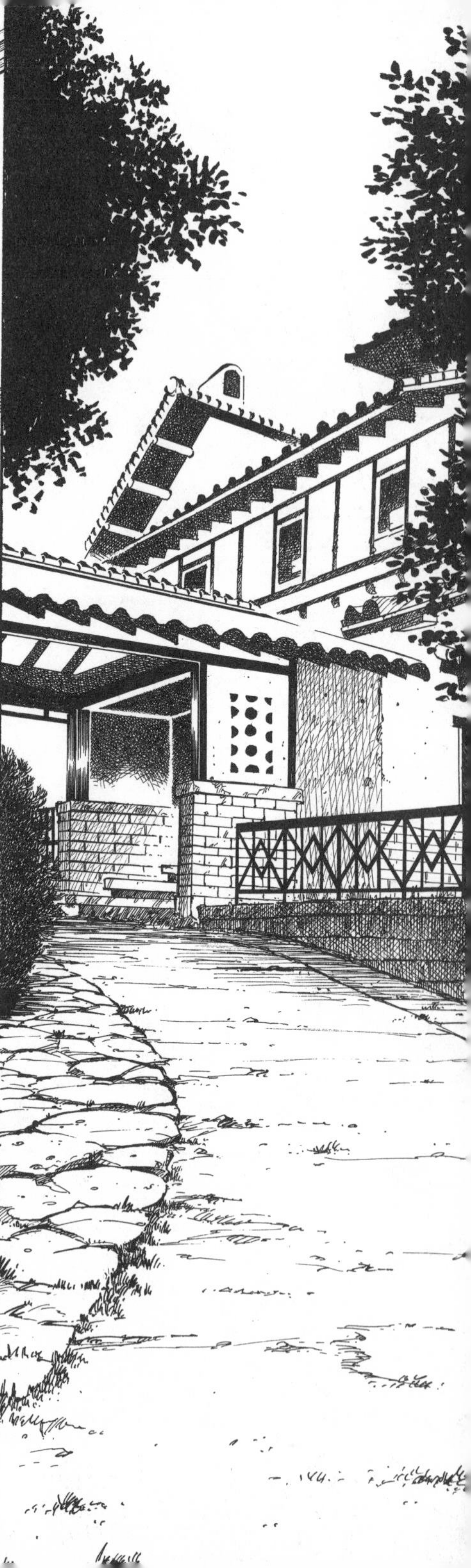

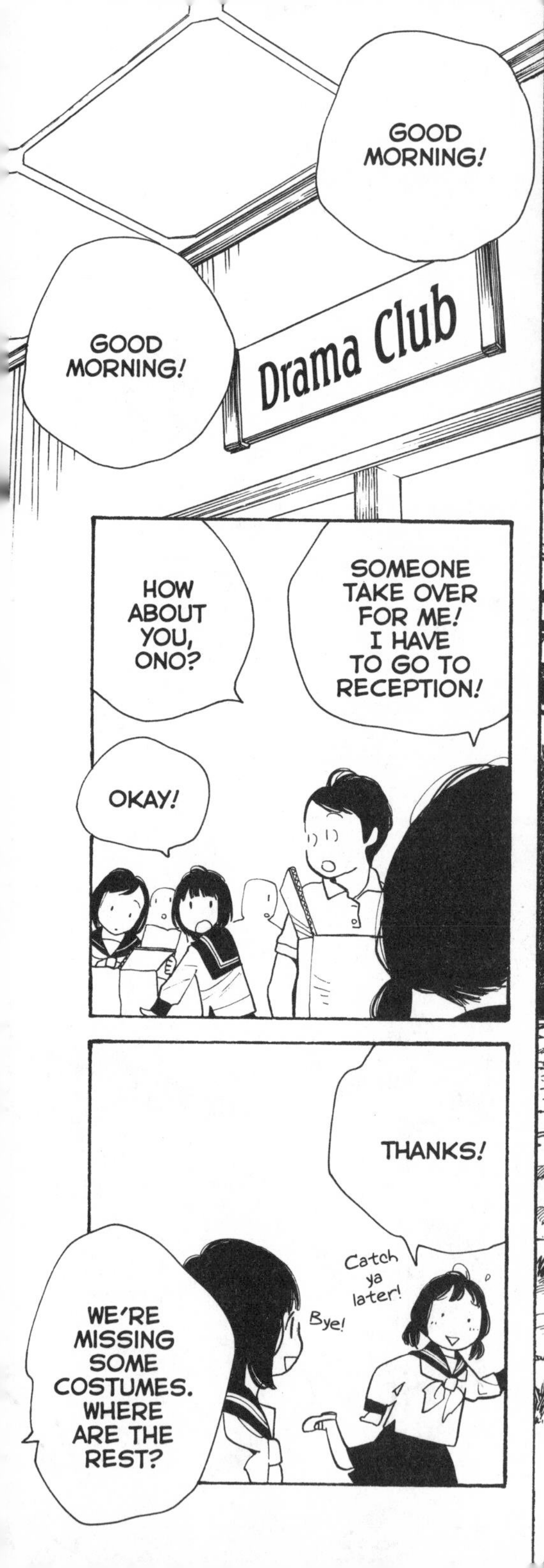
GOOD MORNING!
Drama Club
GOOD MORNING!
SOMEONE TAKE OVER FOR ME! I HAVE TO GO TO RECEPTION!
HOW ABOUT YOU, ONO?
OKAY!
THANKS!
Catch ya later!
Bye!
WE'RE MISSING SOME COSTUMES. WHERE ARE THE REST?

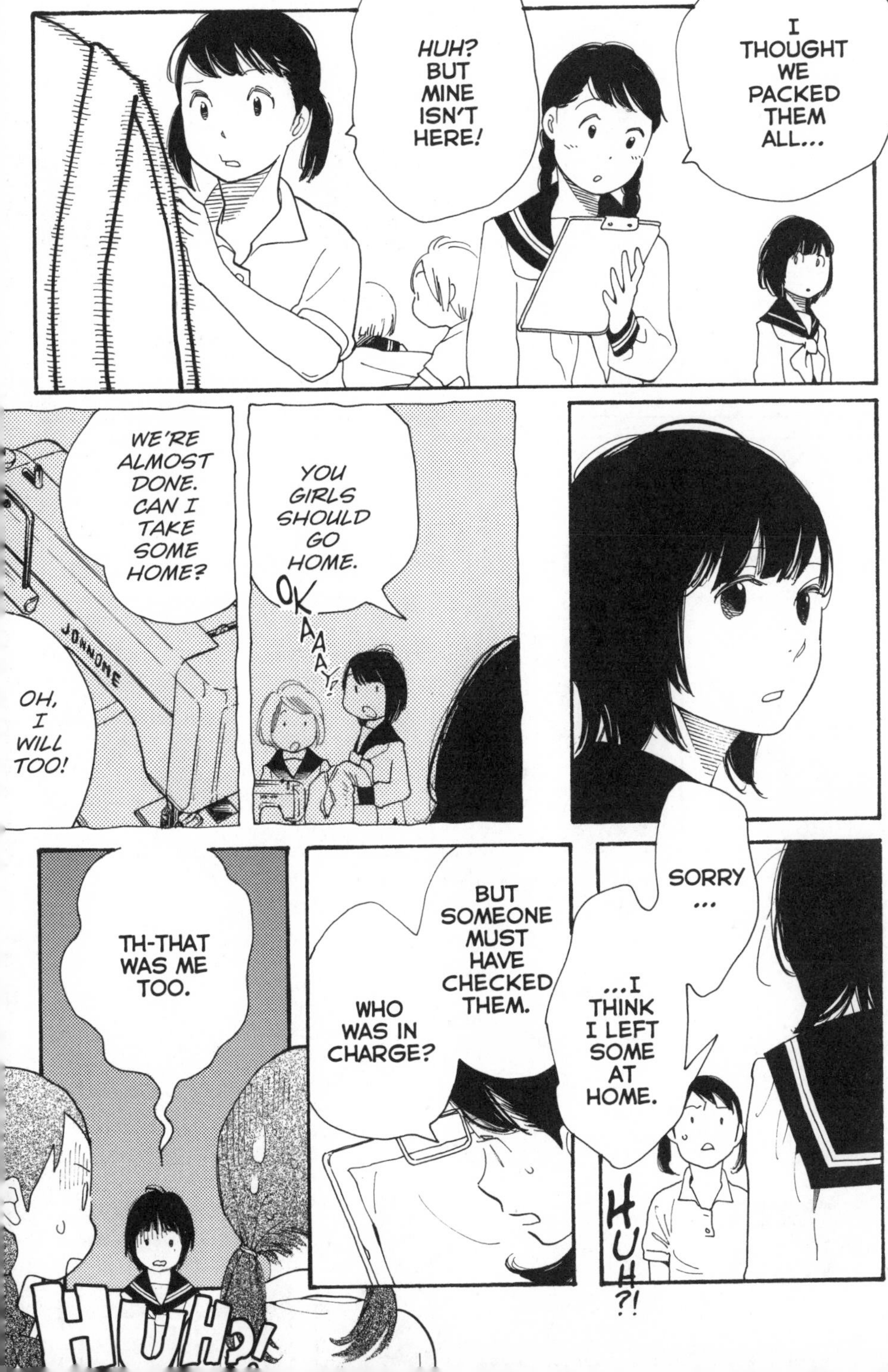
I THOUGHT WE PACKED THEM ALL...
HUH? BUT MINE ISN'T HERE!
YOU GIRLS SHOULD GO HOME.
OKAAAY?!
WE'RE ALMOST DONE. CAN I TAKE SOME HOME?
JONNOME
OH, I WILL TOO!
SORRY...
...I THINK I LEFT SOME AT HOME.
HUH?!
BUT SOMEONE MUST HAVE CHECKED THEM.
WHO WAS IN CHARGE?
TH-THAT WAS ME TOO.
HUH?!

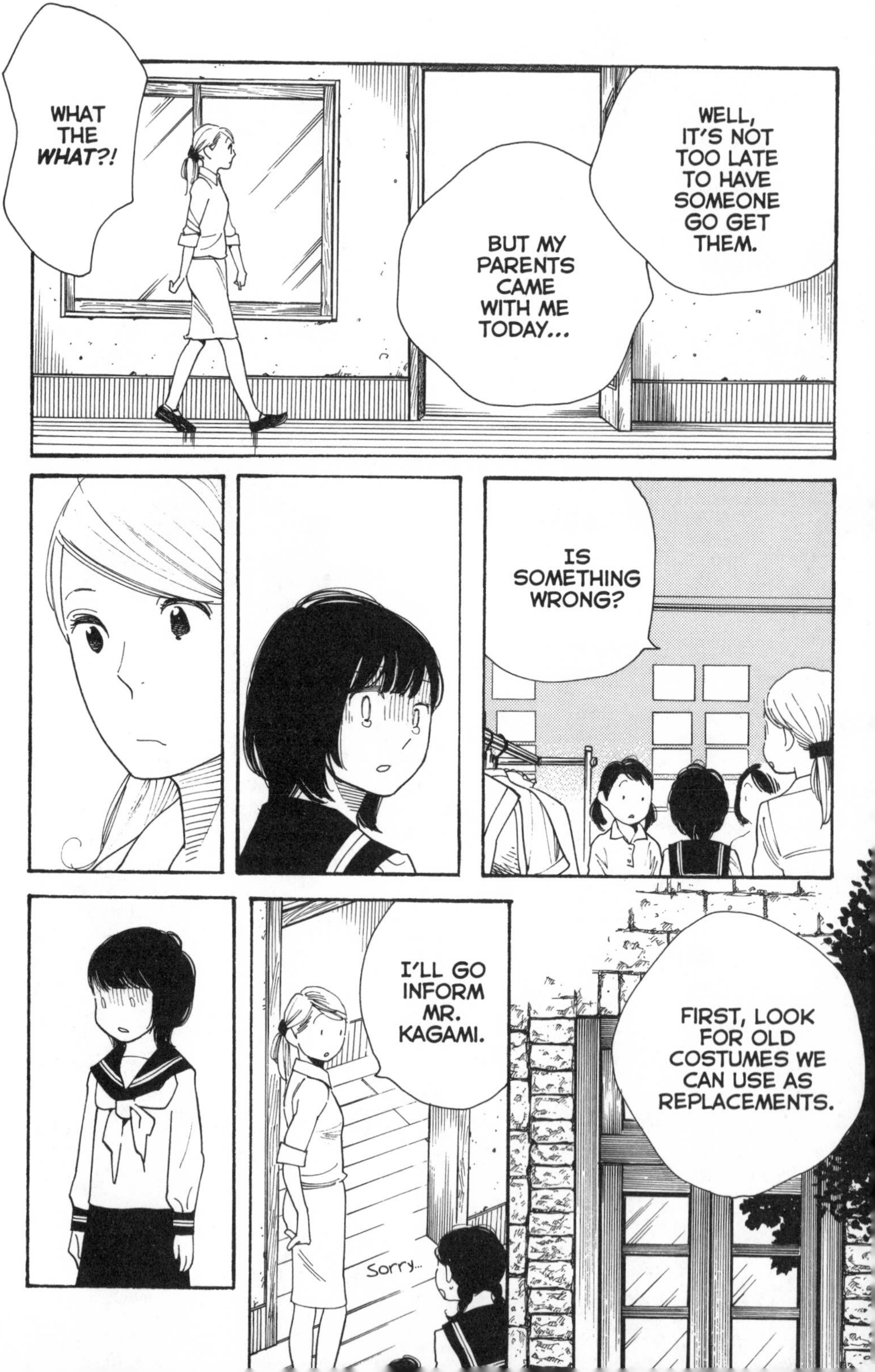
WELL, IT'S NOT TOO LATE TO HAVE SOMEONE GO GET THEM.
BUT MY PARENTS CAME WITH ME TODAY...
WHAT THE *WHAT?!*
IS SOMETHING WRONG?
FIRST, LOOK FOR OLD COSTUMES WE CAN USE AS REPLACEMENTS.
I'LL GO INFORM MR. KAGAMI.
Sorry...

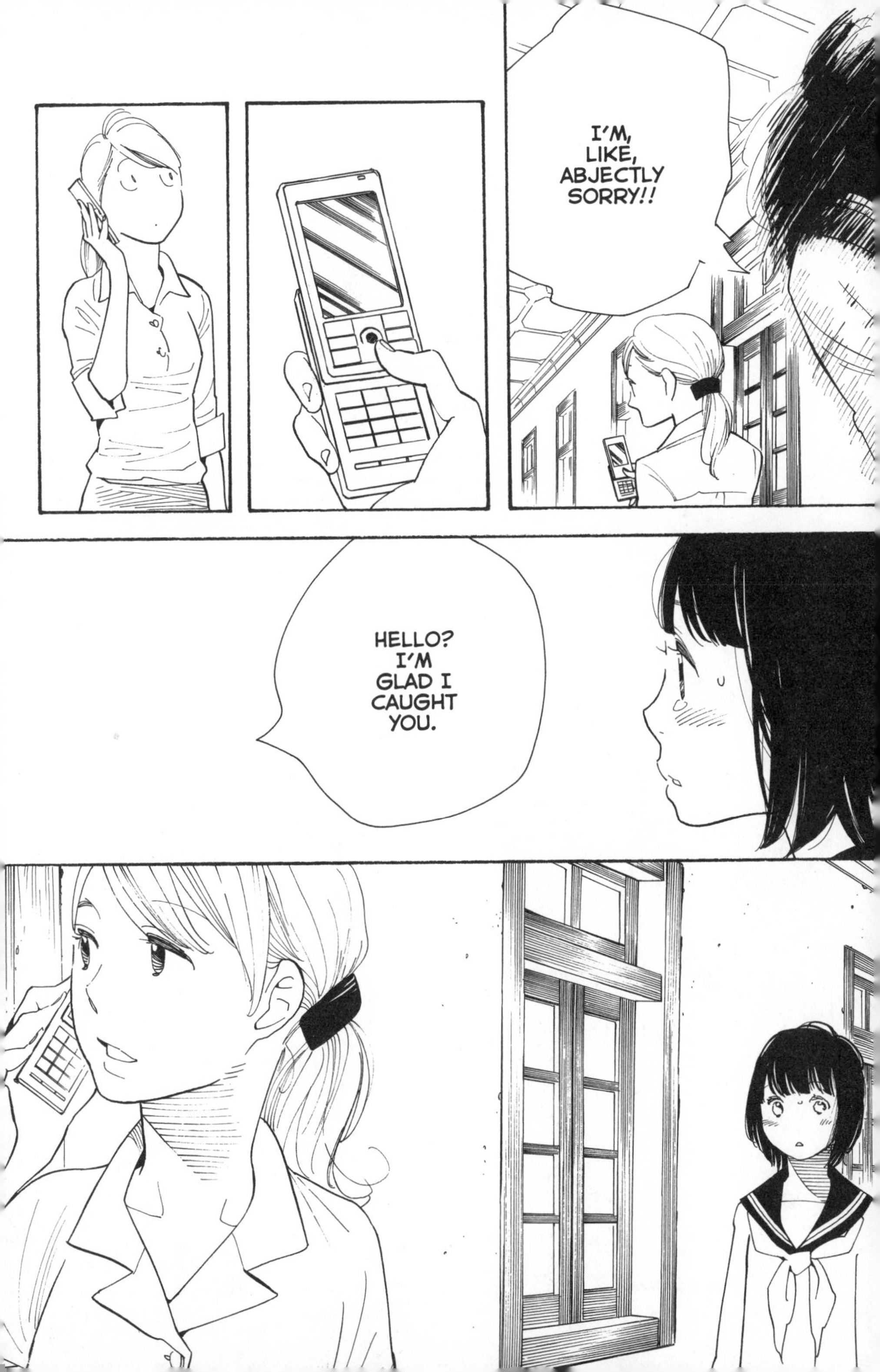
I'M, LIKE, ABJECTLY SORRY!!
HELLO? I'M GLAD I CAUGHT YOU.

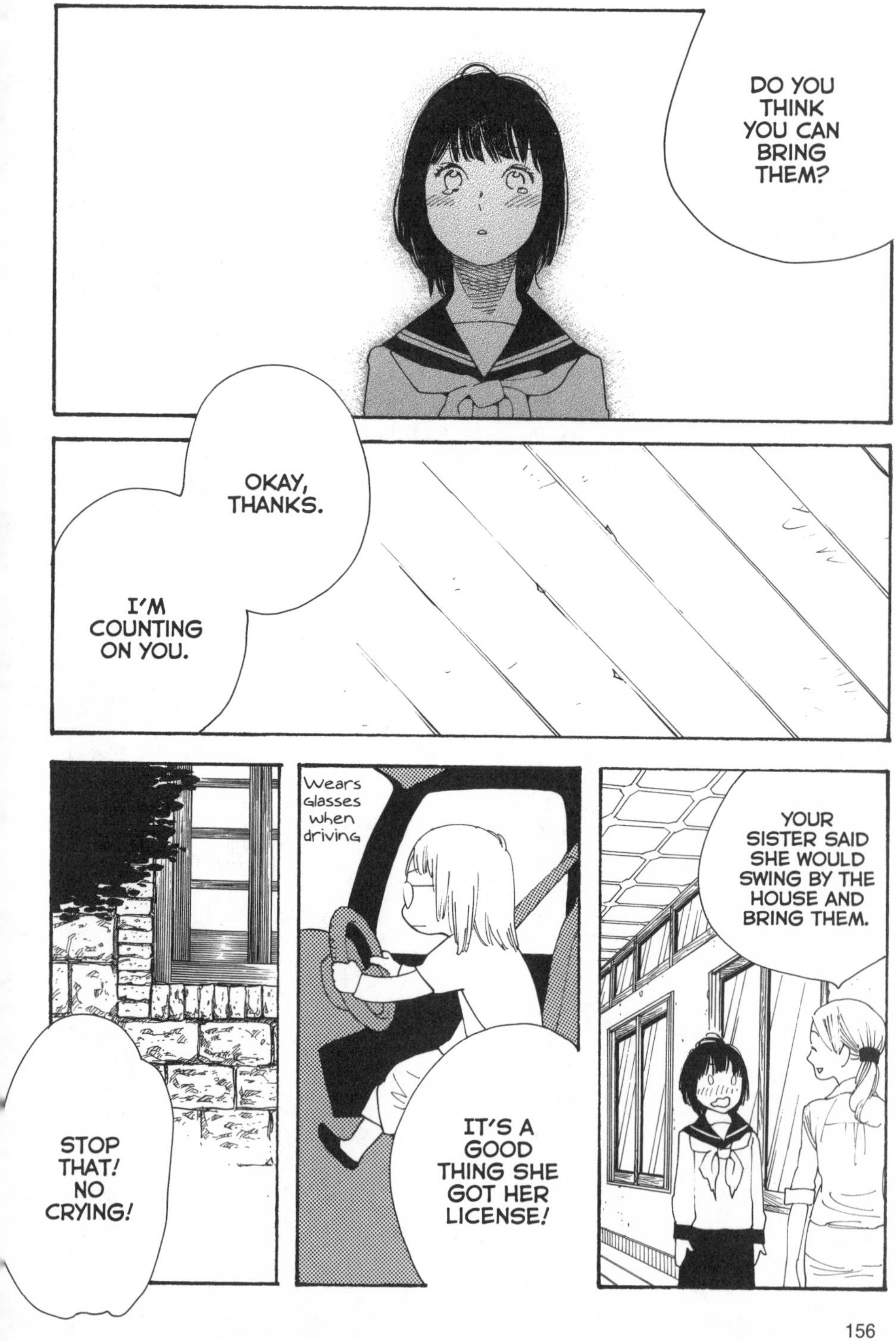
DO YOU THINK YOU CAN BRING THEM?
OKAY, THANKS.
I'M COUNTING ON YOU.
YOUR SISTER SAID SHE WOULD SWING BY THE HOUSE AND BRING THEM.
Wears glasses when driving
IT'S A GOOD THING SHE GOT HER LICENSE!
STOP THAT! NO CRYING!

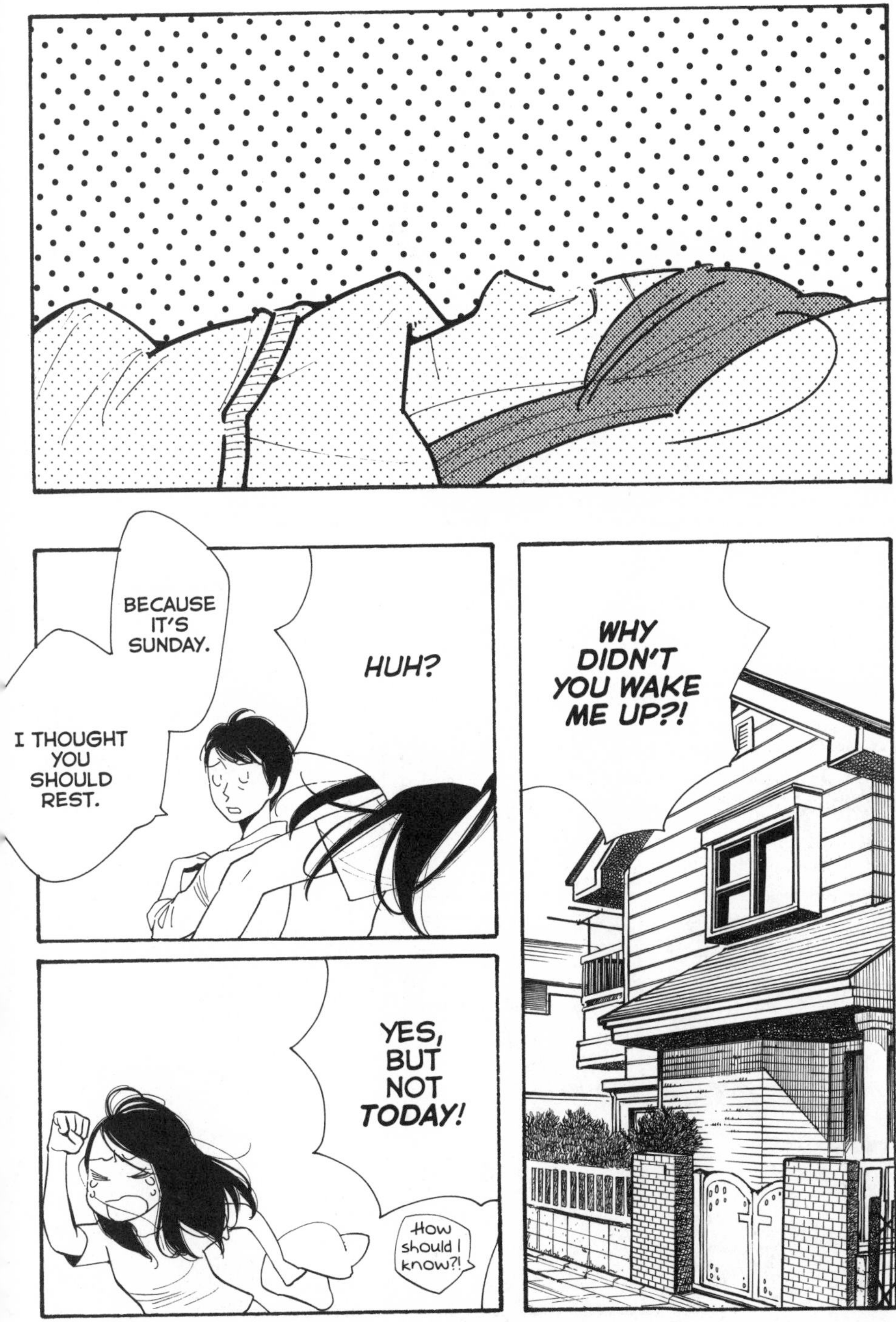
WHY DIDN'T YOU WAKE ME UP?!
HUH?
BECAUSE IT'S SUNDAY.
I THOUGHT YOU SHOULD REST.
YES, BUT NOT TODAY!
How should I know?!

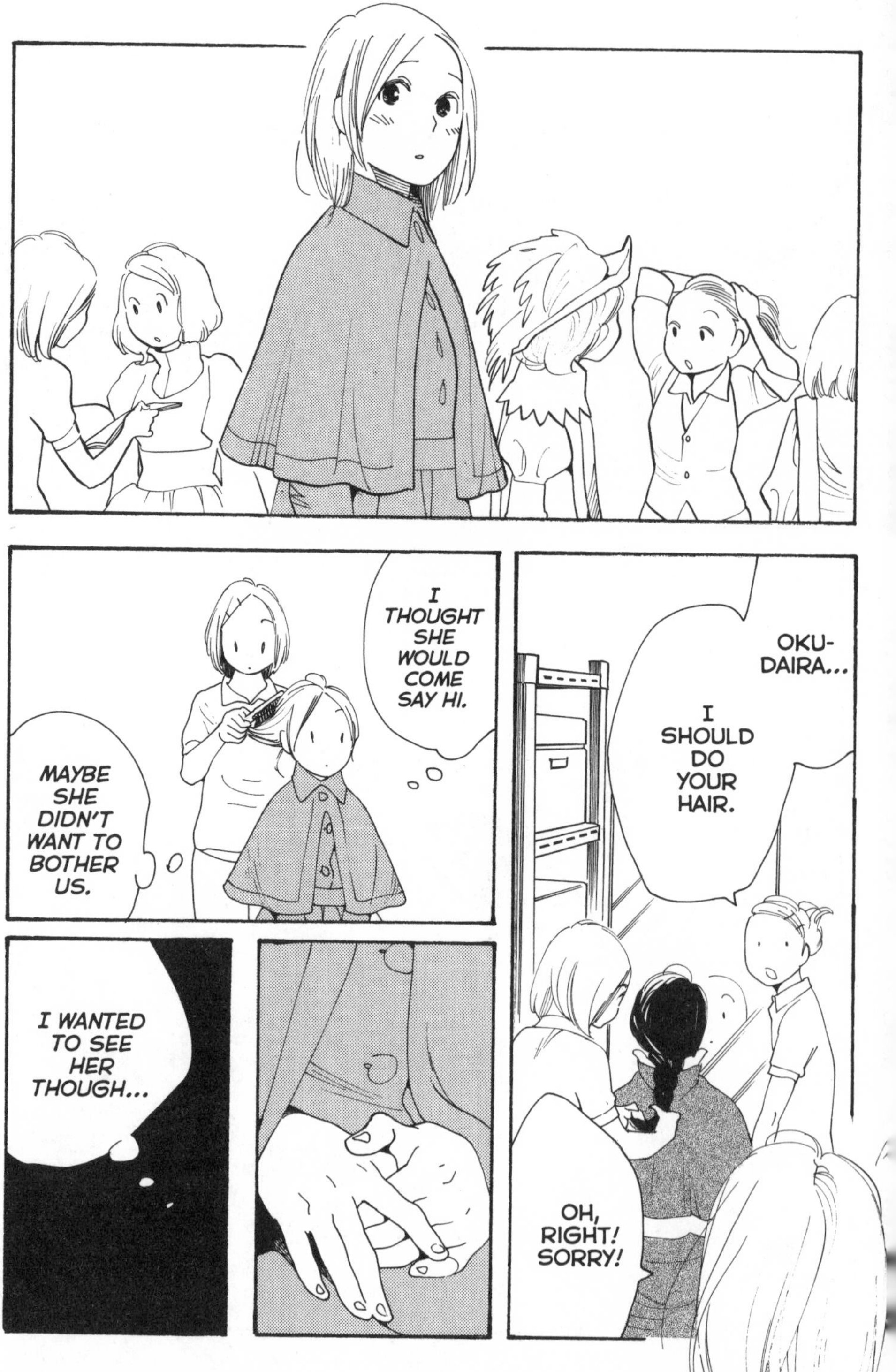
OKU-DAIRA...
I SHOULD DO YOUR HAIR.
OH, RIGHT! SORRY!
I THOUGHT SHE WOULD COME SAY HI.
MAYBE SHE DIDN'T WANT TO BOTHER US.
I WANTED TO SEE HER THOUGH...

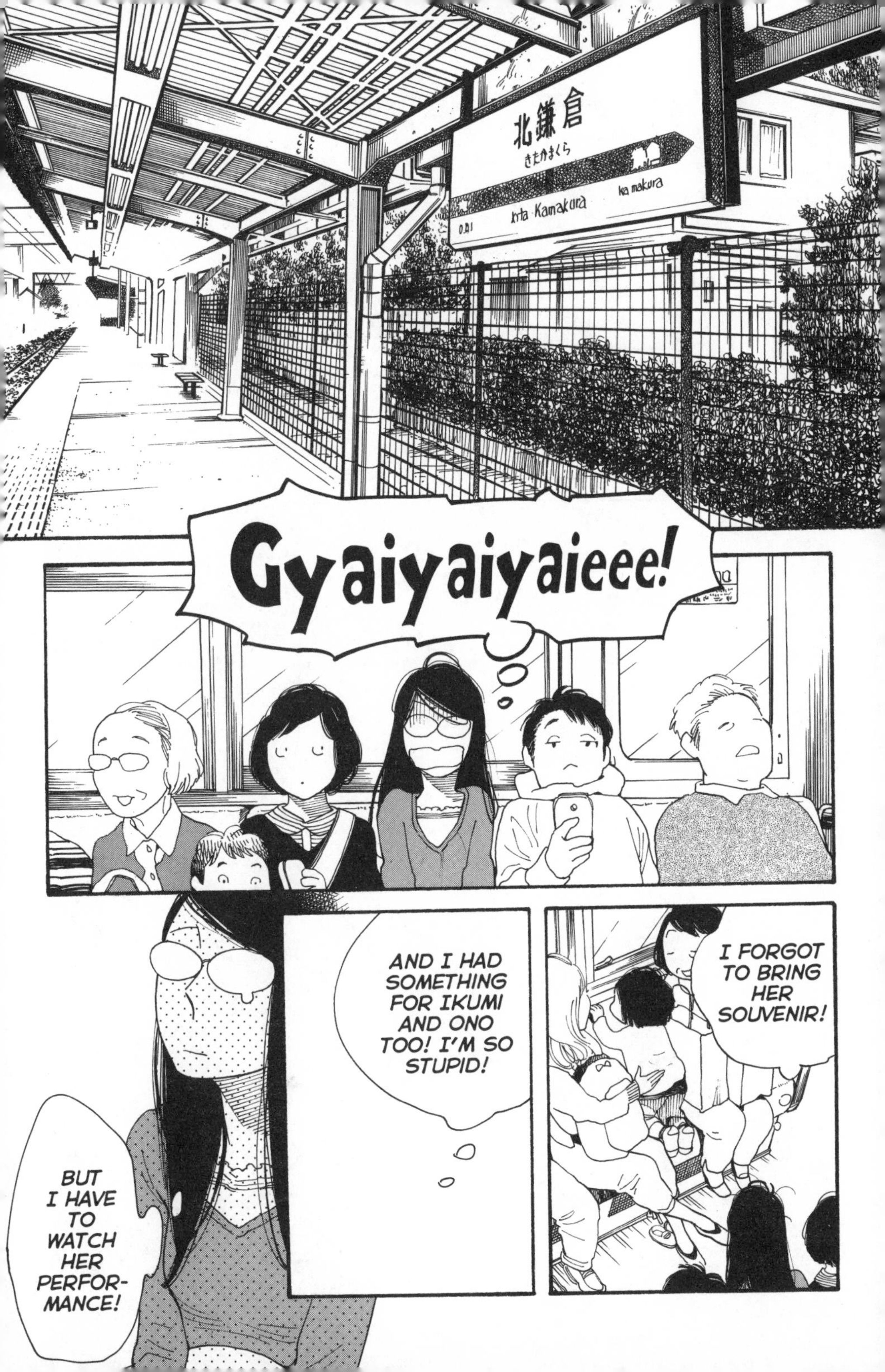
北鎌倉
きたかまくら
Kita Kamakura
Gyaiyaiyaieee!
I FORGOT TO BRING HER SOUVENIR!
AND I HAD SOMETHING FOR IKUMI AND ONO TOO! I'M SO STUPID!
BUT I HAVE TO WATCH HER PERFORMANCE!

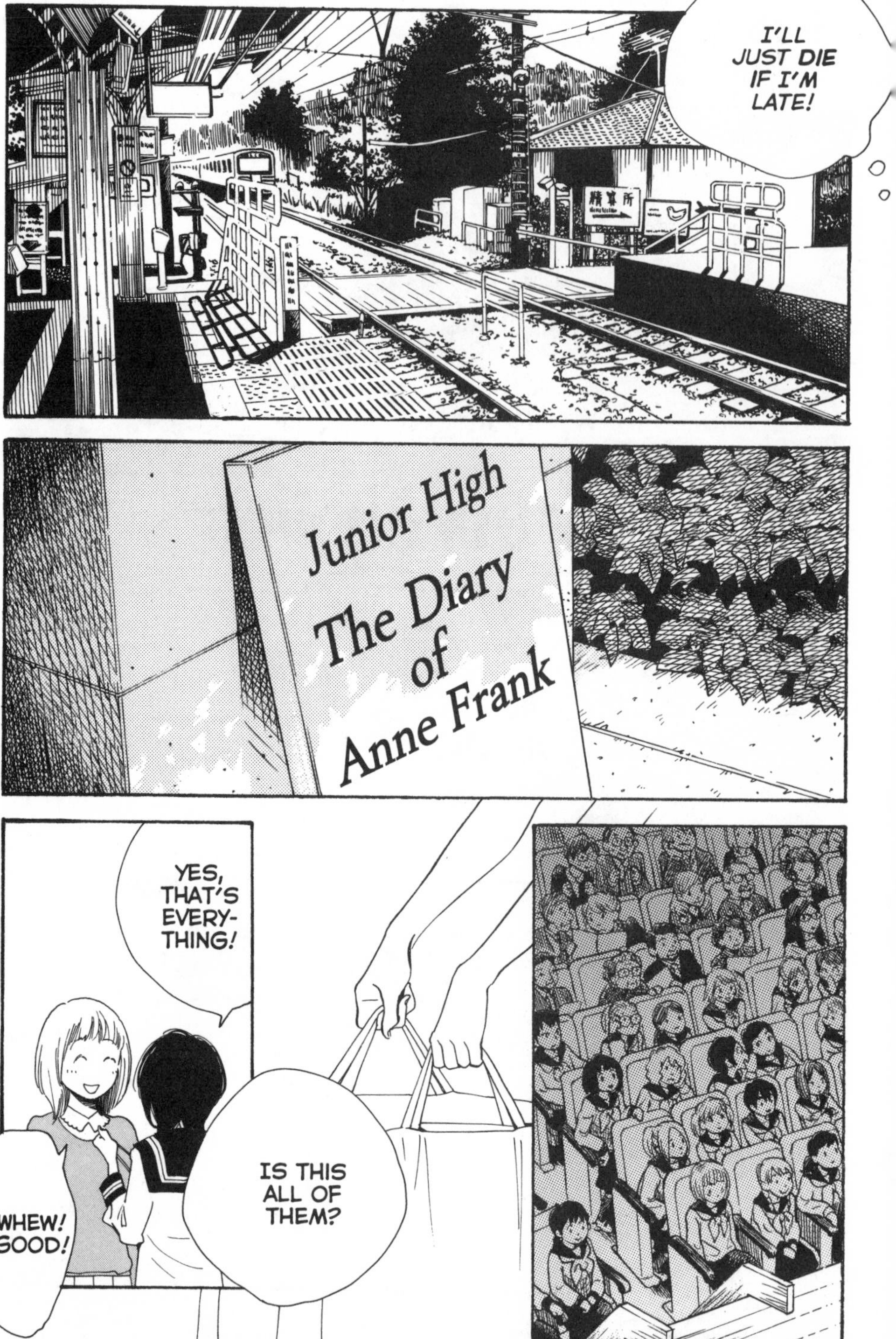
I'LL JUST DIE IF I'M LATE!
精算所
Junior High
The Diary of Anne Frank
IS THIS ALL OF THEM?
YES, THAT'S EVERYTHING!
WHEW! GOOD!

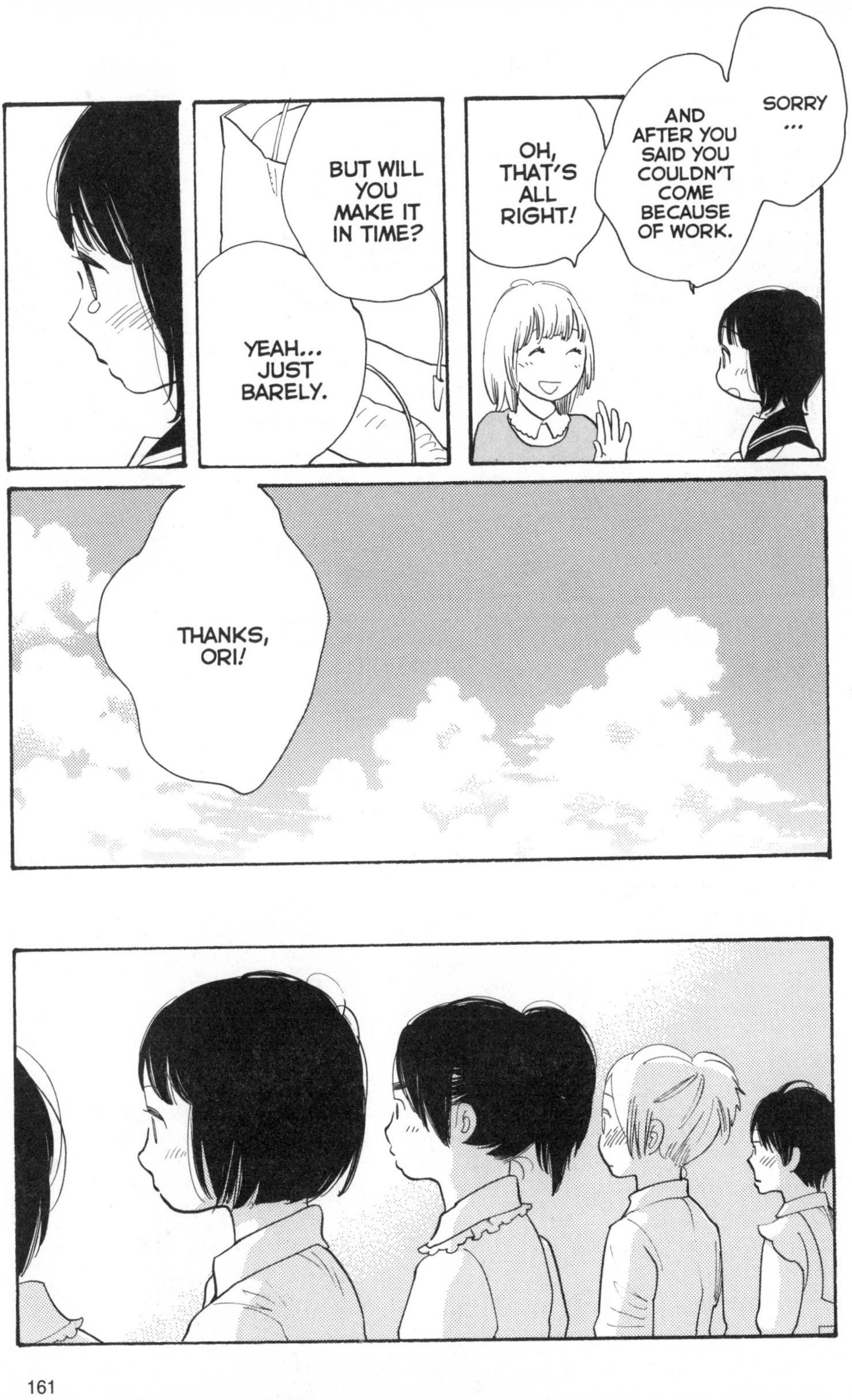
SORRY...
AND AFTER YOU SAID YOU COULDN'T COME BECAUSE OF WORK.
OH, THAT'S ALL RIGHT!
BUT WILL YOU MAKE IT IN TIME?
YEAH... JUST BARELY.
THANKS, ORI!

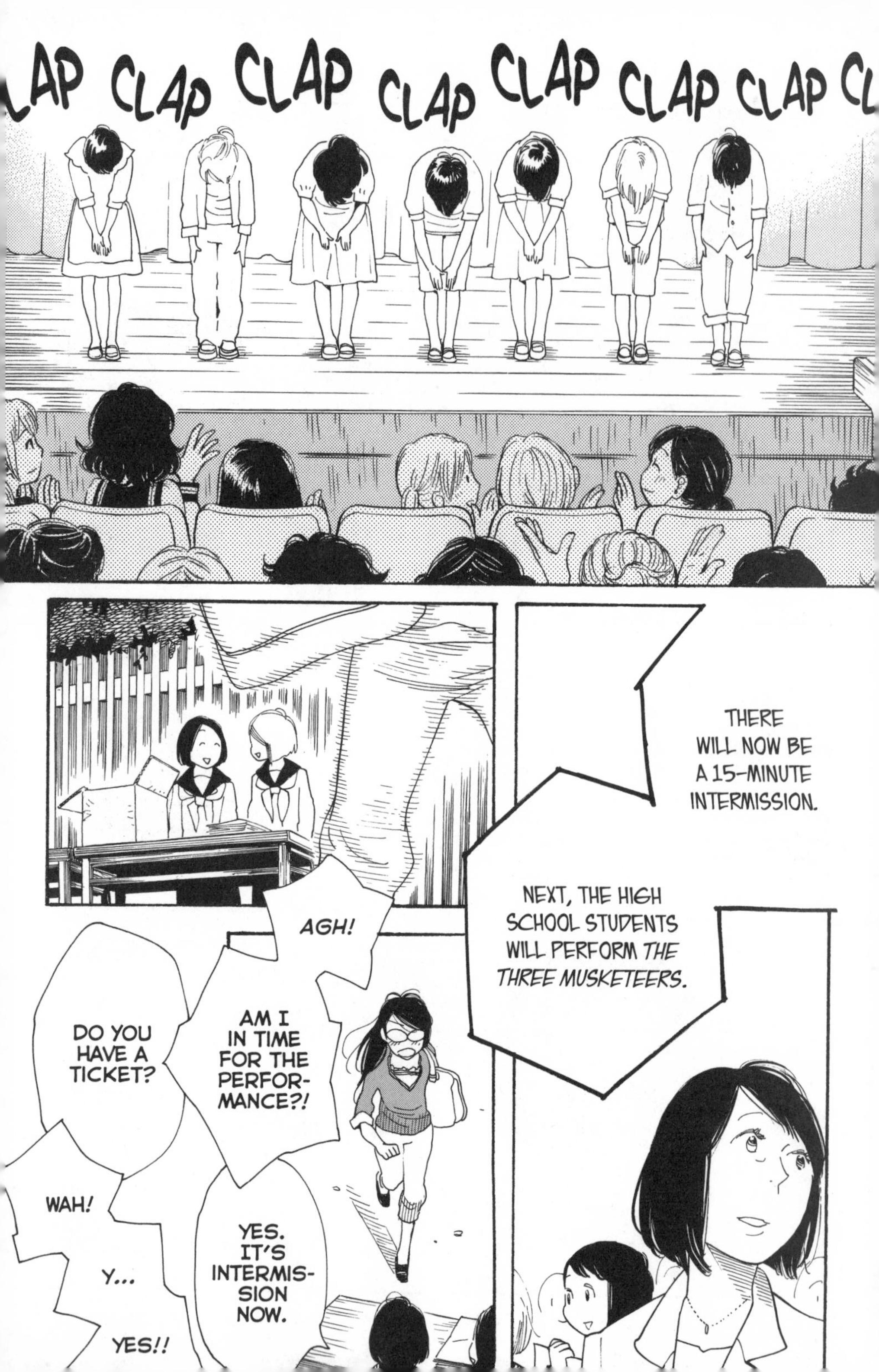
CLAP CLAP CLAP CLAP CLAP CLAP CLAP CL
THERE WILL NOW BE A 15-MINUTE INTERMISSION.
NEXT, THE HIGH SCHOOL STUDENTS WILL PERFORM *THE THREE MUSKETEERS.*
AGH!
AM I IN TIME FOR THE PERFOR-MANCE?!
DO YOU HAVE A TICKET?
YES. IT'S INTERMIS-SION NOW.
WAH!
Y...
YES!!

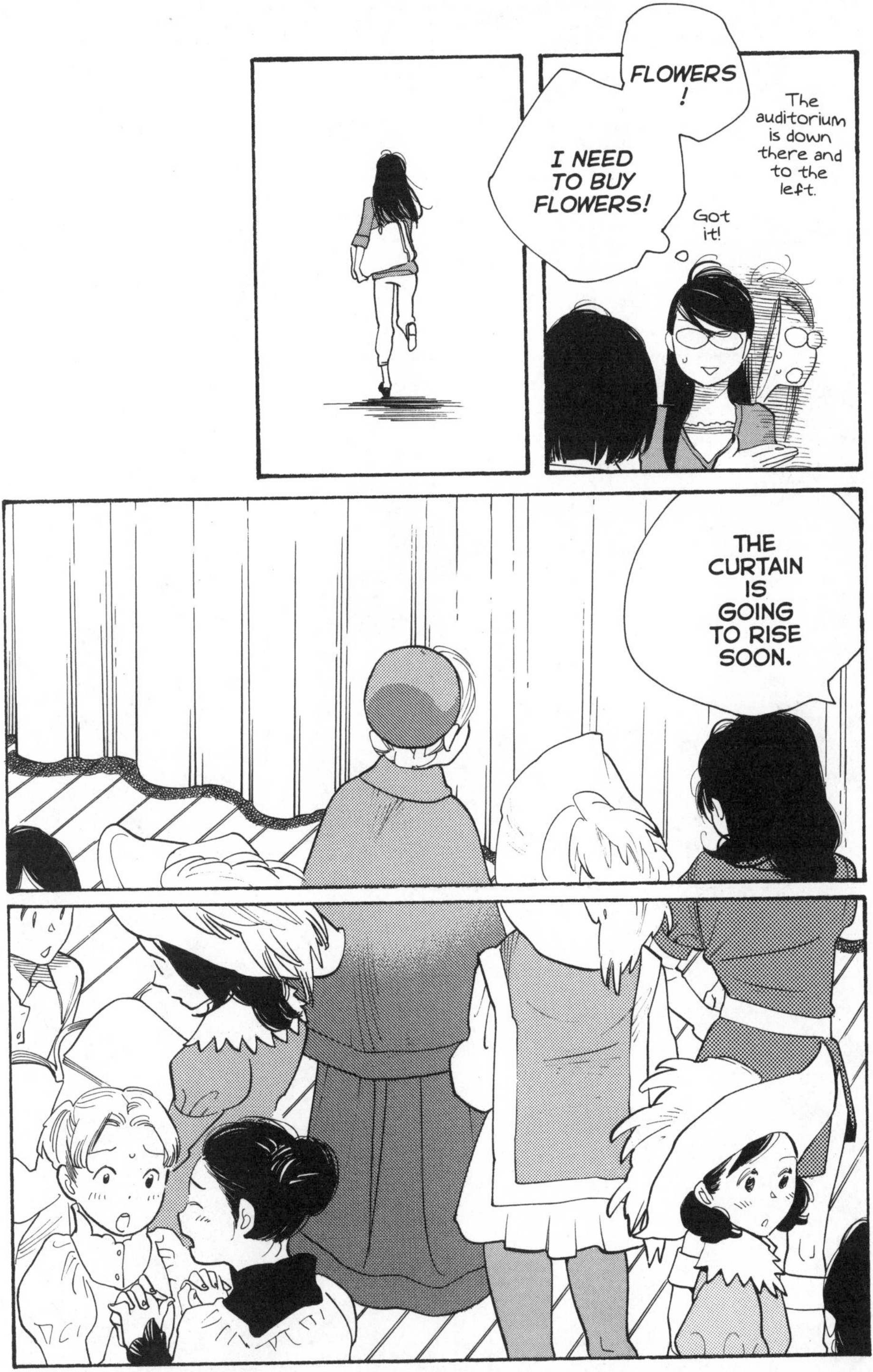
The auditorium is down there and to the left.
Got it!
FLOWERS!
I NEED TO BUY FLOWERS!
THE CURTAIN IS GOING TO RISE SOON.

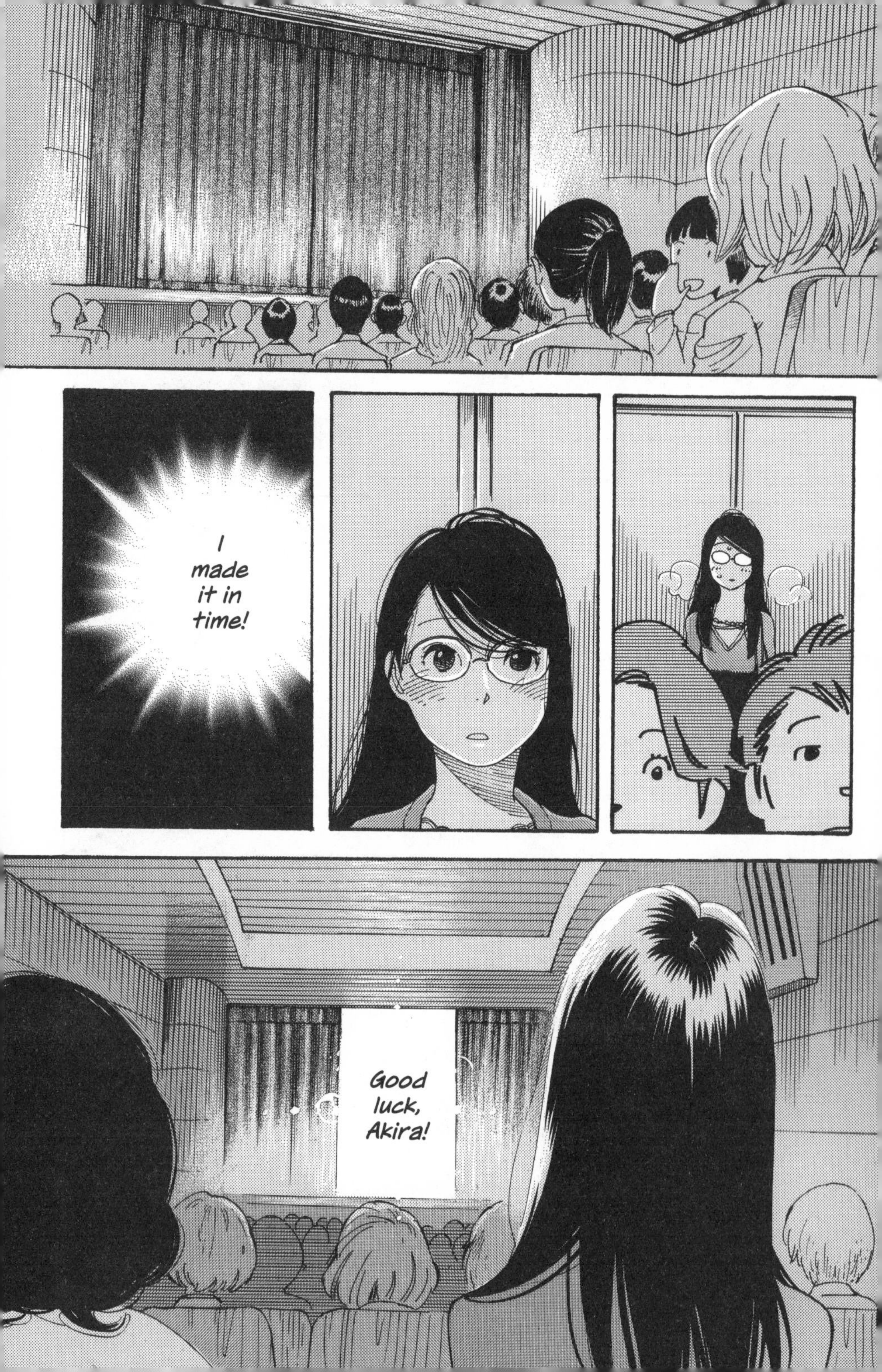
I made it in time!
Good luck, Akira!

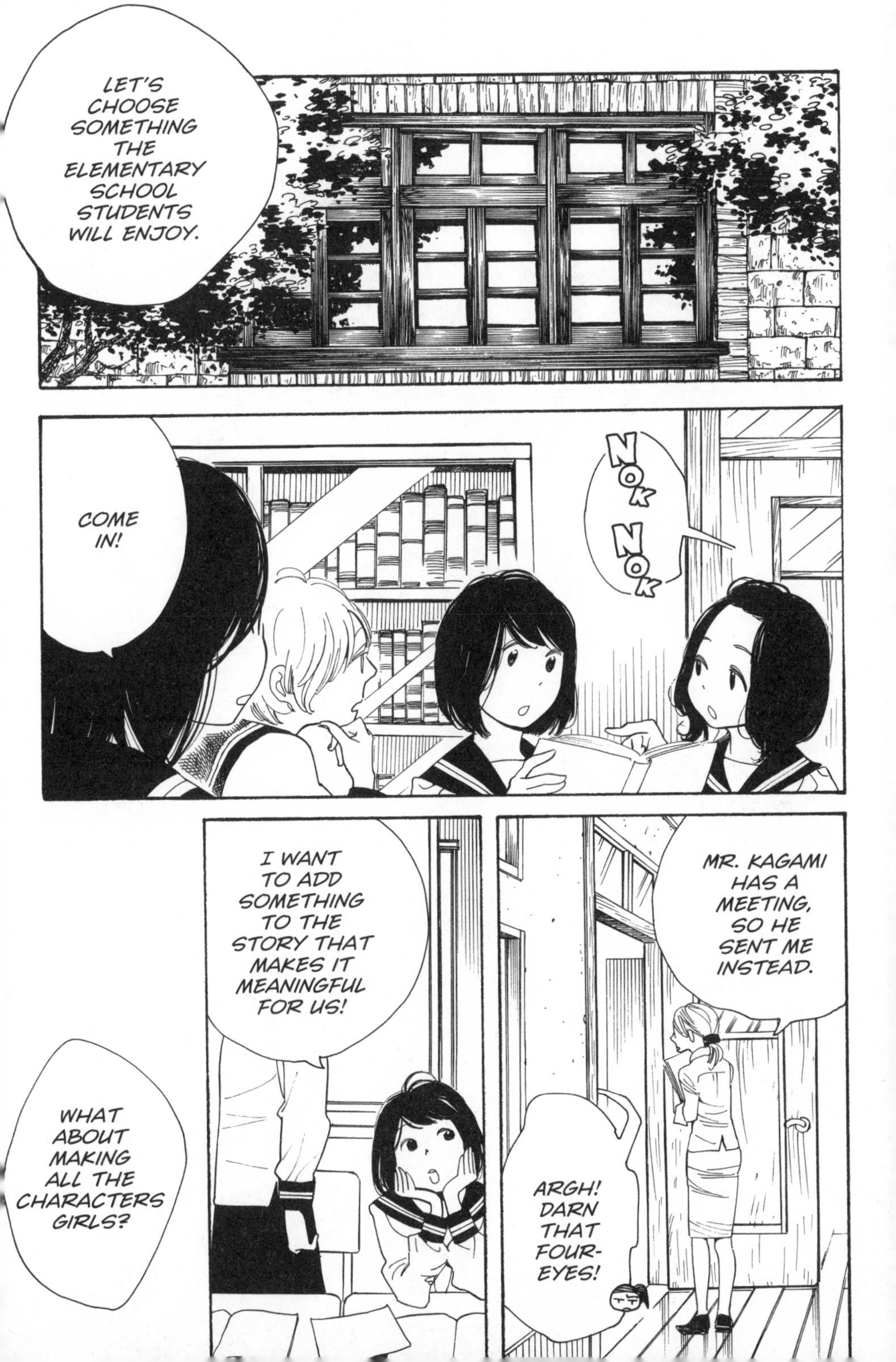
LET'S CHOOSE SOMETHING THE ELEMENTARY SCHOOL STUDENTS WILL ENJOY.
NOK NOK NOK
COME IN!
MR. KAGAMI HAS A MEETING, SO HE SENT ME INSTEAD.
ARGH! DARN THAT FOUR-EYES!
I WANT TO ADD SOMETHING TO THE STORY THAT MAKES IT MEANINGFUL FOR US!
WHAT ABOUT MAKING ALL THE CHARACTERS GIRLS?

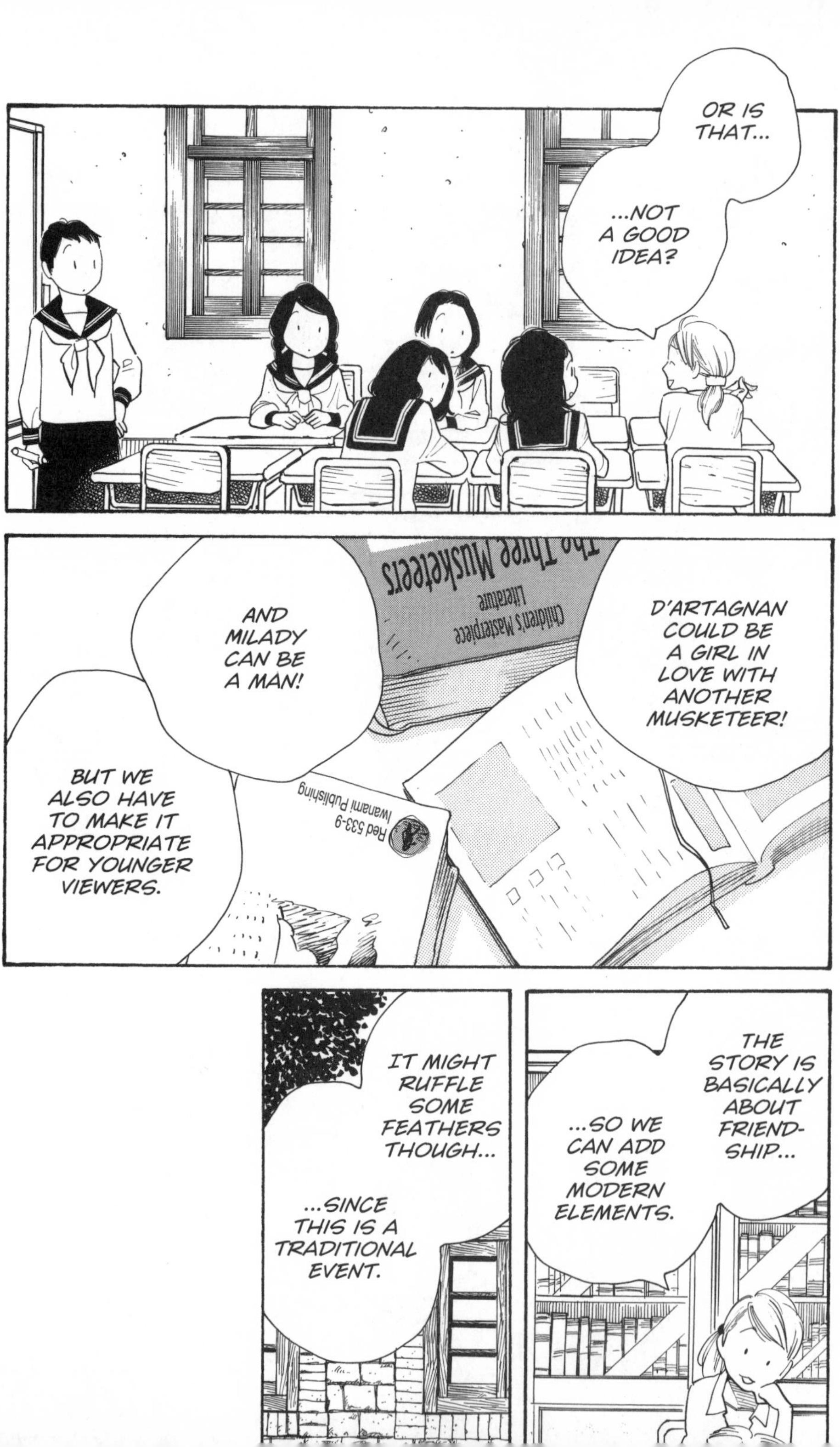
OR IS THAT...
...NOT A GOOD IDEA?
D'ARTAGNAN COULD BE A GIRL IN LOVE WITH ANOTHER MUSKETEER!
The Three Musketeers
Children's Masterpiece Literature
AND MILADY CAN BE A MAN!
Red 533-9
Iwanami Publishing
BUT WE ALSO HAVE TO MAKE IT APPROPRIATE FOR YOUNGER VIEWERS.
THE STORY IS BASICALLY ABOUT FRIEND-SHIP...
...SO WE CAN ADD SOME MODERN ELEMENTS.
IT MIGHT RUFFLE SOME FEATHERS THOUGH...
...SINCE THIS IS A TRADITIONAL EVENT.

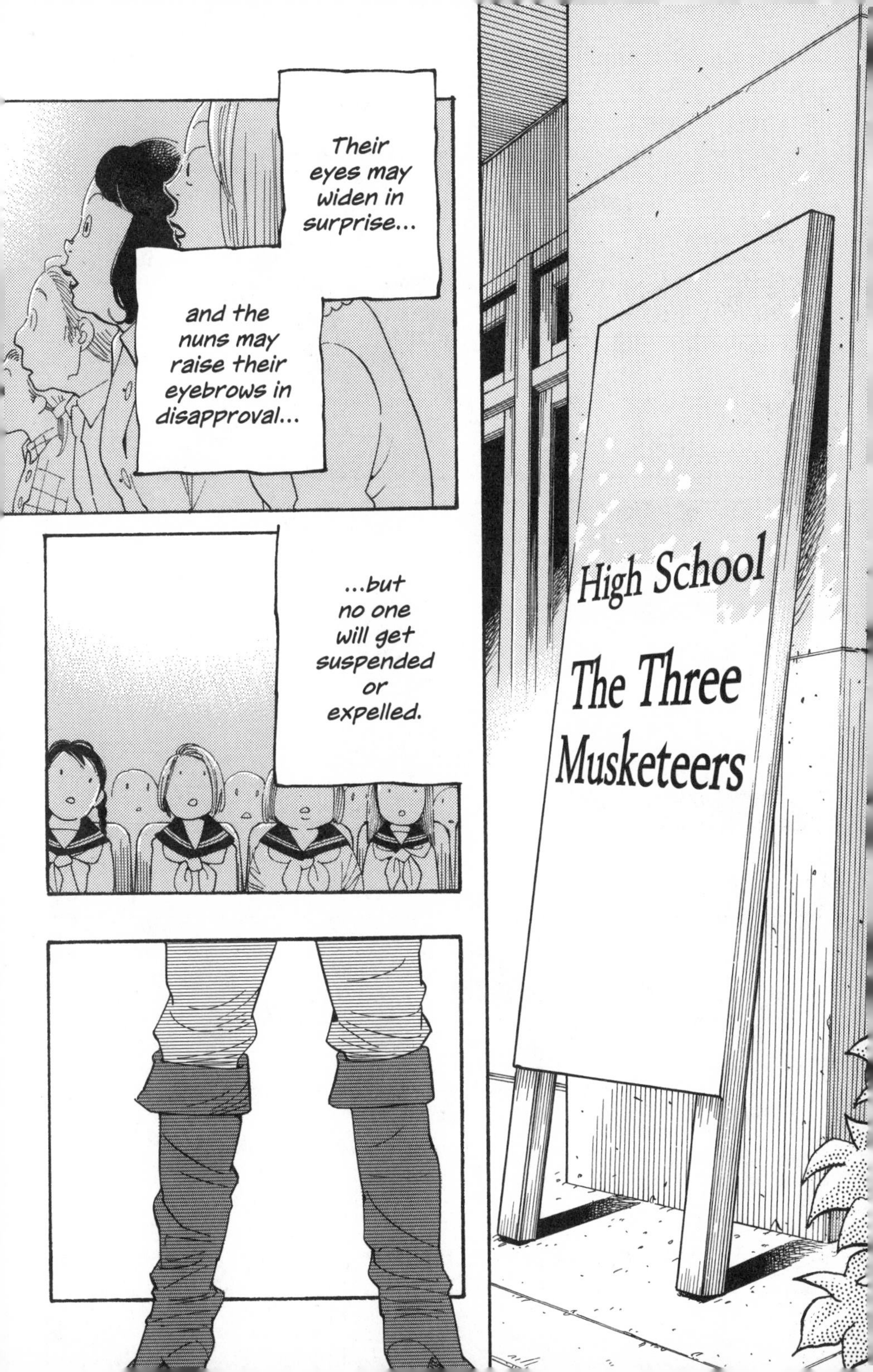
High School
The Three Musketeers
Their eyes may widen in surprise...
and the nuns may raise their eyebrows in disapproval...
...but no one will get suspended or expelled.

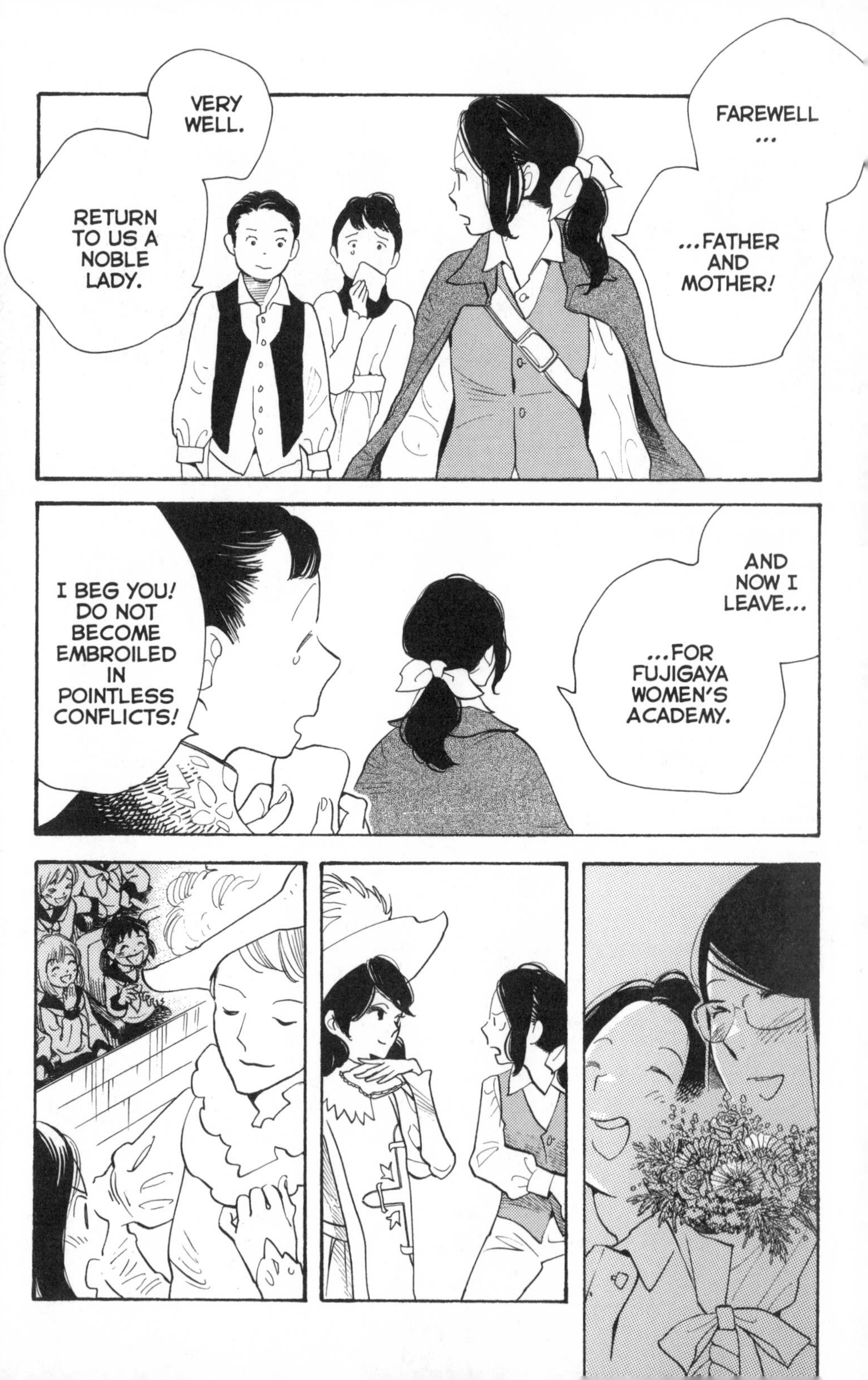
FAREWELL ...
...FATHER AND MOTHER!
VERY WELL.
RETURN TO US A NOBLE LADY.
AND NOW I LEAVE...
...FOR FUJIGAYA WOMEN'S ACADEMY.
I BEG YOU! DO NOT BECOME EMBROILED IN POINTLESS CONFLICTS!

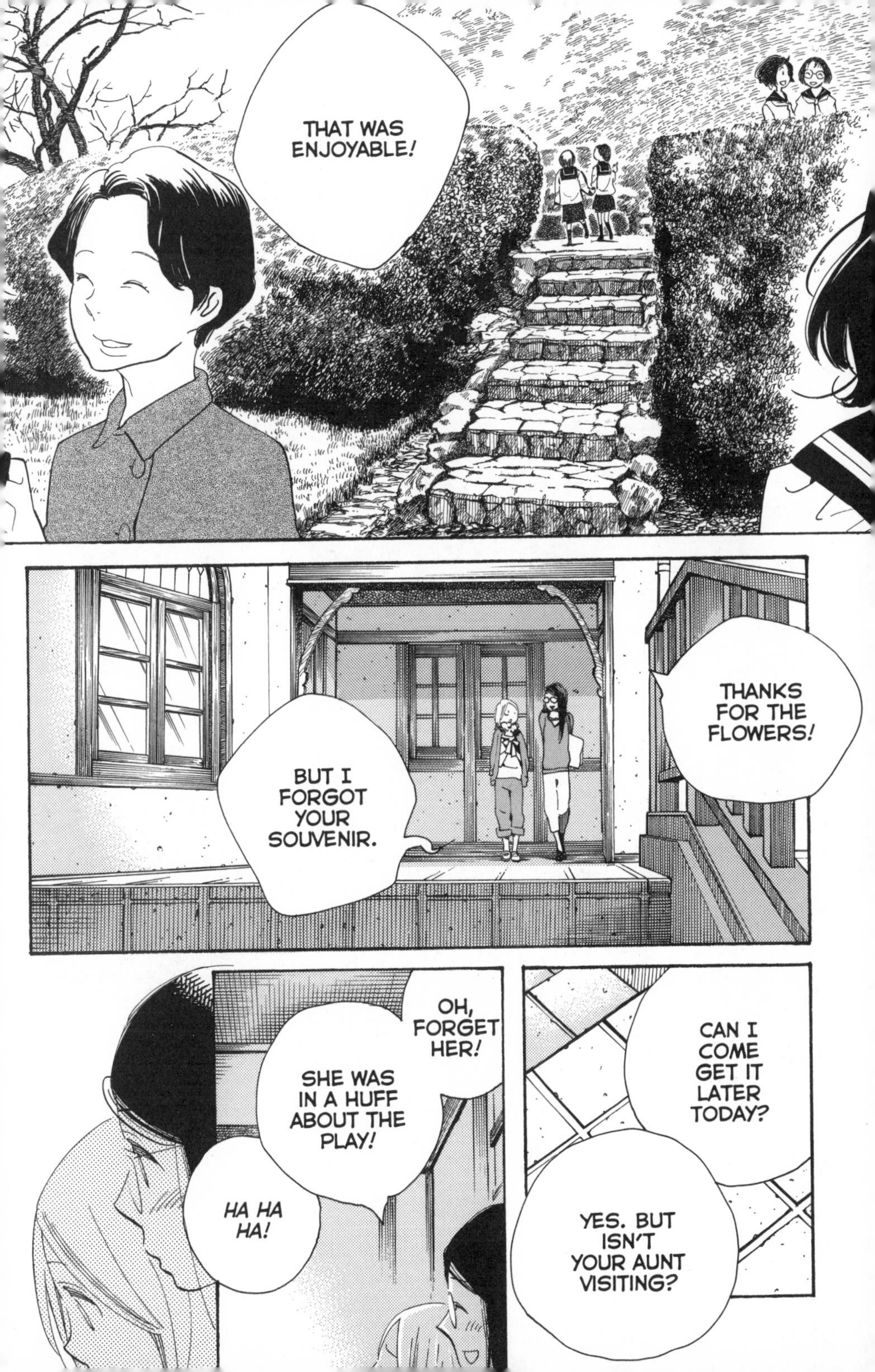
THAT WAS ENJOYABLE!
THANKS FOR THE FLOWERS!
BUT I FORGOT YOUR SOUVENIR.
CAN I COME GET IT LATER TODAY?
YES. BUT ISN'T YOUR AUNT VISITING?
OH, FORGET HER!
SHE WAS IN A HUFF ABOUT THE PLAY!
HA HA HA!

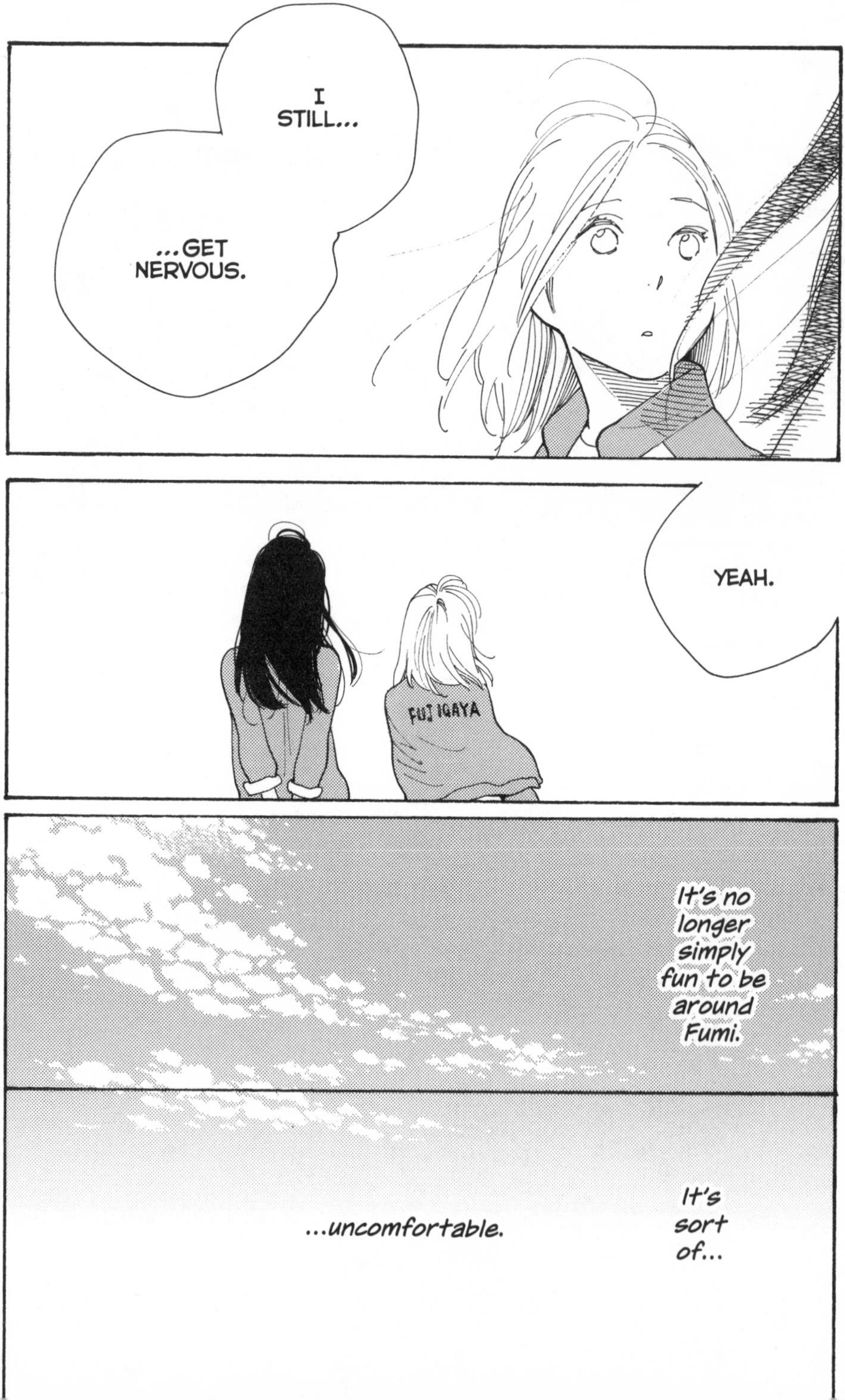
I STILL...
...GET NERVOUS.
YEAH.
FUJIGAYA
It's no longer simply fun to be around Fumi.
It's sort of...
...uncomfortable.

Sweet **Blue**
Flowers

Little Women

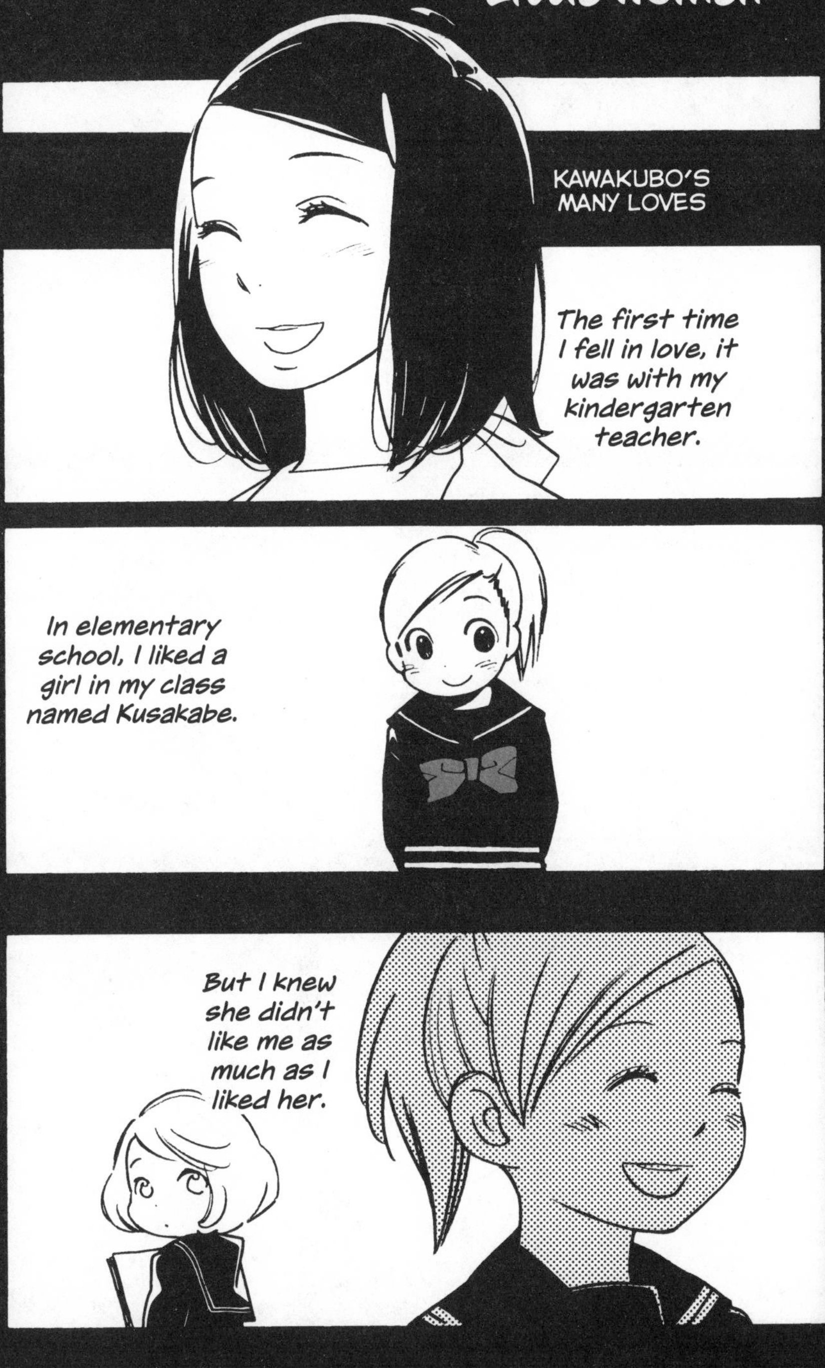
KAWAKUBO'S MANY LOVES
The first time I fell in love, it was with my kindergarten teacher.
In elementary school, I liked a girl in my class named Kusakabe.
But I knew she didn't like me as much as I liked her.

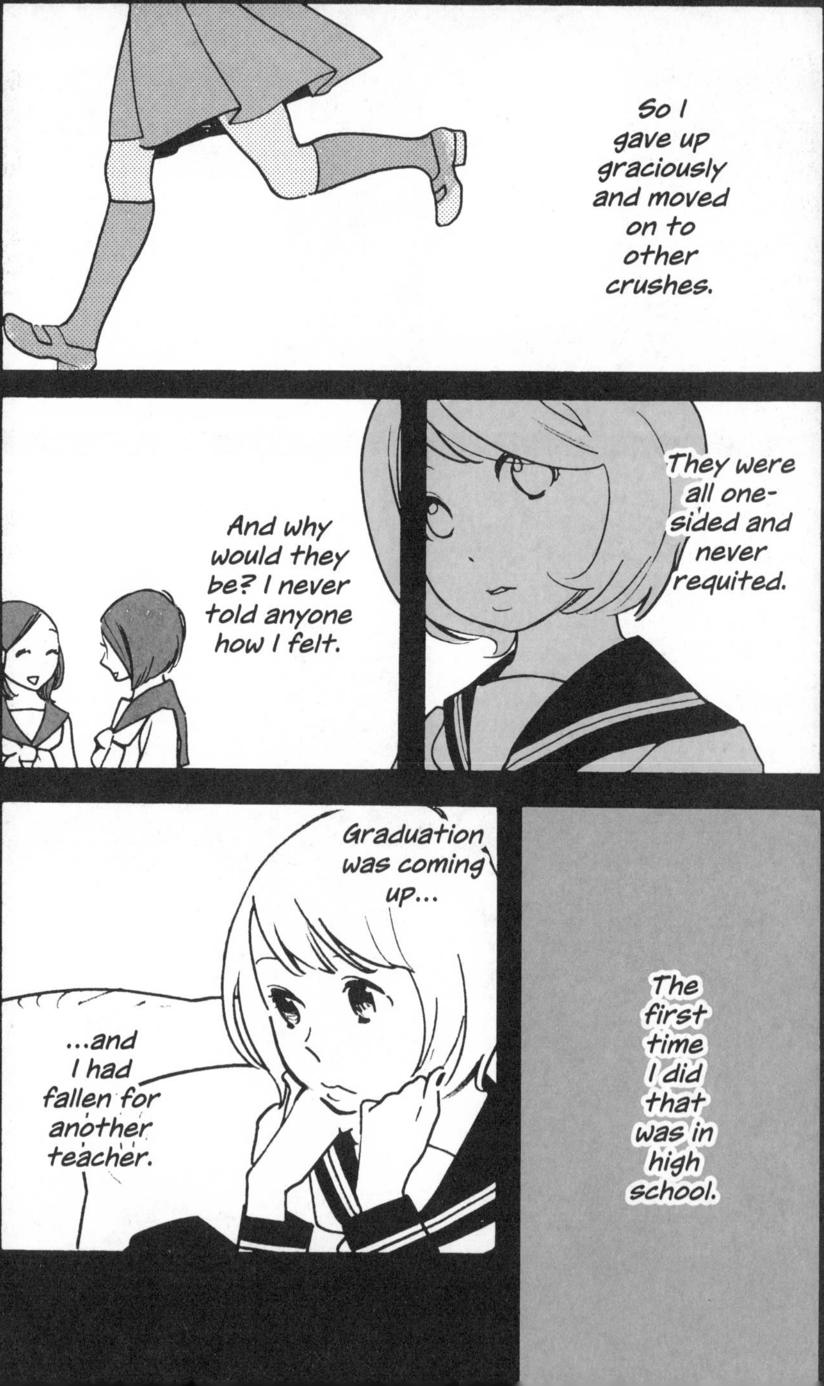
So I gave up graciously and moved on to other crushes.
They were all one-sided and never requited.
And why would they be? I never told anyone how I felt.
The first time I did that was in high school.
Graduation was coming up...
...and I had fallen for another teacher.

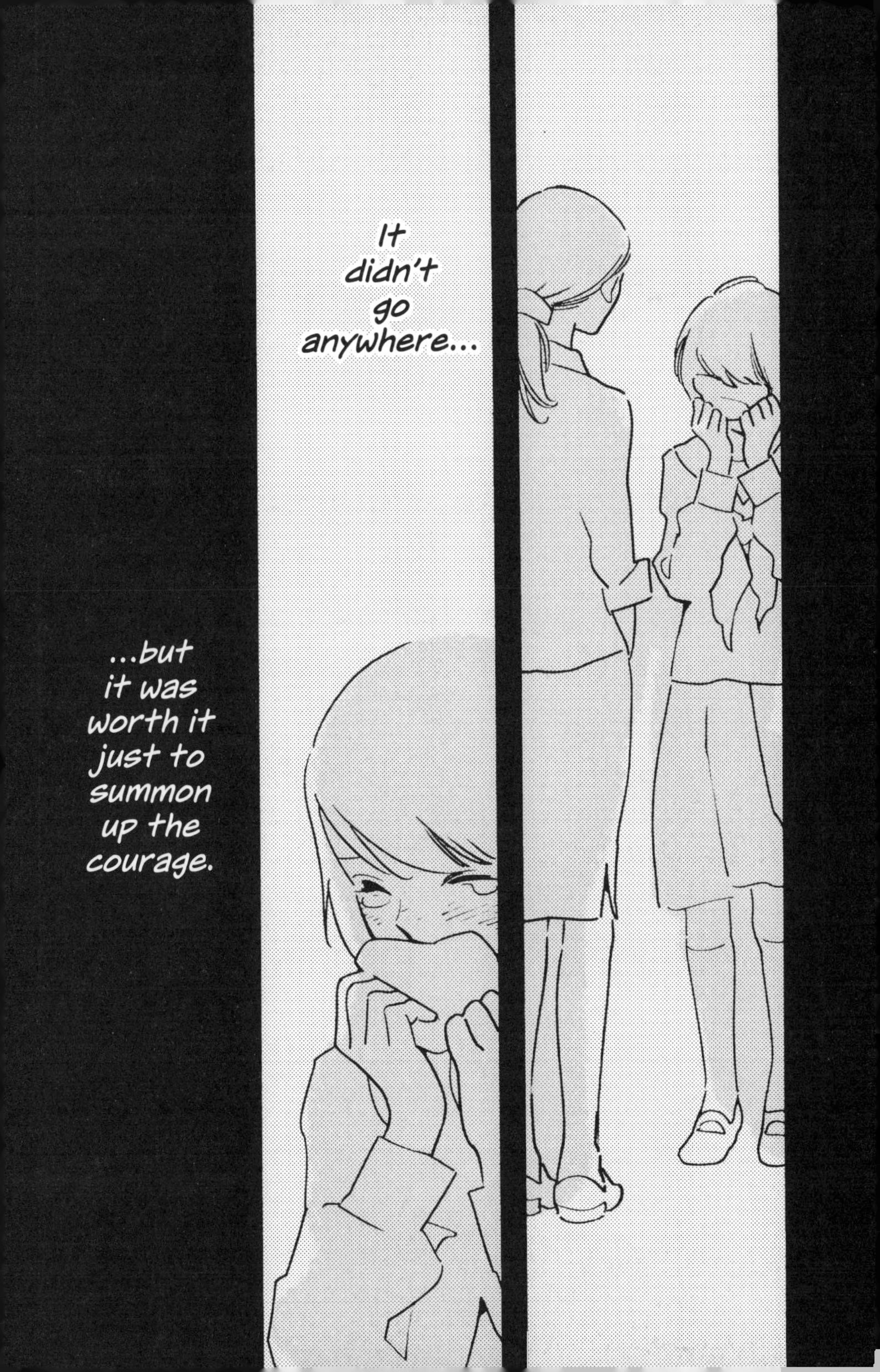
It didn't go anywhere...
...but it was worth it just to summon up the courage.

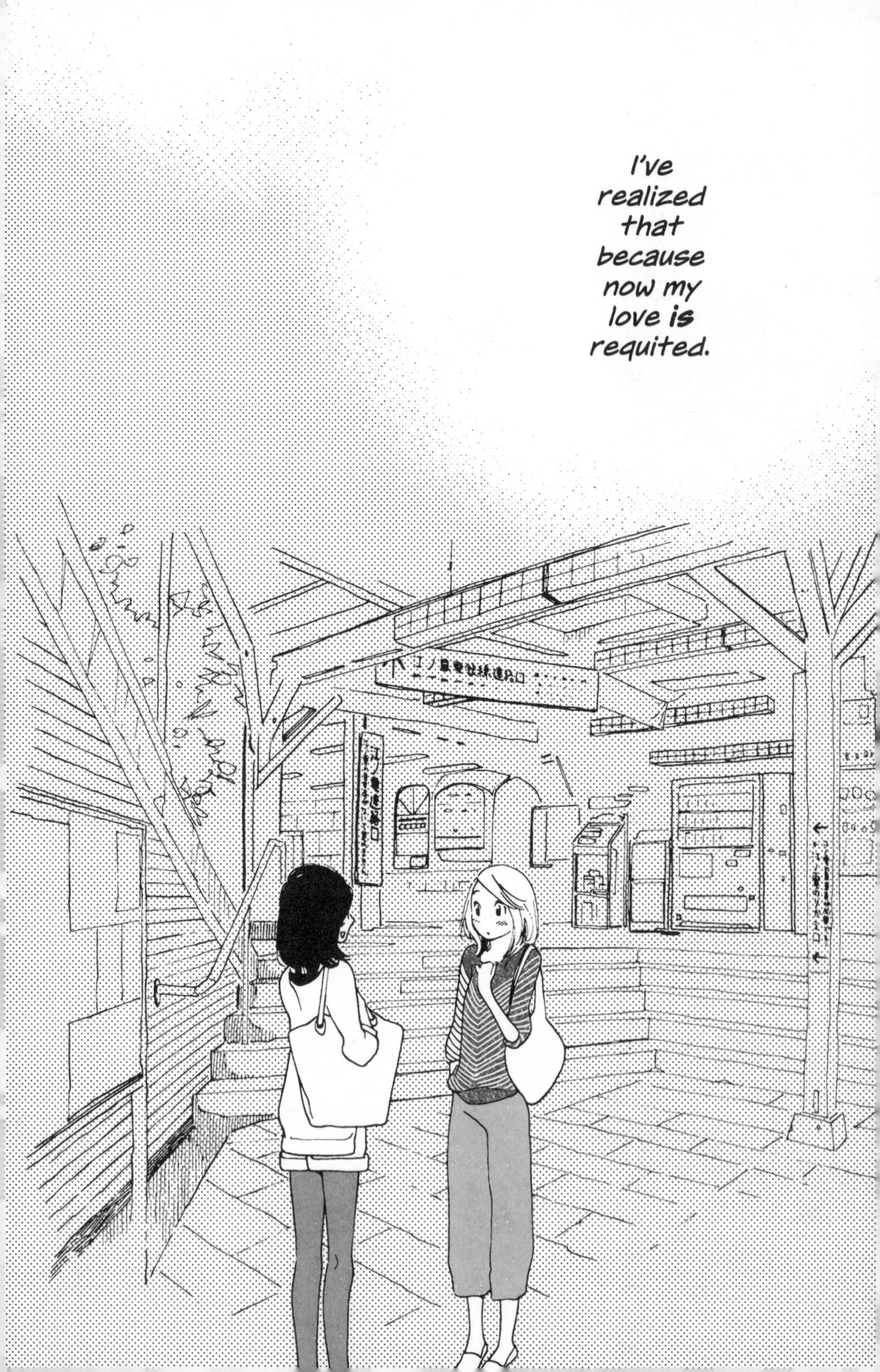
I've realized that because now my love is requited.

Sweet Blue
Flowers

Sweet Blue Flowers

Part Eight

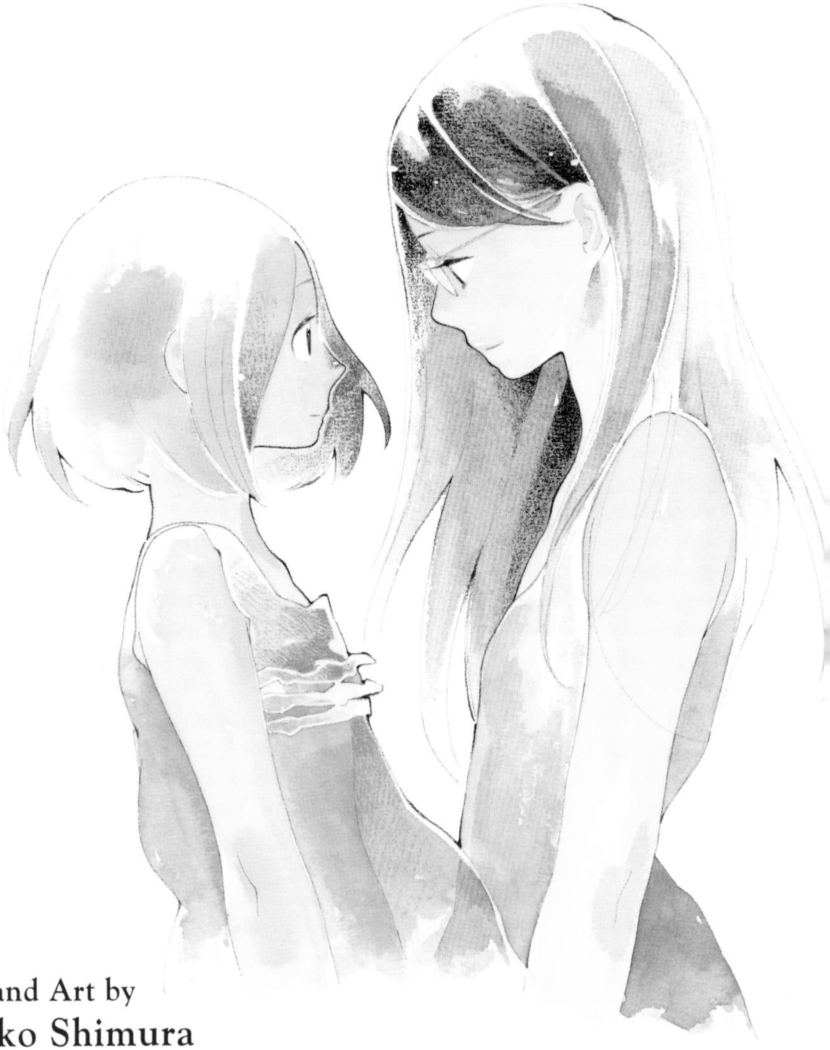

Story and Art by
Takako Shimura

Sweet Blue Flowers
Part Eight

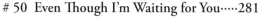

Sweet Blue Flowers

Characters

Fujigaya Women's Academy High School

Kyoko Ikumi

Year 3. Like Akira, she's a member of the Drama Club. The other girls admire her for her maturity. She had a one-sided crush on Yasuko Sugimoto, but her feelings changed after seeing how serious her fiancé Ko Sawanoi is about her.

Akira Okudaira

Year 3. She's small, innocent and honest, and has yet to experience love. She feels uncomfortable when her childhood friend Fumi tells her she likes her, but after giving it serious thought, she decides to start dating her.

Hinako Yamashina

Science teacher. She is Akira's homeroom teacher and a graduate of Fujigaya. Her girlfriend is Haruka Ono's older sister Orie.

Haruka Ono

Year 2. She's an energetic girl who joined the Drama Club because she admires theater, and now she's becoming good friends with a lot of older students.

Ryoko Ueda

Year 3. She's in the same class as Akira. She's a member of the Library Club, but she wins acclaim when she makes a guest appearance onstage at the Fujigaya Theater Festival.

Matsuoka Girls' High School

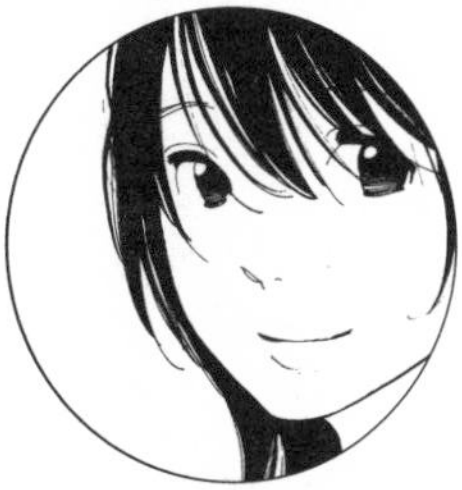

Yasuko Sugimoto

During her time as a student at Matsuoka, she was the popular princely type as well as the captain of the basketball team. She dated Fumi, but the relationship fell apart after a few months. Currently, she is studying in England with her friend Kawasaki.

Fumi Manjome

Year 3. She's tall and pretty—and a worrywart crybaby. She recently realized that her close friend Akira was her first love. After they start dating, she experiences both joy and unease.

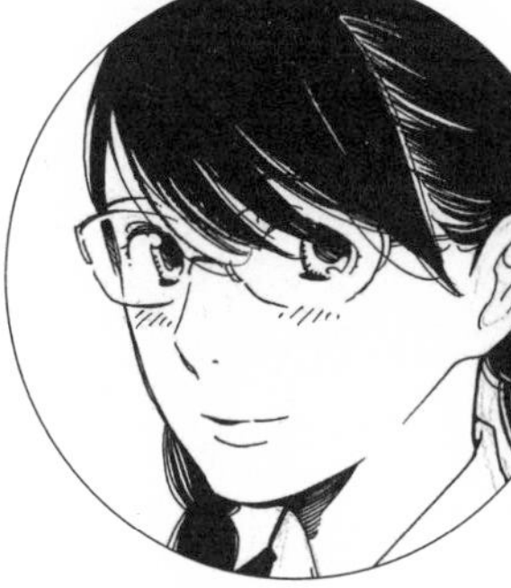

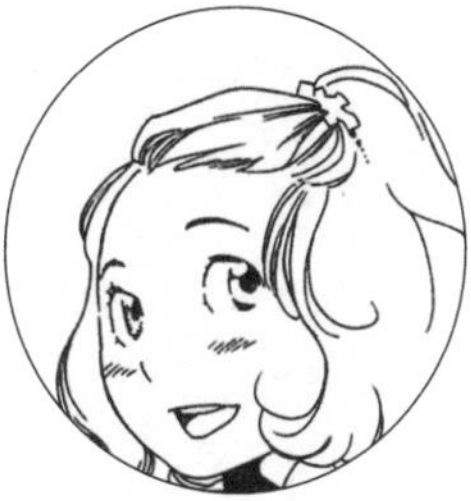

Miwa Motegi

Year 3. Nickname: Mogi. She's a quiet girl who is a member of the school's small Drama Club. She's dating Akira's older brother Shinobu.

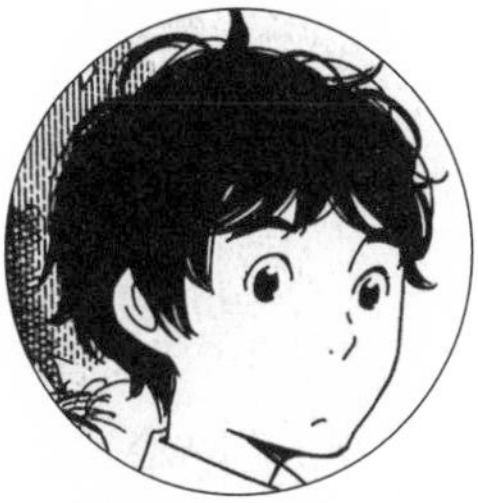

Misako Yasuda

Year 3. Nickname: Yassan. She's the hardworking head of the school's small Drama Club.

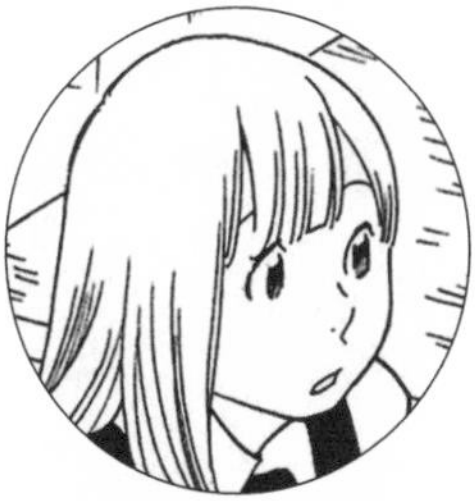

Yoko Honatsugi

Year 3. Nickname: Pon. She's a member of the school's small Drama Club. She has a bright personality and isn't afraid of anything.

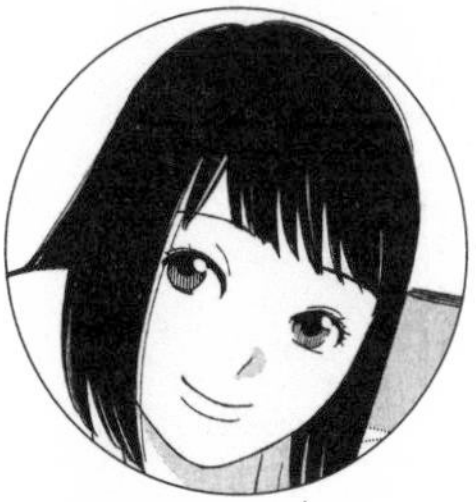

Chizu Hanashiro

Fumi's cousin on her mother's side. She was Fumi's first girlfriend, but she surprised Fumi by getting married.

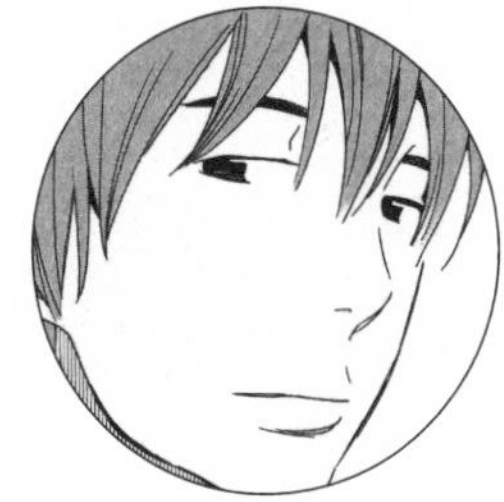

Ko Sawanoi

Kyoko Ikumi's fiancé. He's in his third year at university. He has a gentle and considerate personality, and he's serious about Kyoko.

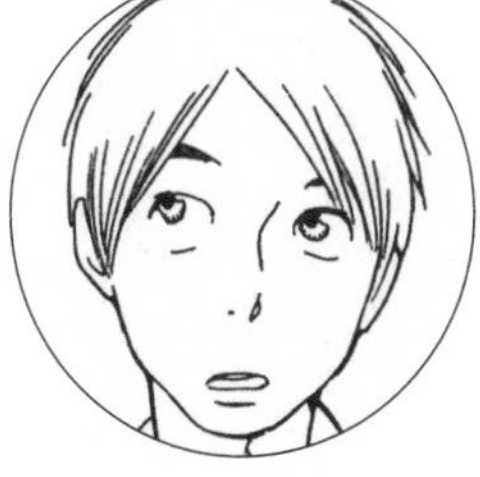

Shinobu Okudaira

Akira's brother. He's in his fourth year at university. He has a serious sister complex, but maybe he's beginning to change now that he's dating Miwa Motegi?

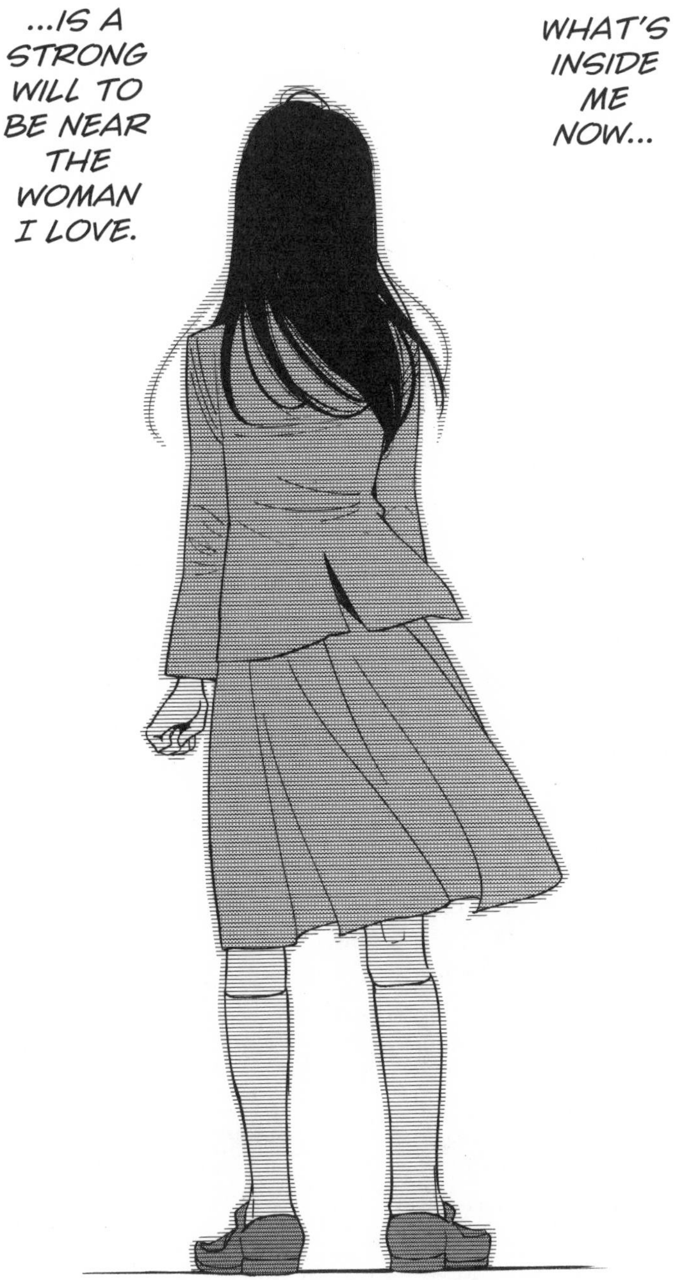
WHAT'S INSIDE ME NOW...
...IS A STRONG WILL TO BE NEAR THE WOMAN I LOVE.

Sweet Blue Flowers

#46 Heavenly Creatures

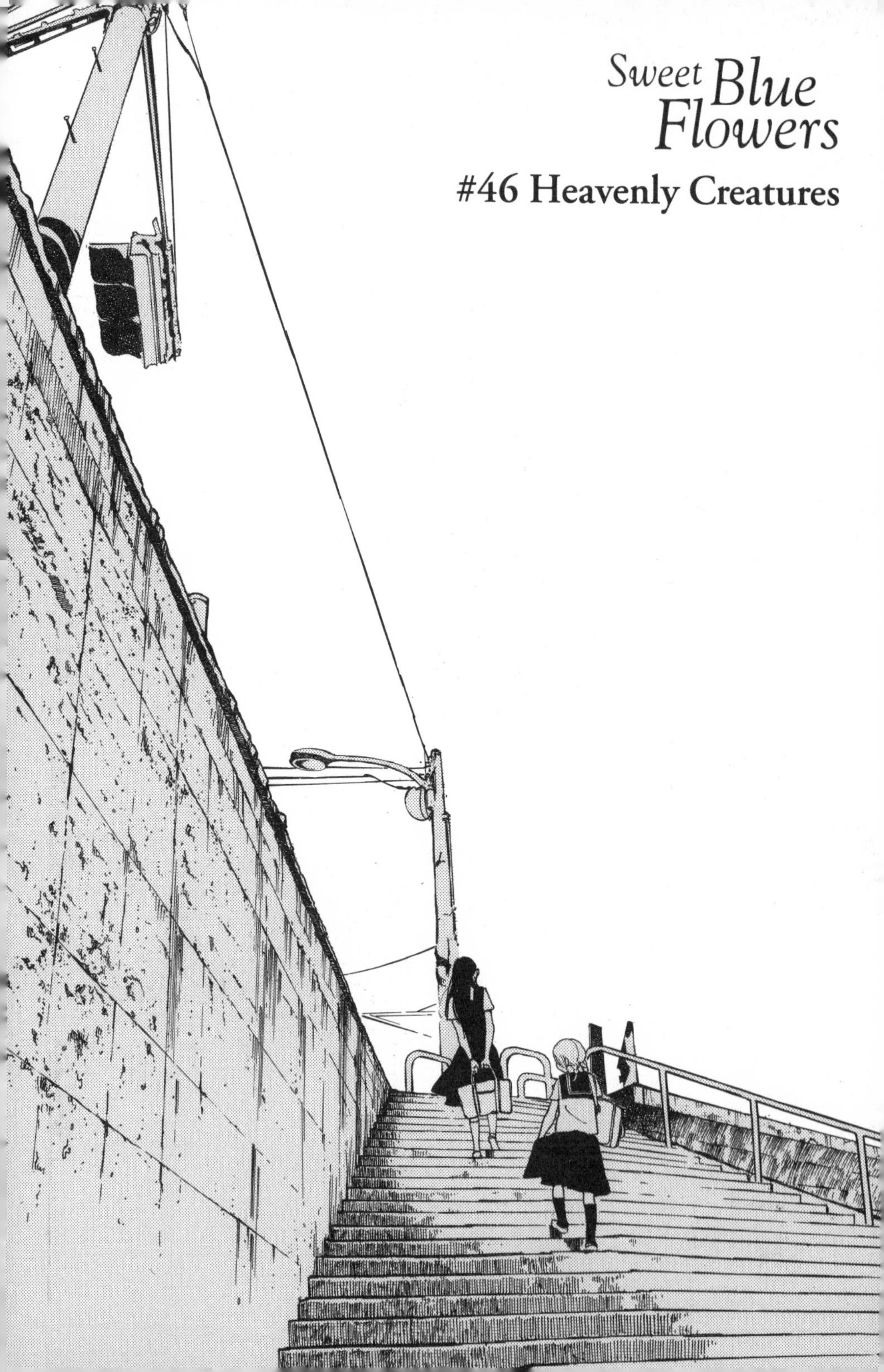

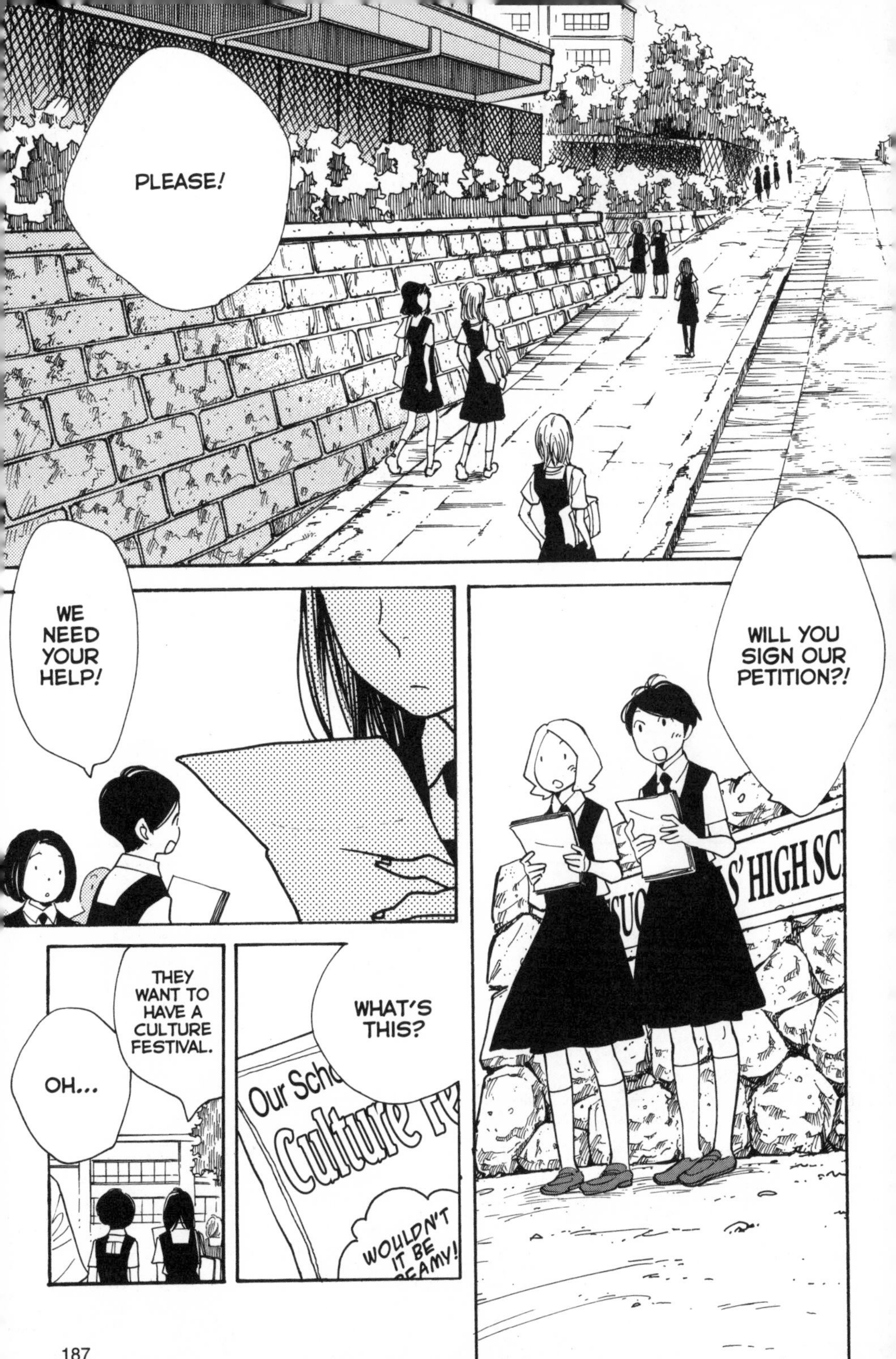
PLEASE!
WILL YOU SIGN OUR PETITION?!
WE NEED YOUR HELP!
WHAT'S THIS?
WOULDN'T IT BE
THEY WANT TO HAVE A CULTURE FESTIVAL.
OH...

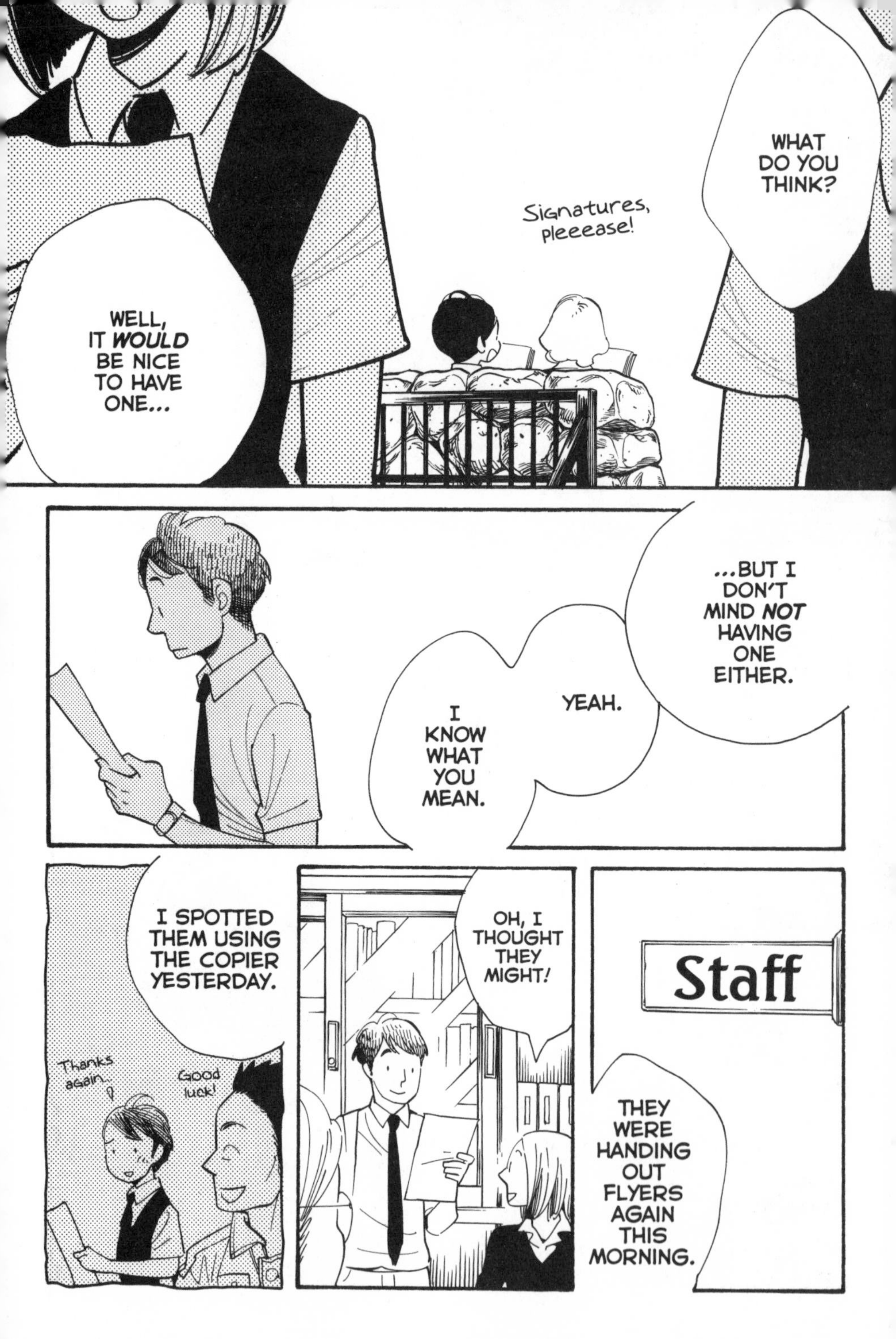
WHAT DO YOU THINK?
Signatures, pleeease!
WELL, IT *WOULD* BE NICE TO HAVE ONE...
...BUT I DON'T MIND *NOT* HAVING ONE EITHER.
YEAH.
I KNOW WHAT YOU MEAN.
Staff
THEY WERE HANDING OUT FLYERS AGAIN THIS MORNING.
OH, I THOUGHT THEY MIGHT!
I SPOTTED THEM USING THE COPIER YESTERDAY.
Good luck!
Thanks again...

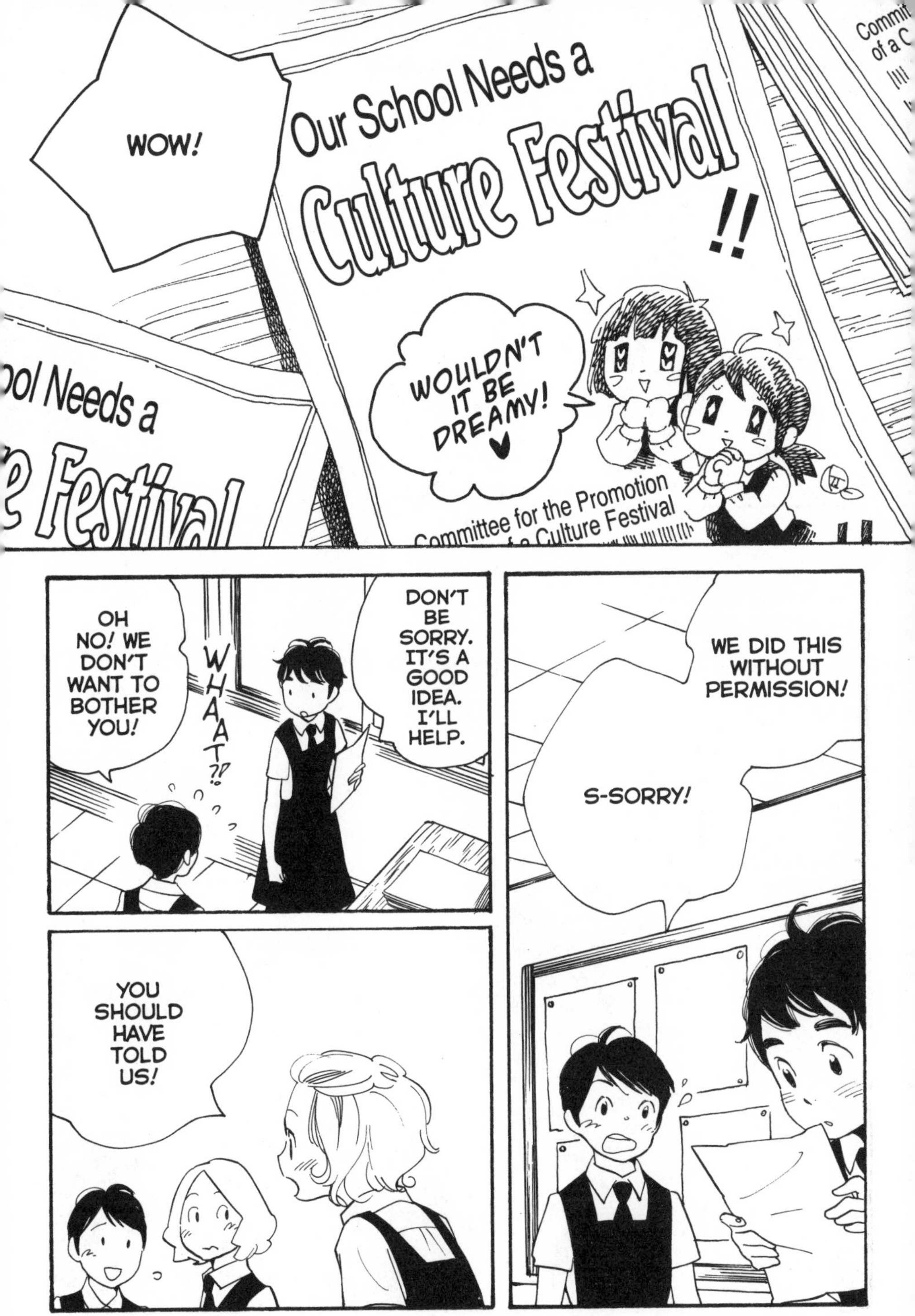
Our School Needs a
Culture Festival!!
WOULDN'T IT BE DREAMY!
Committee for the Promotion
Culture Festival
WOW!
WE DID THIS WITHOUT PERMISSION!
S-SORRY!
DON'T BE SORRY. IT'S A GOOD IDEA. I'LL HELP.
WHAAT?!
OH NO! WE DON'T WANT TO BOTHER YOU!
YOU SHOULD HAVE TOLD US!

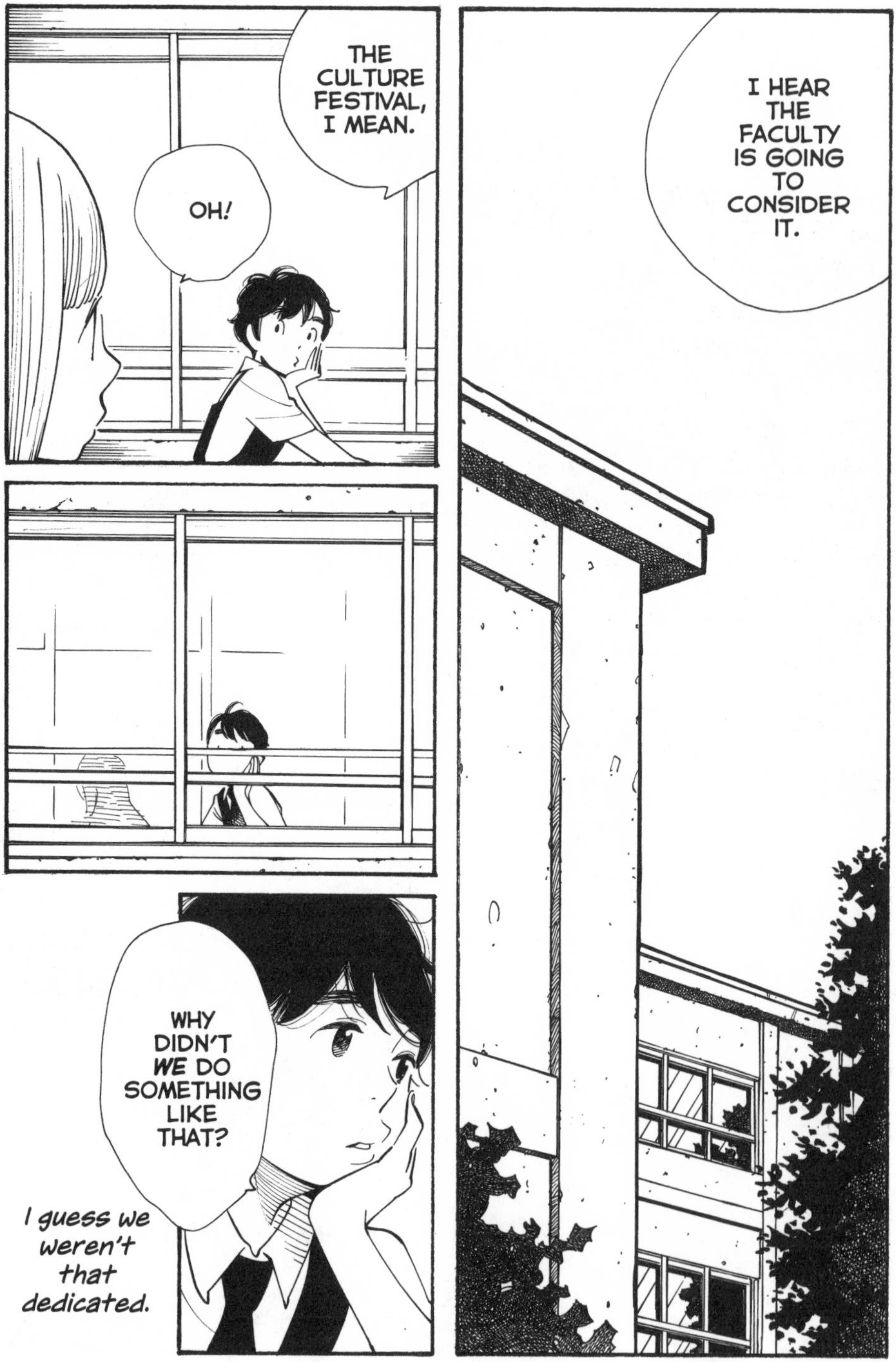
I HEAR THE FACULTY IS GOING TO CONSIDER IT.
THE CULTURE FESTIVAL, I MEAN.
OH!
WHY DIDN'T *WE* DO SOMETHING LIKE THAT?
I guess we weren't that dedicated.

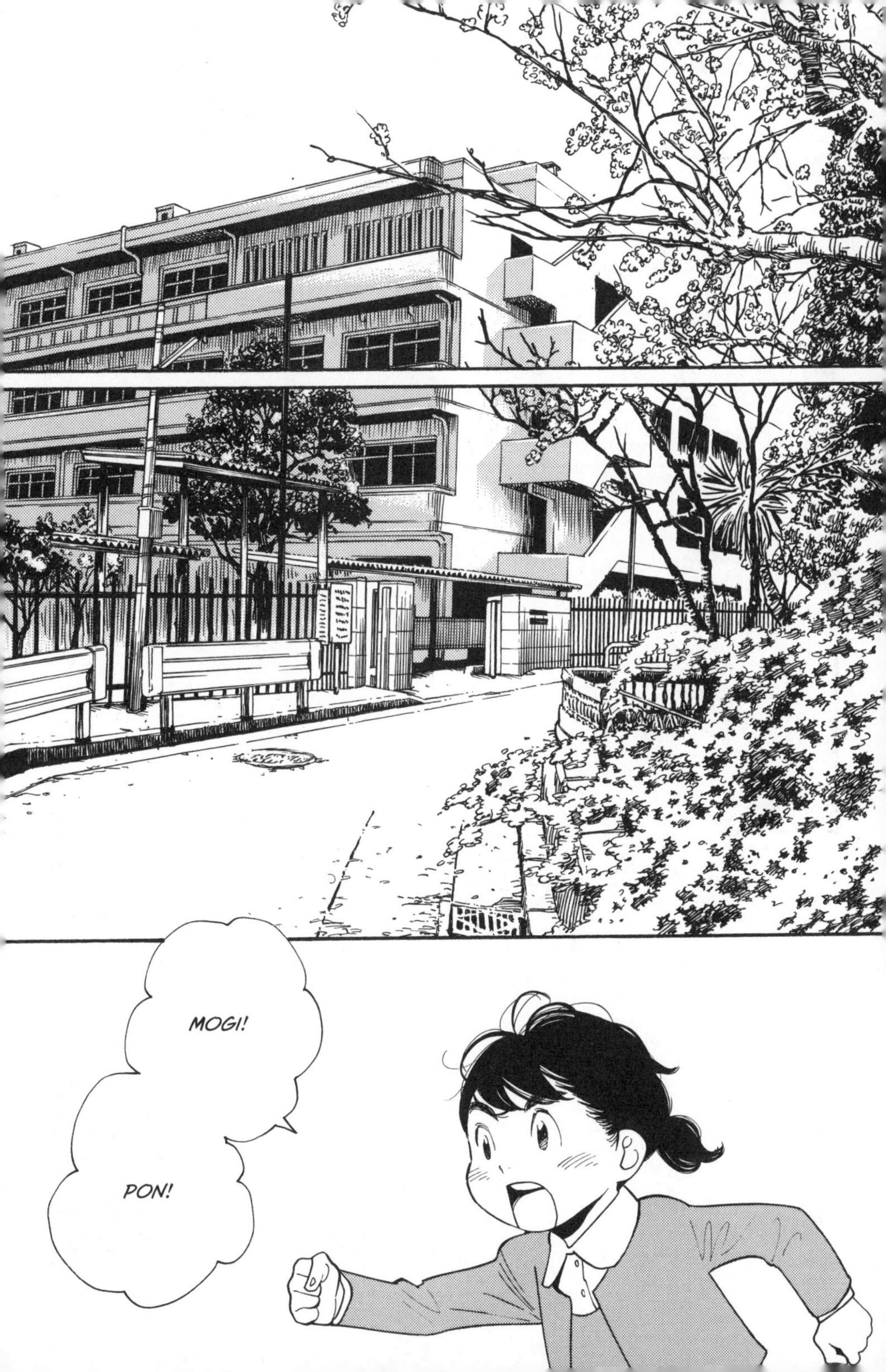
MOGI!
PON!

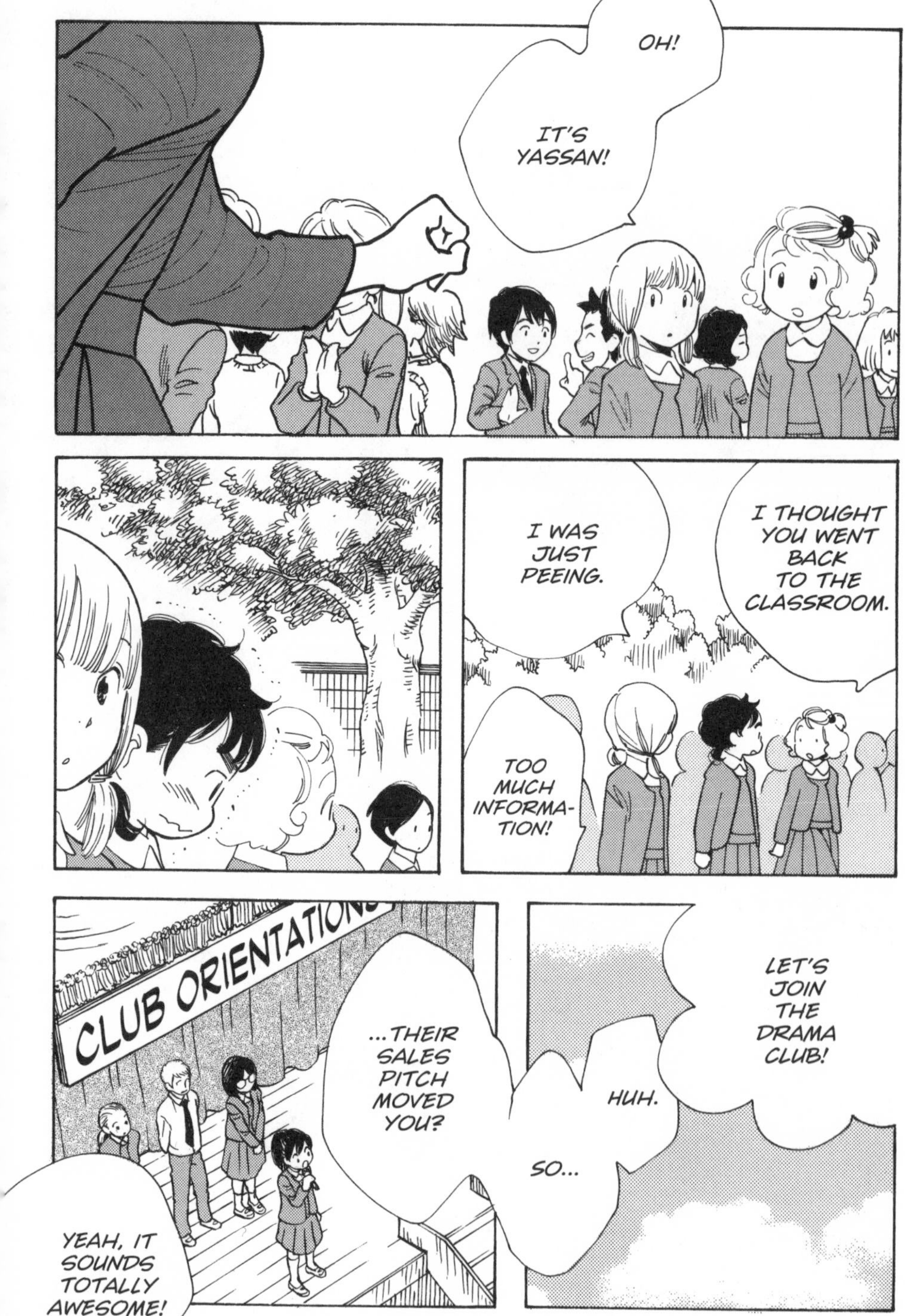
OH!
IT'S YASSAN!
I THOUGHT YOU WENT BACK TO THE CLASSROOM.
I WAS JUST PEEING.
TOO MUCH INFORMATION!
LET'S JOIN THE DRAMA CLUB!
HUH.
SO...
...THEIR SALES PITCH MOVED YOU?
CLUB ORIENTATIONS
YEAH, IT SOUNDS TOTALLY AWESOME!

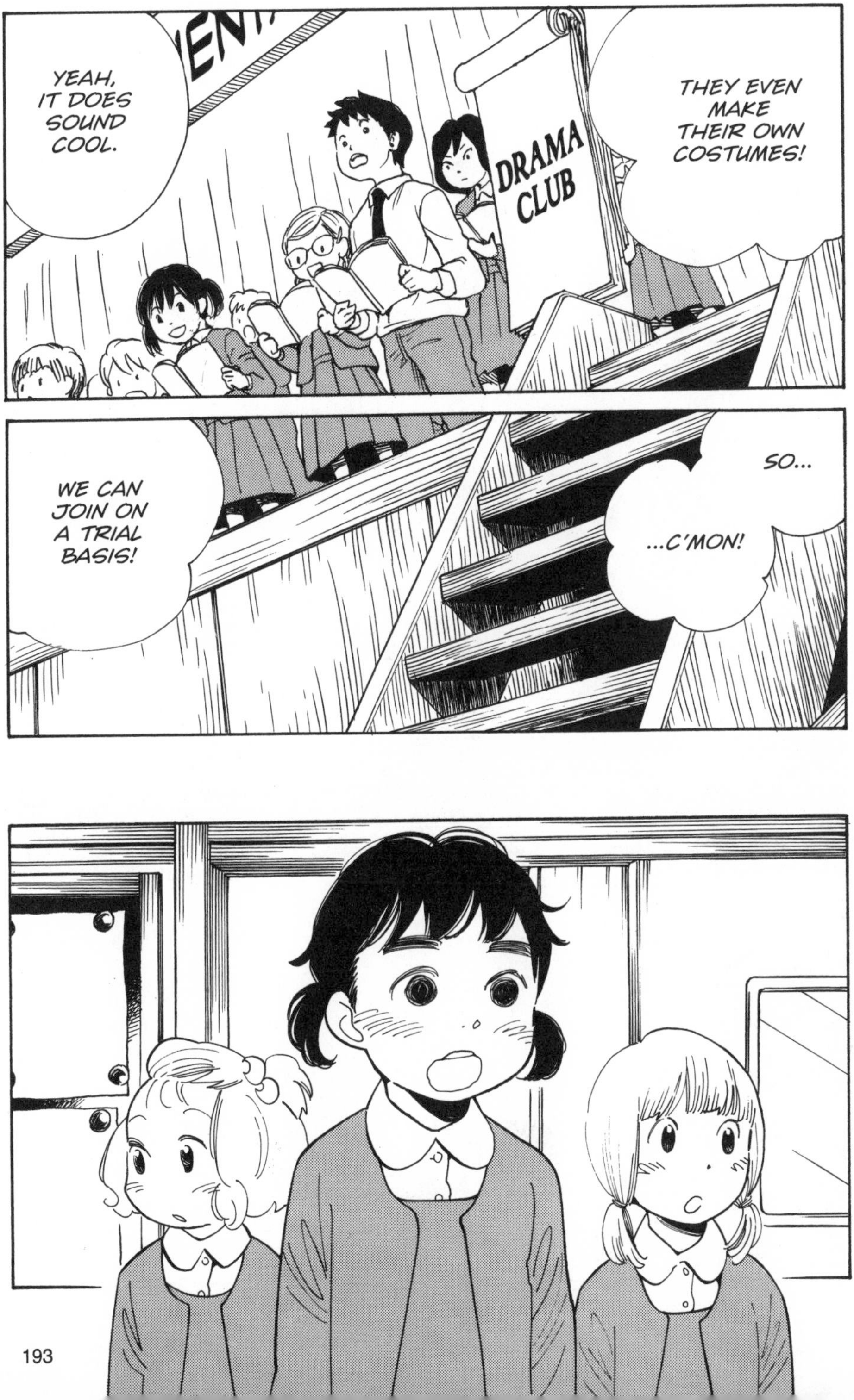
THEY EVEN MAKE THEIR OWN COSTUMES!
DRAMA CLUB
YEAH, IT DOES SOUND COOL.
SO...
...C'MON!
WE CAN JOIN ON A TRIAL BASIS!

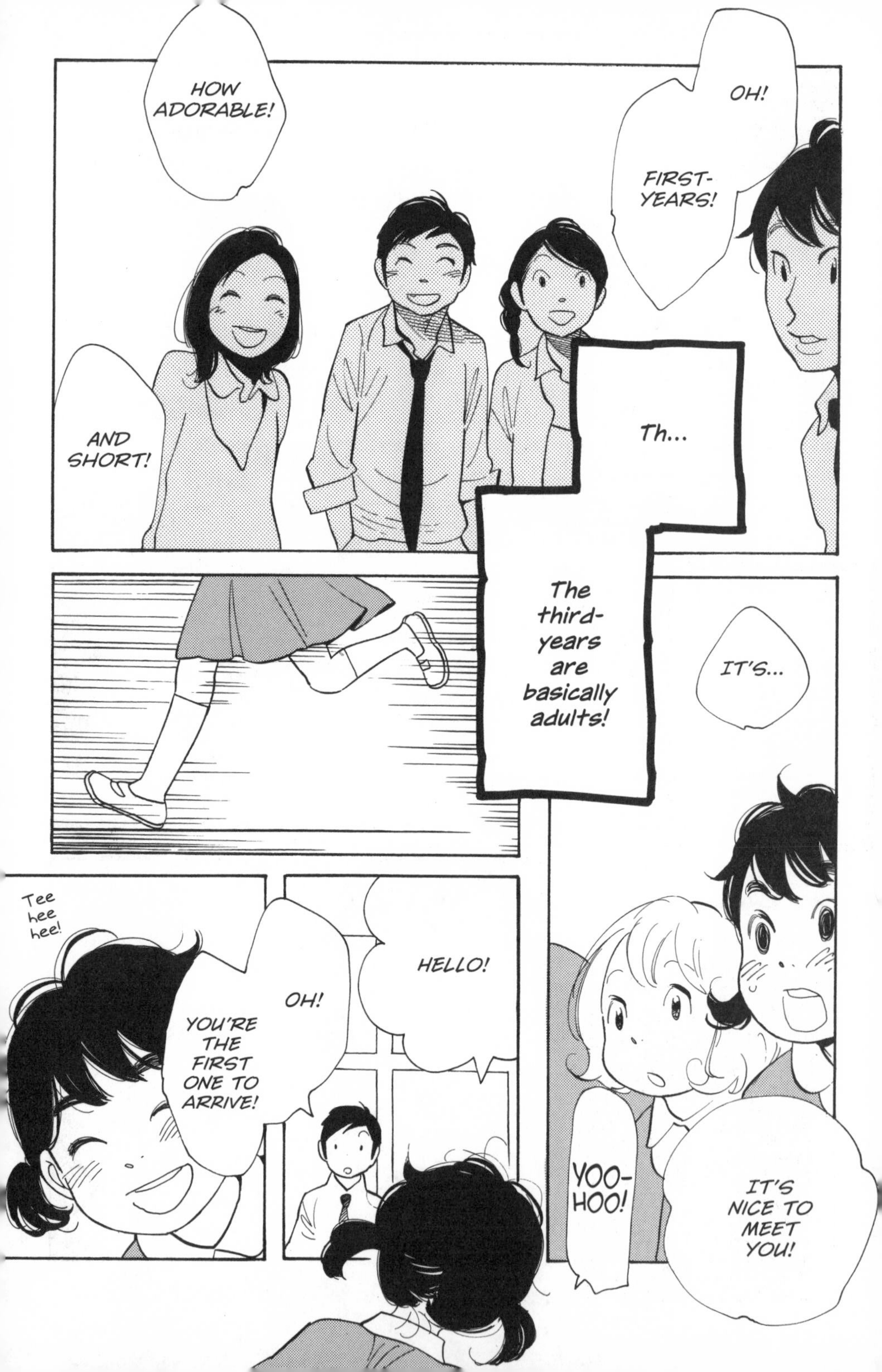

OH!
FIRST-YEARS!
HOW ADORABLE!
AND SHORT!
Th...
The third-years are basically adults!
IT'S...
IT'S NICE TO MEET YOU!
YOO-HOO!
HELLO!
OH!
YOU'RE THE FIRST ONE TO ARRIVE!
Tee hee hee!

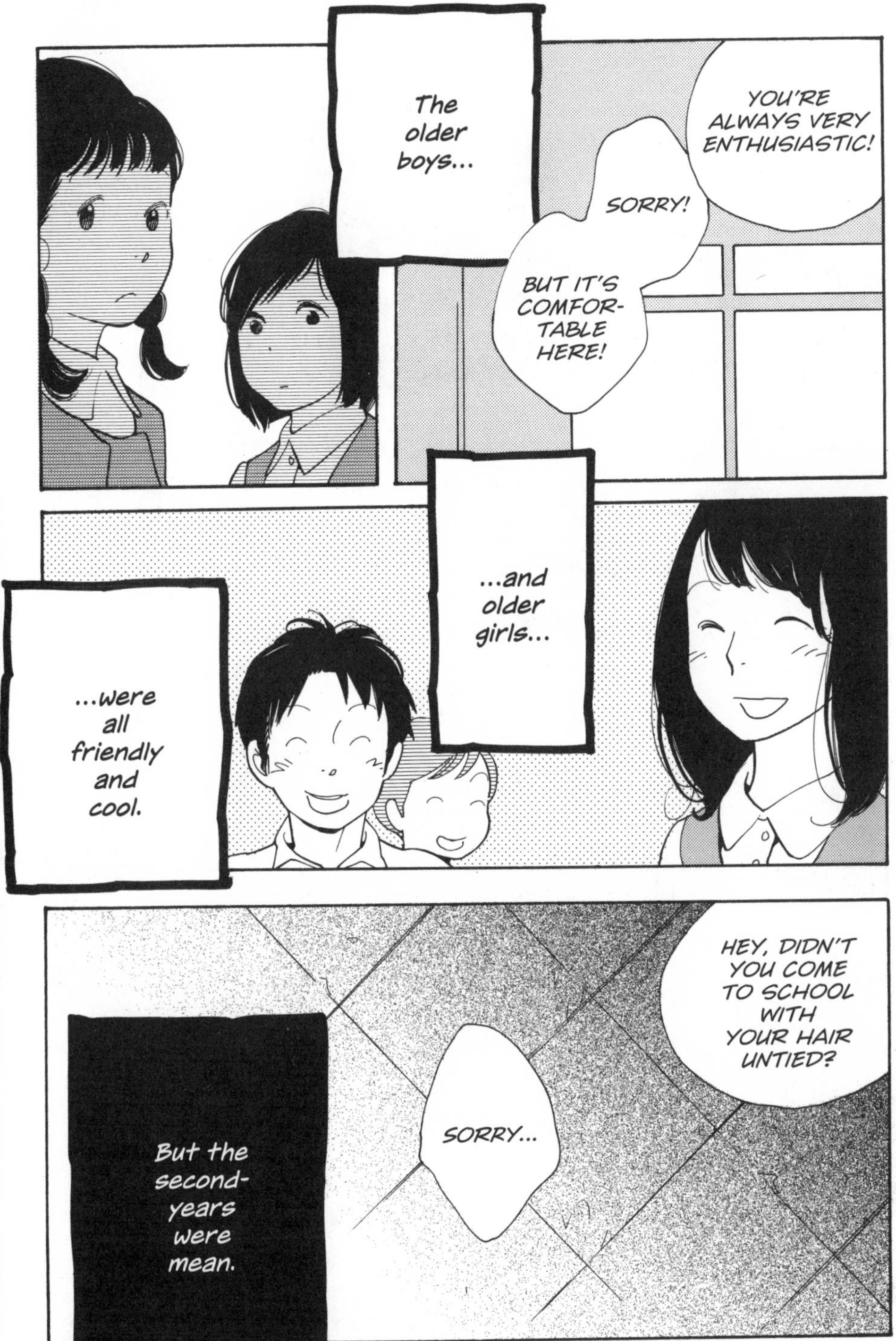
The older boys...
YOU'RE ALWAYS VERY ENTHUSIASTIC!
SORRY!
BUT IT'S COMFORTABLE HERE!
...and older girls...
...were all friendly and cool.
HEY, DIDN'T YOU COME TO SCHOOL WITH YOUR HAIR UNTIED?
SORRY...
But the second-years were mean.

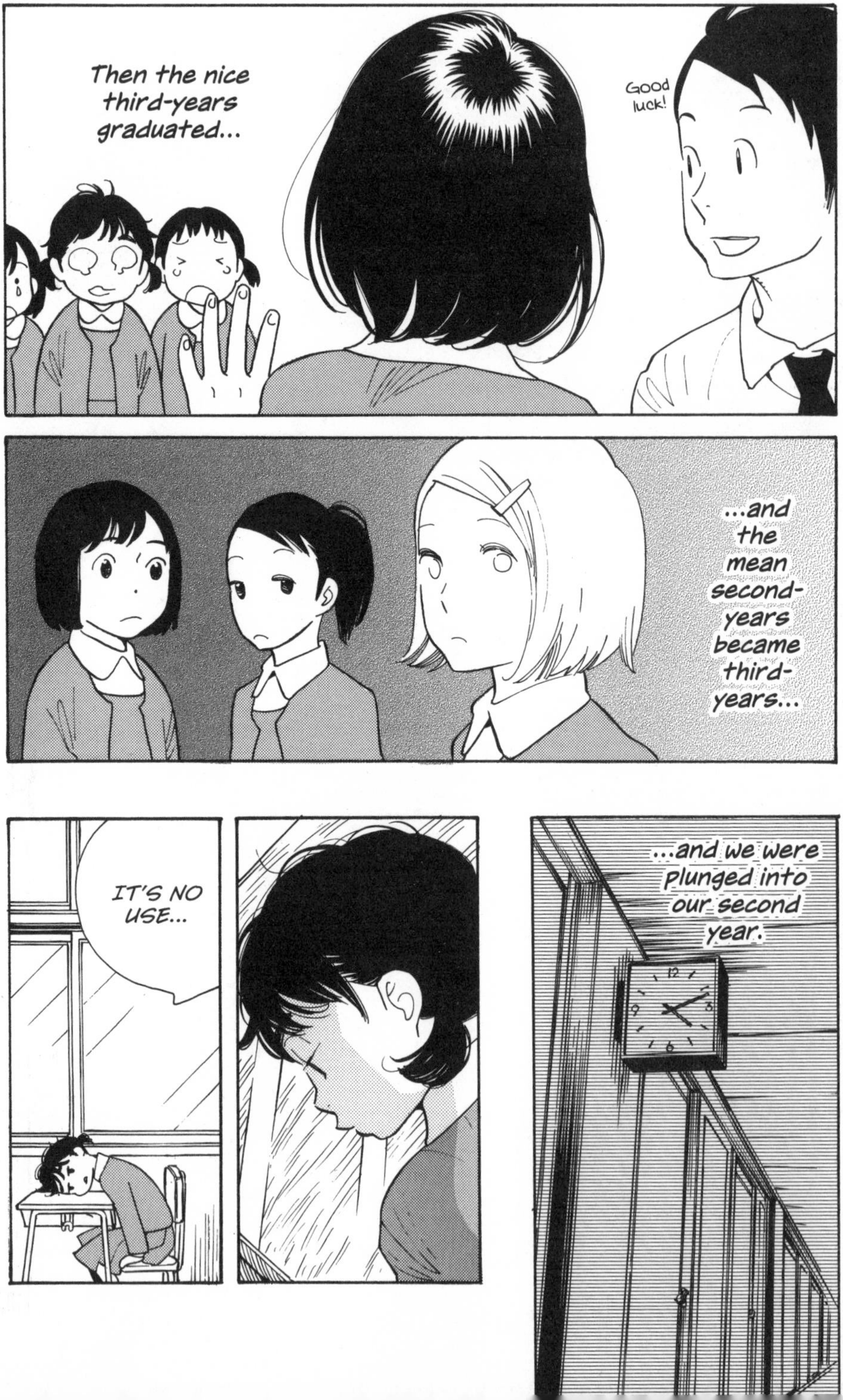
Good luck!
Then the nice third-years graduated...
...and the mean second-years became third-years...
...and we were plunged into our second year.
IT'S NO USE...

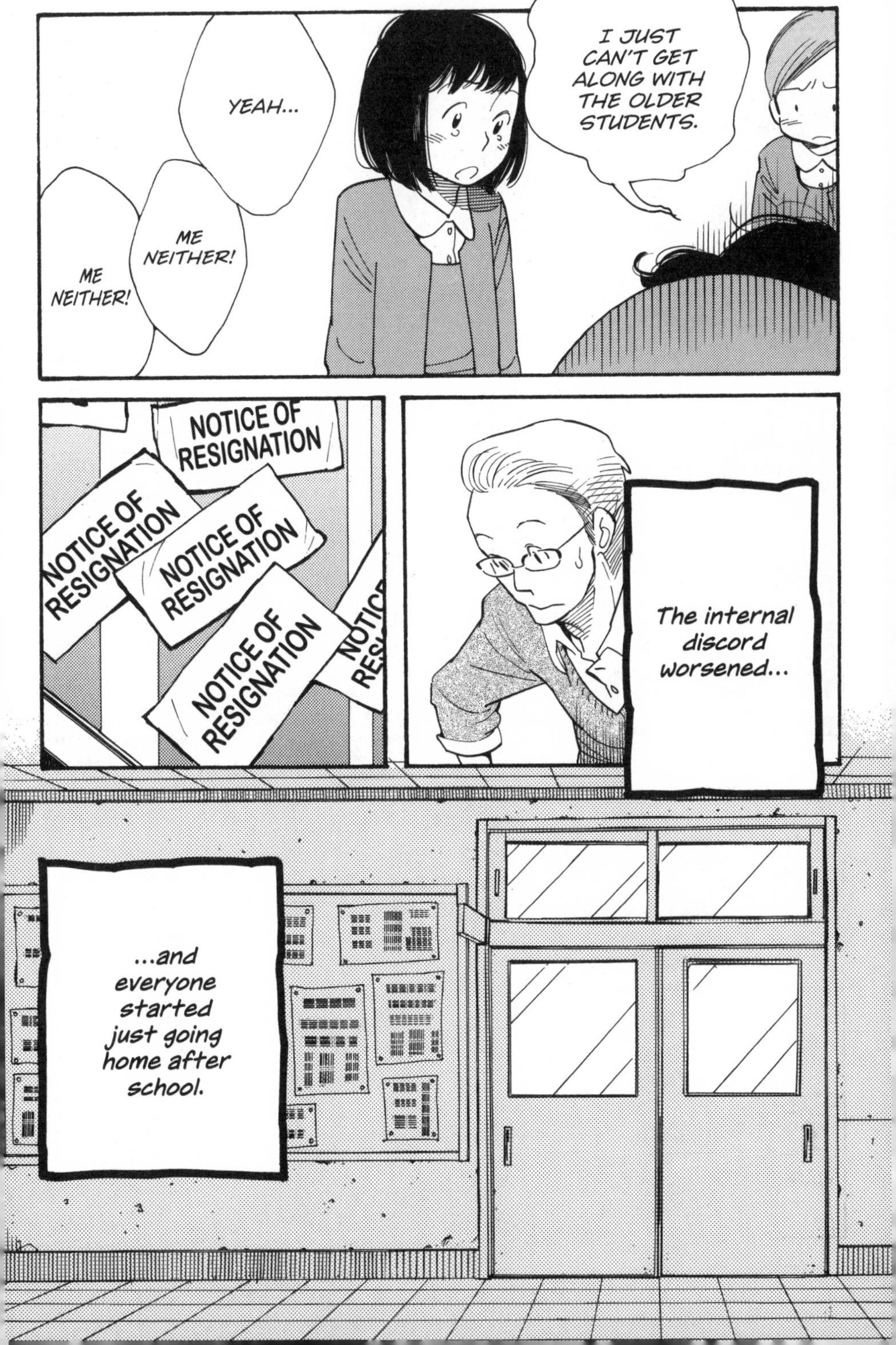
I JUST CAN'T GET ALONG WITH THE OLDER STUDENTS.
YEAH...
ME NEITHER!
ME NEITHER!
The internal discord worsened...
NOTICE OF RESIGNATION
NOTICE OF RESIGNATION
NOTICE OF RESIGNATION
NOTICE OF RESIGNATION
...and everyone started just going home after school.

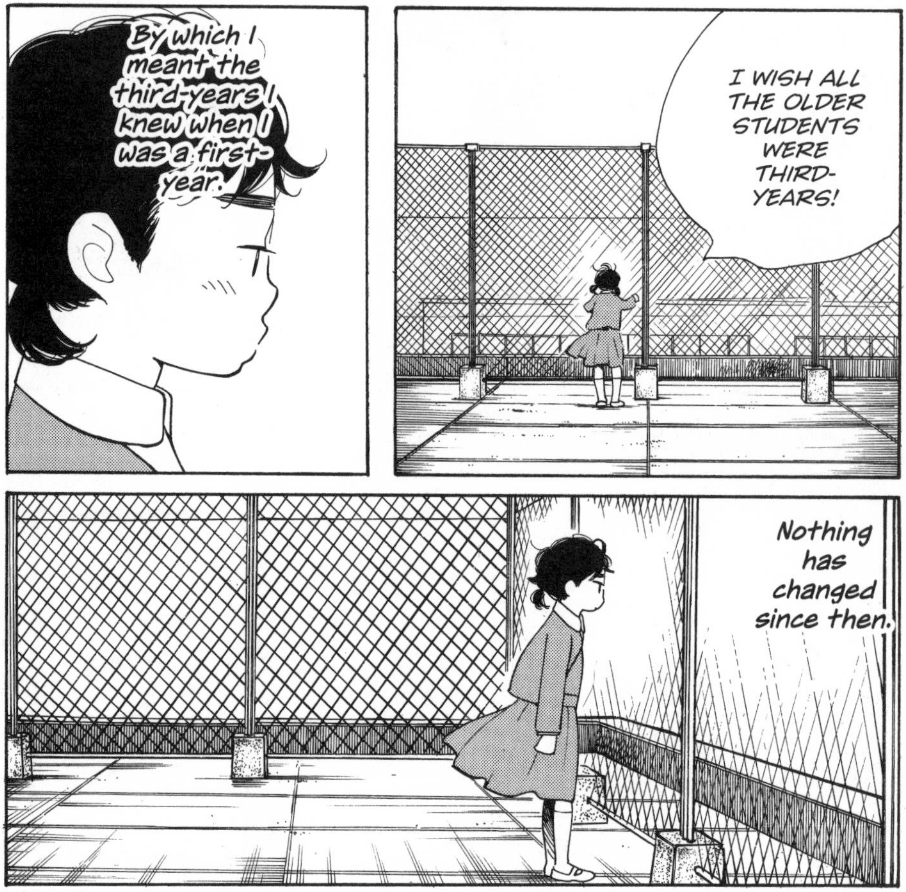
I WISH ALL THE OLDER STUDENTS WERE THIRD-YEARS!
By which I meant the third-years I knew when I was a first-year.
Nothing has changed since then.

When I heard there was no culture festival in high school, I just gave up.

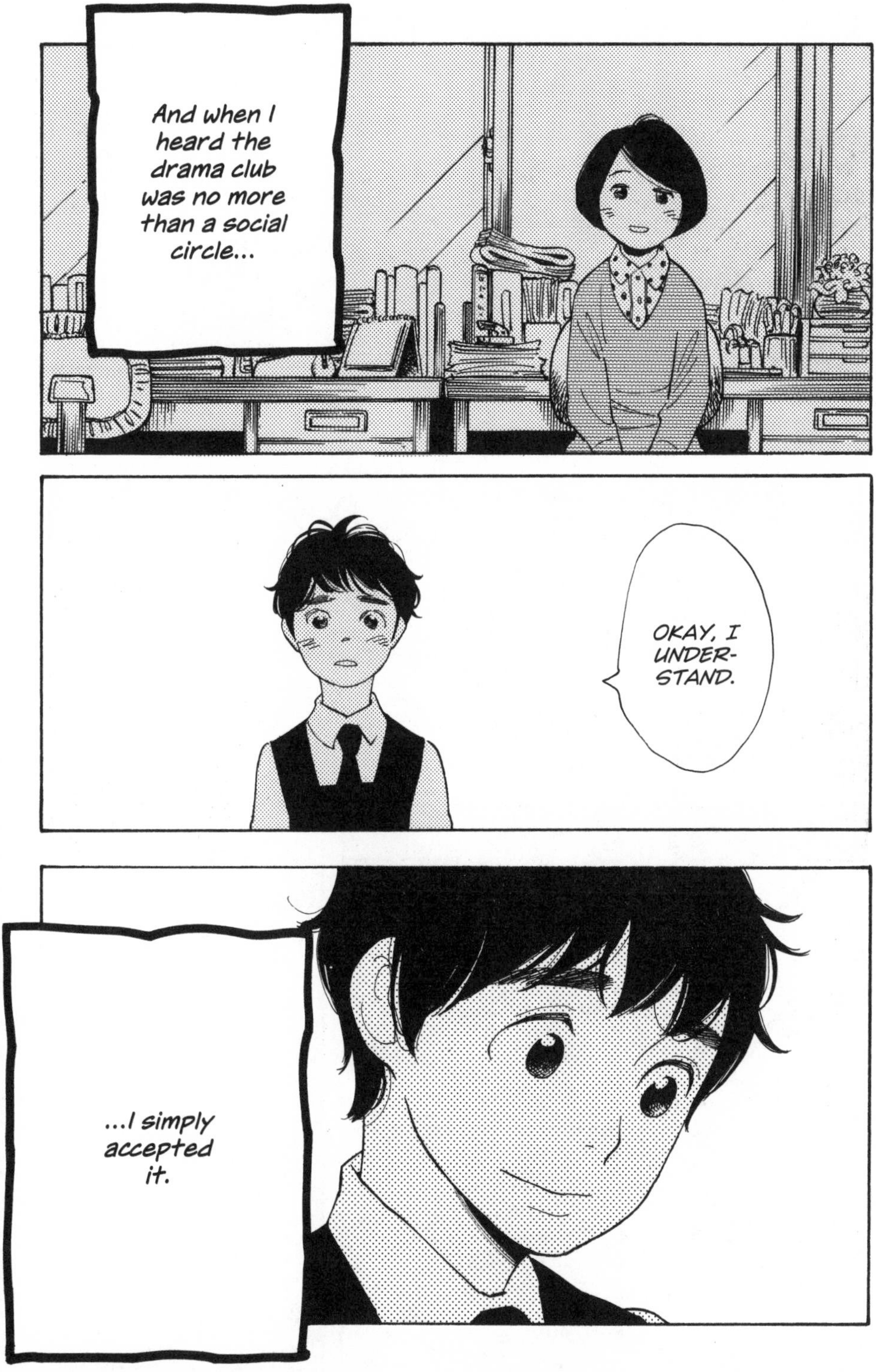
And when I heard the drama club was no more than a social circle...
OKAY, I UNDER-STAND.
...I simply accepted it.

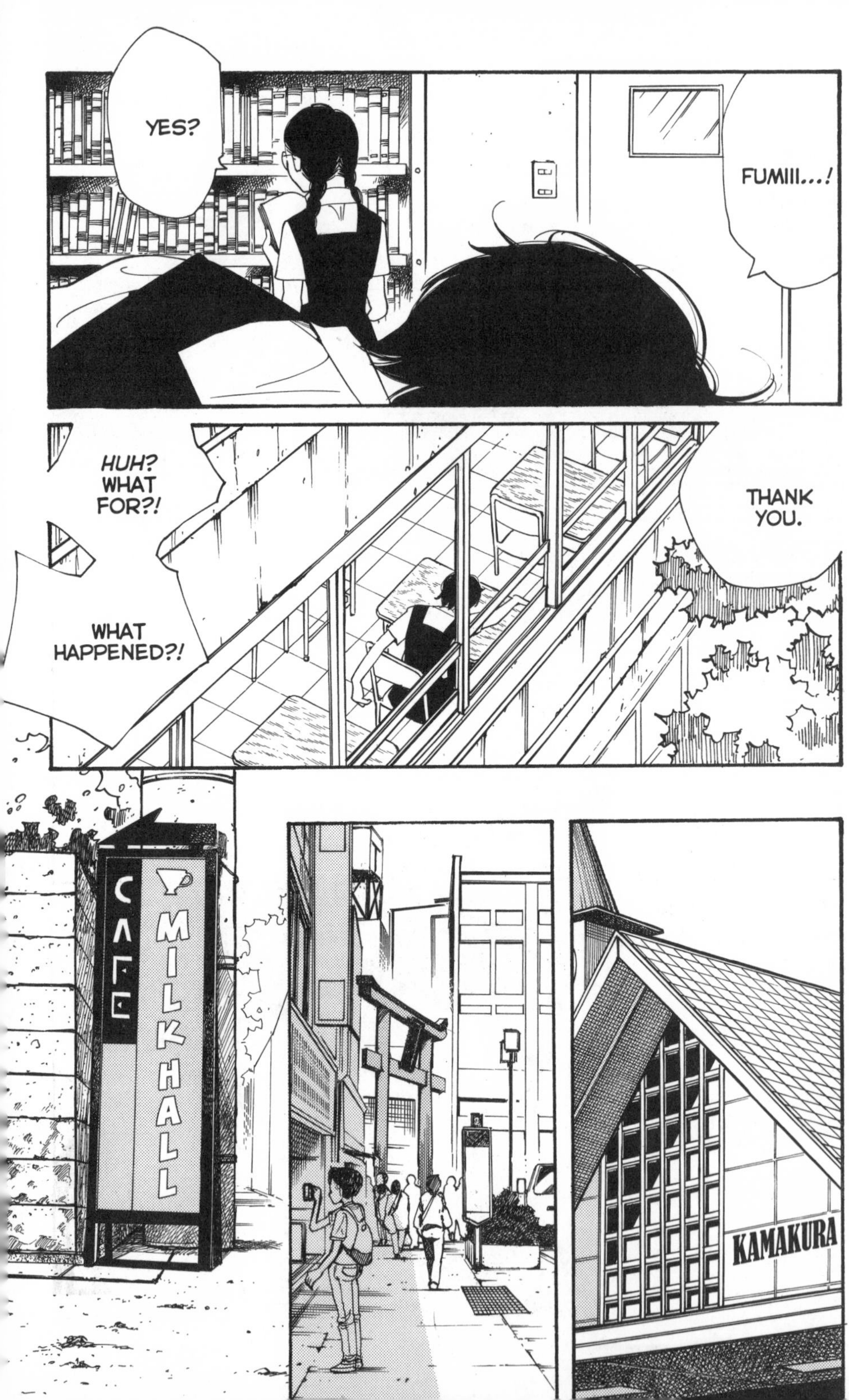
FUMIII...!
YES?
THANK YOU.
HUH? WHAT FOR?!
WHAT HAPPENED?!
KAMAKURA
CAFE
MILK HALL

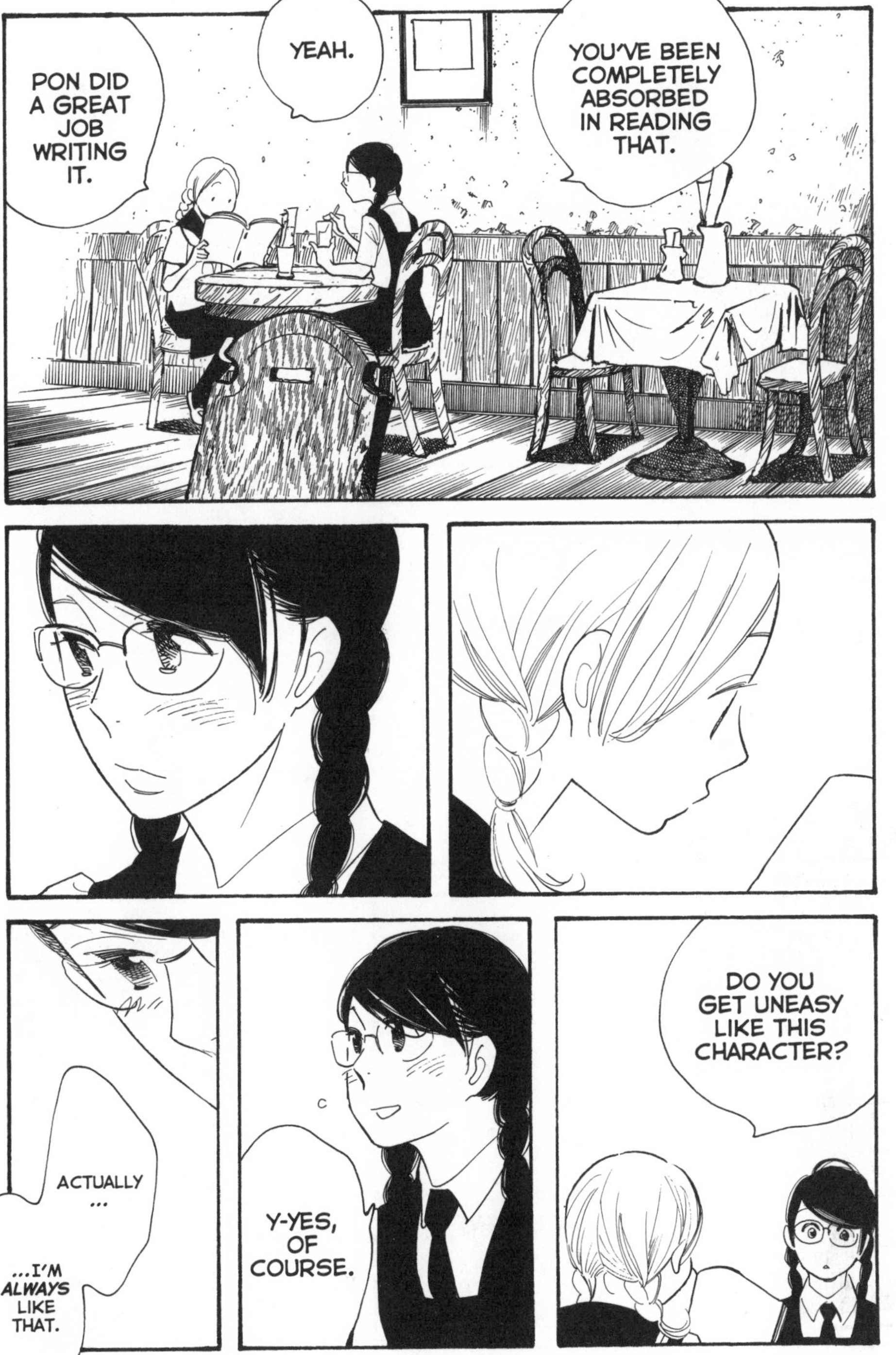
YOU'VE BEEN COMPLETELY ABSORBED IN READING THAT.
YEAH.
PON DID A GREAT JOB WRITING IT.
DO YOU GET UNEASY LIKE THIS CHARACTER?
Y-YES, OF COURSE.
ACTUALLY ...
...I'M *ALWAYS* LIKE THAT.

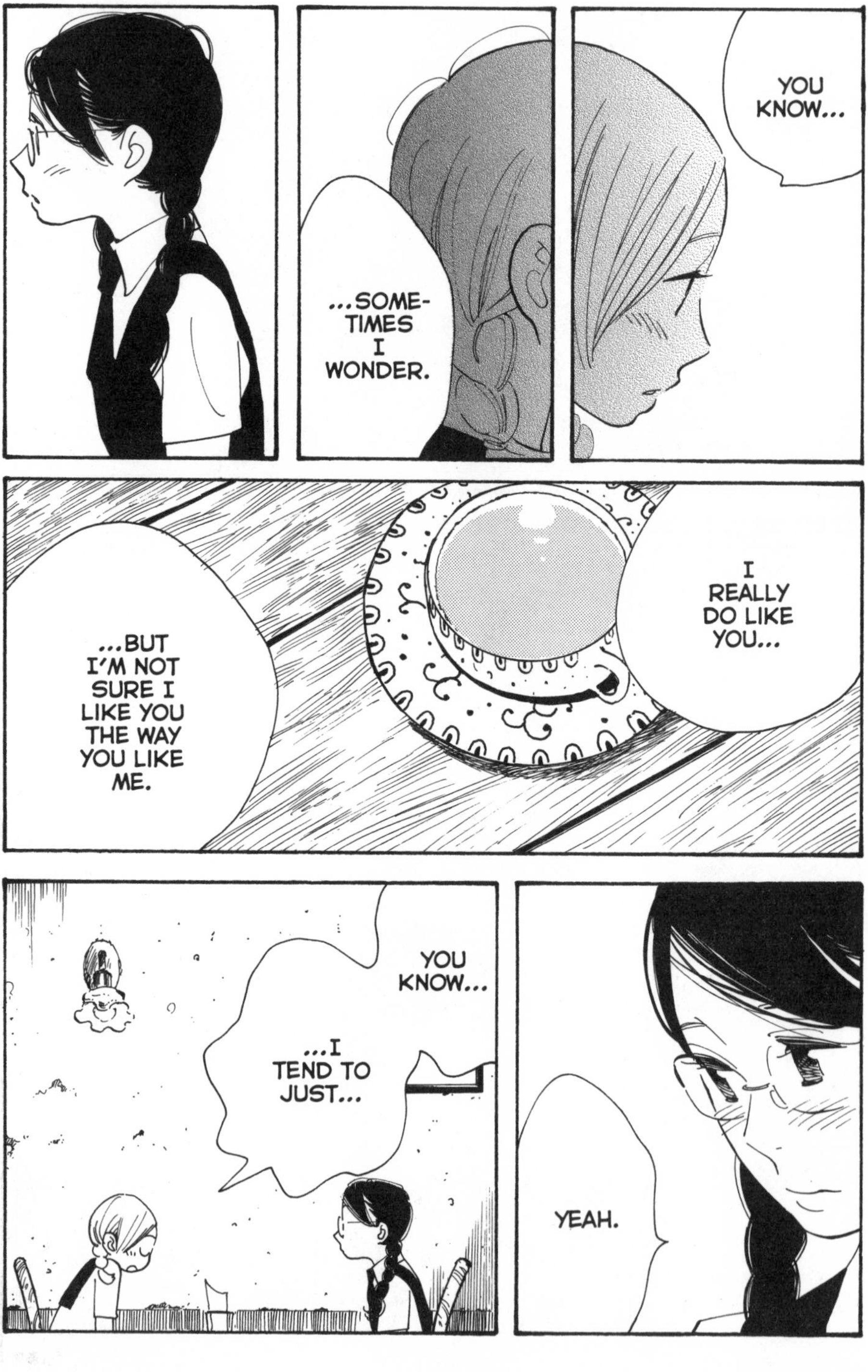
YOU KNOW...
...SOMETIMES I WONDER.
I REALLY DO LIKE YOU...
...BUT I'M NOT SURE I LIKE YOU THE WAY YOU LIKE ME.
YEAH.
YOU KNOW...
...I TEND TO JUST...

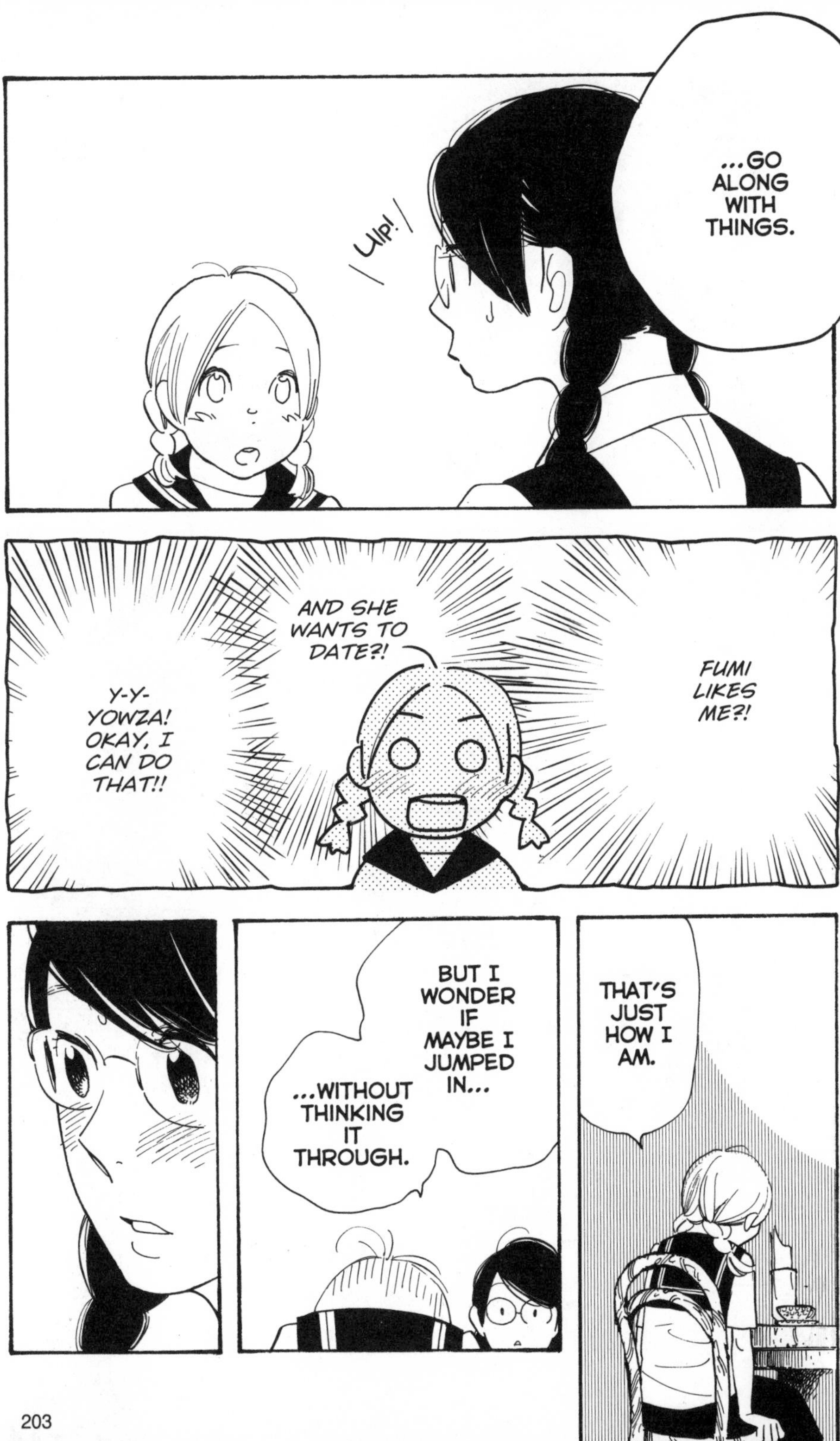
...GO ALONG WITH THINGS.
Ulp!
FUMI LIKES ME?!
AND SHE WANTS TO DATE?!
Y-Y-YOWZA! OKAY, I CAN DO THAT!!
THAT'S JUST HOW I AM.
BUT I WONDER IF MAYBE I JUMPED IN...
...WITHOUT THINKING IT THROUGH.

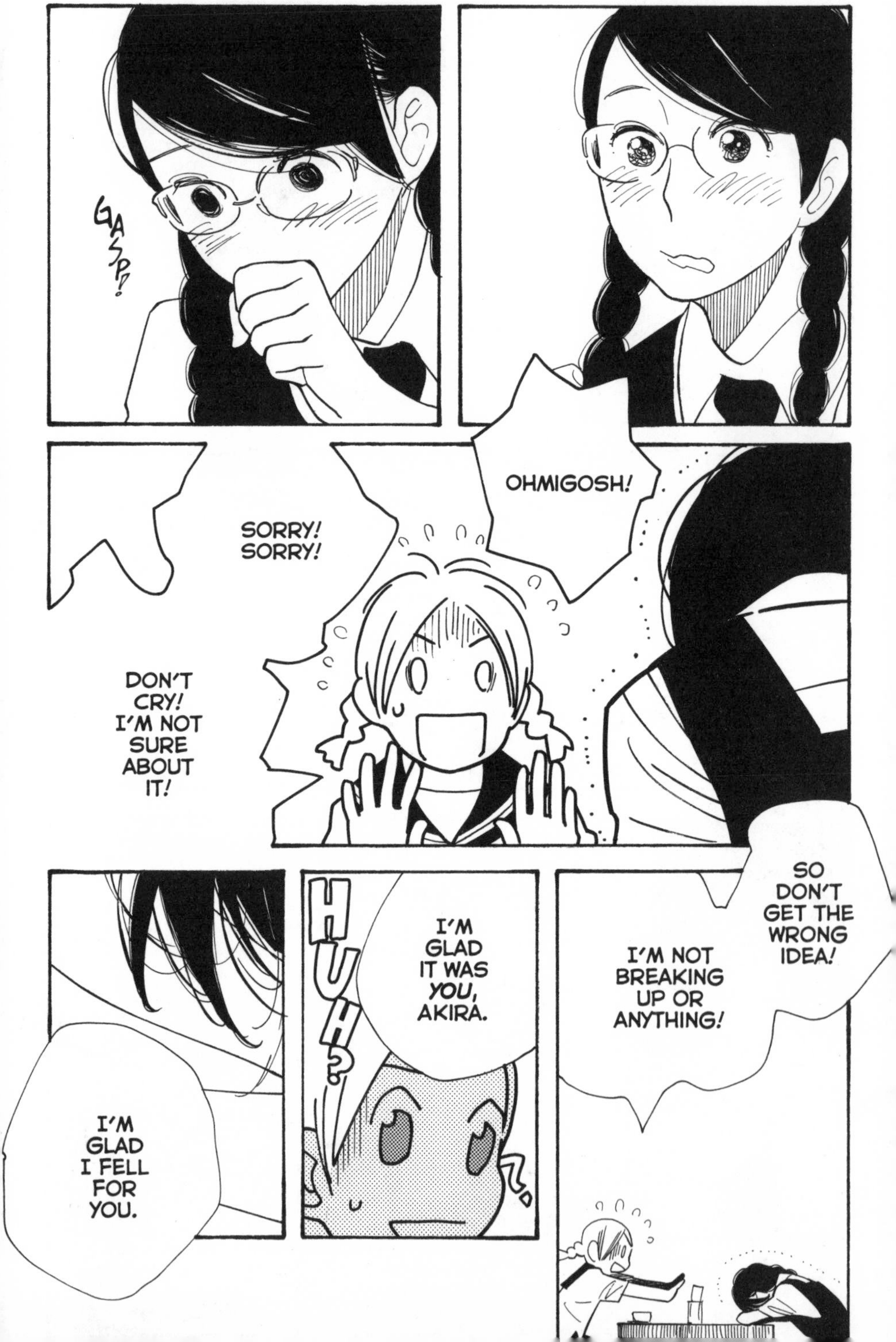
GASP!?
OHMIGOSH!
SORRY! SORRY!
DON'T CRY! I'M NOT SURE ABOUT IT!
SO DON'T GET THE WRONG IDEA!
I'M NOT BREAKING UP OR ANYTHING!
I'M GLAD IT WAS *YOU*, AKIRA.
HUH!?
I'M GLAD I FELL FOR YOU.

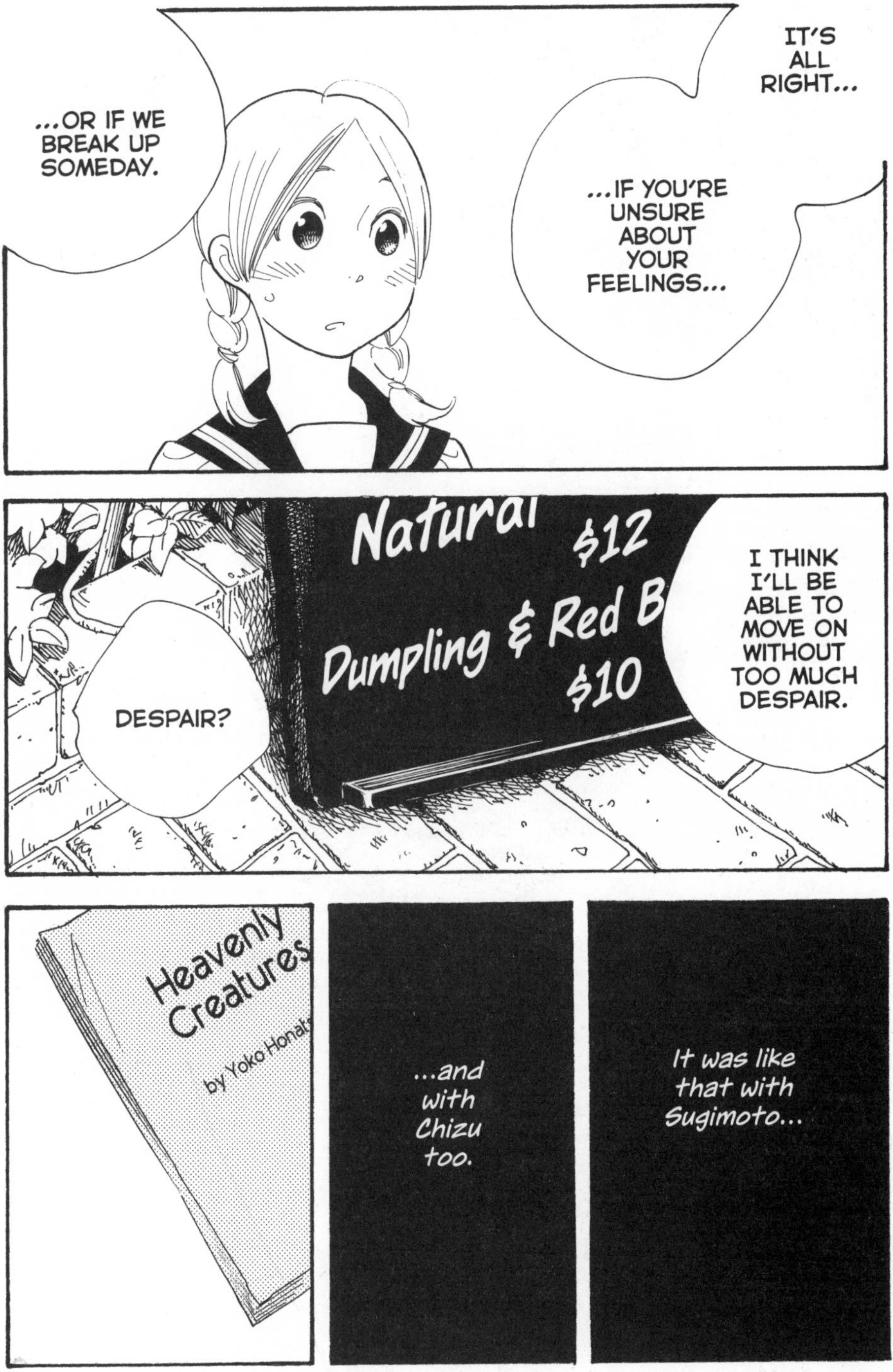
IT'S ALL RIGHT...
...IF YOU'RE UNSURE ABOUT YOUR FEELINGS...
...OR IF WE BREAK UP SOMEDAY.
I THINK I'LL BE ABLE TO MOVE ON WITHOUT TOO MUCH DESPAIR.
Natural $12
Dumpling & Red B
$10
DESPAIR?
It was like that with Sugimoto...
...and with Chizu too.
Heavenly Creatures

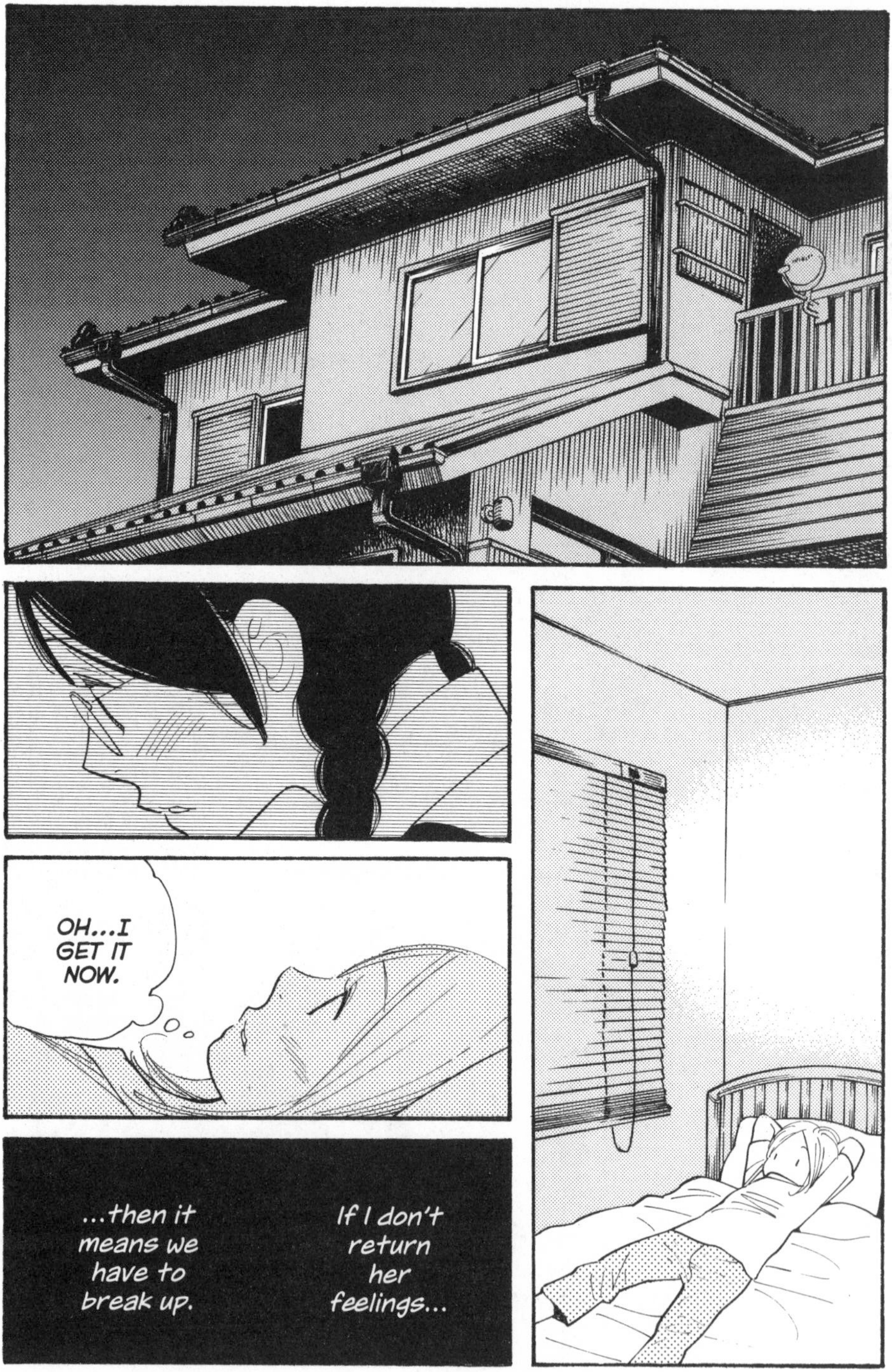
OH...I GET IT NOW.
If I don't return her feelings...
...then it means we have to break up.

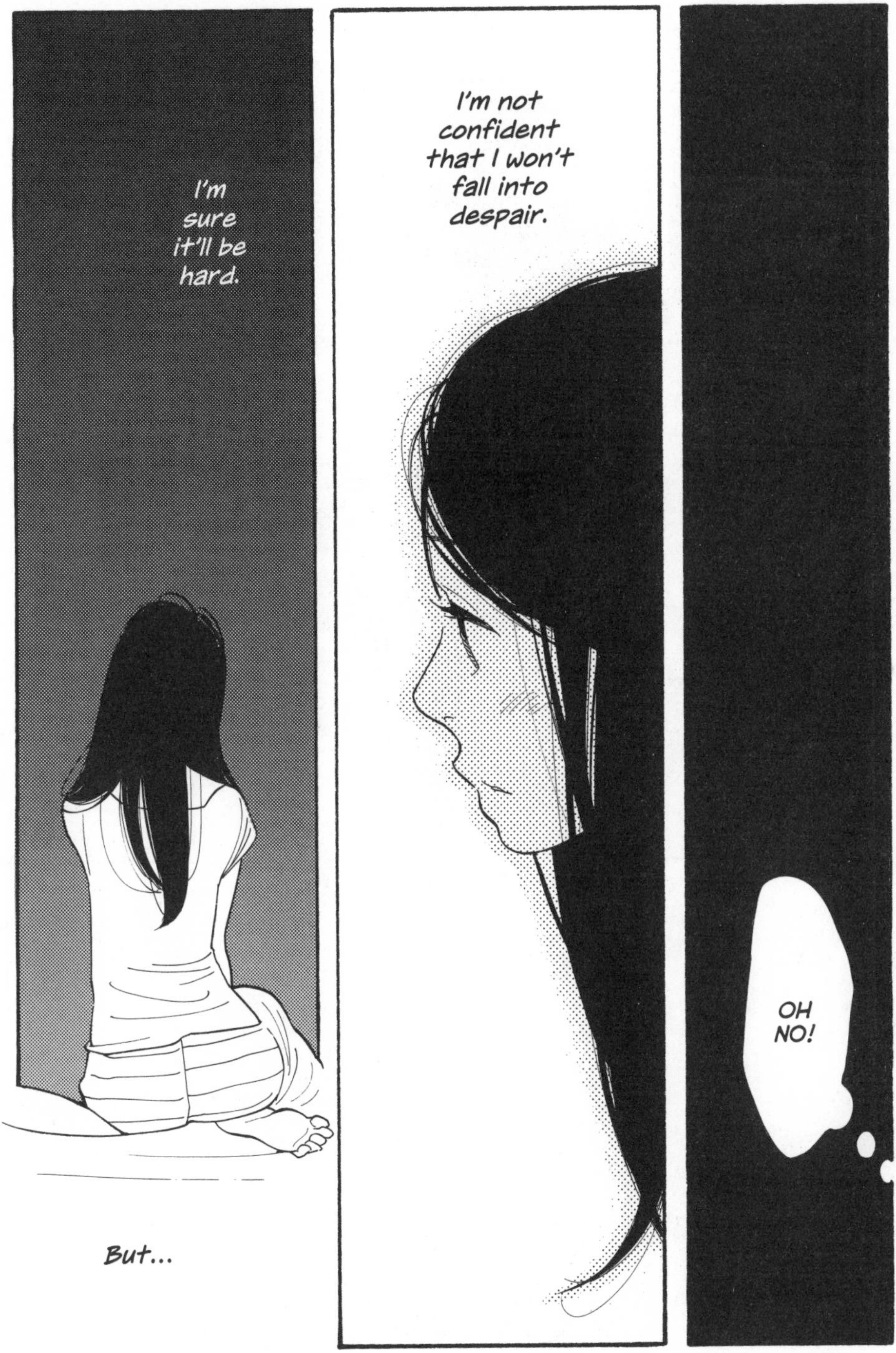
OH NO!
I'm not confident that I won't fall into despair.
I'm sure it'll be hard.
But...

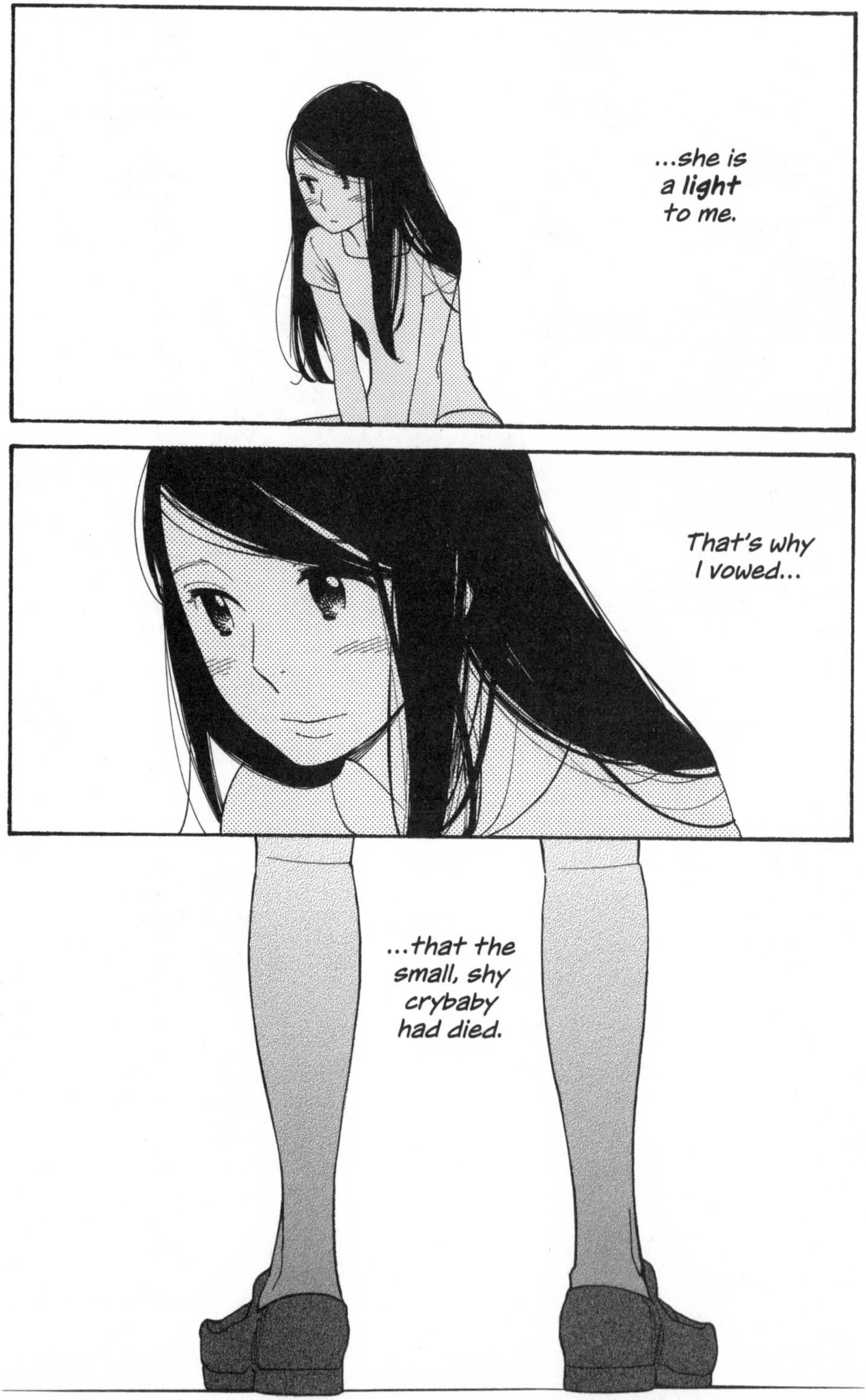
...she is
a light
to me.
That's why
I vowed...
...that the
small, shy
crybaby
had died.

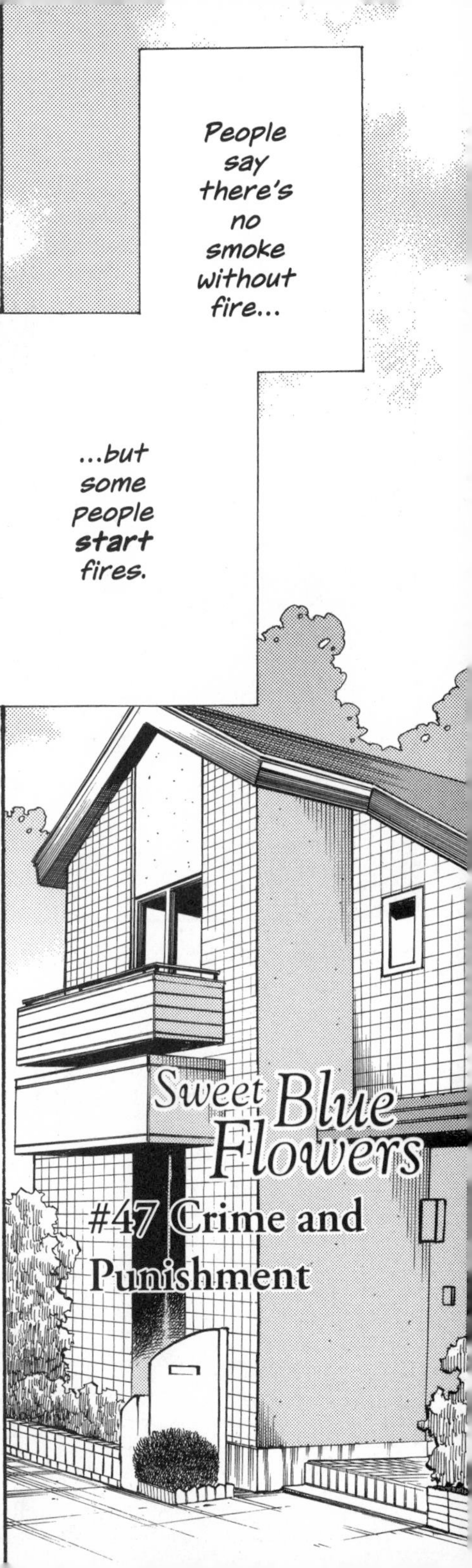
People say there's no smoke without fire...
...but some people **start** fires.
Sweet Blue Flowers
#47 Crime and Punishment

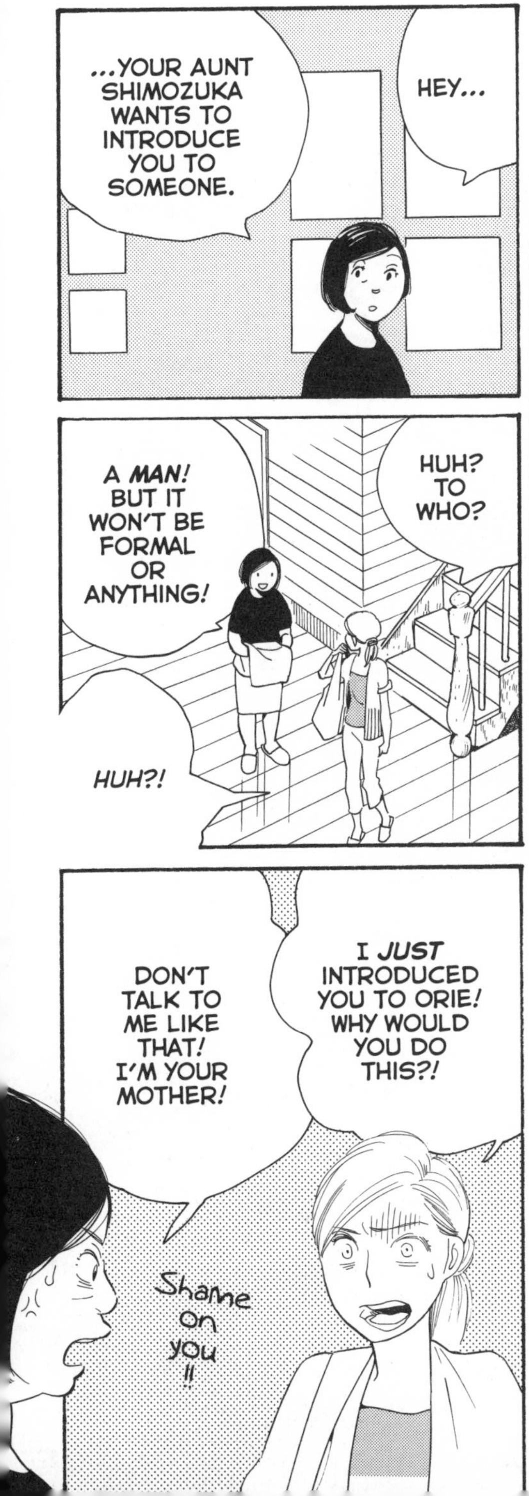
HEY...
...YOUR AUNT SHIMOZUKA WANTS TO INTRODUCE YOU TO SOMEONE.
HUH? TO WHO?
A *MAN*! BUT IT WON'T BE FORMAL OR ANYTHING!
HUH?!
I *JUST* INTRODUCED YOU TO ORIE! WHY WOULD YOU DO THIS?!
DON'T TALK TO ME LIKE THAT! I'M YOUR MOTHER!
Shame on you!!

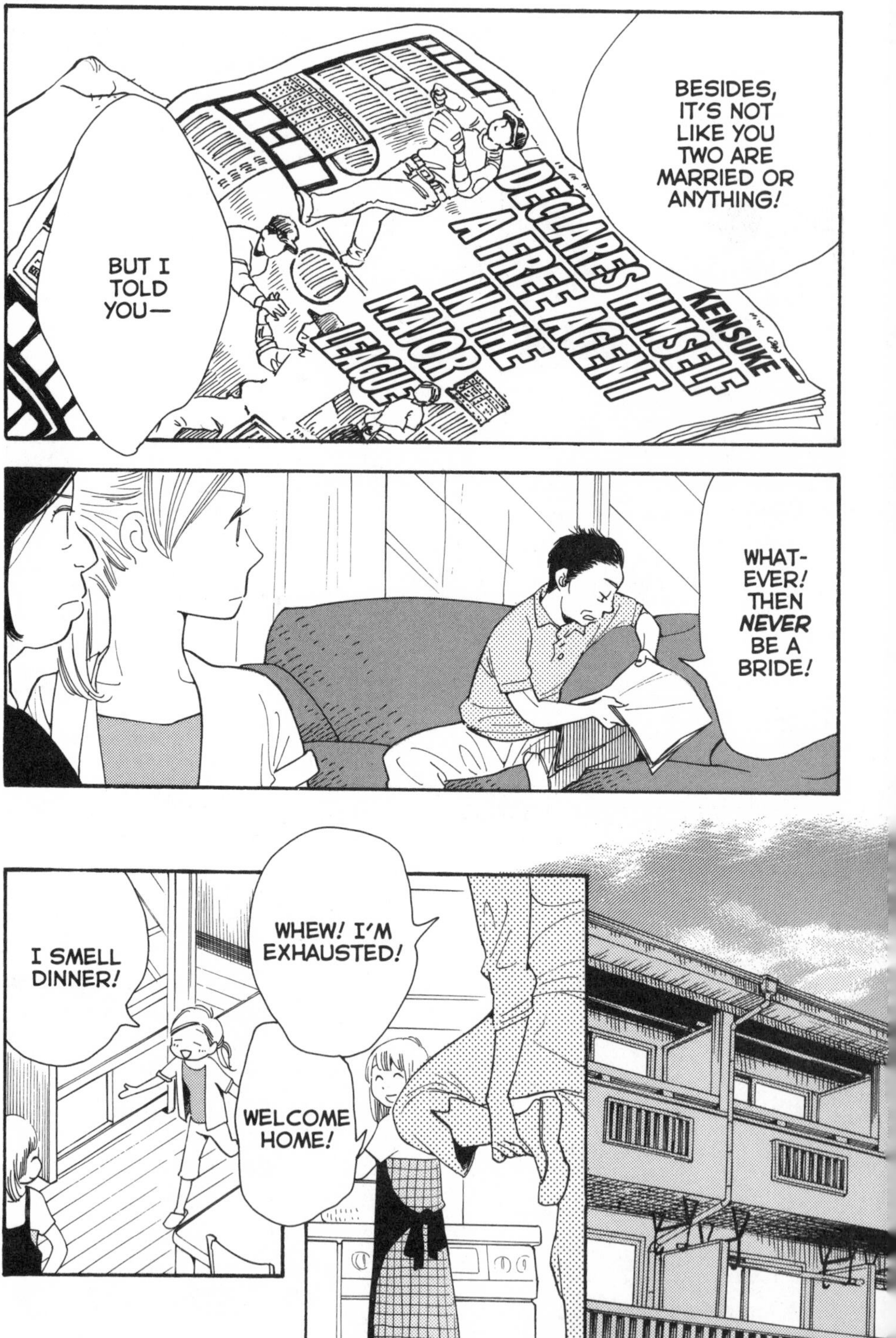
BESIDES, IT'S NOT LIKE YOU TWO ARE MARRIED OR ANYTHING!
KENSUKE DECLARES HIMSELF A FREE AGENT IN THE MAJOR LEAGUE
BUT I TOLD YOU—
WHAT-EVER! THEN *NEVER* BE A BRIDE!
WHEW! I'M EXHAUSTED!
I SMELL DINNER!
WELCOME HOME!

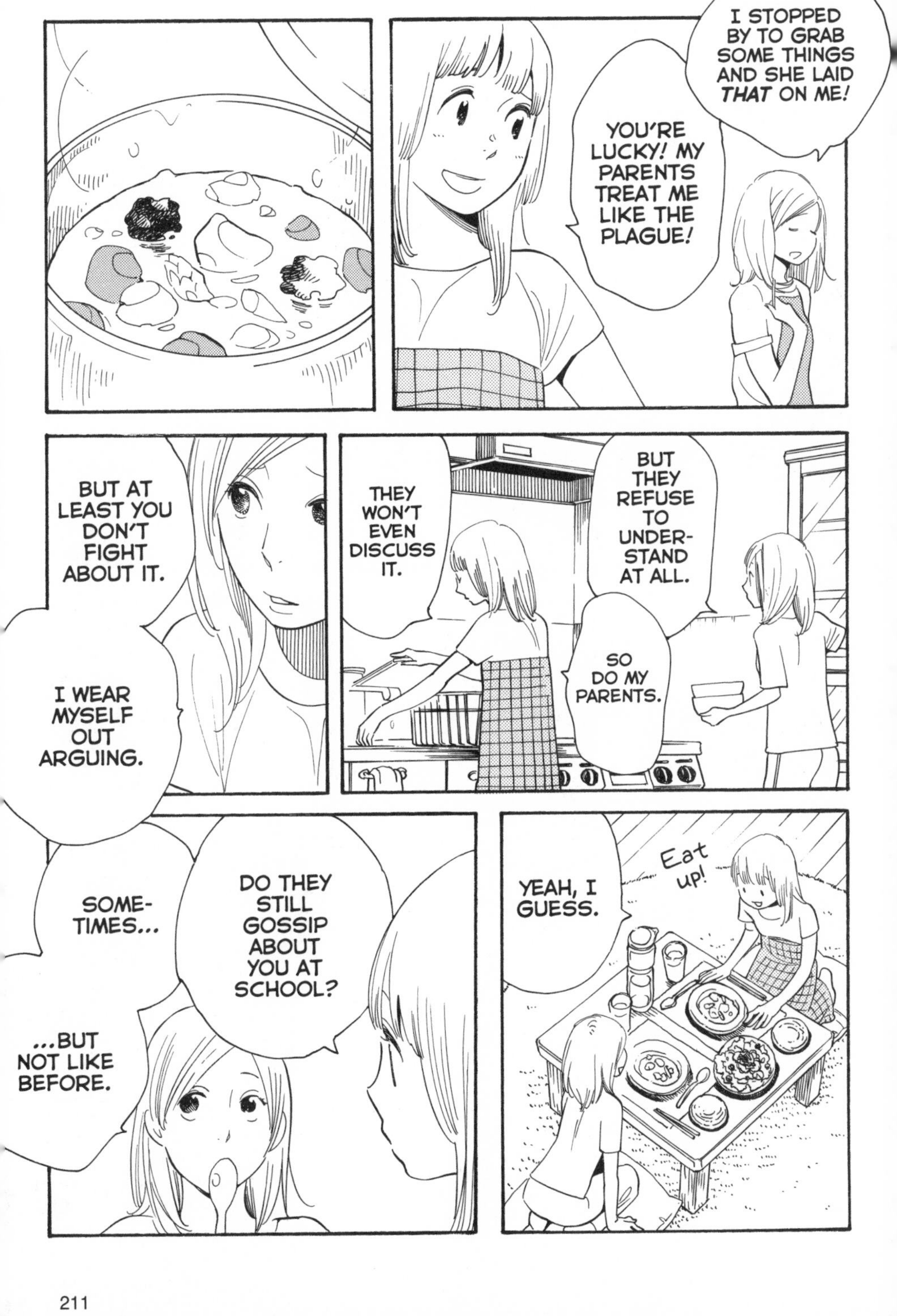
I STOPPED BY TO GRAB SOME THINGS AND SHE LAID *THAT* ON ME!
YOU'RE LUCKY! MY PARENTS TREAT ME LIKE THE PLAGUE!
BUT THEY REFUSE TO UNDER-STAND AT ALL.
THEY WON'T EVEN DISCUSS IT.
SO DO MY PARENTS.
BUT AT LEAST YOU DON'T FIGHT ABOUT IT.
I WEAR MYSELF OUT ARGUING.
Eat up!
YEAH, I GUESS.
DO THEY STILL GOSSIP ABOUT YOU AT SCHOOL?
SOME-TIMES...
...BUT NOT LIKE BEFORE.

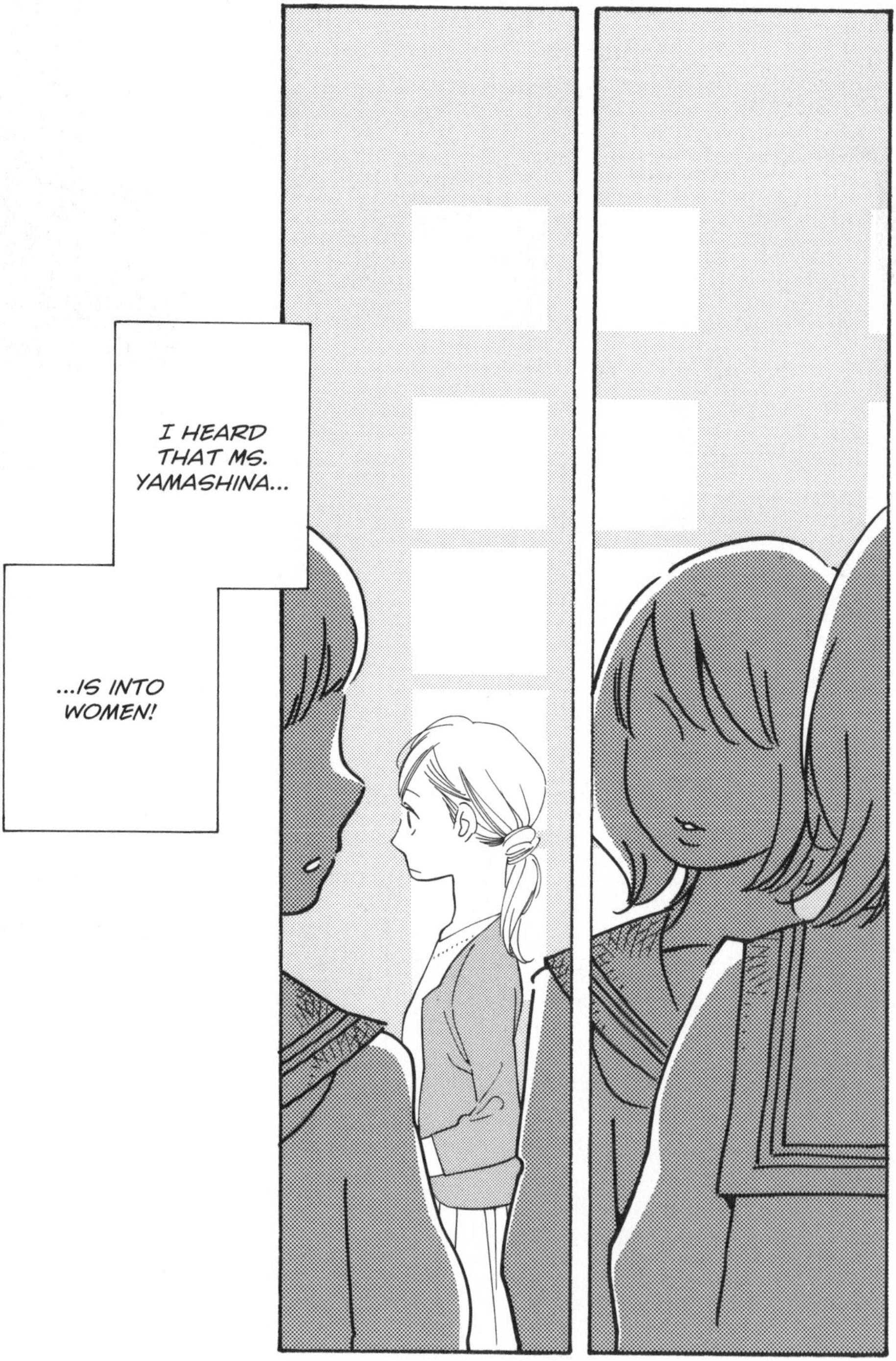
I HEARD THAT MS. YAMASHINA...
...IS INTO WOMEN!

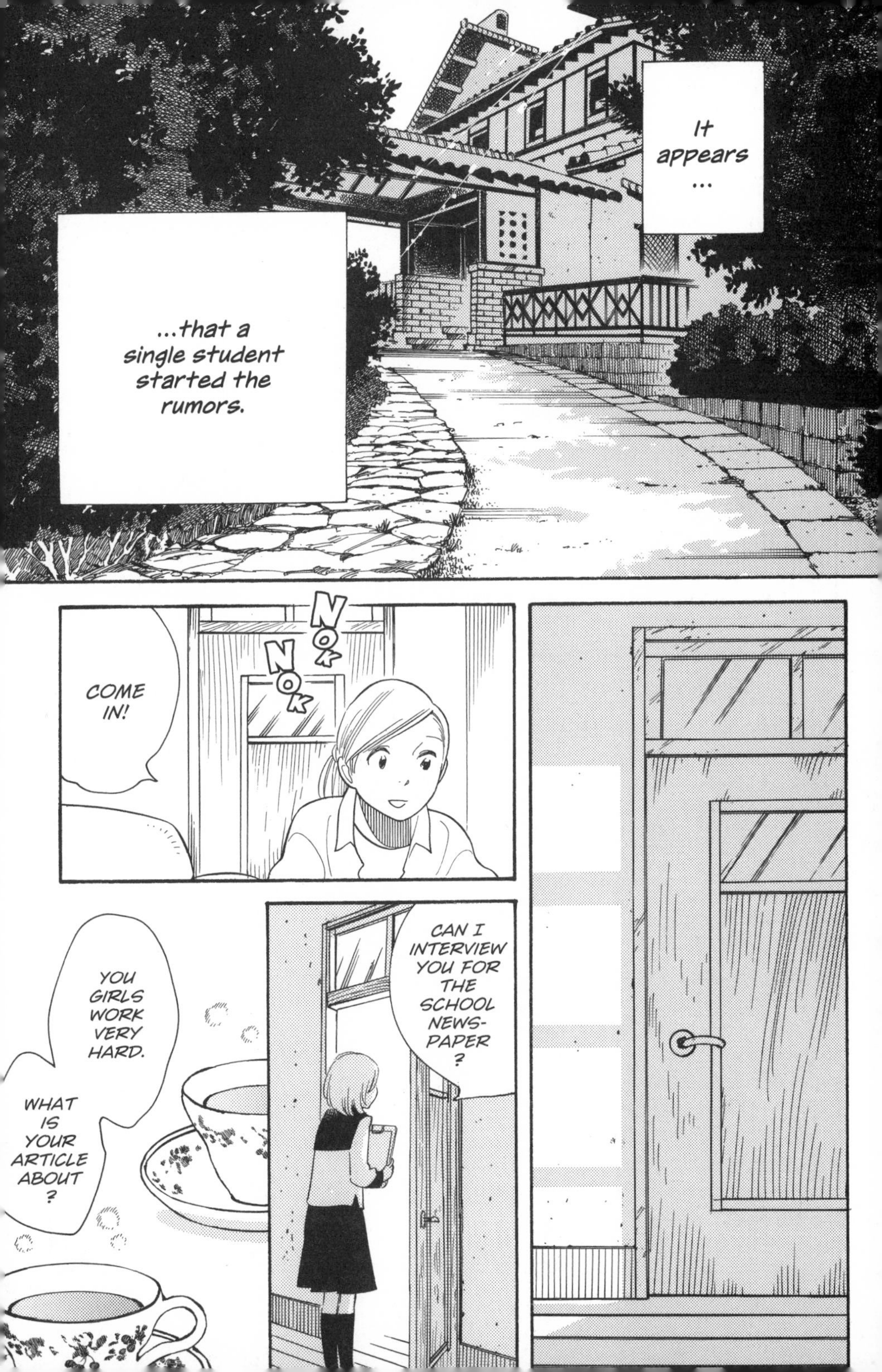
It appears ...
...that a single student started the rumors.
NOK NOK
COME IN!
CAN I INTERVIEW YOU FOR THE SCHOOL NEWS-PAPER?
YOU GIRLS WORK VERY HARD.
WHAT IS YOUR ARTICLE ABOUT?

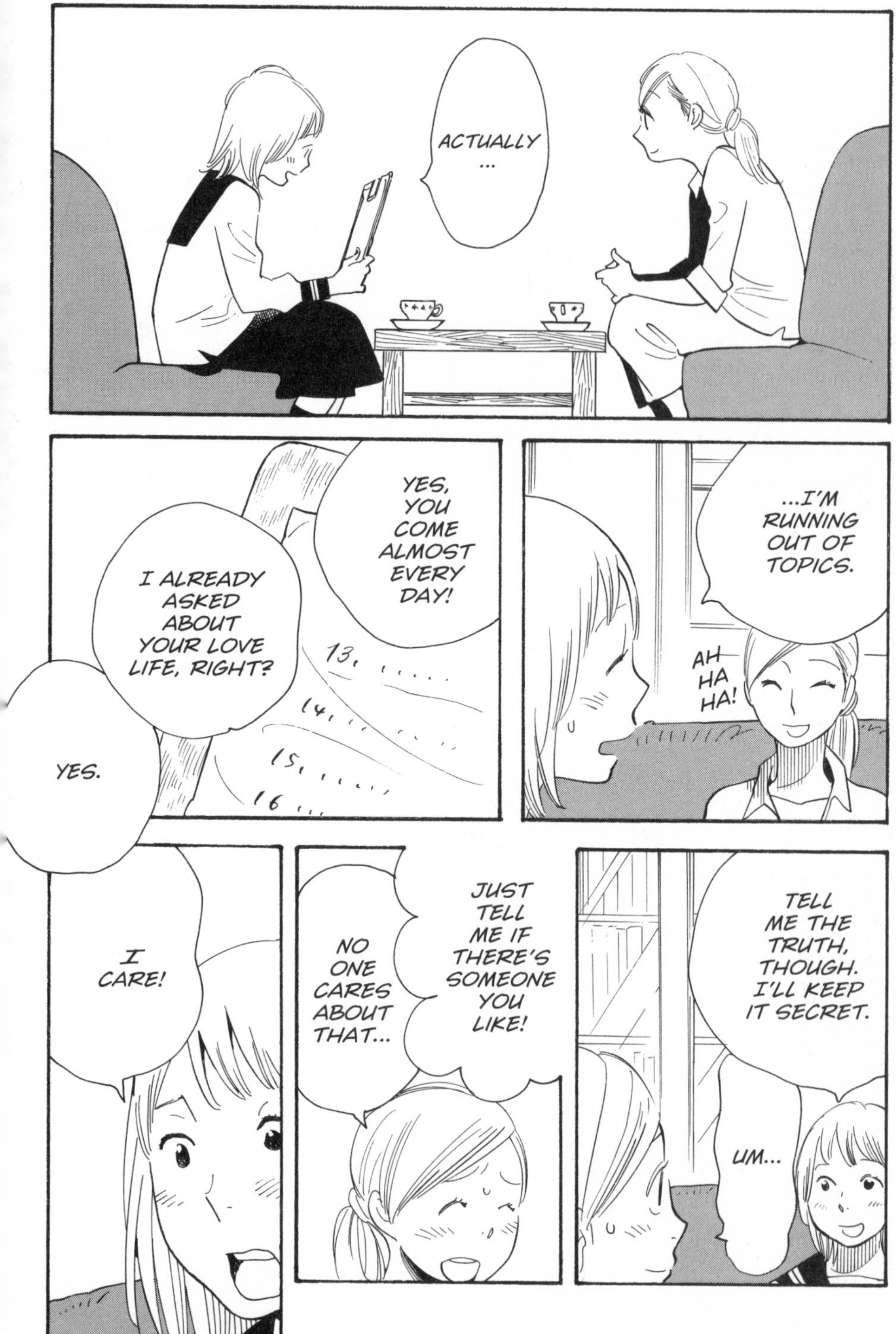
ACTUALLY ...
...I'M RUNNING OUT OF TOPICS.
AH HA HA!
YES, YOU COME ALMOST EVERY DAY!
I ALREADY ASKED ABOUT YOUR LOVE LIFE, RIGHT?
YES.
TELL ME THE TRUTH, THOUGH. I'LL KEEP IT SECRET.
UM...
JUST TELL ME IF THERE'S SOMEONE YOU LIKE!
NO ONE CARES ABOUT THAT...
I CARE!

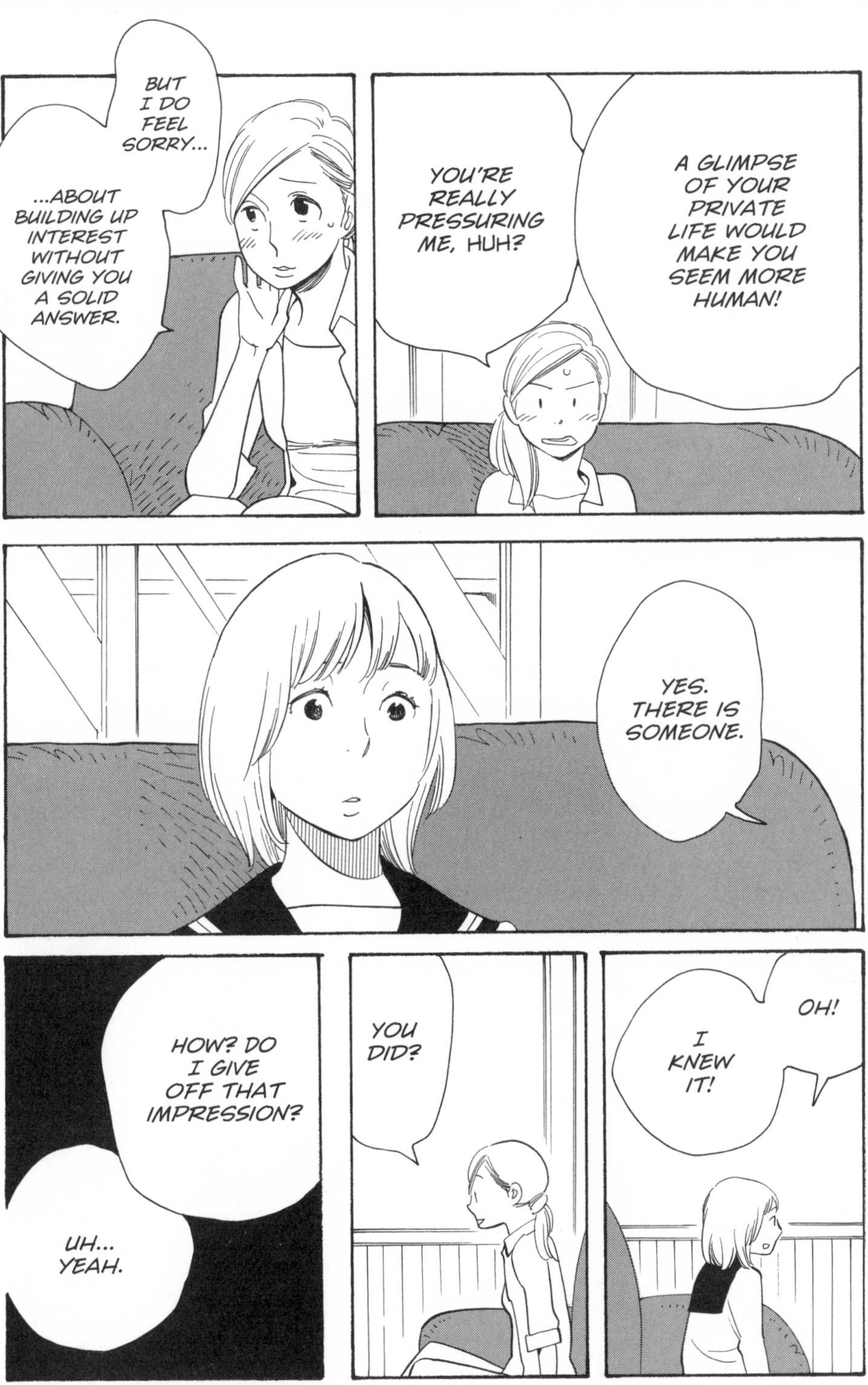
A GLIMPSE OF YOUR PRIVATE LIFE WOULD MAKE YOU SEEM MORE HUMAN!
YOU'RE REALLY PRESSURING ME, HUH?
BUT I DO FEEL SORRY...
...ABOUT BUILDING UP INTEREST WITHOUT GIVING YOU A SOLID ANSWER.
YES. THERE IS SOMEONE.
OH!
I KNEW IT!
YOU DID?
HOW? DO I GIVE OFF THAT IMPRESSION?
UH... YEAH.

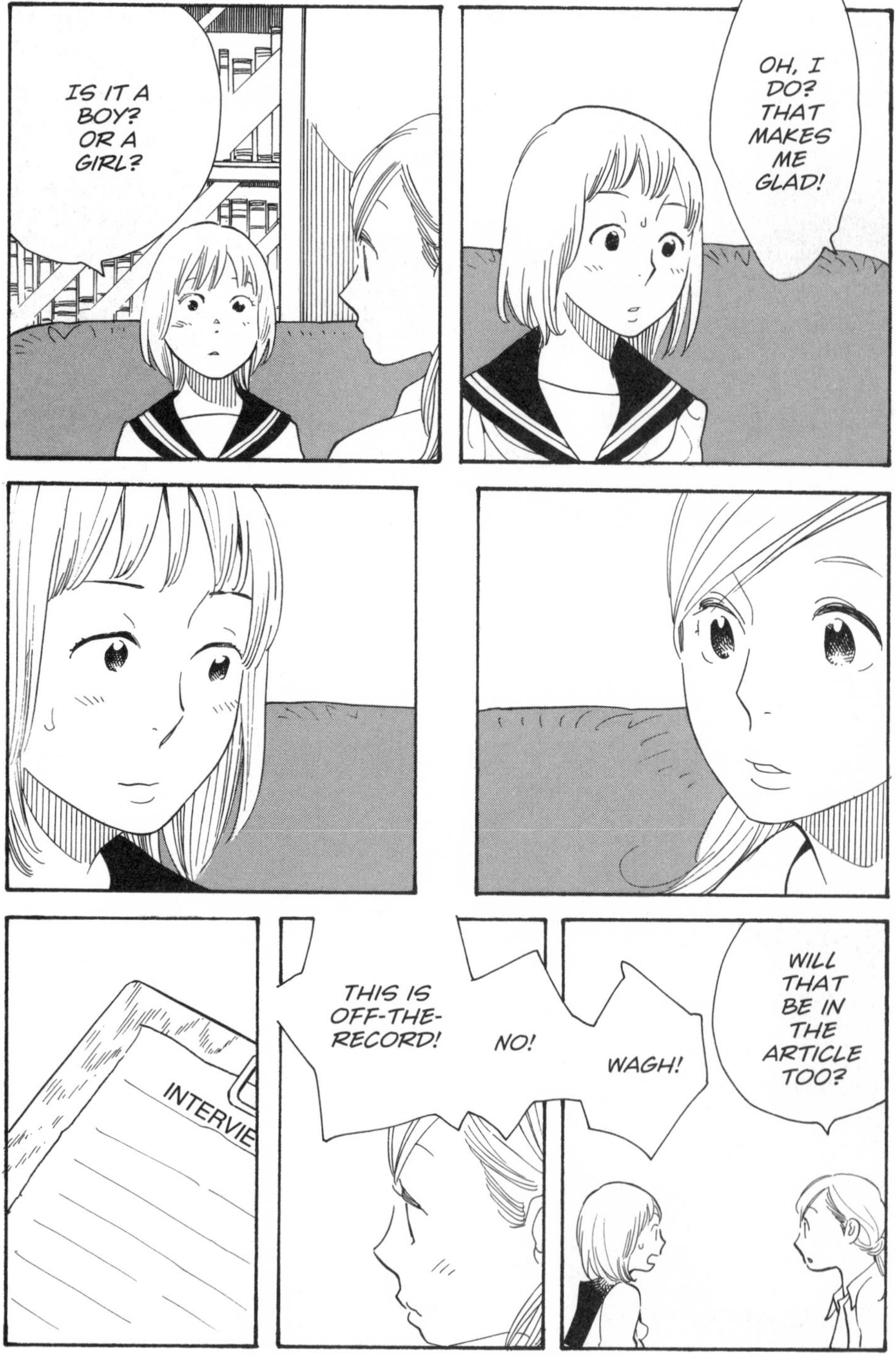
OH, I DO? THAT MAKES ME GLAD!
IS IT A BOY? OR A GIRL?
WILL THAT BE IN THE ARTICLE TOO?
WAGH!
NO!
THIS IS OFF-THE-RECORD!
INTERVIE

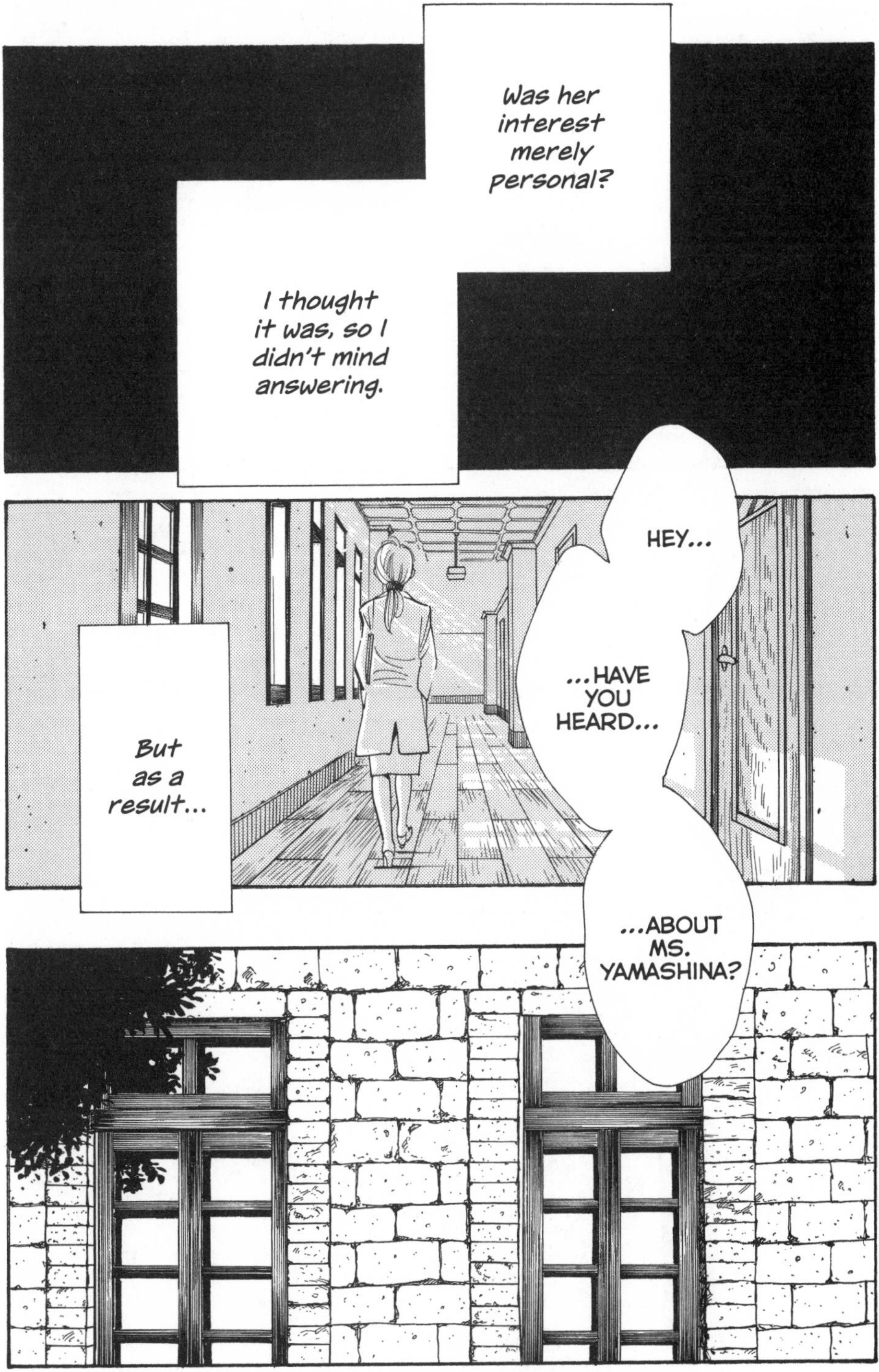
Was her interest merely personal?
I thought it was, so I didn't mind answering.
HEY...
...HAVE YOU HEARD...
...ABOUT MS. YAMASHINA?
But as a result...

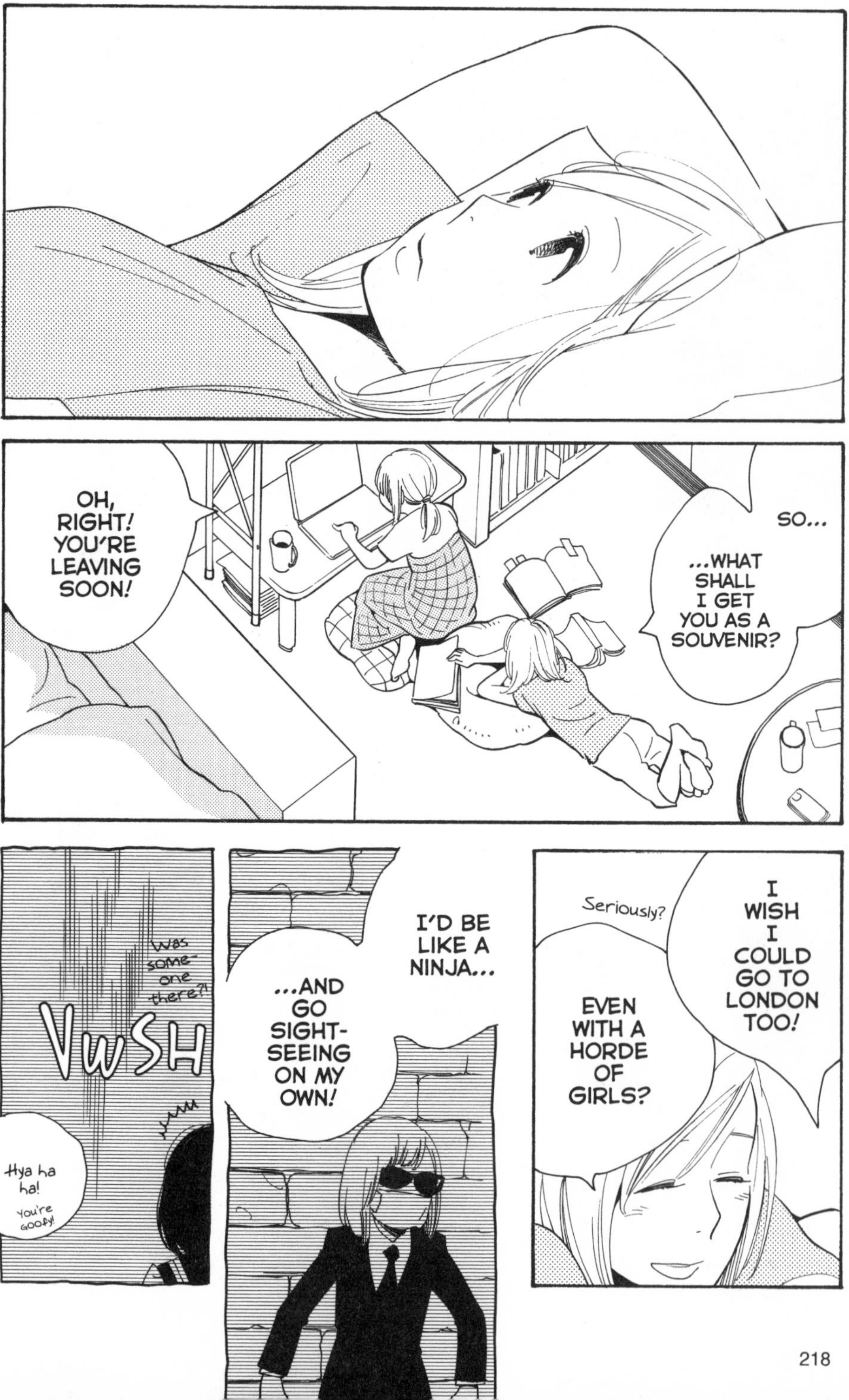
SO...
...WHAT SHALL I GET YOU AS A SOUVENIR?
OH, RIGHT! YOU'RE LEAVING SOON!
I WISH I COULD GO TO LONDON TOO!
Seriously?
EVEN WITH A HORDE OF GIRLS?
I'D BE LIKE A NINJA...
...AND GO SIGHT-SEEING ON MY OWN!
Was someone there?!
VWSH
Hya ha ha!
You're goofy!

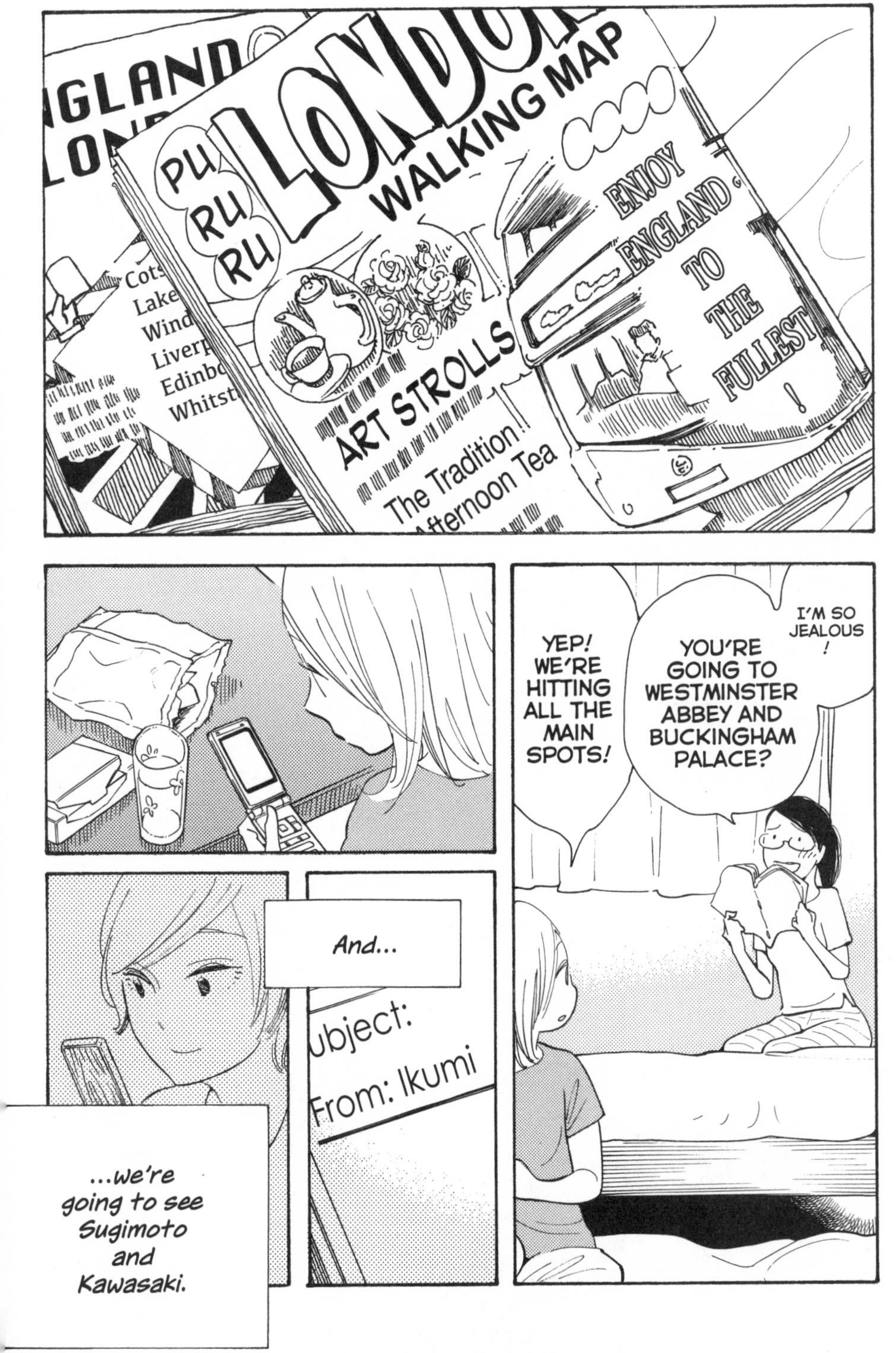

ENJOY ENGLAND TO THE FULLEST!
PU RU RU
LONDON
WALKING MAP
ART STROLLS
The Tradition!
Afternoon Tea
I'M SO JEALOUS!
YOU'RE GOING TO WESTMINSTER ABBEY AND BUCKINGHAM PALACE?
YEP! WE'RE HITTING ALL THE MAIN SPOTS!
And...
From: Ikumi
...we're going to see Sugimoto and Kawasaki.

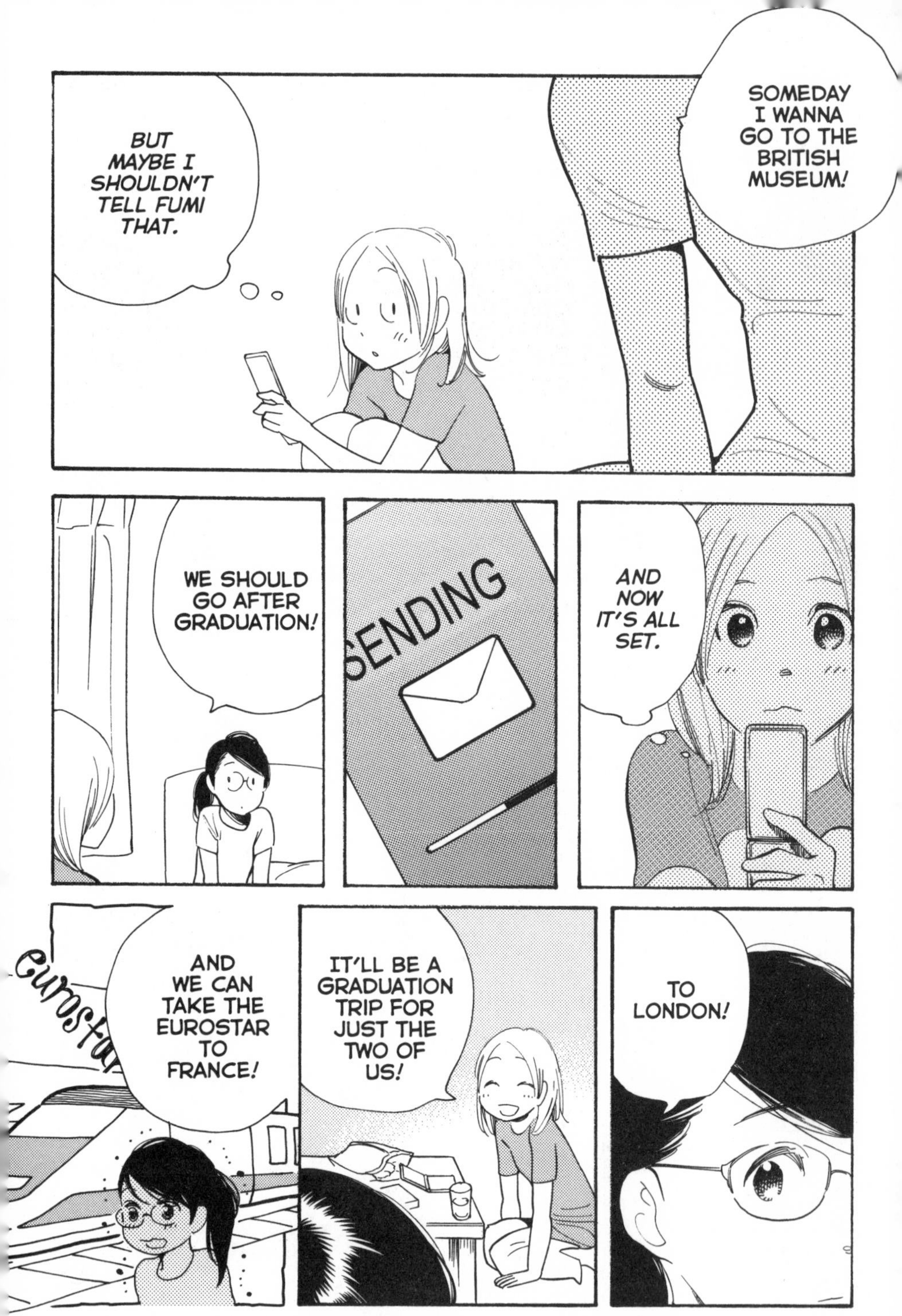
SOMEDAY I WANNA GO TO THE BRITISH MUSEUM!
BUT MAYBE I SHOULDN'T TELL FUMI THAT.
AND NOW IT'S ALL SET.
SENDING
WE SHOULD GO AFTER GRADUATION!
TO LONDON!
IT'LL BE A GRADUATION TRIP FOR JUST THE TWO OF US!
AND WE CAN TAKE THE EUROSTAR TO FRANCE!
eurostar

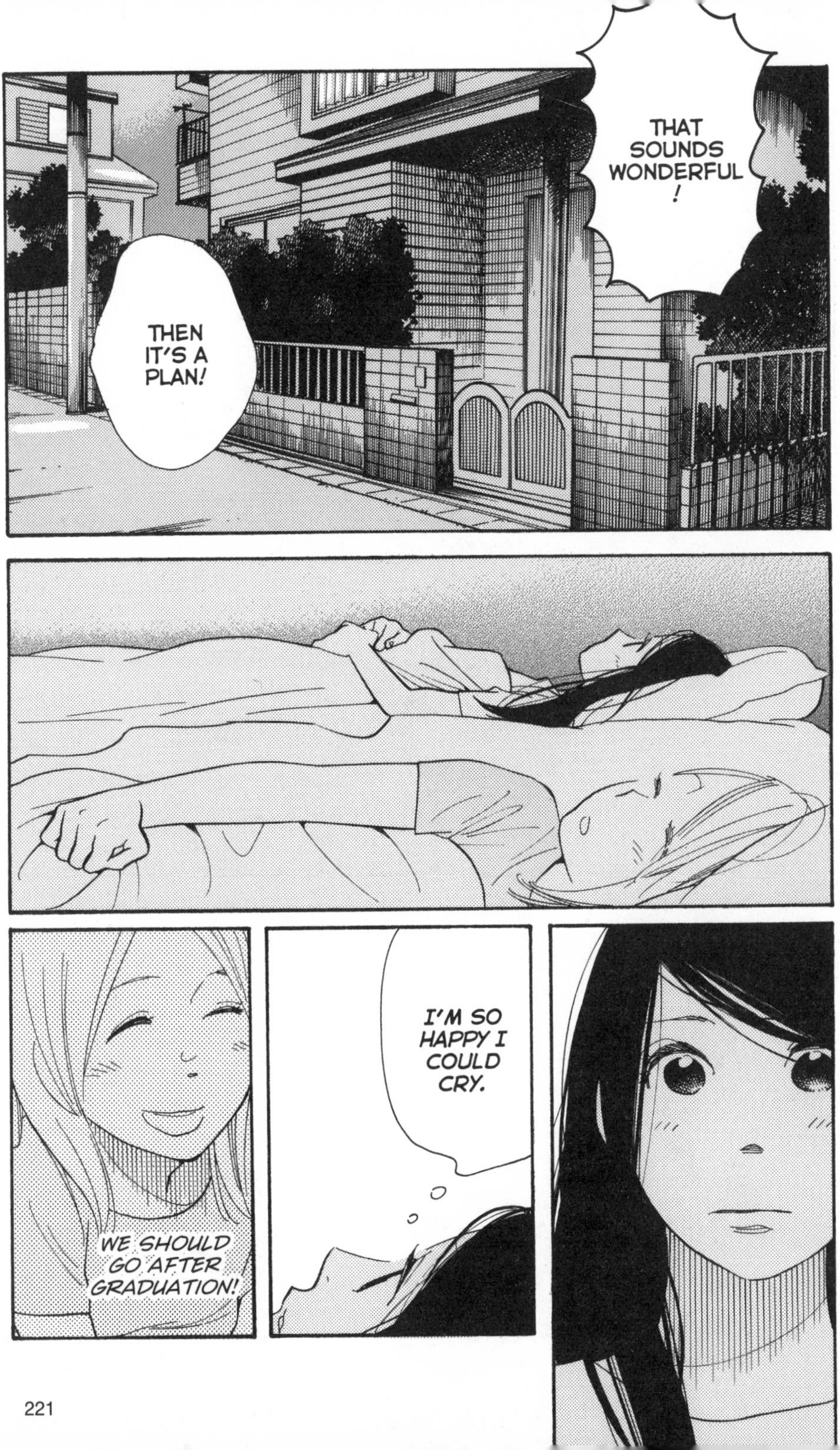
THAT SOUNDS WONDERFUL!
THEN IT'S A PLAN!
I'M SO HAPPY I COULD CRY.
WE SHOULD GO AFTER GRADUATION!

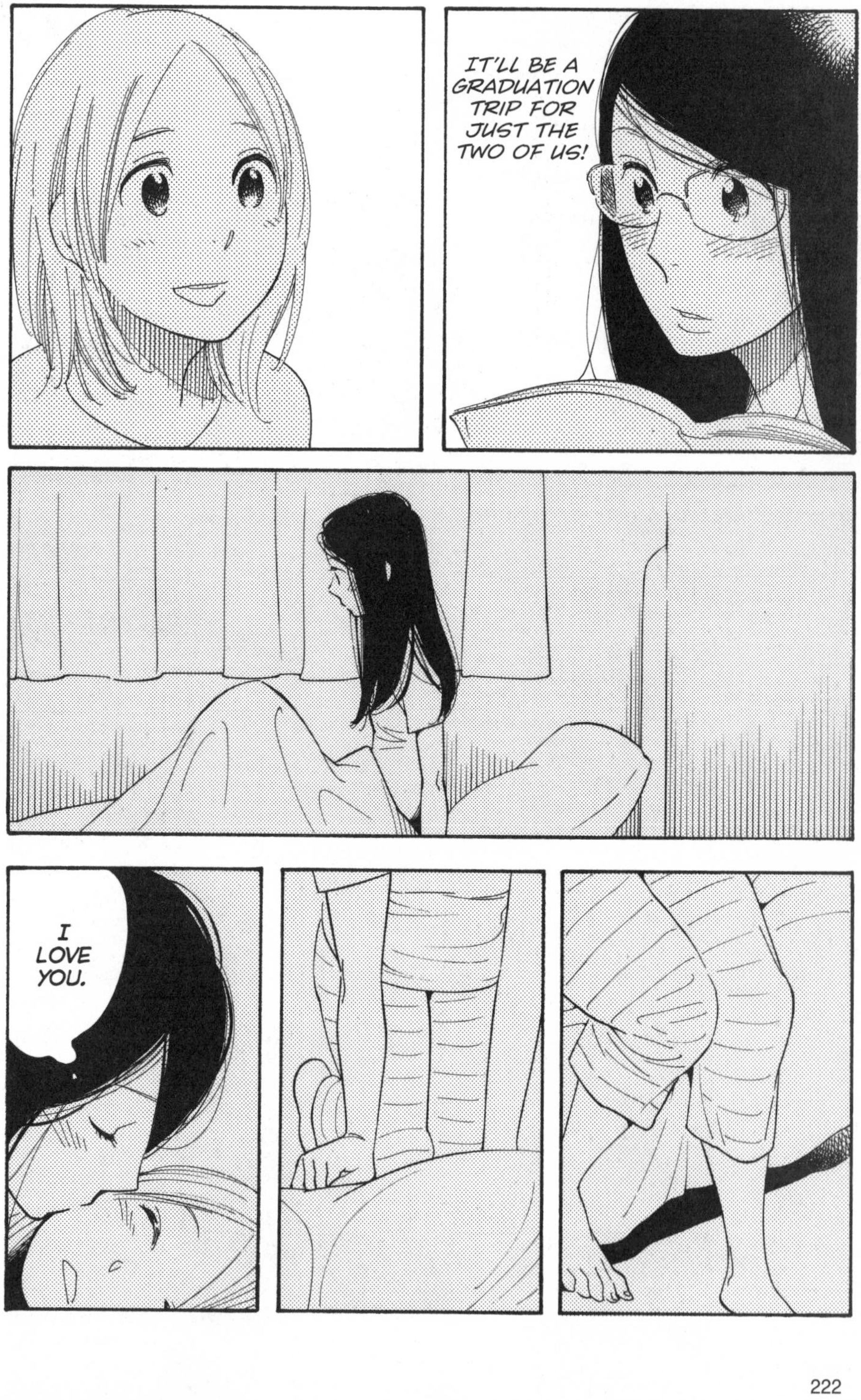
IT'LL BE A GRADUATION TRIP FOR JUST THE TWO OF US!
I LOVE YOU.

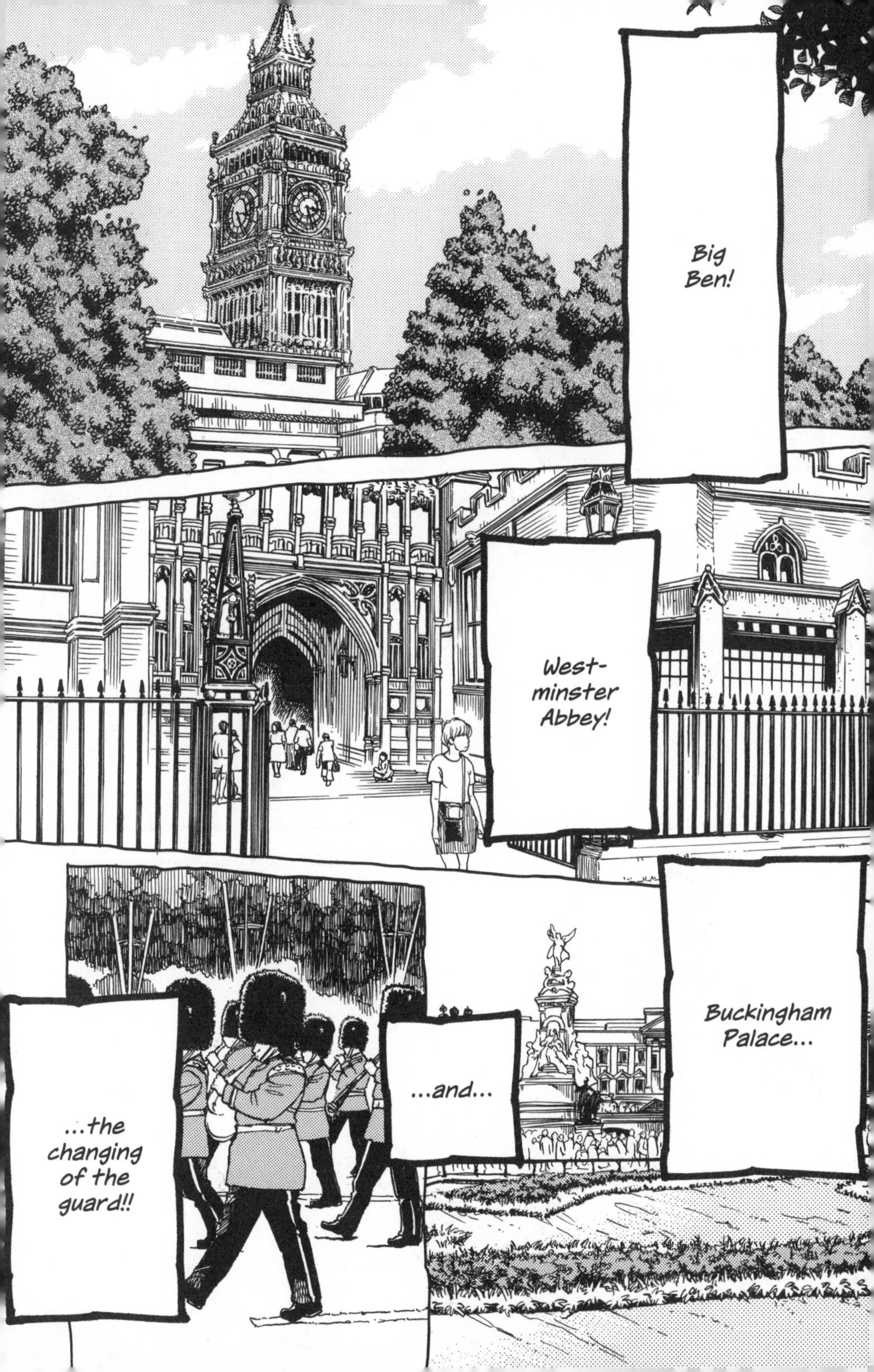
Big Ben!
West-minster Abbey!
Buckingham Palace...
...and...
...the changing of the guard!!

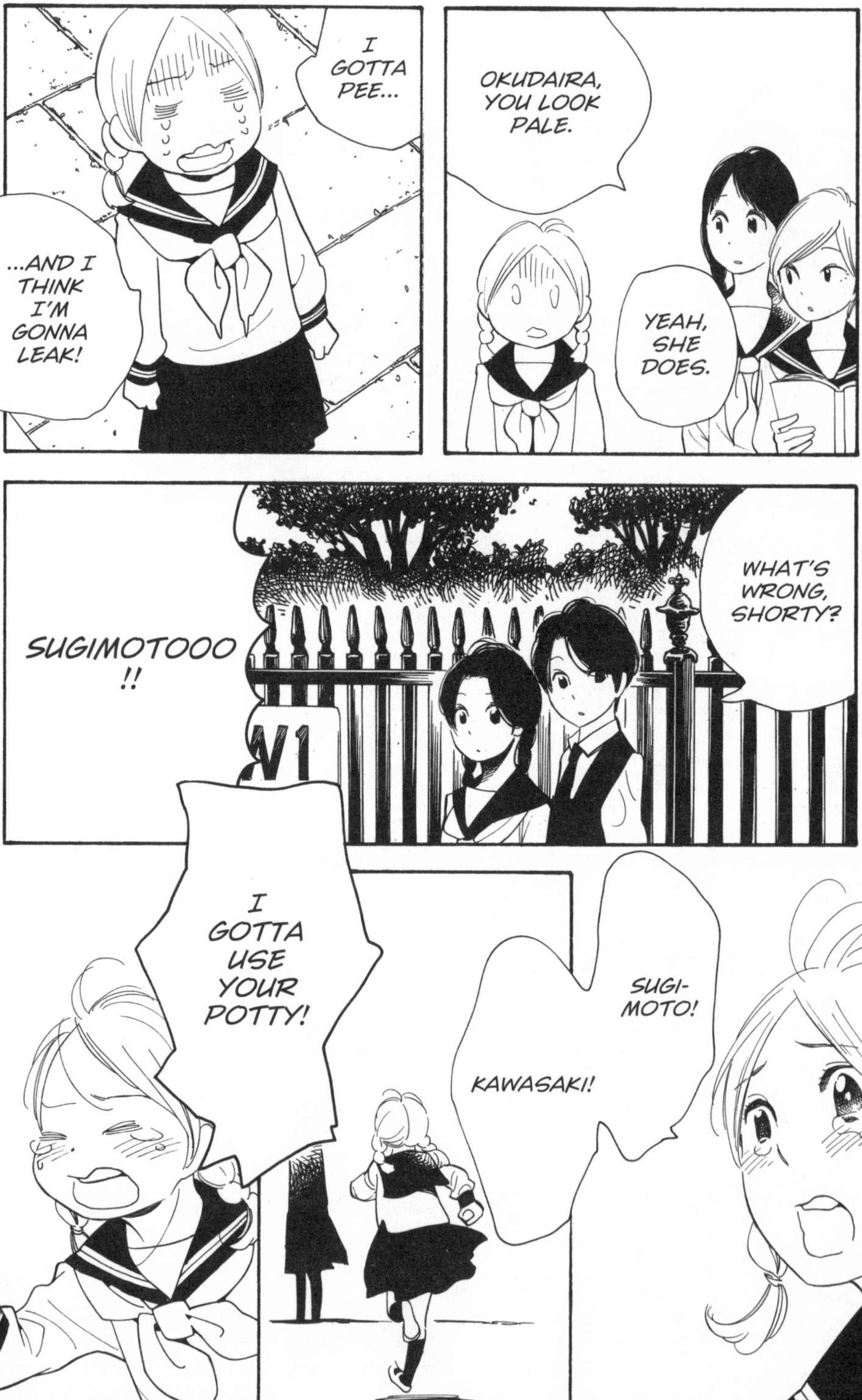
OKUDAIRA, YOU LOOK PALE.
YEAH, SHE DOES.
I GOTTA PEE...
...AND I THINK I'M GONNA LEAK!
WHAT'S WRONG, SHORTY?
SUGIMOTOOO !!
SUGI-MOTO!
KAWASAKI!
I GOTTA USE YOUR POTTY!

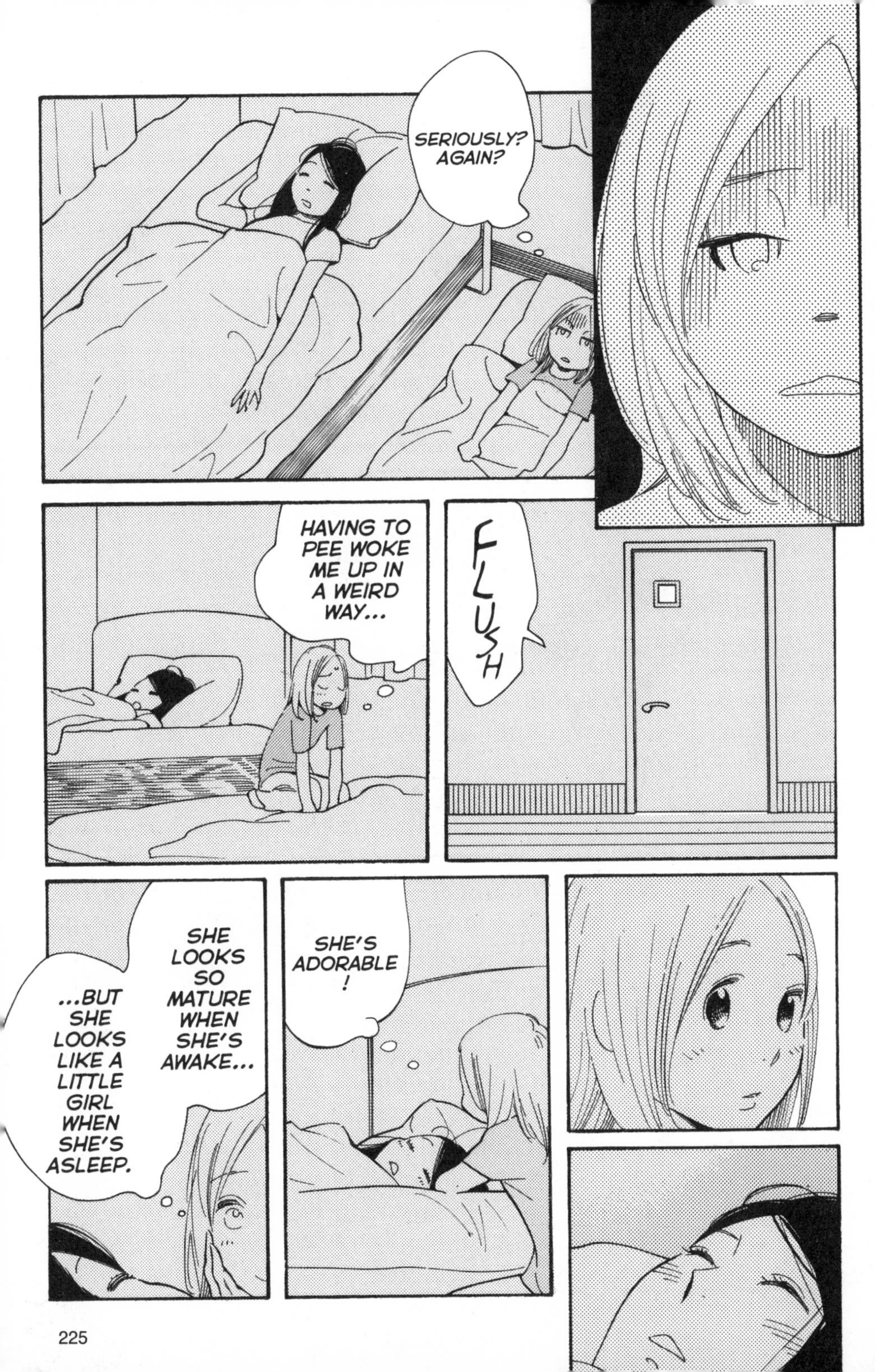
SERIOUSLY? AGAIN?
FLUSH
HAVING TO PEE WOKE ME UP IN A WEIRD WAY...
SHE'S ADORABLE!
SHE LOOKS SO MATURE WHEN SHE'S AWAKE...
...BUT SHE LOOKS LIKE A LITTLE GIRL WHEN SHE'S ASLEEP.

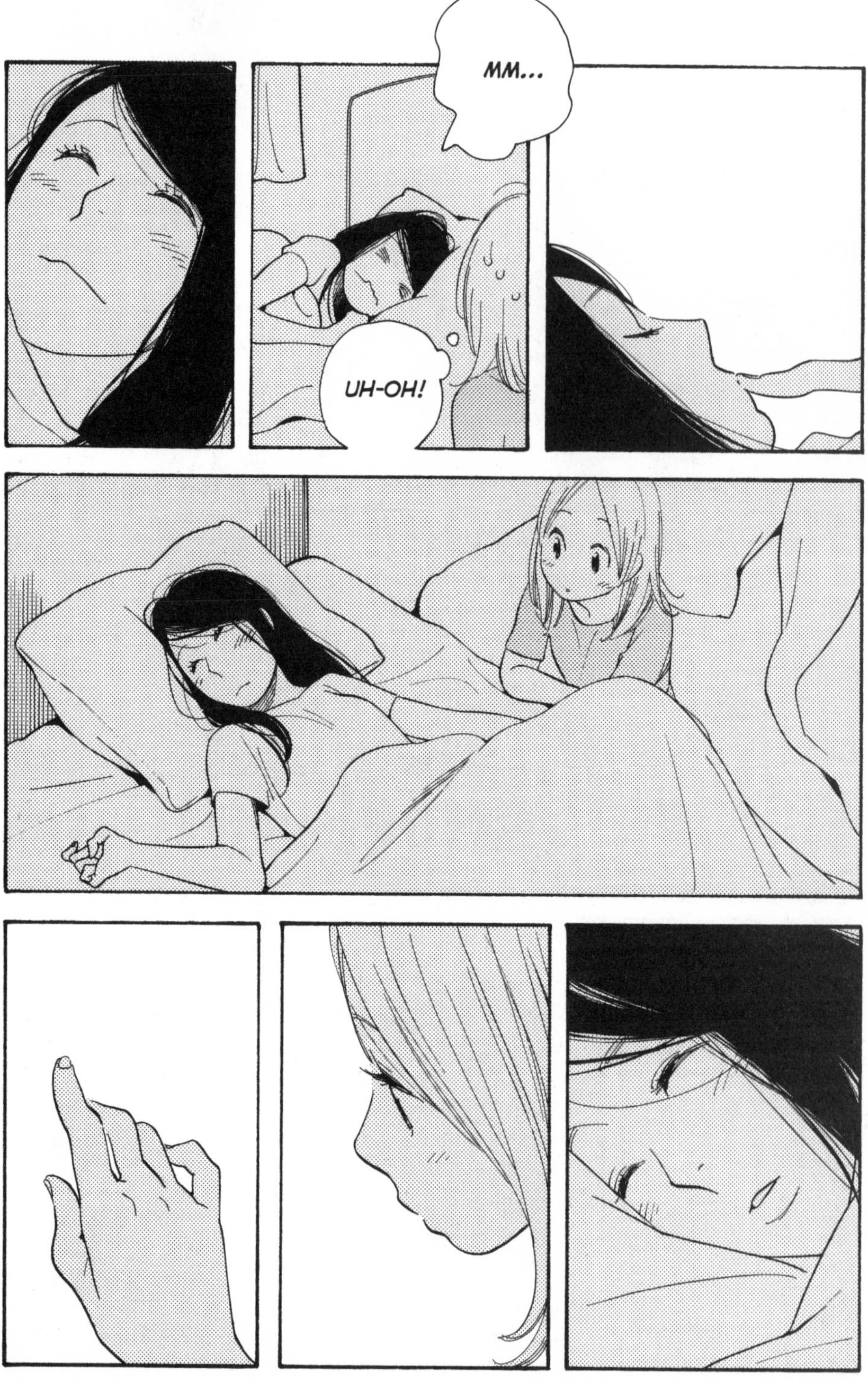
MM...
UH-OH!

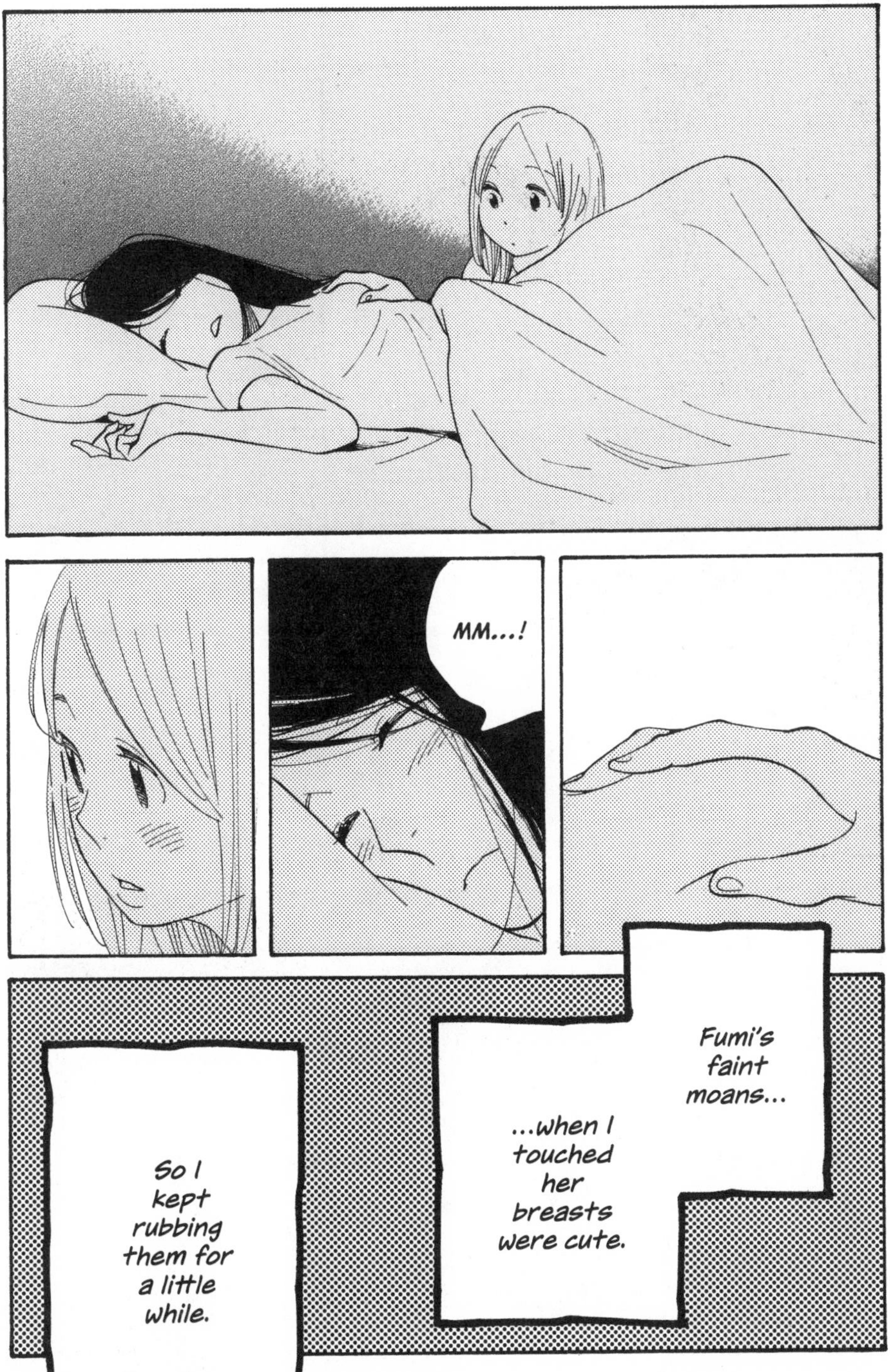
MM...!
Fumi's faint moans...
...when I touched her breasts were cute.
So I kept rubbing them for a little while.

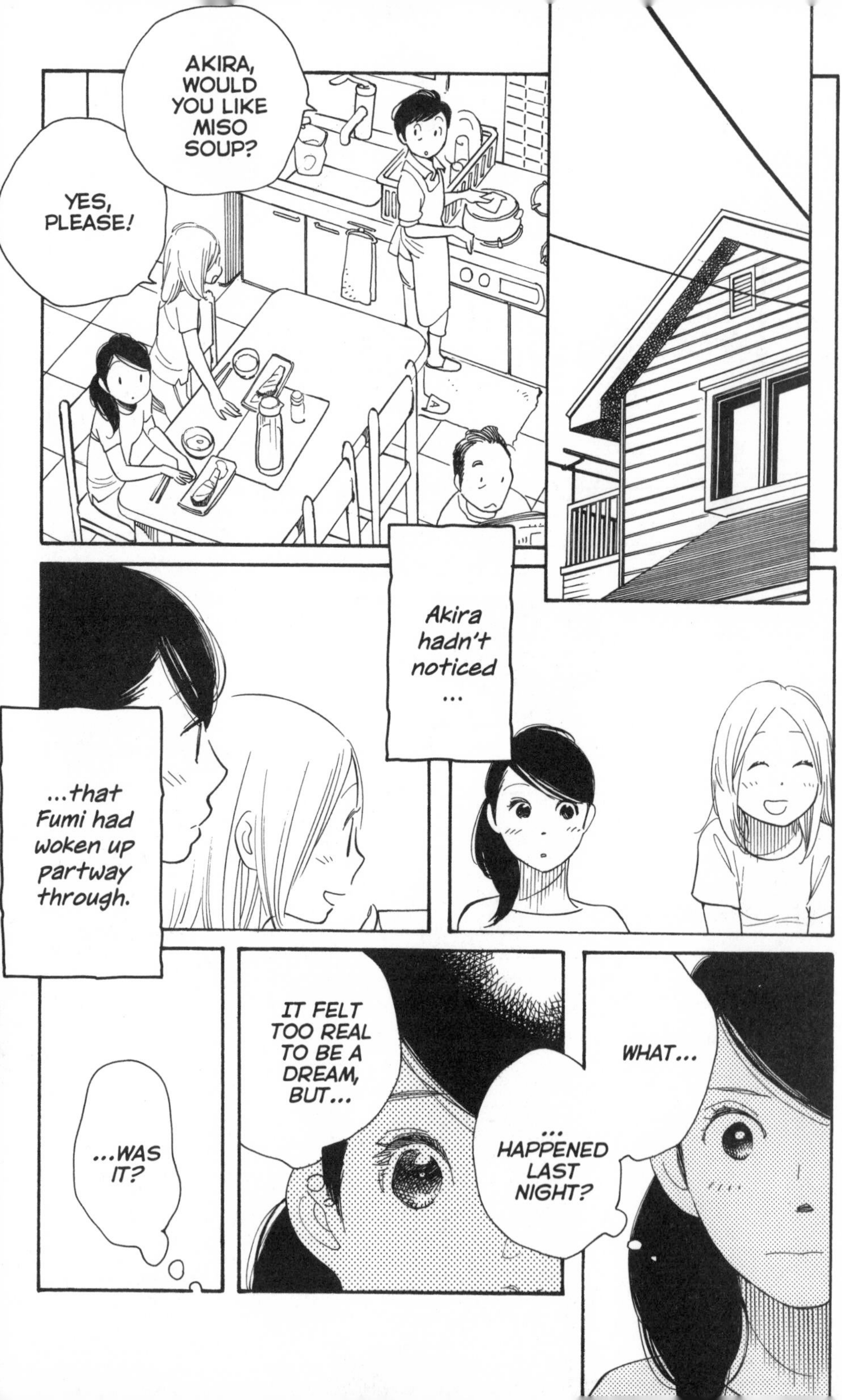
AKIRA, WOULD YOU LIKE MISO SOUP?
YES, PLEASE!
Akira hadn't noticed...
...that Fumi had woken up partway through.
WHAT...
...HAPPENED LAST NIGHT?
IT FELT TOO REAL TO BE A DREAM, BUT...
...WAS IT?

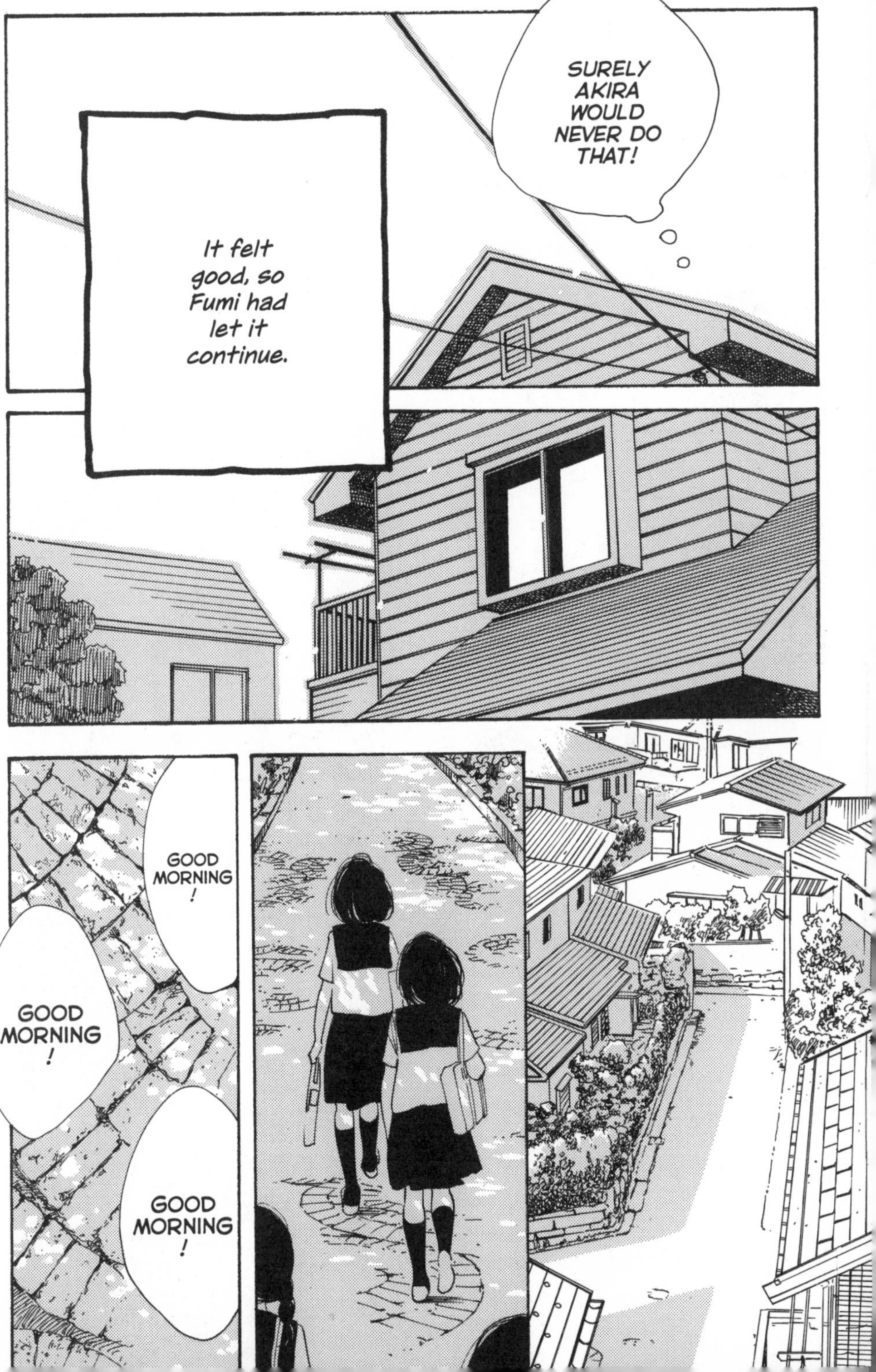
SURELY AKIRA WOULD NEVER DO THAT!
It felt good, so Fumi had let it continue.
GOOD MORNING!
GOOD MORNING!
GOOD MORNING!

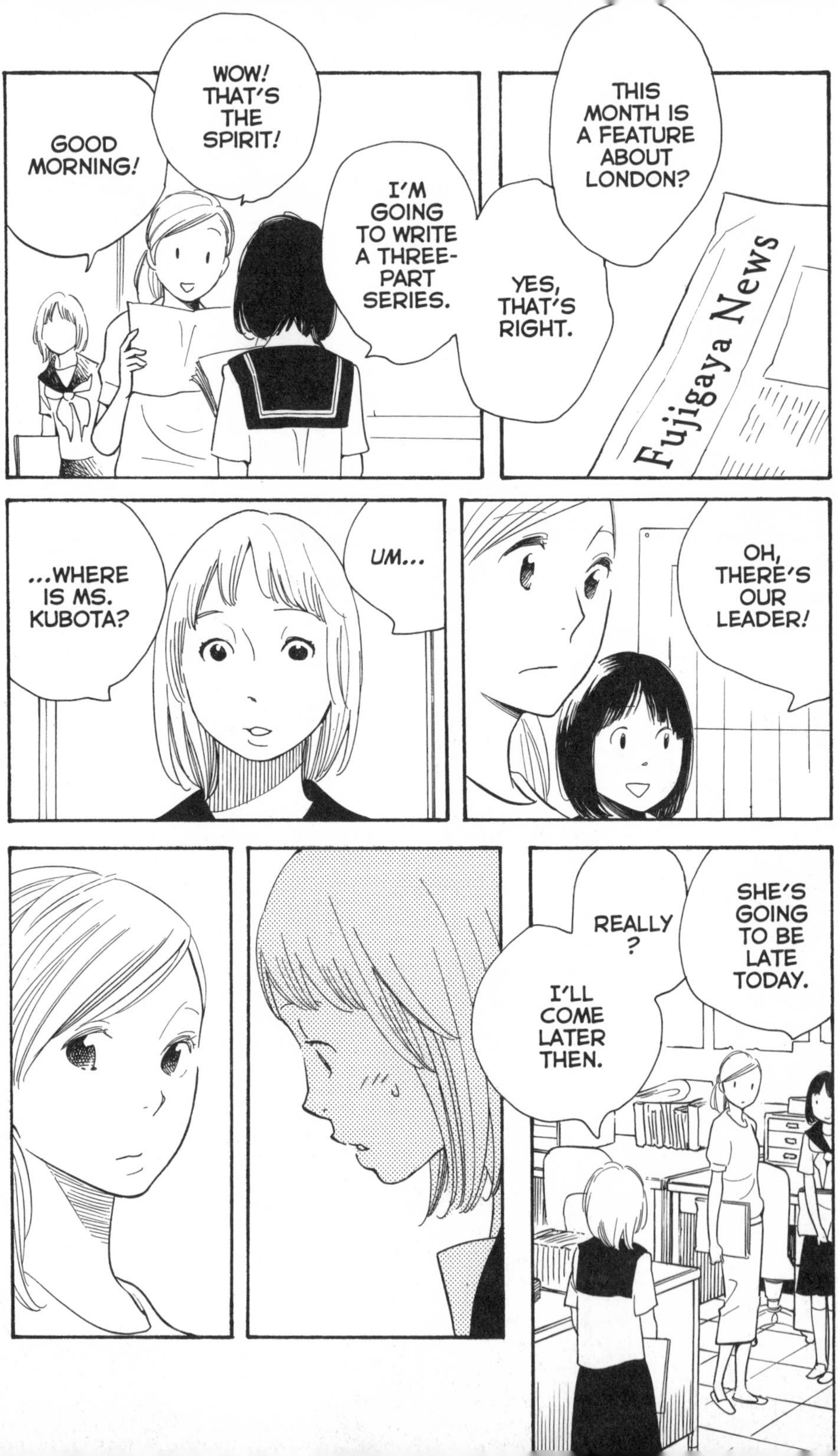
THIS MONTH IS A FEATURE ABOUT LONDON?
YES, THAT'S RIGHT.
Fujigaya News
I'M GOING TO WRITE A THREE-PART SERIES.
WOW! THAT'S THE SPIRIT!
GOOD MORNING!
OH, THERE'S OUR LEADER!
UM...
...WHERE IS MS. KUBOTA?
SHE'S GOING TO BE LATE TODAY.
REALLY?
I'LL COME LATER THEN.

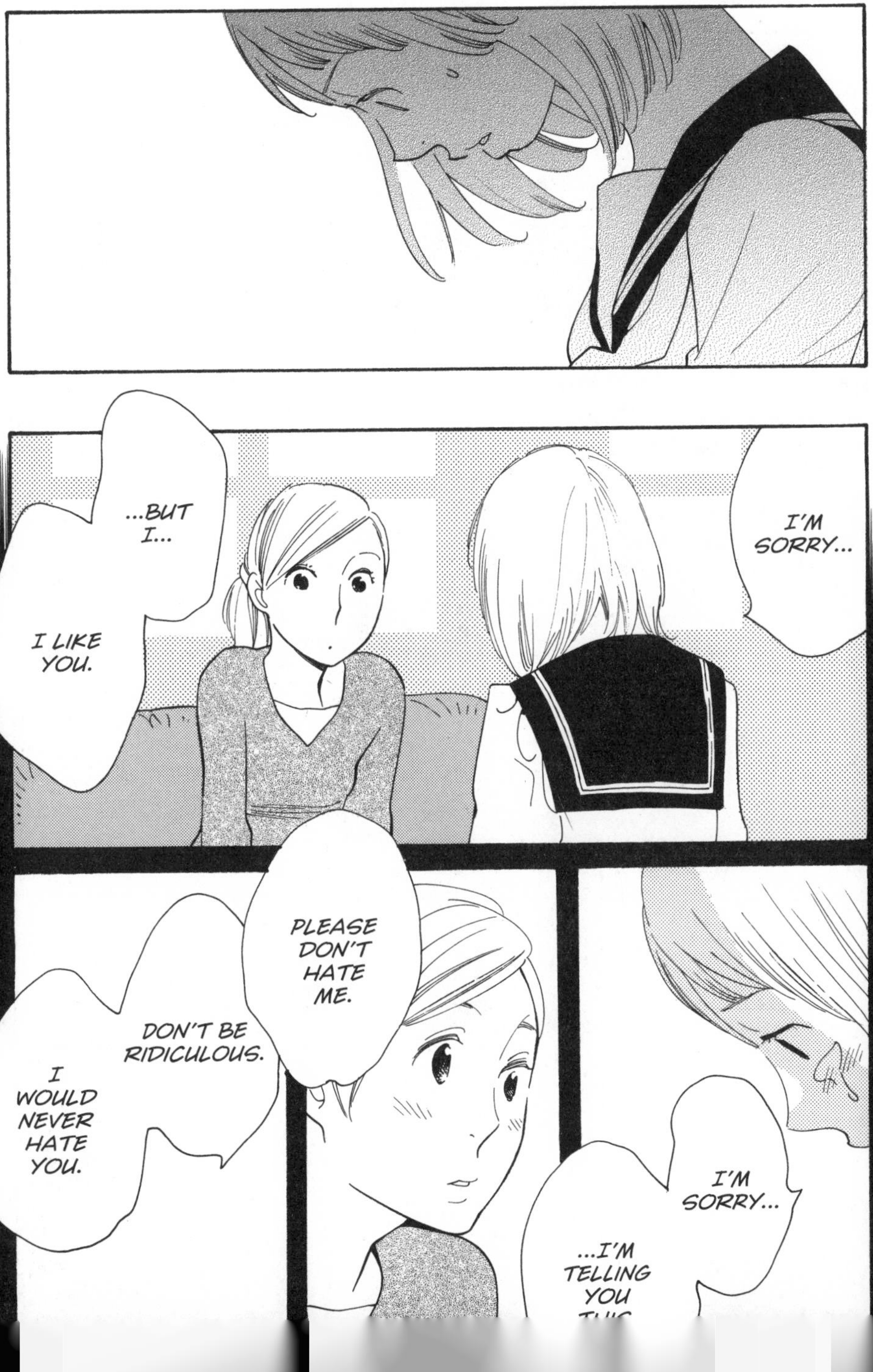
I'M SORRY...
...BUT I...
I LIKE YOU.
I'M SORRY...
...I'M TELLING YOU
PLEASE DON'T HATE ME.
DON'T BE RIDICULOUS.
I WOULD NEVER HATE YOU.

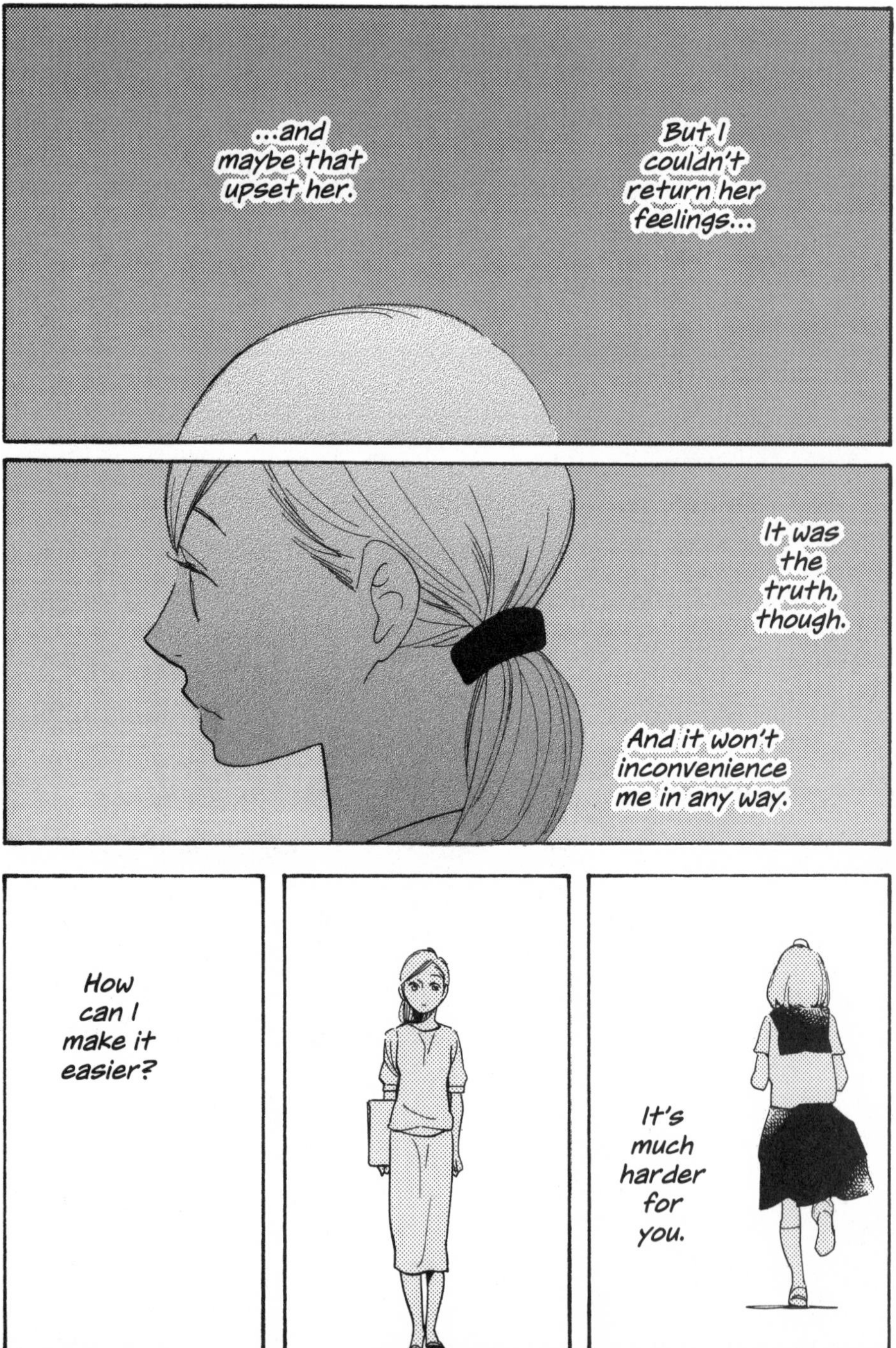
But I couldn't return her feelings...
...and maybe that upset her.
It was the truth, though.
And it won't inconvenience me in any way.
It's much harder for you.
How can I make it easier?

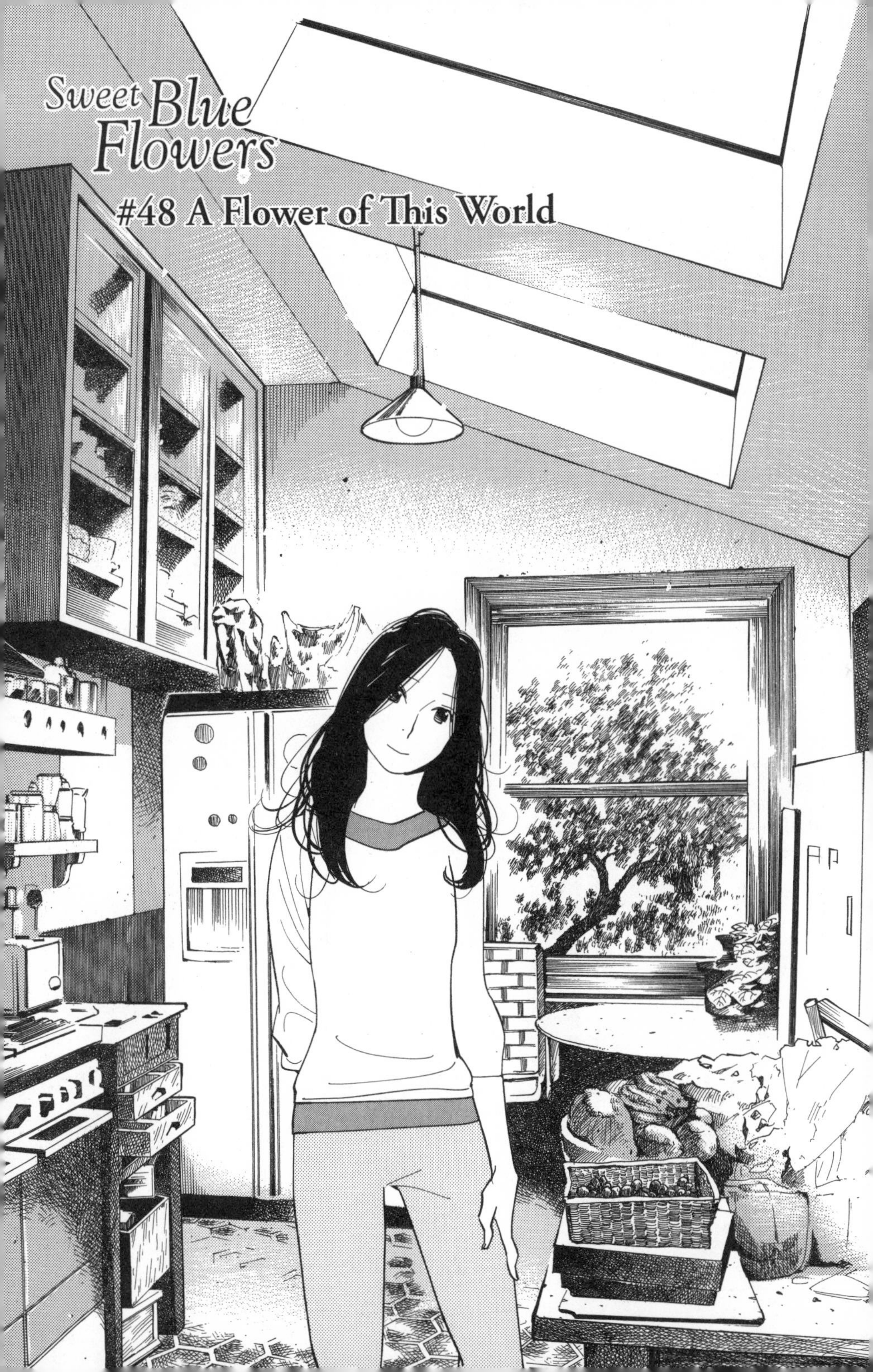
Sweet Blue Flowers
#48 A Flower of This World

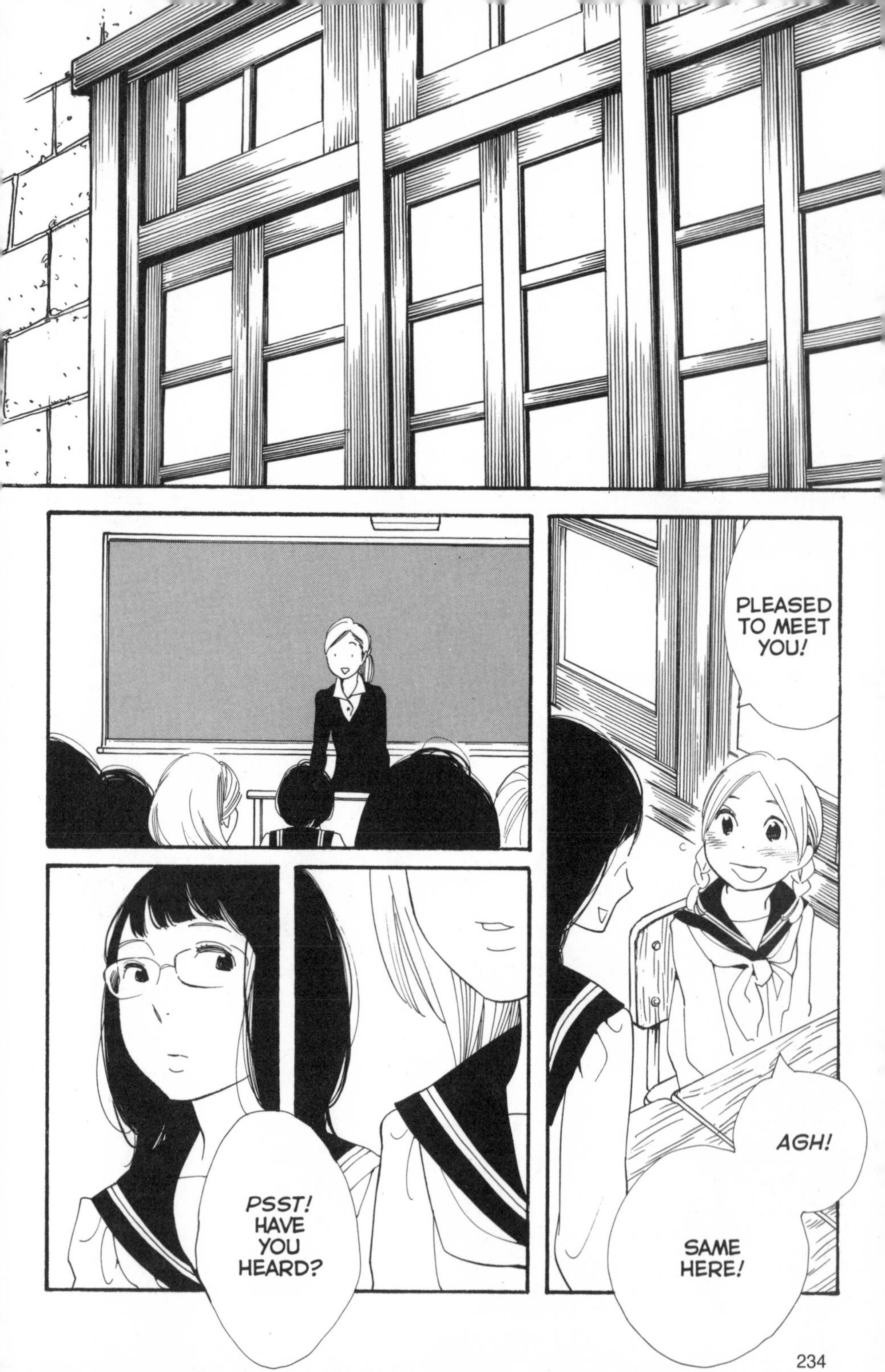
PLEASED TO MEET YOU!
AGH!
SAME HERE!
PSST! HAVE YOU HEARD?

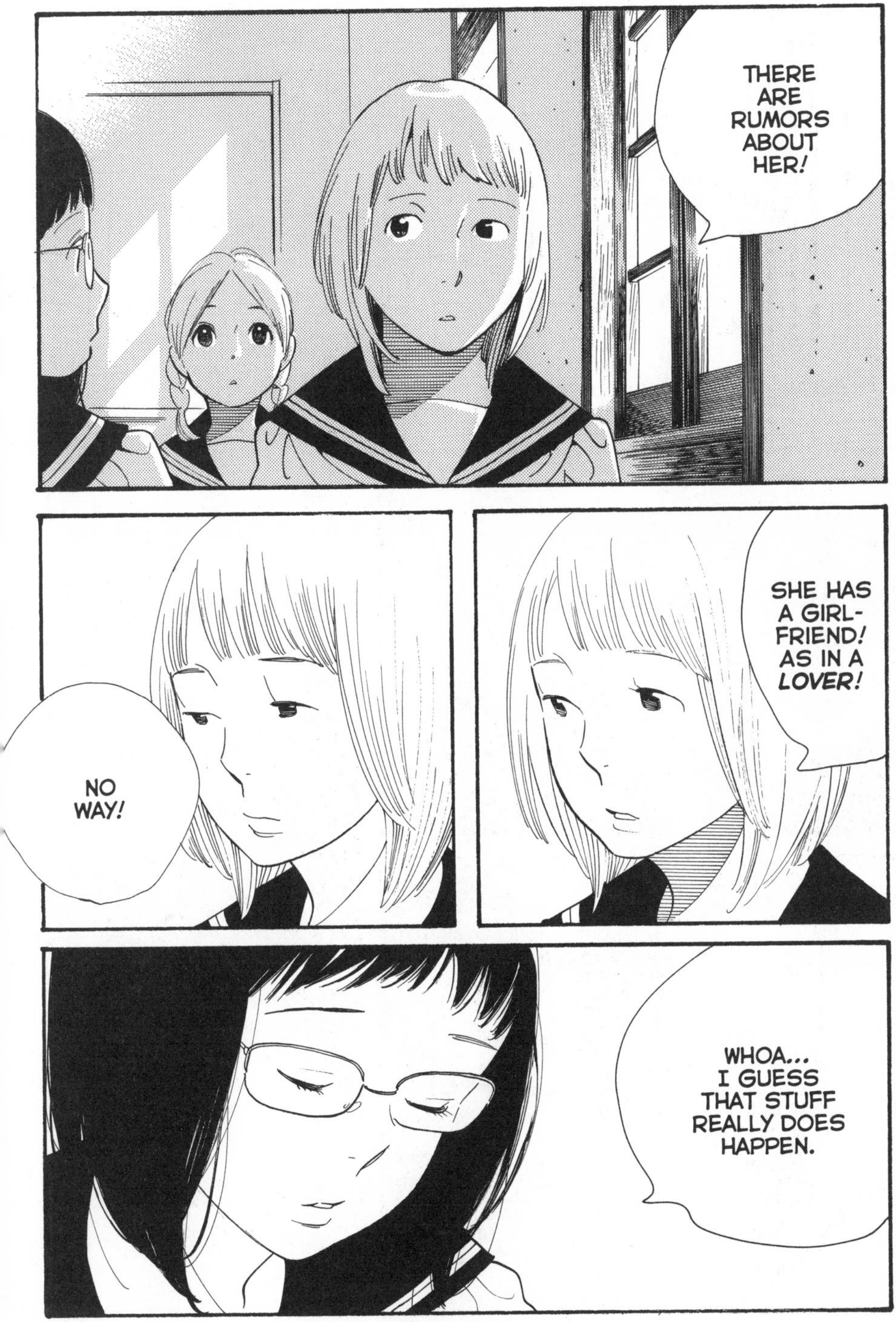
THERE ARE RUMORS ABOUT HER!
SHE HAS A GIRL-FRIEND! AS IN A *LOVER!*
NO WAY!
WHOA... I GUESS THAT STUFF REALLY DOES HAPPEN.

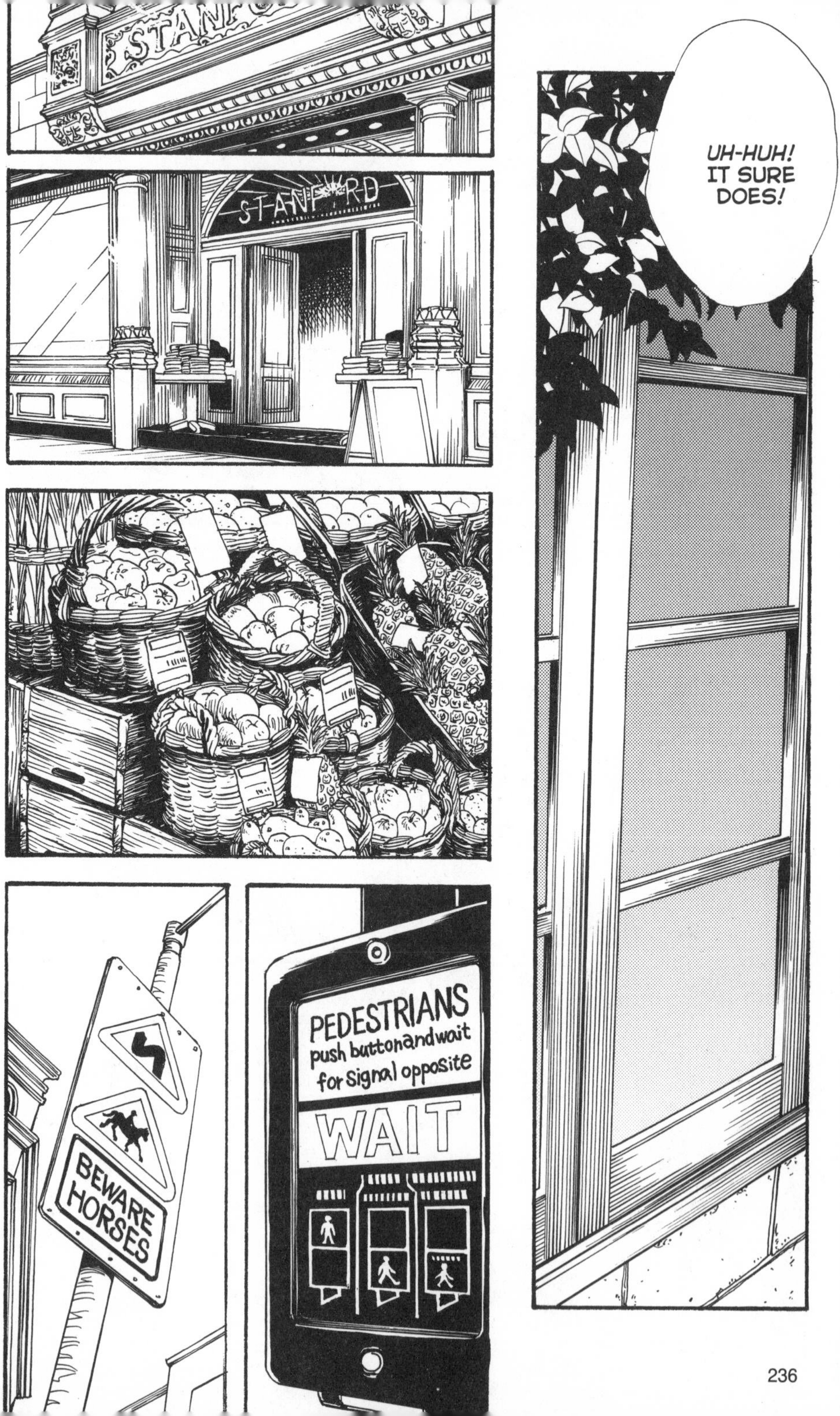
UH-HUH! IT SURE DOES!
PEDESTRIANS push button and wait for signal opposite
WAIT
BEWARE HORSES

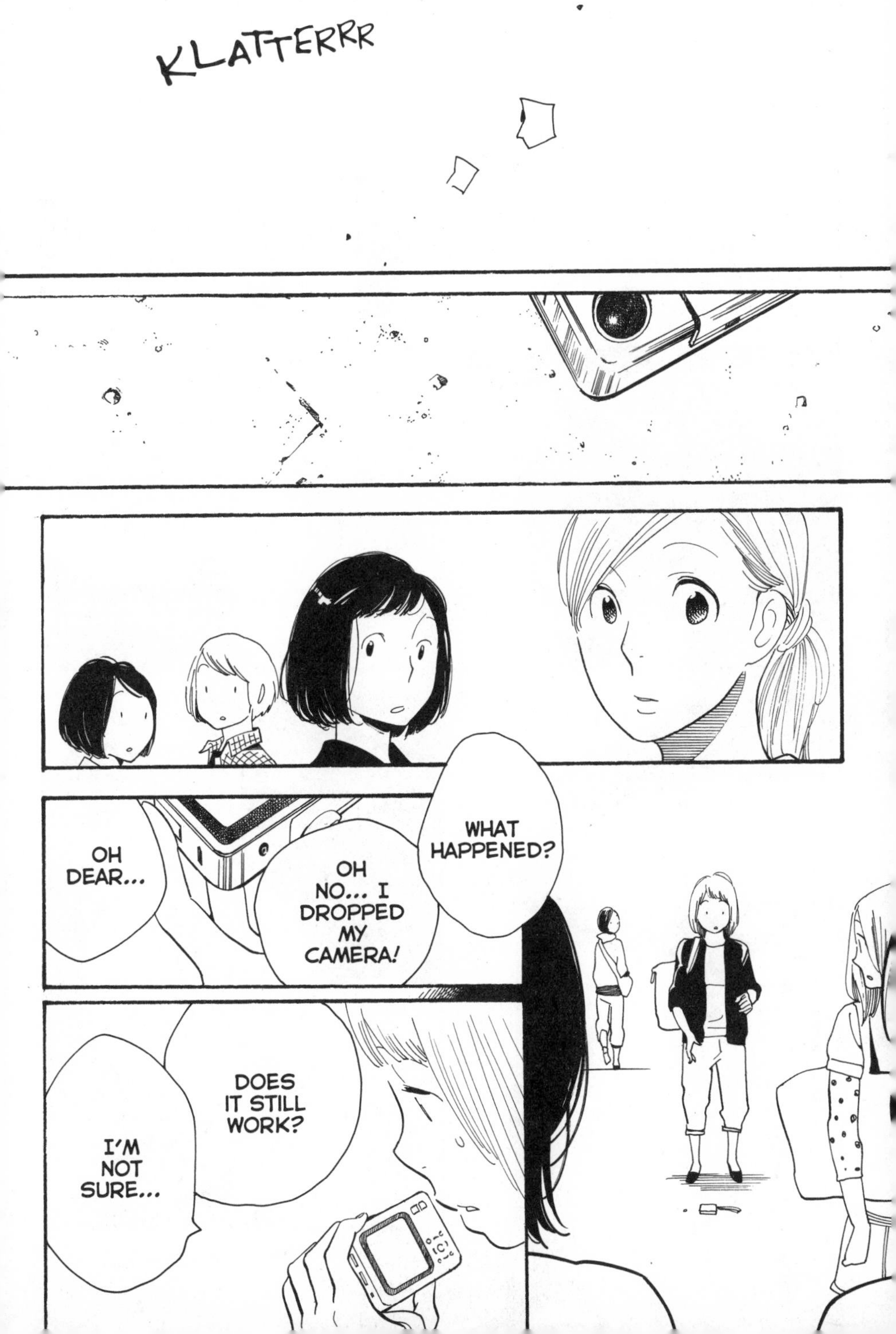
KLATTERRR
WHAT HAPPENED?
OH NO... I DROPPED MY CAMERA!
OH DEAR...
DOES IT STILL WORK?
I'M NOT SURE...

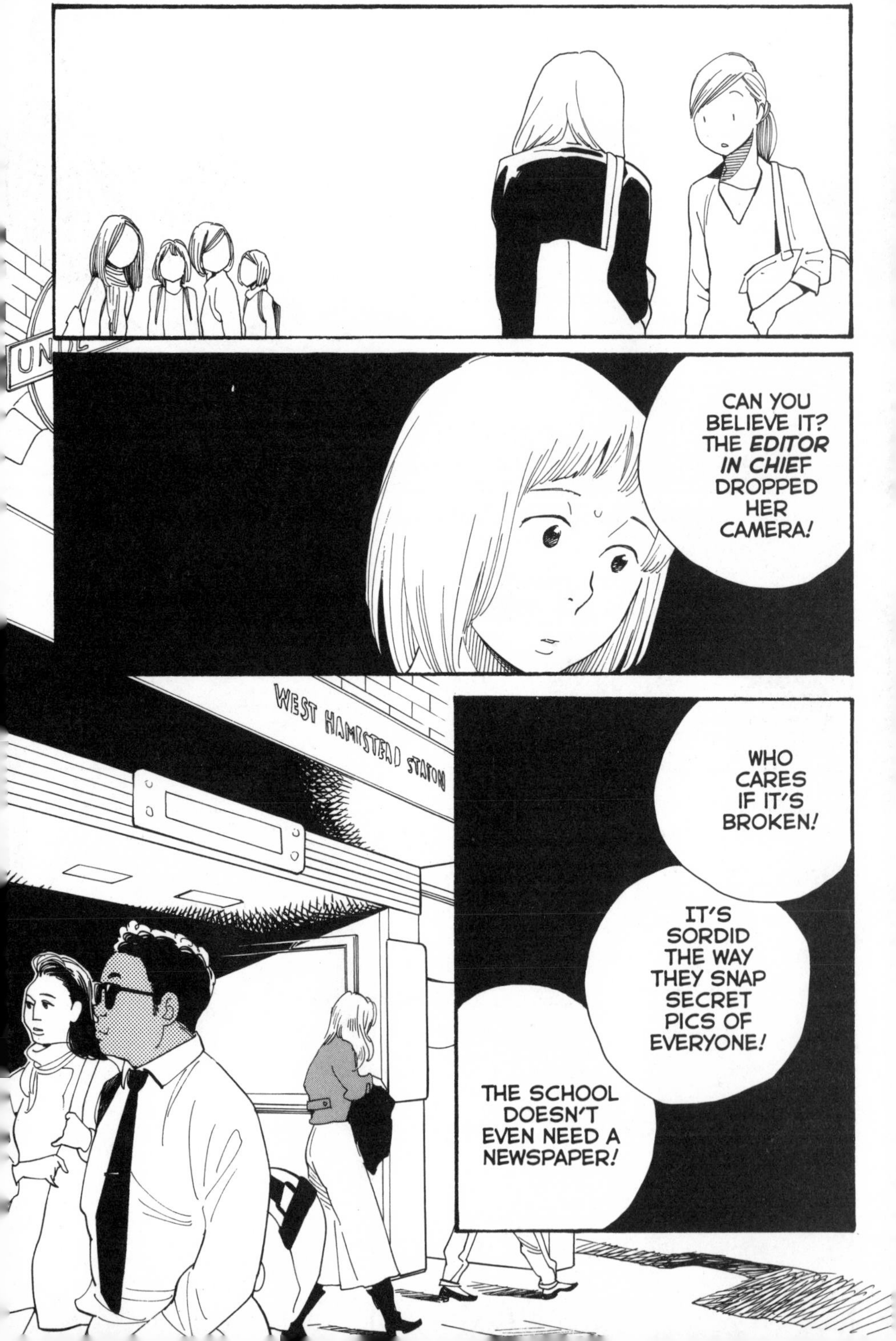
CAN YOU BELIEVE IT? THE *EDITOR IN CHIEF* DROPPED HER CAMERA!
WHO CARES IF IT'S BROKEN!
IT'S SORDID THE WAY THEY SNAP SECRET PICS OF EVERYONE!
THE SCHOOL DOESN'T EVEN NEED A NEWSPAPER!
WEST HAMPSTEAD STATION

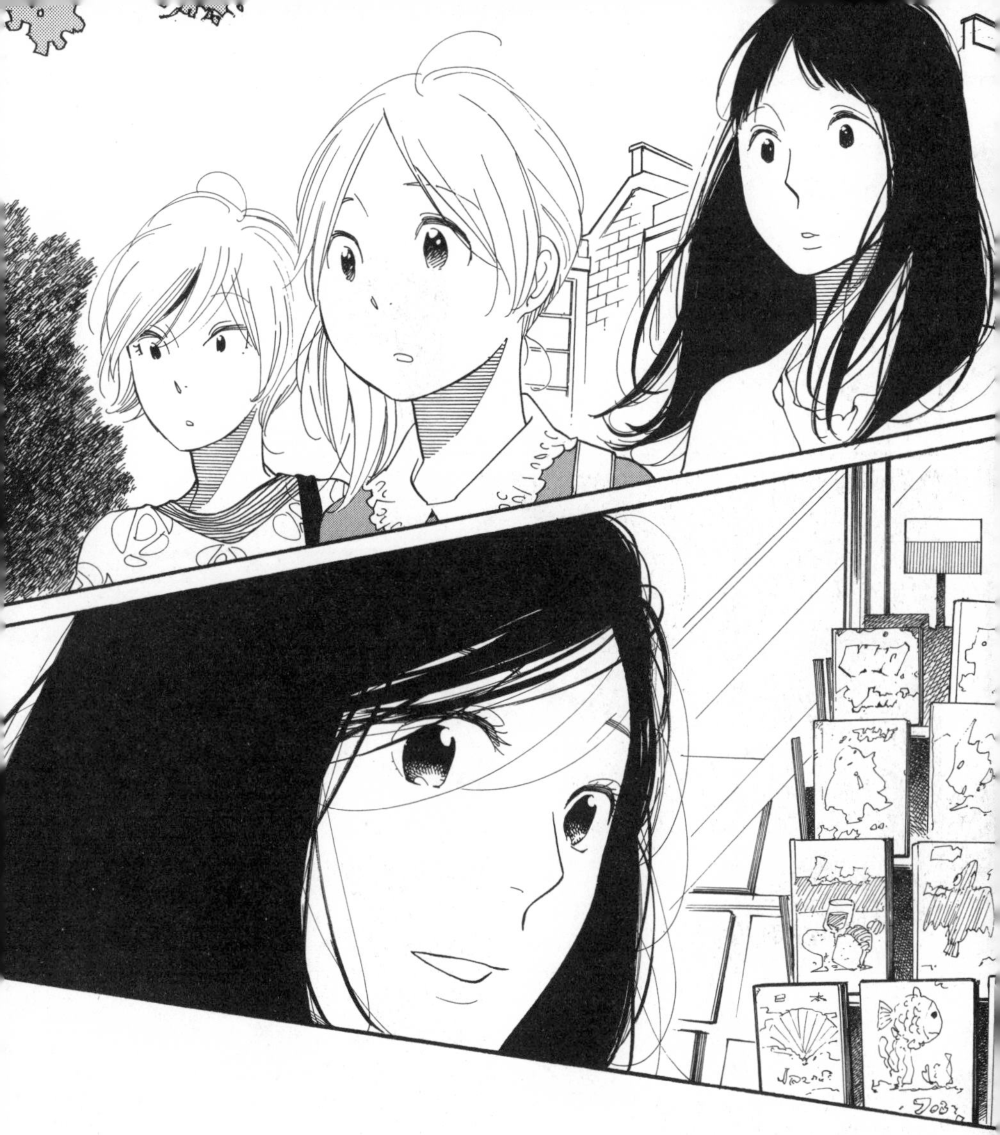

Dear Fumi...

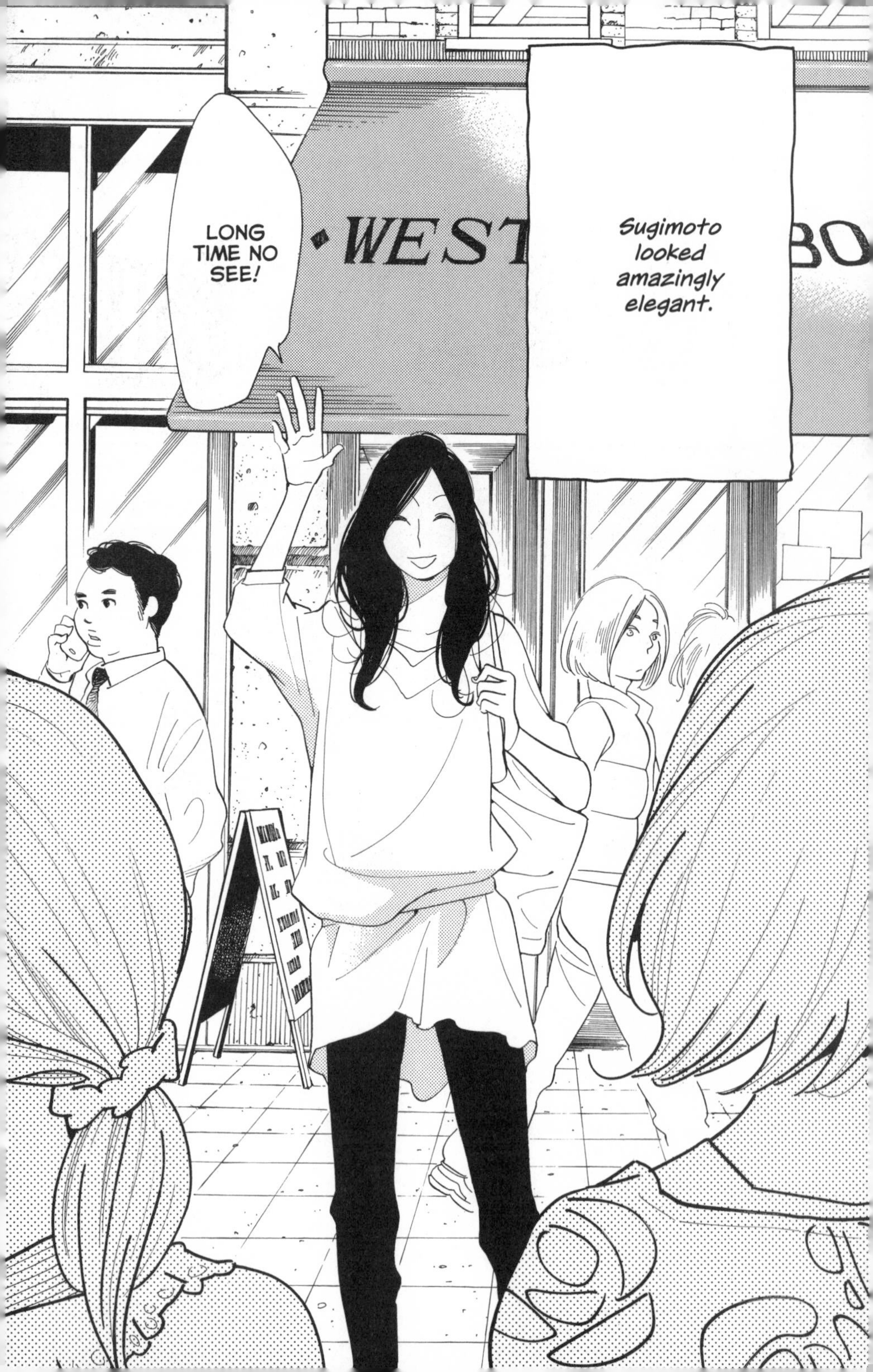
Sugimoto looked amazingly elegant.
LONG TIME NO SEE!
WEST
BO

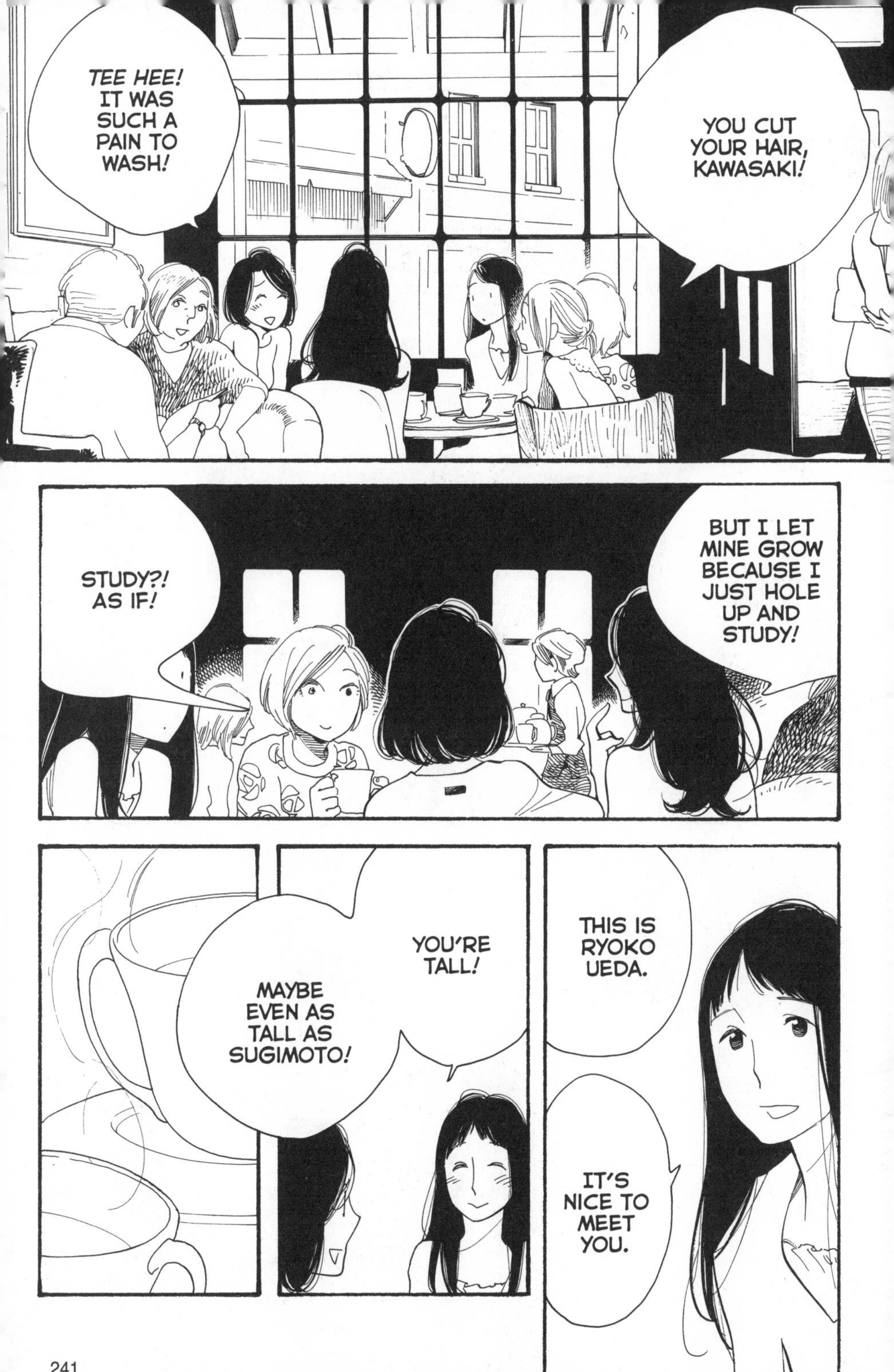
YOU CUT YOUR HAIR, KAWASAKI!
TEE HEE! IT WAS SUCH A PAIN TO WASH!
BUT I LET MINE GROW BECAUSE I JUST HOLE UP AND STUDY!
STUDY?! AS IF!
THIS IS RYOKO UEDA.
IT'S NICE TO MEET YOU.
YOU'RE TALL!
MAYBE EVEN AS TALL AS SUGIMOTO!

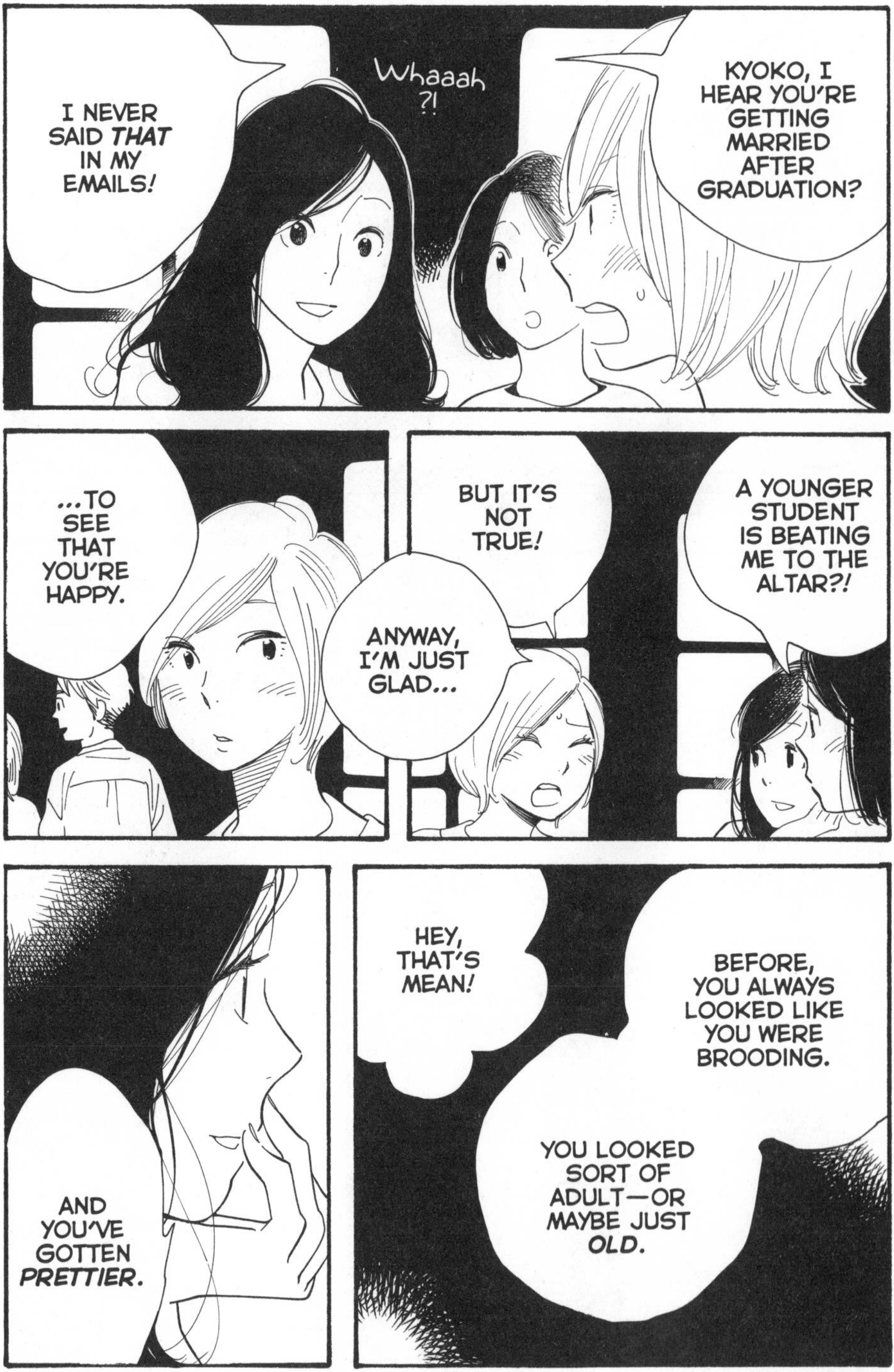
KYOKO, I HEAR YOU'RE GETTING MARRIED AFTER GRADUATION?
Whaaah ?!
I NEVER SAID *THAT* IN MY EMAILS!
A YOUNGER STUDENT IS BEATING ME TO THE ALTAR?!
BUT IT'S NOT TRUE!
ANYWAY, I'M JUST GLAD...
...TO SEE THAT YOU'RE HAPPY.
BEFORE, YOU ALWAYS LOOKED LIKE YOU WERE BROODING.
YOU LOOKED SORT OF ADULT—OR MAYBE JUST ***OLD***.
HEY, THAT'S MEAN!
AND YOU'VE GOTTEN ***PRETTIER***.

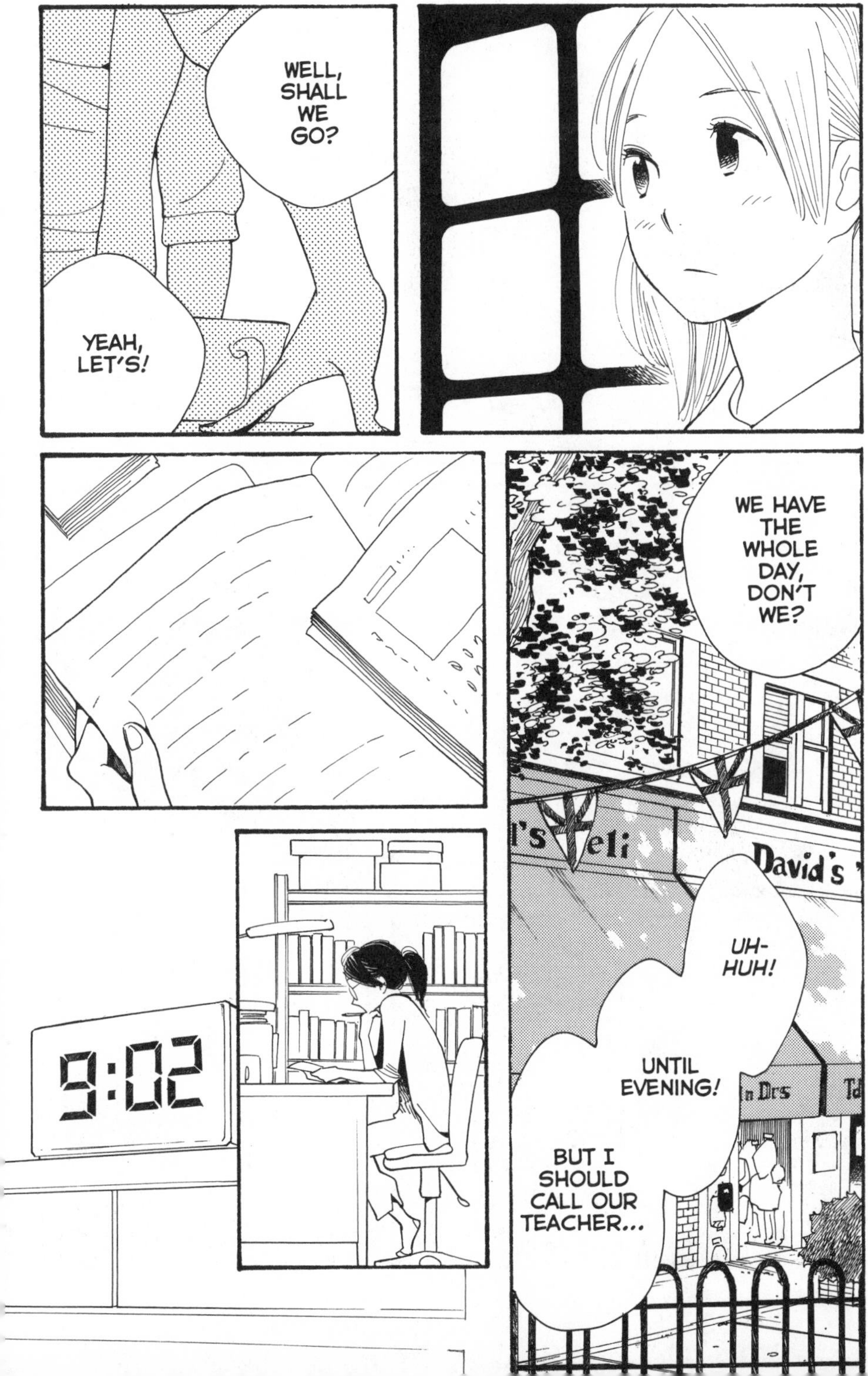
WELL, SHALL WE GO?
YEAH, LET'S!
WE HAVE THE WHOLE DAY, DON'T WE?
David's
UH-HUH!
UNTIL EVENING!
BUT I SHOULD CALL OUR TEACHER...
9:02

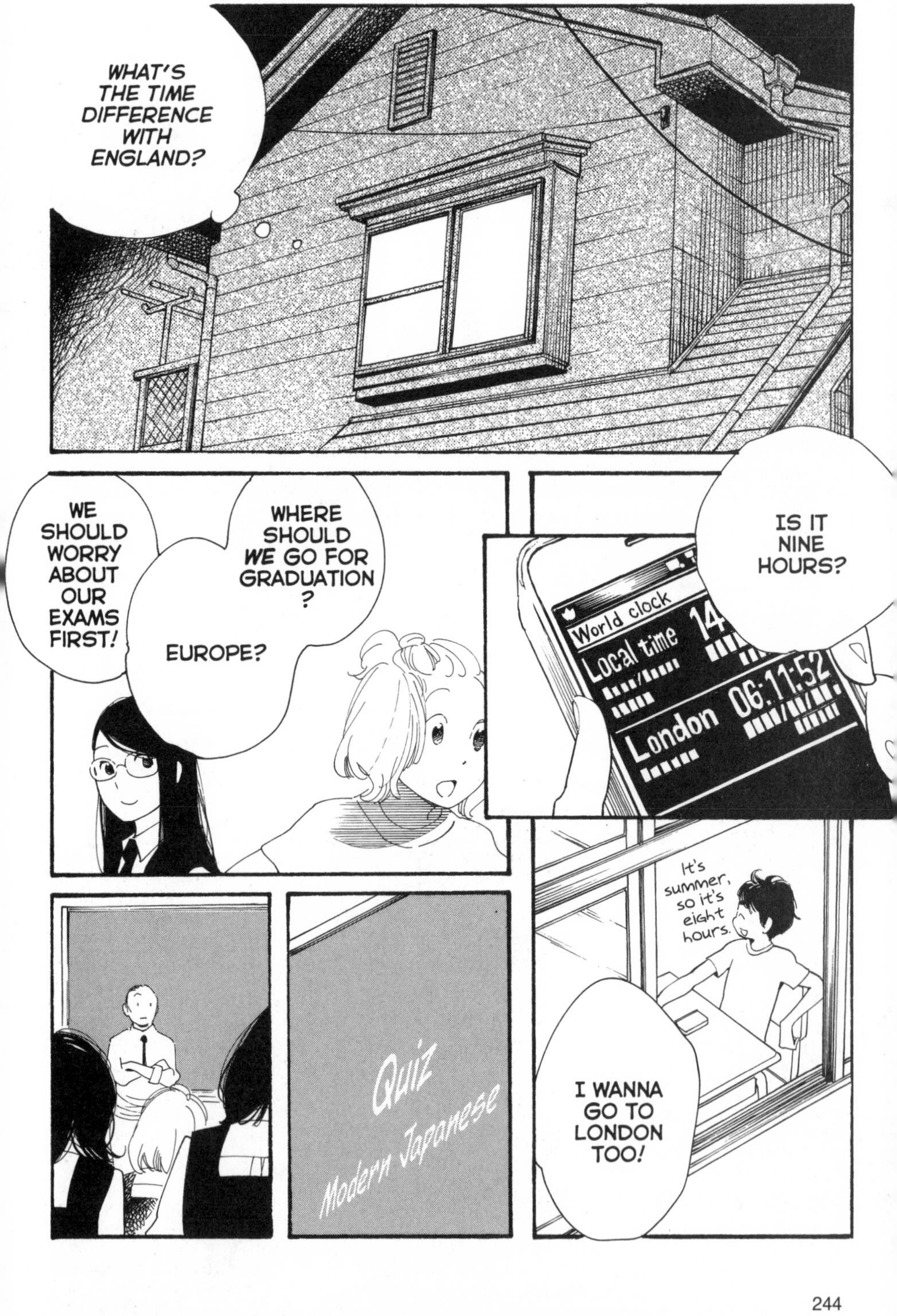
WHAT'S THE TIME DIFFERENCE WITH ENGLAND?
IS IT NINE HOURS?
World clock
Local time 14
London 06:11:52
It's summer, so it's eight hours.
I WANNA GO TO LONDON TOO!
WHERE SHOULD *WE* GO FOR GRADUATION?
EUROPE?
WE SHOULD WORRY ABOUT OUR EXAMS FIRST!
Quiz
Modern Japanese

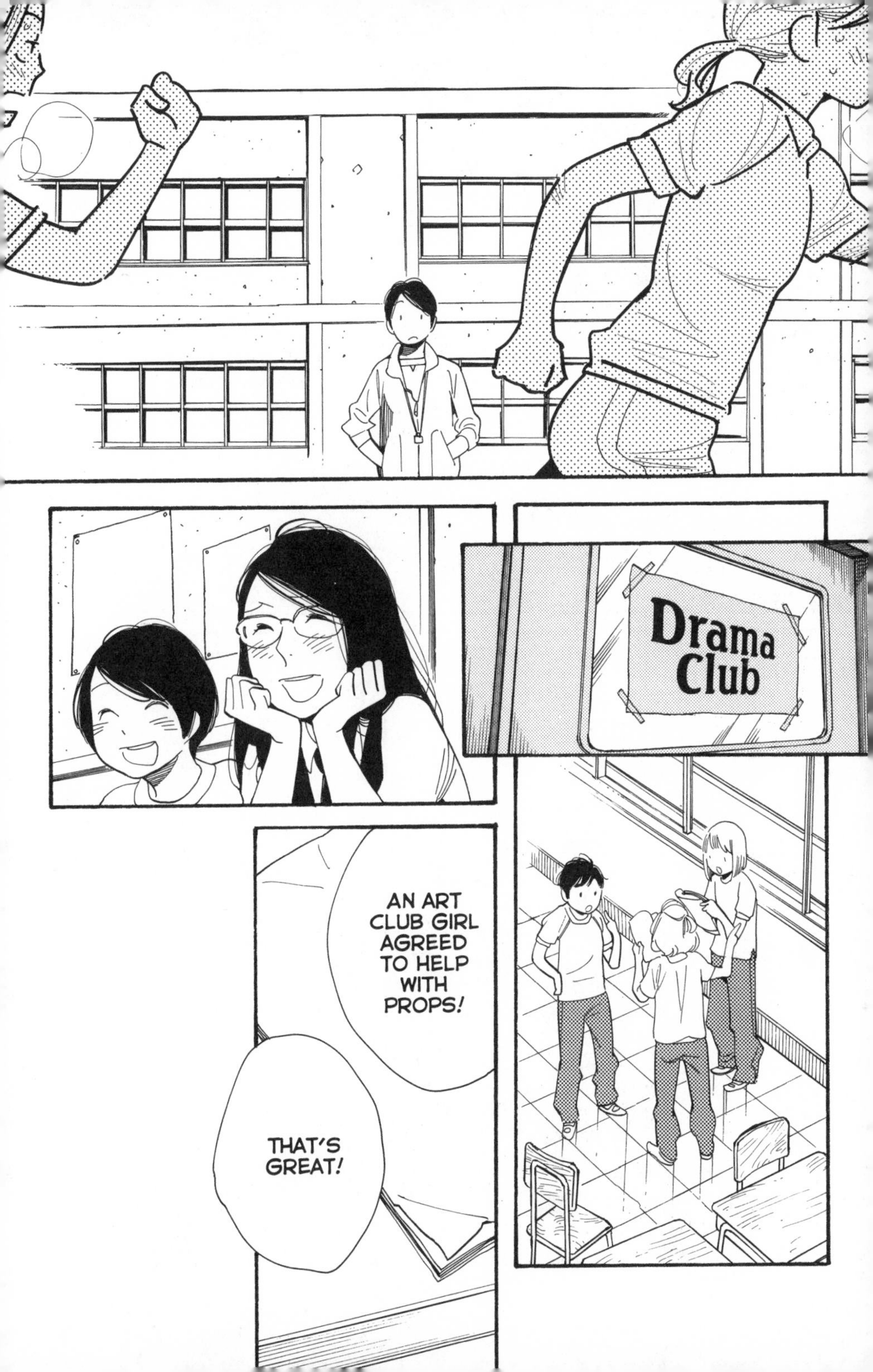
Drama Club
AN ART CLUB GIRL AGREED TO HELP WITH PROPS!
THAT'S GREAT!

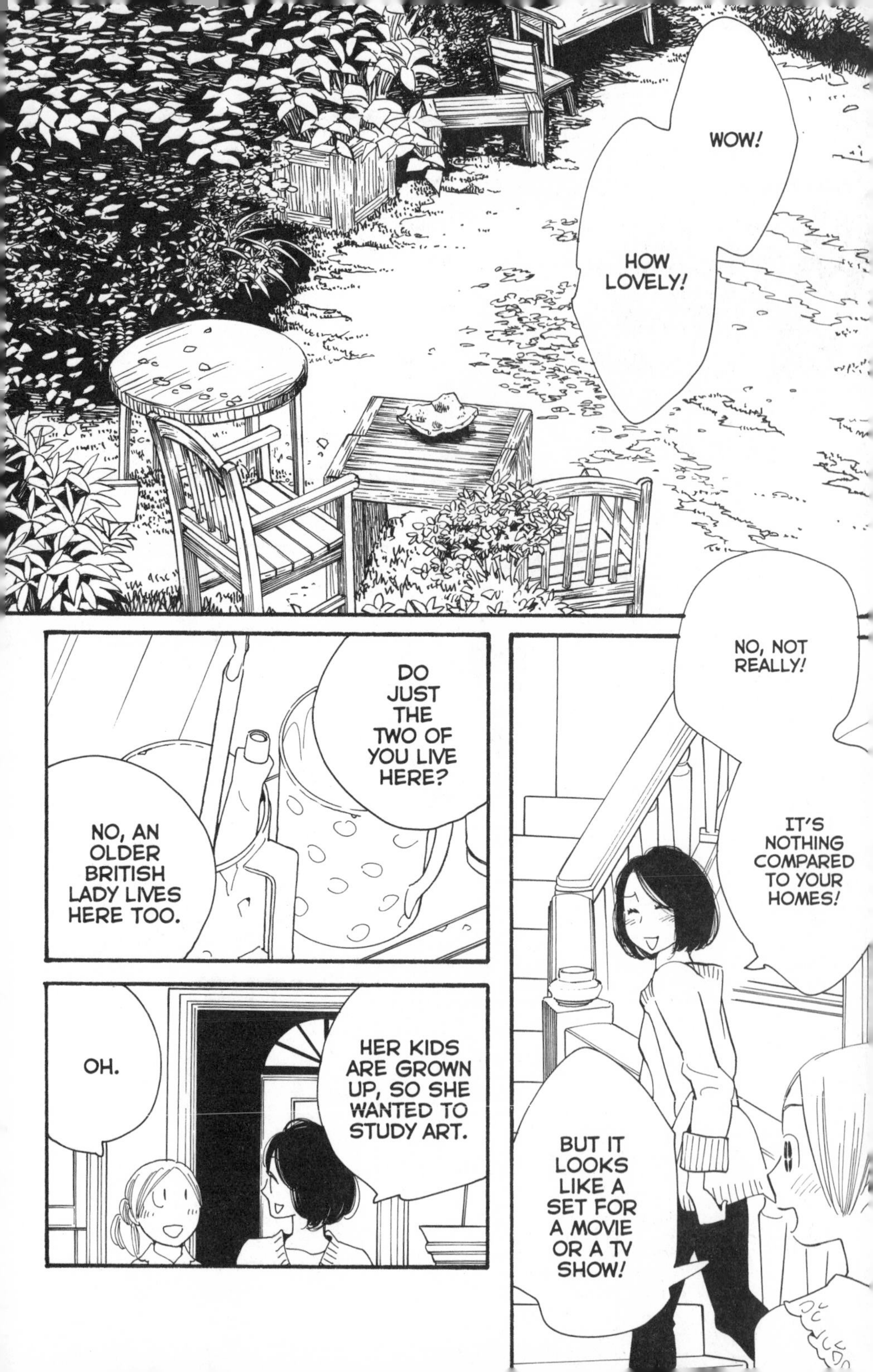
WOW!
HOW LOVELY!
NO, NOT REALLY!
IT'S NOTHING COMPARED TO YOUR HOMES!
BUT IT LOOKS LIKE A SET FOR A MOVIE OR A TV SHOW!
DO JUST THE TWO OF YOU LIVE HERE?
NO, AN OLDER BRITISH LADY LIVES HERE TOO.
HER KIDS ARE GROWN UP, SO SHE WANTED TO STUDY ART.
OH.

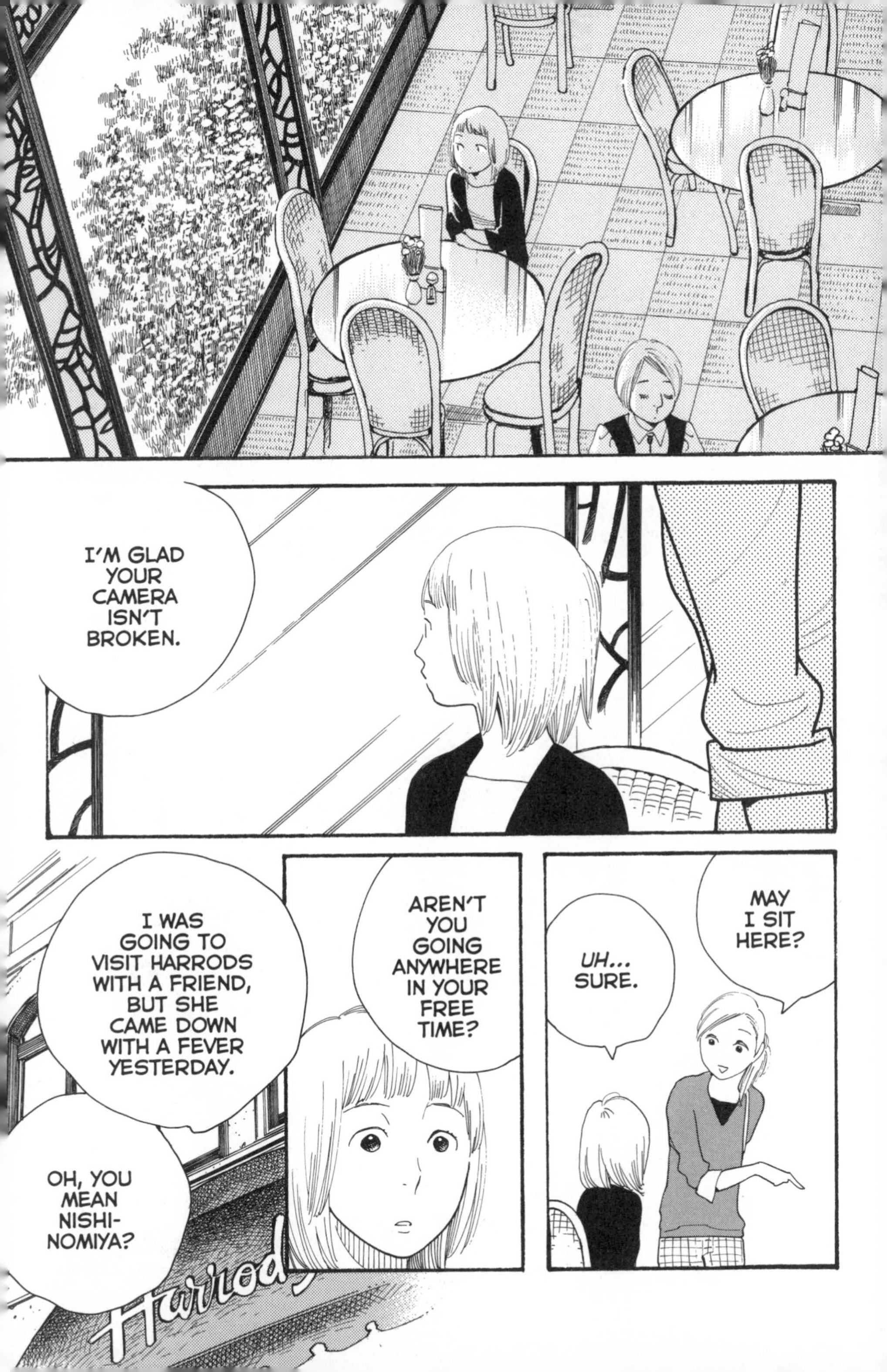
I'M GLAD YOUR CAMERA ISN'T BROKEN.
MAY I SIT HERE?
UH... SURE.
AREN'T YOU GOING ANYWHERE IN YOUR FREE TIME?
I WAS GOING TO VISIT HARRODS WITH A FRIEND, BUT SHE CAME DOWN WITH A FEVER YESTERDAY.
OH, YOU MEAN NISHI-NOMIYA?

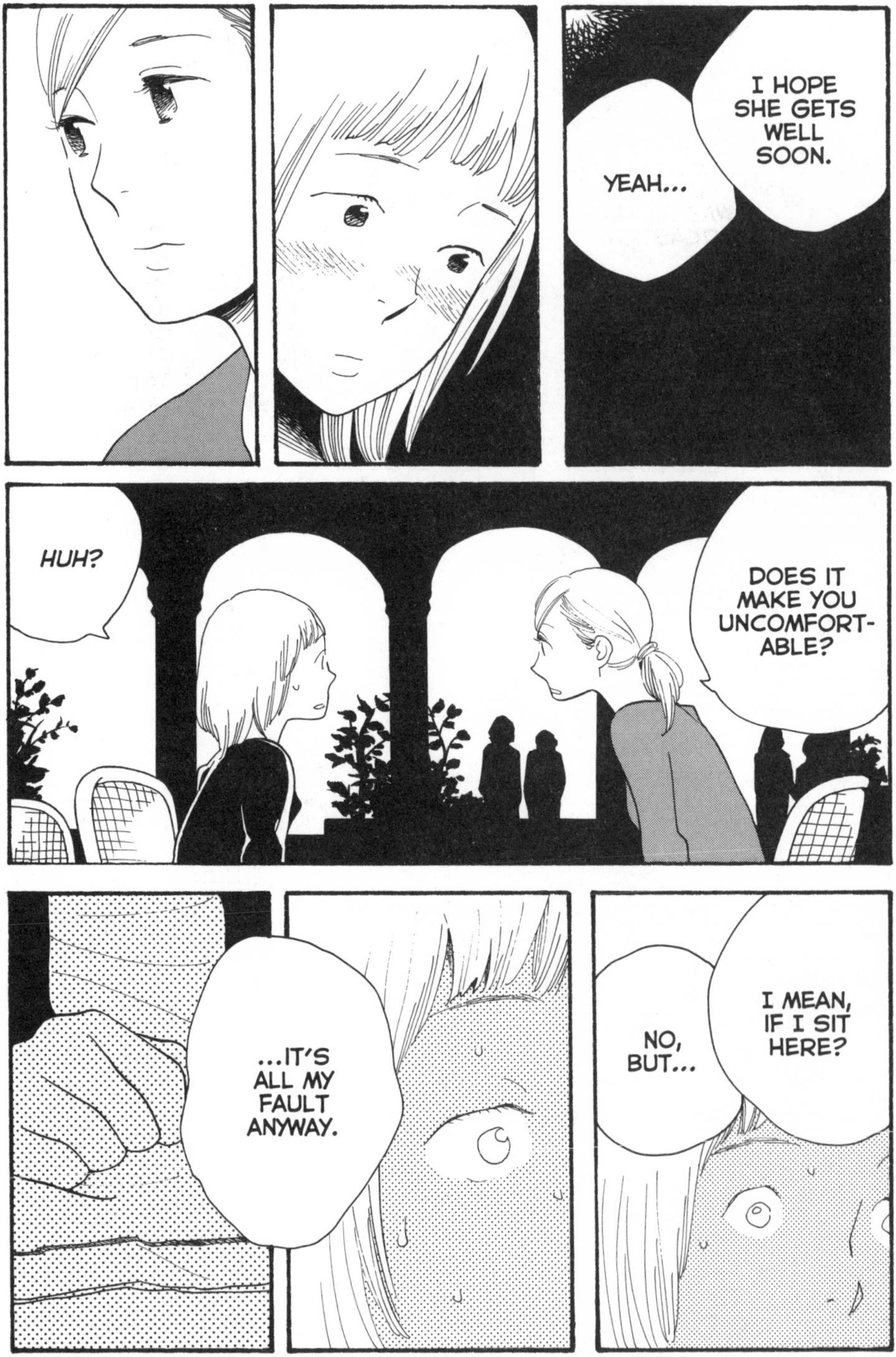
I HOPE SHE GETS WELL SOON.
YEAH...
DOES IT MAKE YOU UNCOMFORT-ABLE?
HUH?
I MEAN, IF I SIT HERE?
NO, BUT...
...IT'S ALL MY FAULT ANYWAY.

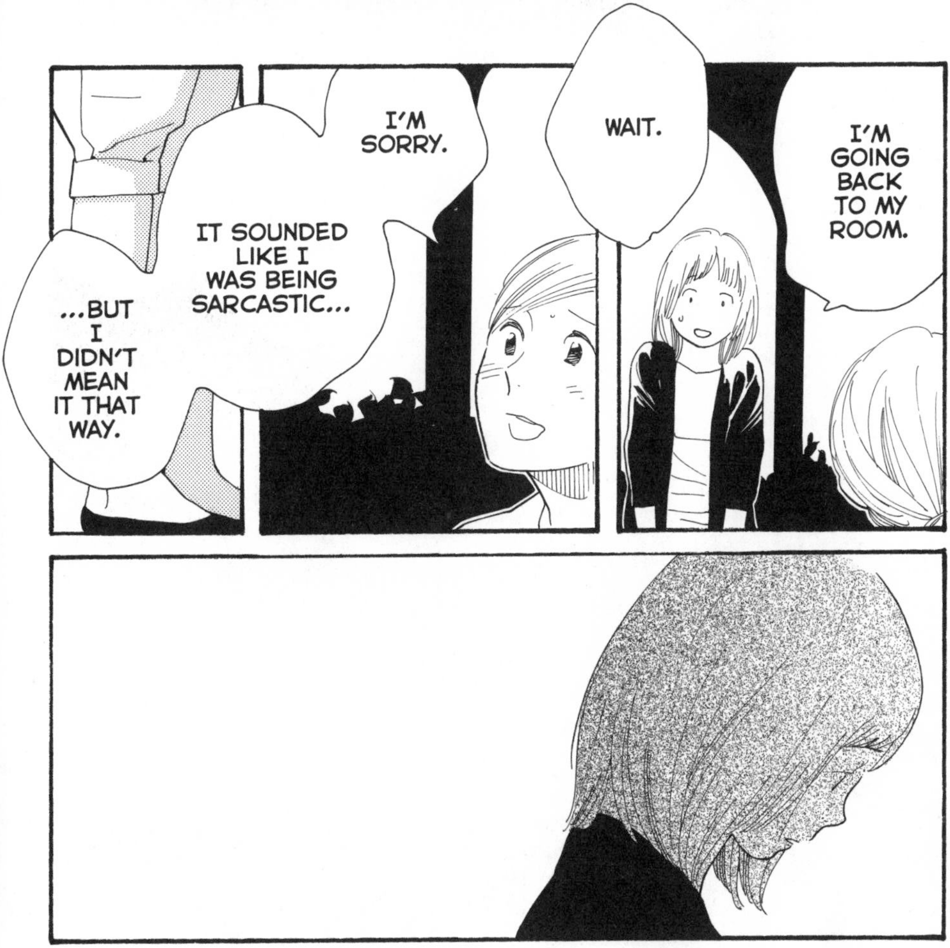
I'M GOING BACK TO MY ROOM.
WAIT.
I'M SORRY.
IT SOUNDED LIKE I WAS BEING SARCASTIC...
...BUT I DIDN'T MEAN IT THAT WAY.

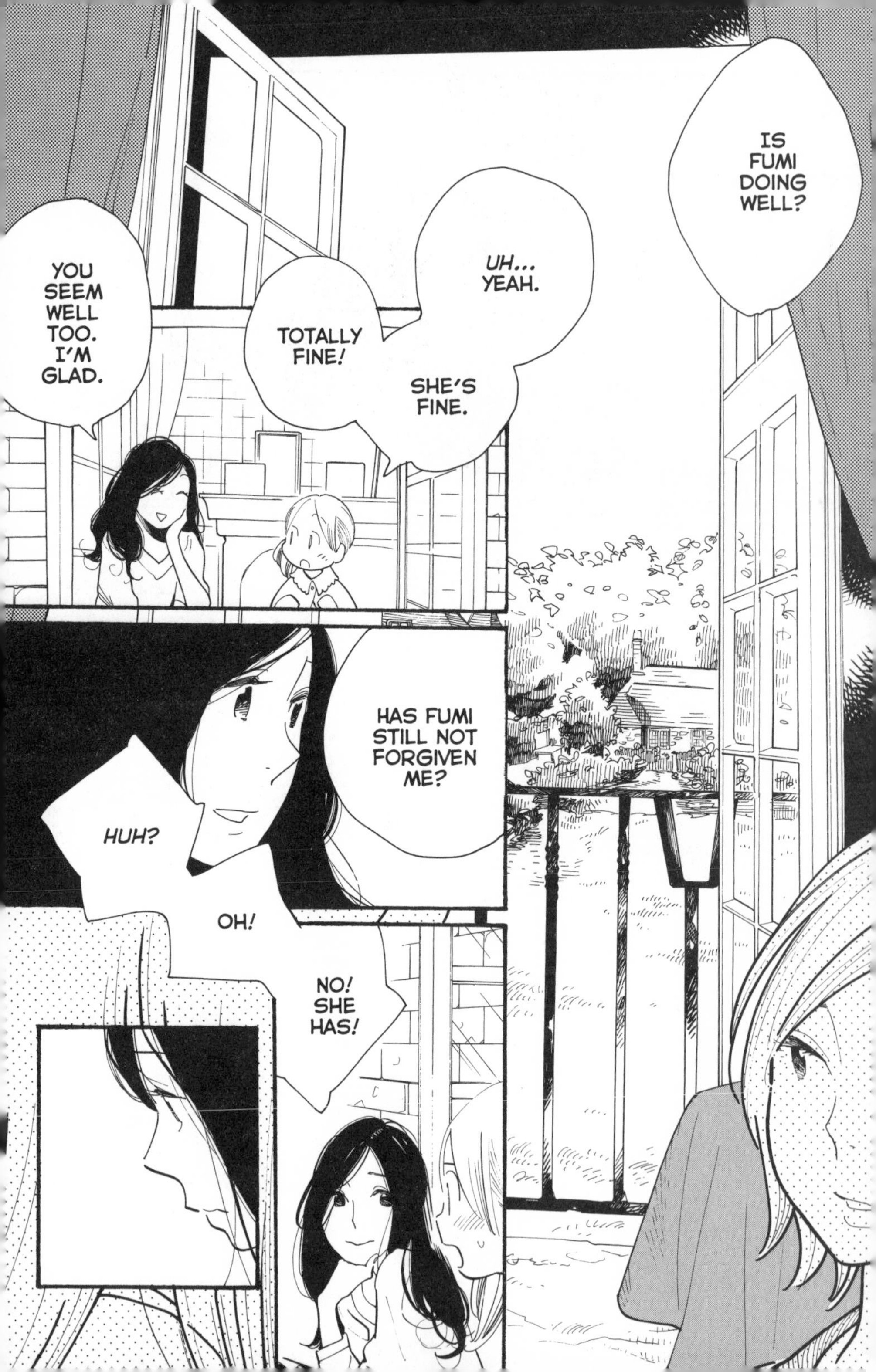
IS FUMI DOING WELL?
UH... YEAH.
SHE'S FINE.
TOTALLY FINE!
YOU SEEM WELL TOO. I'M GLAD.
HAS FUMI STILL NOT FORGIVEN ME?
HUH?
OH!
NO! SHE HAS!

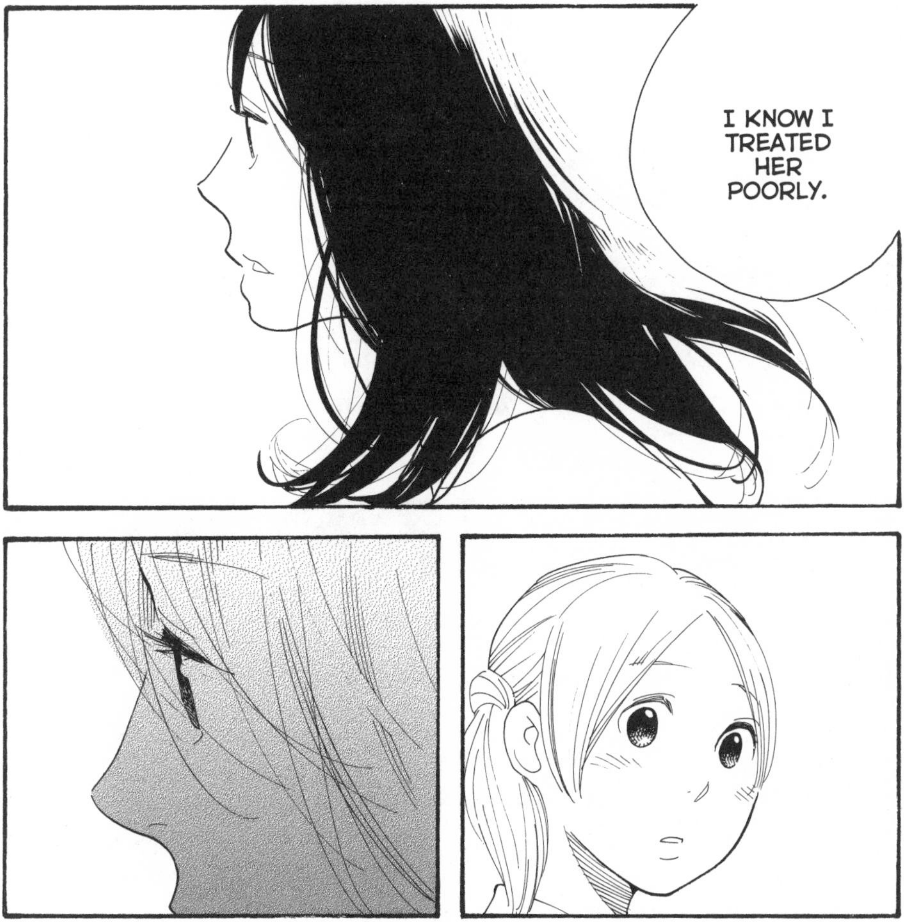
I KNOW I TREATED HER POORLY.

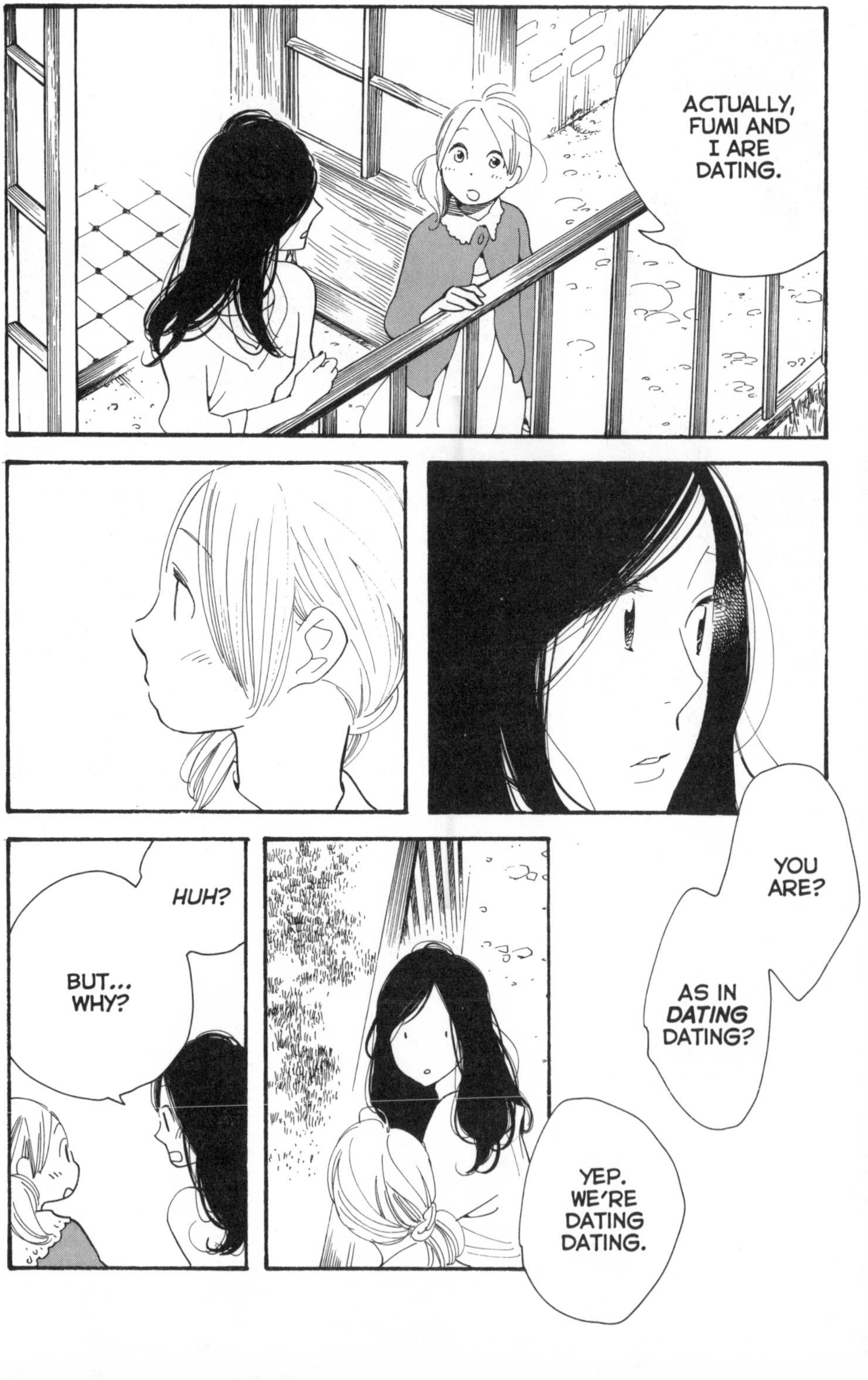

ACTUALLY, FUMI AND I ARE DATING.
YOU ARE?
AS IN *DATING* DATING?
YEP. WE'RE DATING DATING.
HUH?
BUT... WHY?

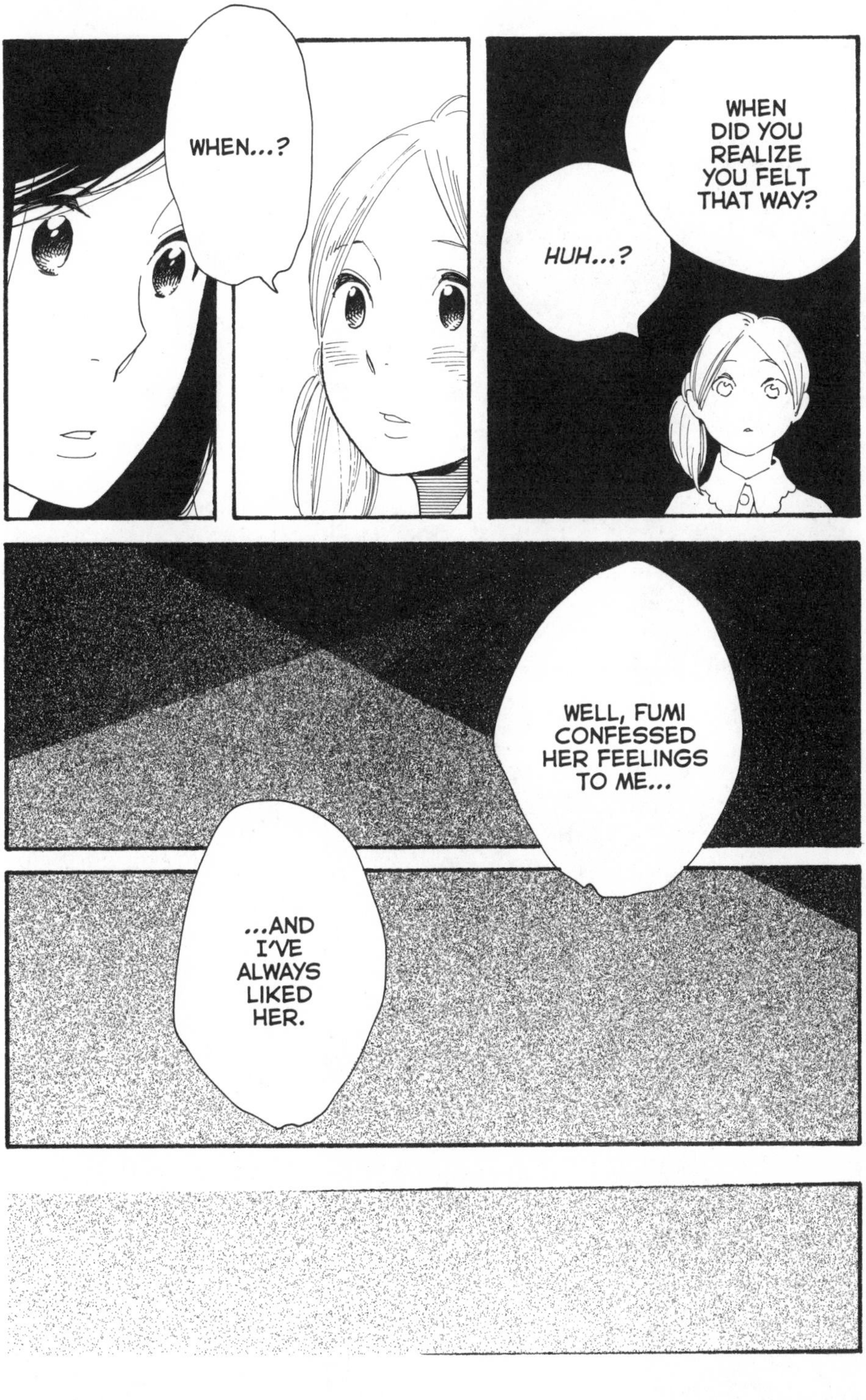
WHEN DID YOU REALIZE YOU FELT THAT WAY?
HUH...?
WHEN...?
WELL, FUMI CONFESSED HER FEELINGS TO ME...
...AND I'VE ALWAYS LIKED HER.

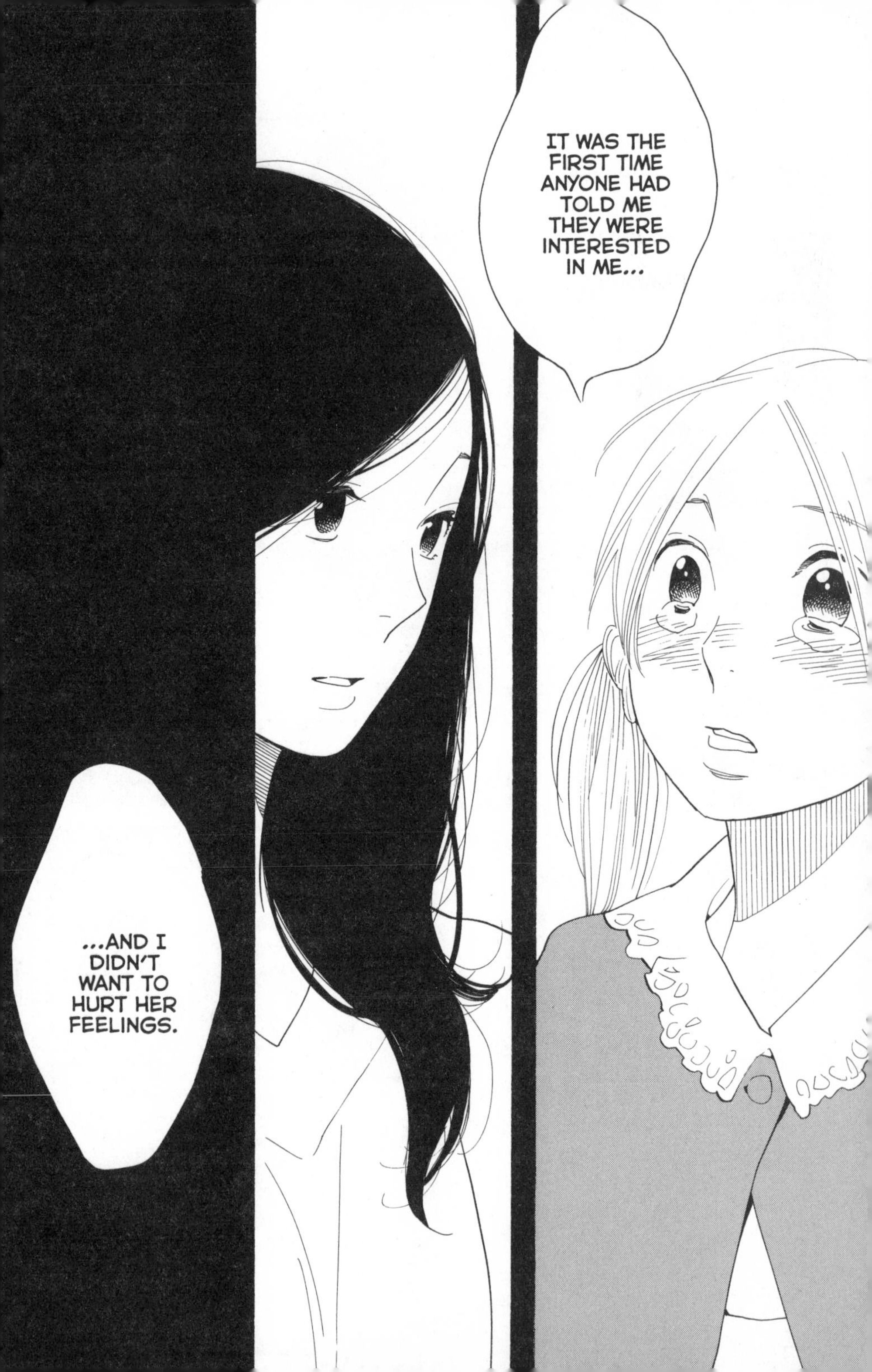
IT WAS THE FIRST TIME ANYONE HAD TOLD ME THEY WERE INTERESTED IN ME...
...AND I DIDN'T WANT TO HURT HER FEELINGS.

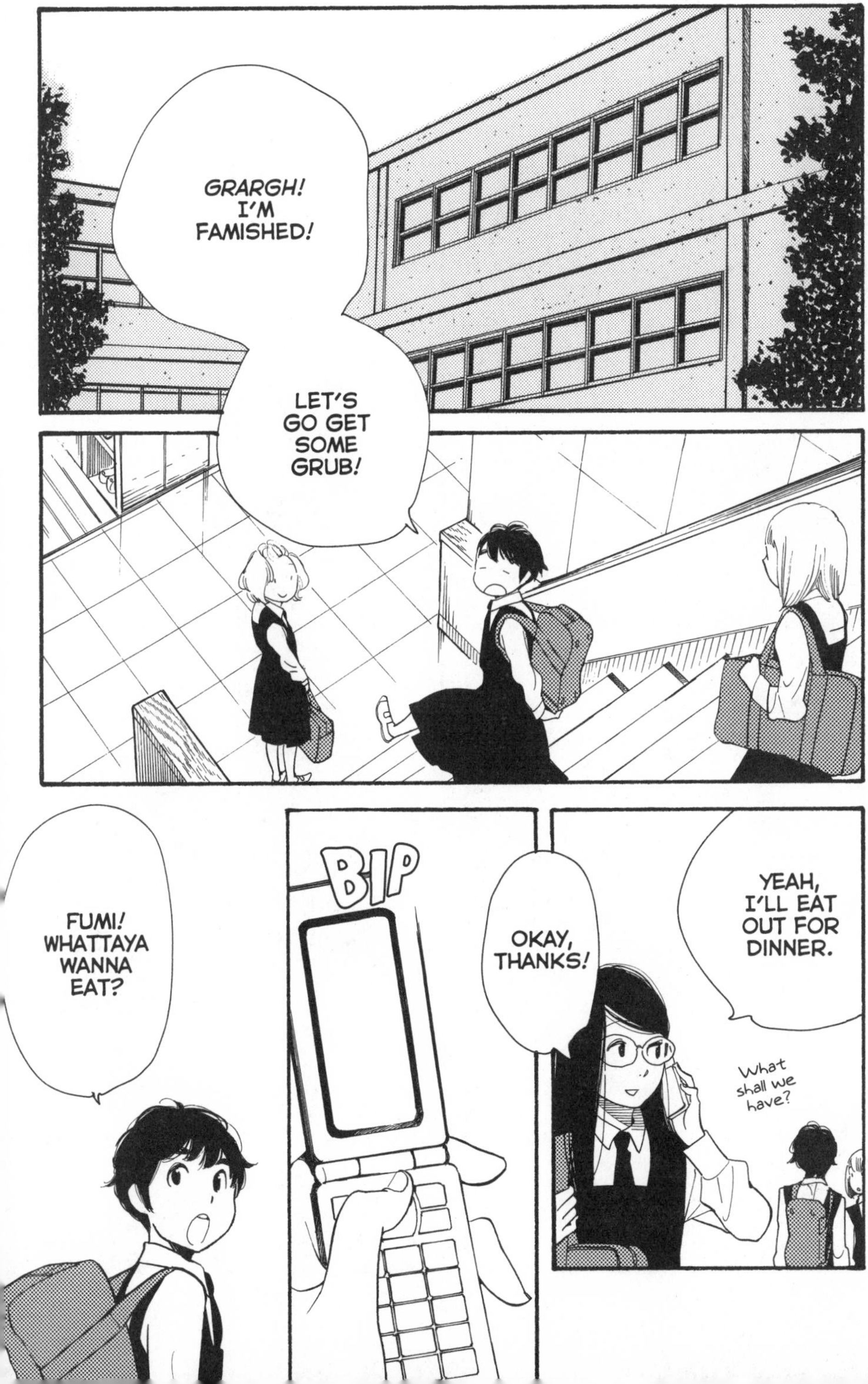
GRARGH! I'M FAMISHED!
LET'S GO GET SOME GRUB!
YEAH, I'LL EAT OUT FOR DINNER.
OKAY, THANKS!
What shall we have?
BIP
FUMI! WHATTAYA WANNA EAT?

Sweet Blue Flowers

#49 Unrequited Love

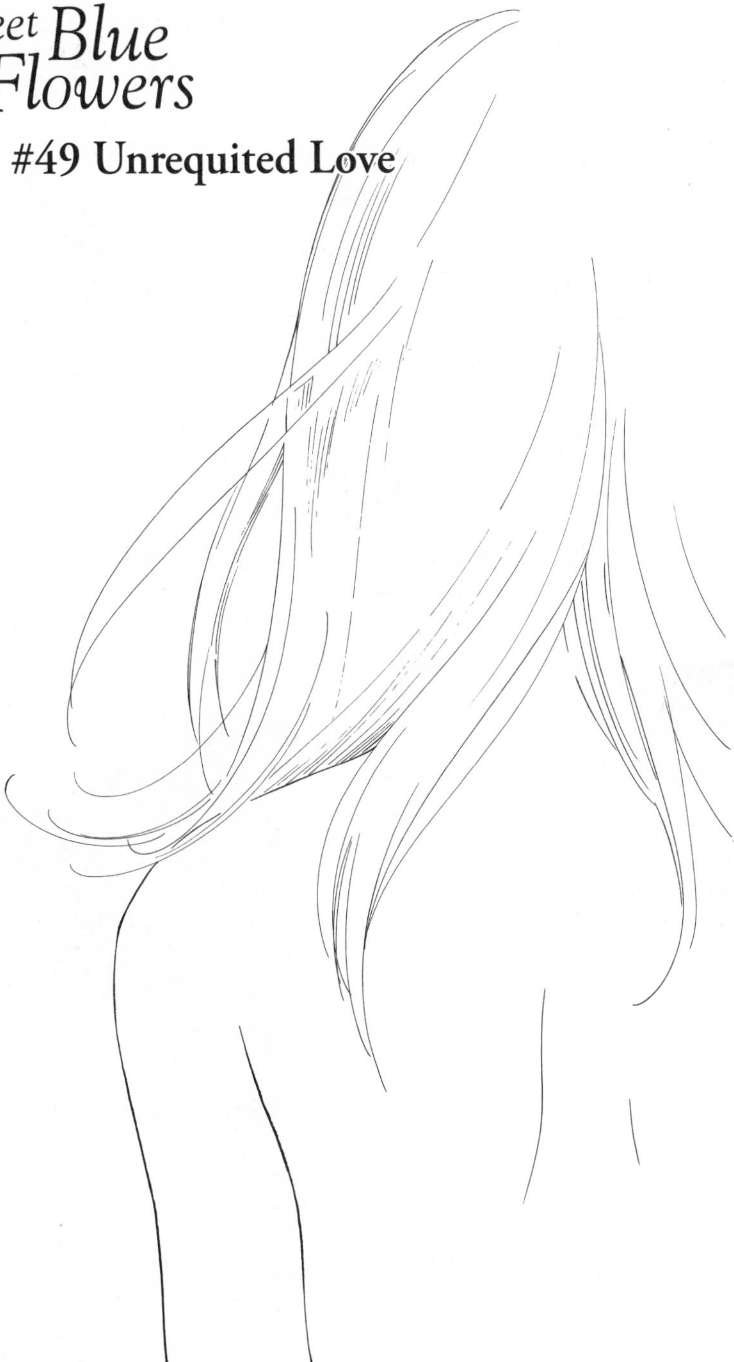

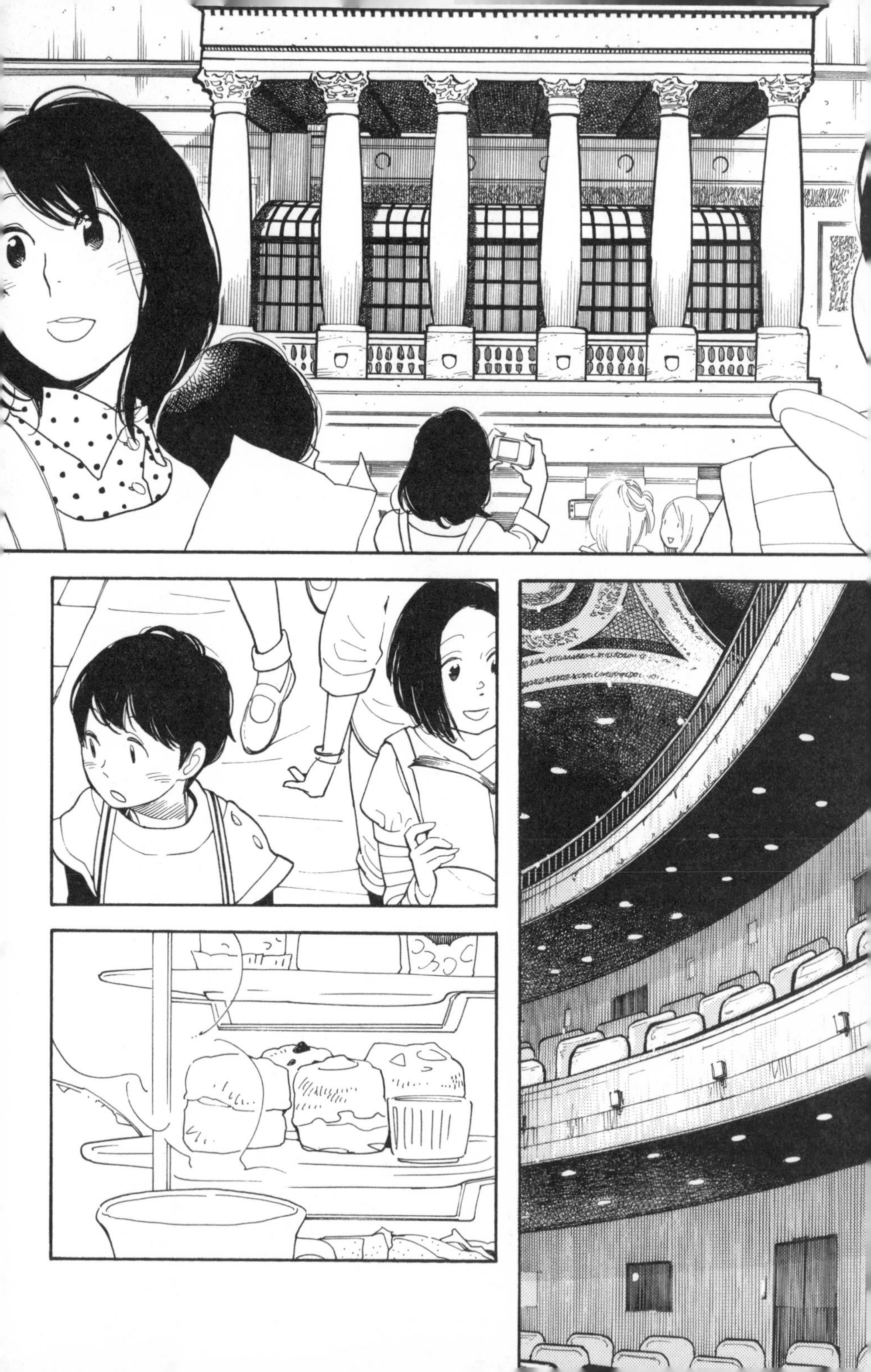

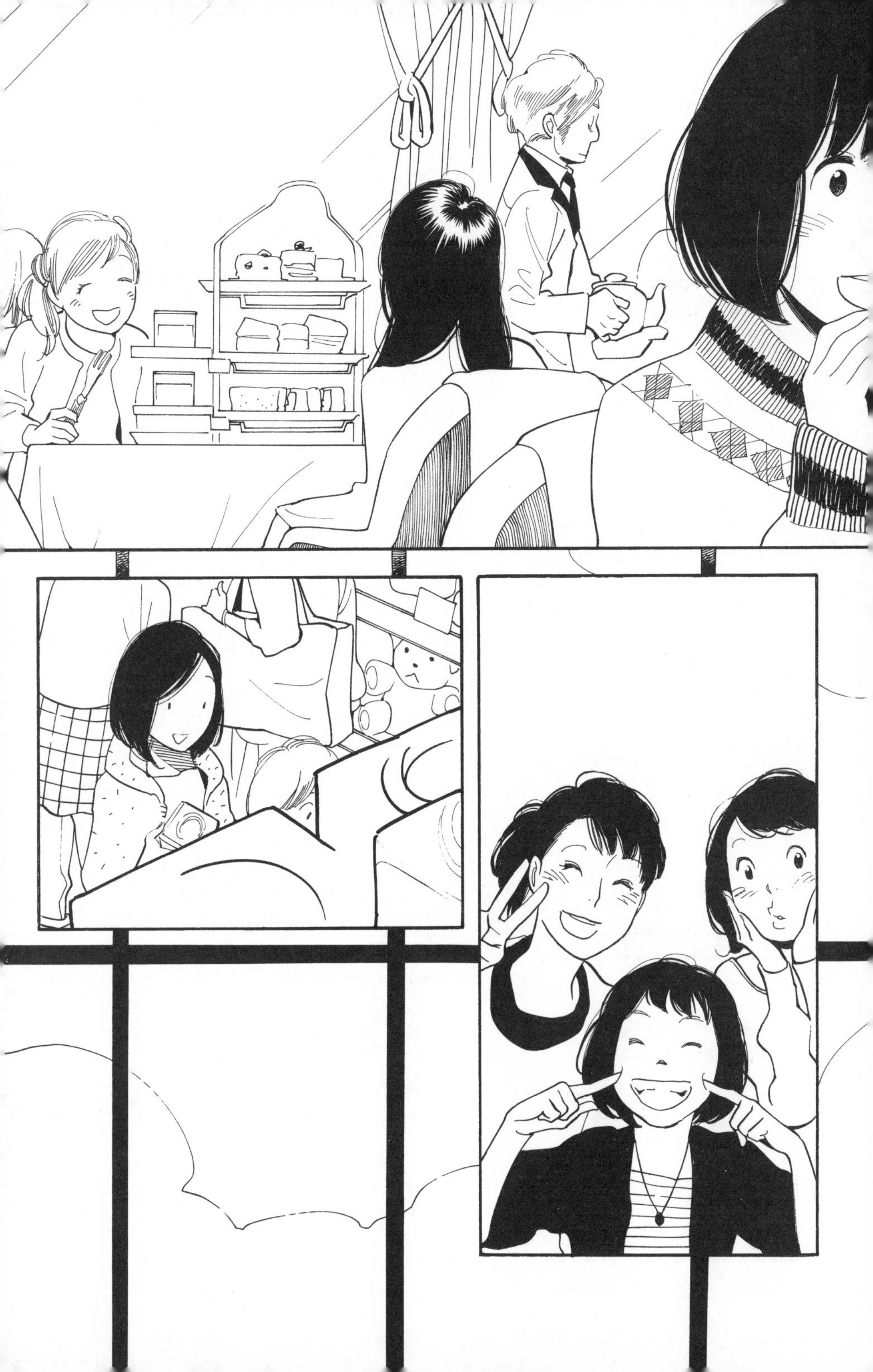

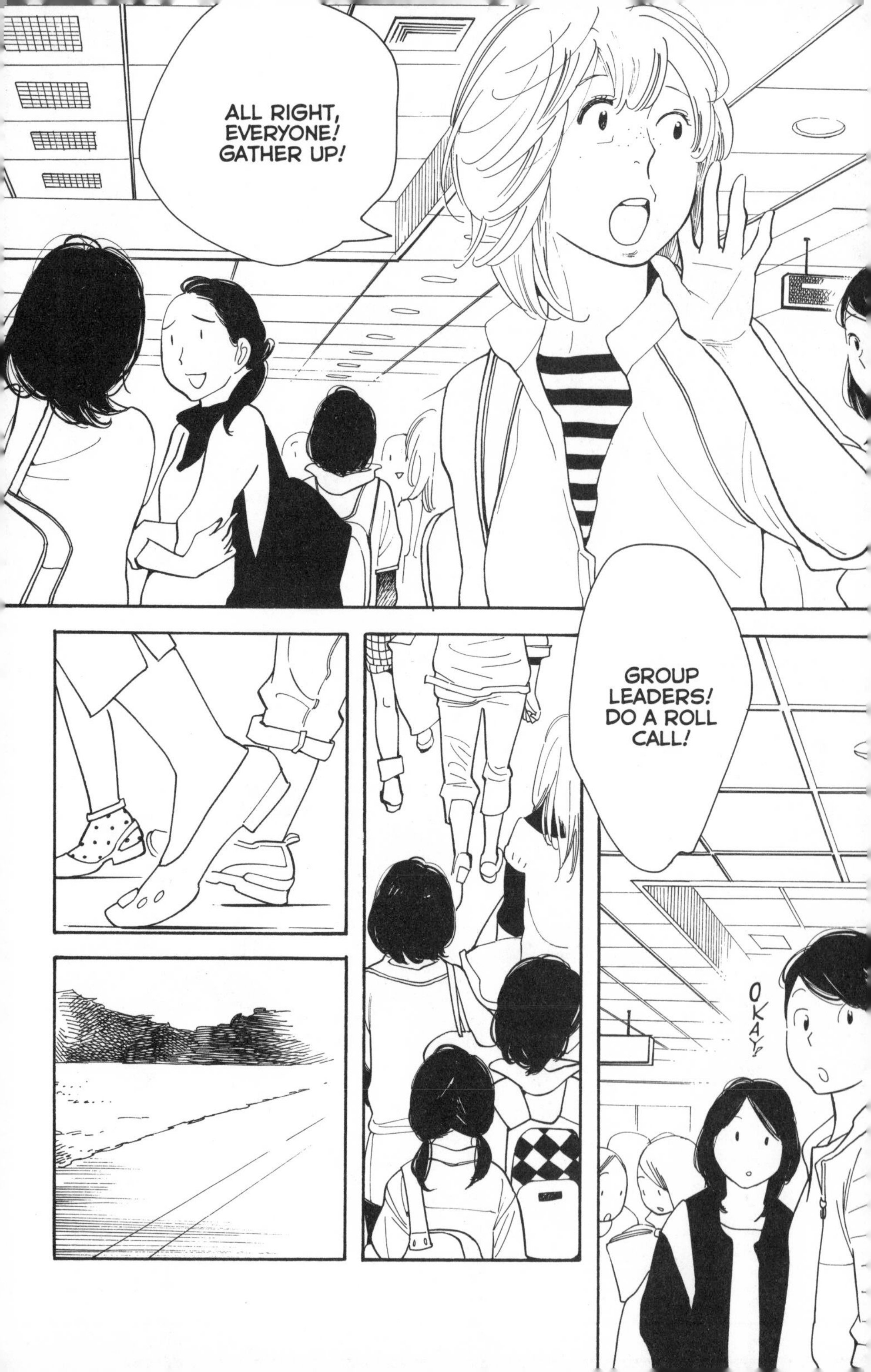
ALL RIGHT, EVERYONE! GATHER UP!
GROUP LEADERS! DO A ROLL CALL!
OKAY!

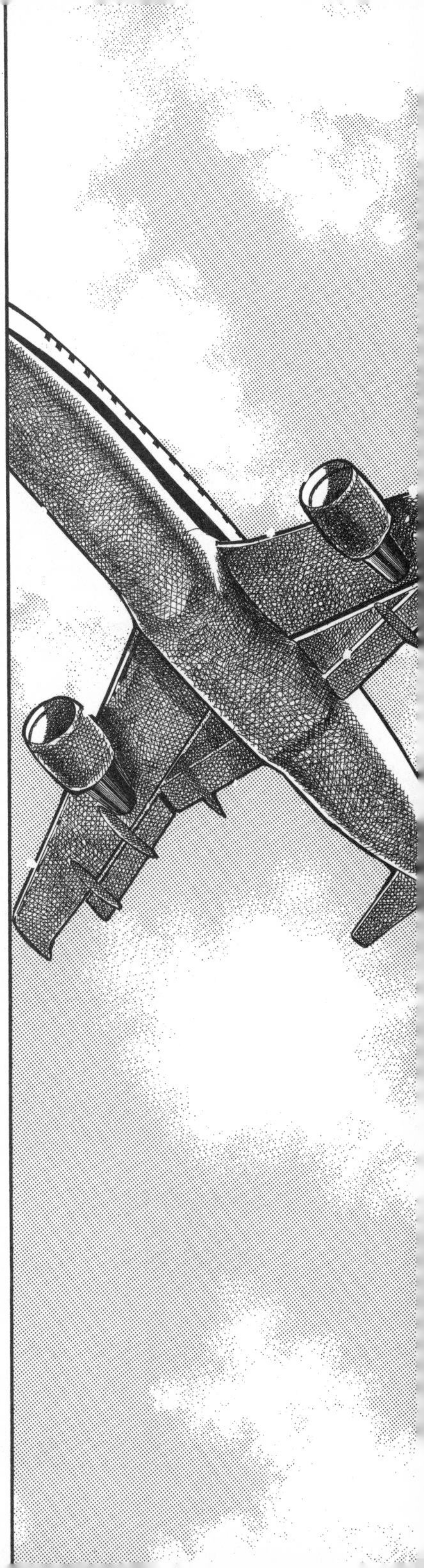
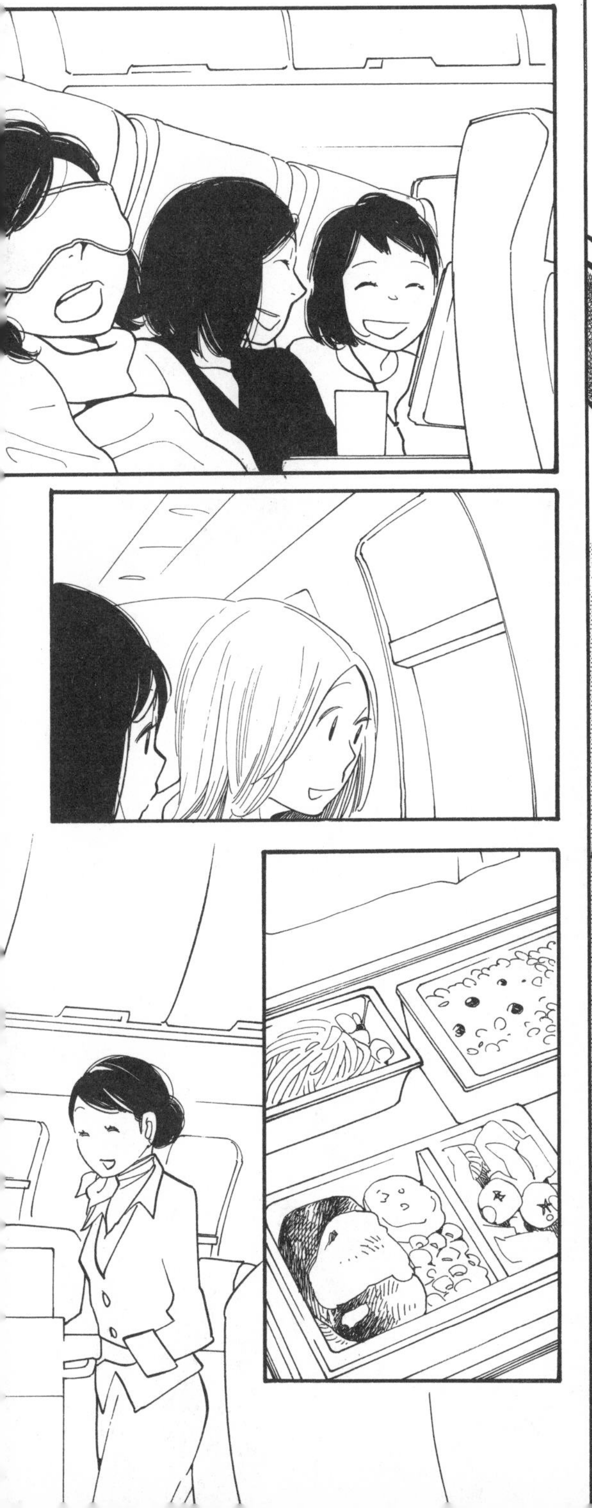

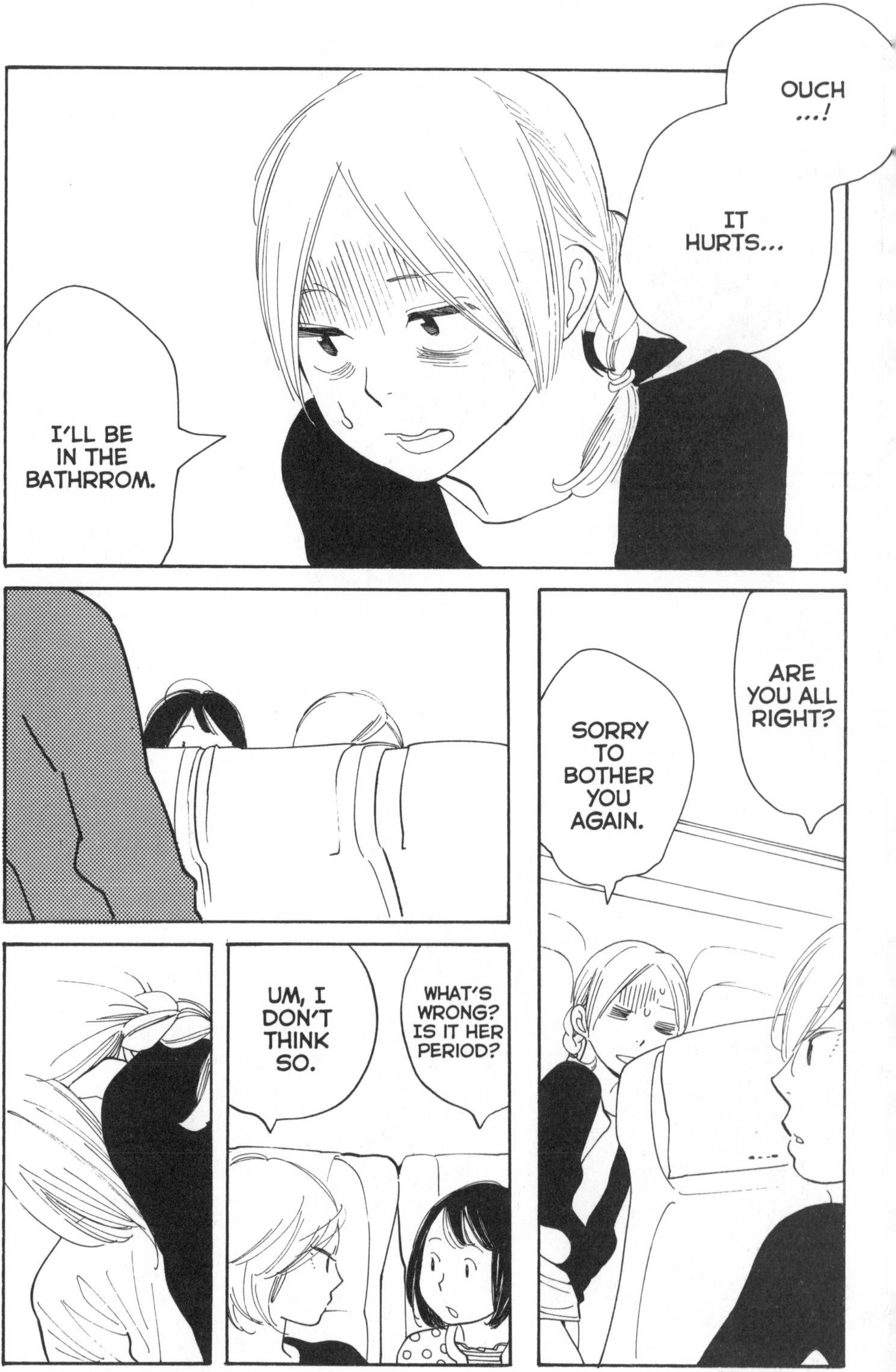
OUCH ...!
IT HURTS...
I'LL BE IN THE BATHRROM.
ARE YOU ALL RIGHT?
SORRY TO BOTHER YOU AGAIN.
WHAT'S WRONG? IS IT HER PERIOD?
UM, I DON'T THINK SO.

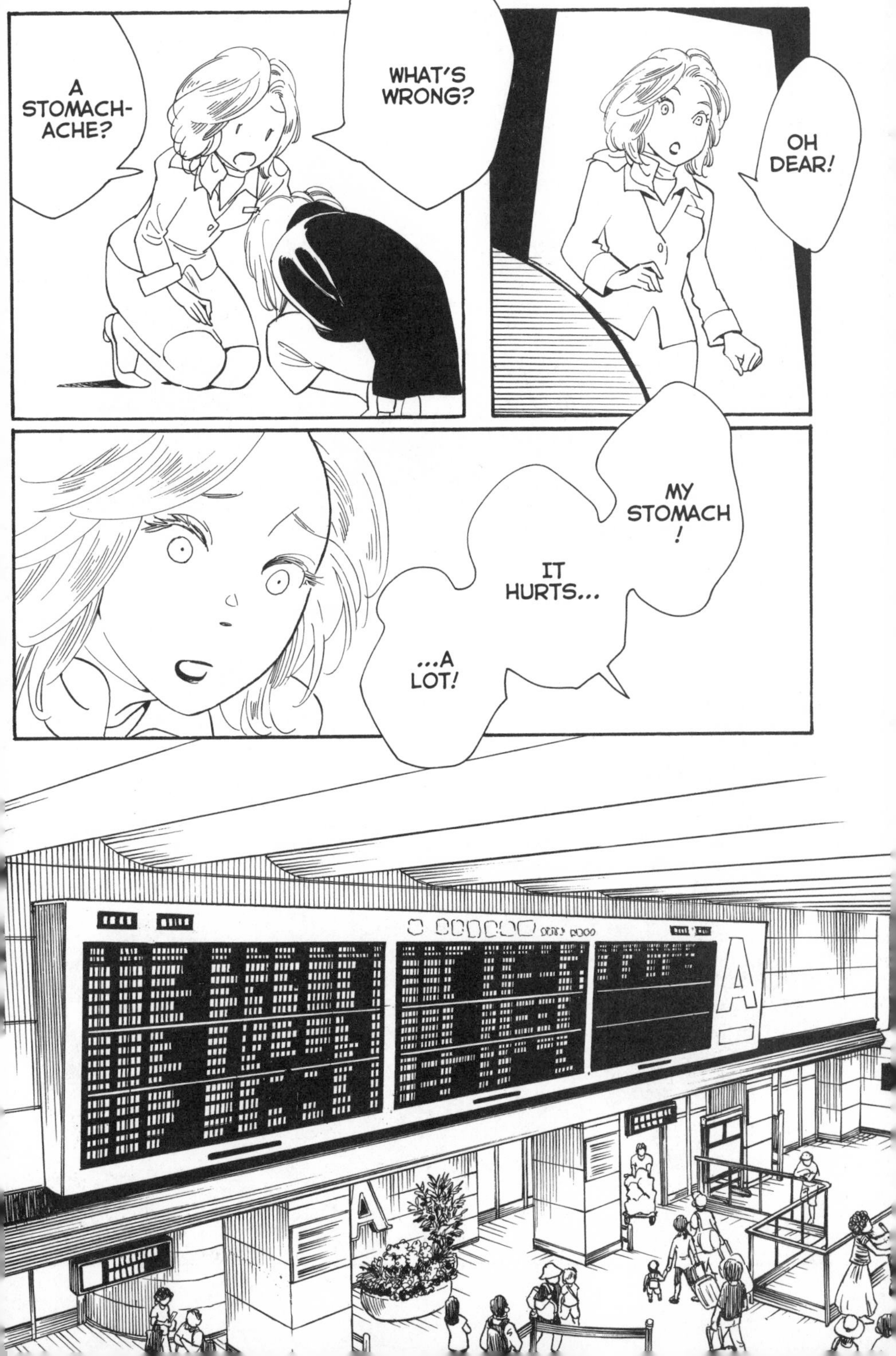
OH DEAR!
WHAT'S WRONG?
A STOMACH-ACHE?
MY STOMACH!
IT HURTS...
...A LOT!

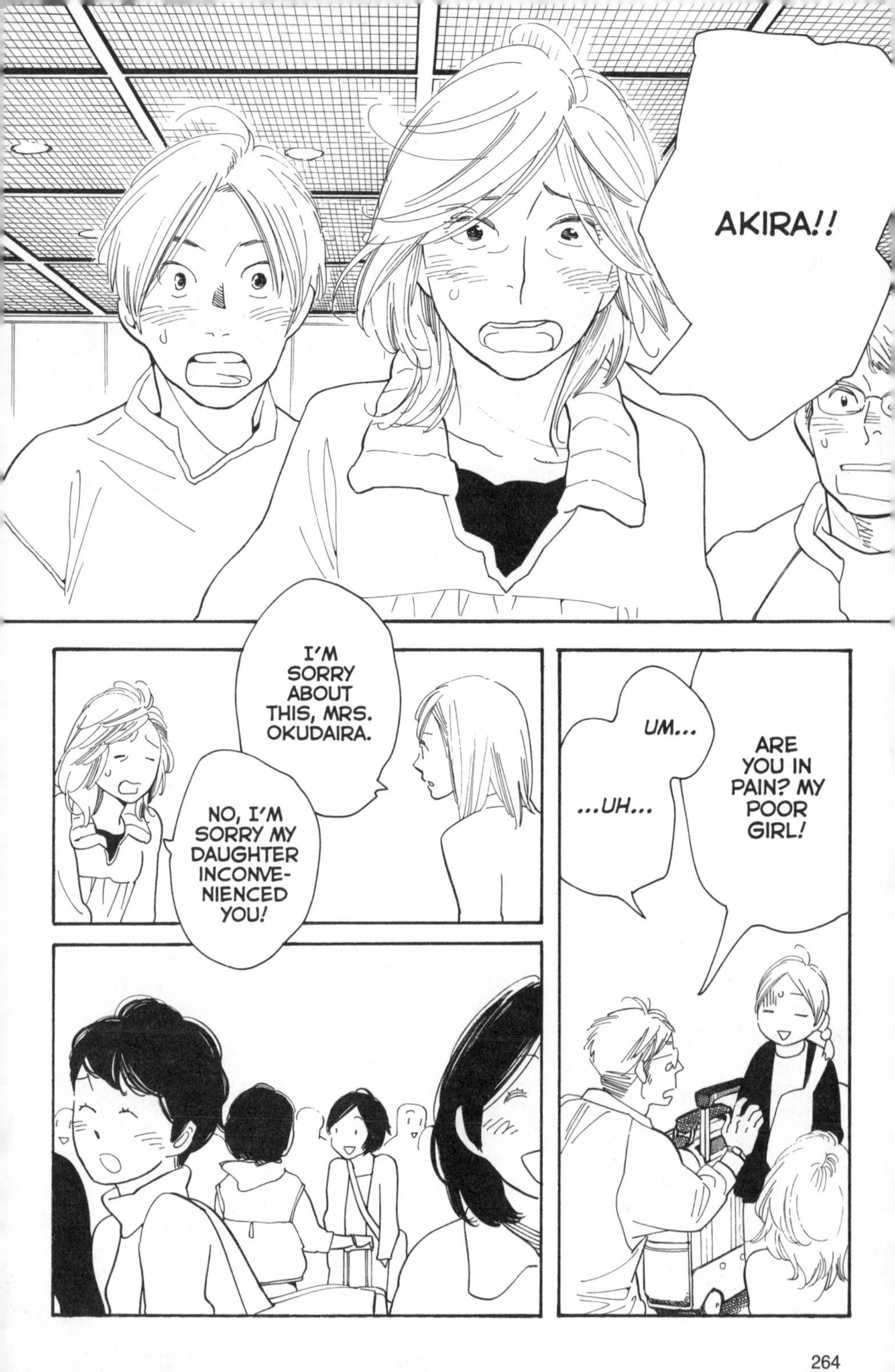
AKIRA!!
ARE YOU IN PAIN? MY POOR GIRL!
UM...
...UH...
I'M SORRY ABOUT THIS, MRS. OKUDAIRA.
NO, I'M SORRY MY DAUGHTER INCONVENIENCED YOU!

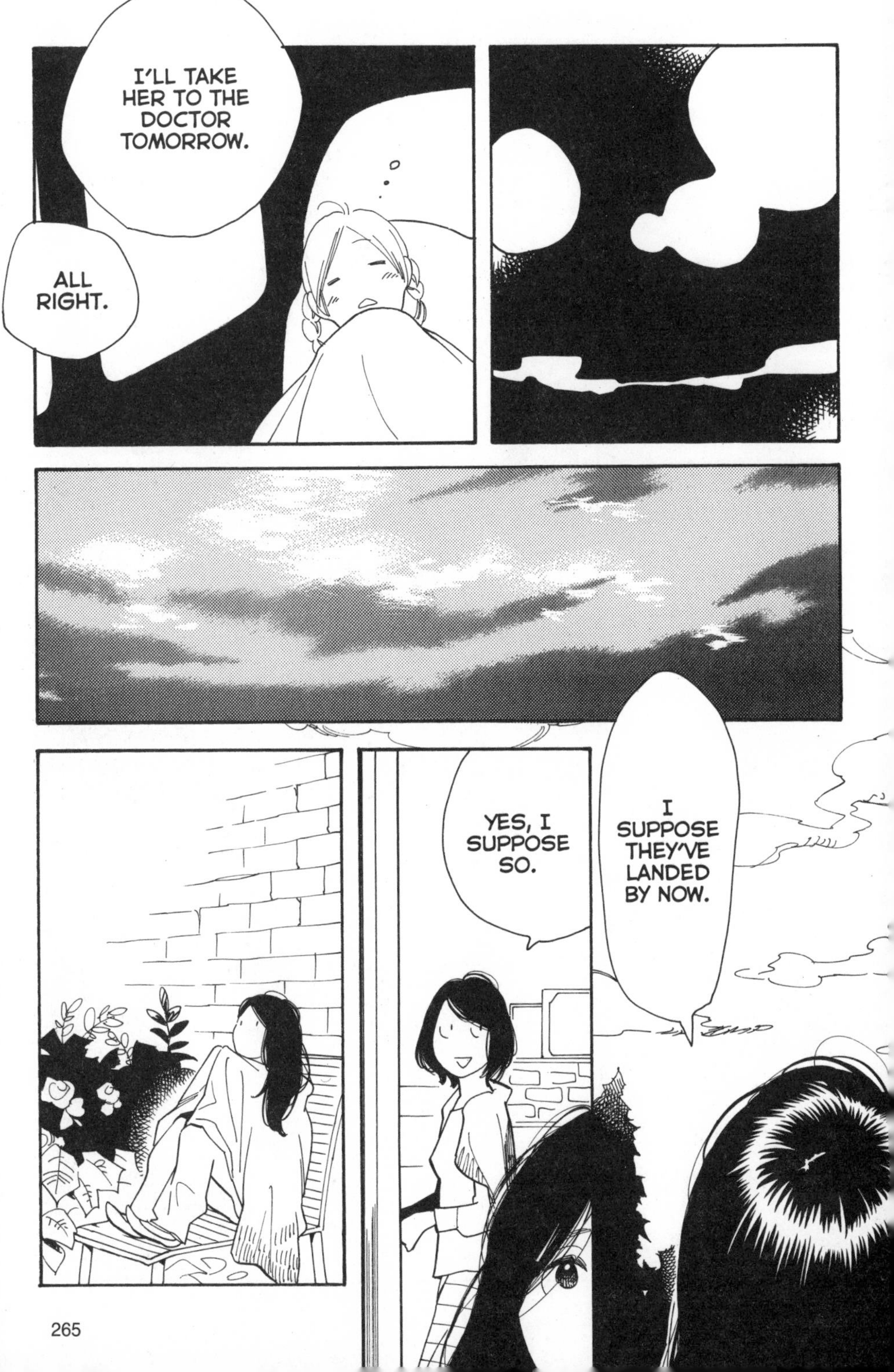
I'LL TAKE HER TO THE DOCTOR TOMORROW.
ALL RIGHT.
I SUPPOSE THEY'VE LANDED BY NOW.
YES, I SUPPOSE SO.

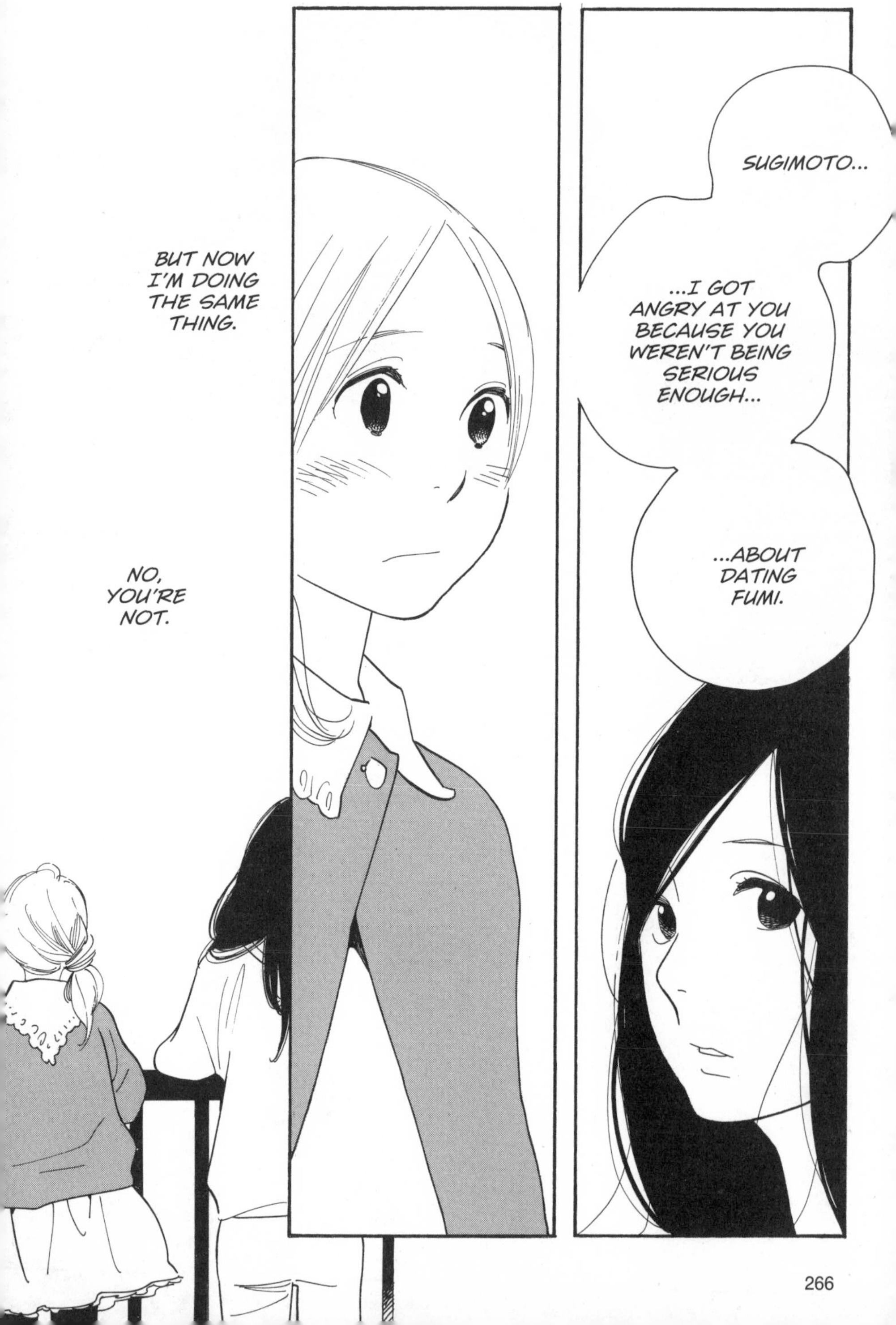
SUGIMOTO...
...I GOT ANGRY AT YOU BECAUSE YOU WEREN'T BEING SERIOUS ENOUGH...
...ABOUT DATING FUMI.
BUT NOW I'M DOING THE SAME THING.
NO, YOU'RE NOT.

THAT'S NOT TRUE, AKIRA.

IT'S NOT TRUE AT ALL.

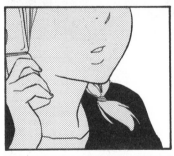

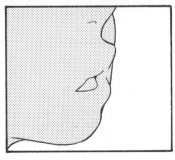

YEAH, I JUST GOT BACK.

AND I HAVE A SOUVENIR FOR YOU!

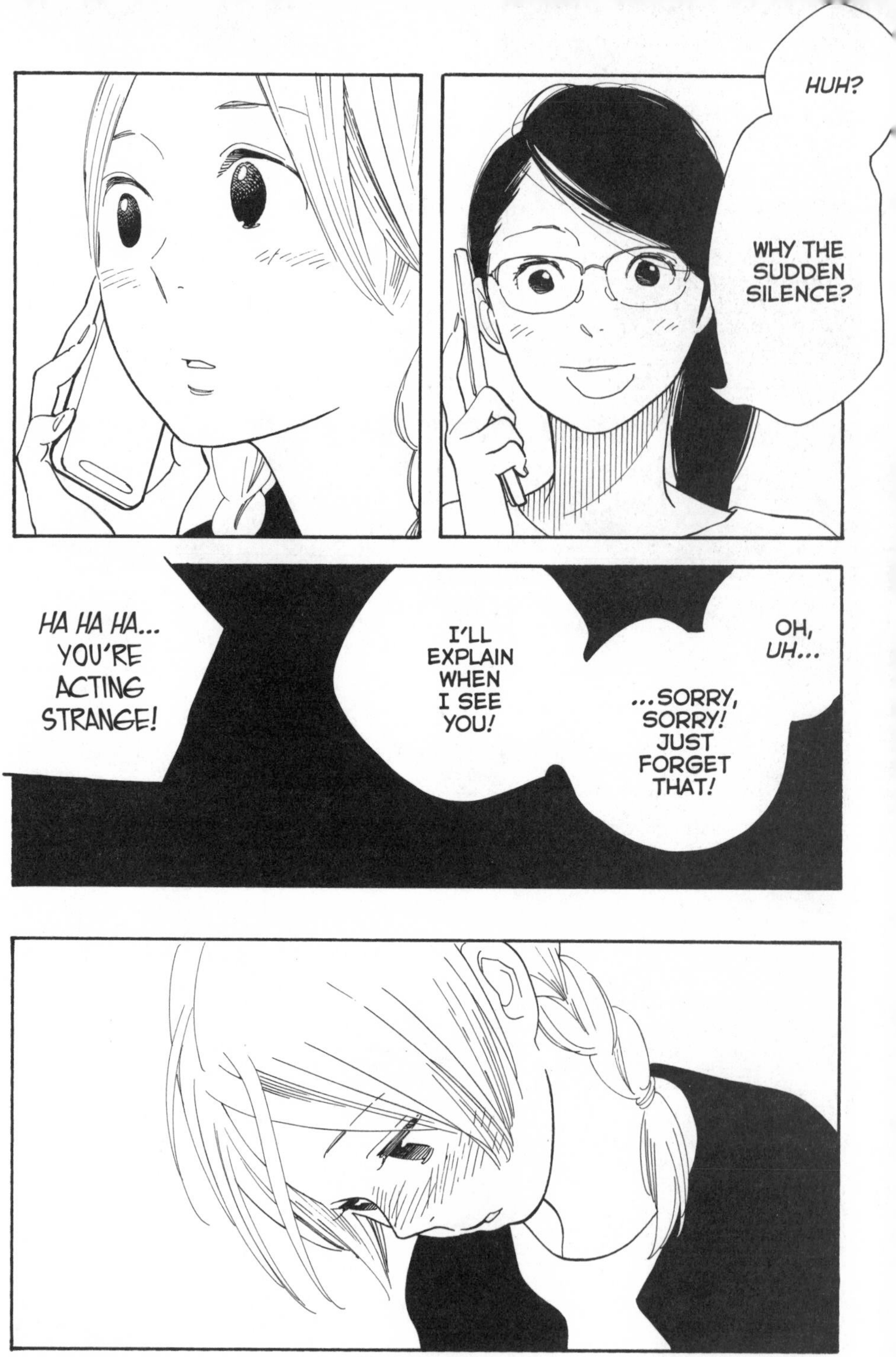
HUH?
WHY THE SUDDEN SILENCE?
OH, UH...
...SORRY, SORRY! JUST FORGET THAT!
I'LL EXPLAIN WHEN I SEE YOU!
HA HA HA... YOU'RE ACTING STRANGE!

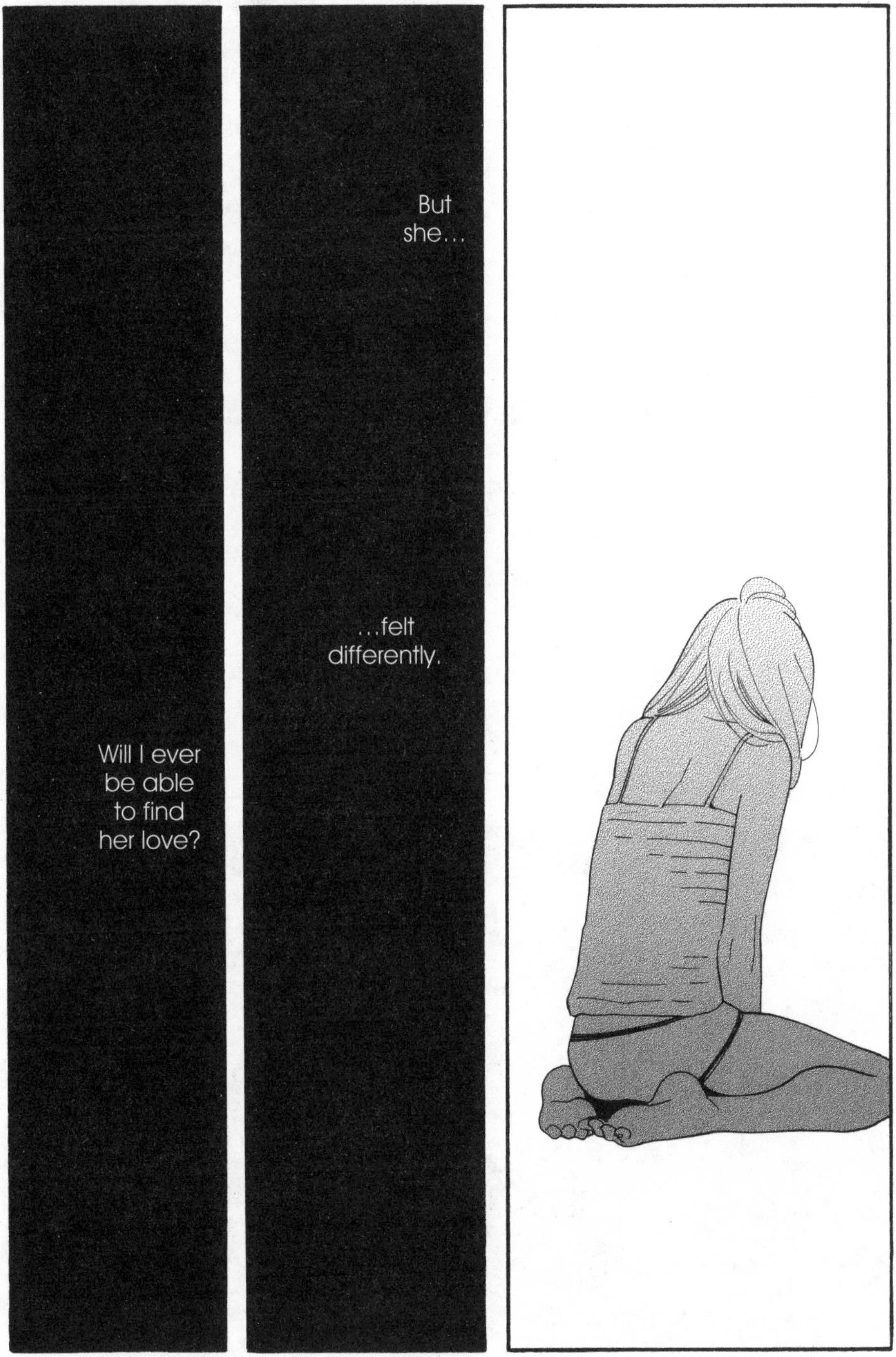
But she…
…felt differently.
Will I ever be able to find her love?

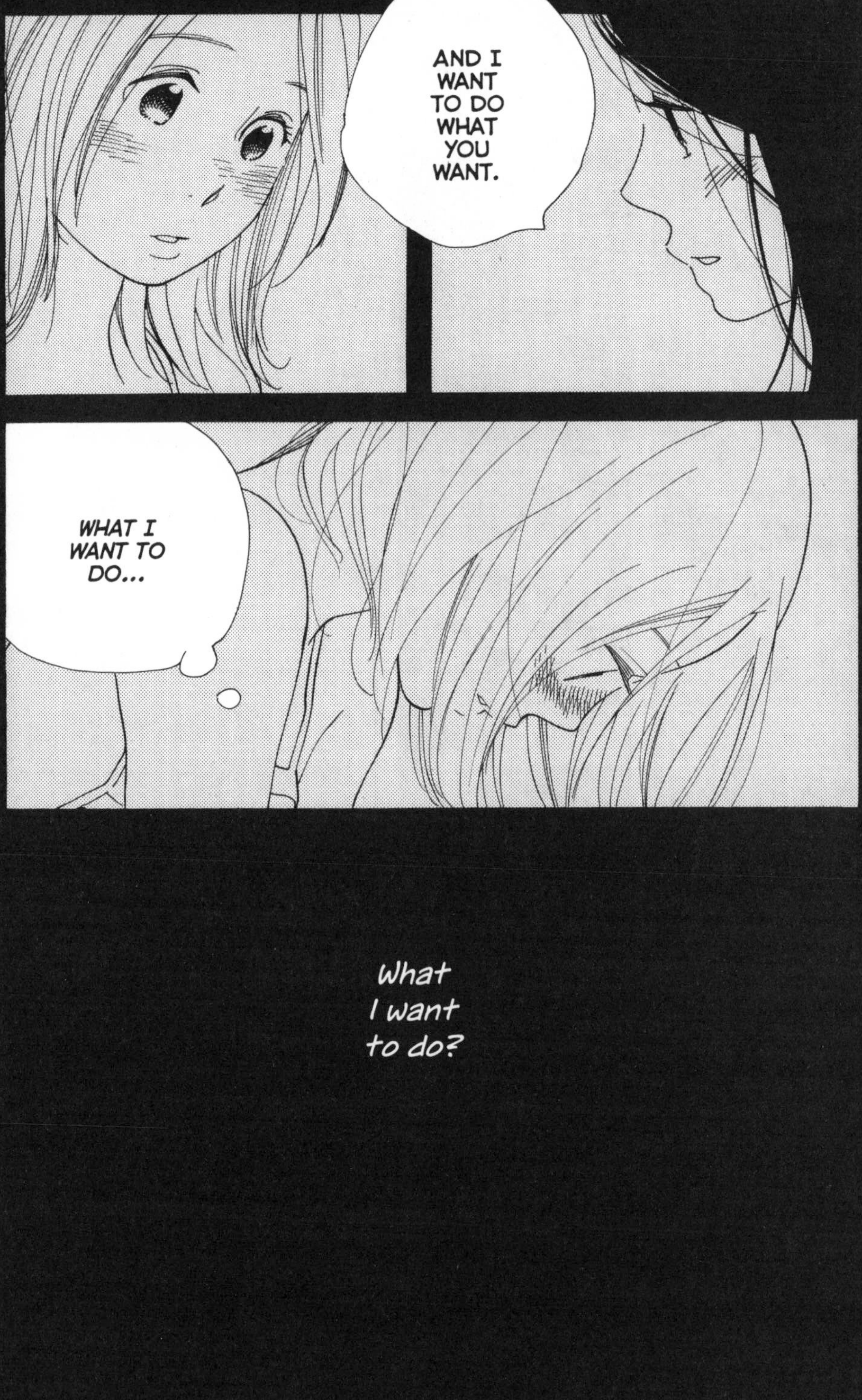
AND I WANT TO DO WHAT YOU WANT.
WHAT I WANT TO DO...
What I want to do?

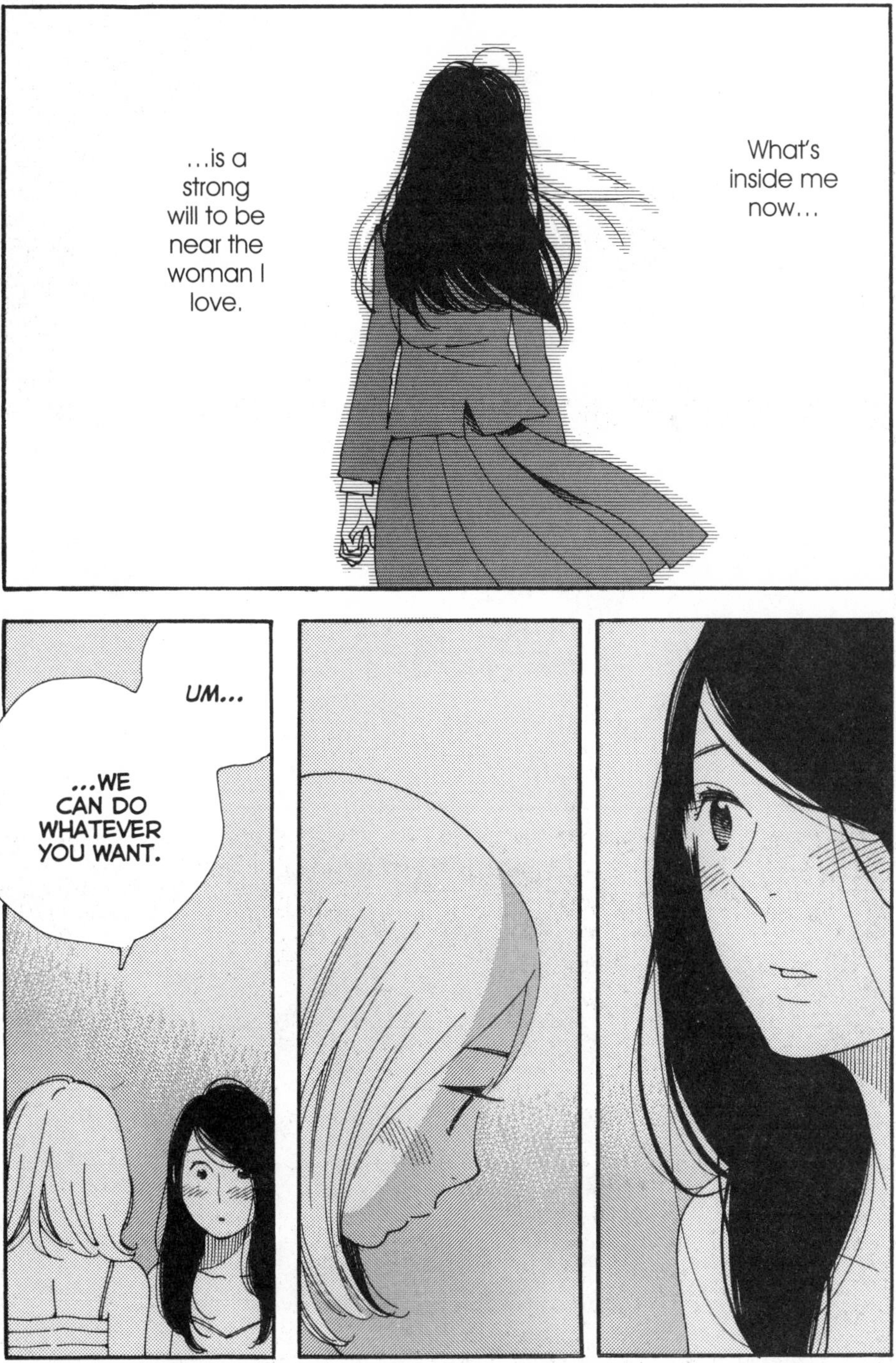
What's inside me now…
…is a strong will to be near the woman I love.
UM…
…WE CAN DO WHATEVER YOU WANT.

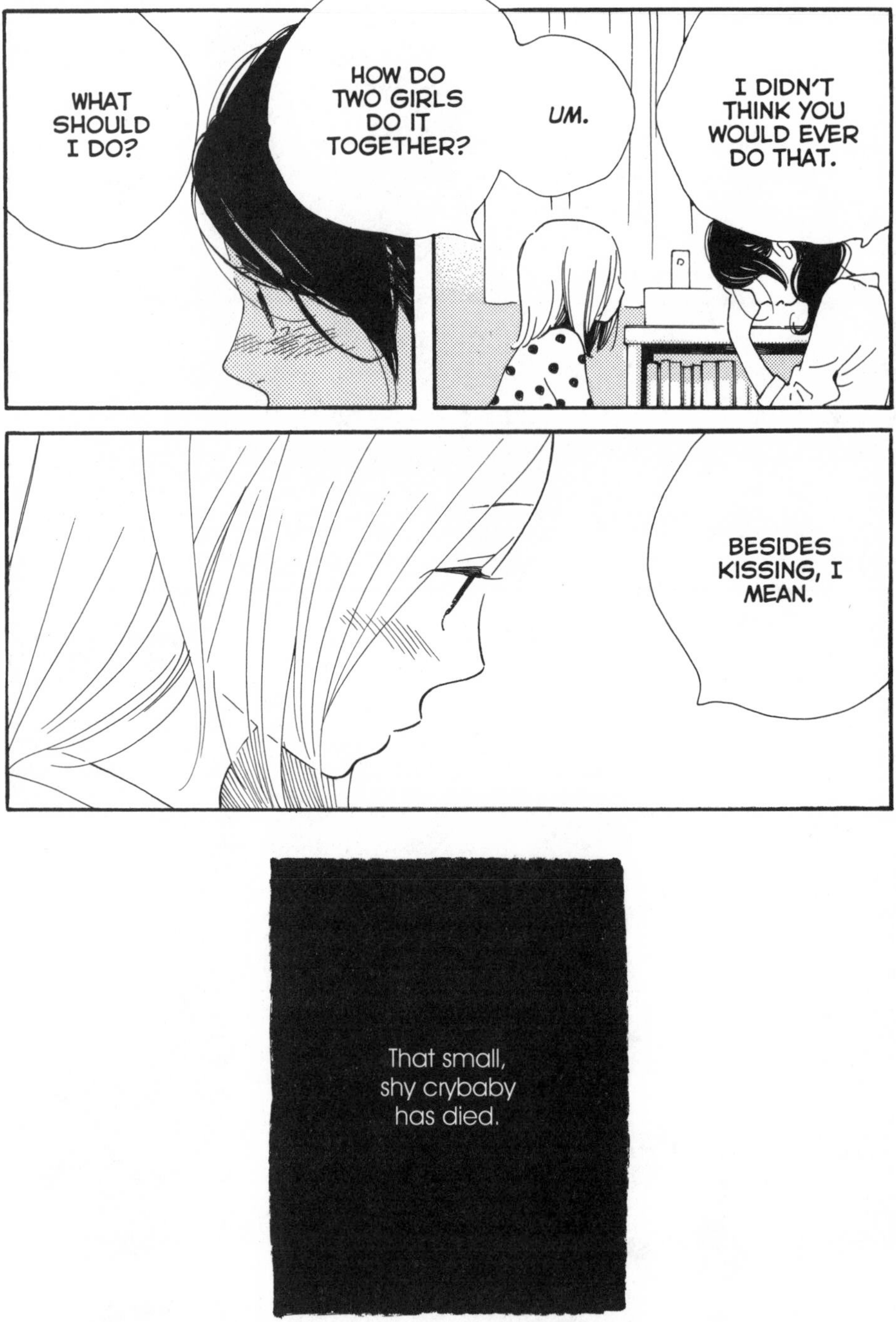
I DIDN'T THINK YOU WOULD EVER DO THAT.
UM.
HOW DO TWO GIRLS DO IT TOGETHER?
WHAT SHOULD I DO?
BESIDES KISSING, I MEAN.
That small, shy crybaby has died.

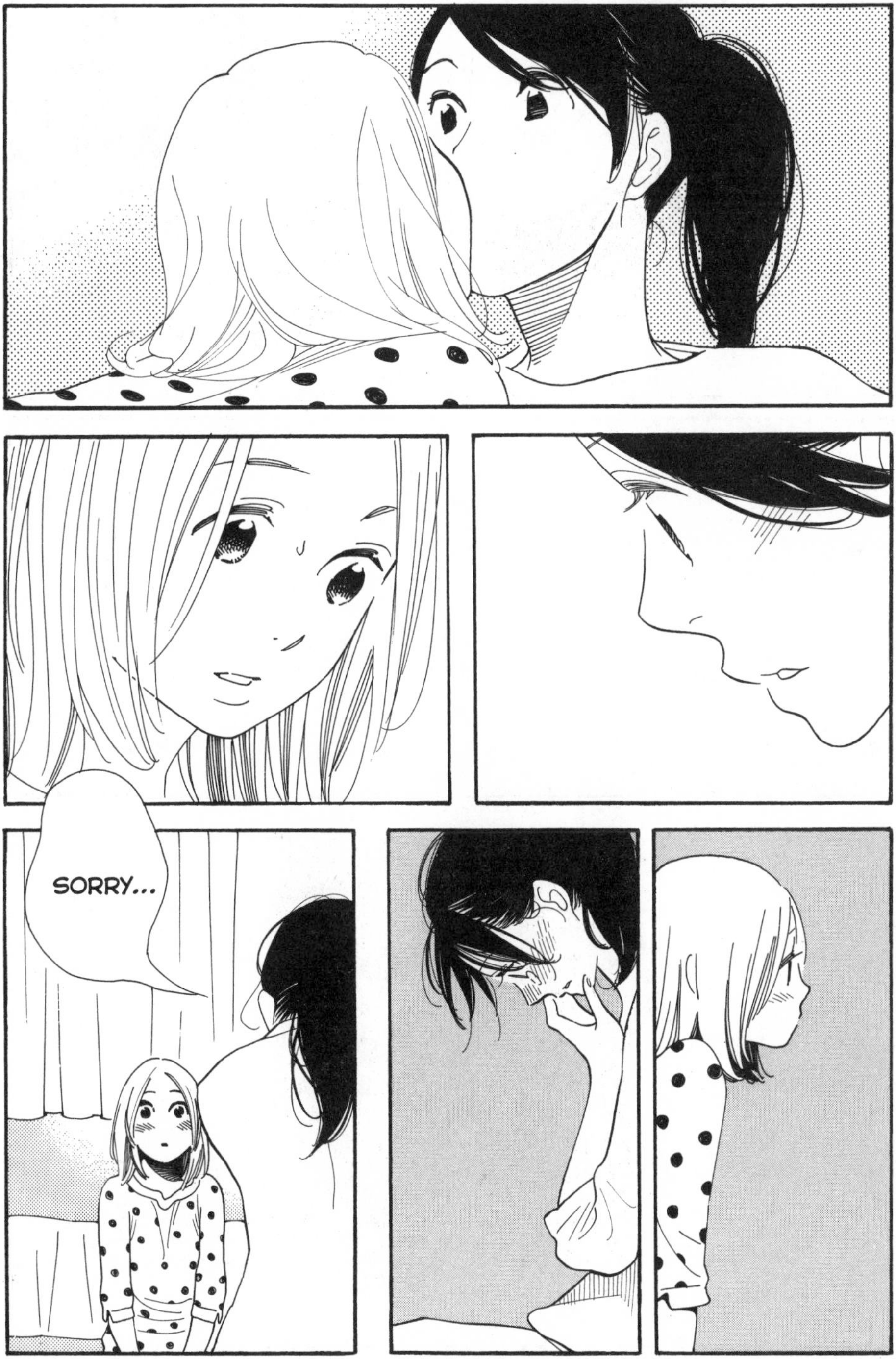
SORRY...

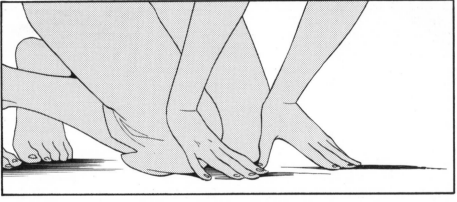

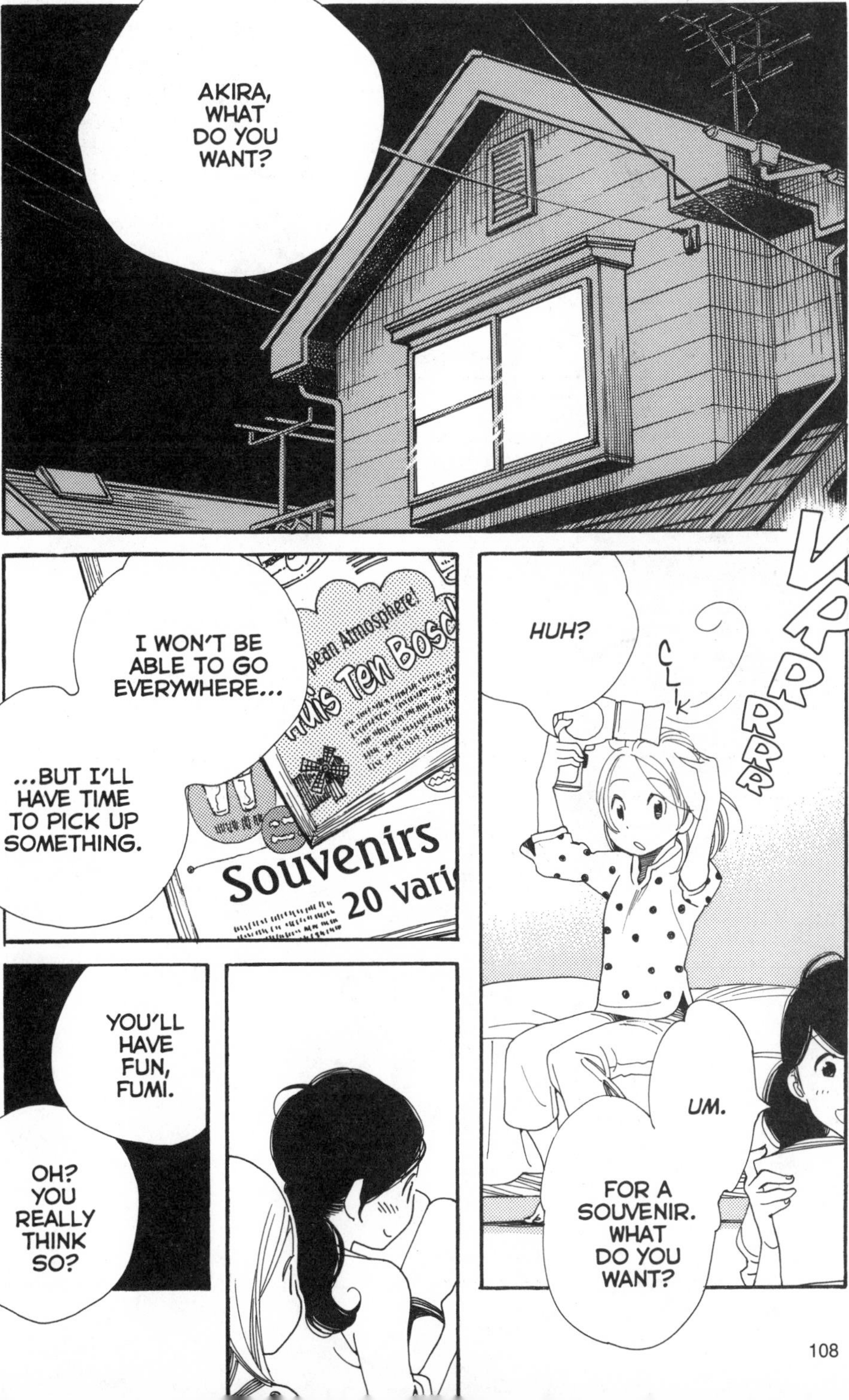
AKIRA, WHAT DO YOU WANT?
HUH?
CLIK
VRRRRRR
UM.
FOR A SOUVENIR. WHAT DO YOU WANT?
I WON'T BE ABLE TO GO EVERYWHERE...
...BUT I'LL HAVE TIME TO PICK UP SOMETHING.
Souvenirs
YOU'LL HAVE FUN, FUMI.
OH? YOU REALLY THINK SO?

It was my first love.
I was a child, and it was all I could think about.
You were everything in the world to me.

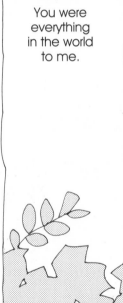

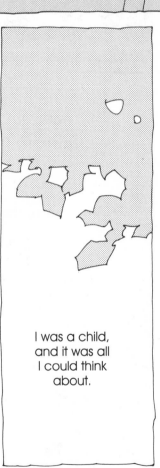

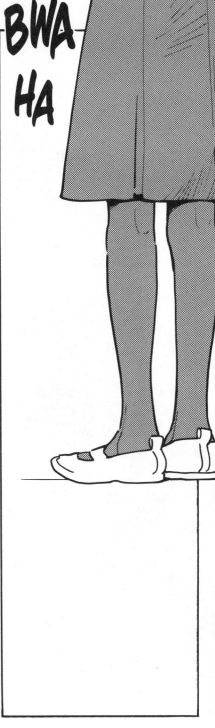

BWA HA

N...

WAS IT SO BAD YOU HAVE TO *LAUGH?*

HUH?

Aw, poor Pon!

NO, NOT AT ALL!

BUT I KEPT READING MYSELF INTO IT!

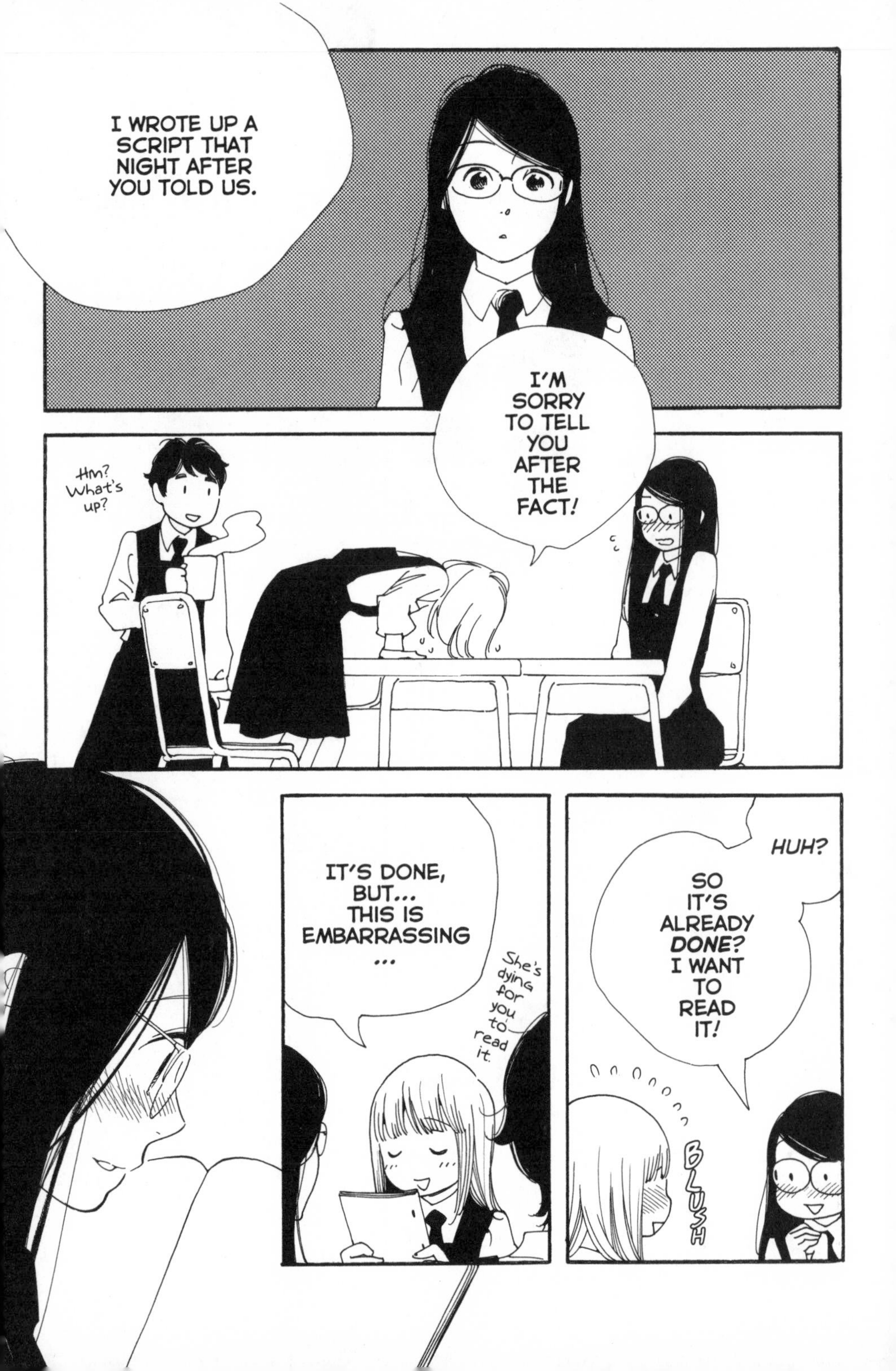
I WROTE UP A SCRIPT THAT NIGHT AFTER YOU TOLD US.
I'M SORRY TO TELL YOU AFTER THE FACT!
Hm? What's up?
HUH?
SO IT'S ALREADY DONE? I WANT TO READ IT!
BLUSH
IT'S DONE, BUT... THIS IS EMBARRASSING...
She's dying for you to read it.

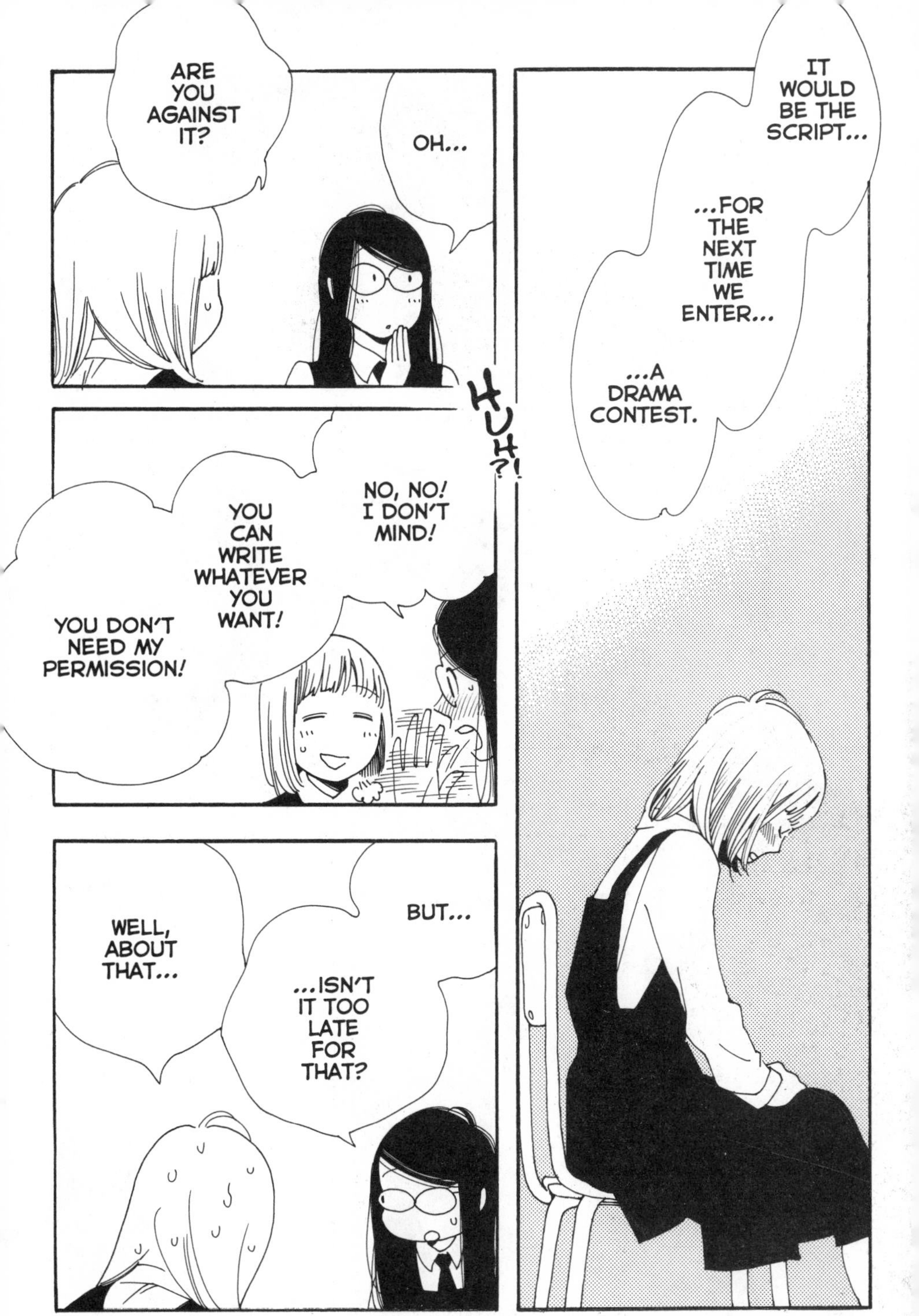

IT WOULD BE THE SCRIPT...
...FOR THE NEXT TIME WE ENTER...
...A DRAMA CONTEST.
OH...
ARE YOU AGAINST IT?
HUH?!
NO, NO! I DON'T MIND!
YOU CAN WRITE WHATEVER YOU WANT!
YOU DON'T NEED MY PERMISSION!
BUT...
...ISN'T IT TOO LATE FOR THAT?
WELL, ABOUT THAT...

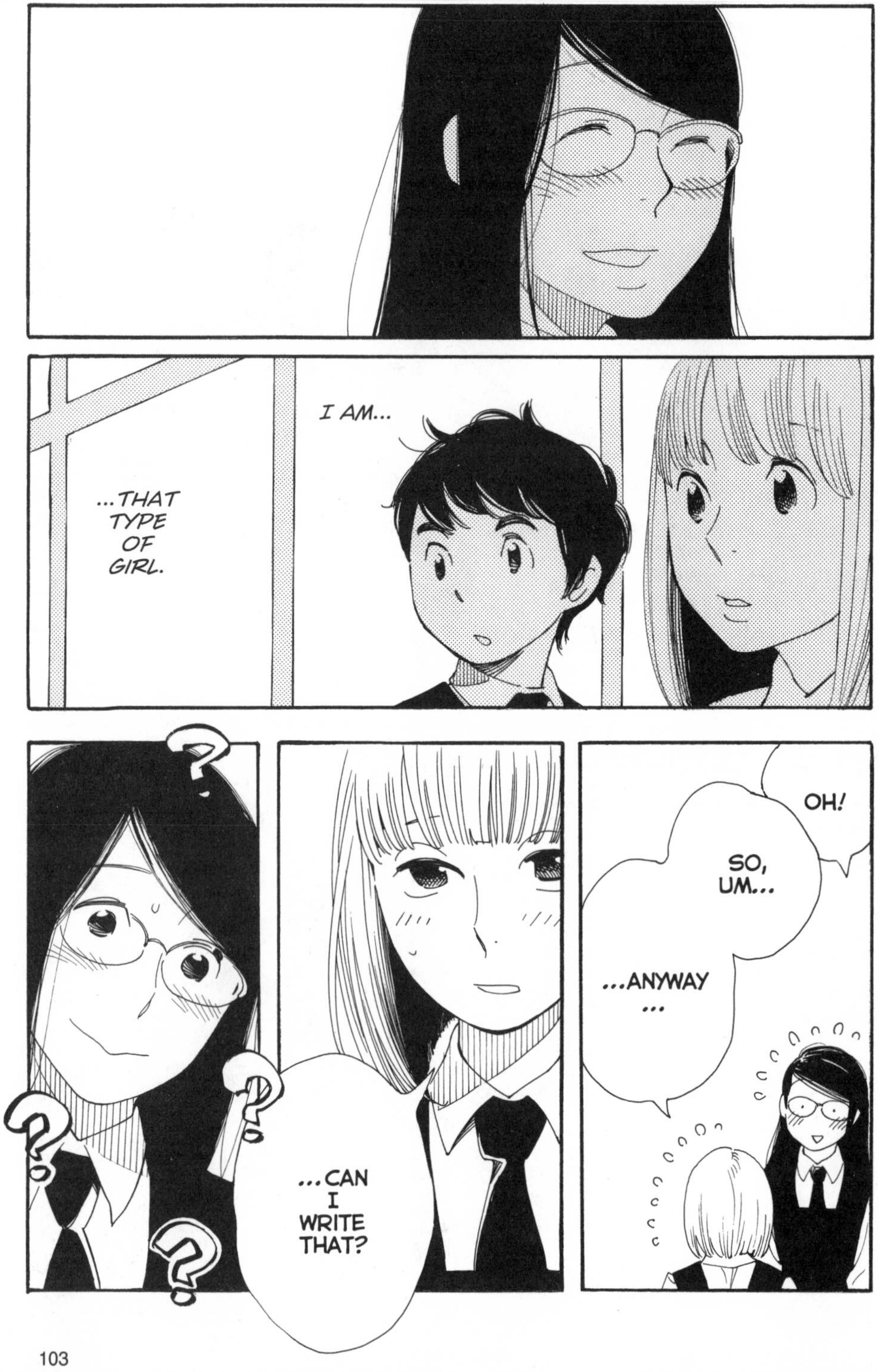
I AM...
...THAT TYPE OF GIRL.
OH!
SO, UM...
...ANYWAY ...
...CAN I WRITE THAT?

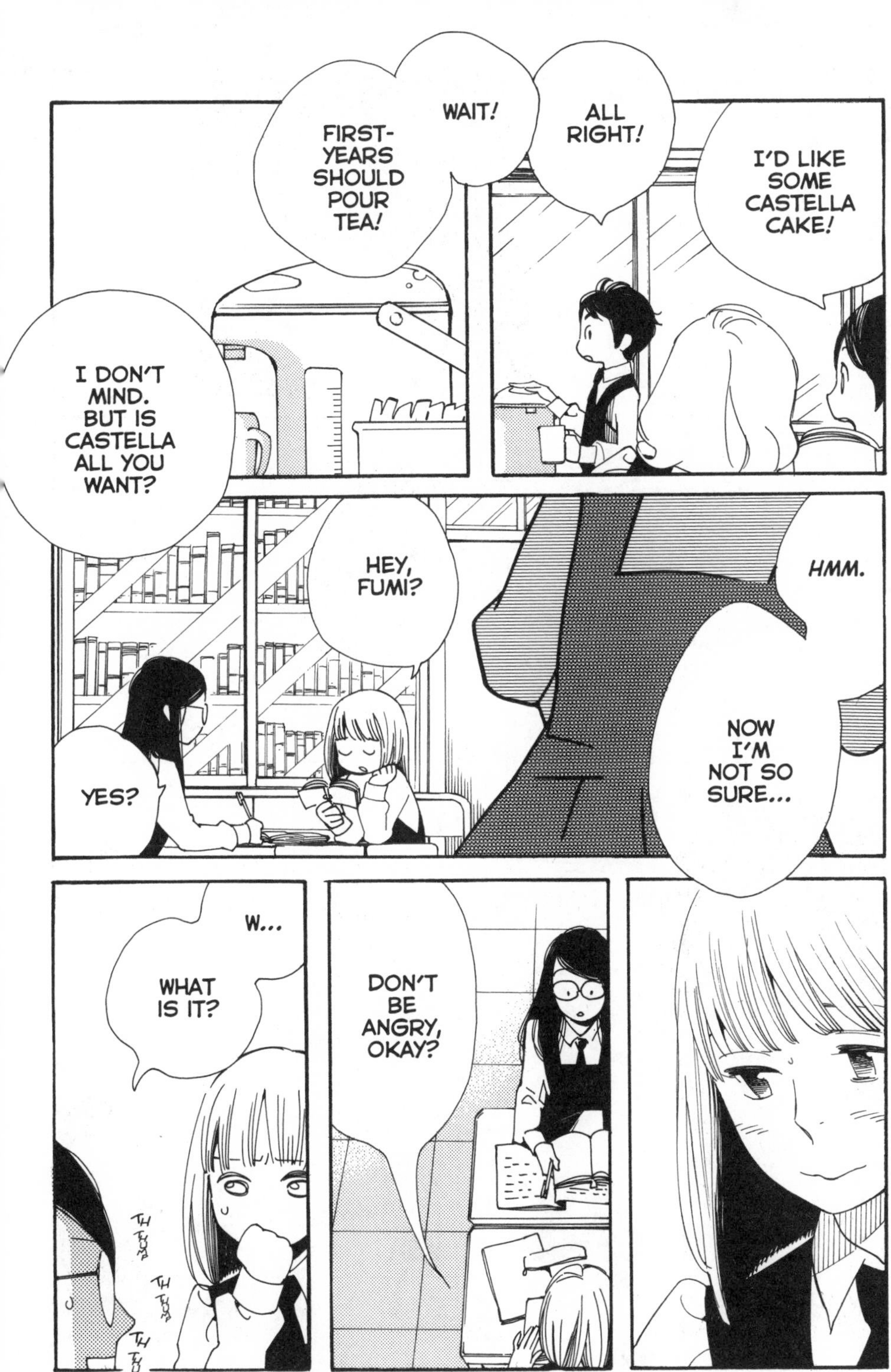
I'D LIKE SOME CASTELLA CAKE!
ALL RIGHT!
WAIT!
FIRST-YEARS SHOULD POUR TEA!
I DON'T MIND. BUT IS CASTELLA ALL YOU WANT?
HMM.
NOW I'M NOT SO SURE...
HEY, FUMI?
YES?
DON'T BE ANGRY, OKAY?
W...
WHAT IS IT?
TH THUMP
TH THUMP
TH THUMP

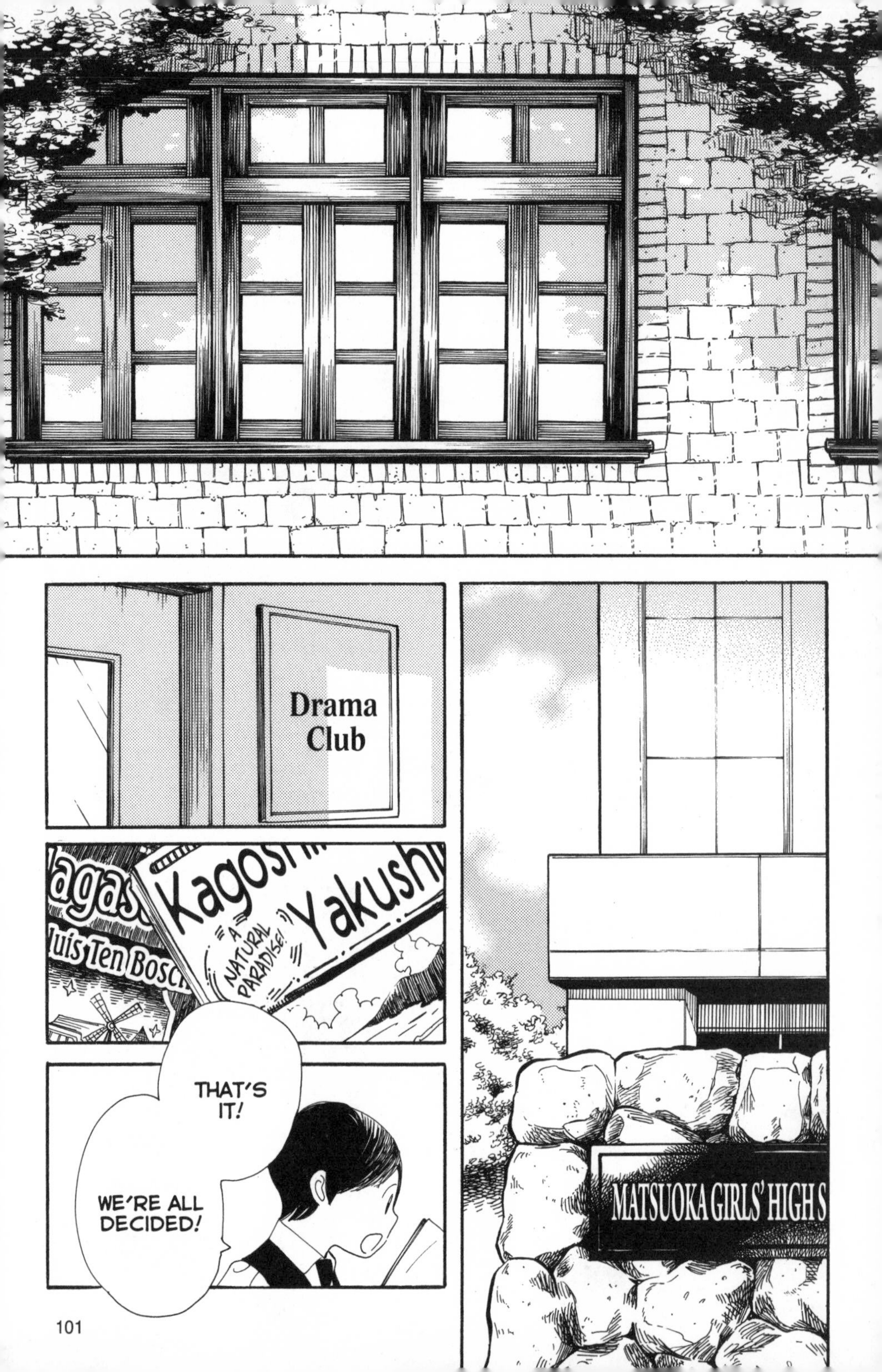
MATSUOKA GIRLS' HIGH S
Drama Club
A NATURAL PARADISE!
THAT'S IT!
WE'RE ALL DECIDED!

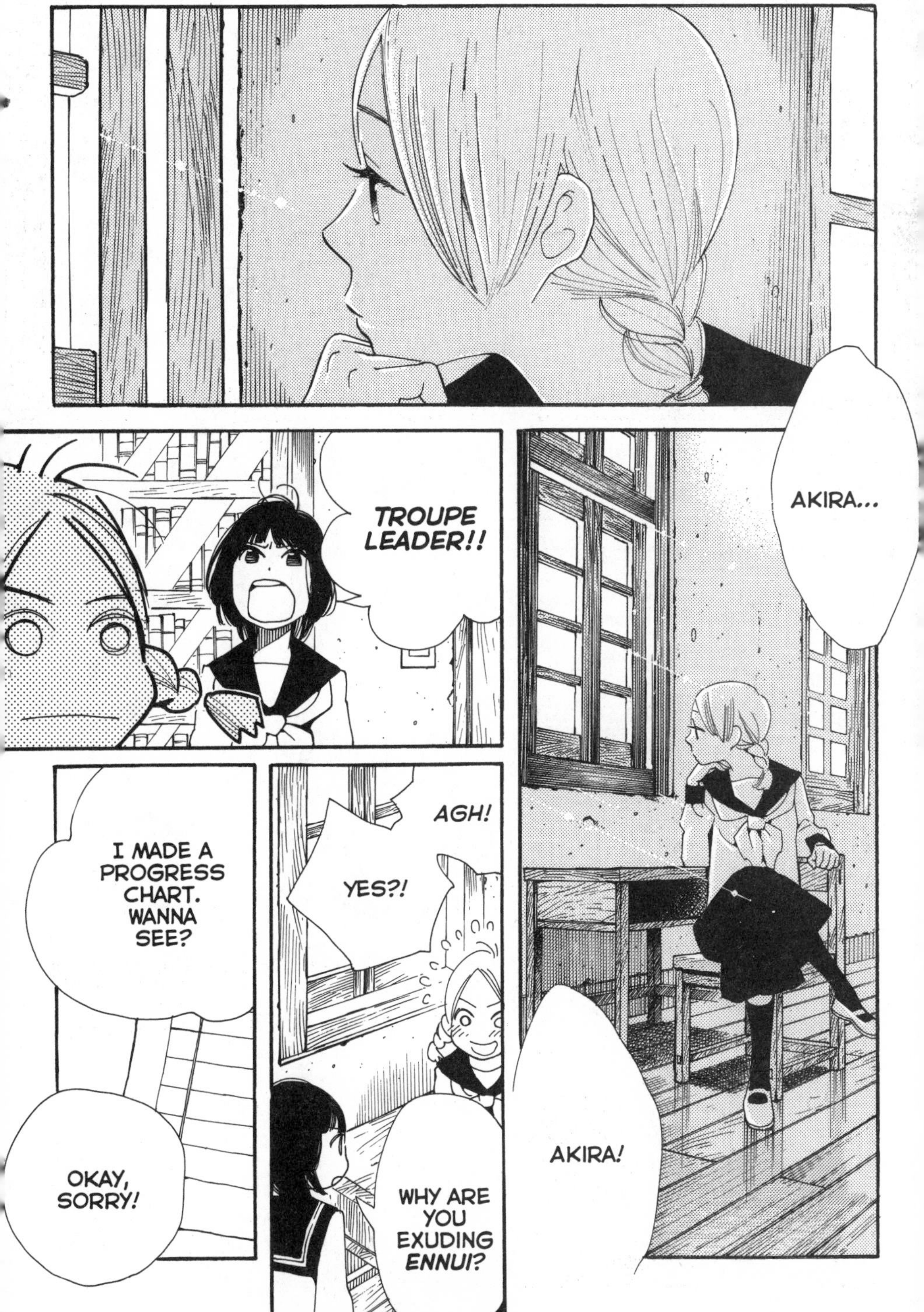
AKIRA...
AKIRA!
TROUPE LEADER!!
AGH!
YES?!
WHY ARE YOU EXUDING ENNUI?
I MADE A PROGRESS CHART. WANNA SEE?
OKAY, SORRY!

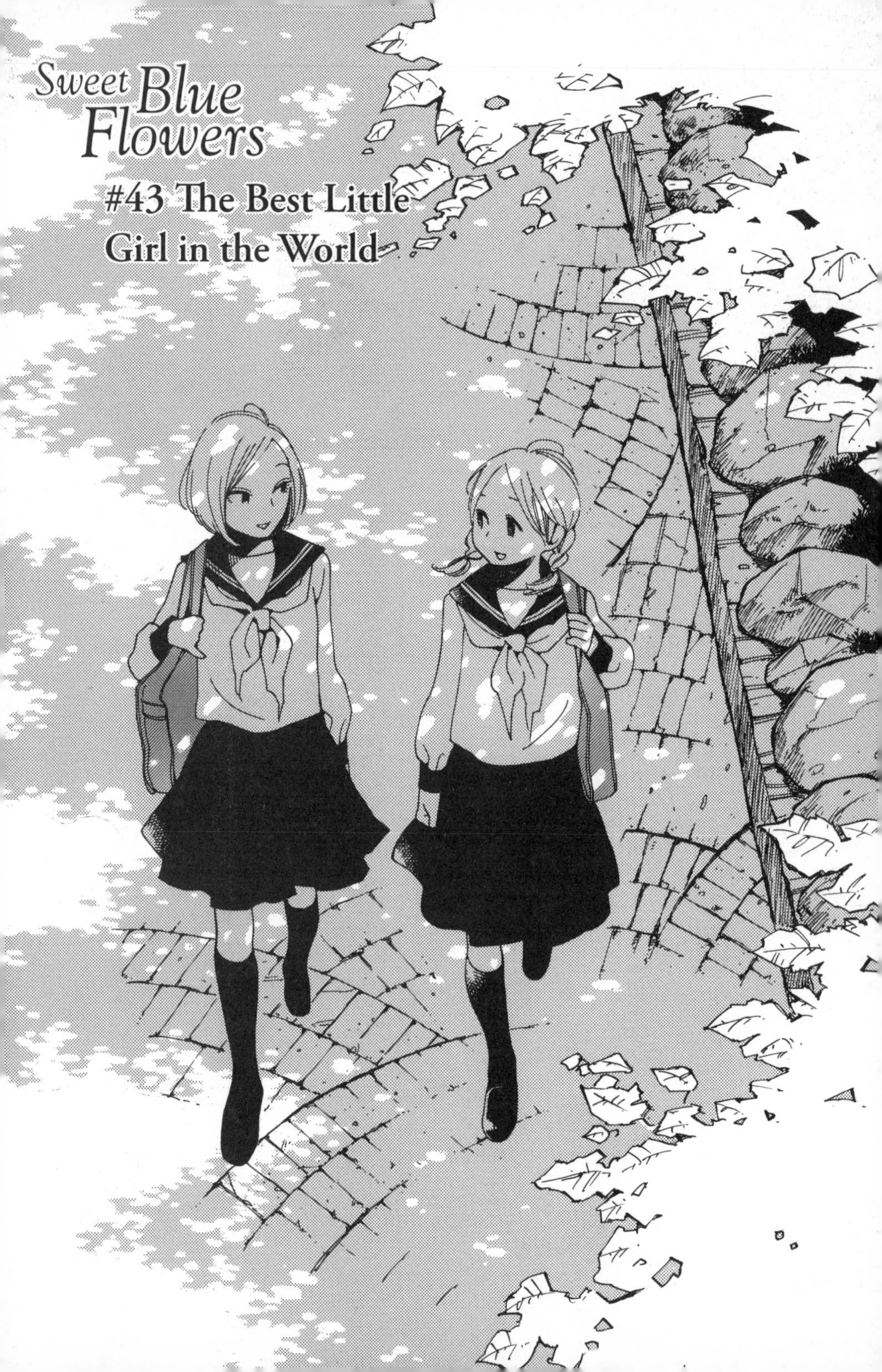
Sweet Blue Flowers
#43 The Best Little Girl in the World

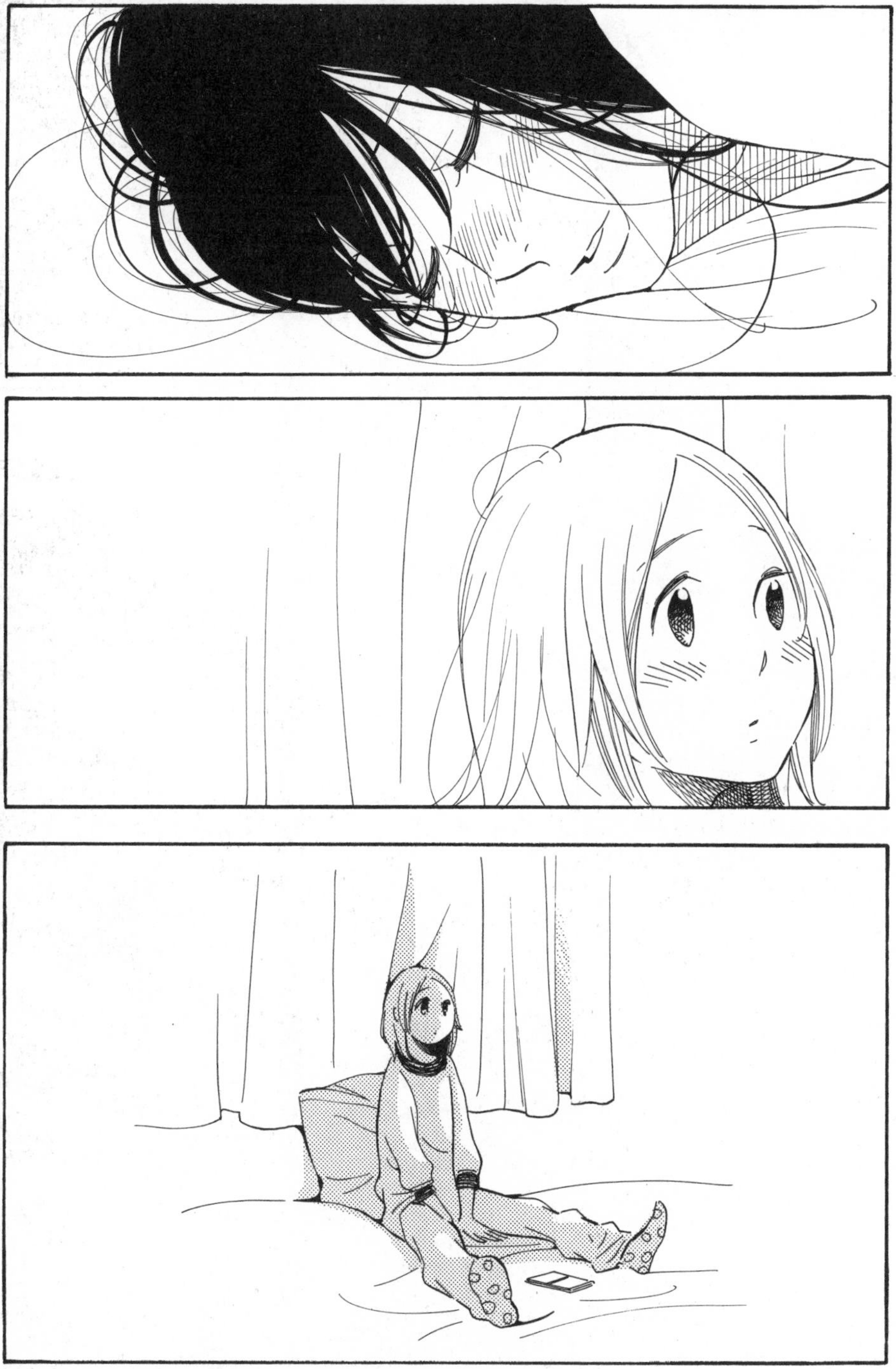

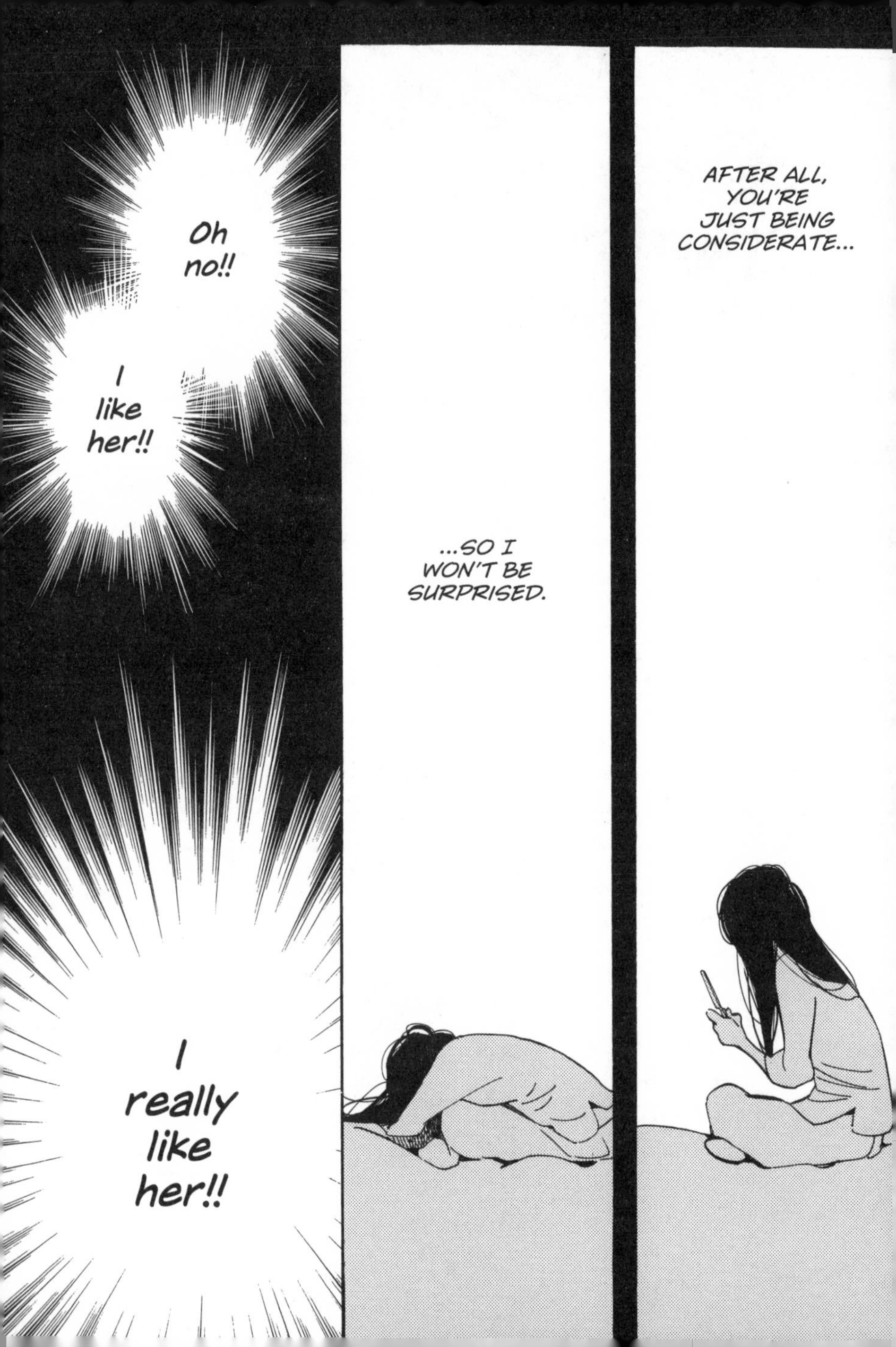
AFTER ALL, YOU'RE JUST BEING CONSIDERATE...
...SO I WON'T BE SURPRISED.
Oh no!!
I like her!!
I really like her!!

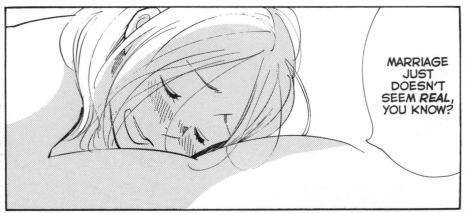

MARRIAGE JUST DOESN'T SEEM *REAL,* YOU KNOW?

YEAH...

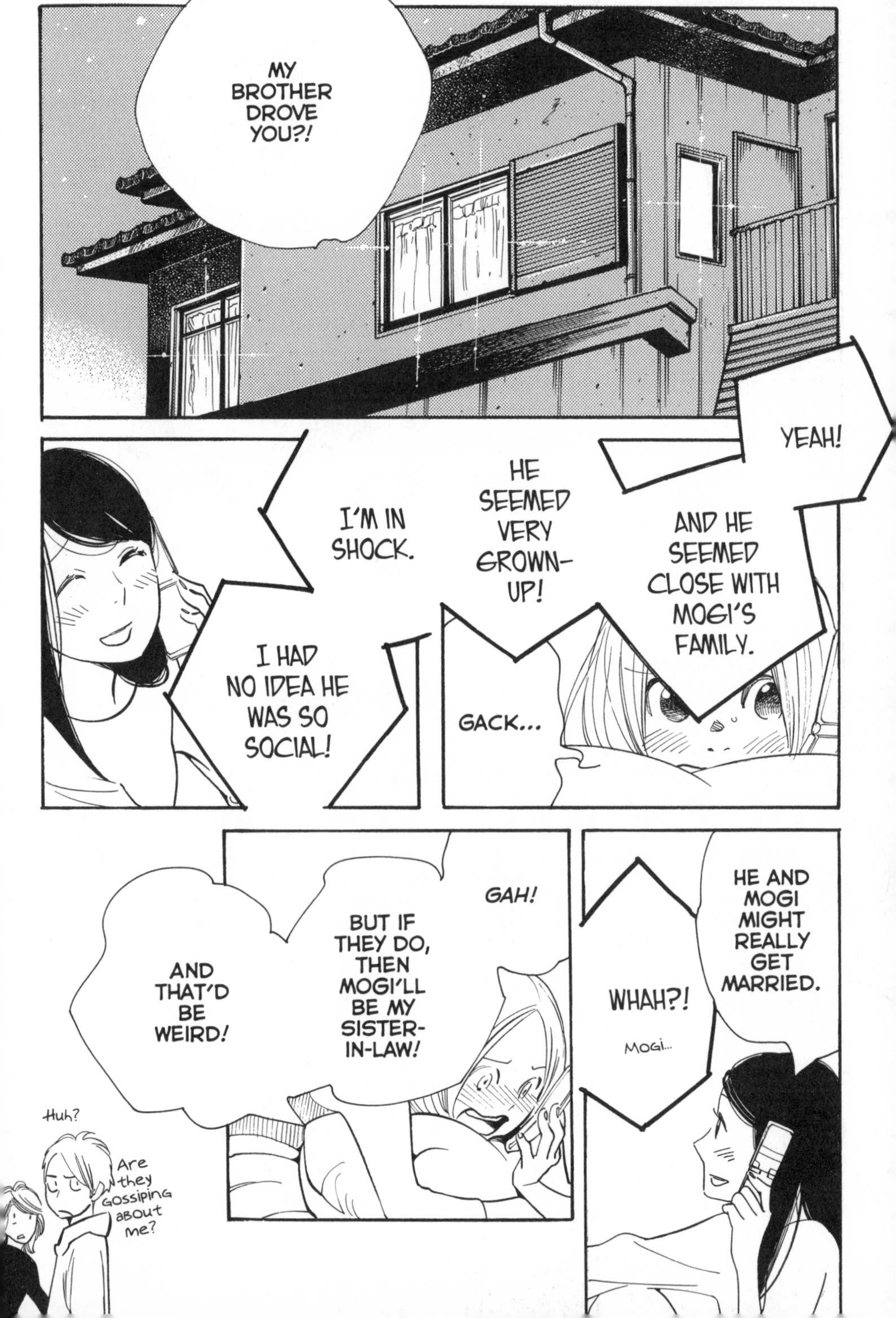
MY BROTHER DROVE YOU?!
YEAH!
AND HE SEEMED CLOSE WITH MOGI'S FAMILY.
HE SEEMED VERY GROWN-UP!
GACK...
I'M IN SHOCK.
I HAD NO IDEA HE WAS SO SOCIAL!
HE AND MOGI MIGHT REALLY GET MARRIED.
WHAH?!
MOGI...
GAH!
BUT IF THEY DO, THEN MOGI'LL BE MY SISTER-IN-LAW!
AND THAT'D BE WEIRD!
Huh?
Are they gossiping about me?

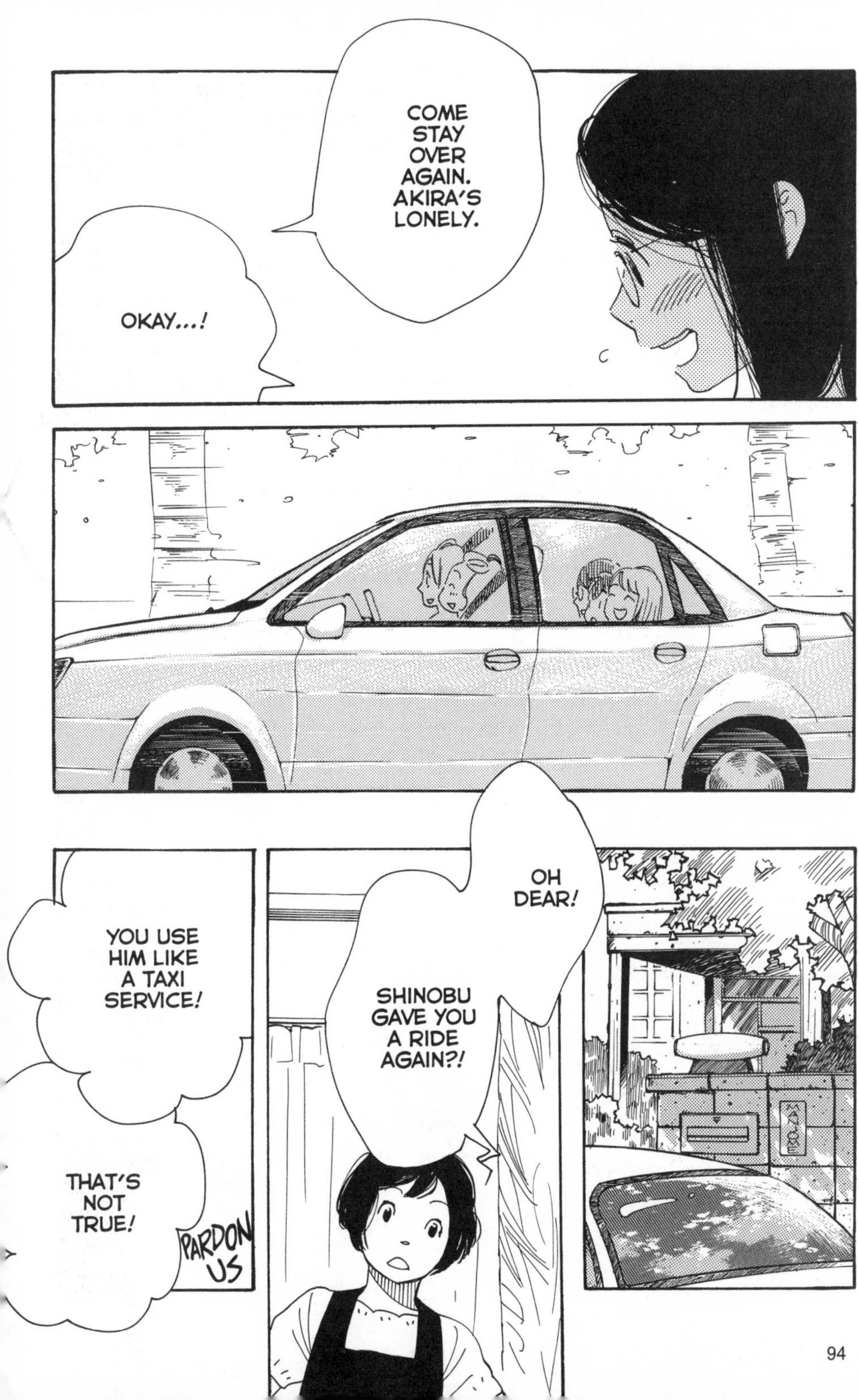
COME STAY OVER AGAIN. AKIRA'S LONELY.
OKAY...!
OH DEAR!
SHINOBU GAVE YOU A RIDE AGAIN?!
YOU USE HIM LIKE A TAXI SERVICE!
THAT'S NOT TRUE!
PARDON US

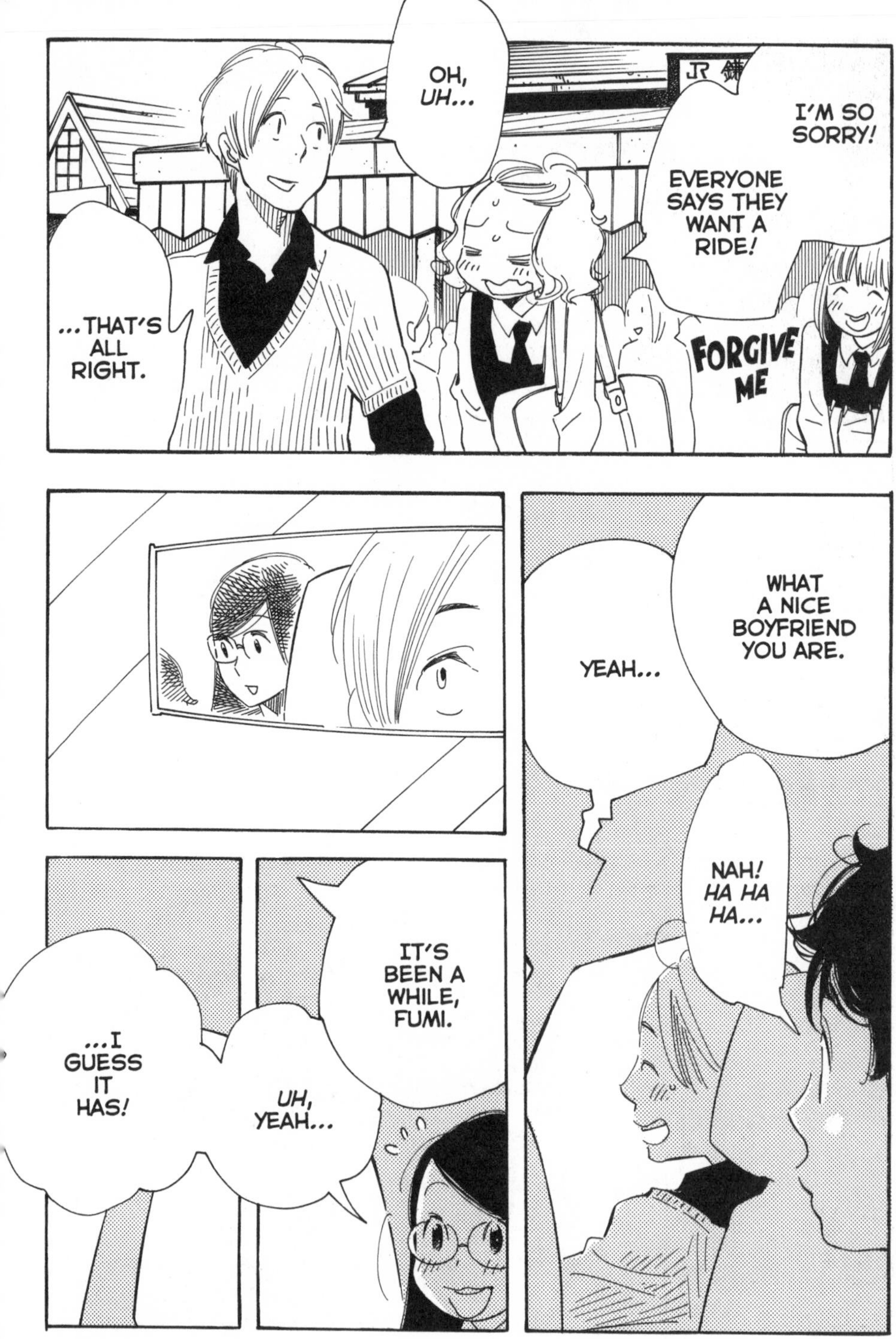
I'M SO SORRY!
EVERYONE SAYS THEY WANT A RIDE!
FORGIVE ME
OH, UH...
...THAT'S ALL RIGHT.
WHAT A NICE BOYFRIEND YOU ARE.
YEAH...
NAH! HA HA HA...
IT'S BEEN A WHILE, FUMI.
UH, YEAH...
...I GUESS IT HAS!

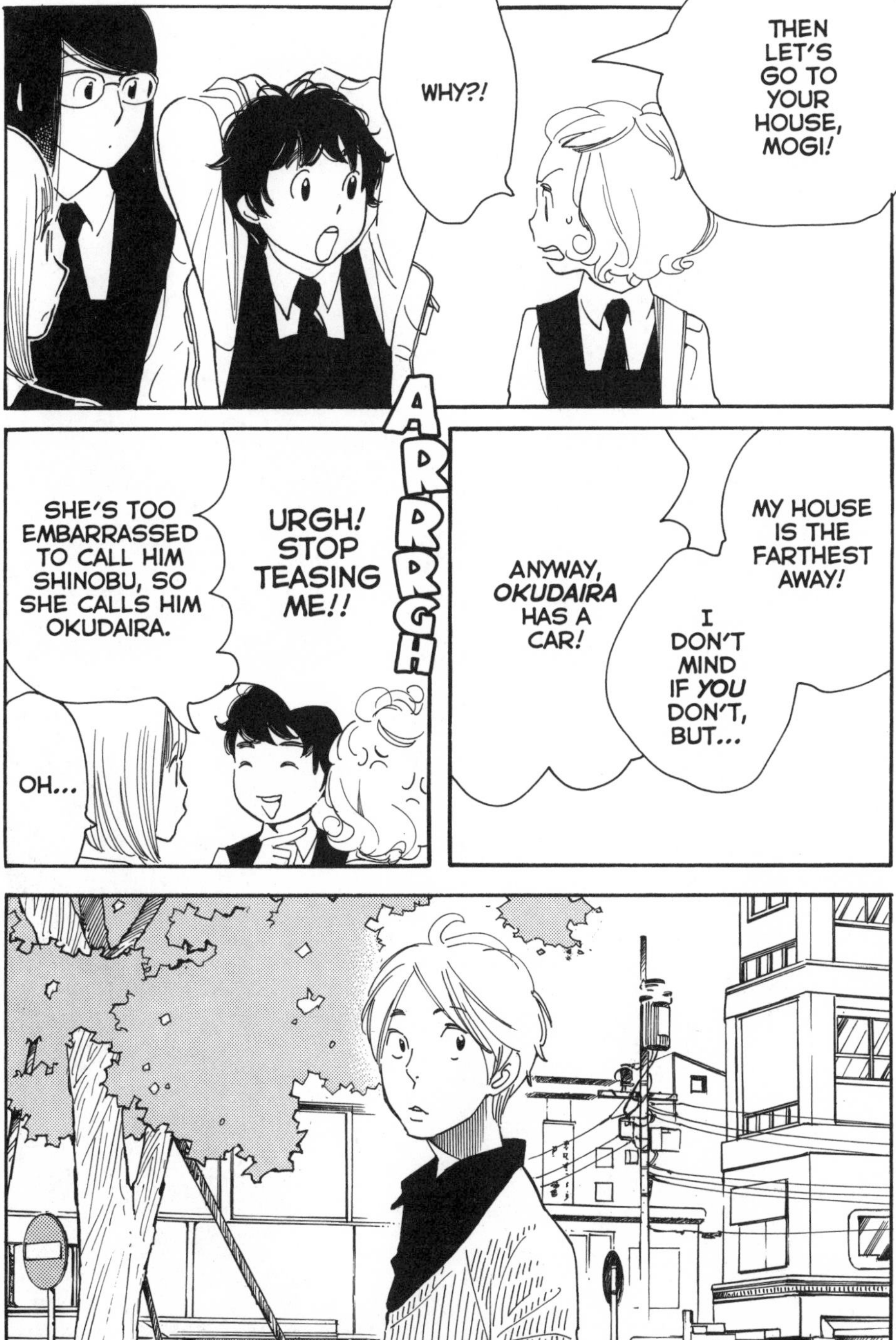
THEN LET'S GO TO YOUR HOUSE, MOGI!
WHY?!
MY HOUSE IS THE FARTHEST AWAY!
I DON'T MIND IF *YOU* DON'T, BUT...
ANYWAY, *OKUDAIRA* HAS A CAR!
ARRRGH
URGH! STOP TEASING ME!!
SHE'S TOO EMBARRASSED TO CALL HIM SHINOBU, SO SHE CALLS HIM OKUDAIRA.
OH...

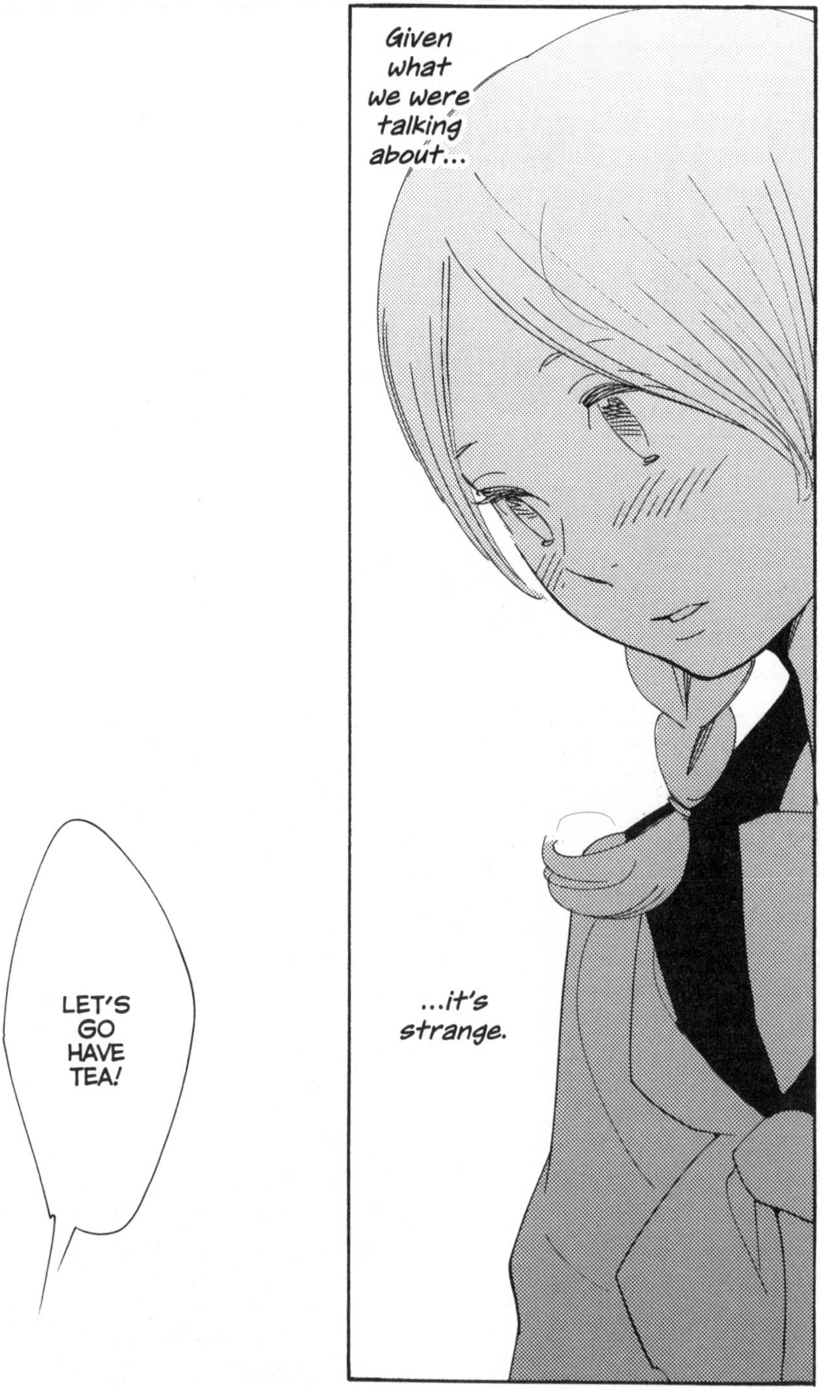
Given what we were talking about...
...it's strange.
LET'S GO HAVE TEA!

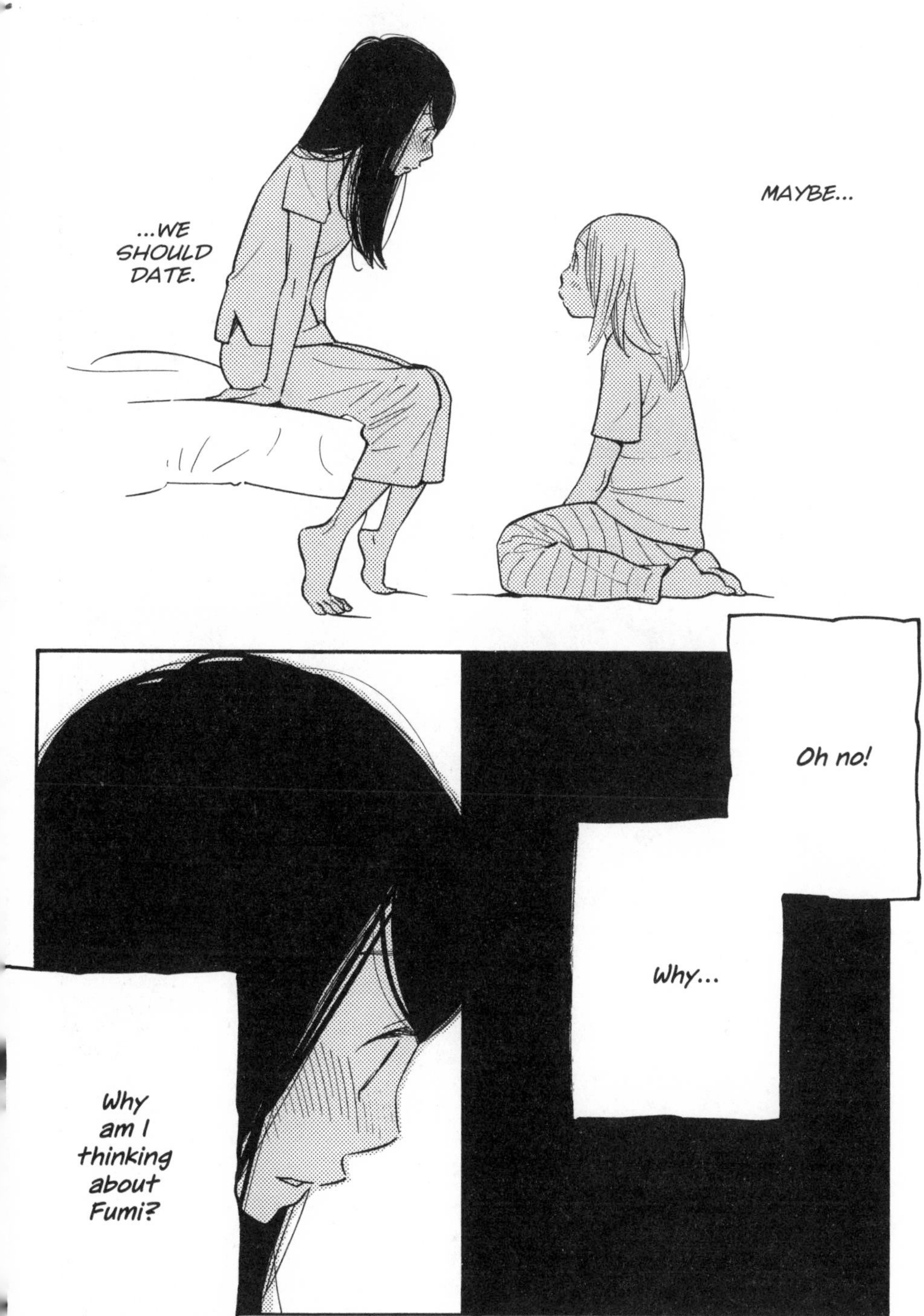
MAYBE...
...WE SHOULD DATE.
Oh no!
Why...
Why am I thinking about Fumi?

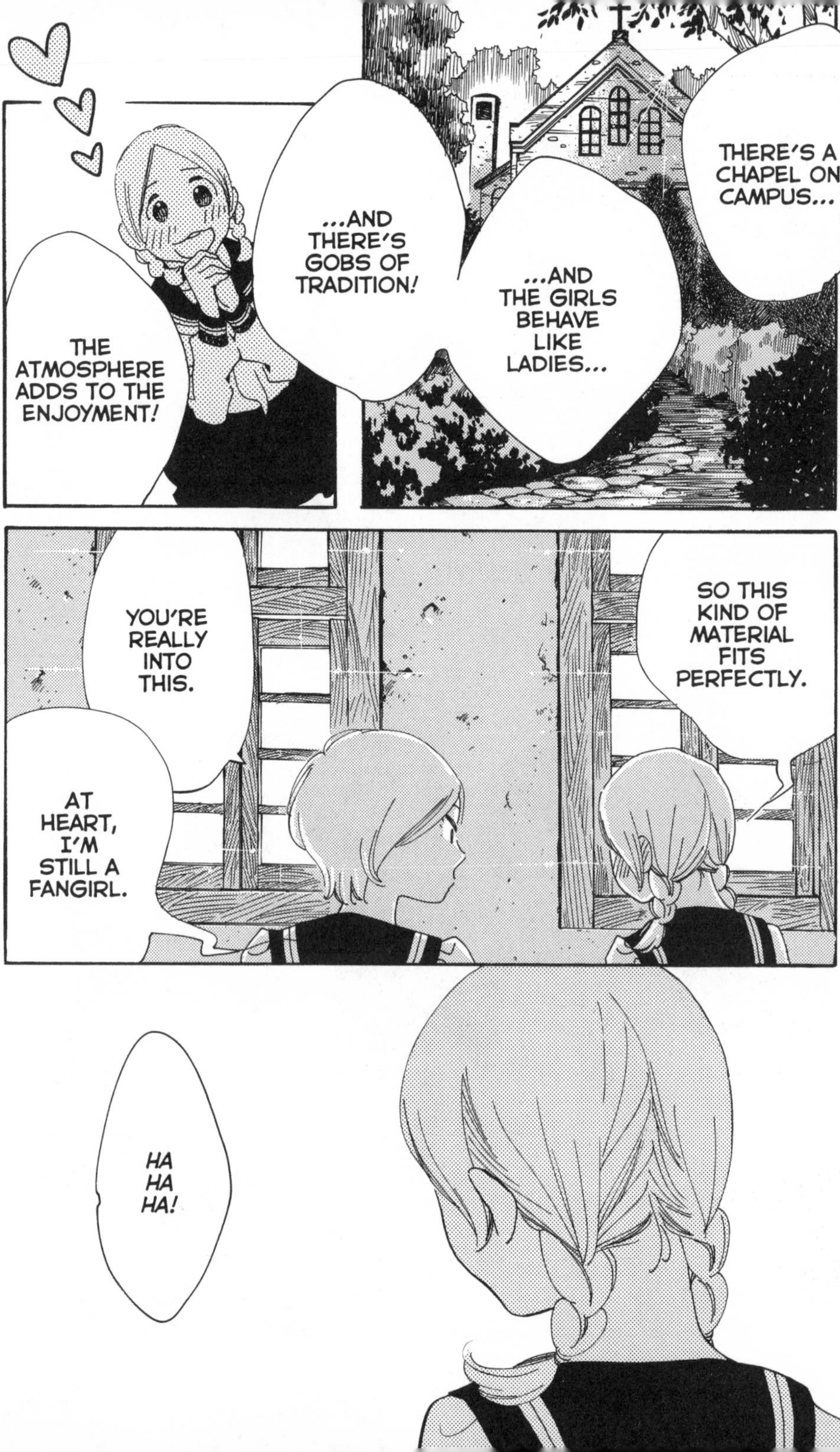
THERE'S A CHAPEL ON CAMPUS...
...AND THE GIRLS BEHAVE LIKE LADIES...
...AND THERE'S GOBS OF TRADITION!
THE ATMOSPHERE ADDS TO THE ENJOYMENT!
SO THIS KIND OF MATERIAL FITS PERFECTLY.
YOU'RE REALLY INTO THIS.
AT HEART, I'M STILL A FANGIRL.
HA HA HA!

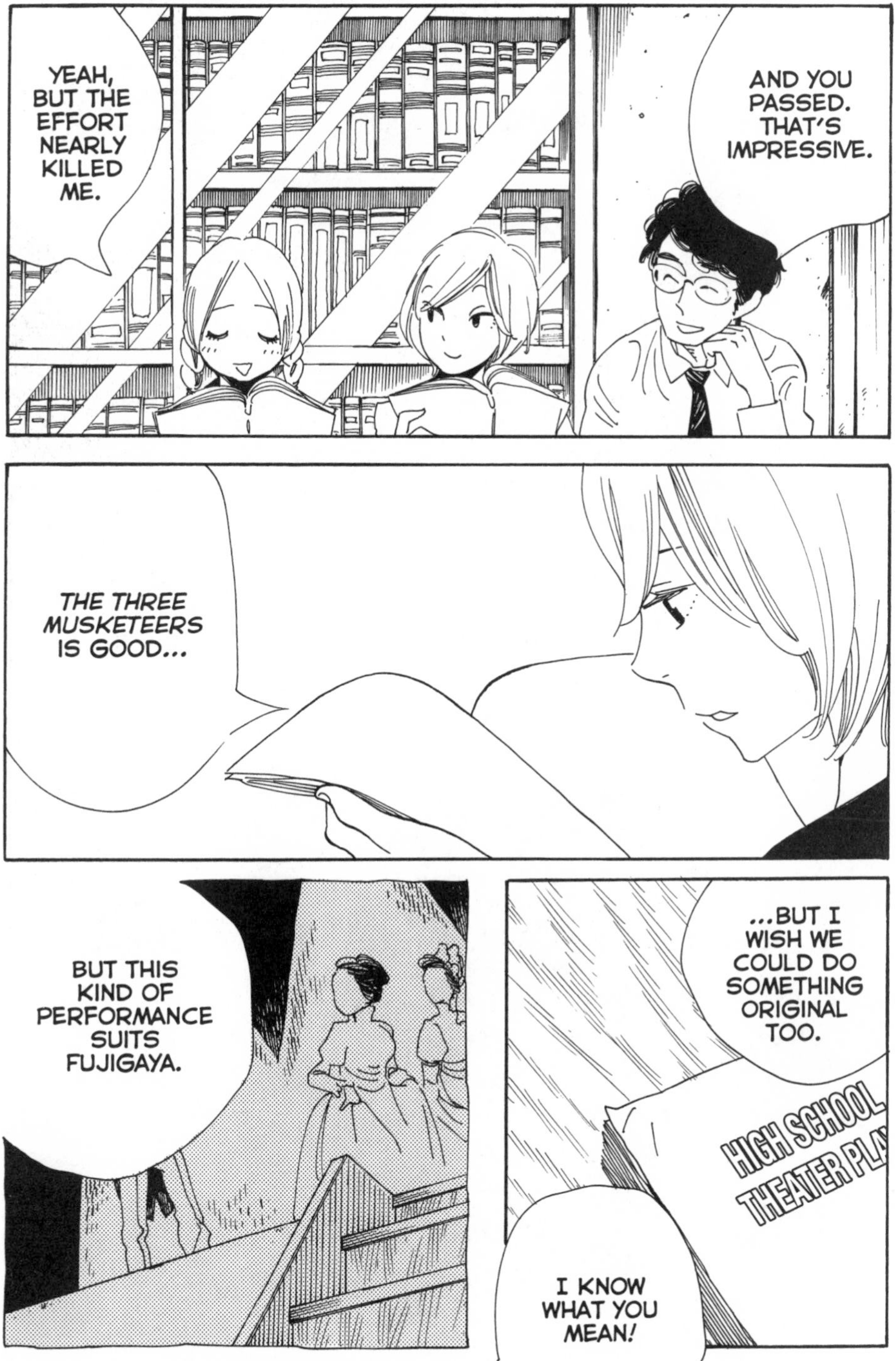
AND YOU PASSED. THAT'S IMPRESSIVE.
YEAH, BUT THE EFFORT NEARLY KILLED ME.
THE THREE MUSKETEERS IS GOOD...
...BUT I WISH WE COULD DO SOMETHING ORIGINAL TOO.
HIGH SCHOOL THEATER PLA
I KNOW WHAT YOU MEAN!
BUT THIS KIND OF PERFORMANCE SUITS FUJIGAYA.

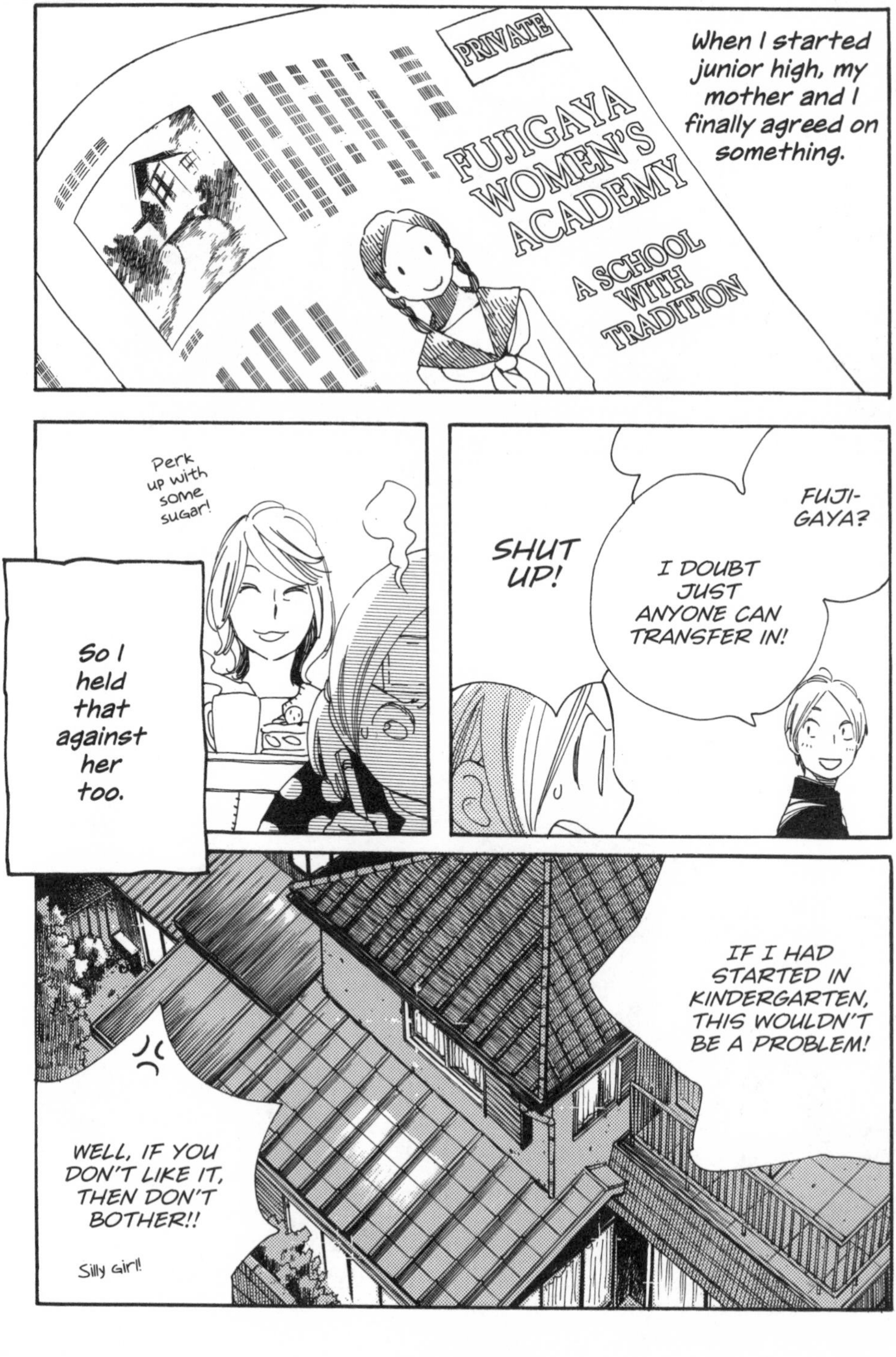
When I started junior high, my mother and I finally agreed on something.
PRIVATE
FUJIGAYA WOMEN'S ACADEMY
A SCHOOL WITH TRADITION
FUJI-GAYA?
I DOUBT JUST ANYONE CAN TRANSFER IN!
SHUT UP!
Perk up with some sugar!
So I held that against her too.
IF I HAD STARTED IN KINDERGARTEN, THIS WOULDN'T BE A PROBLEM!
WELL, IF YOU DON'T LIKE IT, THEN DON'T BOTHER!!
Silly girl!

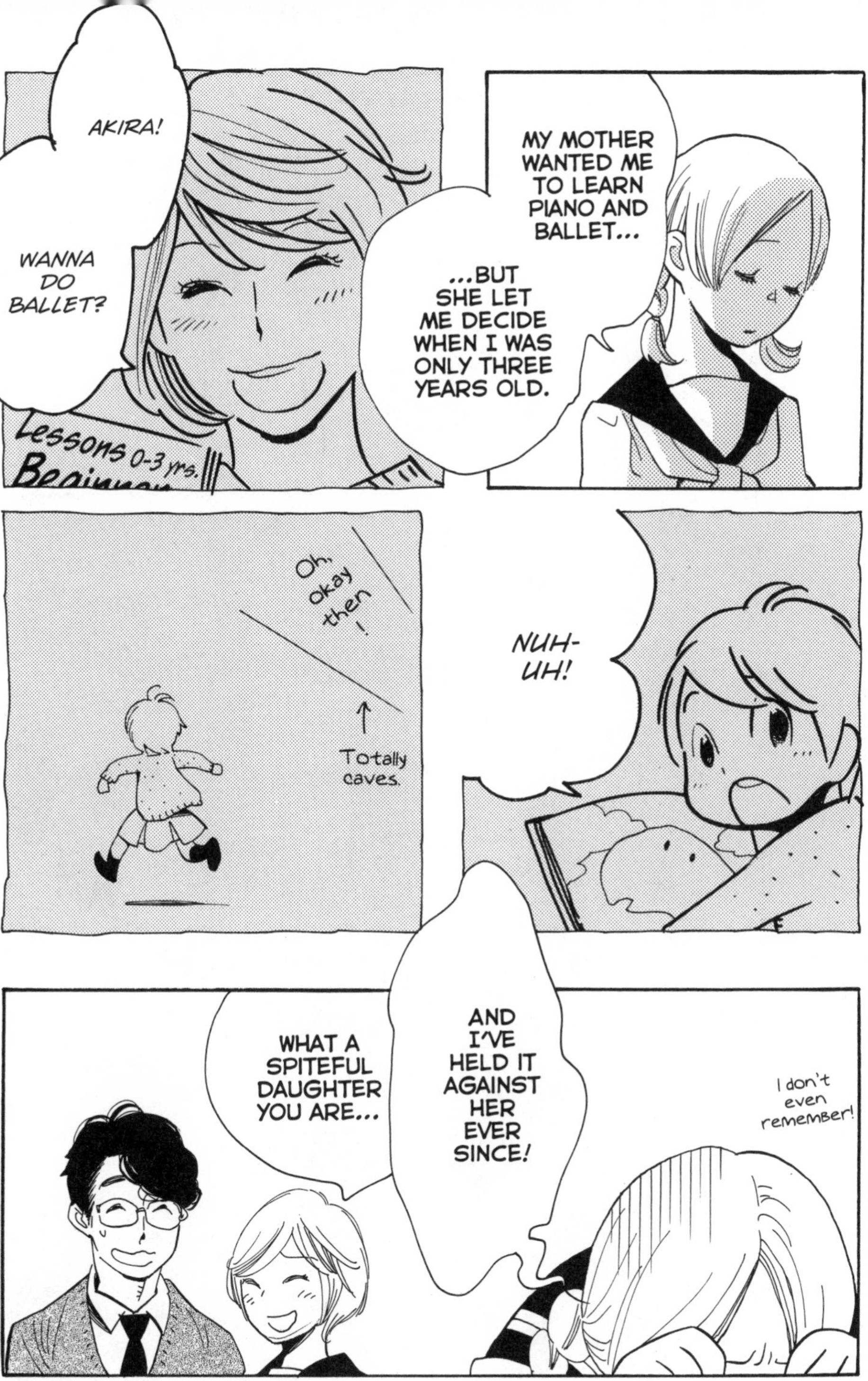
MY MOTHER WANTED ME TO LEARN PIANO AND BALLET...
...BUT SHE LET ME DECIDE WHEN I WAS ONLY THREE YEARS OLD.
AKIRA!
WANNA DO BALLET?
Lessons 0-3 yrs.
NUH-UH!
Oh, okay then!
Totally caves.
AND I'VE HELD IT AGAINST HER EVER SINCE!
I don't even remember!
WHAT A SPITEFUL DAUGHTER YOU ARE...

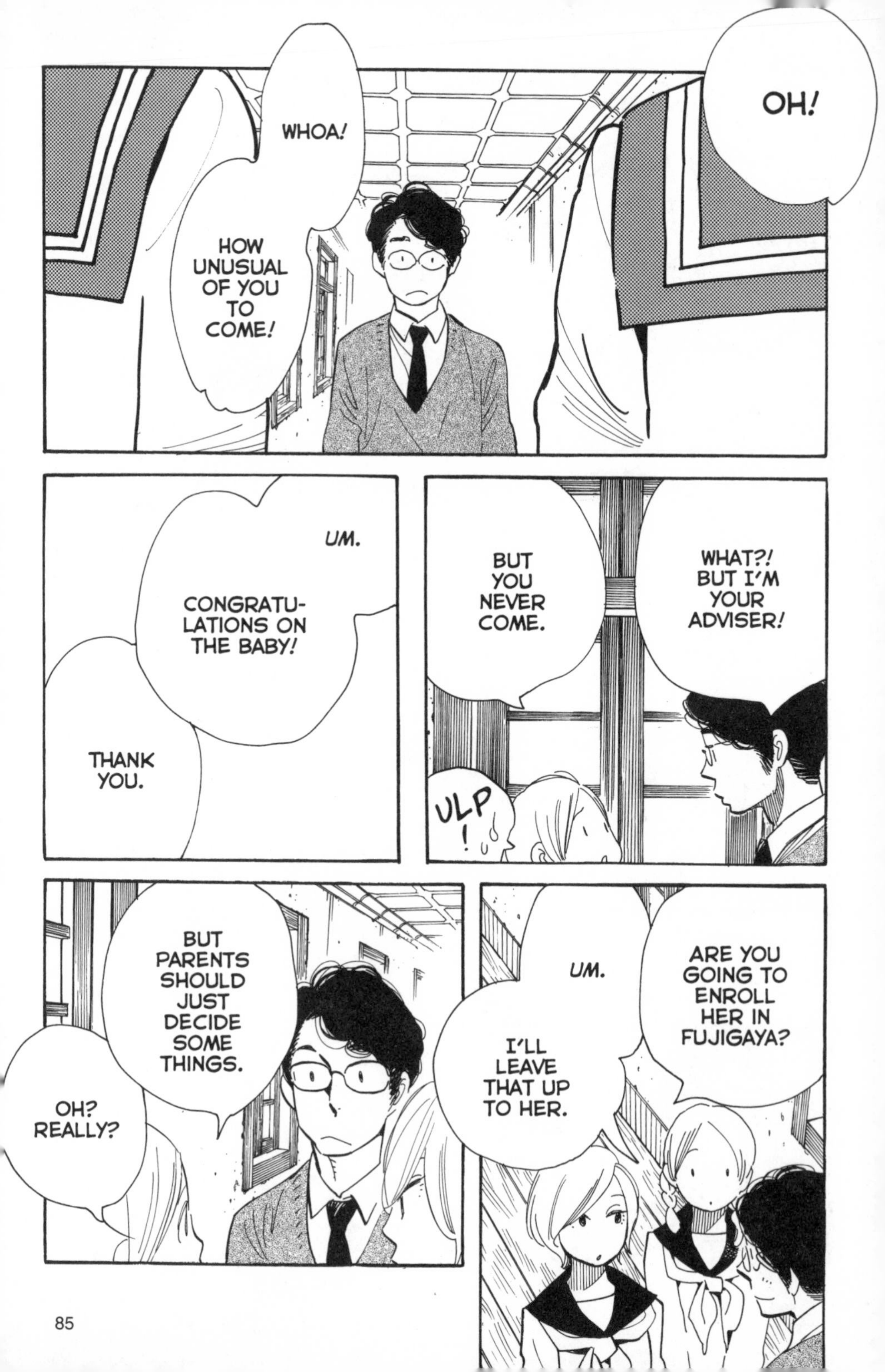
OH!
WHOA!
HOW UNUSUAL OF YOU TO COME!
WHAT?! BUT I'M YOUR ADVISER!
BUT YOU NEVER COME.
ULP!
UM.
CONGRATU-LATIONS ON THE BABY!
THANK YOU.
ARE YOU GOING TO ENROLL HER IN FUJIGAYA?
UM.
I'LL LEAVE THAT UP TO HER.
BUT PARENTS SHOULD JUST DECIDE SOME THINGS.
OH? REALLY?

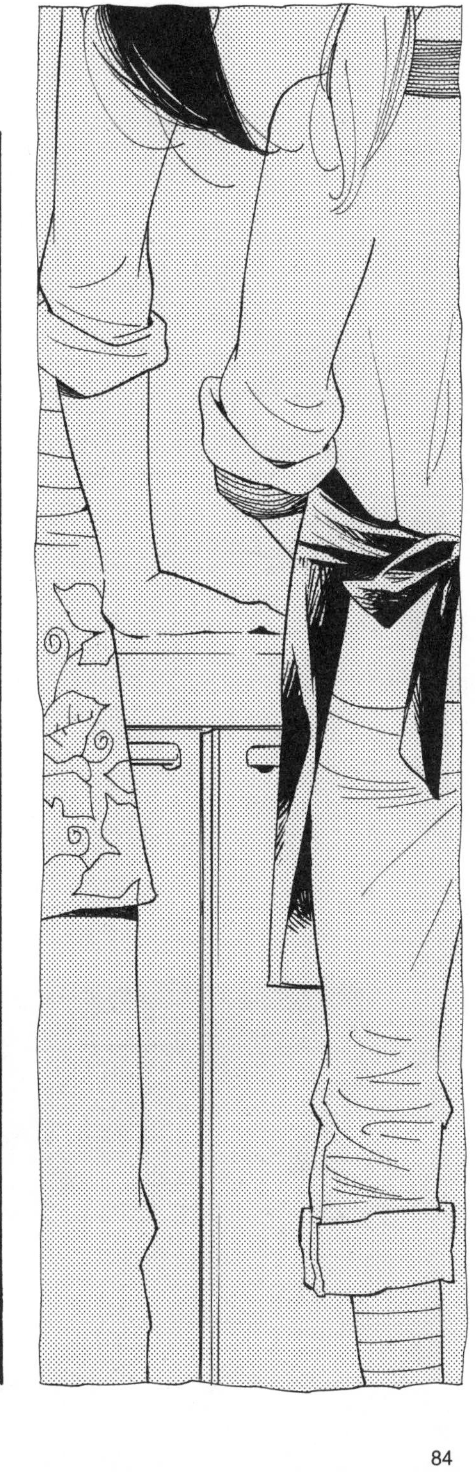

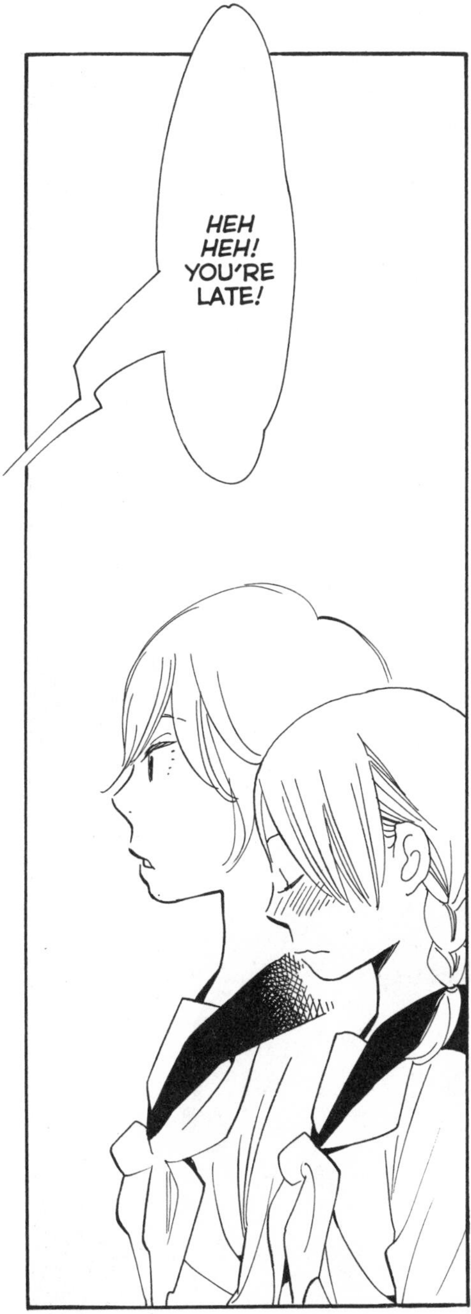
HEH HEH! YOU'RE LATE!

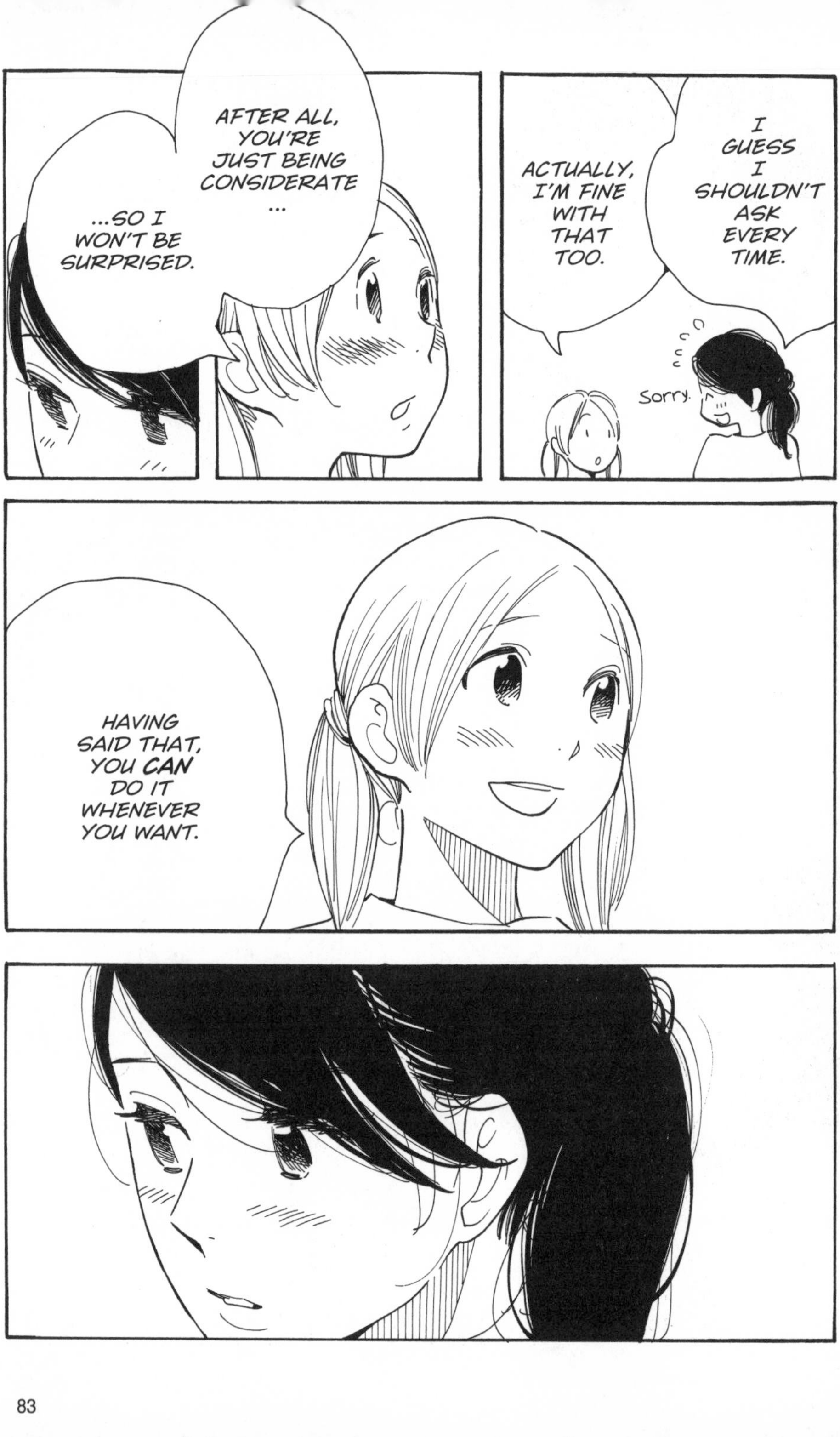
I GUESS I SHOULDN'T ASK EVERY TIME.
ACTUALLY, I'M FINE WITH THAT TOO.
Sorry.
AFTER ALL, YOU'RE JUST BEING CONSIDERATE ...
...SO I WON'T BE SURPRISED.
HAVING SAID THAT, YOU **CAN** DO IT WHENEVER YOU WANT.

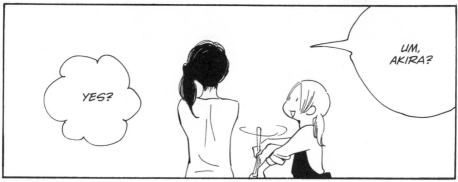

UM, AKIRA?

YES?

I WON'T IF YOU DON'T WANT ME TO!

SORRY!!

...SURE!

UH...

NO, IT'S FINE!

MAY I KISS YOU?

HUH?!

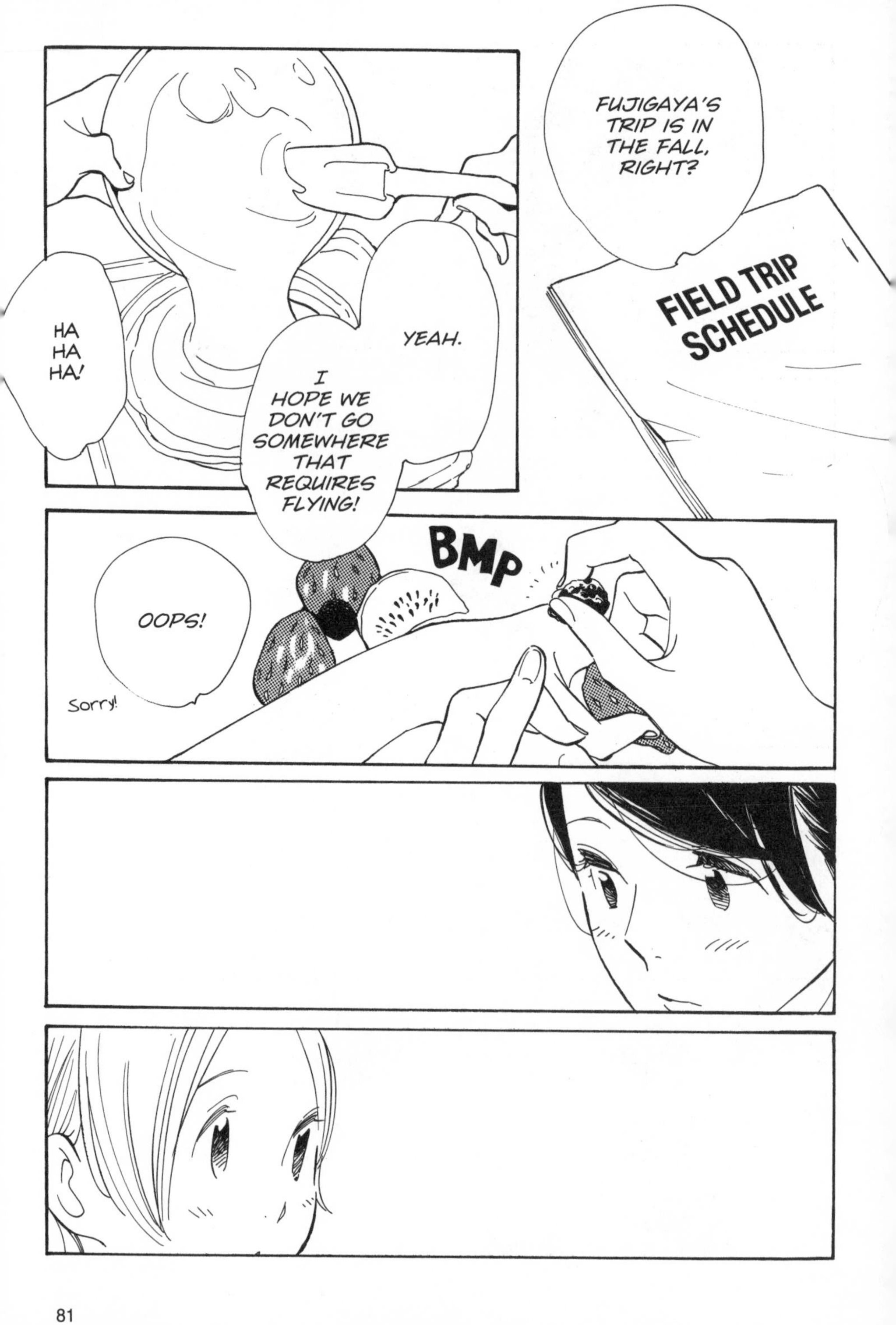
FUJIGAYA'S TRIP IS IN THE FALL, RIGHT?
FIELD TRIP SCHEDULE
YEAH.
I HOPE WE DON'T GO SOMEWHERE THAT REQUIRES FLYING!
HA HA HA!
BMP
OOPS!
Sorry!

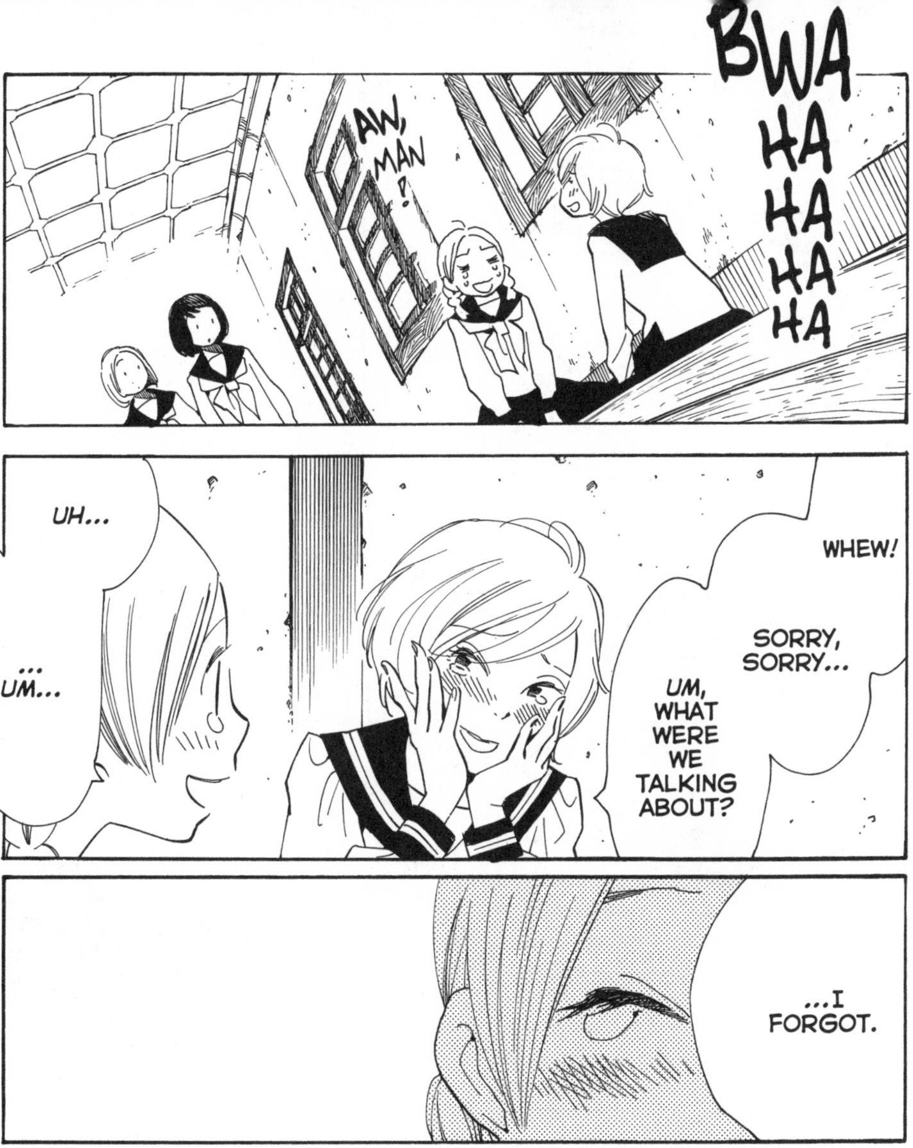
BWA HA HA HA HA
AW, MAN!
WHEW!
SORRY, SORRY...
UM, WHAT WERE WE TALKING ABOUT?
UH...
...UM...
...I FORGOT.

I was going to ask if she's ever kissed anyone.

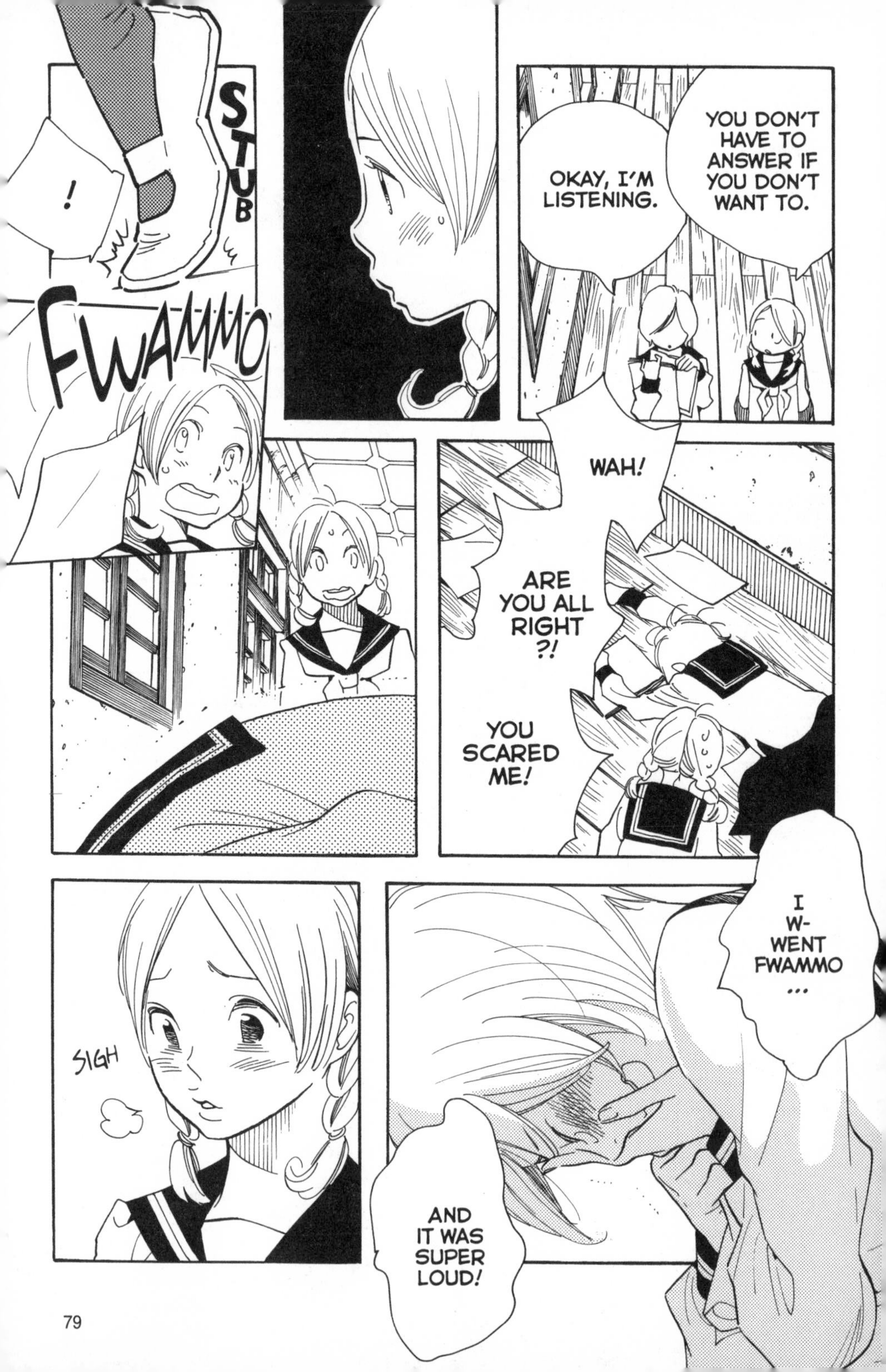
YOU DON'T HAVE TO ANSWER IF YOU DON'T WANT TO.
OKAY, I'M LISTENING.
STUB
!
FWAMMO
WAH!
ARE YOU ALL RIGHT?!
YOU SCARED ME!
I W-WENT FWAMMO...
AND IT WAS SUPER LOUD!
SIGH

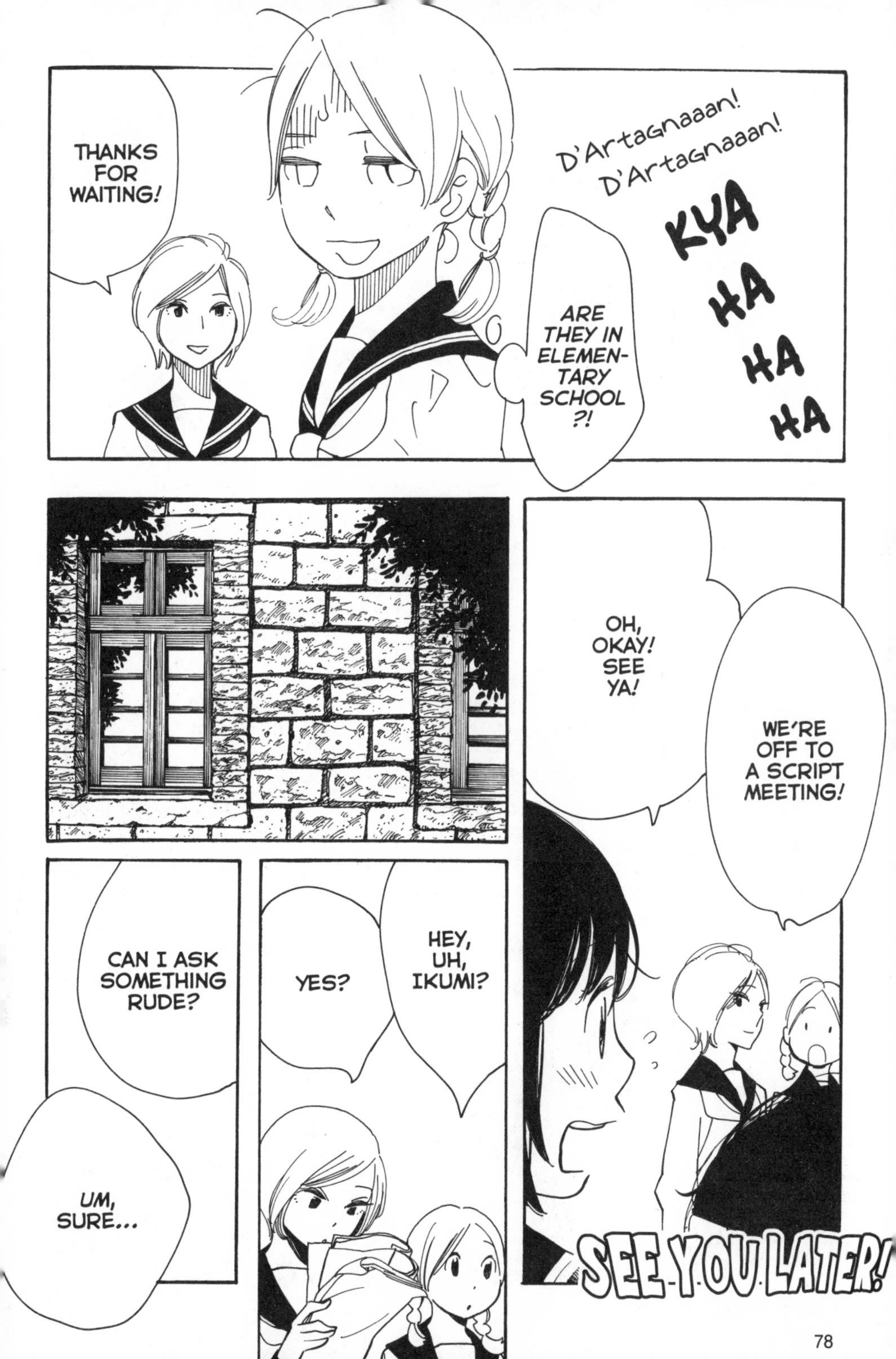
D'Artagnaaan! D'Artagnaaan!
KYA HA HA HA HA
ARE THEY IN ELEMENTARY SCHOOL ?!
THANKS FOR WAITING!
WE'RE OFF TO A SCRIPT MEETING!
OH, OKAY! SEE YA!
SEE YOU LATER!
HEY, UH, IKUMI?
YES?
CAN I ASK SOMETHING RUDE?
UM, SURE...

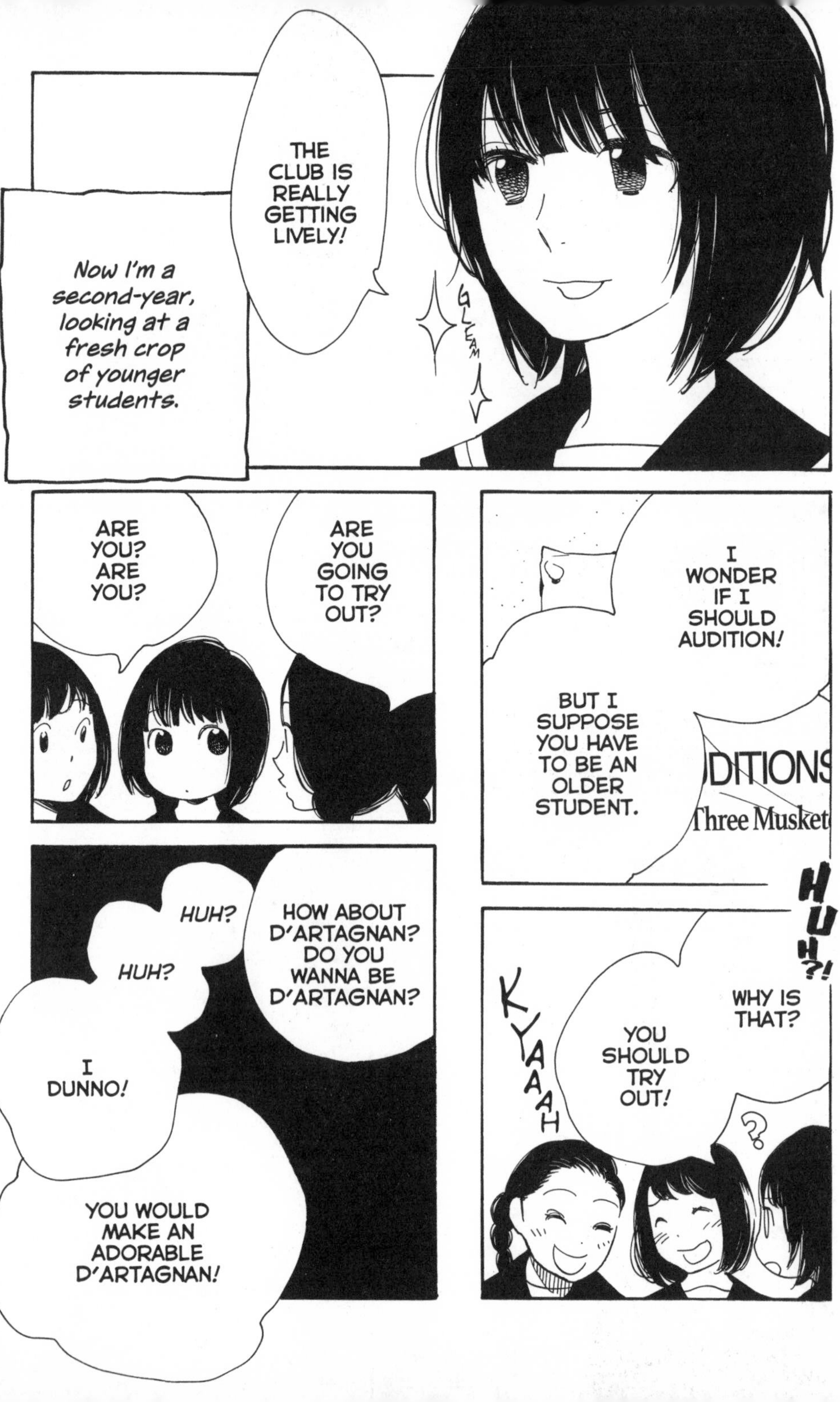
THE CLUB IS REALLY GETTING LIVELY!
GLEAM
Now I'm a second-year, looking at a fresh crop of younger students.
I WONDER IF I SHOULD AUDITION!
BUT I SUPPOSE YOU HAVE TO BE AN OLDER STUDENT.
DITIONS
Three Musket
ARE YOU GOING TO TRY OUT?
ARE YOU? ARE YOU?
HUH?!
WHY IS THAT?
YOU SHOULD TRY OUT!
KYAAAH
HOW ABOUT D'ARTAGNAN? DO YOU WANNA BE D'ARTAGNAN?
HUH?
HUH?
I DUNNO!
YOU WOULD MAKE AN ADORABLE D'ARTAGNAN!

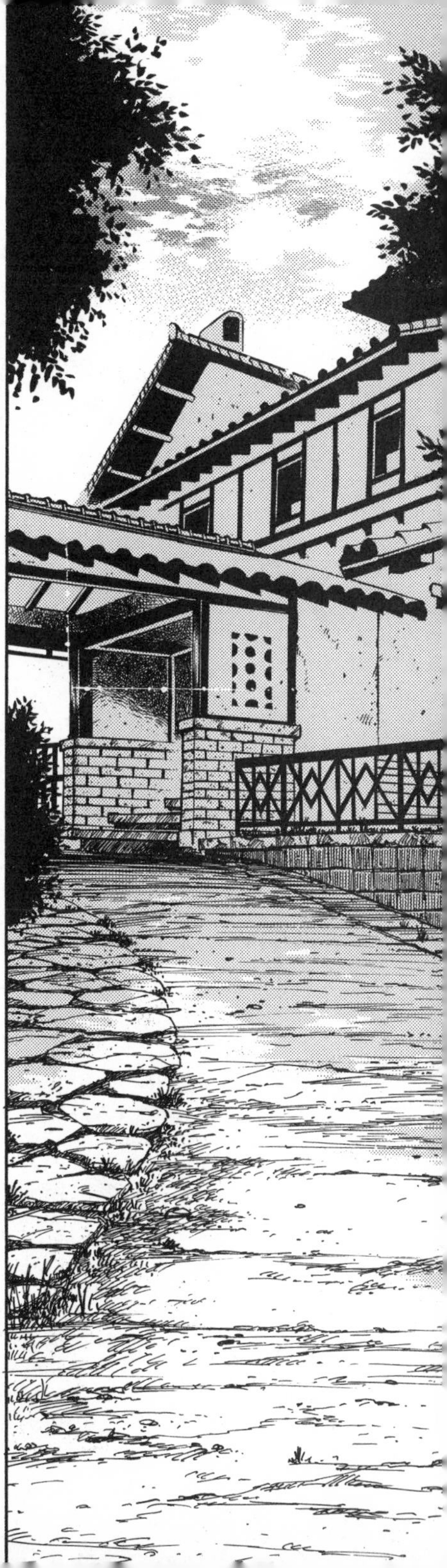

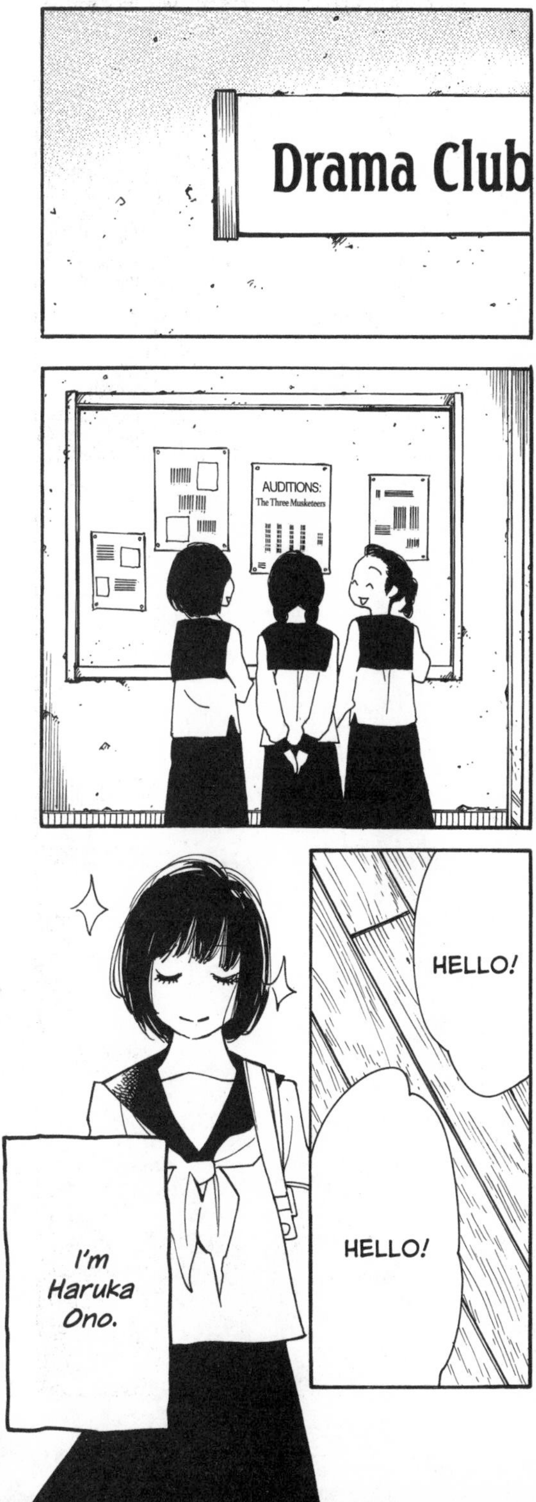
Drama Club
AUDITIONS:
The Three Musketeers
HELLO!
HELLO!
I'm Haruka Ono.

Sweet Blue Flowers

#42 Froth on the Daydream

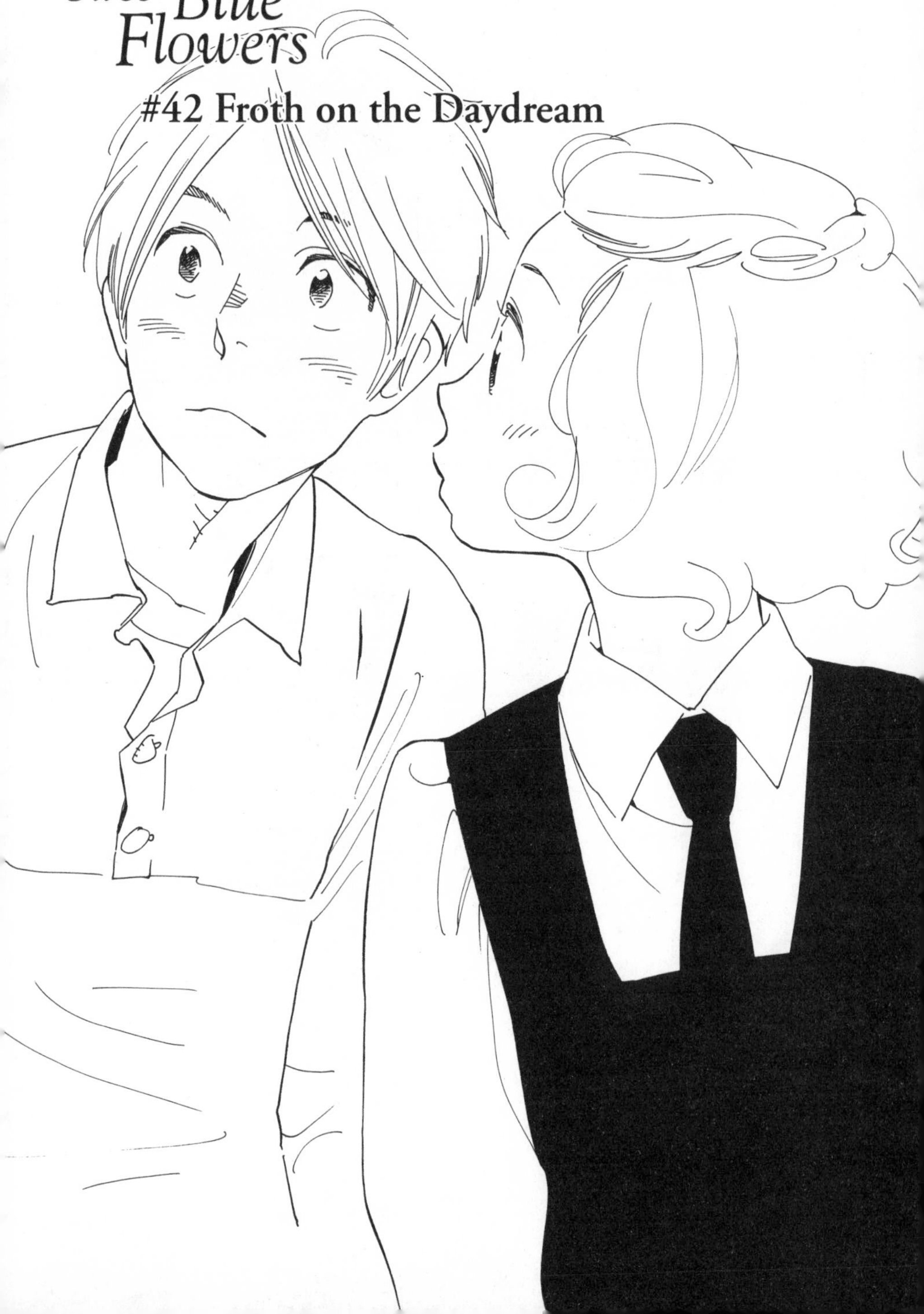

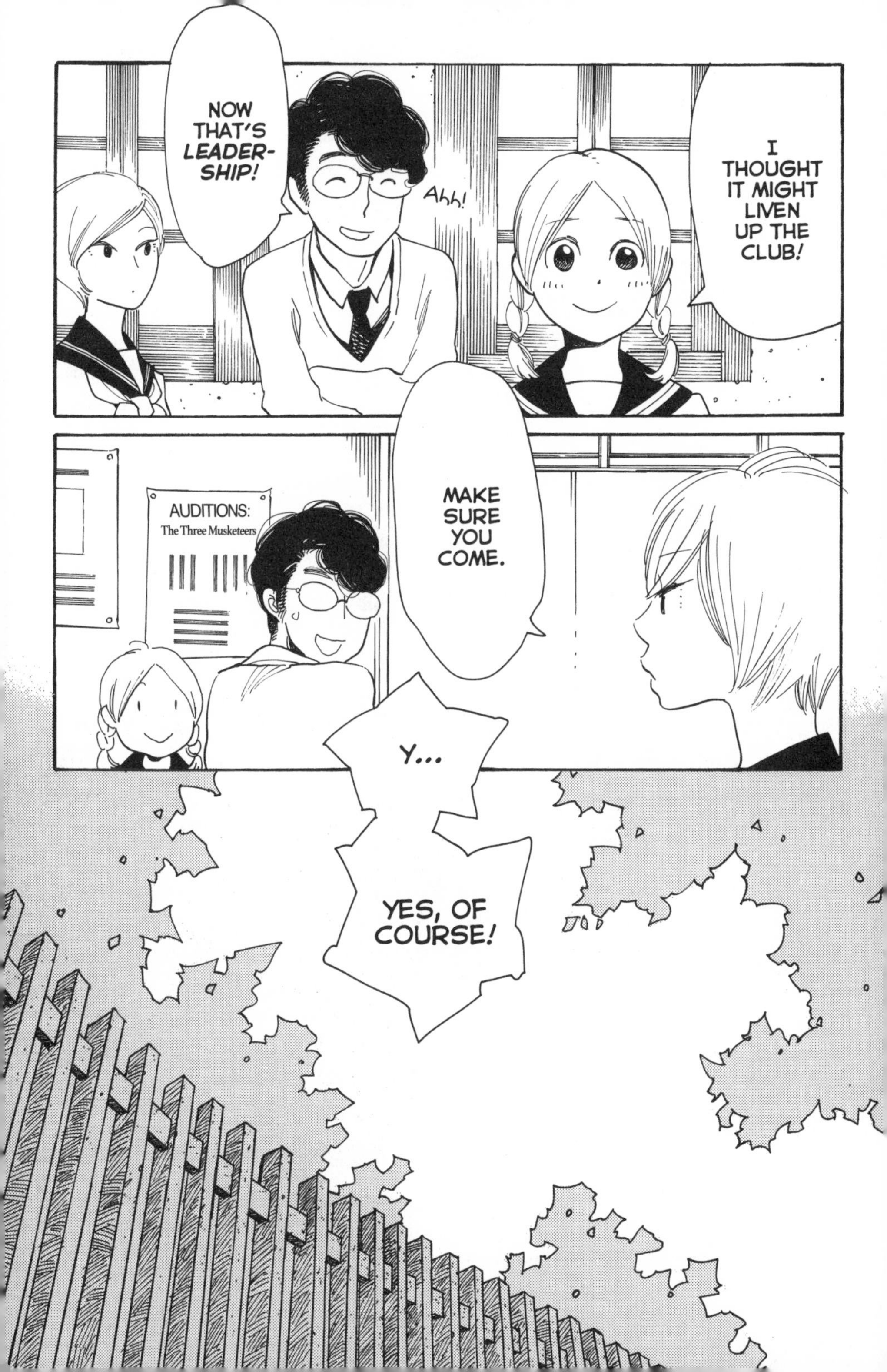
I THOUGHT IT MIGHT LIVEN UP THE CLUB!
NOW THAT'S LEADERSHIP!
Ahh!
MAKE SURE YOU COME.
AUDITIONS: The Three Musketeers
Y...
YES, OF COURSE!

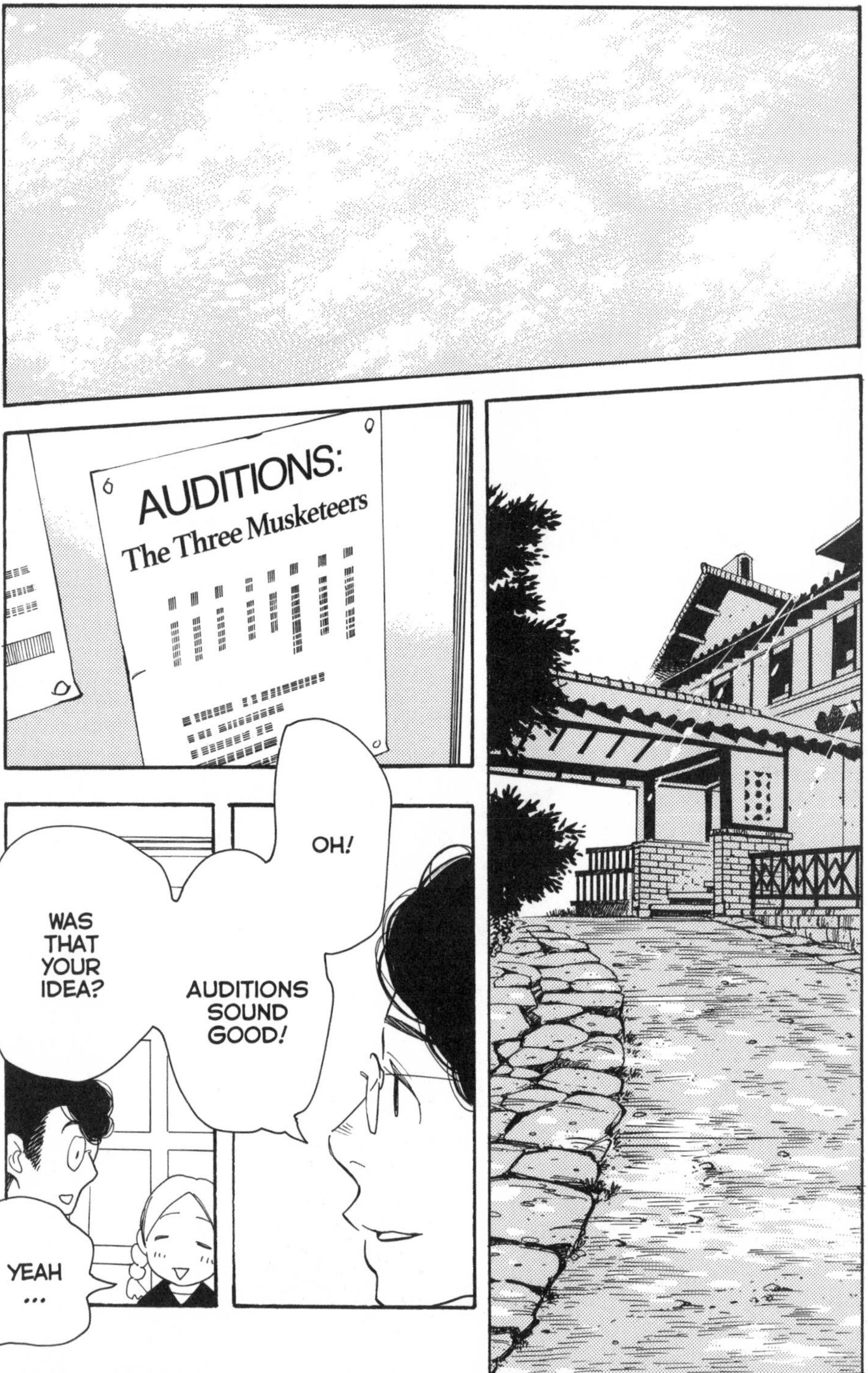
AUDITIONS:
The Three Musketeers
OH!
AUDITIONS SOUND GOOD!
WAS THAT YOUR IDEA?
YEAH ...

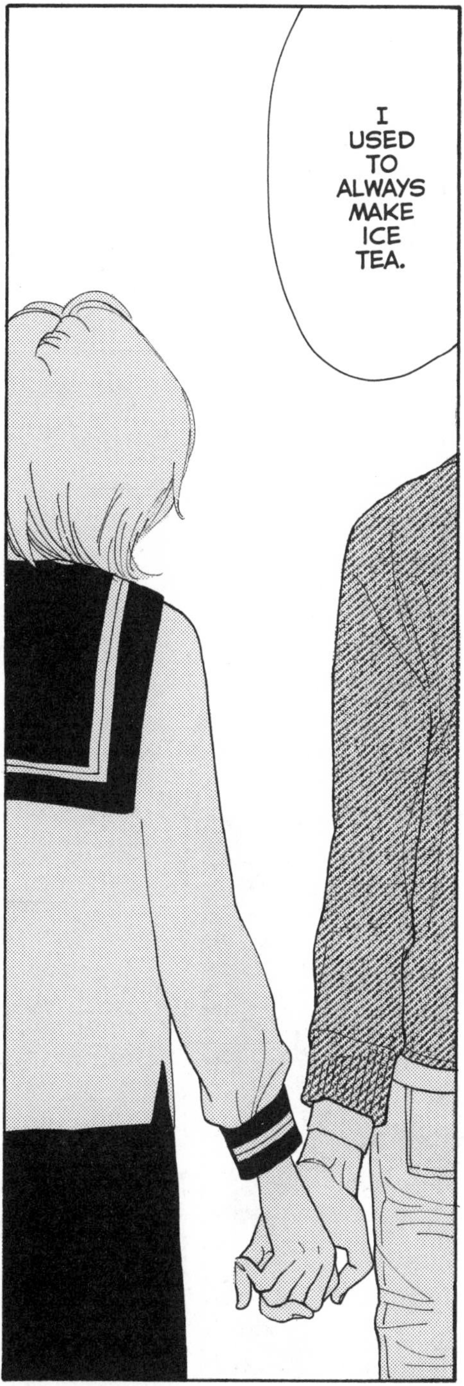
I USED TO ALWAYS MAKE ICE TEA.
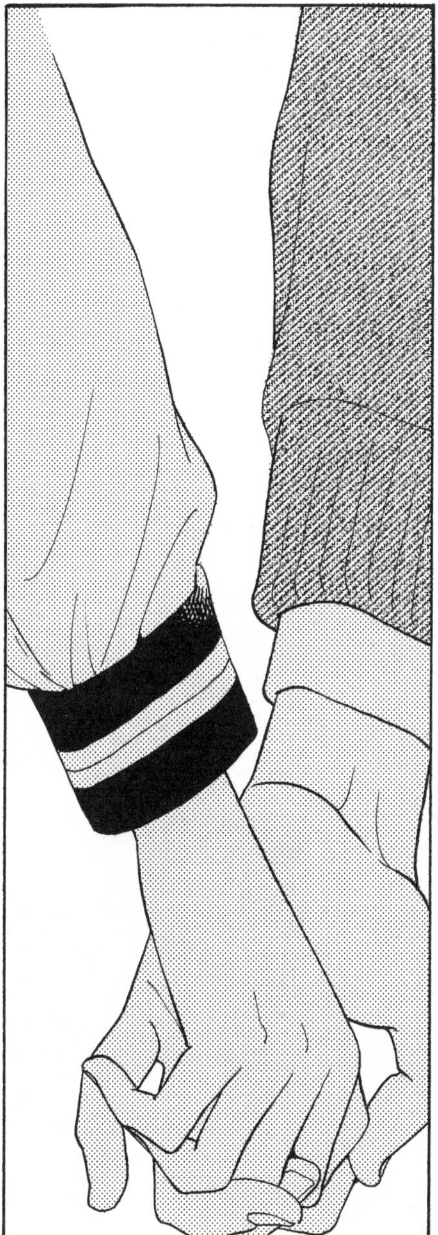

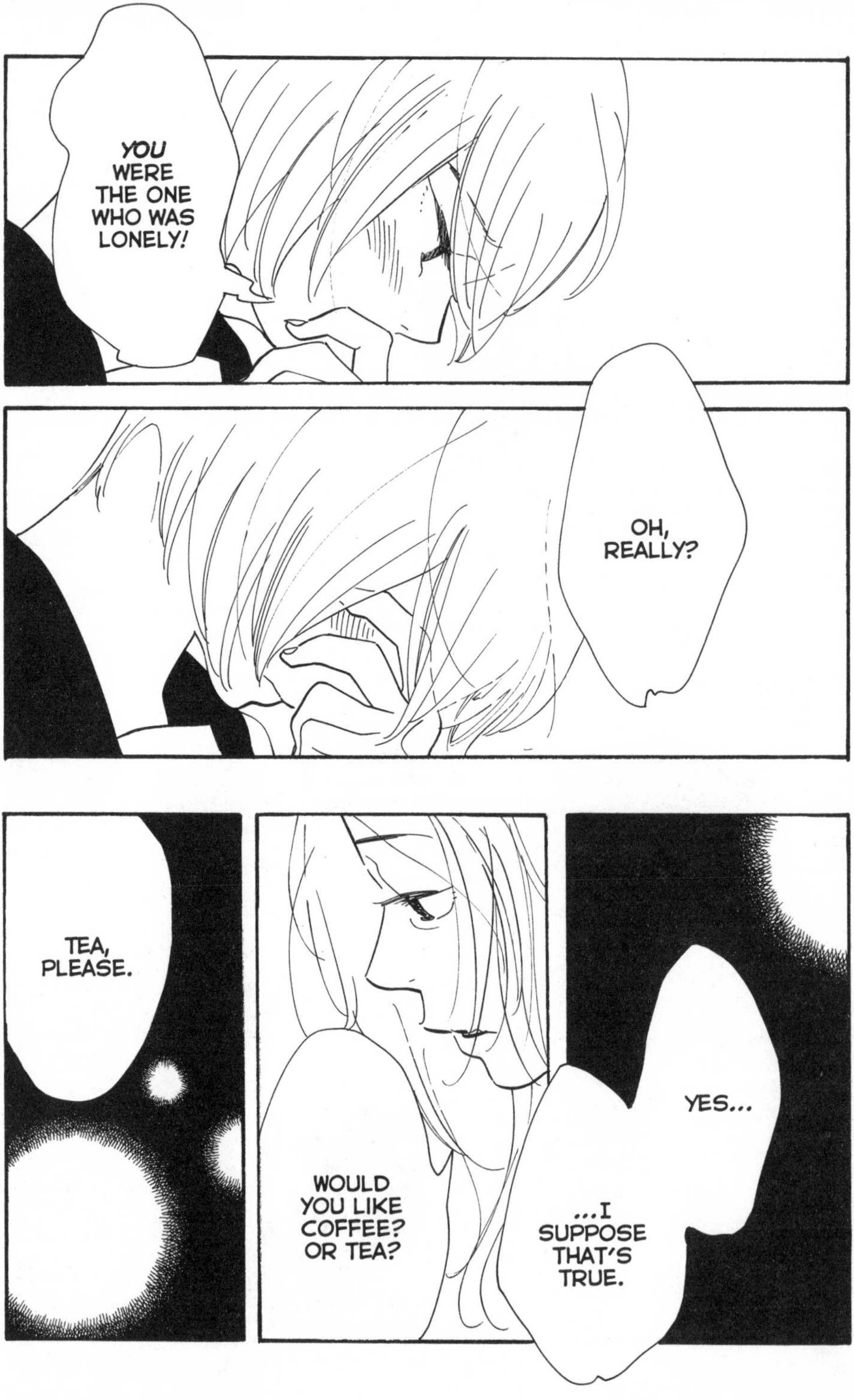
YOU WERE THE ONE WHO WAS LONELY!
OH, REALLY?
YES...
...I SUPPOSE THAT'S TRUE.
WOULD YOU LIKE COFFEE? OR TEA?
TEA, PLEASE.

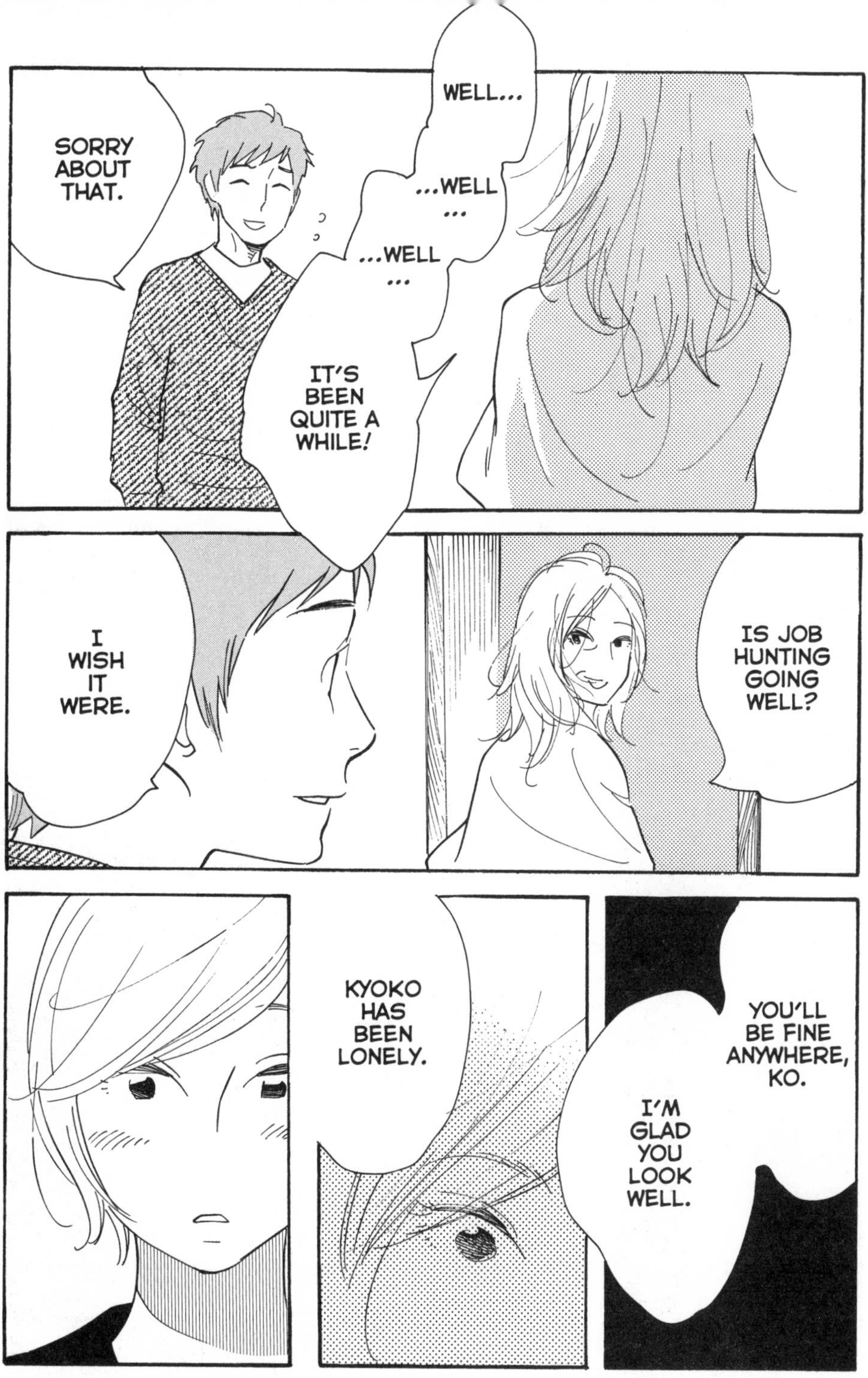
WELL...
...WELL ...
...WELL ...
IT'S BEEN QUITE A WHILE!
SORRY ABOUT THAT.
IS JOB HUNTING GOING WELL?
I WISH IT WERE.
YOU'LL BE FINE ANYWHERE, KO.
I'M GLAD YOU LOOK WELL.
KYOKO HAS BEEN LONELY.

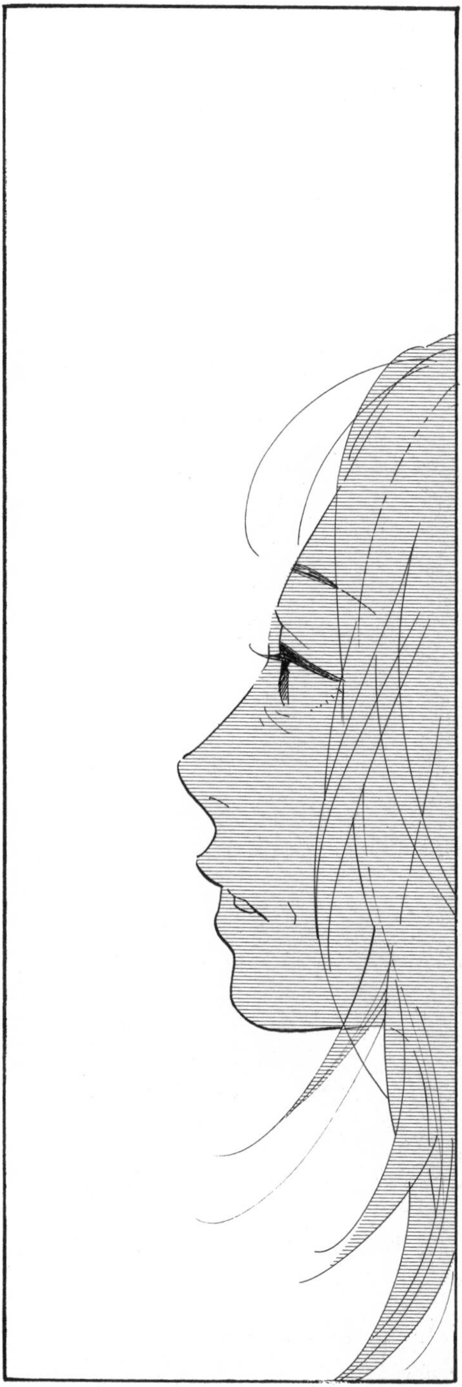
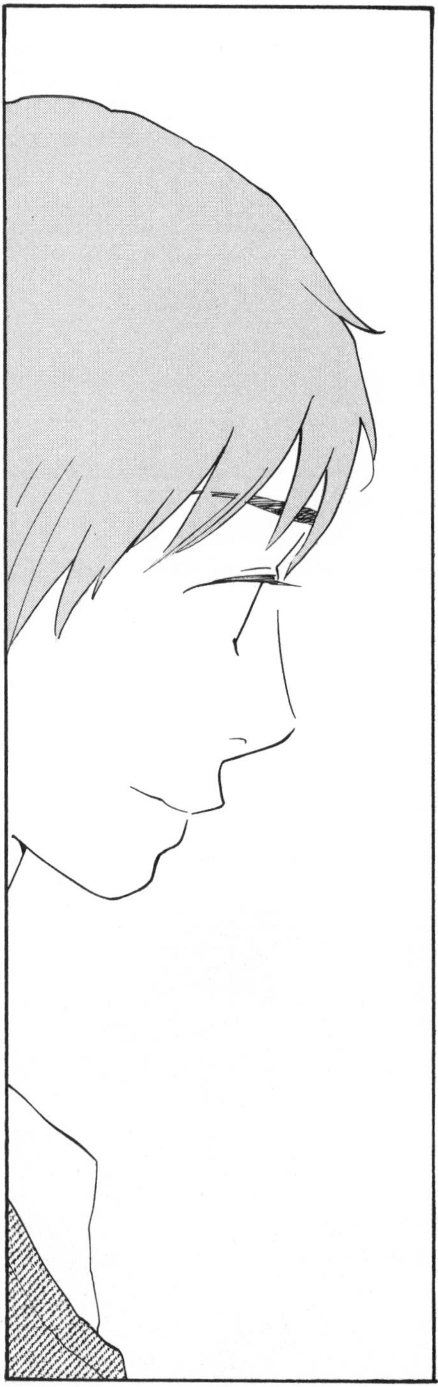

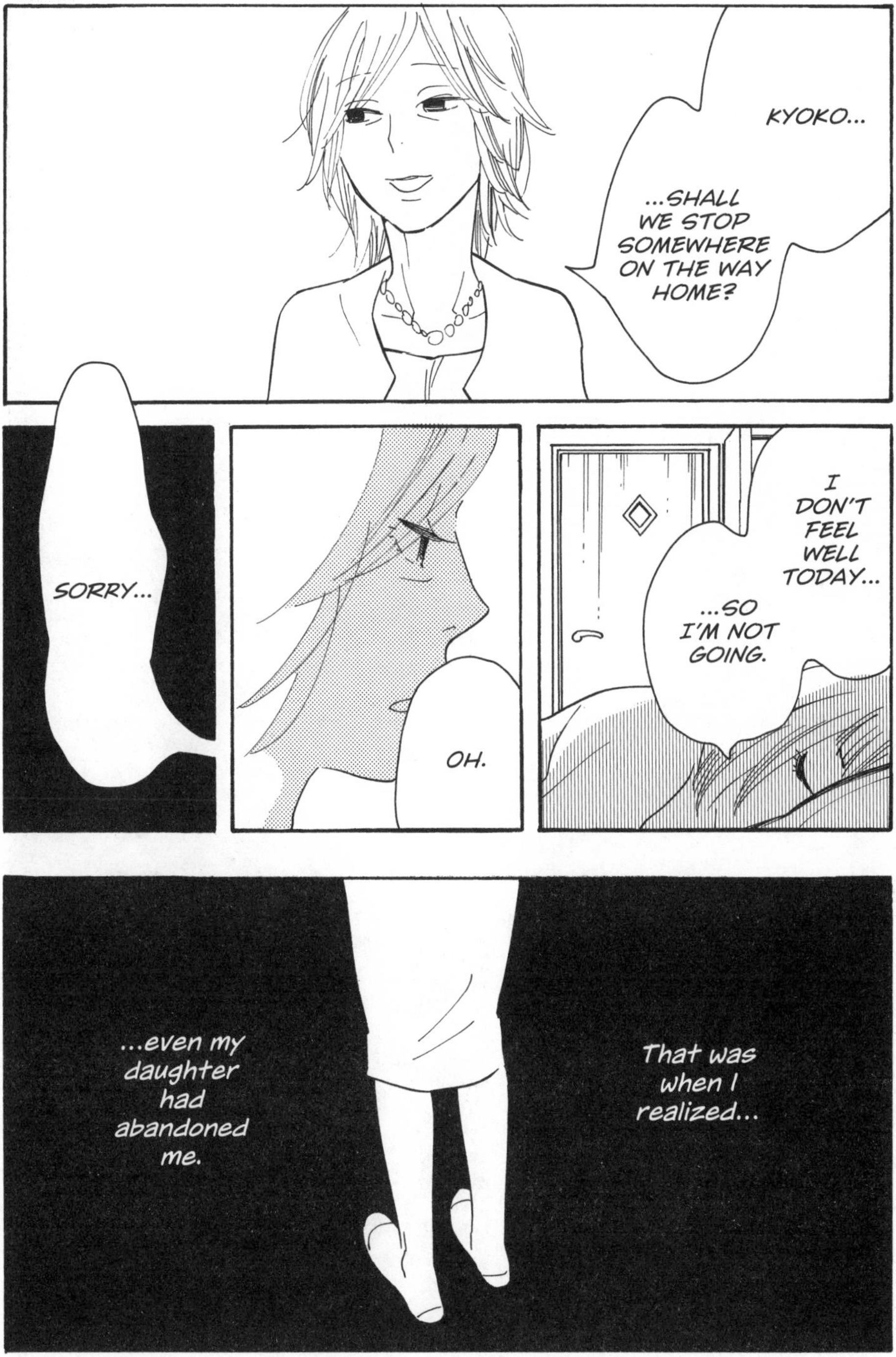
KYOKO...
...SHALL WE STOP SOMEWHERE ON THE WAY HOME?
I DON'T FEEL WELL TODAY...
...SO I'M NOT GOING.
OH.
SORRY...
That was when I realized...
...even my daughter had abandoned me.

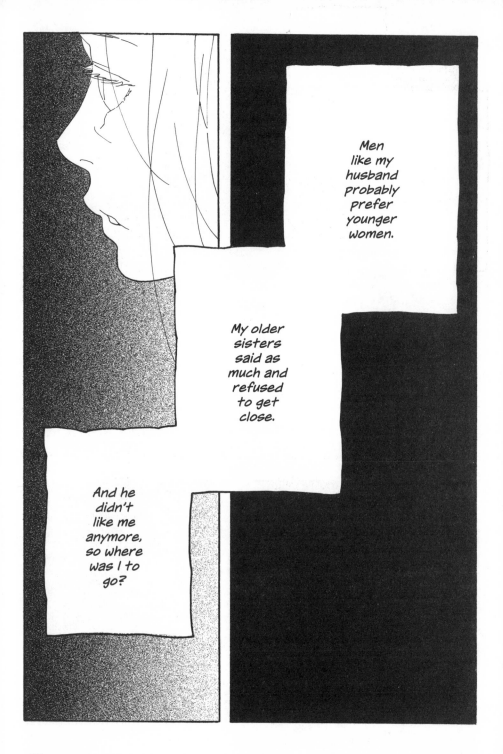

Men like my husband probably prefer younger women.

My older sisters said as much and refused to get close.

And he didn't like me anymore, so where was I to go?

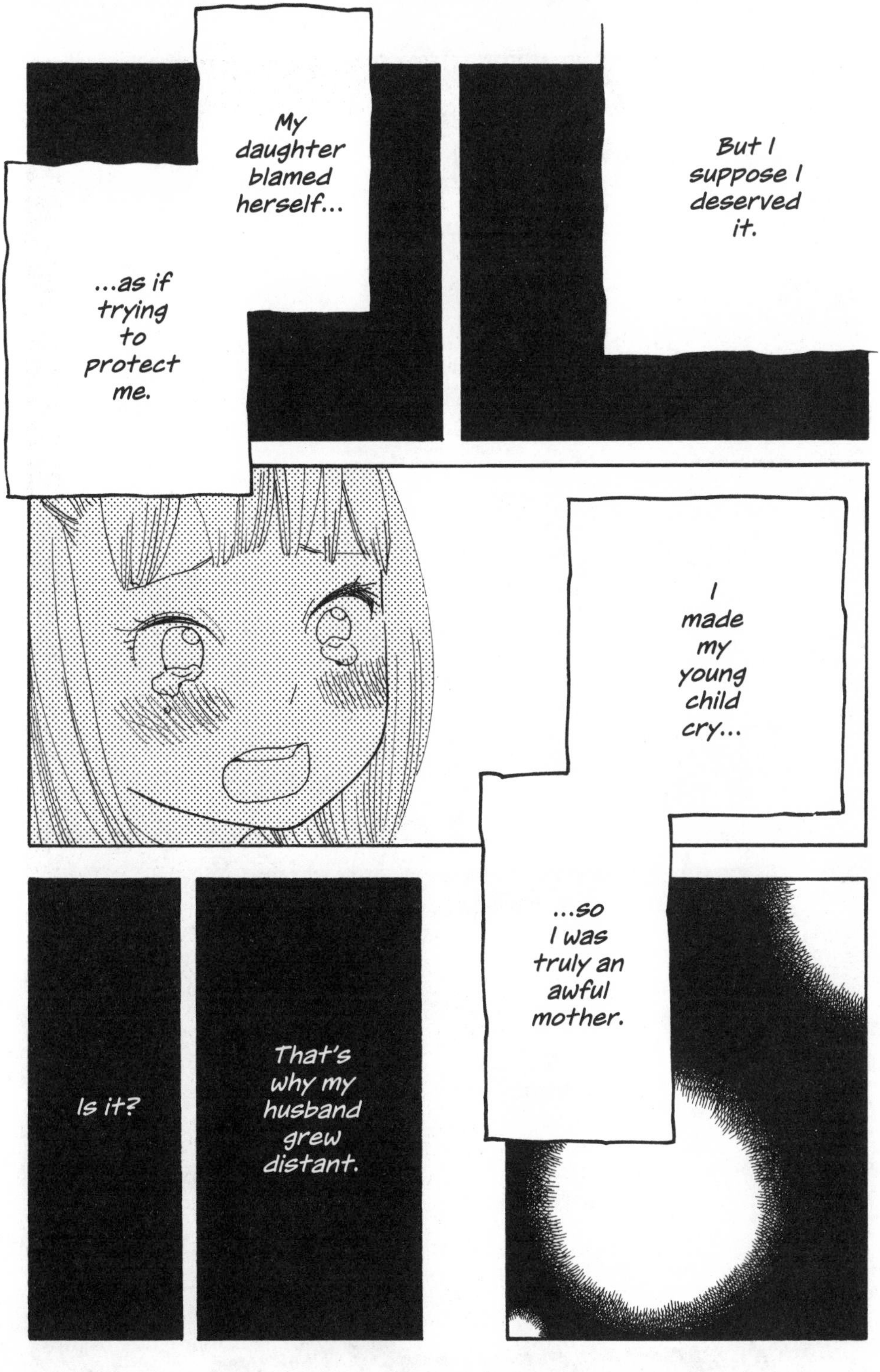
But I suppose I deserved it.
My daughter blamed herself...
...as if trying to protect me.
I made my young child cry...
...so I was truly an awful mother.
That's why my husband grew distant.
Is it?

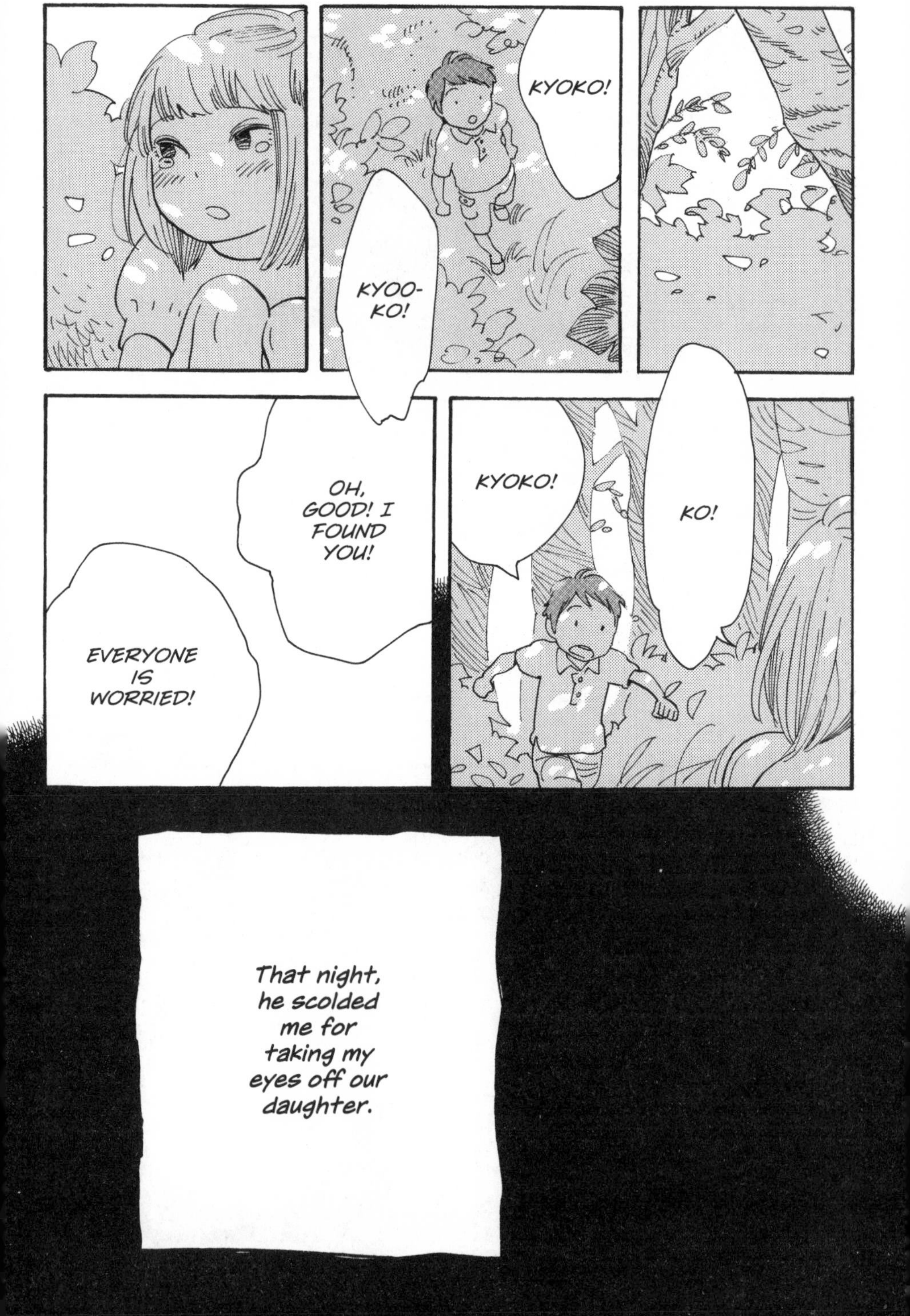
KYOKO!
KYOO-KO!
KO!
KYOKO!
OH, GOOD! I FOUND YOU!
EVERYONE IS WORRIED!
That night, he scolded me for taking my eyes off our daughter.

KYOKO...

...IT'S
DANGEROUS,
SO DON'T GO
TOO FAR!

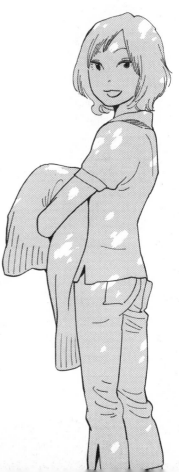

He was openly thrilled to learn I was a virgin.

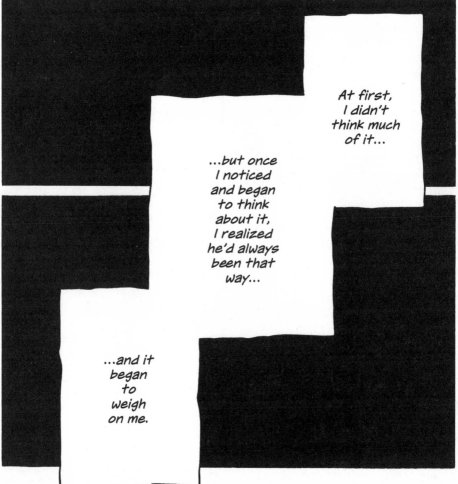

At first, I didn't think much of it...

...but once I noticed and began to think about it, I realized he'd always been that way...

...and it began to weigh on me.

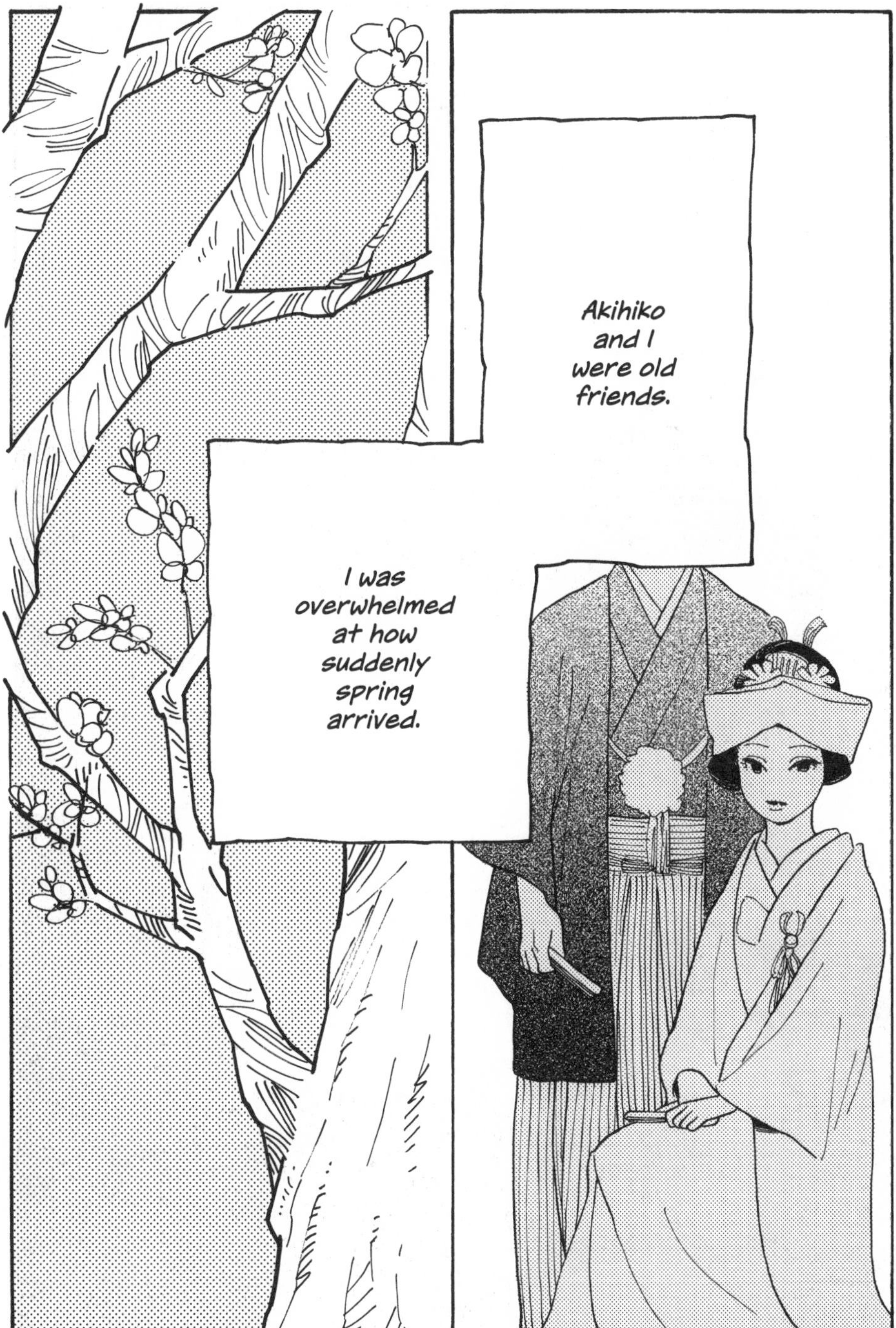
Akihiko and I were old friends.
I was overwhelmed at how suddenly spring arrived.

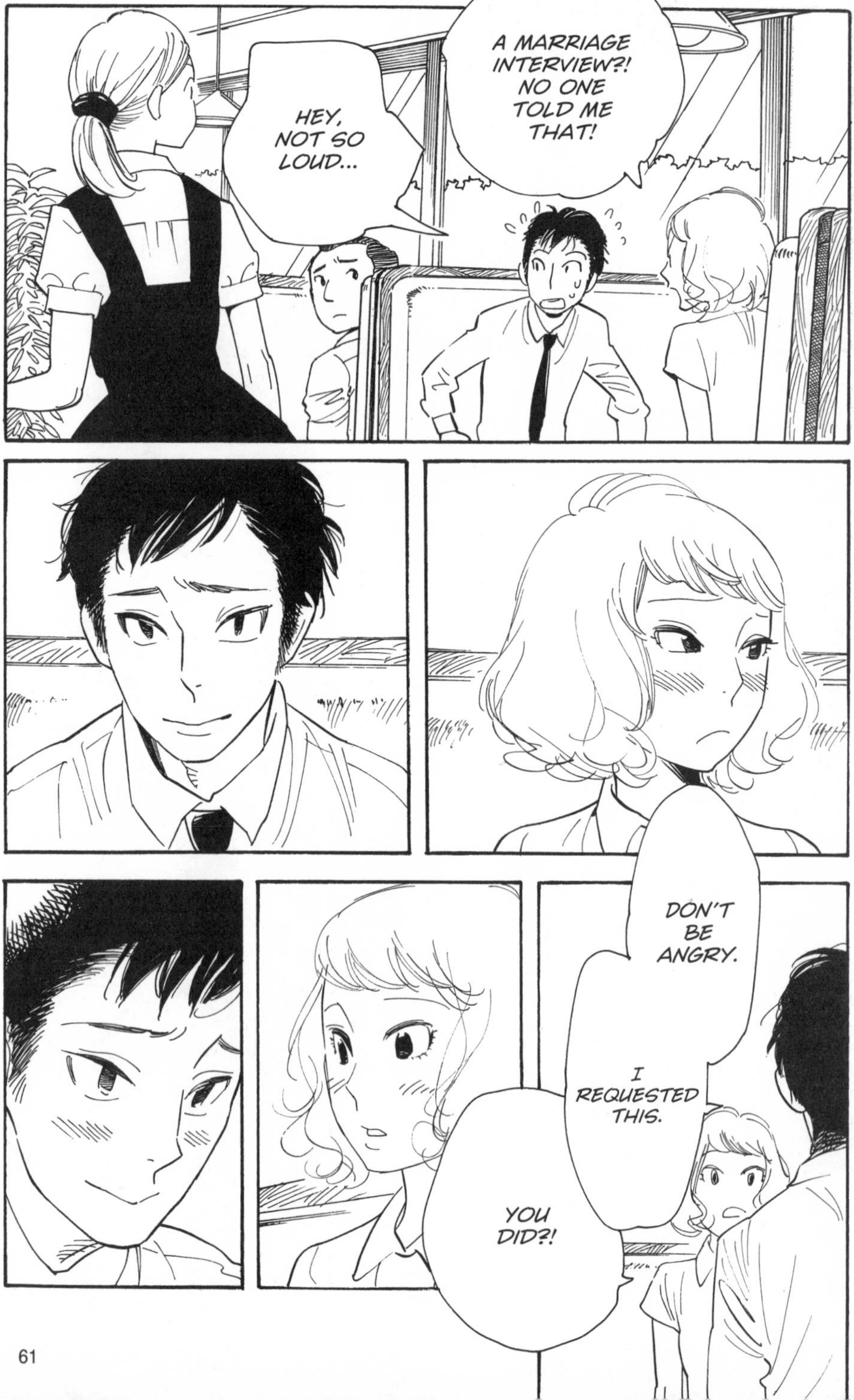
A MARRIAGE INTERVIEW?! NO ONE TOLD ME THAT!
HEY, NOT SO LOUD...
DON'T BE ANGRY.
I REQUESTED THIS.
YOU DID?!

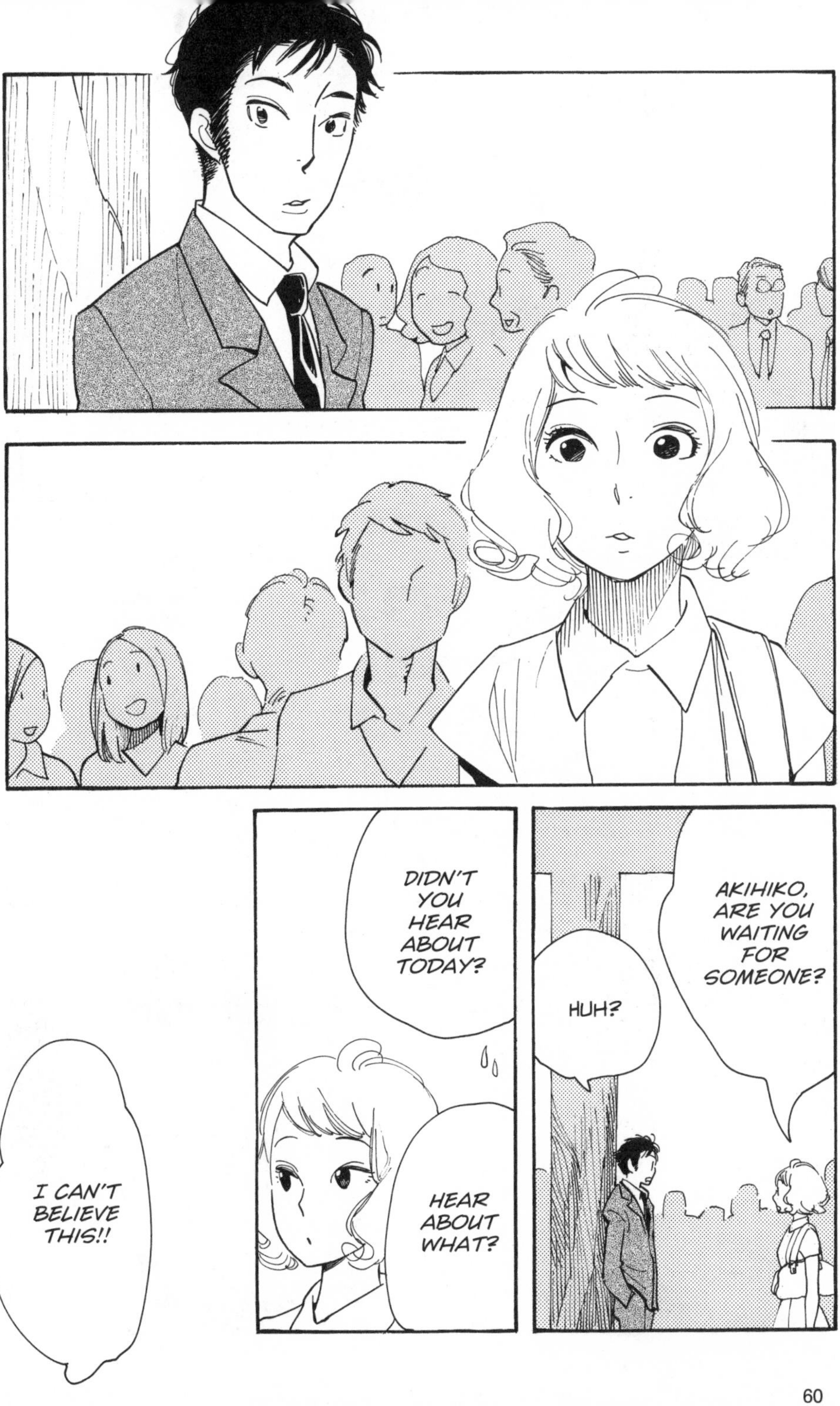
AKIHIKO, ARE YOU WAITING FOR SOMEONE?
HUH?
DIDN'T YOU HEAR ABOUT TODAY?
HEAR ABOUT WHAT?
I CAN'T BELIEVE THIS!!

MAKE
SURE
YOU
DELIVER
THE
GIFT!

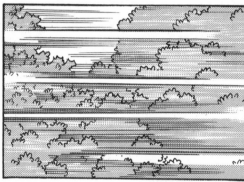

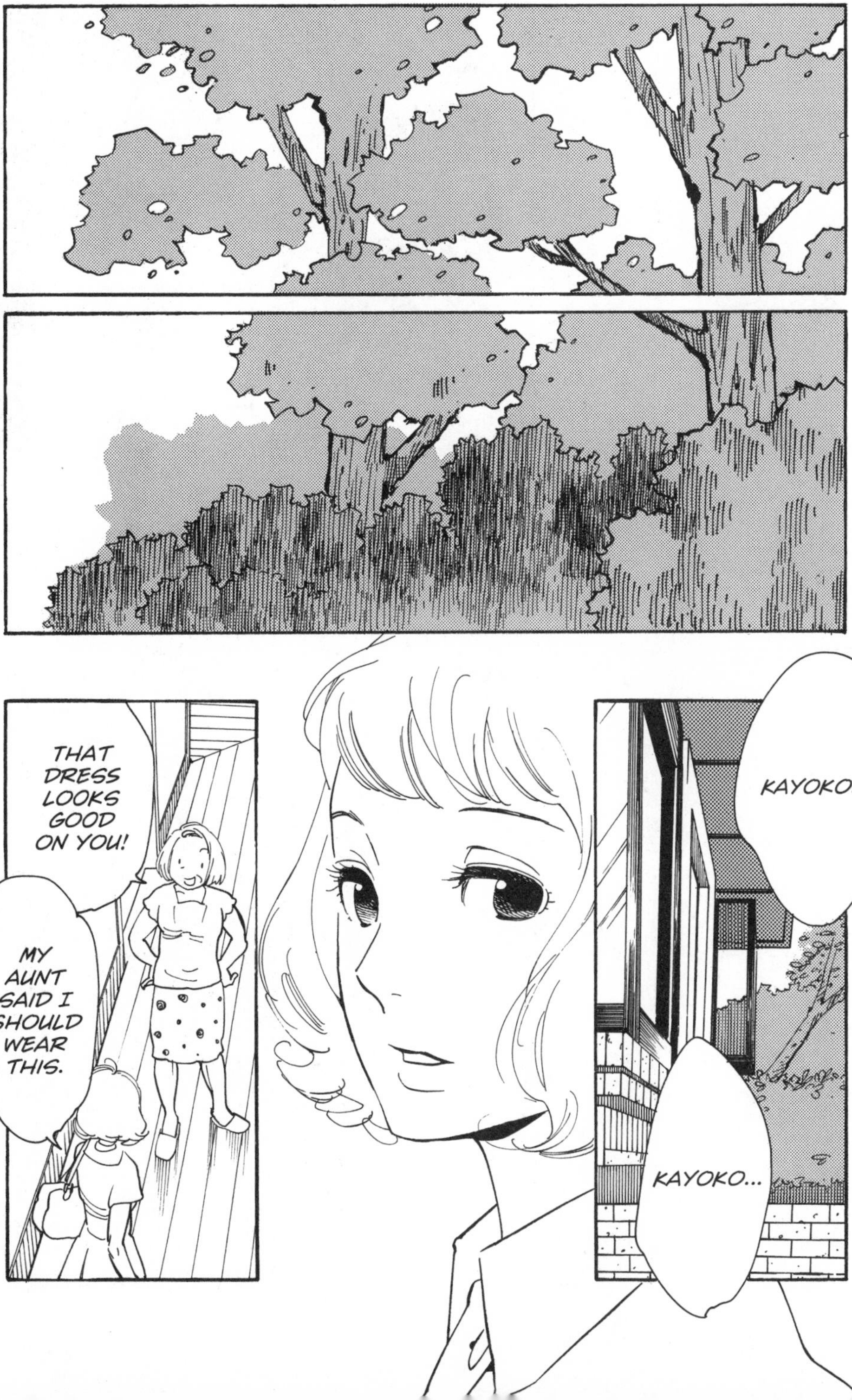
KAYOKO...
KAYOKO...
THAT DRESS LOOKS GOOD ON YOU!
MY AUNT SAID I SHOULD WEAR THIS.

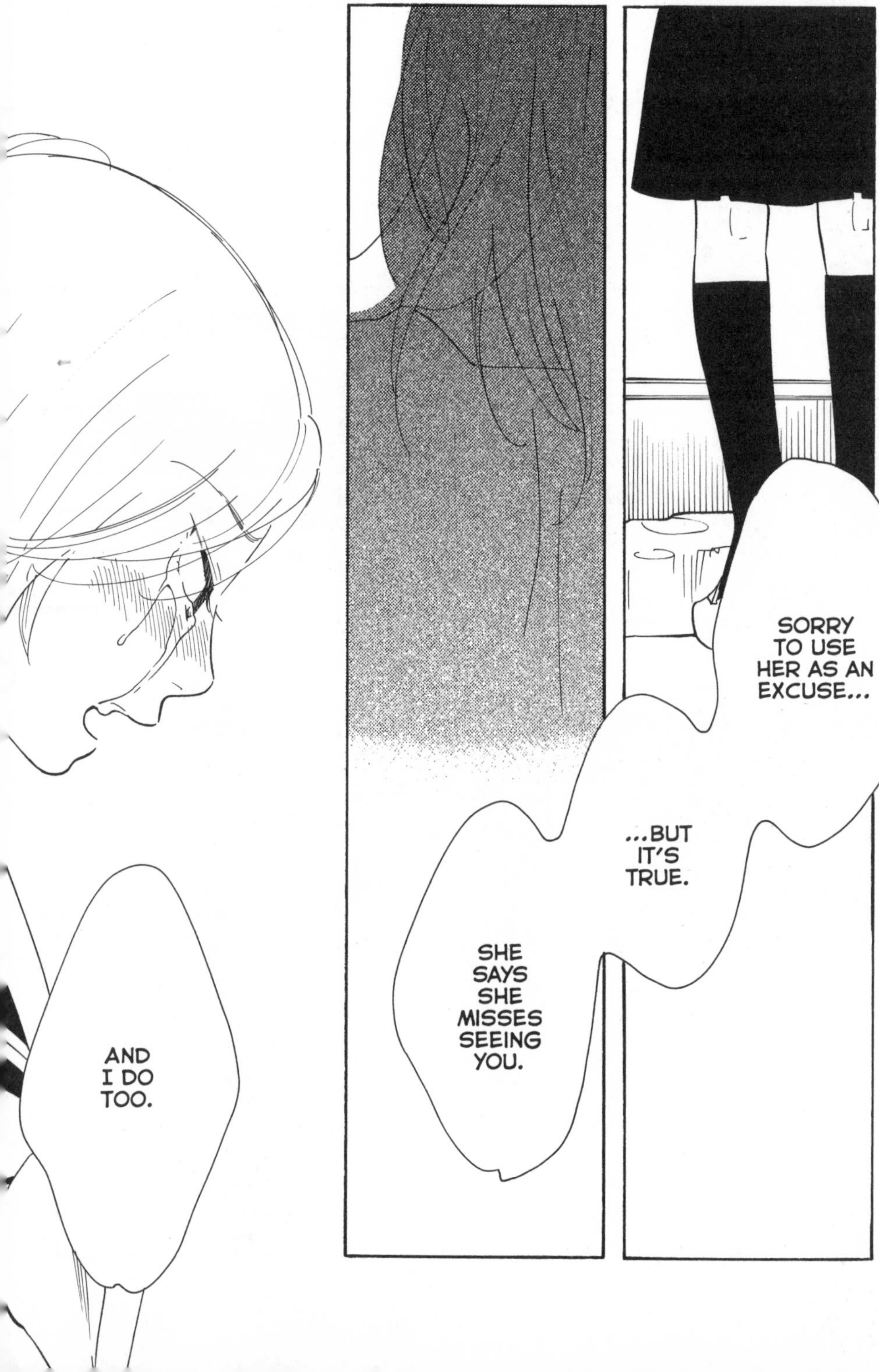
SORRY TO USE HER AS AN EXCUSE...
...BUT IT'S TRUE.
SHE SAYS SHE MISSES SEEING YOU.
AND I DO TOO.

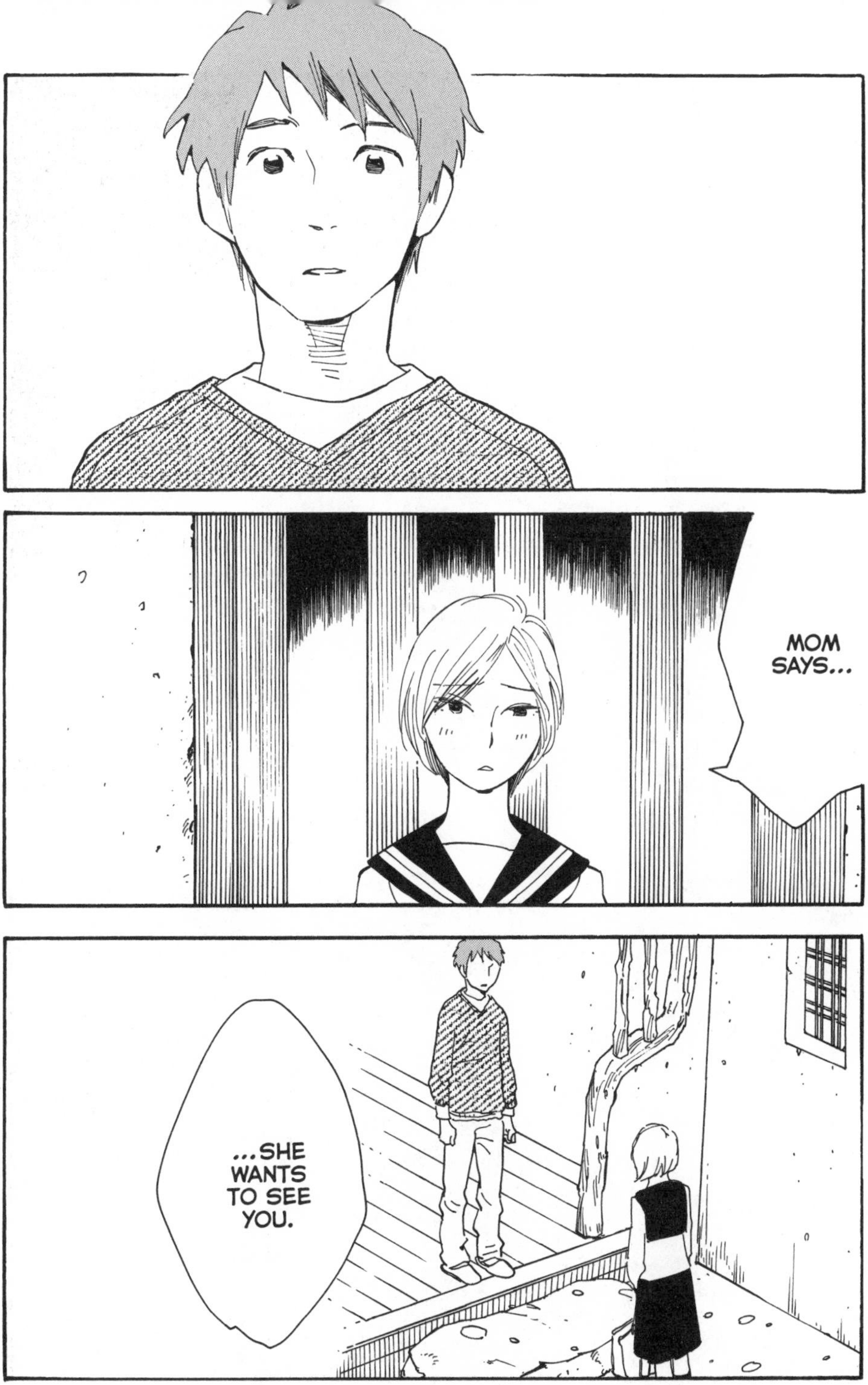
MOM SAYS...
...SHE WANTS TO SEE YOU.

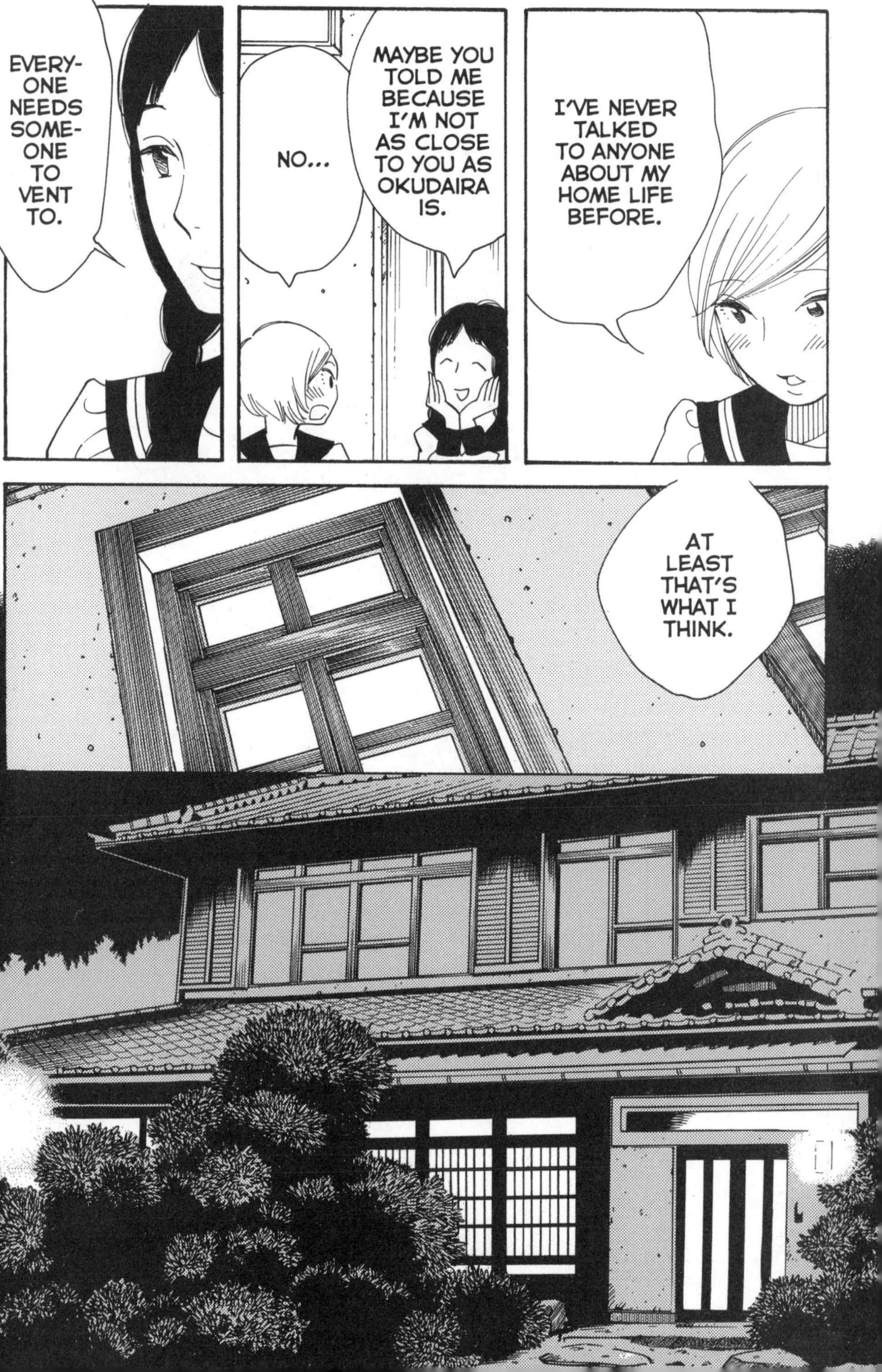
I'VE NEVER TALKED TO ANYONE ABOUT MY HOME LIFE BEFORE.
MAYBE YOU TOLD ME BECAUSE I'M NOT AS CLOSE TO YOU AS OKUDAIRA IS.
NO...
EVERY-ONE NEEDS SOME-ONE TO VENT TO.
AT LEAST THAT'S WHAT I THINK.

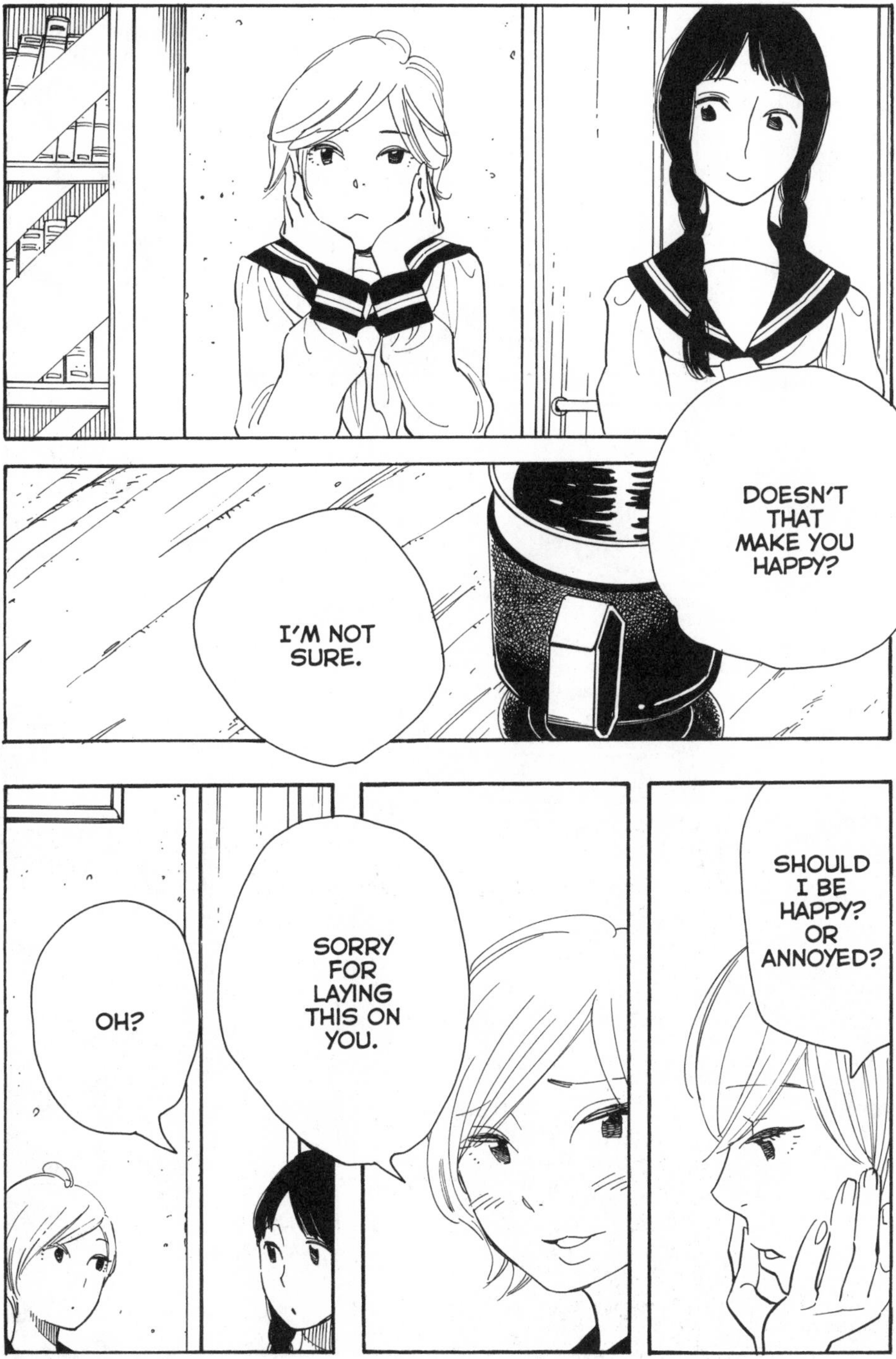
DOESN'T THAT MAKE YOU HAPPY?
I'M NOT SURE.
SHOULD I BE HAPPY? OR ANNOYED?
SORRY FOR LAYING THIS ON YOU.
OH?

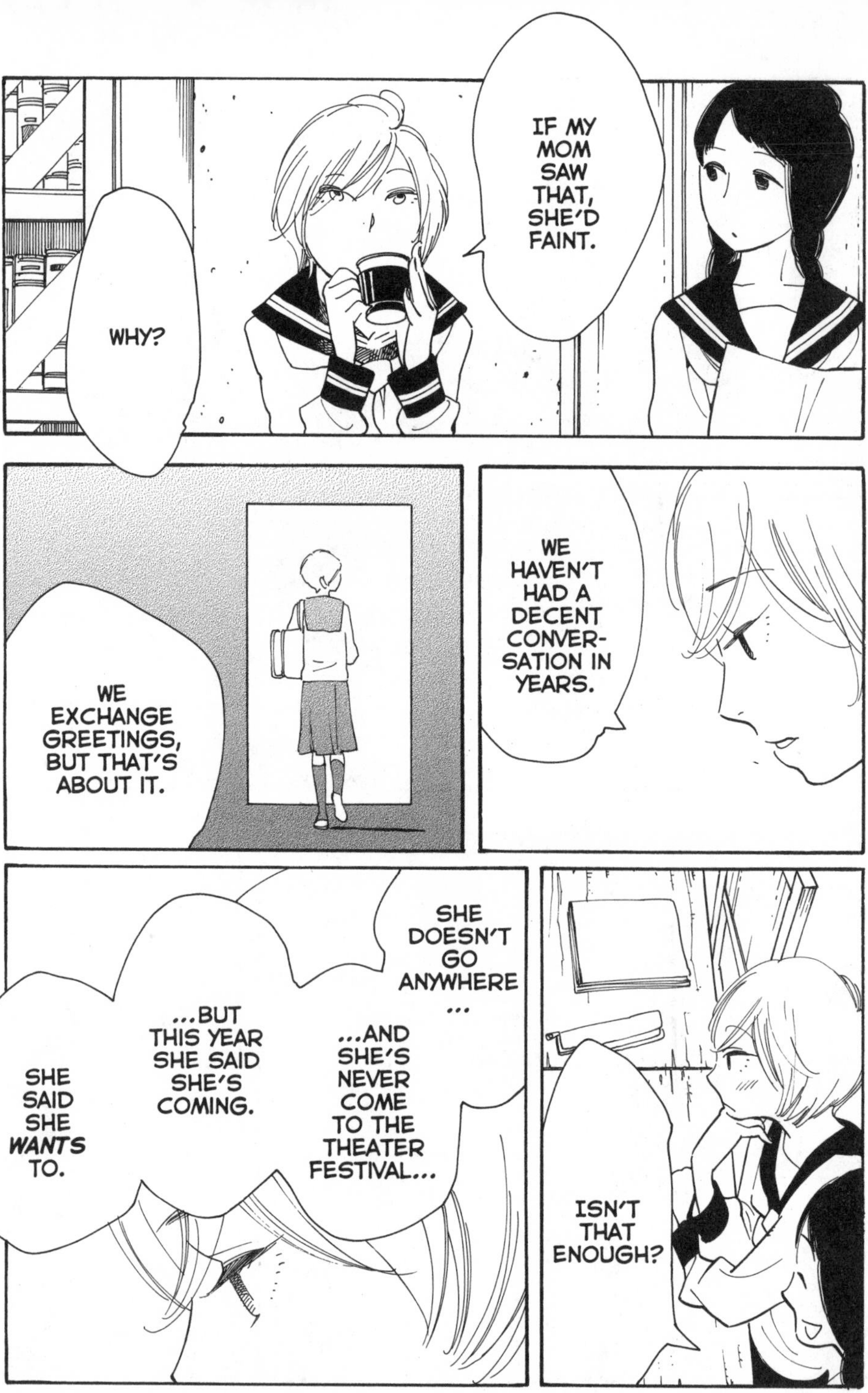
IF MY MOM SAW THAT, SHE'D FAINT.
WHY?
WE HAVEN'T HAD A DECENT CONVERSATION IN YEARS.
WE EXCHANGE GREETINGS, BUT THAT'S ABOUT IT.
ISN'T THAT ENOUGH?
SHE DOESN'T GO ANYWHERE...
...AND SHE'S NEVER COME TO THE THEATER FESTIVAL...
...BUT THIS YEAR SHE SAID SHE'S COMING.
SHE SAID SHE *WANTS* TO.

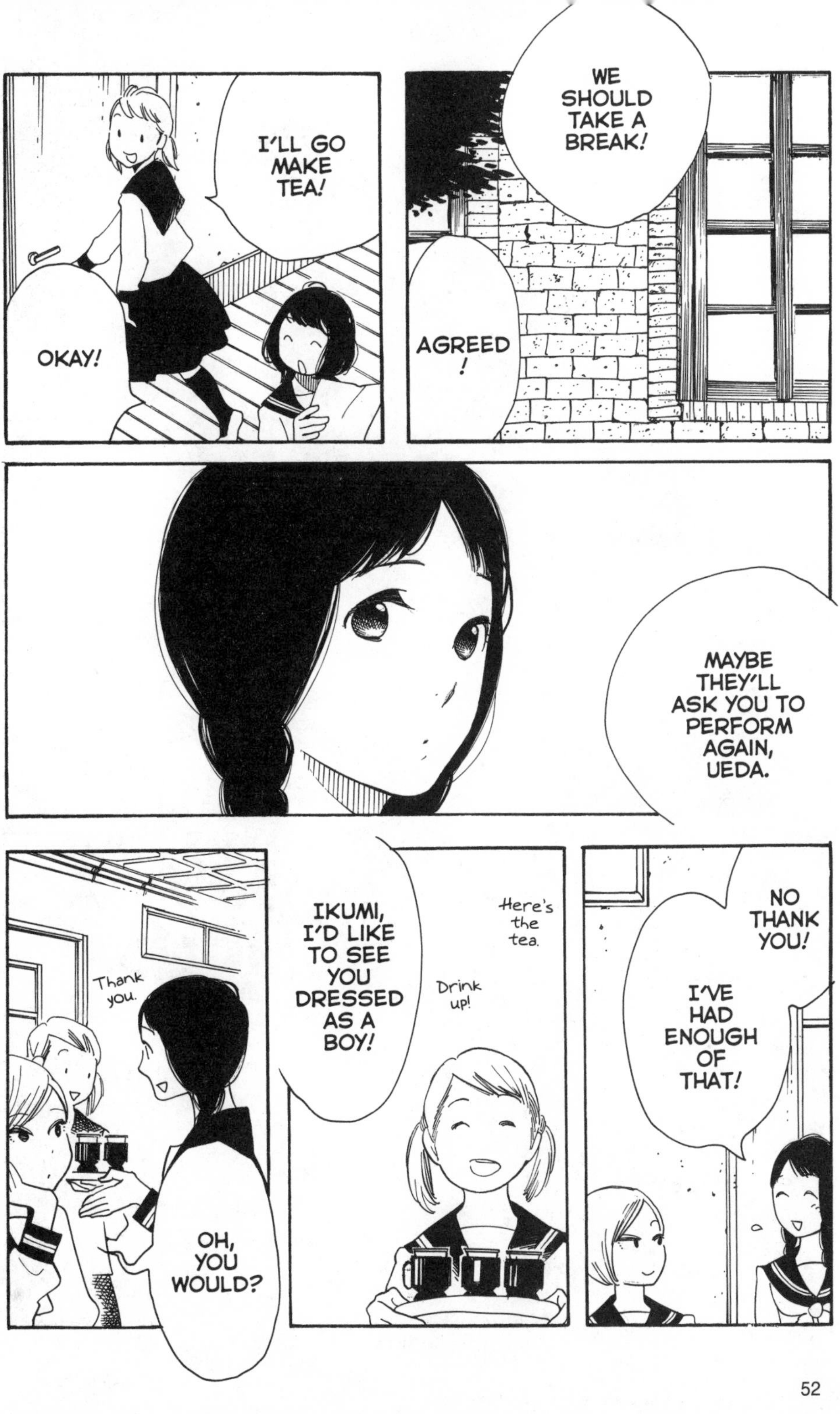
WE SHOULD TAKE A BREAK!
AGREED!
I'LL GO MAKE TEA!
OKAY!
MAYBE THEY'LL ASK YOU TO PERFORM AGAIN, UEDA.
NO THANK YOU!
I'VE HAD ENOUGH OF THAT!
Here's the tea.
IKUMI, I'D LIKE TO SEE YOU DRESSED AS A BOY!
Drink up!
Thank you.
OH, YOU WOULD?

Sweet Blue Flowers

#41 Melody, Part 2

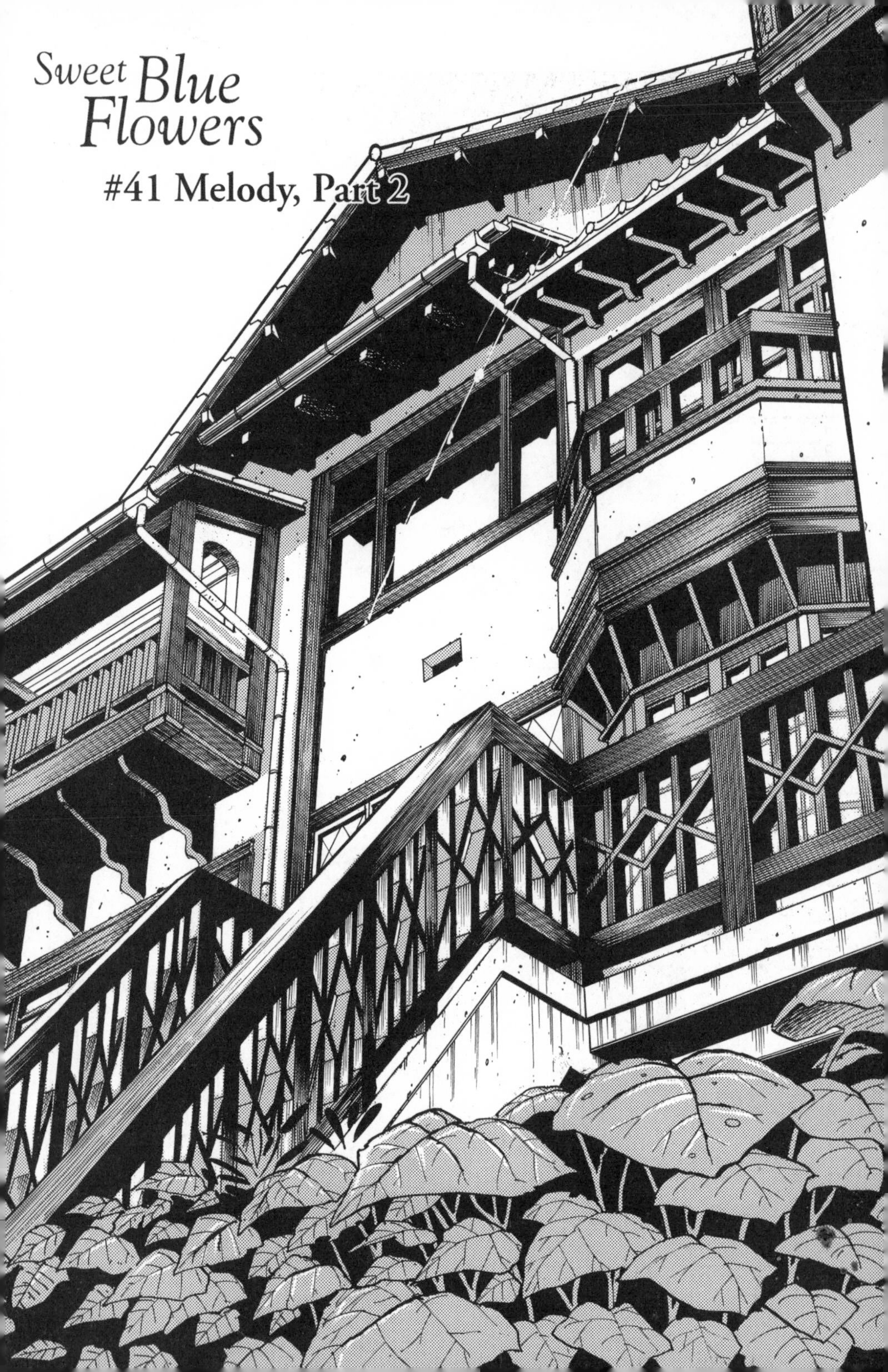

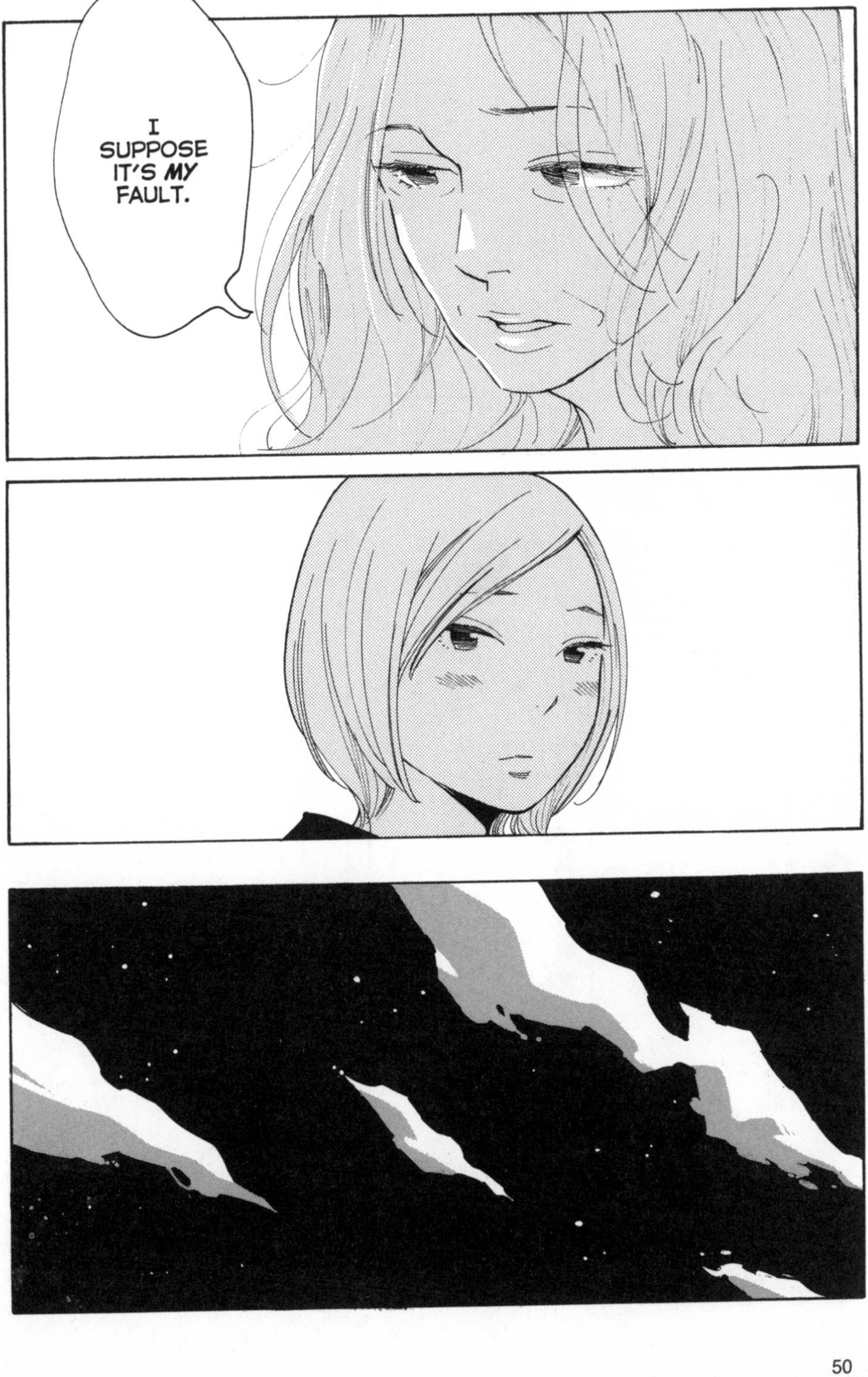
I SUPPOSE IT'S *MY* FAULT.

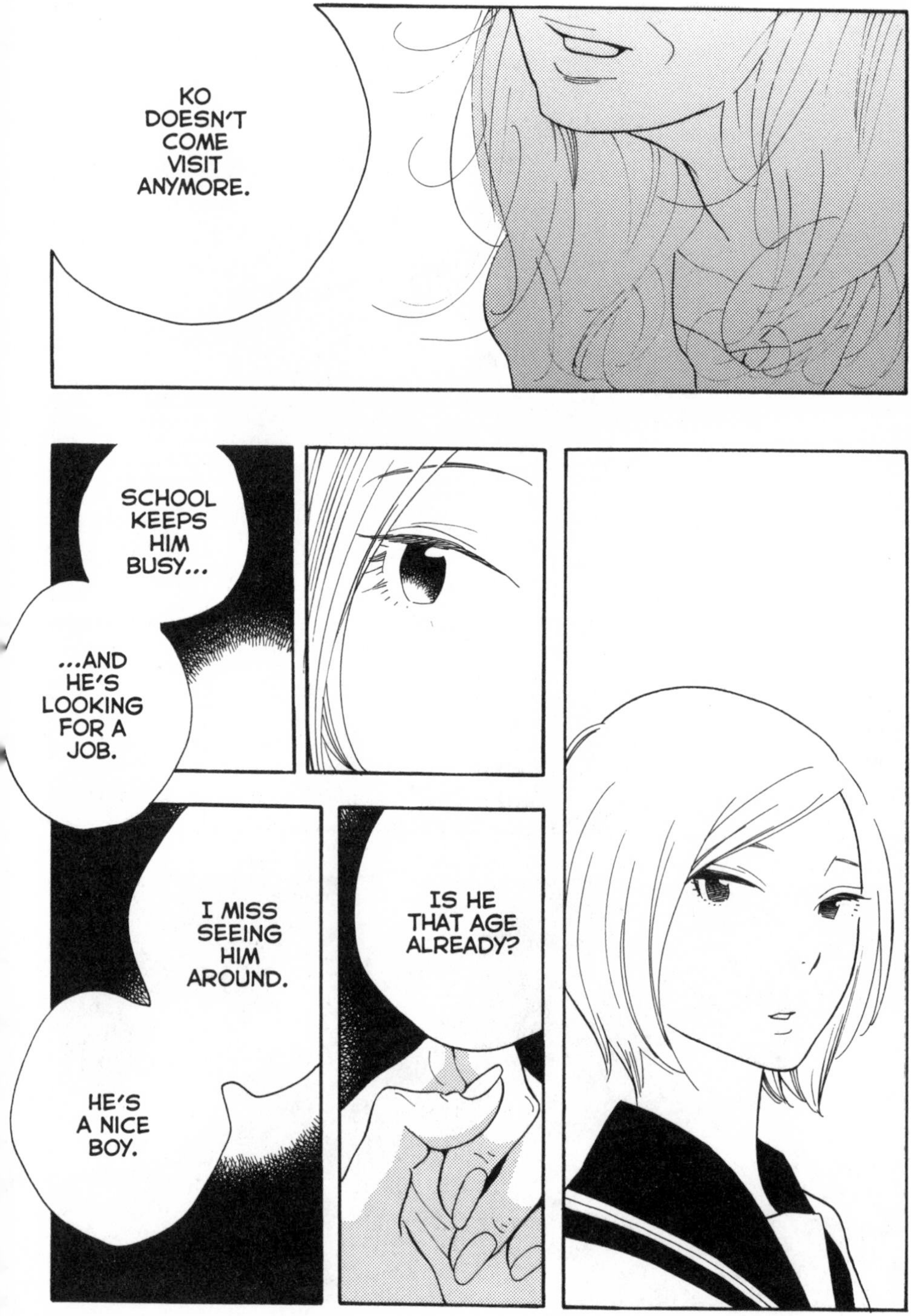
KO DOESN'T COME VISIT ANYMORE.
SCHOOL KEEPS HIM BUSY...
...AND HE'S LOOKING FOR A JOB.
IS HE THAT AGE ALREADY?
I MISS SEEING HIM AROUND.
HE'S A NICE BOY.

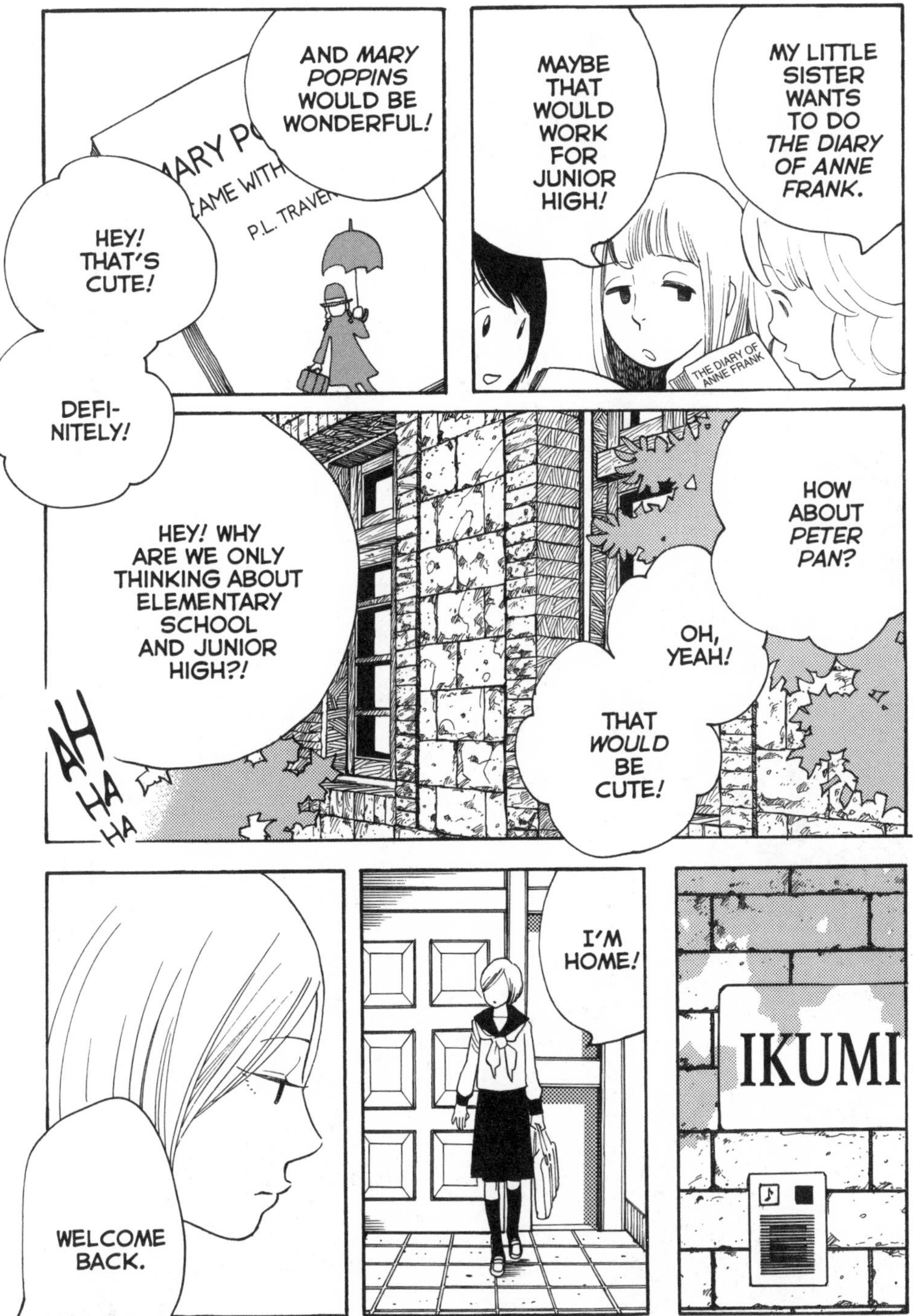

MY LITTLE SISTER WANTS TO DO *THE DIARY OF ANNE FRANK.*
MAYBE THAT WOULD WORK FOR JUNIOR HIGH!
THE DIARY OF ANNE FRANK
AND *MARY POPPINS* WOULD BE WONDERFUL!
HEY! THAT'S CUTE!
DEFI-NITELY!
HOW ABOUT *PETER PAN*?
OH, YEAH!
THAT *WOULD* BE CUTE!
HEY! WHY ARE WE ONLY THINKING ABOUT ELEMENTARY SCHOOL AND JUNIOR HIGH?!
AH HA HA HA
IKUMI
I'M HOME!
WELCOME BACK.

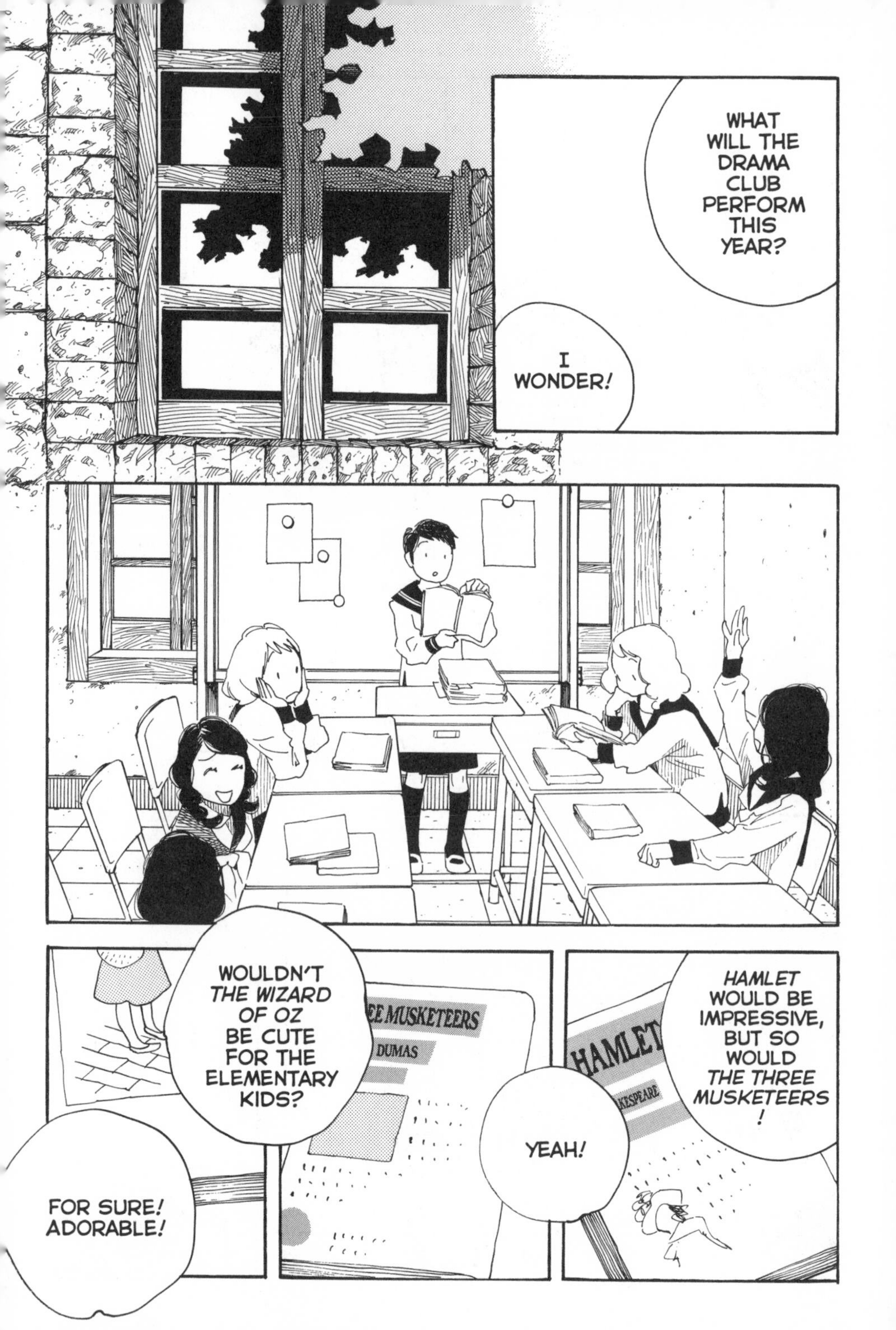
WHAT WILL THE DRAMA CLUB PERFORM THIS YEAR?
I WONDER!
HAMLET WOULD BE IMPRESSIVE, BUT SO WOULD *THE THREE MUSKETEERS*!
HAMLET
YEAH!
DUMAS
WOULDN'T *THE WIZARD OF OZ* BE CUTE FOR THE ELEMENTARY KIDS?
FOR SURE! ADORABLE!

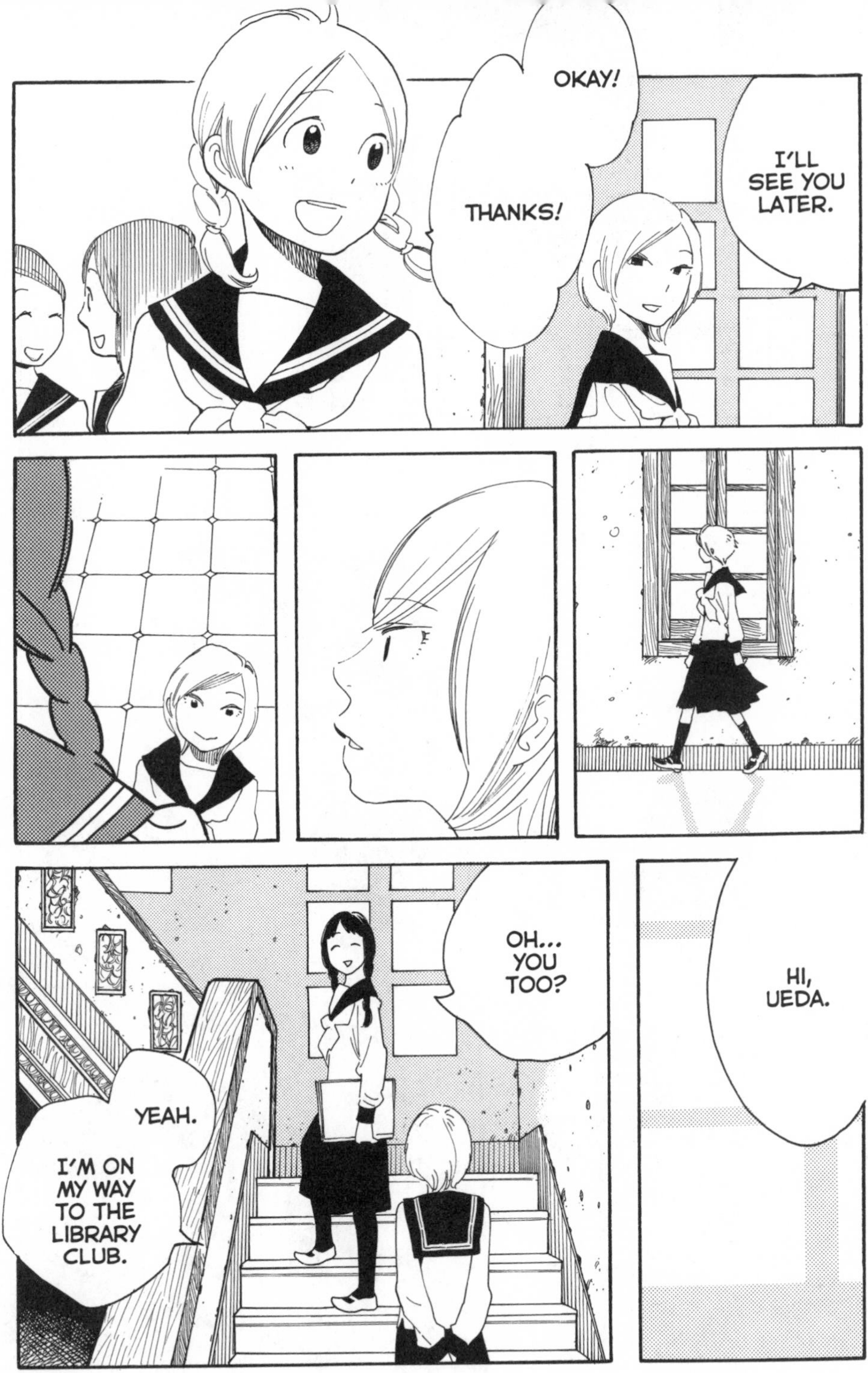
I'LL SEE YOU LATER.
OKAY!
THANKS!
HI, UEDA.
OH... YOU TOO?
YEAH.
I'M ON MY WAY TO THE LIBRARY CLUB.

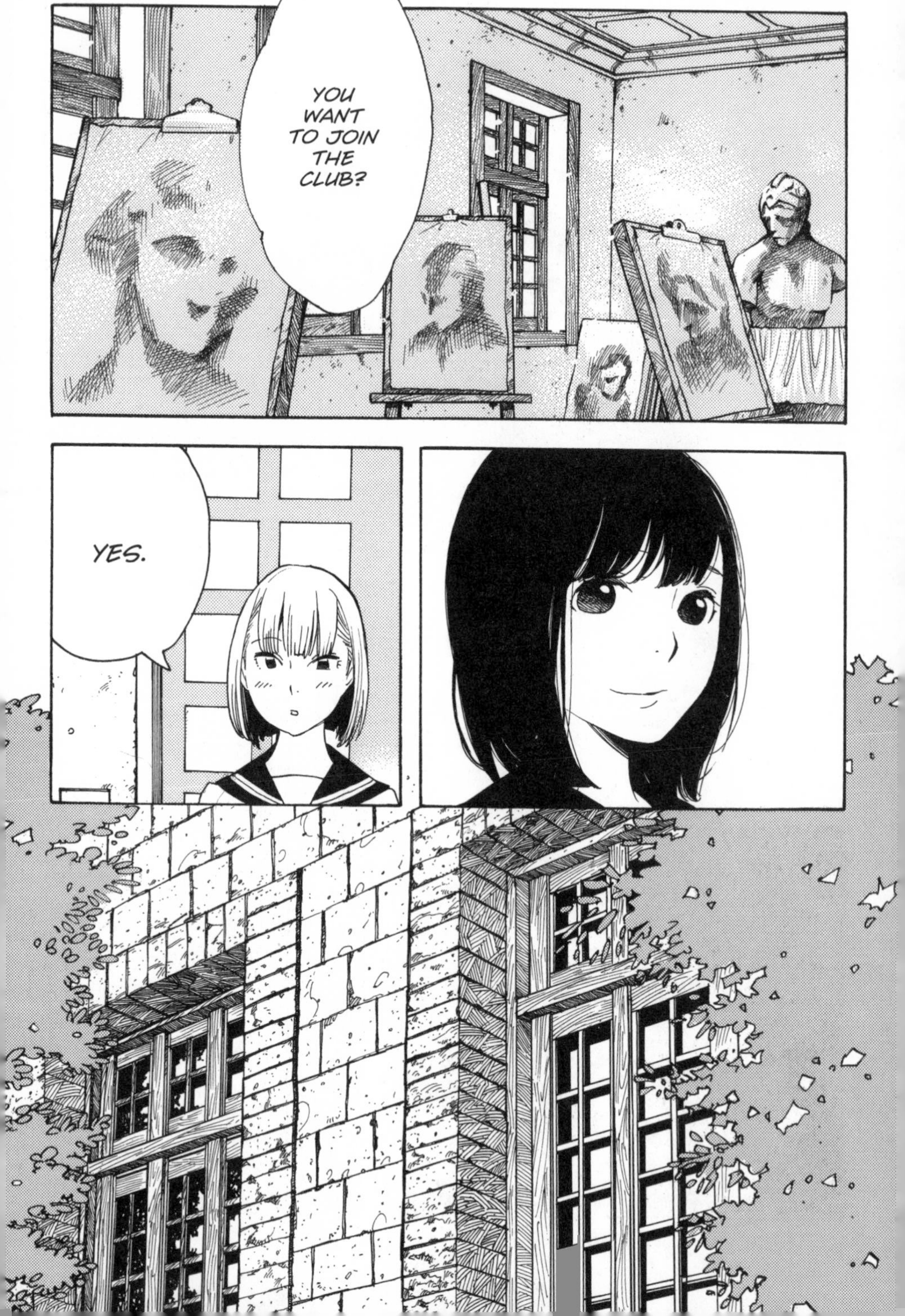
YOU WANT TO JOIN THE CLUB?
YES.

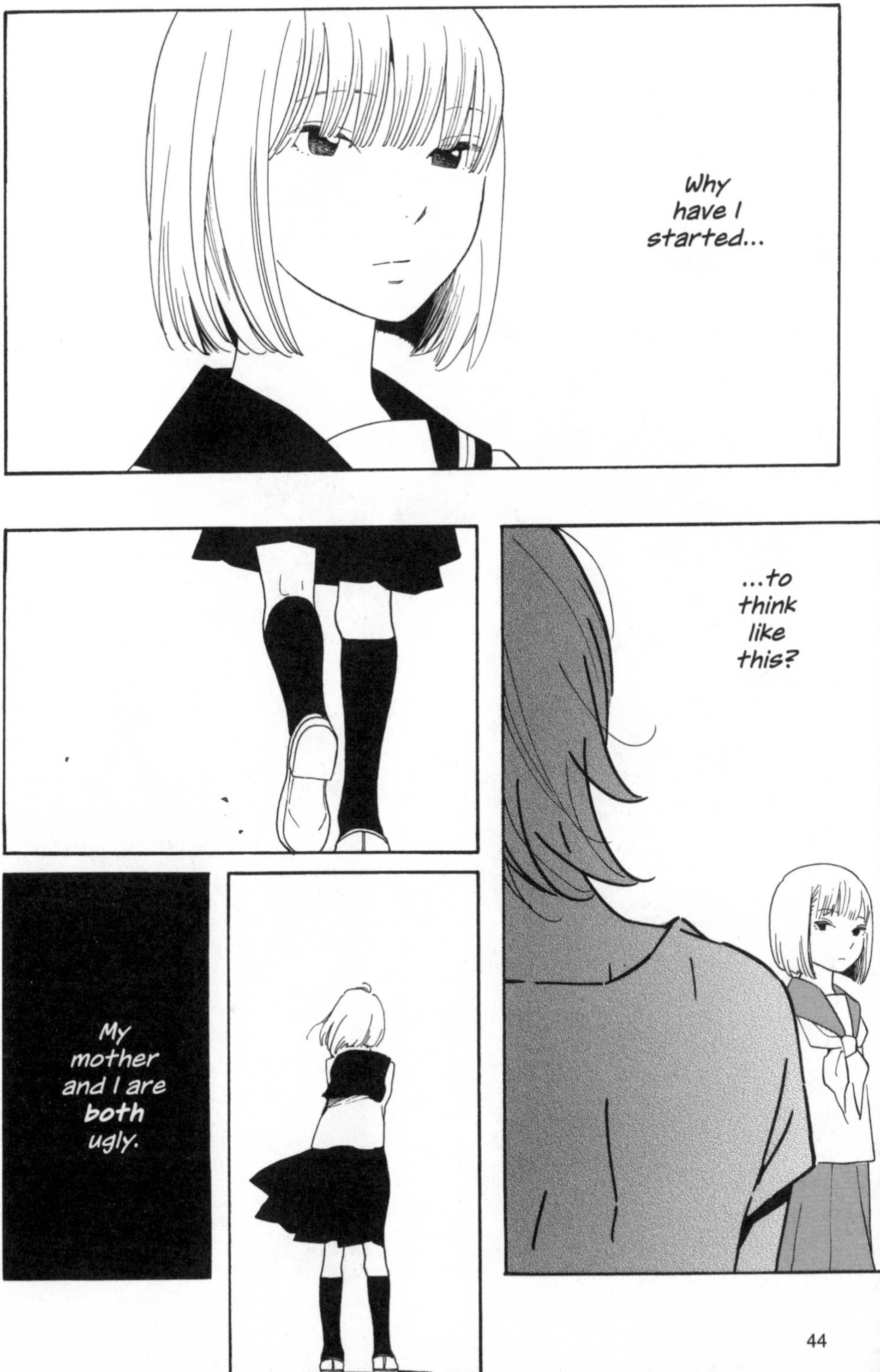
Why have I started...
...to think like this?
My mother and I are both ugly.

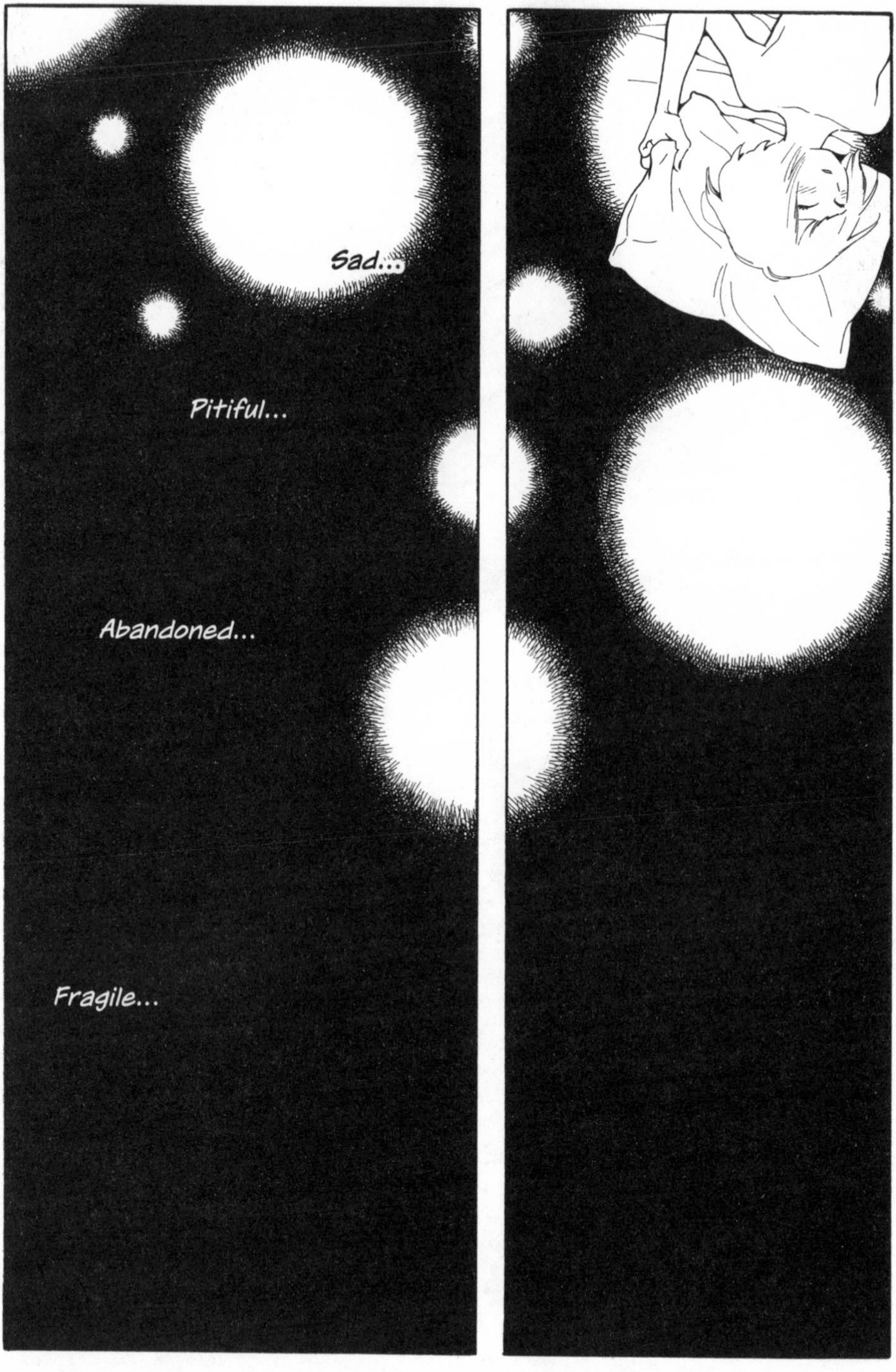
Sad...
Pitiful...
Abandoned...
Fragile...

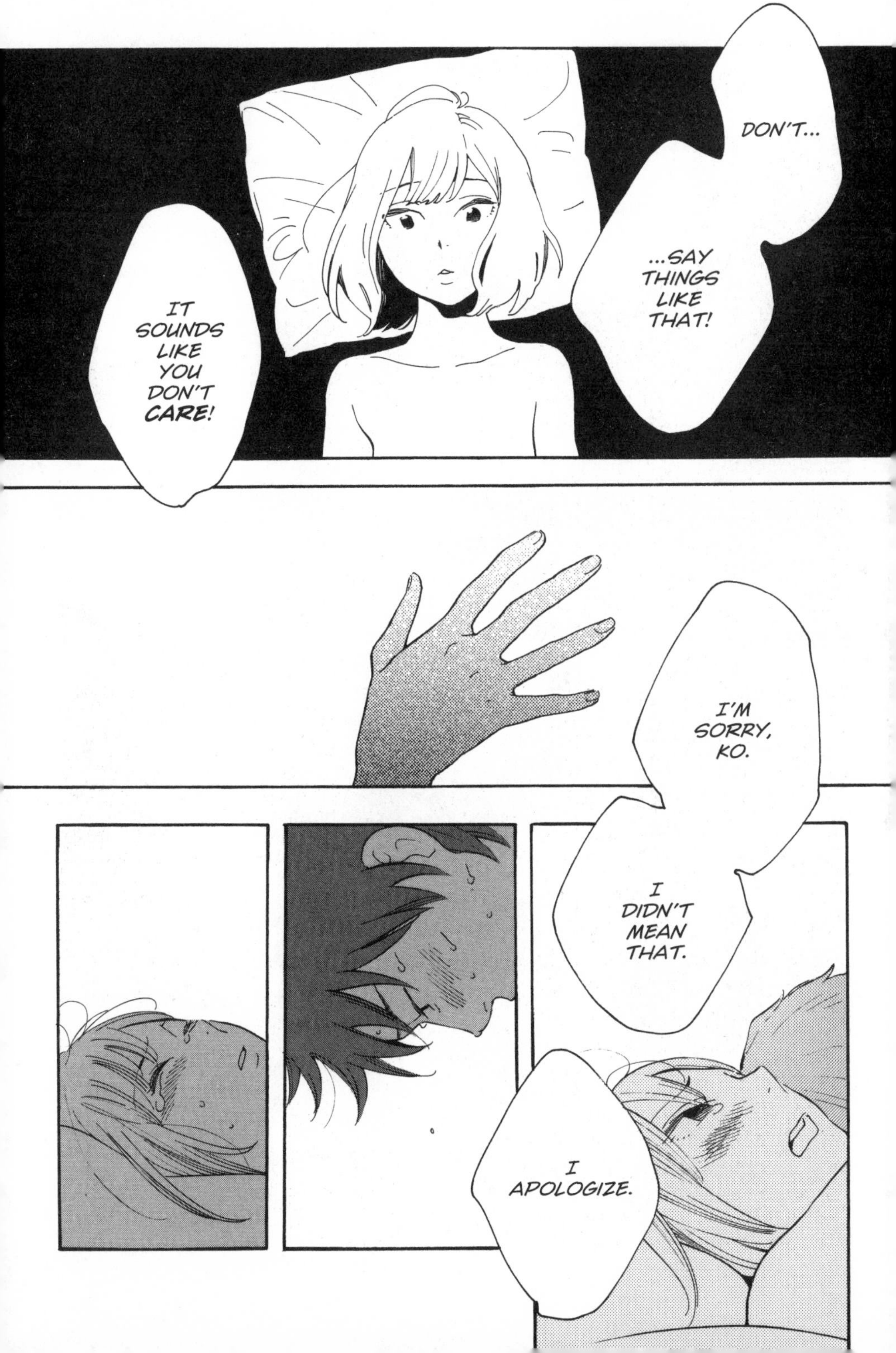
DON'T...
...SAY THINGS LIKE THAT!
IT SOUNDS LIKE YOU DON'T CARE!
I'M SORRY, KO.
I DIDN'T MEAN THAT.
I APOLOGIZE.

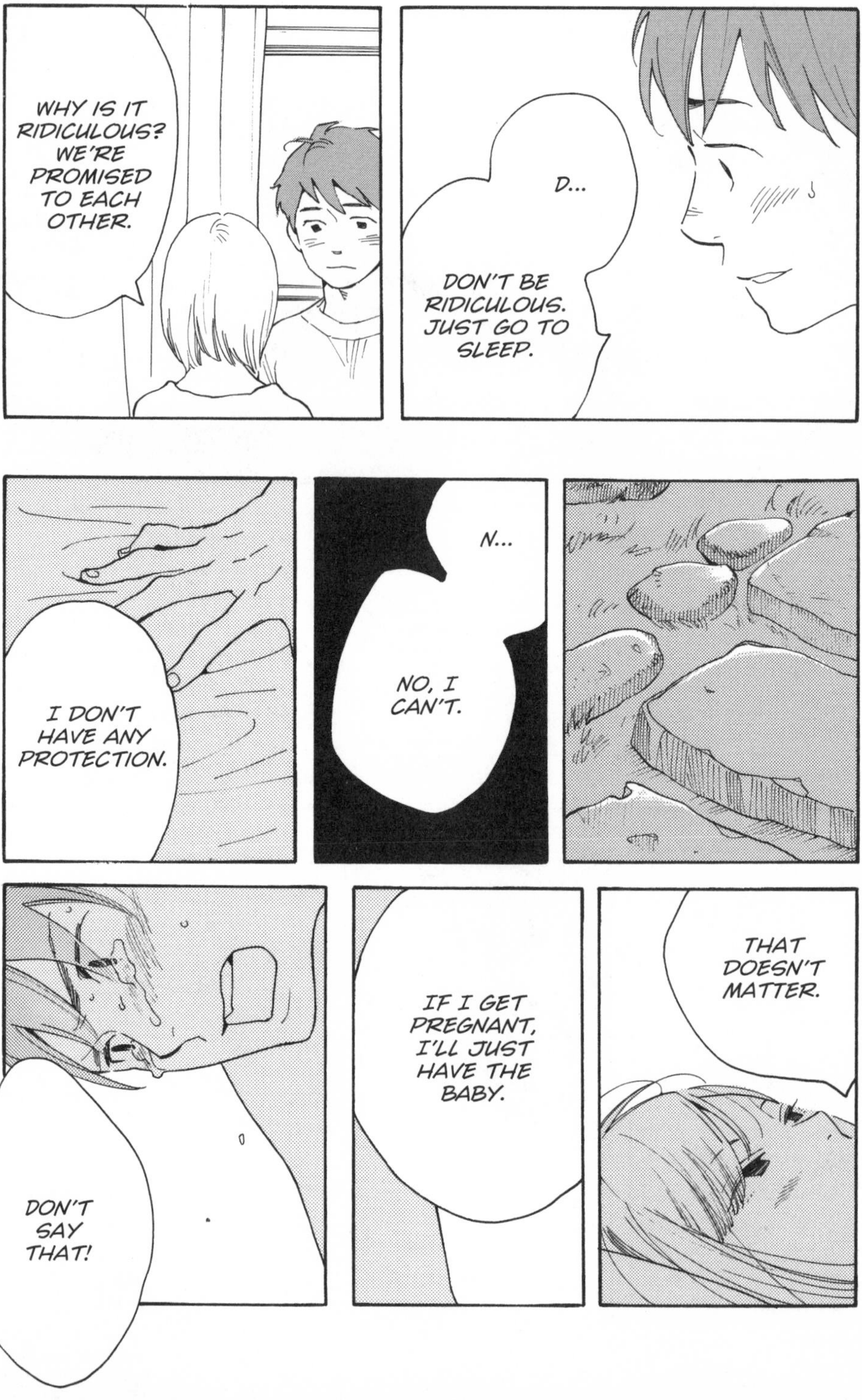
D...
DON'T BE RIDICULOUS. JUST GO TO SLEEP.
WHY IS IT RIDICULOUS? WE'RE PROMISED TO EACH OTHER.
N...
NO, I CAN'T.
I DON'T HAVE ANY PROTECTION.
THAT DOESN'T MATTER.
IF I GET PREGNANT, I'LL JUST HAVE THE BABY.
DON'T SAY THAT!

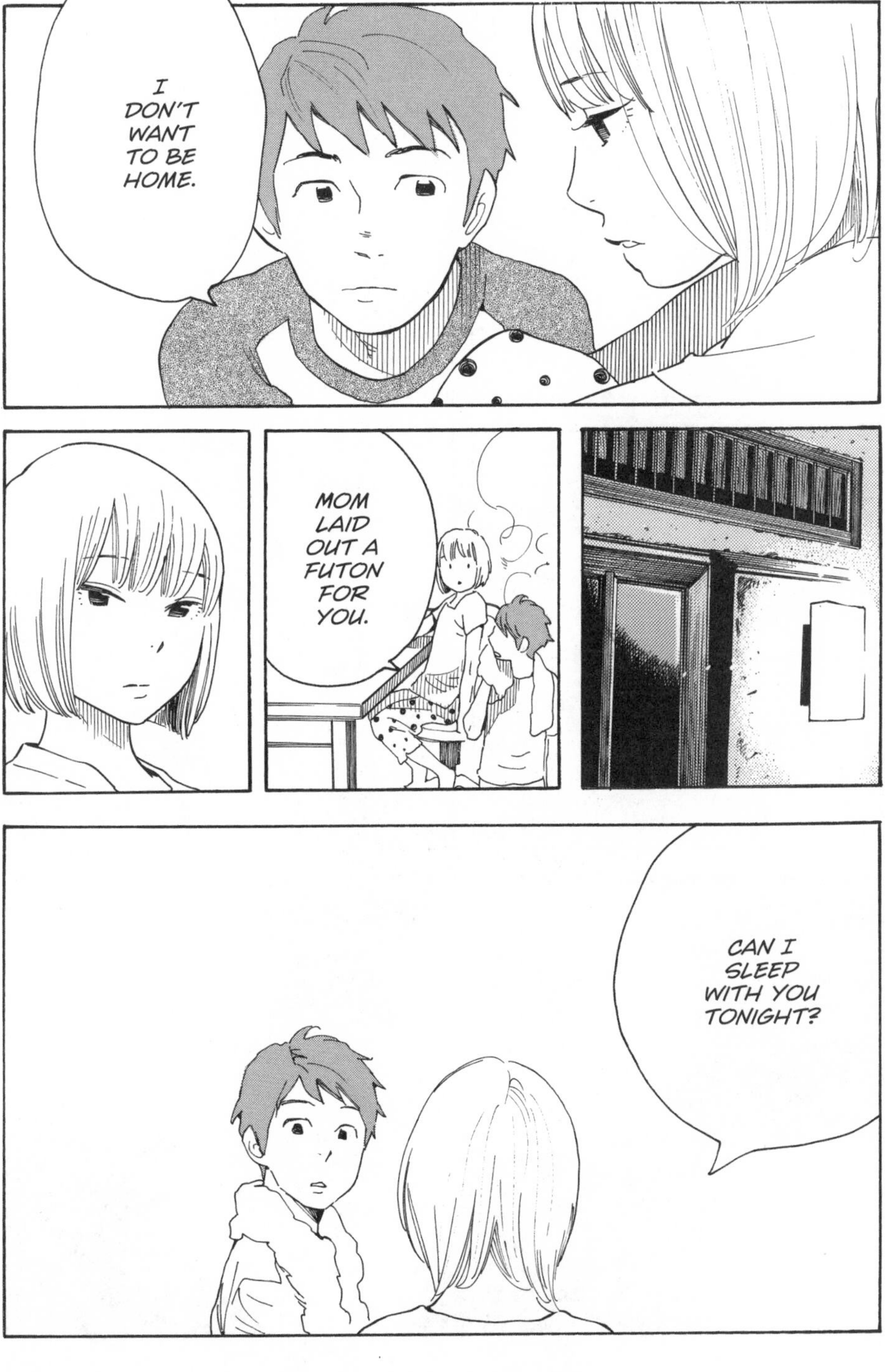
I DON'T WANT TO BE HOME.
MOM LAID OUT A FUTON FOR YOU.
CAN I SLEEP WITH YOU TONIGHT?

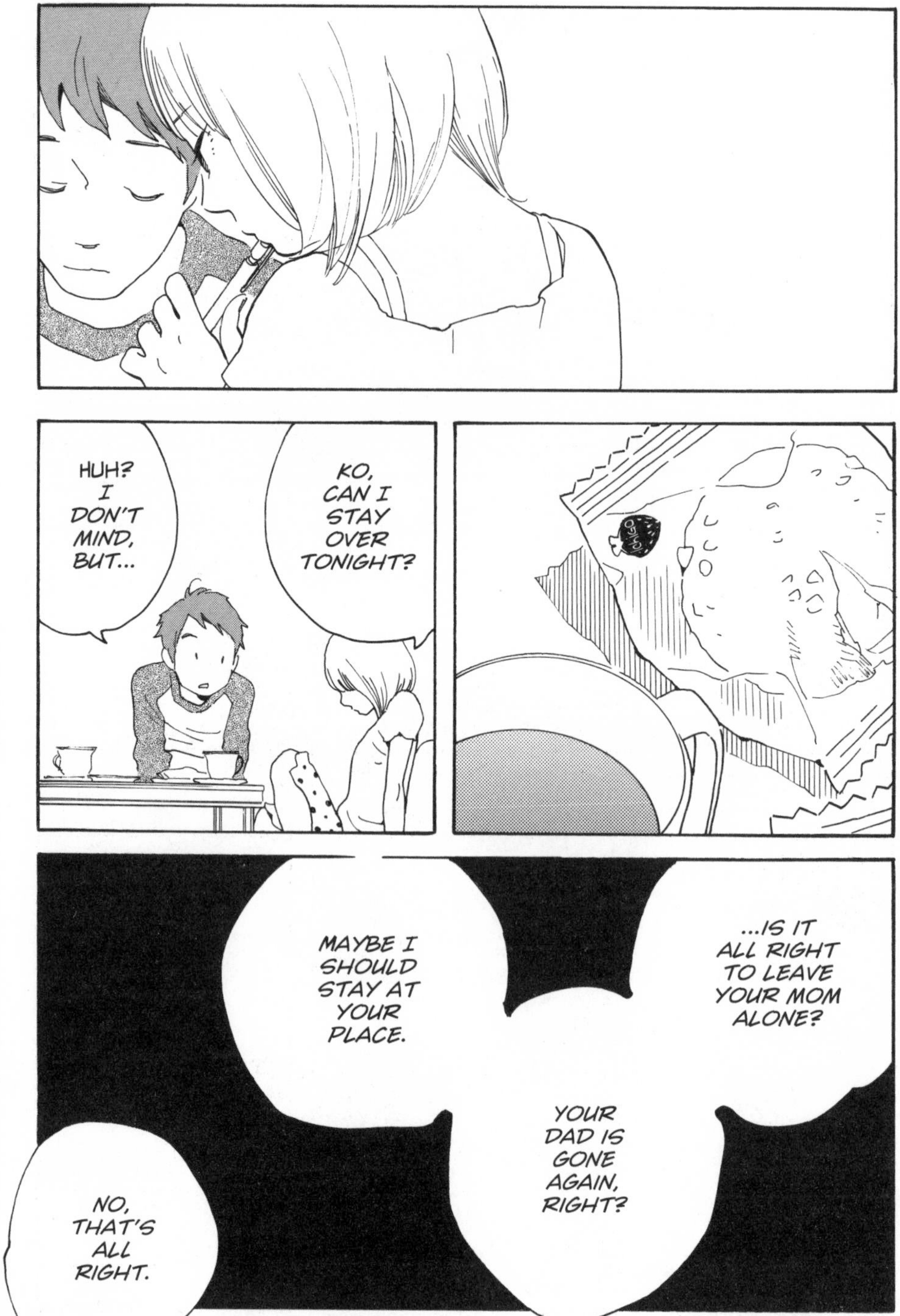
ICHIGO
KO, CAN I STAY OVER TONIGHT?
HUH? I DON'T MIND, BUT...
...IS IT ALL RIGHT TO LEAVE YOUR MOM ALONE?
MAYBE I SHOULD STAY AT YOUR PLACE.
YOUR DAD IS GONE AGAIN, RIGHT?
NO, THAT'S ALL RIGHT.

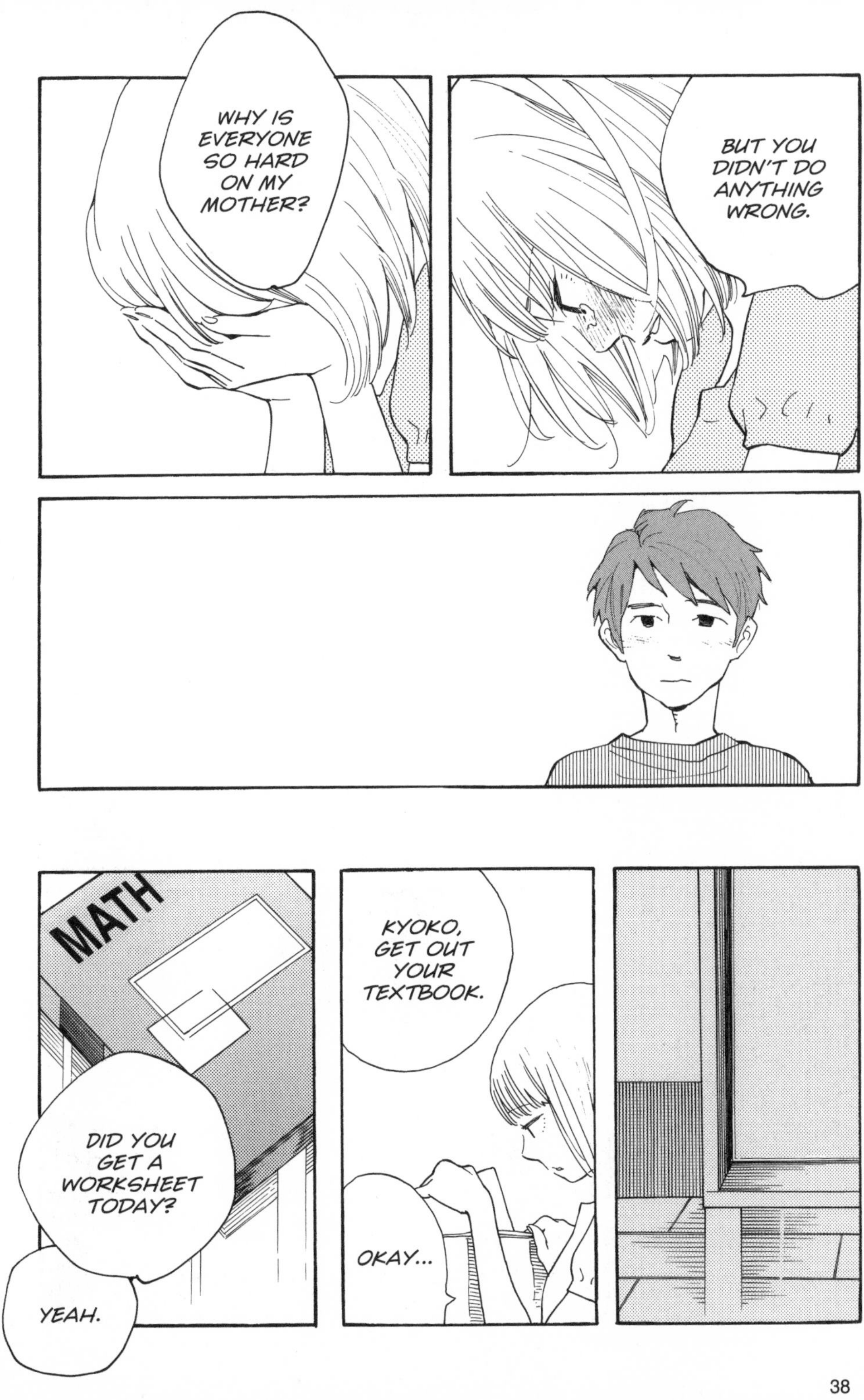
BUT YOU DIDN'T DO ANYTHING WRONG.
WHY IS EVERYONE SO HARD ON MY MOTHER?
KYOKO, GET OUT YOUR TEXTBOOK.
OKAY...
MATH
DID YOU GET A WORKSHEET TODAY?
YEAH.

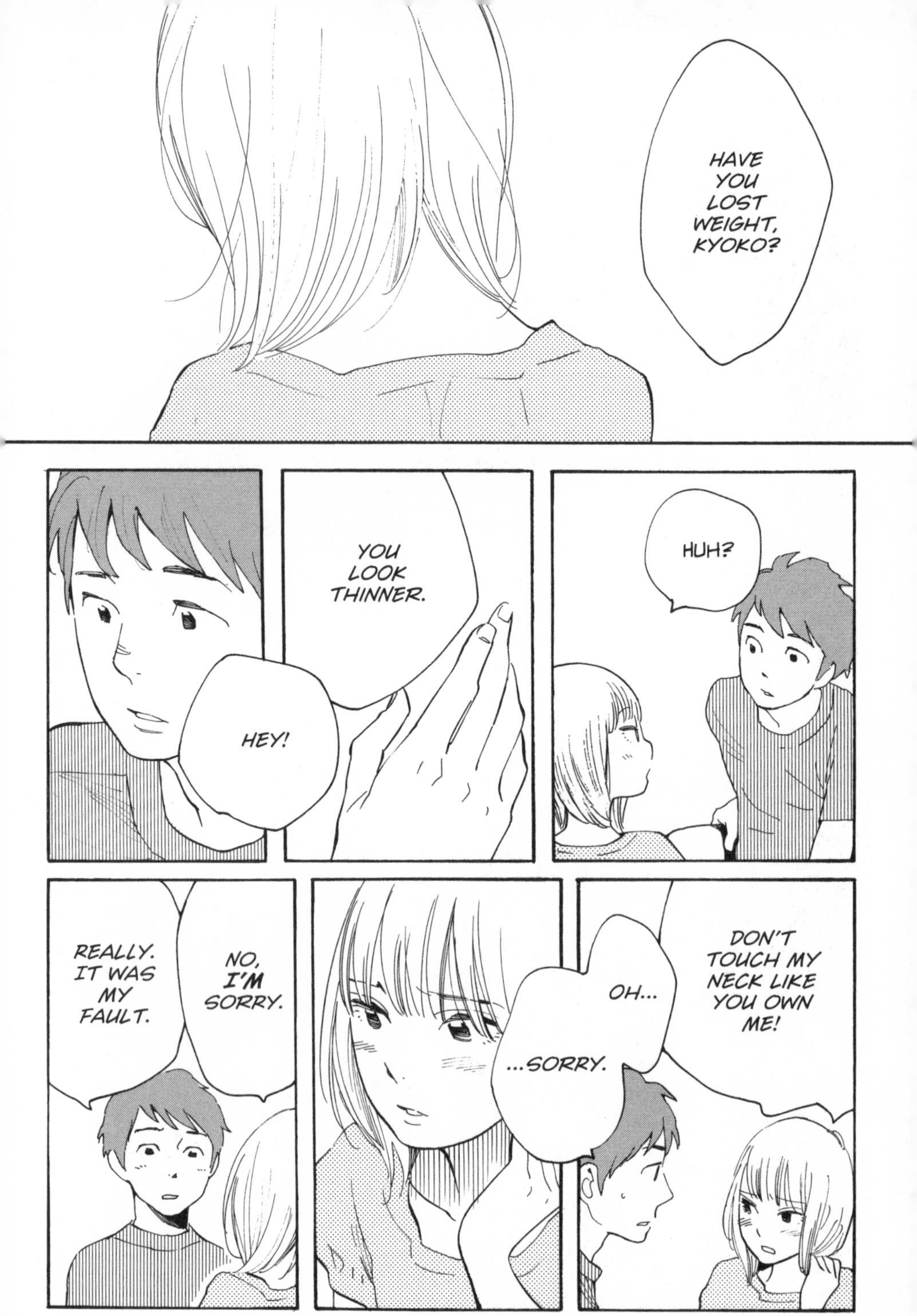
HAVE YOU LOST WEIGHT, KYOKO?
HUH?
YOU LOOK THINNER.
HEY!
DON'T TOUCH MY NECK LIKE YOU OWN ME!
OH... ...SORRY.
NO, I'M SORRY.
REALLY. IT WAS MY FAULT.

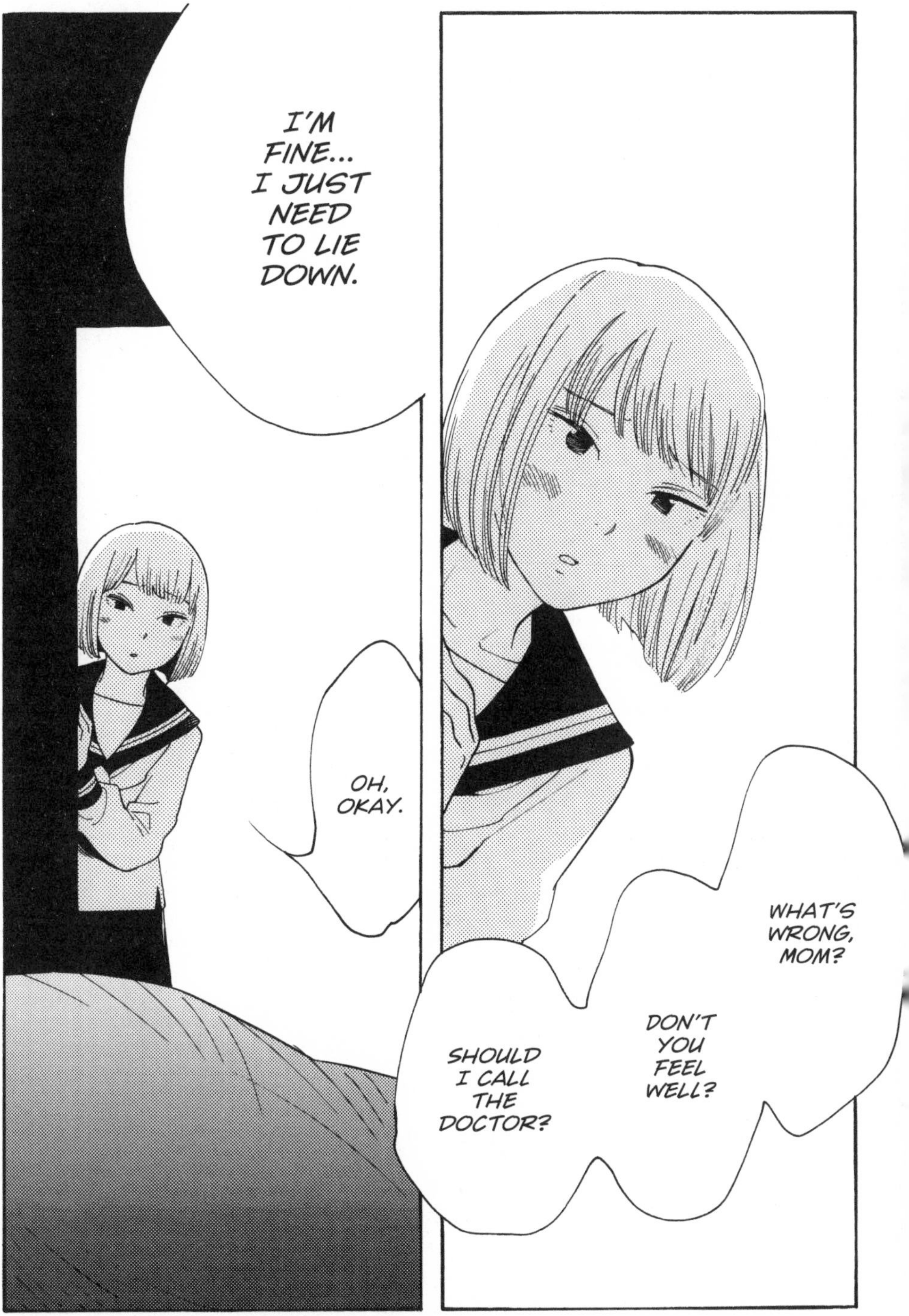
WHAT'S WRONG, MOM?
DON'T YOU FEEL WELL?
SHOULD I CALL THE DOCTOR?
I'M FINE... I JUST NEED TO LIE DOWN.
OH, OKAY.

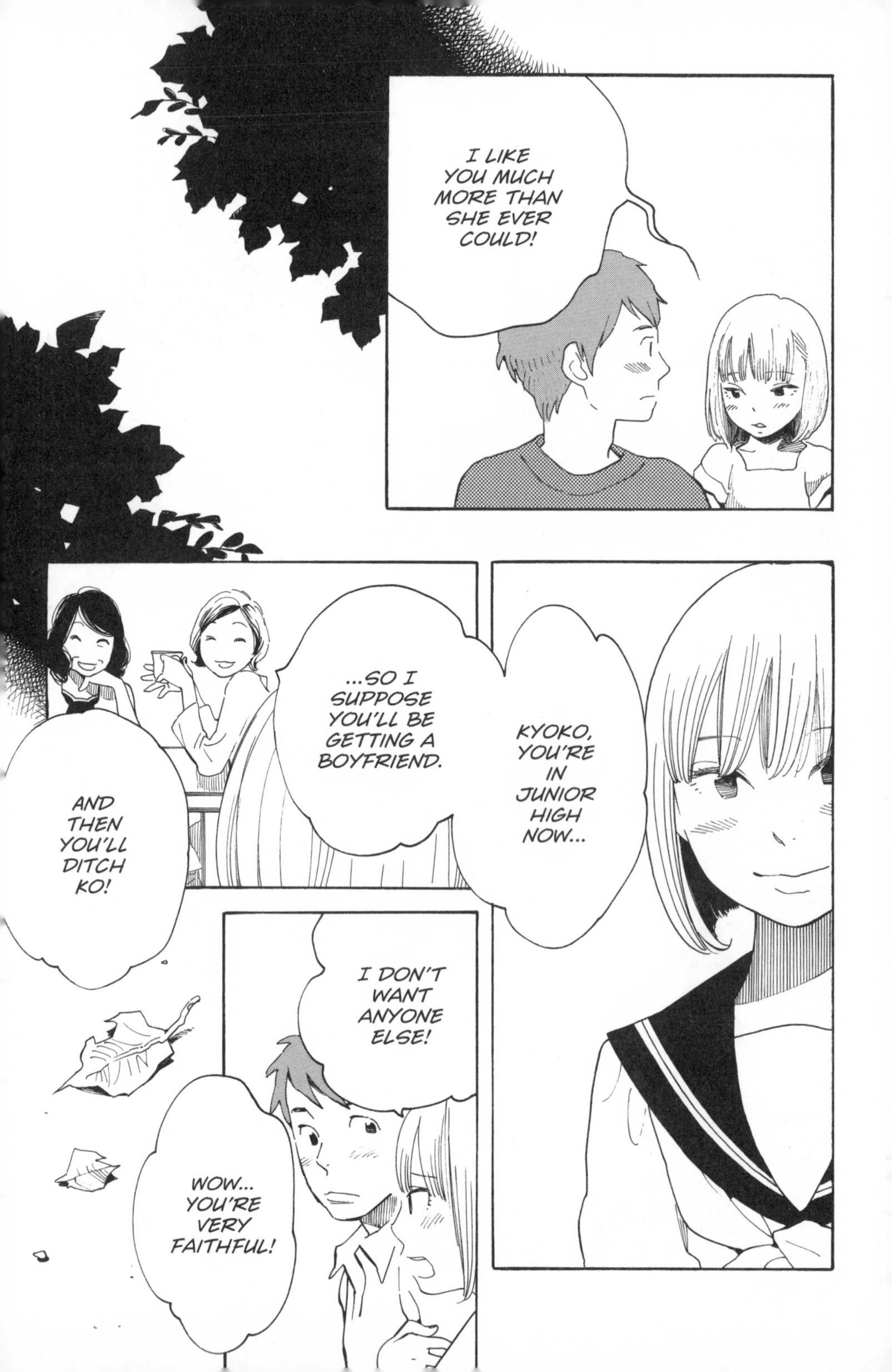
I LIKE YOU MUCH MORE THAN SHE EVER COULD!
KYOKO, YOU'RE IN JUNIOR HIGH NOW...
...SO I SUPPOSE YOU'LL BE GETTING A BOYFRIEND.
AND THEN YOU'LL DITCH KO!
I DON'T WANT ANYONE ELSE!
WOW... YOU'RE VERY FAITHFUL!

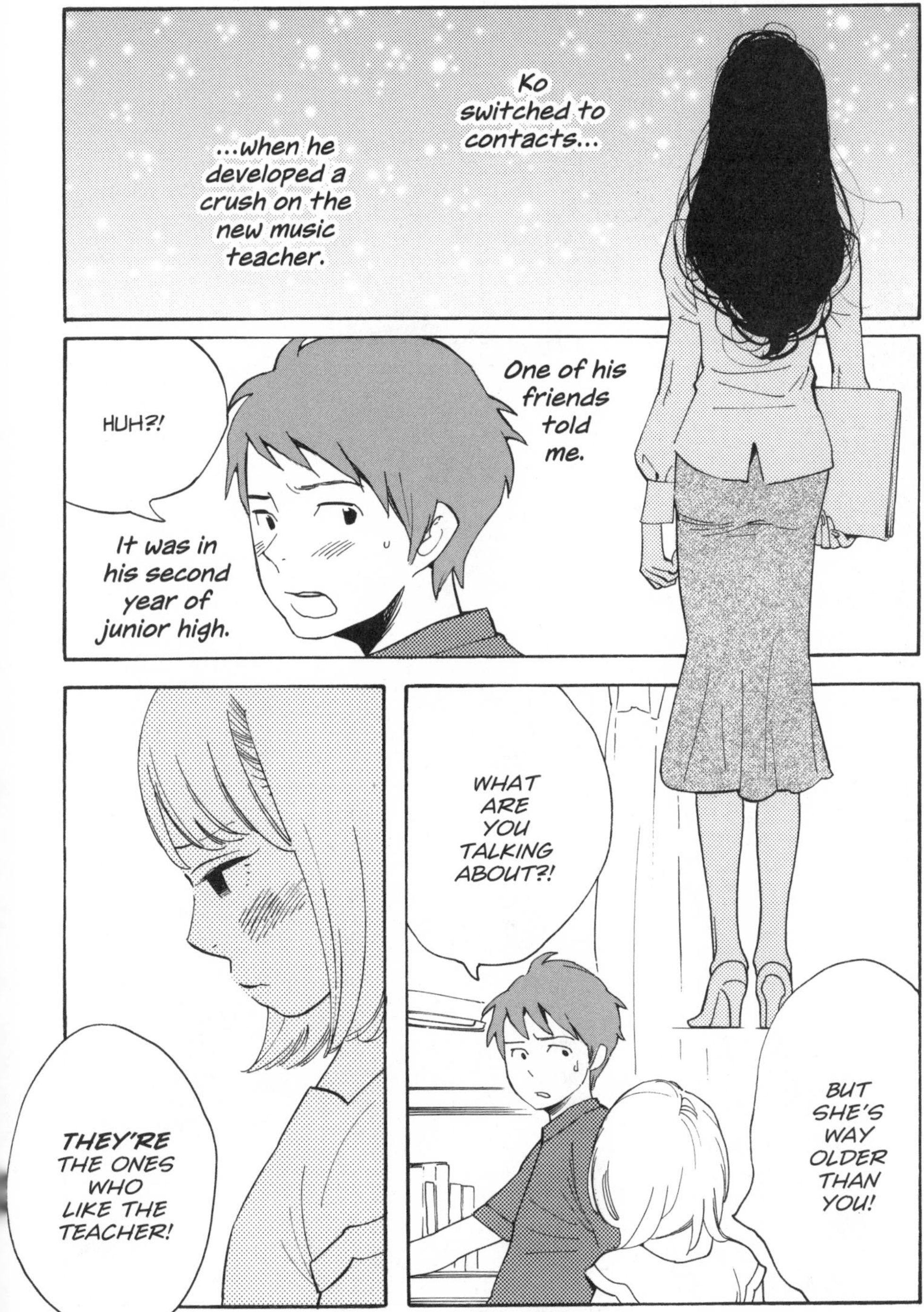
Ko switched to contacts...
...when he developed a crush on the new music teacher.
One of his friends told me.
HUH?!
It was in his second year of junior high.
WHAT ARE YOU TALKING ABOUT?!
BUT SHE'S WAY OLDER THAN YOU!
THEY'RE THE ONES WHO LIKE THE TEACHER!

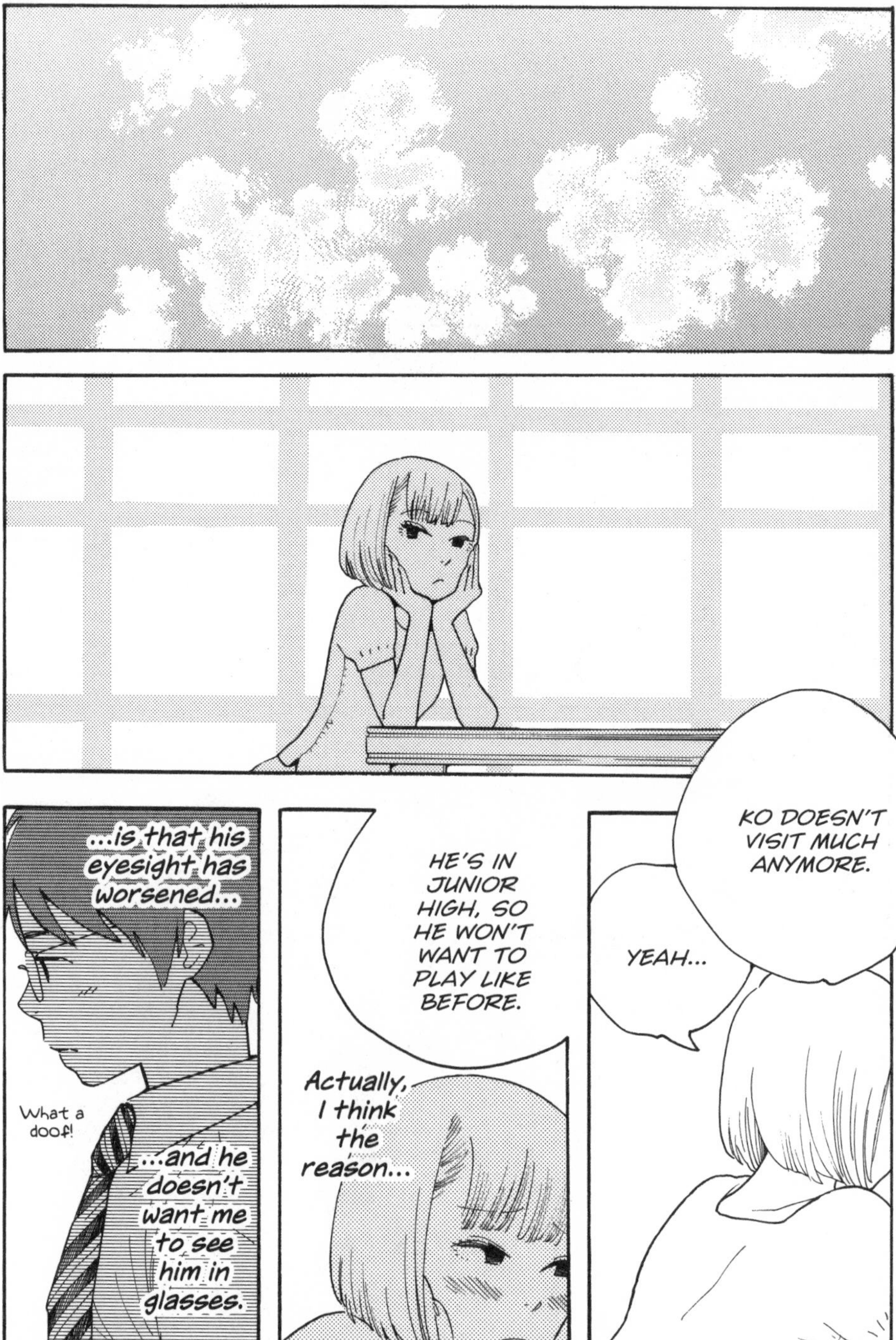
KO DOESN'T VISIT MUCH ANYMORE.
YEAH...
HE'S IN JUNIOR HIGH, SO HE WON'T WANT TO PLAY LIKE BEFORE.
Actually, I think the reason...
...is that his eyesight has worsened...
What a doof!
...and he doesn't want me to see him in glasses.

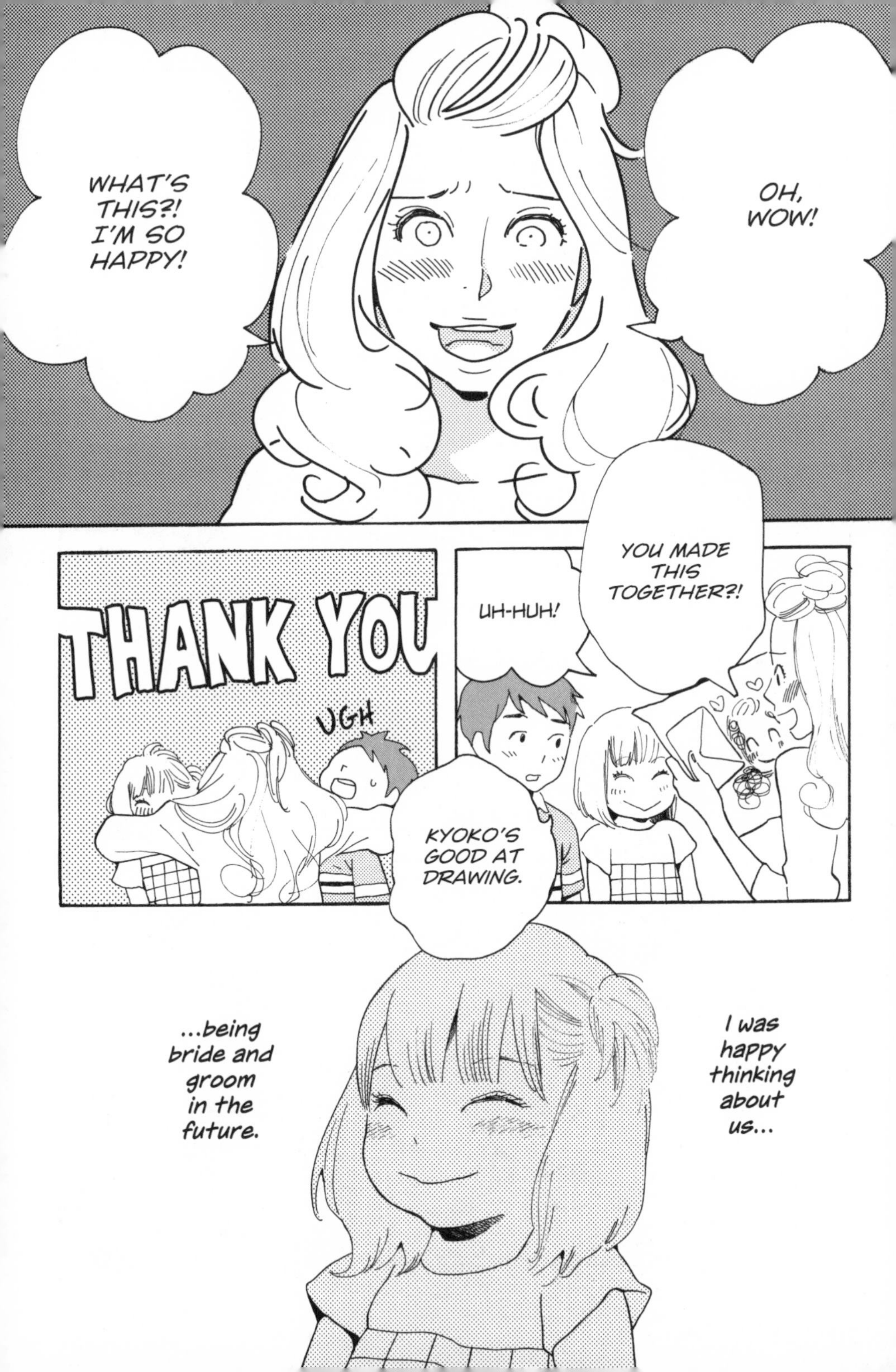
OH, WOW!
WHAT'S THIS?! I'M SO HAPPY!
YOU MADE THIS TOGETHER?!
UH-HUH!
THANK YOU
UGH
KYOKO'S GOOD AT DRAWING.
I was happy thinking about us...
...being bride and groom in the future.

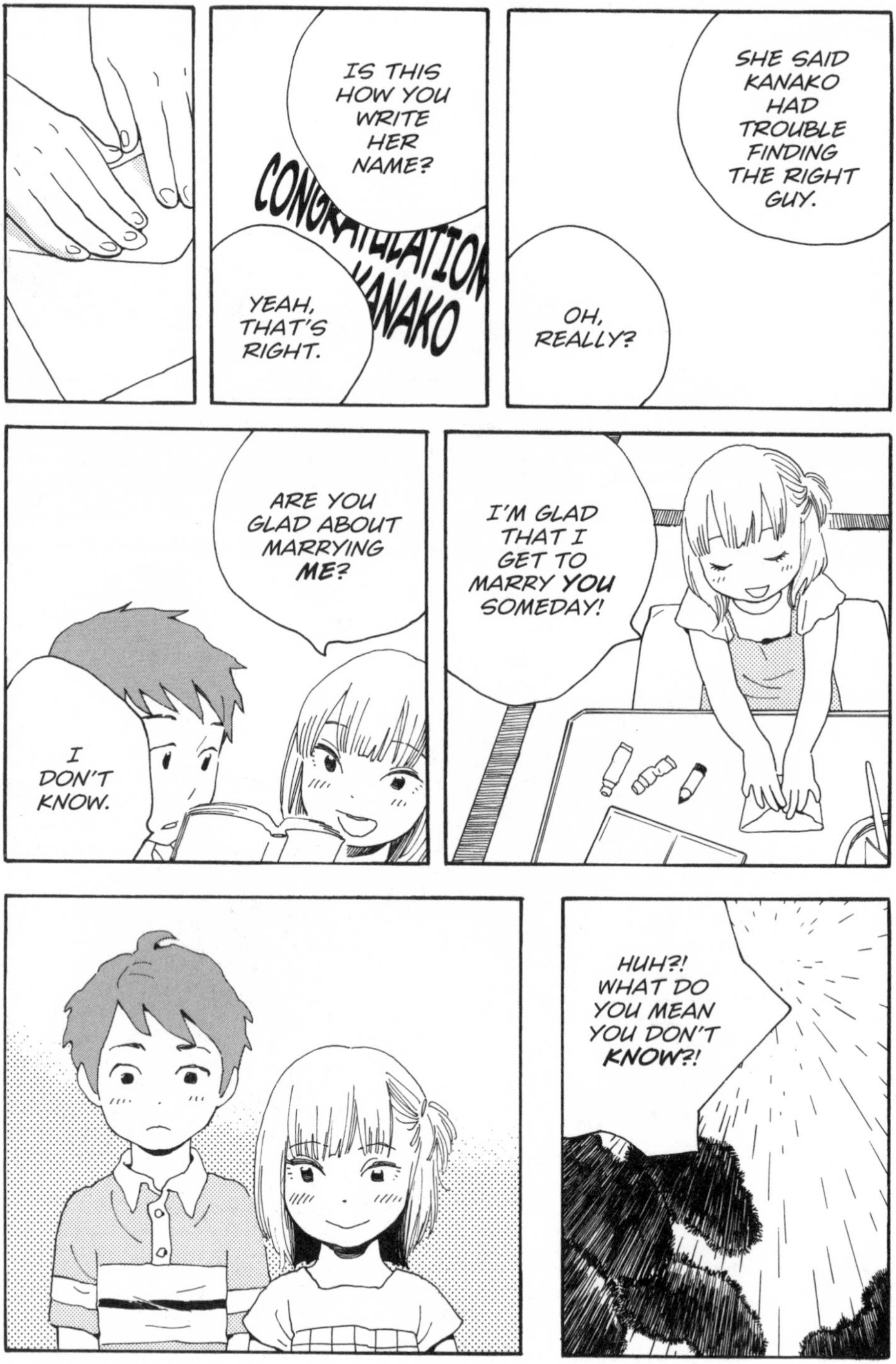
SHE SAID KANAKO HAD TROUBLE FINDING THE RIGHT GUY.
OH, REALLY?
IS THIS HOW YOU WRITE HER NAME?
CONGRATULATION
KANAKO
YEAH, THAT'S RIGHT.
I'M GLAD THAT I GET TO MARRY **YOU** SOMEDAY!
ARE YOU GLAD ABOUT MARRYING **ME**?
I DON'T KNOW.
HUH?! WHAT DO YOU MEAN YOU DON'T **KNOW**?!

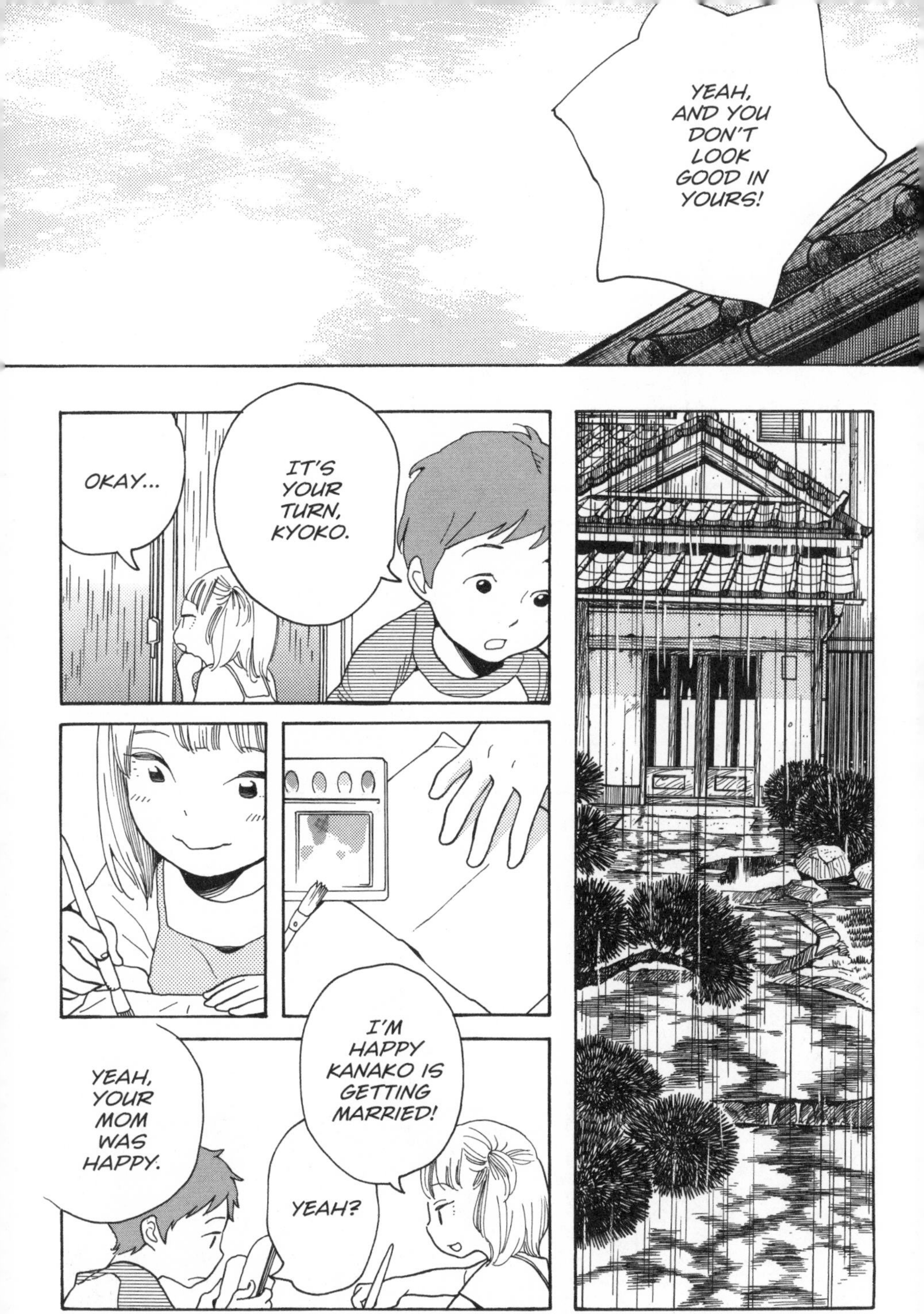
YEAH, AND YOU DON'T LOOK GOOD IN YOURS!
IT'S YOUR TURN, KYOKO.
OKAY...
I'M HAPPY KANAKO IS GETTING MARRIED!
YEAH, YOUR MOM WAS HAPPY.
YEAH?

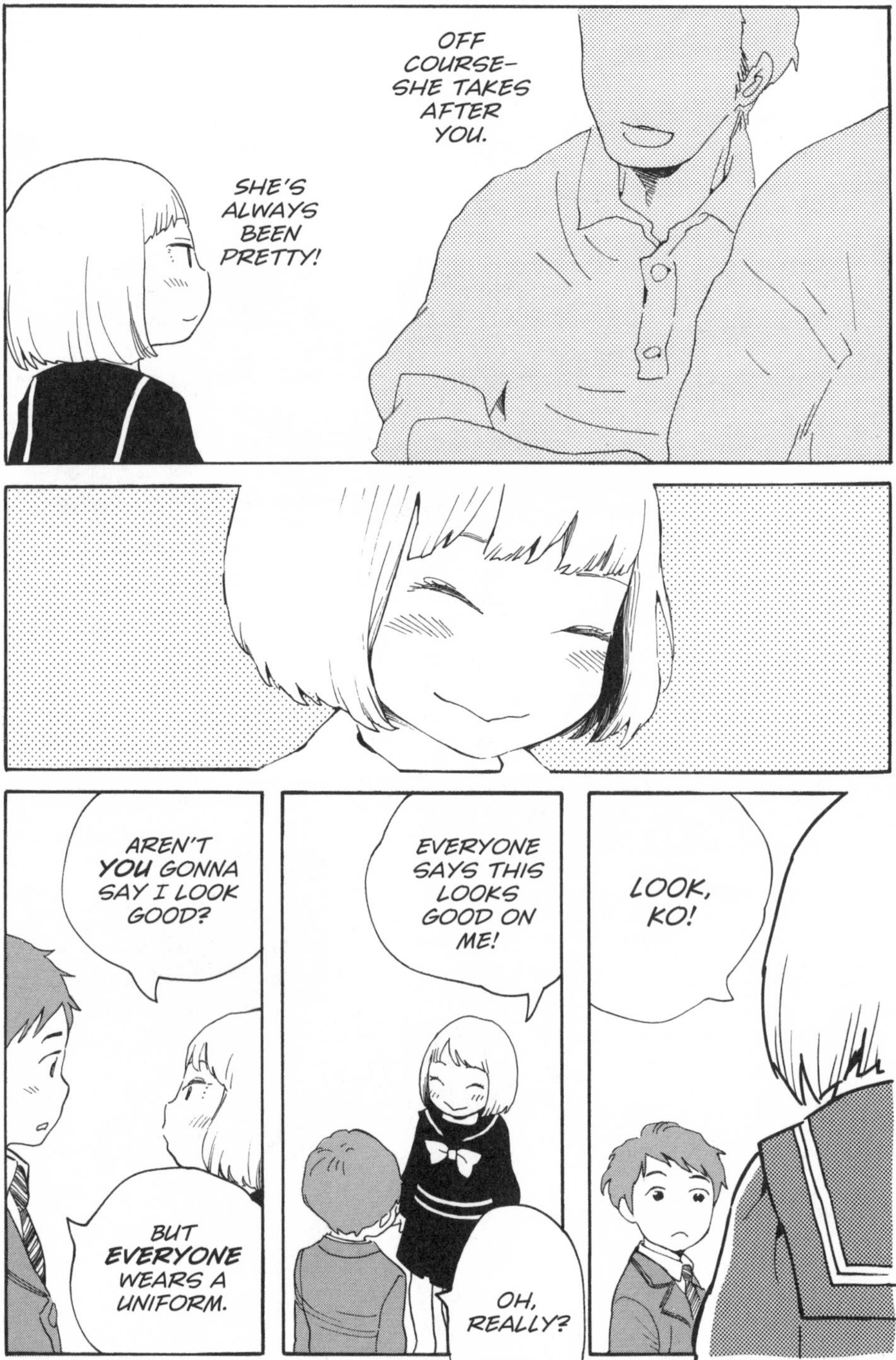
OFF COURSE-SHE TAKES AFTER YOU.
SHE'S ALWAYS BEEN PRETTY!
LOOK, KO!
EVERYONE SAYS THIS LOOKS GOOD ON ME!
OH, REALLY?
AREN'T YOU GONNA SAY I LOOK GOOD?
BUT EVERYONE WEARS A UNIFORM.

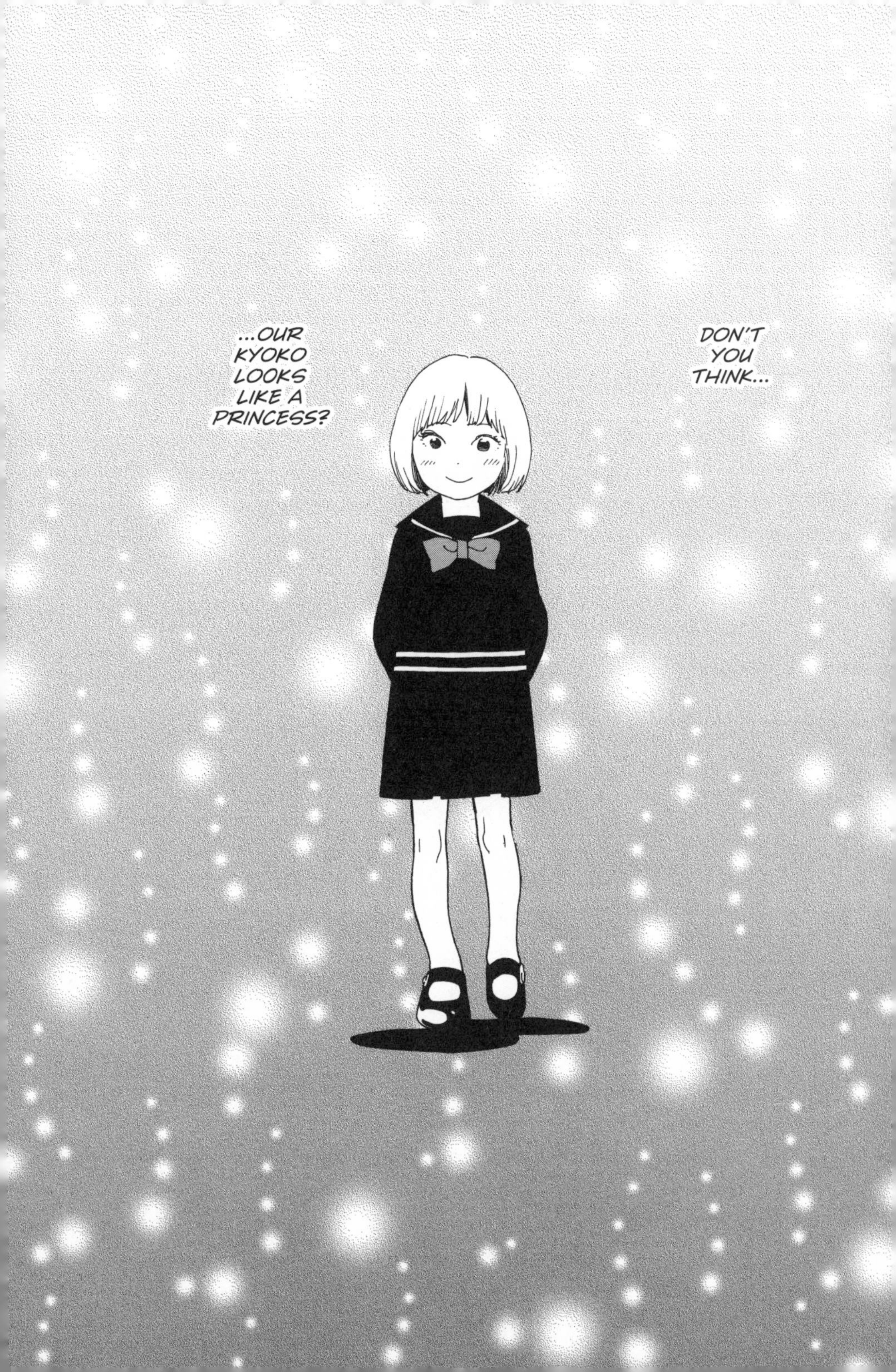
DON'T YOU THINK...
...OUR KYOKO LOOKS LIKE A PRINCESS?

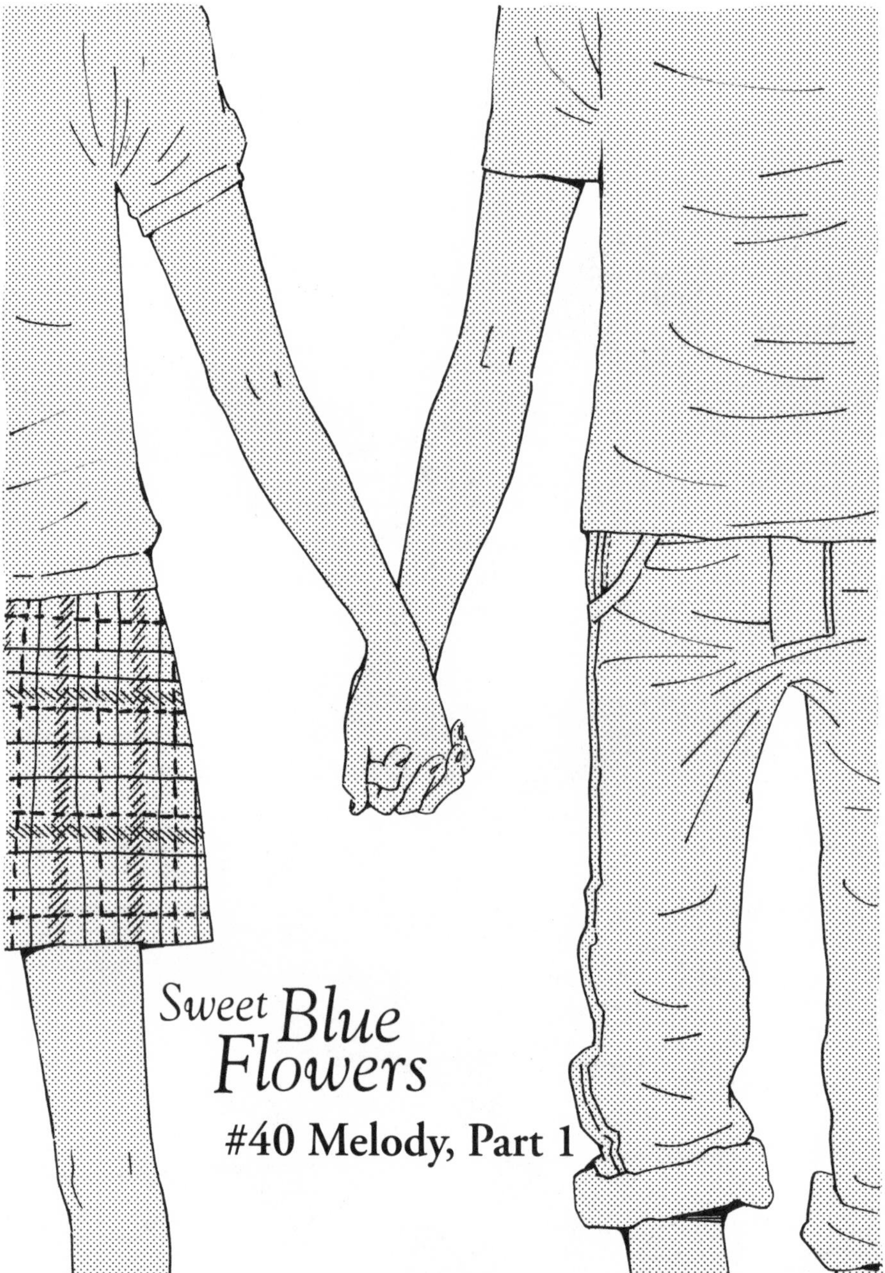
Sweet Blue Flowers
#40 Melody, Part 1

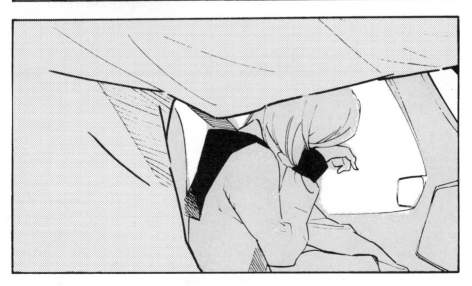

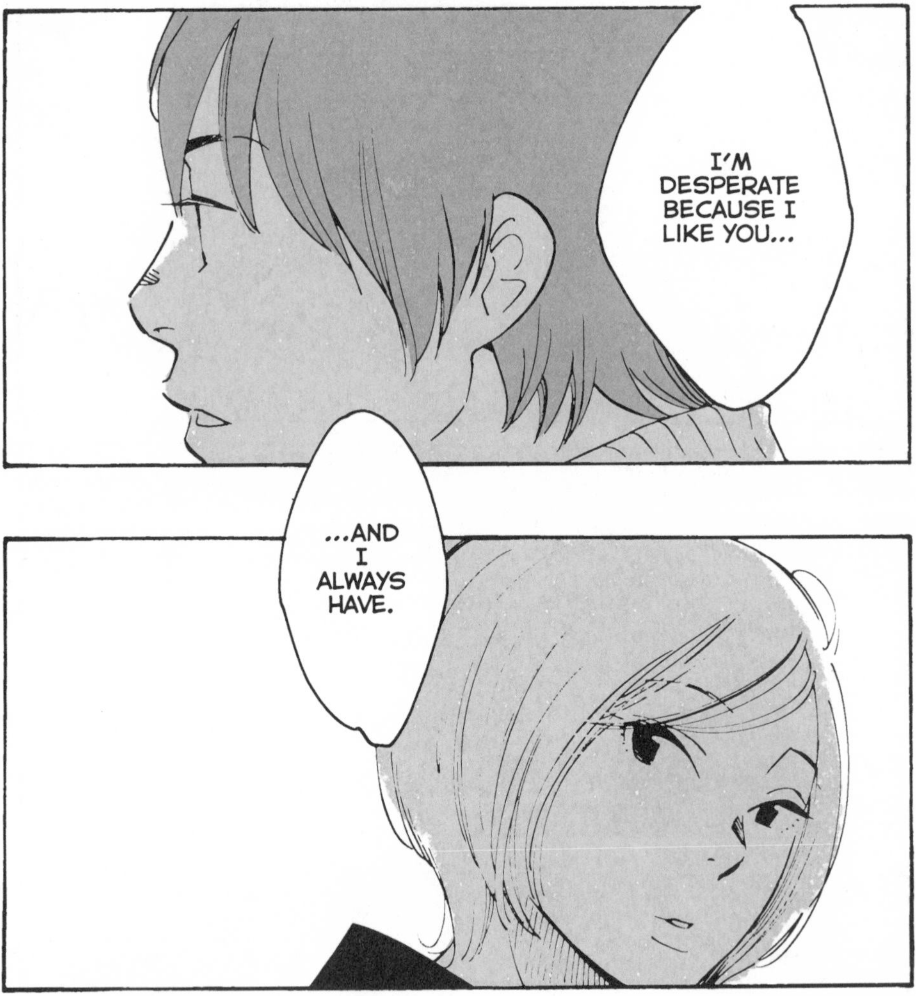
I'M DESPERATE BECAUSE I LIKE YOU...
...AND I ALWAYS HAVE.

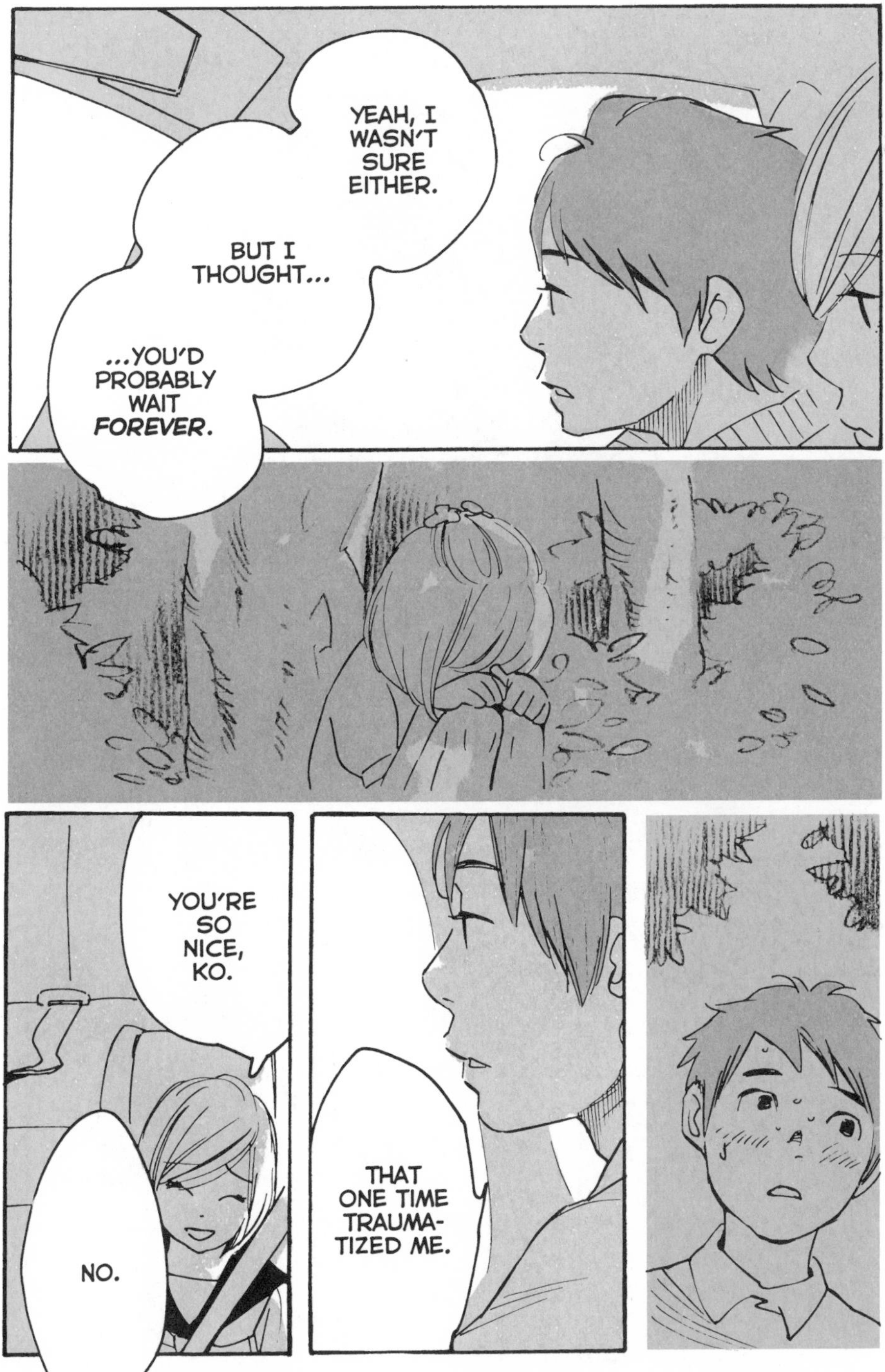
YEAH, I WASN'T SURE EITHER.
BUT I THOUGHT...
...YOU'D PROBABLY WAIT *FOREVER*.
THAT ONE TIME TRAUMA-TIZED ME.
YOU'RE SO NICE, KO.
NO.

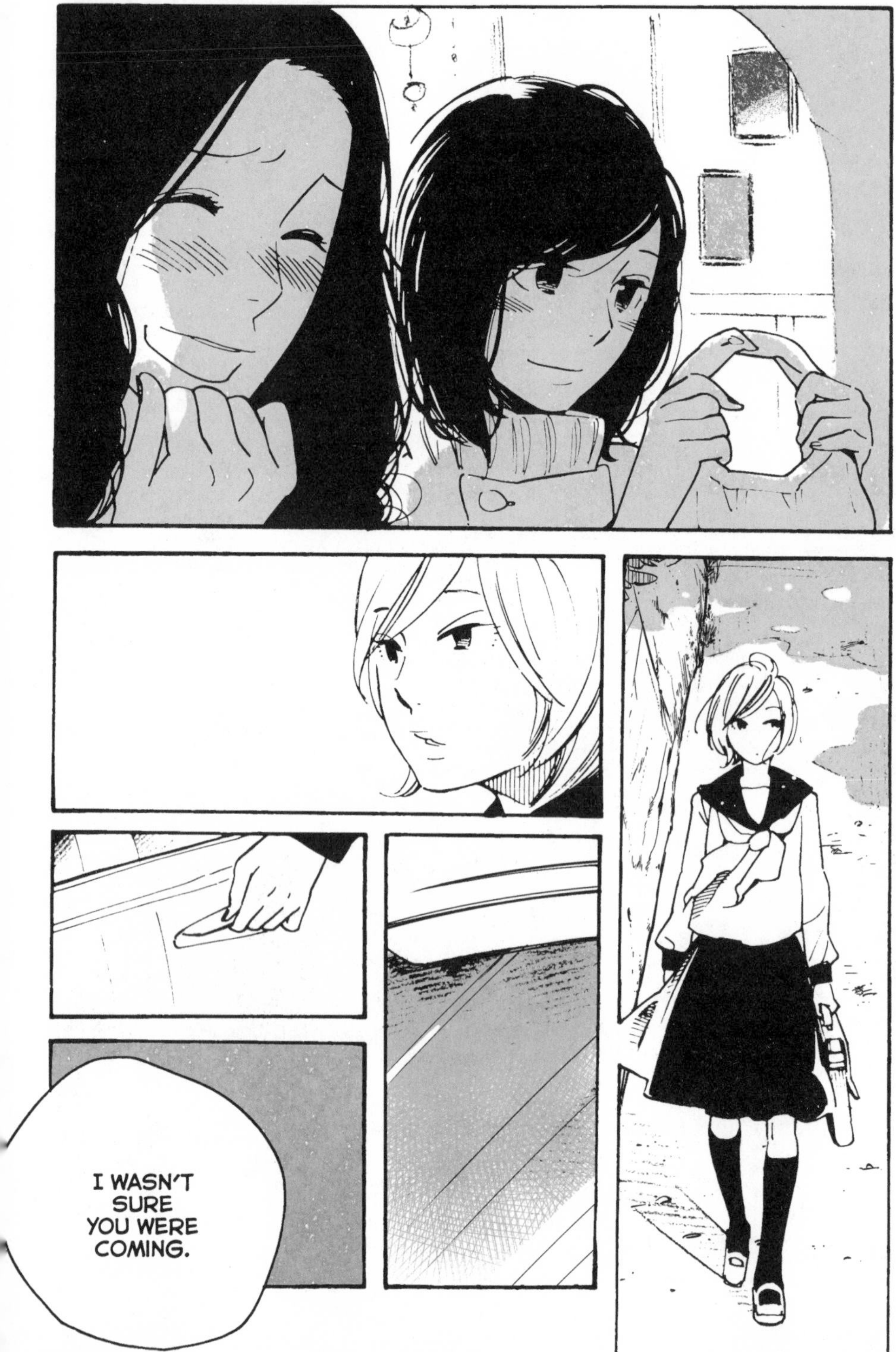
I WASN'T SURE YOU WERE COMING.

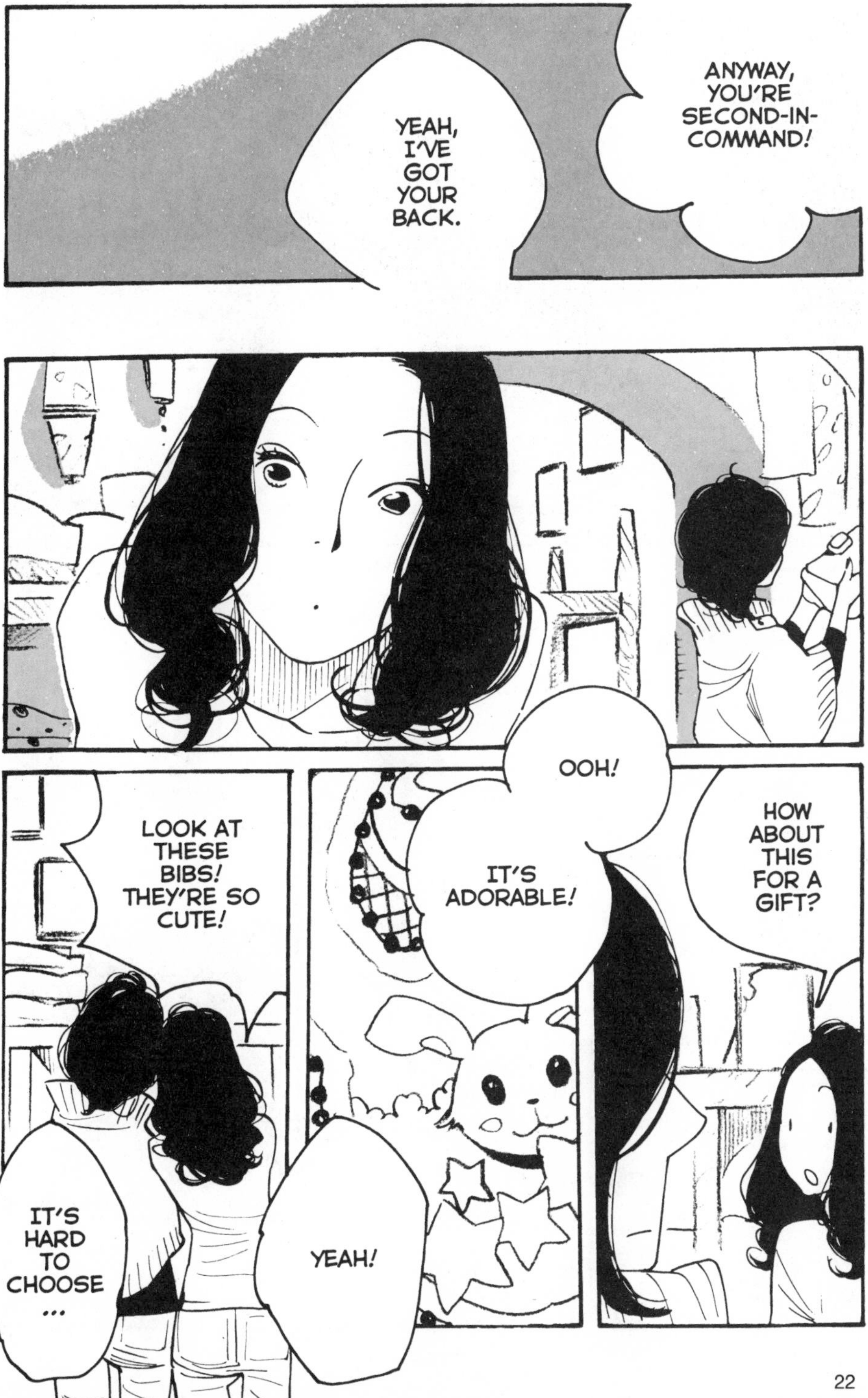
ANYWAY, YOU'RE SECOND-IN-COMMAND!
YEAH, I'VE GOT YOUR BACK.
HOW ABOUT THIS FOR A GIFT?
OOH!
IT'S ADORABLE!
YEAH!
LOOK AT THESE BIBS! THEY'RE SO CUTE!
IT'S HARD TO CHOOSE...

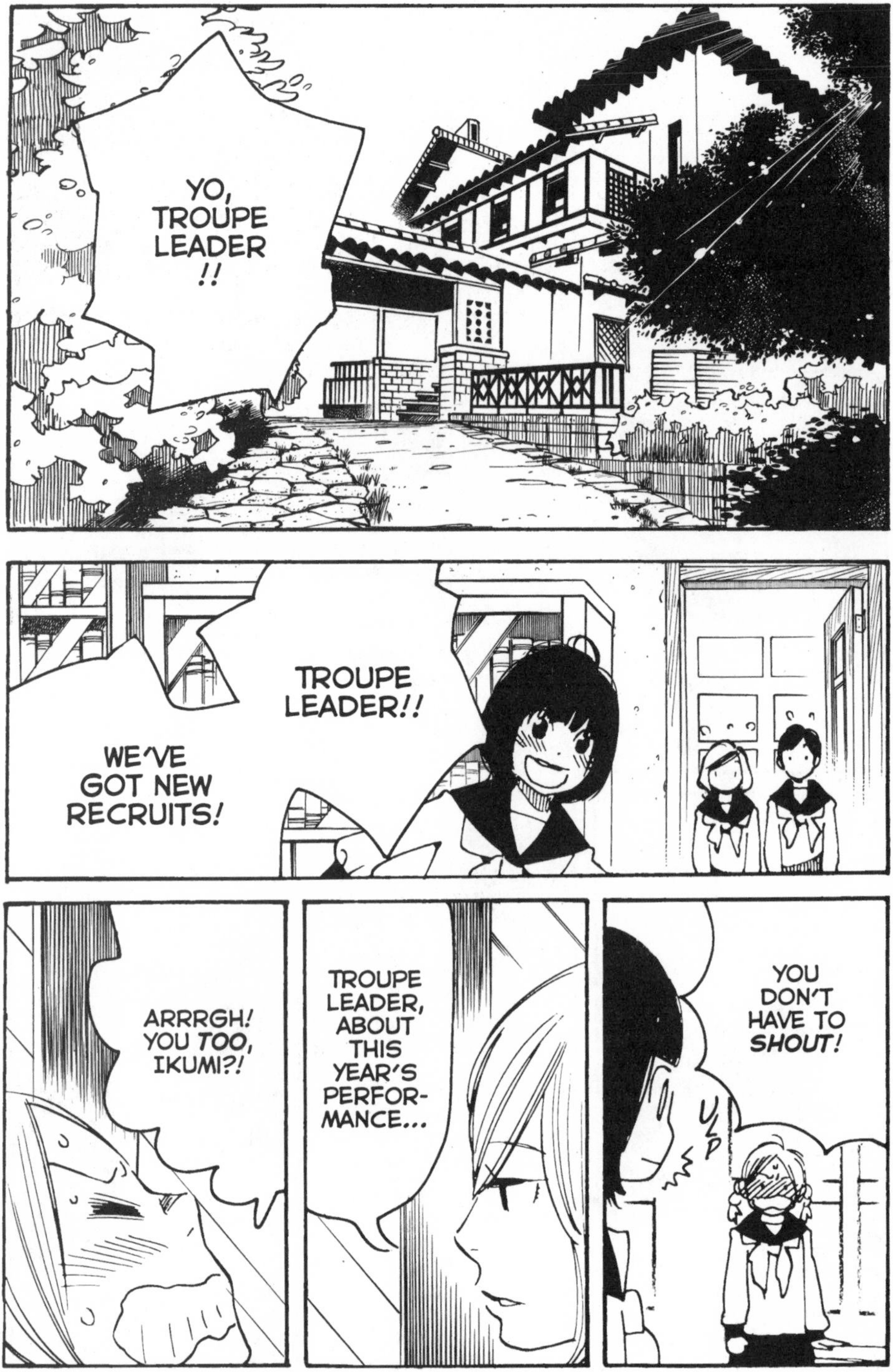
YO, TROUPE LEADER!!
TROUPE LEADER!!
WE'VE GOT NEW RECRUITS!
YOU DON'T HAVE TO *SHOUT*!
ULP
TROUPE LEADER, ABOUT THIS YEAR'S PERFOR-MANCE...
ARRRGH! YOU *TOO*, IKUMI?!

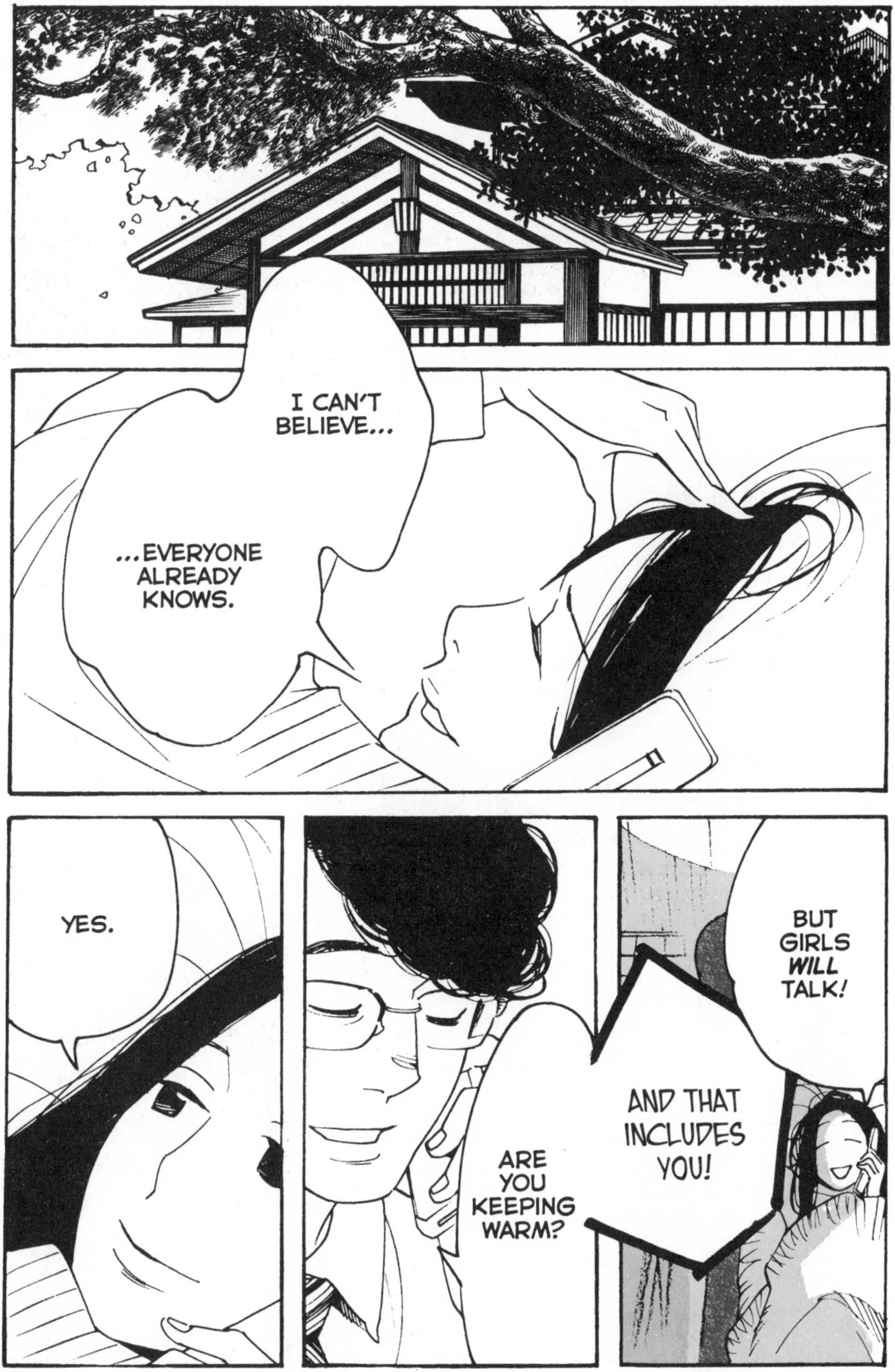
I CAN'T BELIEVE...
...EVERYONE ALREADY KNOWS.
BUT GIRLS *WILL* TALK!
AND THAT INCLUDES YOU!
ARE YOU KEEPING WARM?
YES.

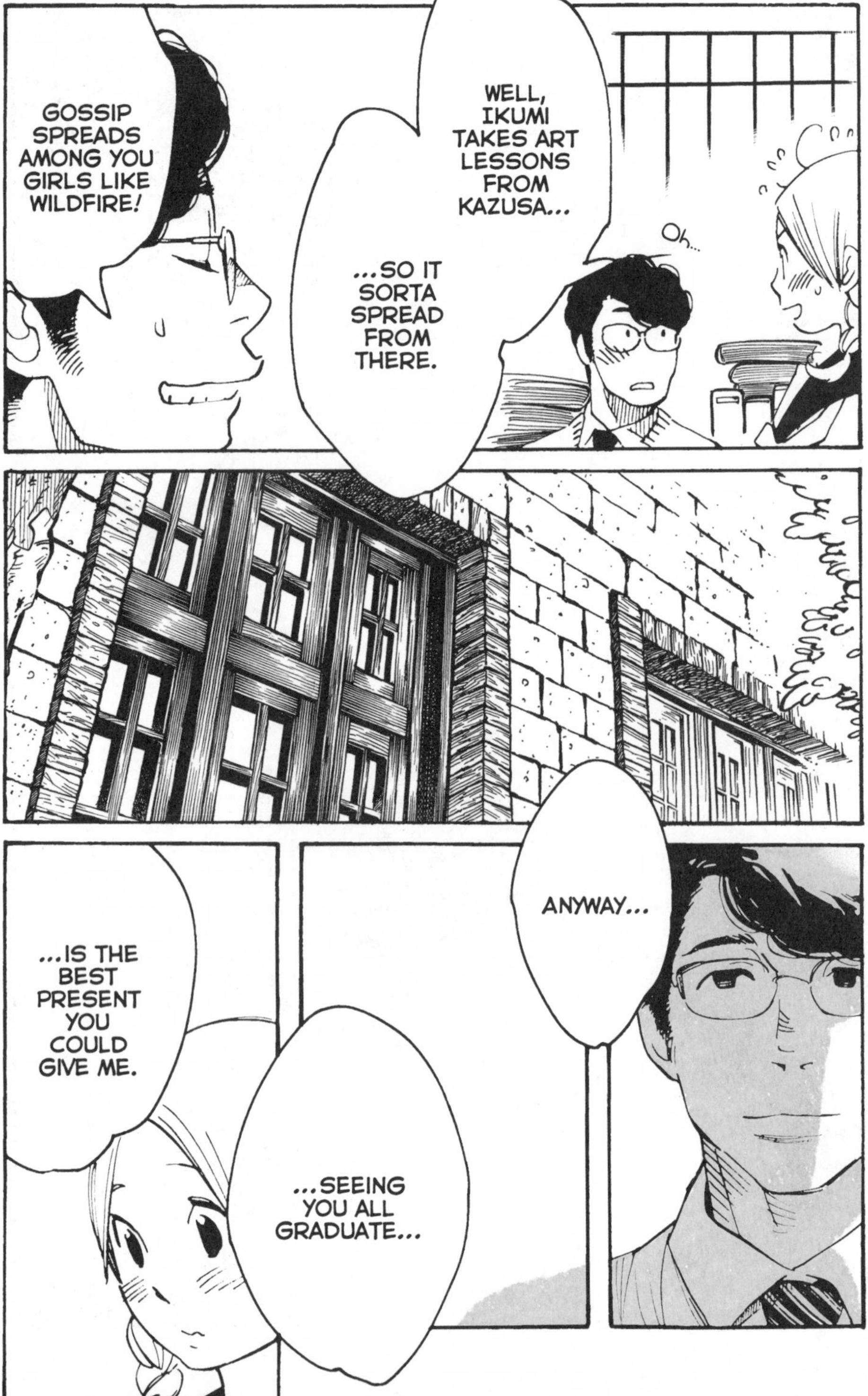
WELL, IKUMI TAKES ART LESSONS FROM KAZUSA...
Oh...
...SO IT SORTA SPREAD FROM THERE.
GOSSIP SPREADS AMONG YOU GIRLS LIKE WILDFIRE!
ANYWAY...
...SEEING YOU ALL GRADUATE...
...IS THE BEST PRESENT YOU COULD GIVE ME.

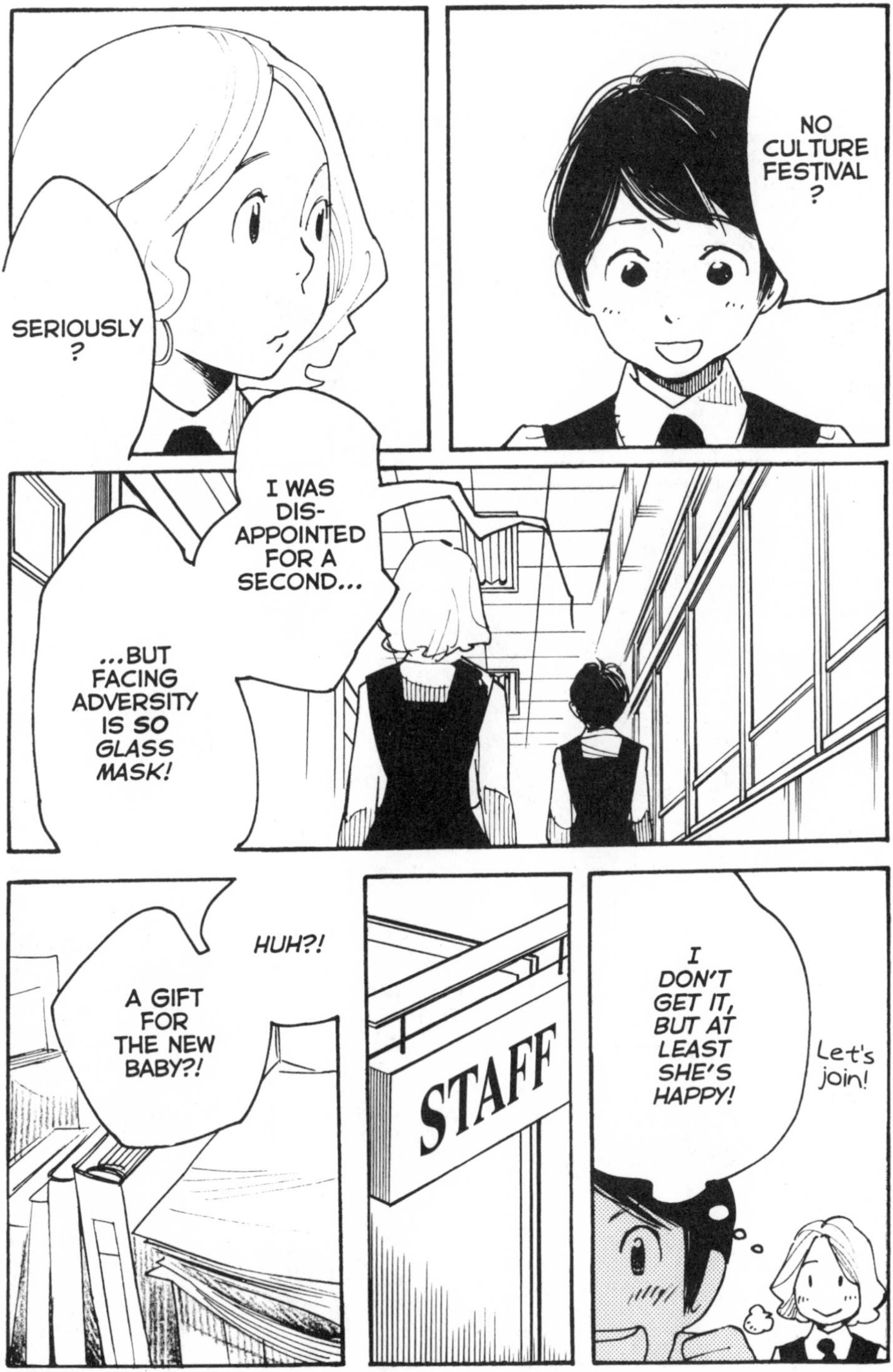
NO CULTURE FESTIVAL ?
SERIOUSLY ?
I WAS DIS-APPOINTED FOR A SECOND...
...BUT FACING ADVERSITY IS SO GLASS MASK!
I DON'T GET IT, BUT AT LEAST SHE'S HAPPY!
Let's join!
STAFF
HUH?!
A GIFT FOR THE NEW BABY?!

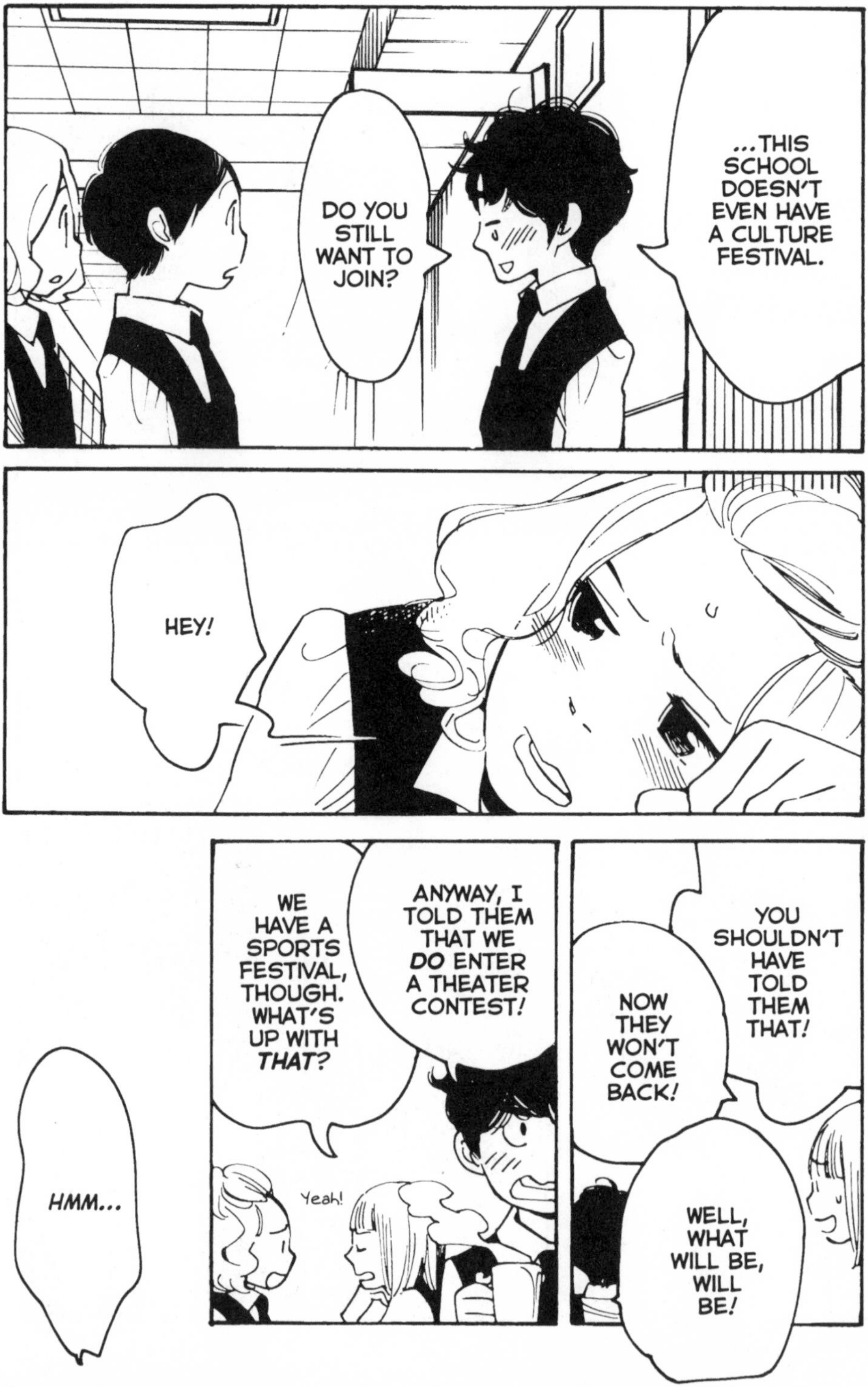
...THIS SCHOOL DOESN'T EVEN HAVE A CULTURE FESTIVAL.
DO YOU STILL WANT TO JOIN?
HEY!
YOU SHOULDN'T HAVE TOLD THEM THAT!
NOW THEY WON'T COME BACK!
WELL, WHAT WILL BE, WILL BE!
ANYWAY, I TOLD THEM THAT WE *DO* ENTER A THEATER CONTEST!
WE HAVE A SPORTS FESTIVAL, THOUGH. WHAT'S UP WITH *THAT*?
Yeah!
HMM...

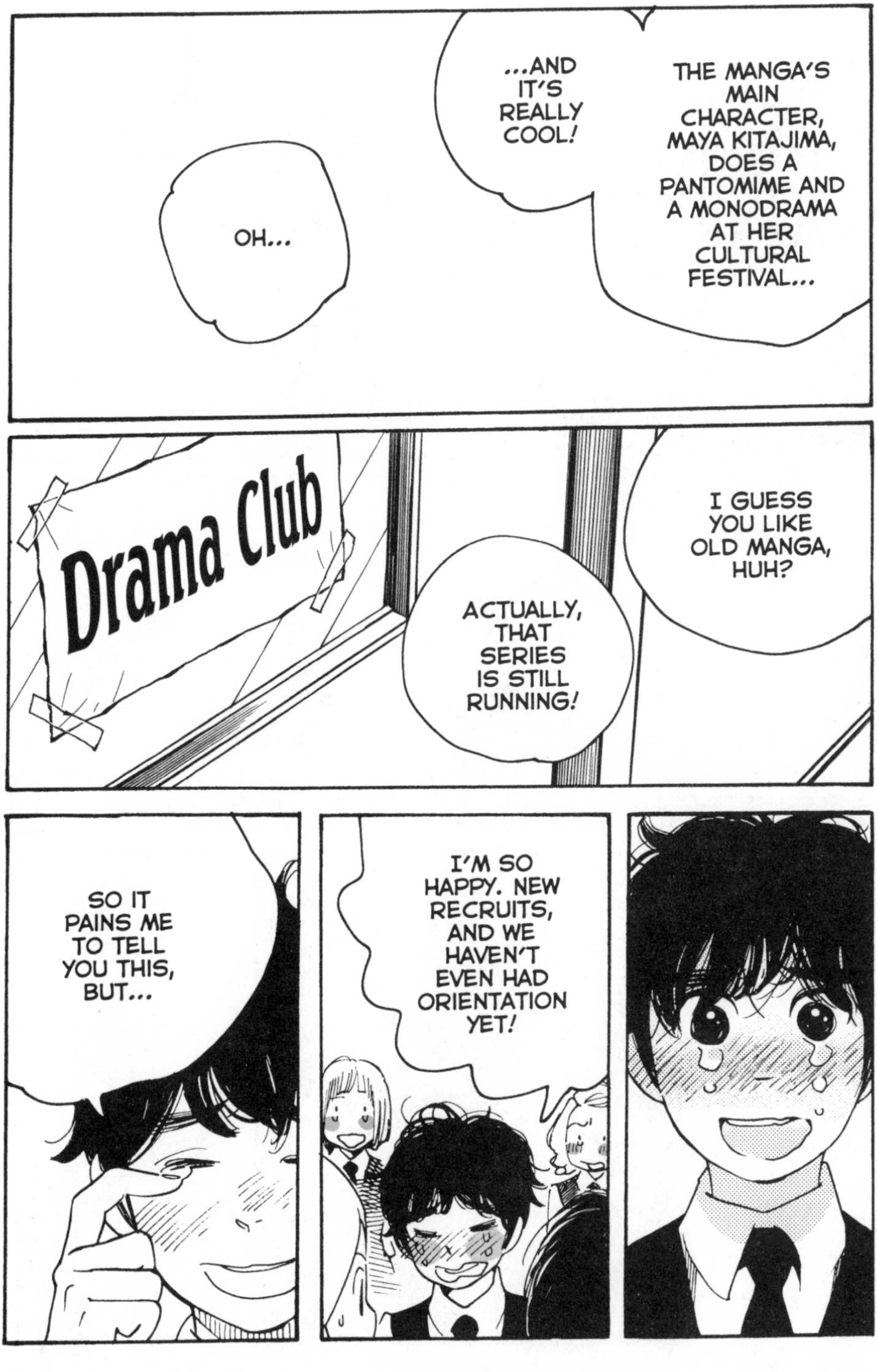
THE MANGA'S MAIN CHARACTER, MAYA KITAJIMA, DOES A PANTOMIME AND A MONODRAMA AT HER CULTURAL FESTIVAL...
...AND IT'S REALLY COOL!
OH...
I GUESS YOU LIKE OLD MANGA, HUH?
ACTUALLY, THAT SERIES IS STILL RUNNING!
Drama Club
I'M SO HAPPY. NEW RECRUITS, AND WE HAVEN'T EVEN HAD ORIENTATION YET!
SO IT PAINS ME TO TELL YOU THIS, BUT...

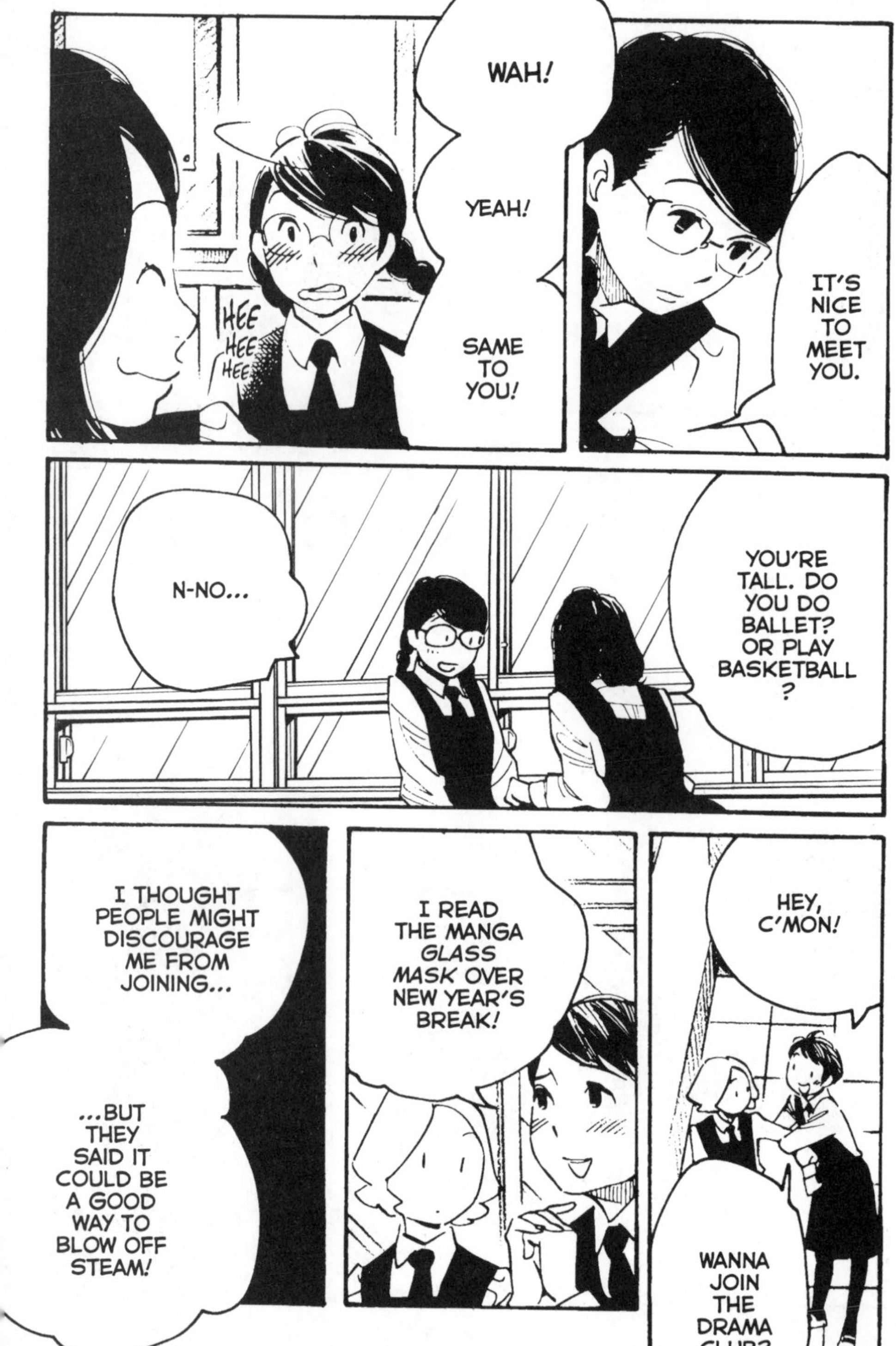
IT'S NICE TO MEET YOU.
WAH!
YEAH!
SAME TO YOU!
HEE HEE HEE
YOU'RE TALL. DO YOU DO BALLET? OR PLAY BASKETBALL?
N-NO...
HEY, C'MON!
WANNA JOIN THE DRAMA CLUB?
I READ THE MANGA *GLASS MASK* OVER NEW YEAR'S BREAK!
I THOUGHT PEOPLE MIGHT DISCOURAGE ME FROM JOINING...
...BUT THEY SAID IT COULD BE A GOOD WAY TO BLOW OFF STEAM!

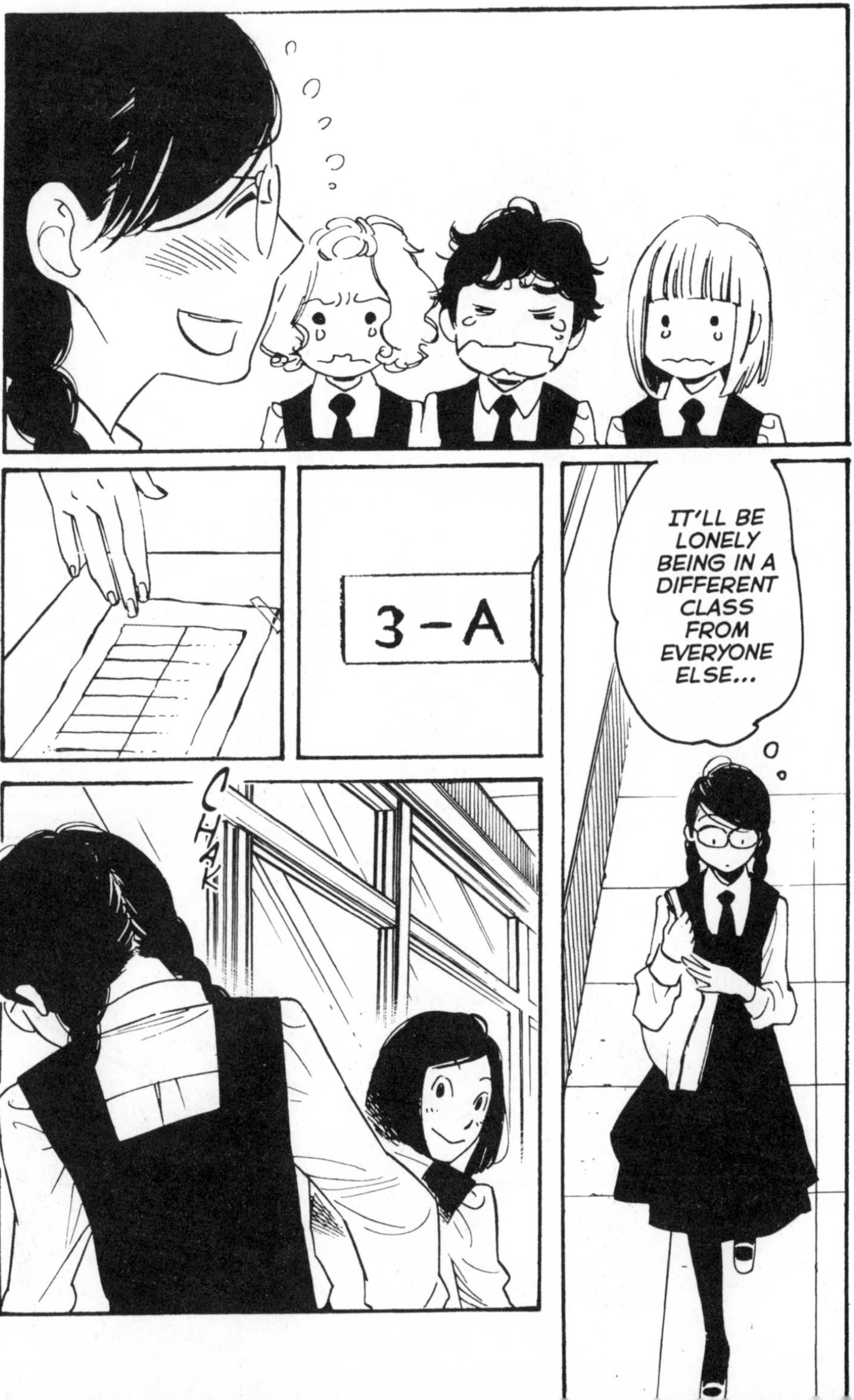

IT'LL BE LONELY BEING IN A DIFFERENT CLASS FROM EVERYONE ELSE...
3-A
CHAK

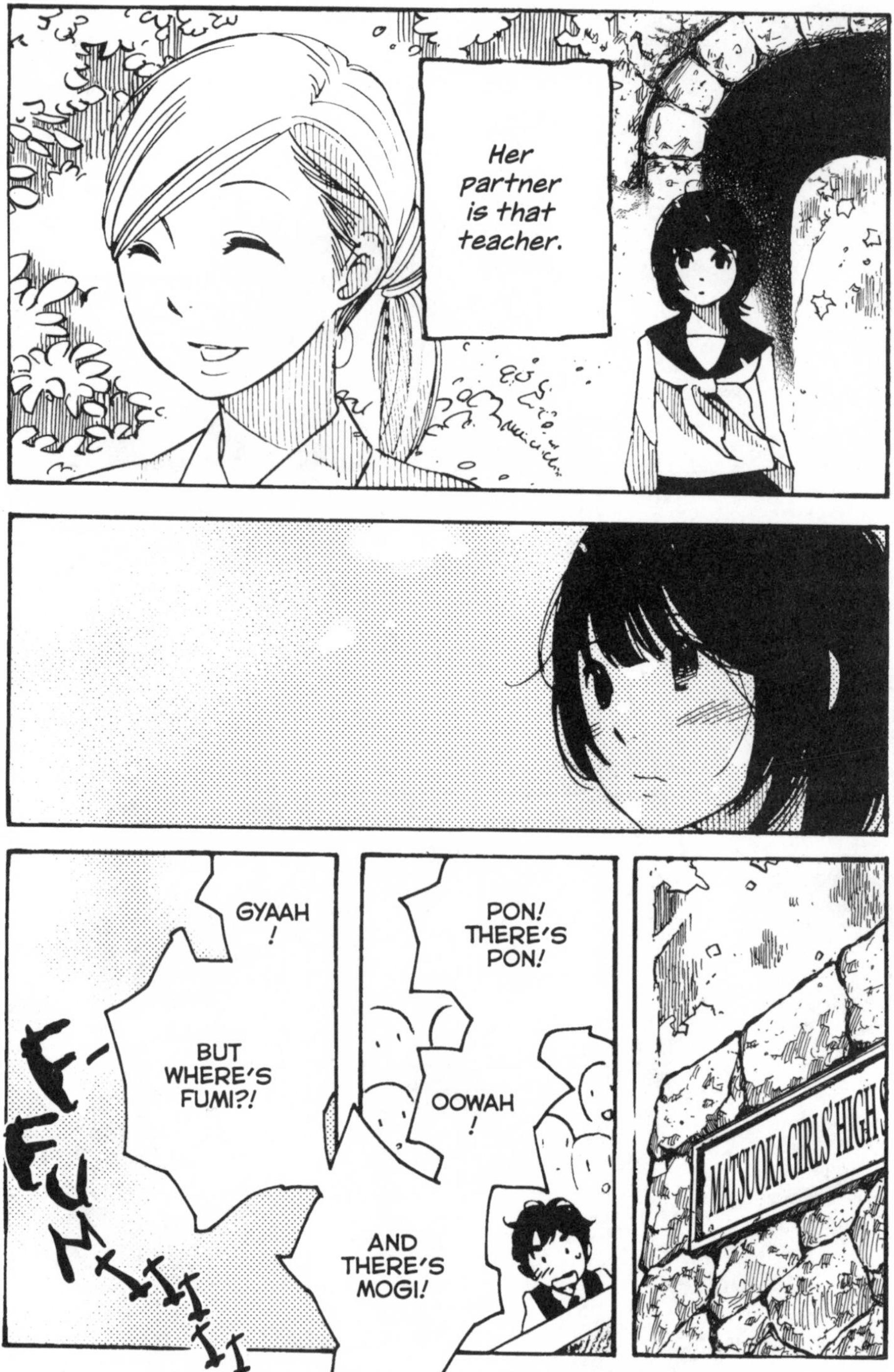
Her partner is that teacher.
MATSUOKA GIRLS' HIGH S
PON! THERE'S PON!
OOWAH!
AND THERE'S MOGI!
GYAAH!
BUT WHERE'S FUMI?!
F-FUMIIIIII...

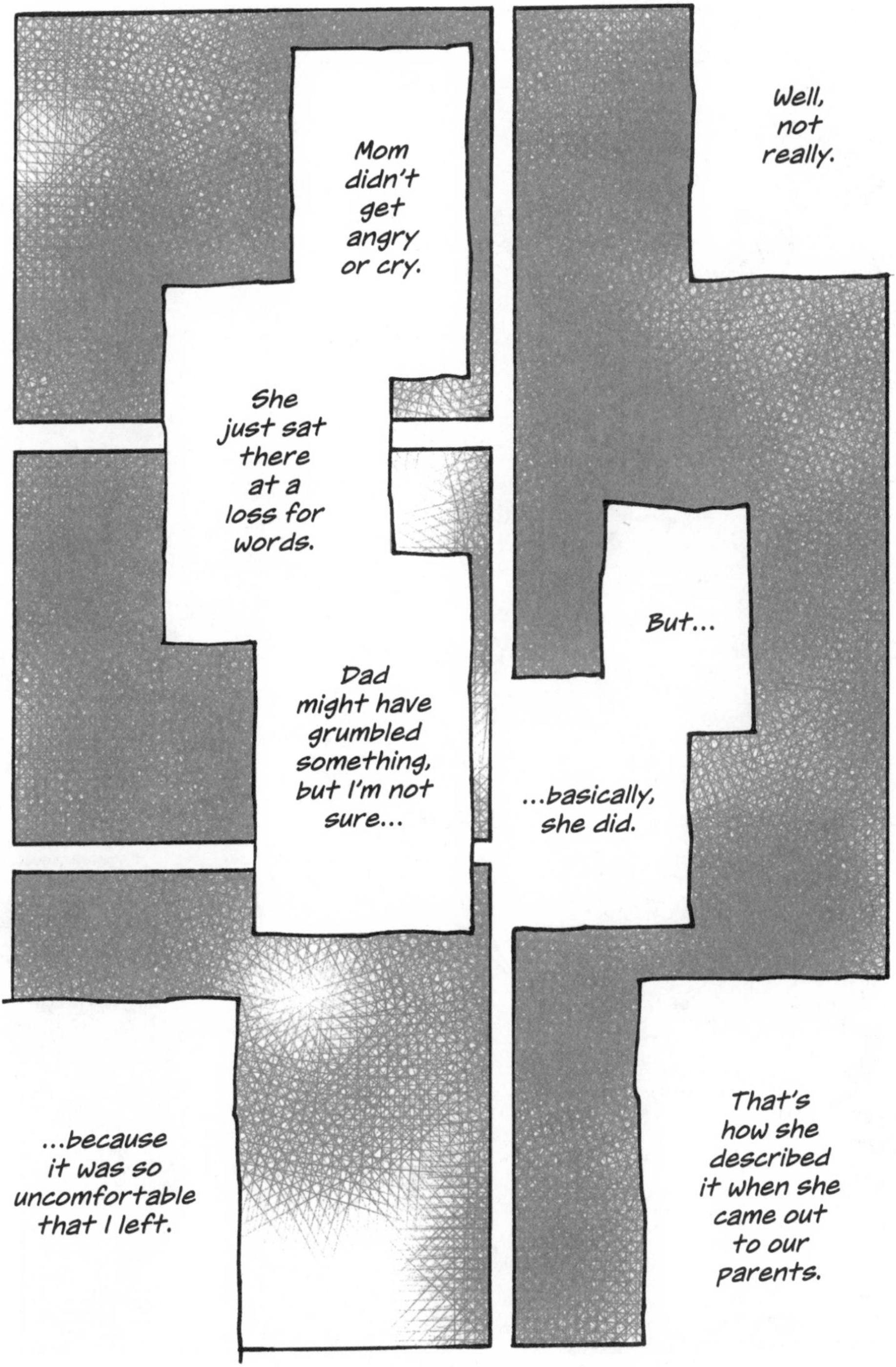
Well, not really.
Mom didn't get angry or cry.
She just sat there at a loss for words.
Dad might have grumbled something, but I'm not sure...
...because it was so uncomfortable that I left.
But...
...basically, she did.
That's how she described it when she came out to our parents.

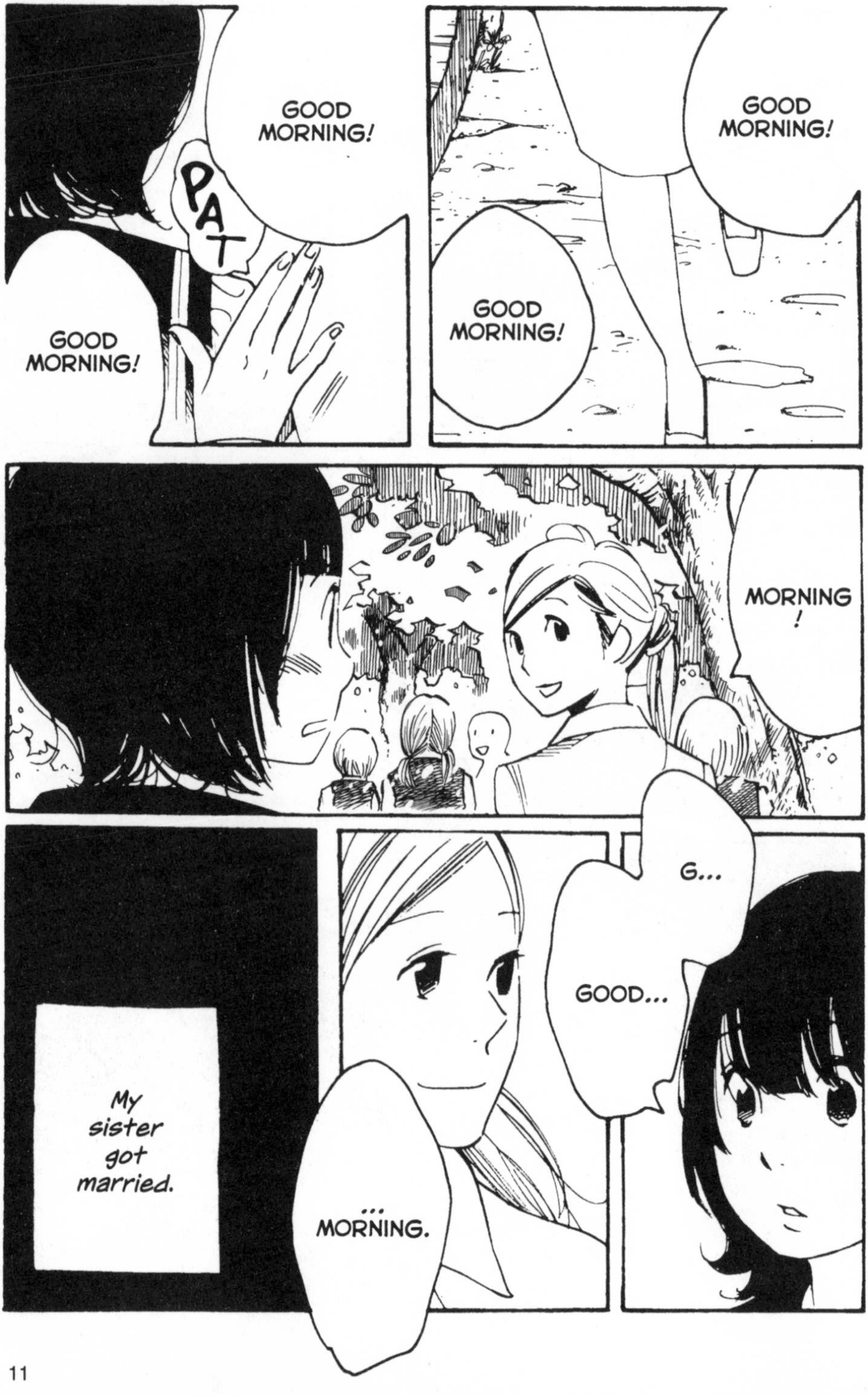
GOOD MORNING!
GOOD MORNING!
GOOD MORNING!
PAT
GOOD MORNING!
MORNING!
G...
GOOD...
...MORNING.
My sister got married.

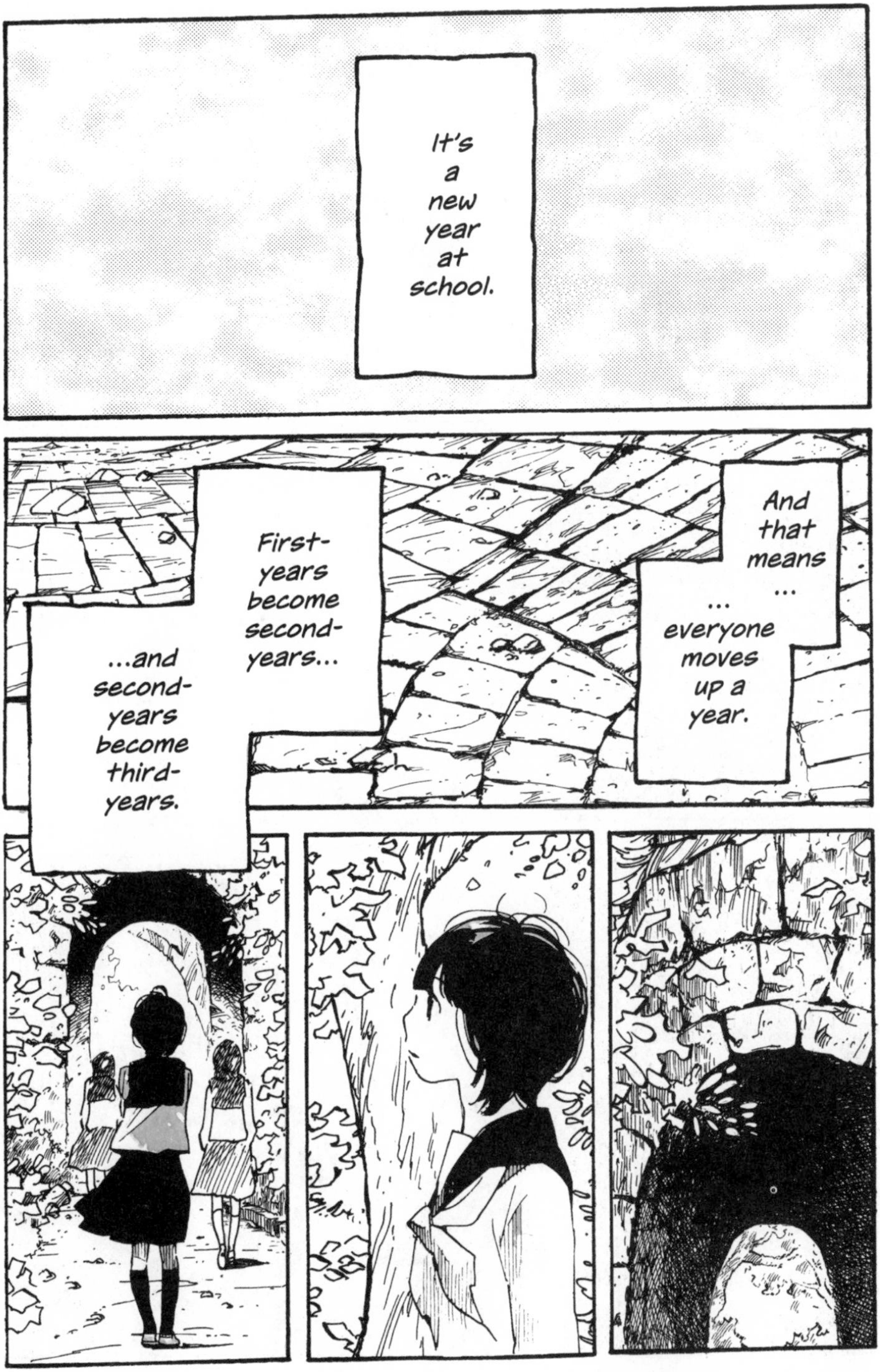
It's a new year at school.
And that means ...
... everyone moves up a year.
First-years become second-years...
...and second-years become third-years.

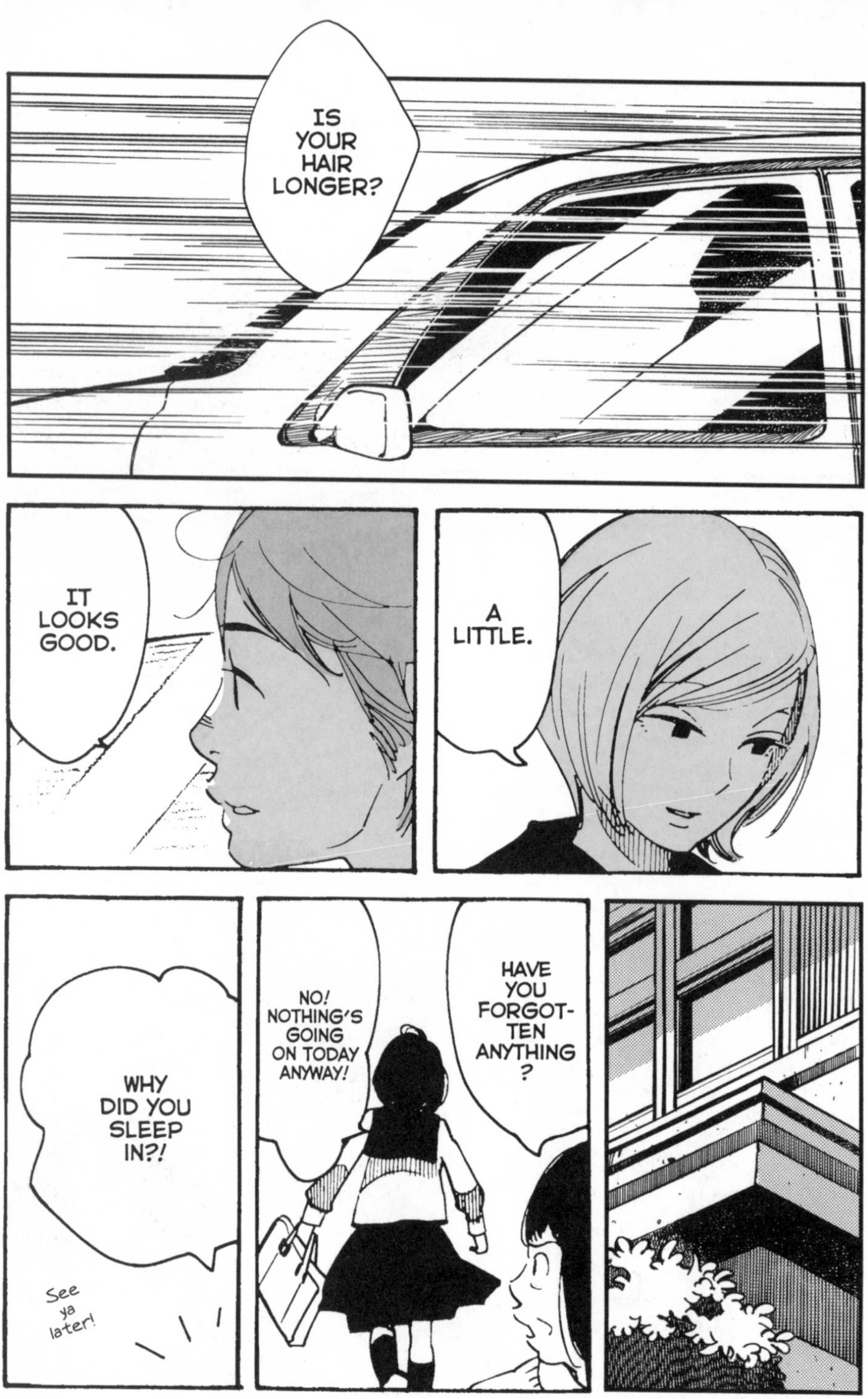
IS YOUR HAIR LONGER?
A LITTLE.
IT LOOKS GOOD.
HAVE YOU FORGOTTEN ANYTHING?
NO! NOTHING'S GOING ON TODAY ANYWAY!
WHY DID YOU SLEEP IN?!
See ya later!

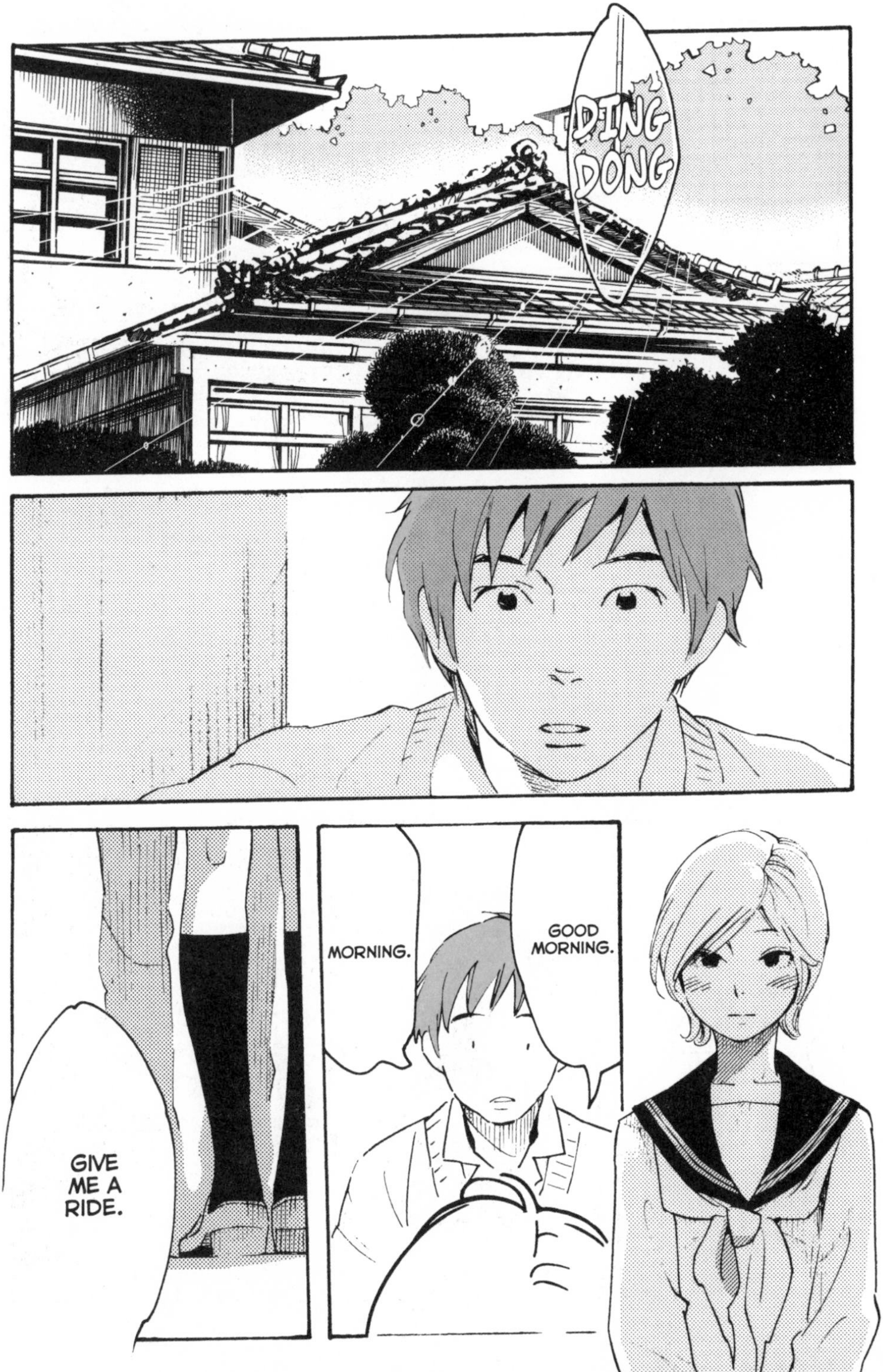
DING DONG
GOOD MORNING.
MORNING.
GIVE ME A RIDE.

Sweet Blue Flowers

#39 A Little Princess

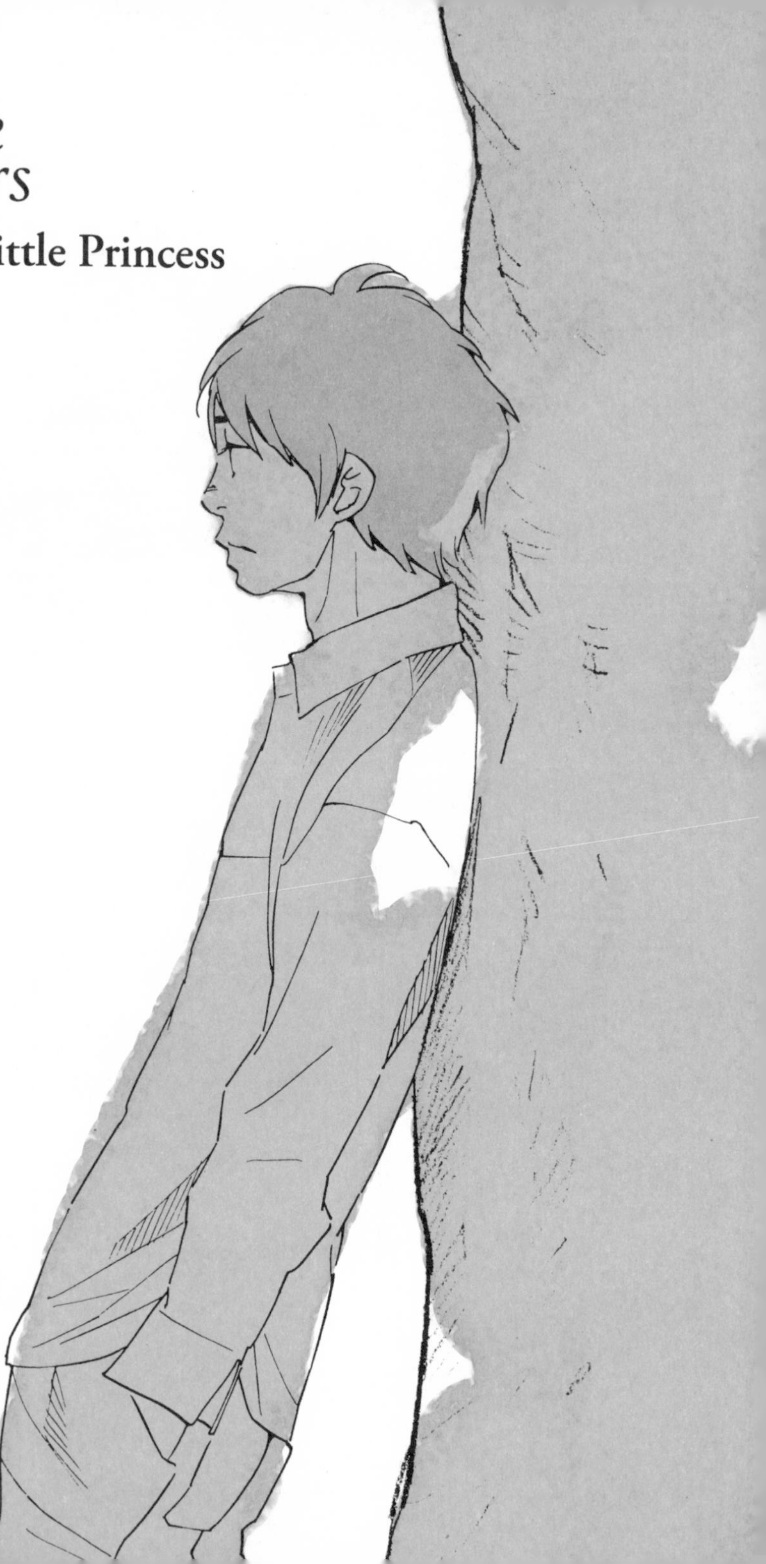

Matsuoka Girls' High School

Yasuko Sugimoto
During her time as a student at Matsuoka, she was the popular princely type as well as the captain of the basketball team. She dated Fumi, but the relationship fell apart after a few months. Currently, she is studying in England with her friend Kawasaki.

Fumi Manjome
Year 3. She's tall and pretty—and a worrywart crybaby. She recently realized that her close friend Akira was her first love. After they start dating, she experiences both joy and unease.

Miwa Motegi
Year 3. Nickname: Mogi. She's a quiet girl who is a member of the school's small Drama Club. She's dating Akira's older brother Shinobu.

Misako Yasuda
Year 3. Nickname: Yassan. She's the hardworking head of the school's small Drama Club.

Yoko Honatsugi
Year 3. Nickname: Pon. She's a member of the school's small Drama Club. She has a bright personality and isn't afraid of anything.

Chizu Hanashiro
Fumi's cousin on her mother's side. She was Fumi's first girlfriend, but she surprised Fumi by getting married.

Ko Sawanoi
Kyoko Ikumi's fiancé. He's in his third year at university. He has a gentle and considerate personality, and he's serious about Kyoko.

Shinobu Okudaira
Akira's brother. He's in his fourth year at university. He has a serious sister complex, but maybe he's beginning to change now that he's dating Miwa Motegi?

Characters

Fujigaya Women's Academy High School

Kyoko Ikumi
Year 3. Like Akira, she's a member of the Drama Club. The other girls admire her for her maturity. She had a one-sided crush on Yasuko Sugimoto, but her feelings changed after seeing how serious her fiancé Ko Sawanoi is about her.

Akira Okudaira
Year 3. She's small, innocent and honest, and has yet to experience love. She feels uncomfortable when her childhood friend Fumi tells her she likes her, but after giving it serious thought, she decides to start dating her.

Hinako Yamashina
Science teacher. She is Akira's homeroom teacher and a graduate of Fujigaya. Her girlfriend is Haruka Ono's older sister Orie.

Haruka Ono
Year 2. She's an energetic girl who joined the Drama Club because she admires theater, and now she's becoming good friends with a lot of older students.

Ryoko Ueda
Year 3. She's in the same class as Akira. She's a member of the Library Club, but she wins acclaim when she makes a guest appearance onstage at the Fujigaya Theater Festival.

Sweet **Blue**
Flowers

CHILDREN OF THE WHALES

In this postapocalyptic fantasy, a sea of sand swallows everything but the past.

In an endless sea of sand drifts the Mud Whale, a floating island city of clay and magic. In its chambers a small community clings to survival, cut off from its own history by the shadows of the past.

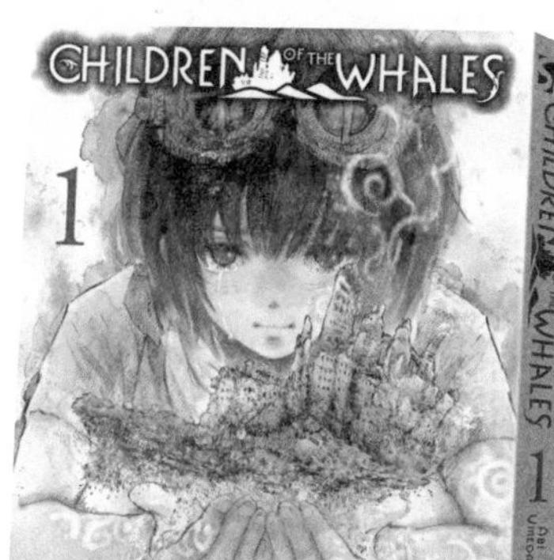
CHILDREN OF THE WHALES
1
ABI UMEDA
VIZ

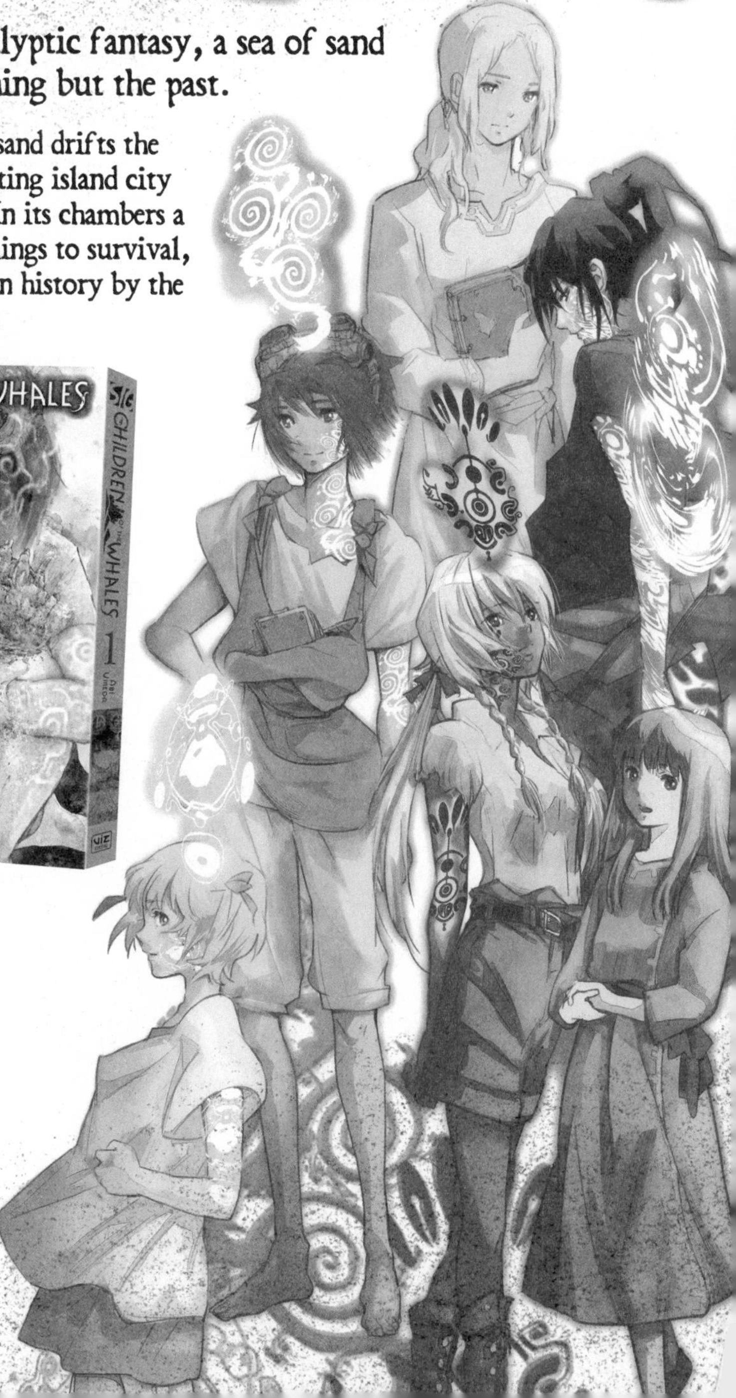

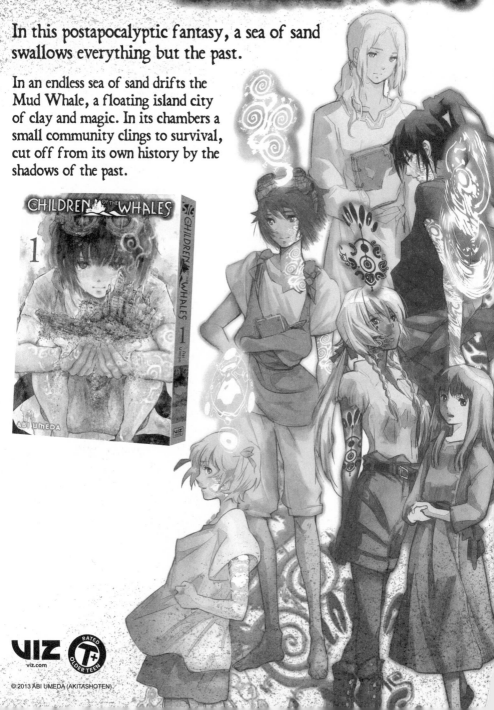

This is the last page. *Sweet Blue Flowers*
has been printed in the original Japanese
format to preserve the orientation
of the original artwork.